1,001 Praxis® Core Practice Questions

for
dummies®
A Wiley Brand

1,001 Praxis® Core Practice Questions

for dummies®
A Wiley Brand

by Carla Kirkland and Chan Cleveland

for dummies®
A Wiley Brand

1,001 Praxis® Core Practice Questions For Dummies®

Published by: **John Wiley & Sons, Inc.,** 111 River Street, Hoboken, NJ 07030-5774, www.wiley.com

Copyright © 2017 by John Wiley & Sons, Inc., Hoboken, New Jersey

Published simultaneously in Canada

For general information on our other products and services, please contact our Customer Care Department within the U.S. at 877-762-2974, outside the U.S. at 317-572-3993, or fax 317-572-4002. For technical support, please visit https://hub.wiley.com/community/support/dummies.

Wiley publishes in a variety of print and electronic formats and by print-on-demand. Some material included with standard print versions of this book may not be included in e-books or in print-on-demand. If this book refers to media such as a CD or DVD that is not included in the version you purchased, you may download this material at http://booksupport.wiley.com. For more information about Wiley products, visit www.wiley.com.

Library of Congress Control Number: 2016949223

ISBN 978-1-119-26388-3 (pbk); ISBN 978-1-119-26395-1 (ebk); ISBN 978-1-119-26398-2 (ebk)

Manufactured in the United States of America

10 9 8 7 6 5 4 3 2 1

Contents at a Glance

Table of Contents

Introduction

Welcome to *1,001 Praxis Core Practice Questions For Dummies*. Don't take the *dummies* thing literally — you're obviously smart and capable. You've chosen to shape the minds of future generations through education. And on that quest, you will encounter obstacles. At least one of those is a Praxis exam.

This book is designed to give you lots of exposure to the kinds of questions you'll see on the very first test for teachers: the Praxis Core Academic Skills for Educators exam (referred to as Praxis or Praxis Core from here on). To clear this hurdle, you need some practice and pointers on how best to answer the questions. This book provides that and more: It goes beyond providing relevant practice questions by showing simple and effective ways to solve challenging Praxis problems.

What You'll Find

The Praxis Core practice problems in this book are divided into four chapters based on skills involving Math, Reading, Writing, and Essays. Questions are adjusted and repeated to give you practice and mastery. If you struggle with one question, you can find a group of similar questions to practice and hone your skills. This book serves as an effective standalone refresher of Praxis basics or as an excellent companion to the latest edition of *Praxis Core For Dummies* (Wiley). Either way, this book helps you identify subject areas you need to work on so you can practice them until you're a pro and thus prepare for test day.

If you get a problem wrong, don't just read the answer explanation and move on. Instead, come back to the problem and solve it again, this time avoiding the mistake you made the first time. This is how you improve your skills and figure out how to solve the problems correctly and easily.

Whatever you do, stay positive. The challenging problems in this book aren't meant to discourage you; they're meant to show you how to solve and master them.

How This Book Is Organized

The first part of this book gives you questions covering math, reading, and writing. All the answers and explanations are in the second part of the book.

The math subtest covers the following topics:

» **Number and quantity:** These questions focus on your understanding of order among integers, the representation of a number in more than one way, place value, whole number properties, equivalent computational procedures, ratios, proportions, and percentages.

» **Algebra and functions:** These questions assess your ability to handle equations and inequalities, recognize various ways to solve a problem, determine the relationship between verbal and symbolic expressions, and interpret graphs. In this section, you also encounter questions that test your knowledge of basic function definitions and the relationship between the domain and range of any given function.

» **Geometry:** These questions assess your the understanding and application of the characteristics and properties of geometric shapes, the Pythagorean theorem, transformations, and the use of symmetry to analyze mathematical situations. (Knowledge of basic U.S. and metric systems of measurement is assumed.)

» **Statistics and probability:** These questions assess your ability to read and interpret the visual display of quantitative information; understand the correspondence between data and graph; make inferences from a given data display; determine mean, median, and mode; and assign probability to an outcome.

The reading questions in this book cover the following topics:

» **Key ideas and details:** These questions require you to read text closely, make logical inferences, connect specific details, address author differences, and determine uncertain matters.

» **Craft, structure, and language skills:** These questions require you to interpret words and phrases, recognize the tone of word choices, analyze text structure, assess points of view, and apply language knowledge to determine fact or opinion, determine word meanings, and understand a range of words and their nuances.

» **Integration of knowledge and ideas:** These questions require you to analyze diverse media content, evaluate arguments in texts, and analyze how two or more texts address similar themes.

On the writing subtest, you find these types of questions:

» **Text types, purposes, and production:** These questions require you to edit and revise text passages.

» **Language skills:** These questions require you to demonstrate command of English grammar, usage, capitalization, and punctuation.

» **Research skills:** These questions assess your understanding of doing research and citing sources.

As part of the writing subtest, you'll also be required to demonstrate knowledge and research skills by writing two essays based on information presented. One is an argumentative essay; the other is an explanation of a topic.

Beyond the Book

Your purchase of this book gives you so much more than a thousand (and one) problems to work on to improve your skills with the Praxis Core. It also comes with a free, one-year subscription to hundreds of practice questions online. Not only can you access this digital content anytime you want, on whichever device is available to you, but you can also track your progress and view personalized reports that show which concepts you need to study the most.

What you'll find online

The online practice that comes free with this book offers you the same questions and answers that are available here. Of course, the real beauty of the online problems is your ability to customize your practice. In other words, you get to choose the types of problems and the number of problems you want to tackle. The online program tracks how many questions you answer correctly or incorrectly so that you can get an immediate sense of which topics require more of your attention.

This product also comes with an online Cheat Sheet that helps you increase your odds of performing well on the Praxis Core. To get the Cheat Sheet, simply go to www.dummies.com and type "1,001 Praxis Core Practice Questions For Dummies Cheat Sheet" in the Search box. (No access code required. You can benefit from this info even before you register.)

How to register

To gain access to practice online, all you have to do is register. Just follow these simple steps:

1. **Find your PIN access code:**

   - **Print-book users:** If you purchased a print copy of this book, look at the inside of the front cover of your book to find your access code.

   - **E-book users:** If you purchased this book as an e-book, you can get your access code by registering your e-book at www.dummies.com/go/getaccess. Once on this website, find your book and click it, and then answer the security questions to verify your purchase. You'll receive an email with your access code.

2. Go to Dummies.com and click *Activate Now.*

3. Find your product (*1,001 Praxis Core Practice Questions For Dummies*) and then follow the on-screen prompts to activate your PIN.

Now you're ready to go! You can come back to the program as often as you want — simply log in with the username and password you created during your initial login. No need to enter the access code a second time.

TIP

For Technical Support, please visit http://wiley.custhelp.com or call Wiley at 1-800-762-2974 (U.S.) or +1-317-572-3994 (international).

Where to Go for Additional Help

The solutions to the practice problems in this book are meant to walk you through how to get the right answers; they're not meant to teach the material. If certain concepts are unfamiliar to you, you can find help at www.dummies.com. Just type "1,001 Praxis Core" into the Search box to turn up a wealth of Praxis-related information.

If you need more detailed instruction, check out *Praxis Core For Dummies*, also by Carla Kirkland and Chan Cleveland.

1 The Questions

Chapter 1

Math

The math test of the Praxis Core exam includes 56 questions in four major areas of math. This part of the book explores each of those areas and the general math topics that are covered on the test. In this chapter, you can gain further understanding of the skills you need and get perspective on an array of questions and approaches to various math topics.

The Problems You'll Work On

Math questions may be multiple choice, fill-in, or select all that apply. When working through the questions in this chapter, be prepared to answer questions on these topics:

» **Number and quantity,** including topics such as basic operations, number form conversions, order of operations, number order, sequences, word problems, and measurement

» **Algebra,** which includes combining like terms, using given variable values, solving equations and inequalities, and solving algebraic word problems

» **Geometry,** which covers basic geometric building blocks, angles, polygons and circles, three-dimensional figures, and the coordinate plane

» **Statistics and probability,** involving representations of data, central tendencies, probability calculations, and scientific notation

What to Watch Out For

Various types of mistakes can occur when you're working math problems. Be on the lookout for common errors such as these:

» Overlooking part of a rule or confusing one rule with another

» Misusing the four-function online calculator

» Confusing one mathematical term with another

» Using the incorrect expression to represent what's described

» Assuming all geometric figures are drawn to scale

» Stopping before answering the final question in a multi-step problem

Number and Quantity

1. What is the value of the following sum?

   $-3 + 14 - (-7)$

   (A) 24
   (B) −10
   (C) 4
   (D) −24
   (E) 18

2. What is the sum of −5, −10, 4, and −7?
   (A) −18
   (B) −26
   (C) 18
   (D) −4
   (E) 26

3. Which of the following is the value of this product?

   $(5)(-1)(3)(-2)(1)(-3)(-1)$

   (A) 45
   (B) −90
   (C) −45
   (D) 90
   (E) 30

4. What is the value of $(-1)^{379}$?
   (A) 379
   (B) 1
   (C) −379
   (D) −1
   (E) 378

5. Which of the following is a factor of 63?
   (A) 31
   (B) 21
   (C) 13
   (D) 16
   (E) 6

6. Which of the following is NOT a factor of 42?
   (A) 7
   (B) 6
   (C) 14
   (D) 21
   (E) 18

7. All of the following are multiples of 53 EXCEPT
   (A) 106
   (B) 265
   (C) 370
   (D) 159
   (E) 318

8. Ninety is NOT a multiple of which of the following?
   (A) 30
   (B) 5
   (C) 15
   (D) 23
   (E) 3

9. What number is the greatest common factor of 28 and 72?
   (A) 4
   (B) 1
   (C) 7
   (D) 2
   (E) 14

10. Which of the following is NOT a common factor of 84 and 144?
   (A) 12
   (B) 6
   (C) 1
   (D) 24
   (E) 21

11. What is the least common multiple of 18 and 24?

(A) 48

(B) 72

(C) 144

(D) 432

(E) 6

12. Twenty-four is the least common multiple of 8 and which of the following numbers?

(A) 12

(B) 36

(C) 4

(D) 16

(E) 2

13. What is the cube of 5?

(A) 25

(B) 15

(C) 625

(D) 125

(E) 50

14. Which of the following numbers to the 4th power is 81?

(A) 27

(B) 3

(C) 9

(D) 36

(E) 13

15. What is the square root of 576?

(A) 34

(B) 56

(C) 24

(D) 44

(E) 26

16. If the cube root of 64 is multiplied by the greatest common factor of 20 and 45, what is the result?

(A) 100

(B) 20

(C) 80

(D) 60

(E) 40

17. What is half the square of the least common multiple of 14 and 21?

(A) 882

(B) 98

(C) 1,764

(D) 220.5

(E) 196

18. Which of the following is the value of this expression?

$$\left(\left(2\right)^{3}\right)^{2}$$

(A) 8

(B) 16

(C) 32

(D) 72

(E) 64

19. What is the greatest common factor of the square of 6 and the least common multiple of 8 and 9?

(A) 72

(B) 6

(C) 24

(D) 36

(E) 18

20. Which of the following is a counterexample to this statement?

With the exception of 1, the common factors of 24 and 120 are even.

(A) 3

(B) 12

(C) 10

(D) 9

(E) 6

21. Which of the following is the simplified form of $\frac{12}{16}$?

(A) $\frac{4}{3}$

(B) $\frac{3}{4}$

(C) $\frac{6}{8}$

(D) $\frac{12}{16}$

(E) $\frac{2}{3}$

22. What is $\frac{20}{70}$ in simplest form?

(A) $\frac{4}{5}$

(B) $\frac{27}{77}$

(C) $\frac{2}{7}$

(D) $\frac{3}{8}$

(E) $\frac{4}{14}$

23. The fraction $\frac{4}{7}$ is the simplified form of which of the following fractions?

(A) $\frac{5}{30}$

(B) $\frac{16}{26}$

(C) $\frac{28}{49}$

(D) $\frac{6}{15}$

(E) $\frac{8}{15}$

24. If $\frac{55}{99}$ of the songs played on a radio station in a year were rock and roll songs, which of the following also represents the portion of rock and roll songs that were played on the station?

(A) $\frac{15}{19}$

(B) $\frac{50}{91}$

(C) $\frac{18}{35}$

(D) $\frac{8}{13}$

(E) $\frac{5}{9}$

25. Which of the following is $\frac{324}{918}$ in simplest form?

(A) $\frac{5}{18}$

(B) $\frac{6}{17}$

(C) $\frac{7}{16}$

(D) $\frac{8}{15}$

(E) $\frac{5}{13}$

26. Is $\frac{84}{96}$ equal to $\frac{14}{16}$?

(A) Yes

(B) No

27. Which of the following fractions is equal to $8\frac{2}{5}$?

(A) $\frac{17}{2}$

(B) $\frac{42}{13}$

(C) $\frac{42}{5}$

(D) $\frac{48}{5}$

(E) $\frac{5}{42}$

28. What is $9\frac{3}{8}$ in simplified fraction form? Write your answer.

29. What fraction is the simplified form of $-4\frac{3}{10}$?

(A) $-\frac{37}{10}$

(B) $-\frac{41}{10}$

(C) $-\frac{21}{5}$

(D) $-\frac{47}{10}$

(E) $-\frac{43}{10}$

30. Which of the following mixed numbers is equal to $\frac{81}{8}$?

(A) $9\frac{1}{8}$

(B) $1\frac{1}{8}$

(C) $10\frac{1}{4}$

(D) $10\frac{1}{8}$

(E) $11\frac{1}{4}$

31. Which of the following is equal to $\frac{37}{2}$?

(A) $16\frac{1}{2}$

(B) $15\frac{2}{5}$

(C) $15\frac{1}{2}$

(D) $16\frac{2}{7}$

(E) $18\frac{1}{2}$

32. The fraction $\frac{77}{11}$ is equal to which of the following?

(A) $7\frac{1}{7}$

(B) $6\frac{6}{7}$

(C) 7

(D) $7\frac{7}{11}$

(E) $8\frac{1}{7}$

33. Which of the following is the sum of $\frac{2}{5}$ and $3\frac{1}{5}$?

(A) $3\frac{2}{5}$

(B) $4\frac{1}{5}$

(C) 4

(D) $3\frac{3}{10}$

(E) $3\frac{3}{5}$

34. Which of the following equals the value of this expression?

$$5\frac{2}{3} - 7\frac{4}{5}$$

(A) $1\frac{7}{15}$

(B) $-2\frac{2}{15}$

(C) $2\frac{1}{15}$

(D) -2

(E) $-1\frac{7}{15}$

35. What is the product of $2\frac{5}{8}$ and $-1\frac{5}{7}$?

(A) $-4\frac{5}{9}$

(B) $-2\frac{5}{8}$

(C) $-3\frac{2}{7}$

(D) $-4\frac{1}{2}$

(E) $-2\frac{3}{7}$

36. What is the quotient?

$$\frac{4}{9} \div 11\frac{4}{5}$$

(A) $\frac{20}{531}$

(B) $\frac{3}{201}$

(C) $\frac{37}{58}$

(D) $\frac{531}{20}$

(E) $\frac{21}{25}$

37. What is the value of $-9\frac{7}{8}$ divided by $-10\frac{5}{12}$?

38. Which of the following is $\frac{4}{5}$ in decimal form?

(A) 0.8

(B) 0.4

(C) 0.5

(D) 0.1

(E) 0.2

39. Which of the following is equal to $\frac{1}{8}$?

(A) 0.2

(B) 0.8

(C) 0.7

(D) 0.125

(E) 0.15

40. Which of the following is 0.34 expressed as a fraction in simplest form?

(A) $\frac{17}{50}$

(B) $\frac{17}{100}$

(C) $\frac{34}{100}$

(D) $\frac{1}{34}$

(E) $\frac{34}{1}$

41. The number 0.75 can be expressed as which percent?

(A) 0.075%

(B) 750%

(C) 0.75%

(D) 0.0075%

(E) 75%

42. The fraction $\frac{1}{4}$ can be represented as what percent?

(A) 2.5%

(B) 0.25%

(C) 250%

(D) 25%

(E) 0.025%

43. Which of the following is 42% in simplest fraction form?

(A) $\frac{21}{100}$

(B) $\frac{42}{100}$

(C) $\frac{21}{50}$

(D) $\frac{100}{42}$

(E) $\frac{2}{5}$

44. What is 34.848% in decimal form?

(A) 34.848

(B) 3,484.8

(C) 3.4848

(D) 348.48

(E) 0.34848

45. Which of the following is 496.032% expressed as a decimal number?

(A) 496032.0

(B) 49.6032

(C) 49,603.2

(D) 496.032

(E) 4.96032

46. What is $-2\frac{1}{8}$ in decimal form?

(A) −2.125

(B) −2.25

(C) −2.1

(D) −2.8

(E) −2.012

47. Which of the following is $8\frac{2}{5}$ expressed as a percent?

(A) 8.2%

(B) 8.4%

(C) 0.08%

(D) 80.4%

(E) 840%

48. What is the sum of $\frac{1}{12}$ and 3.178, rounded to the nearest thousandth?

(A) 3.3

(B) 3.26

(C) 3.262

(D) 3.026

(E) 3.261

49. Which of the following is the sum of this expression, rounded to the nearest tenth?

$46.893\% + 15.0723$

(A) 15.54123

(B) 15.6

(C) 4,704.4

(D) 15.5

(E) 4,704.3

50. Which of the following is the product of $\frac{3}{20}$ and -14.4?

(A) 2.16

(B) -2

(C) -2.16

(D) 2

(E) -2.07

51. Which of these numbers is greater?

(A) $\frac{3}{4}$

(B) 0.76

52. Which of these numbers has the greatest value?

$\frac{25}{8}$ $3\frac{1}{9}$ 3.1   3.11 $\frac{16}{5}$

(A) $\frac{25}{8}$

(B) $3\frac{1}{9}$

(C) 3.1

(D) 3.11

(E) $\frac{16}{5}$

53. Which of these numbers has the lowest absolute value?

$-\frac{3}{8}$ $\frac{23}{50}$ -0.47 0.471 $\frac{5}{12}$

(A) $-\frac{3}{8}$

(B) $\frac{23}{50}$

(C) -0.47

(D) 0.471

(E) $\frac{5}{12}$

54. Which of the following is the correct order of these numbers from least to greatest?

$\frac{27}{20}$ $1\frac{9}{20}$ 134%   1.36 $1\frac{7}{10}$

(A) $1\frac{7}{10}$, 1.36, 134%, 1.36, $1\frac{7}{10}$

(B) $\frac{27}{20}$, $1\frac{9}{20}$, 1.36, 134%, $1\frac{7}{10}$

(C) 134%, $\frac{27}{20}$, 1.36, $1\frac{9}{20}$, $1\frac{7}{10}$

(D) $\frac{27}{20}$, $1\frac{9}{20}$, 134%, 1.36, $1\frac{7}{10}$

(E) $1\frac{7}{10}$, $1\frac{9}{20}$, 1.36, $\frac{27}{20}$, 134%

55. Which of the following is the correct order of these numbers from greatest to least?

4.1 $\frac{411}{100}$ $\frac{105}{25}$ $4\frac{3}{20}$ 409%

(A) 409%, 4.1, $\frac{411}{100}$, $4\frac{3}{20}$, $\frac{105}{25}$

(B) $\frac{105}{25}$, $4\frac{3}{20}$, 4.1, $\frac{411}{100}$, 409%

(C) 409%, 4.1, $4\frac{3}{20}$, $\frac{411}{100}$, $\frac{105}{25}$

(D) $\frac{105}{25}$, 409%, $4\frac{3}{20}$, $\frac{411}{100}$, 4.1

(E) $\frac{105}{25}$, $4\frac{3}{20}$, $\frac{411}{100}$, 4.1, 409%

56. Which of the following numbers has a greater magnitude than $-12\frac{5}{8}$?

(A) 1,250%

(B) $-12\frac{11}{16}$

(C) $12\frac{13}{24}$

(D) -12.51

(E) $\frac{23}{2}$

57. What is the correct order of absolute value for these numbers, from greatest to least?

$$5.14 \qquad -5\frac{4}{25} \qquad -\frac{128}{25}$$

(A) $-5\frac{4}{25}, 5.14, -\frac{128}{25}$

(B) $-\frac{128}{25}, 5.14, -5\frac{4}{25}$

(C) $-5\frac{4}{25}, -\frac{128}{25}, 5.14$

(D) $5.14, -\frac{128}{25}, -5\frac{4}{25}$

(E) $-\frac{128}{25}, -5\frac{4}{25}, 5.14$

58. The distance from one labeled coordinate to the next on the number line is the same in every case. What is the value of y?

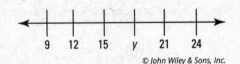

© John Wiley & Sons, Inc.

(A) 17.5

(B) 18.5

(C) 17

(D) 16

(E) 18

59. For the number line, if D is halfway between C and E, what is the coordinate of D?

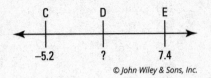

© John Wiley & Sons, Inc.

(A) 2.2

(B) 2.4

(C) 1.2

(D) 1.6

(E) 1.1

60. For this number line, the distance from P to Q is half the distance from Q to R, and that distance is half the distance from R to S. The coordinate of P is 4, and the coordinate of R is 10. What is the coordinate of S?

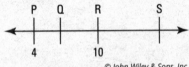

© John Wiley & Sons, Inc.

(A) 18

(B) 16

(C) 20

(D) 24

(E) 14

61. A number line contains the points $A, B, C,$ and D. C is half the distance from B to D, and B is half the distance from A to C. Which of the following statements is true?

(A) The distance from A to B is greater than the distance from C to D.

(B) The distance from A to B is less than the distance from C to D.

(C) The distance from B to D is greater than the distance from A to C.

(D) The distance from B to D is equal to the distance from A to B.

(E) The distance from A to B is equal to the distance from C to D.

62. For this number line, T is halfway between M and W. What is the coordinate of T?

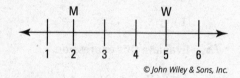

© John Wiley & Sons, Inc.

(A) 3.5

(B) 3

(C) 4

(D) 3.25

(E) 3.75

63. What is the seventh term of this sequence?

5, 9, 13, 17, . . .

(A) 21

(B) 20

(C) 29

(D) 24

(E) 33

64. What term belongs in the blank in this sequence?

14, 17, ___, 23, . . .

(A) 18

(B) 20

(C) 26

(D) 22

(E) 29

65. What is the first term in this sequence?

___, 6, 12, 24, . . .

(A) 5

(B) 2

(C) 4

(D) 3

(E) 1

66. The first term of a geometric sequence is 1. The fifth term is 81. How many times greater is each term, after the first term, than the preceding term?

(A) 2

(B) 9

(C) 4

(D) 18

(E) 3

67. Is this sequence arithmetic or geometric?

10, 15, 20, 25, 30, . . .

(A) Arithmetic

(B) Geometric

68. What is the value of this expression?

$2 + 3 \times 4 + 1$

(A) 25

(B) 20

(C) 21

(D) 15

(E) 24

69. Which of the following is the first operation that should be performed in evaluating the expression?

$$7 - 2(3 + 5 \times 2)^2$$

(A) Multiplying 5 by 2

(B) Adding 3 and 5

(C) Subtracting 2 from 7

(D) Squaring 2

(E) Multiplying 2 by 3

70. Which of the following is the value of this expression?

$$(3 \times 8 + 2^2 - 4 \times 6) \times (-1) + 1$$

(A) 11

(B) −143

(C) 5

(D) 0

(E) −3

71. What is the value of this expression?

$$-5 \times 4 \div 2 + 1 + (-3) - 24 \div 4 \times 3$$

(A) −14

(B) 12

(C) −30

(D) 1

(E) −3

72. What is the value of this expression?

$$\frac{3 \times 2 - 1 + 3}{9 - (6 \times 2 - 5)}$$

(A) 2

(B) 4

(C) $\frac{3}{4}$

(D) 8

(E) $\frac{8}{27}$

73. What number results from a correct evaluation of this expression?

$$4\left(8 - (2 \times 4 - 7)^3 - 5\right)^2 + 5$$

(A) 16

(B) 13

(C) 3

(D) 26

(E) 21

74. What is the value of this expression?

$$15 \div 3 + 2 \times 5$$

(A) 15

(B) $\frac{3}{5}$

(C) 12.5

(D) $\frac{15}{13}$

(E) 3

75. Evaluate this expression.

$$\frac{2}{3} + \frac{3}{4}(10 \times 3 + 10)$$

(A) $\frac{170}{3}$

(B) $\frac{9}{2}$

(C) $30\frac{2}{3}$

(D) $\frac{70}{12}$

(E) $5\frac{1}{2}$

76. Evaluate this expression.

$$\frac{1}{2} + \frac{5}{8} \times \frac{2}{5}$$

(A) $\frac{9}{20}$

(B) $\frac{3}{4}$

(C) $\frac{2}{3}$

(D) $\frac{6}{25}$

(E) $\frac{1}{3}$

77. What is the value of this expression?

$$3 + 4 - 5 \times 6 \div 3 - 2 + 4 \div 2 - 7$$

(A) −5

(B) 4

(C) −12

(D) −10

(E) 7

78. At a school, 110 of the students are boys and 122 of the students are girls. What percent, rounded to the nearest hundredth, of the students are girls?

(A) 92.423%

(B) 52.59%

(C) 90.16%

(D) 190.16%

(E) 52.586%

79. The number of records in Joe's record collection went from 400 to 408. By what percent did Joe's record collection increase?

(A) 16%

(B) 8%

(C) 5%

(D) 4%

(E) 2%

80. The number of cookies in a box went from 40 to 30. Which of the following accurately describes the change in the number of cookies in the box?

(A) 1.33% increase

(B) 0.25% increase

(C) 25% decrease

(D) 0.25% decrease

(E) 2.5% increase

81. If $\frac{2}{5}$ of the flowers in a garden are daisies, what percent of the flowers in the garden are daisies?

(A) 40%

(B) 4%

(C) 2%

(D) 20%

(E) 50%

82. At a police department, 14% of the officers are rookies. What is the ratio, in simplest form, of officers who are rookies to the total number of officers?

(A) $\frac{7}{50}$

(B) $\frac{50}{7}$

(C) $\frac{43}{50}$

(D) $\frac{50}{43}$

(E) $\frac{1}{6}$

83. Sebastian ran 42 miles in a week. The next week, he ran 48 miles. Which of the following accurately represents the ratio of the number of miles Sebastian ran the first week to the number of miles he ran the second week?

(A) $\frac{7}{8}$

(B) $\frac{8}{7}$

(C) $\frac{1}{6}$

(D) $\frac{1}{8}$

(E) $\frac{3}{4}$

84. Two U.S. states are not on the country's mainland. The U.S. has a total of 50 states. What is the ratio of U.S. states NOT on its mainland to U.S. states that are on the country's mainland?

(A) $\frac{1}{25}$

(B) $\frac{1}{50}$

(C) $\frac{2}{25}$

(D) $\frac{1}{24}$

(E) $\frac{1}{48}$

85. Luca is 12 years old, and Dave is 66 years old. What is the ratio of Dave's age to Luca's age, in simplest form?

(A) $\frac{66}{12}$

(B) $\frac{11}{2}$

(C) $\frac{12}{66}$

(D) $\frac{2}{11}$

(E) $\frac{54}{1}$

86. In a game of golf, Johnny scored 78. The next day, Johnny played another game of golf and scored 72. What is the ratio of Johnny's golf score on the first day to his score on the second day, in simplest form?

(A) $\frac{13}{12}$

(B) $\frac{12}{13}$

(C) $\frac{78}{72}$

(D) $\frac{72}{78}$

(E) $\frac{13}{78}$

87. Trace's video collection includes 132 comedy videos and 144 drama videos. What is the ratio of comedy videos to drama videos in the collection?

(A) $\frac{12}{11}$

(B) $\frac{132}{144}$

(C) $\frac{11}{12}$

(D) $\frac{144}{132}$

(E) $\frac{1}{11}$

88. In a classroom, 8 of the 30 students are football players. In another classroom, 3 of the 10 students are football players. What is the sum of the ratios of football players to students who do not play football for the two classrooms?

(A) $\frac{8}{30}$

(B) $\frac{4}{15}$

(C) $\frac{3}{10}$

(D) $\frac{13}{30}$

(E) $\frac{61}{77}$

89. The ratio of cashews to other nuts in Jar 1 is $\frac{1}{5}$. The ratio of cashews to other nuts in Jar 2 is $\frac{1}{3}$. How much greater is the ratio of cashews to other nuts in Jar 2 than the ratio of cashews to other nuts in Jar 1?

(A) $\frac{5}{15}$

(B) $\frac{2}{15}$

(C) $\frac{3}{15}$

(D) $\frac{1}{5}$

(E) $\frac{1}{3}$

90. In a town with a population of 2,400, 41% of the residents drive trucks. How many of the residents drive trucks?

(A) 1,124
(B) 984
(C) 1,492
(D) 432
(E) 587

91. On a track team, 11 of the 22 members are honor roll students. What percent of the members of the track team are honor roll students?

(A) 200%
(B) 50%
(C) 25%
(D) 75%
(E) 2%

92. What number results from tripling the sum of 4 and 7?

(A) 11
(B) 3
(C) 22
(D) 19
(E) 33

93. If 17 is decreased by 8 and the difference is multiplied by 2 more than itself, what is the result?

(A) 72
(B) 11
(C) 20
(D) 99
(E) 20

94. A group of 400 people went camping for a weekend. On Saturday, each camper engaged in one of the activities listed in the table. The table shows the percentages of campers who engaged in each activity. According to the table, which of the following statements is true?

ACTIVITY	PERCENT
Canoeing	34%
Hiking	21%
Rock Climbing	38%
Birdwatching	17%

(A) Sixty-eight campers went canoeing.
(B) Twice as many campers went bird-watching as the number that went canoeing.
(C) Eighty-two campers went hiking.
(D) Sixteen more campers went rock climbing than canoeing.
(E) Twenty-one more campers went rock climbing than birdwatching.

95. The table shows the percentages of political party affiliation at a college for eccentric students. The number of students attending the college is 2,850. How many more students are in a political party NOT listed in the table than students in a political party that is listed in the table?

POLITICAL PARTY MEMBERSHIP	PERCENT
People's Party of Utopia	22%
Anarchist Party of Not Voting	16%
Party of Free Market Communism	8%
Other	54%

(A) 8
(B) 1,539
(C) 627
(D) 228
(E) 1,311

96. An island had a population of 824 pen-guins. One-fourth of the island's penguin population moved to another island. The remaining population increased by $\frac{1}{2}$ and has remained the same since then. How many penguins are now on the island?

(A) 927

(B) 824

(C) 618

(D) 206

(E) 309

97. A bakery had 42 rolls on a shelf. A cus-tomer bought $\frac{4}{7}$ of the rolls on the shelf. How many rolls did the customer buy?

(A) 42

(B) 7

(C) 16

(D) 24

(E) 32

98. Karen read $\frac{5}{9}$ of the pages in a book the day she bought it. The next day, she read another $\frac{1}{5}$ of the book. What portion of the book had Karen read by the end of the day after she bought it?

(A) $\frac{25}{45}$

(B) $\frac{34}{45}$

(C) $\frac{9}{45}$

(D) $\frac{5}{45}$

(E) $\frac{5}{9}$

99. A soccer team has a uniform design with 5 stripes on the shirt. Each stripe has 4 stars. The team has 34 members. If every member of the team stands in the same room, how many uniform stars are in the room?

(A) 43

(B) 680

(C) 54

(D) 720

(E) 870

100. In an organization, $\frac{2}{9}$ of the members are from Texas. Three-sevenths of those members are women. Of those women, $\frac{5}{8}$ ride a bus to work. What portion of the members of the organization are women from Texas who ride a bus to work?

(A) $\frac{5}{54}$

(B) $\frac{191}{504}$

(C) $\frac{13}{54}$

(D) $\frac{12}{95}$

(E) $\frac{5}{84}$

101. The number of customers in a grocery store at 4:15 p.m. was 37. An hour later, the number of customers was 5 times as many. At the decoration store across the street, the number of customers in the store at 4:15 p.m. on the same day was 12. An hour later, the number of customers in the decoration store was $3\frac{1}{2}$ times as many. At 5:15 p.m. on that day, what was the sum of the number of customers in the grocery store and the decoration store?

(A) 185

(B) 42

(C) 188

(D) 240

(E) 227

102. Edward opened a savings account and put $500 in it. The interest on the account is 12% per year. If no money is deposited in or taken out of the account, how much money will Edward have in the account exactly a year after he put in $500?

(A) $560

(B) $60

(C) $6,000

(D) $440

(E) $620

103. Virgie buys a hat for $56. If the tax on the hat is 8%, what is the total price of the hat?

(A) $4.48

(B) $51.52

(C) $60.48

(D) $62.58

(E) $58.72

104. A governor wants $\frac{3}{11}$ of a state construction project finished by the end of the month. The construction supervisor wants $\frac{9}{33}$ of the project finished by the end of the month. Do the governor and the construction supervisor want the same portion of the project finished by the end of the month?

(A) Yes

(B) No

105. How many meters are in 14.8 centimeters?

(A) 14

(B) 1.4

(C) 0.014

(D) 140

(E) 0.148

106. How many deciliters are in 0.571 hectoliters?

(A) 5.71

(B) 571

(C) 57.1

(D) 5,710

(E) 0.571

107. A rock has a mass of 4.9327 deka-grams. What is the mass of the rock in centigrams?

(A) 4,932.7

(B) 49.327

(C) 0.49327

(D) 0.049327

(E) 493.27

108. Alexia drove 54 kilometers on the Natchez Trace. How many millimeters did she drive?

(A) 540

(B) 5,400

(C) 0.000054

(D) 0.00054

(E) 54,000,000

109. The amount of rainwater in a bucket is 0.38 liters. How many kiloliters of rain water are in the bucket?

(A) 380

(B) 0.00038

(C) 0.038

(D) 3,800

(E) 3.8

110. How many inches are in 4 feet?

(A) $\frac{1}{3}$

(B) 3

(C) 8

(D) 48

(E) 12

111. How many feet are in 4 inches?

(A) $\frac{1}{3}$

(B) 3

(C) 8

(D) 48

(E) 12

112. How many cups are in 4.5 gallons?

(A) 0.28125

(B) 3.56

(C) 20.5

(D) 72

(E) 11.5

113. How many gallons are in 4.5 cups?

(A) 0.28125

(B) 3.56

(C) 20.5

(D) 72

(E) 11.5

114. Simon walked 3 kilometers down a trail. He then got on another trail and walked 456 meters. What is the total distance Simon walked, in kilometers?

(A) 3.456

(B) 3,456

(C) 459

(D) 34.56

(E) 345.6

115. Dr. Richard has 5.382 kiloliters of a chemical in a drum. He pours out 42.79 hectoliters of the chemical. How much of the chemical remains in the drum?

(A) 48.172 kL

(B) 1.103 kL

(C) 4.8172 kL

(D) 4.9541 kL

(E) 374.08 kL

116. A baby frog had a mass of 4.07 decigrams. It now has an extra 0.08 kilograms of mass. Which of the following correctly represents the mass of the frog?

(A) 4.15 decigrams

(B) 804.07 decigrams

(C) 399 decigrams

(D) 0.080407 decigrams

(E) 1,207 decigrams

117. The height of a tower is 15 feet plus another 7 yards. Which of the following is a true representation of the height of the tower?

(A) 22 feet

(B) 66 feet

(C) 36 feet

(D) 52 feet

(E) 24 feet

118. A snail moved 2,088 inches north and then turned around and moved 72 yards south. Which of the following correctly represents the position of the snail in relation to its starting point?

(A) 42 feet north

(B) 58 feet north

(C) 42 feet south

(D) 58 feet south

(E) 2,016 feet north

119. Jake has 3.5 gallons of water in a jug for his football team. Each player has a 2-pint bottle. How many 2-pint bottles can be filled by the water in the jug?

(A) 28

(B) 56

(C) 14

(D) 7

(E) 112

120. Stefan ran 15 miles at a constant speed in 3 hours. What was his speed?

(A) 45 miles per hour

(B) 15 miles per hour

(C) 5 miles per hour

(D) 3 miles per hour

(E) $\frac{1}{5}$ mile per hour

121. Two trains start at the same place and move in opposite directions. One train moves at a constant speed of 56 kilometers per hour, and the other train moves at a constant speed of 72 kilometers per hour. How many hours will it take for the trains to be 729.6 kilometers apart?

(A) 10.13

(B) 13

(C) 601.6

(D) 5.7

(E) 0.175

122. What is 41 yards per minute expressed in inches per second?

(A) 24.6 inches per second

(B) 1,476 inches per second

(C) 123 inches per second

(D) 2.05 inches per second

(E) 8.2 inches per second

123. Herschel ran 40 yards in 4.2 seconds. What was his average speed in feet per minute, rounded to the nearest hundredth?

(A) 28.57 feet per minute

(B) 571.43 feet per minute

(C) 8.40 feet per minute

(D) 9.52 feet per minute

(E) 1,714.29 feet per minute

Algebra

124. What is the sum of $12xy$ and $14xy$?

(A) $26x^2y^2$

(B) $26xy$

(C) $2xy$

(D) 26

(E) $\frac{26x}{y}$

125. Which of the following is the product of $w-2$ and $w+5$?

(A) w^2-10

(B) $w^2-3w+10$

(C) $w+3$

(D) w^2-7

(E) $w^2+3w-10$

126. If a represents 2 pounds and b represents 4 ounces, which of the following represents 8 pounds and 12 ounces?

(A) $4a+3b$

(B) $3a+4b$

(C) $2a+4b$

(D) $a+b$

(E) $8a+12b$

127. Which of the following is the sum of $3p^3q^5r$ and $-7p^3q^5r$?

(A) $4p^3q^5r$

(B) $-4p^6q^{10}r^2$

(C) -4

(D) $-4p^3q^5r$

(E) $4p^6q^{10}r^2$

128. Which of the following is equal to $j\left(\left(wx^2y\right)^3\right)^5$?

(A) $j^5w^3x^3y^3$

(B) $jw^{15}x^{30}y^{15}$

(C) $j^3w^{15}x^{30}y^{15}$

(D) $jw^{25}x^{10}y^5$

(E) $5jw^{15}x^{30}y^{15}$

129. All of the following are like terms to $-17x^4y^2$ EXCEPT

(A) $8x^4y^2$

(B) x^4y^2

(C) $-17x^2y^2$

(D) $17x^4y^2$

(E) $\frac{4}{17}x^4y^2$

130. What is the product of $\frac{2}{5}ab$ and $\frac{3}{7}ab$?

(A) $\frac{29}{35}a^2b^2$

(B) $\frac{5}{12}a^2b^2$

(C) $\frac{6}{35}ab$

(D) $\frac{6}{35}a^2b^2$

(E) $\frac{5}{35}ab$

131. Which of the following is equal to this expression?

$$\left(9f^4g^4h^7\right)\left(8f^5g^5\right)$$

(A) $72f^9g^9h^7$

(B) $72f^5g^5h^7$

(C) $17f^9g^9h^7$

(D) $17f^9g^9h^7$

(E) $f^4g^4h^7$

132. If j, k, and m are consecutive integers, listed in order from least to greatest, what is one-third of their sum?

(A) $\frac{j}{2}$

(B) k

(C) $\frac{j}{m}$

(D) $\frac{k}{3}$

(E) $3j$

133. Bill's age is represented by xy, and Michael's age is represented by xyz. Which of the following represents the product of Bill and Michael's ages?

(A) $2xyz$

(B) $2x^2y^2z$

(C) $4xyz$

(D) x^2y^2z

(E) y

134. Which of the following binomials can be multiplied by $p-7$ to get a product of $pq+4p-7q-28$?

(A) $q+4$

(B) $q-4$

(C) $pq-4$

(D) $q-4p$

(E) $4p+q$

135. Which of the following is equal to the product of $4g^3h^2j^6$ and $-11g^5h^2j^8$?

(A) $-11\left(2g^4h^3j^{14}g^4h\right)$

(B) $-22\left(2g^4h^3j^{14}g^4h\right)$

(C) $-44g^4h^3j^{13}g^4h$

(D) $-11\left(4g^4h^2j^{14}g^4h\right)$

(E) $-4\left(11g^4h^3j^{14}g^4h^2\right)$

136. If the ratio $p:q$ is equal to the ratio $q:r$, which of the following is true?

(A) $pr=q$

(B) $\sqrt{q}=pr$

(C) $p^2=qr$

(D) $p=r$

(E) $\sqrt{pr}=\pm q$

137. Which of the following terms is equal to this expression?

$5m-m+m-m-2m$

(A) $9m$

(B) $6m$

(C) $4m$

(D) $-9m$

(E) $2m$

138. If j is an even number and k is an odd number, which of the following represents an odd number?

(A) $3jk - 7$

(B) $j - 2k$

(C) $4j + 8k$

(D) $3j - 2k$

(E) $j + 3k - k$

139. Which of the following is the complete factorization of $c^2 + 7c + 12$?

(A) $(c + 12)(c - 5)$

(B) $(c + 4)(c + 3)$

(C) $(c + 5)(c + 2)$

(D) $(c - 3)(c - 4)$

(E) $(c + 6)(c + 2)$

140. Which of the following is the full factorization of $50x^3y^2 - 10xy^3 + 40xy$?

(A) $10xy(5x^2y + y^2 + 10)$

(B) $10xy(5x^2y - y^2 + 4)$

(C) $10xy(5x^2 - y^2 + 10)$

(D) $5xy(10x^2y - y^2 + 10)$

(E) $10x(5x^2y - y^2 + 10y)$

141. What is the greatest common factor of $35a^4b^7c^{12}$ and $20a^8b^3c^{10}$?

(A) $7a^4b^3c^{10}$

(B) $5a^4b^7c^{12}$

(C) $10a^4b^3c^{10}$

(D) $5a^4b^3c^{10}$

(E) $10a^8b^8c^{12}$

142. Which of the following is the full factorization of $5h^2 - 45h + 100$?

(A) $(5h - 5)(h - 4)$

(B) $5(h - 5)(h - 4)$

(C) $5(h - 5)(h + 4)$

(D) $(5h + 5)(5h + 4)$

(E) $(5h - 10)(h - 2)$

143. Which of the following is NOT a factor of $18m^8n^{11}p^{15}$?

(A) $2m^7n^{11}p^{15}$

(B) $9m^8n^2p^{14}$

(C) $9m^8n^{14}p^{11}$

(D) $6mnp$

(E) $18m^8n^{11}p^{15}$

144. $4w^4x^7y^3(7wxy^2 - 4w^5x^3y^2)$ is the full factorization of what expression?

145. Which of the following is the full factorization of $q^2 - 4q - 32$?

(A) $(q - 8)(q + 4)$

(B) $(q - 16)(q + 2)$

(C) $(q + 32)(q - 1)$

(D) $(q + 8)(q - 4)$

(E) $(q - 4)(q + 8)$

146. $6xy$ is the greatest common factor of $24x^2y$ and which of the following terms?

(A) $8xy$

(B) $12x$

(C) $24y$

(D) $42xy^2$

(E) $3x^2y$

147. $77a^6b^6 - 55a^5b^2$ is the product of $11a^4b$ and what binomial?

(A) $5a^2b^5 - 7ab$

(B) $7a^2b^4 - 5ab$

(C) $5a^2b^5 - 7ab^2$

(D) $7a^2b^5 + 5ab$

(E) $7a^2b^5 - 5ab$

148. If $12x^7y^8z^9$ is factored out of $48x^8y^9z^{10} + 12x^7y^8z^9$, by which of the following binomials will it be multiplied?

(A) $4xyz + 12$

(B) $4xyz + 1$

(C) $3xyz + 1$

(D) $4xy^2z + 1$

(E) $4xy^2 + 12x^8y^9z^{10}$

149. $3(x-3)(x+8)$ is the full factorization of which of the following trinomials?

(A) $3x^2 + 15x - 72$

(B) $3x^2 + 15x - 24$

(C) $x^2 + 5x - 24$

(D) $x^2 + 15x - 72$

(E) $3x^2 - 5x - 72$

150. Which of the following terms is a factor of $28p^{10}q^7r^{12}$?

Select <u>all</u> that apply.

[A] $14p^7q^8r^{12}$

[B] $2p^{11}q^4r$

[C] $7p^9q^5r$

[D] $28pqrv$

[E] $14p^8q^7r^{11}$

151. The trinomial $y^2 - 16y + 64$ is the square of which of the following binomials?

(A) $y + 8$

(B) $y - 16$

(C) $y + 4$

(D) $y - 8$

(E) $-y + 8$

152. What is the greatest common factor of $27jk^5m^2$ and $54j^{10}k^4m^8$?

(A) $27jk^4m^2$

(B) $9jk^4m^2$

(C) $54jk^4m^2$

(D) $54j^{10}k^5m^8$

(E) $3jkm$

153. Which of the following binomials is a factor of $a^2 + 11a + 28$?

(A) $a + 14$

(B) $a + 2$

(C) $a - 4$

(D) $a + 7$

(E) $a - 2$

154. Which of the following is NOT a factor of $2u^2 - 8u - 42$?

(A) 1

(B) $u - 7$

(C) $u + 3$

(D) $u + 7$

(E) 2

155. Which of the following is the simplified form of this expression?

$19x + 4 - 3x - 8$

(A) $16x - 12$

(B) $16x - 4$

(C) $22x - 4$

(D) $16x + 4$

(E) $22x - 12$

156. Which of the following is the simplified form of the expression $8x^2y - 5xy^2 + 12xy^2 - 3x^2y$?

(A) $5x^2y^2 + 7x^2y$

(B) $3x^2y + 9xy^2$

(C) $5x^2y + 7xy^2$

(D) $5x^2y^2 + 7x^2y^2$

(E) $7x^2y^2 + 5x^2y^2$

157. Which of the following is the simplified form of this rational expression?

$$\frac{4a^7b^5c^8}{20a^3b^2c^5}$$

(A) $\dfrac{5a^7b^5c^8}{a^3b^2c^5}$

(B) $\dfrac{1}{5a^4b^3c^3}$

(C) $\dfrac{5}{a^4b^3c^3}$

(D) $80a^{10}b^7c^{13}$

(E) $\dfrac{a^4b^3c^3}{5}$

158. Which of the following is equal to this rational expression?

$$\frac{x^2+6x-16}{x^2-9x+14}$$

(A) $\dfrac{x+8}{z^2-9x+14}$

(B) $\dfrac{x+8}{x-7}$

(C) $\dfrac{x^2+6x-16}{x-7}$

(D) $\dfrac{x-8}{x+7}$

(E) $x+8$

159. Which of the following is the simplified form of this expression?

$$9pq-7pq$$

(A) $-2pq$

(B) 2

(C) $16pq$

(D) -2

(E) $2pq$

160. Which of the following represents this expression in simplified form?

$$12x^2-3x+4-\left(8x^2+2x-8\right)$$

(A) $4x^2-x-4$

(B) $4x^2-x-8$

(C) $4x^2-5x+12$

(D) $20x^2-5x+12$

(E) $4x^2-x+12$

161. Which of the following is the simplified form of $\dfrac{u^2+13u+40}{u^2+8u+15}$?

(A) $\dfrac{u+3}{u+8}$

(B) $\dfrac{1}{u+3}$

(C) $u+8$

(D) $\dfrac{u+8}{u+3}$

(E) $\dfrac{u^2+13u+40}{u^2+8u+15}$

162. Which of the following is this expression in simplest form?

$$8x-7+2y+9x-5y+2$$

(A) $x-12+4$

(B) $-x-3y-3$

(C) $17x-7y-5$

(D) $17x+3y-5$

(E) $17x-3y-5$

163. Which of the following is the value of this expression?

$$\frac{w-1}{1-w}$$

(A) -1

(B) 1

(C) $w-1$

(D) $-\dfrac{1}{2}$

(E) $\dfrac{1}{1-w}$

164. Which of the following has the same value as $\dfrac{9x^8y^3z^2}{3x^4y^2z^2}$?

(A) $\dfrac{x^8y^3z^2}{3x^4y^2z^2}$

(B) $\dfrac{3}{x^4yz}$

(C) $9x^4y$

(D) $\dfrac{x^4y}{3}$

(E) $3x^4y$

165. Which of the following is the rational expression $\dfrac{p^2+7p+10}{p+5}$ in simplest form?

(A) $p+5$

(B) $\dfrac{1}{p+2}$

(C) $p+2$

(D) $\dfrac{1}{p+5}$

(E) $\dfrac{p^2+7p+10}{p+5}$

166. Which of the following is the simplified form of this rational expression?

$$\frac{8mn}{24n}$$

(A) $3m$

(B) $\dfrac{3}{m}$

(C) $3mn$

(D) $\dfrac{m}{3}$

(E) $3n$

167. Which of the following is the simplified form of this expression?

$$(3x-5y)^2 + 2y - 7(x+4)$$

(A) $9x^2 - 30xy + 2y - 7x - 28$

(B) $9x^2 - 30xy + 25y^2 + 2y - 7x - 28$

(C) $3x^2 - 30xy + 25y^2 + 2y - 7x - 28$

(D) $9x^2 - 30xy + 25y^2 - 7x - 28$

(E) $3x^2 - 30xy + 2y - 7x - 28$

168. Which of the following is this expression in simplest form?

$$\frac{y-5}{y^2 + 2y - 35}$$

(A) $\dfrac{y-5}{y+7}$

(B) $y-5$

(C) $\dfrac{1}{y+7}$

(D) $y+7$

(E) $\dfrac{y+7}{y-5}$

169. Which of the following is the value of the expression $\dfrac{14ab}{2a}$?

(A) $7ab$

(B) $7a$

(C) $\dfrac{1}{7a}$

(D) $7b$

(E) $\dfrac{1}{7b}$

170. What is the value of $a+3$ if $a=2$?

(A) -5

(B) 1

(C) $2a$

(D) -1

(E) 5

171. What is the value of this expression if $x=1$, $y=-5$, and $z=8$?

$$7x - 5y + 4z$$

(A) -8

(B) 103

(C) 64

(D) 36

(E) -71

172. What is the value of $6p^2q(8q-10p)$ if $p=1$ and $q=2$?

(A) 72

(B) -12

(C) 54

(D) 68

(E) -45

173. If $a=3$, $b=2a-7$, and $c=4b+5$, what is the value of $5a - 2b + 7c$?

(A) 42

(B) 24

(C) -34

(D) 7

(E) 17

174. What is the value of this expression if $w=8$, $x=4$, $y=9$, and $z=10$?

$$\frac{w-x}{y+z}$$

(A) $\dfrac{3}{2}$

(B) $\dfrac{5}{17}$

(C) $\dfrac{8}{17}$

(D) 26

(E) $\dfrac{4}{19}$

175. What is the value of this expression if $p = 4$, $q = 5$, and $r = 2$?

$$5(2p - r \cdot q)^2 + pr$$

(A) 24

(B) 15

(C) −2

(D) 28

(E) −31

176. If $x = 5$, $y = x$, and $z = 2y$, what is the value of $3x - 2y + 4z$?

(A) 45

(B) 40

(C) 58

(D) 19

(E) 34

177. If $j = \frac{3}{4}$ and $k = \frac{4}{5}$, what is the value of $2j - 2k$?

(A) $\frac{4}{7}$

(B) $-\frac{1}{10}$

(C) $\frac{9}{16}$

(D) 1

(E) $\frac{3}{2}$

178. What is the value of this expression if $k = -7$, $m = -10$, and $n = 11$?

$$\frac{7k + 4m - 3n}{(5k - 4m)^2 + 7}$$

(A) $\frac{41}{50}$

(B) $\frac{12}{21}$

(C) $-\frac{61}{16}$

(D) $\frac{5}{17}$

(E) $-\frac{5}{4}$

179. What is the value of $5\left(x^y\right)^z$ if $x = 2$, $y = 1$, and $z = 2$?

(A) 40

(B) 20

(C) 10

(D) 50

(E) 60

180. What is the value of x if $3x - 7 = 8$?

(A) $\frac{1}{3}$

(B) 3

(C) 15

(D) 5

(E) 4

181. Which of the following is a solution to this equation?

$$|2u| = 10$$

Select all that apply.

[A] 5

[B] 10

[C] 20

[D] −5

[E] −10

182. If $x + y = 12$ and $x - y = -4$, what is the value of y?

(A) 10

(B) −2

(C) 8

(D) 4

(E) −11

183. If $w = y$, what is the value of $\frac{8wy^2}{w^2 y}$?

(A) $8w$

(B) $\frac{8}{y}$

(C) 1

(D) 8

(E) y

184. If $\frac{a}{b} = \frac{b}{c}$ and $ac = 49$, which of the following could be the value of b?

Select all that apply.

[A] 49

[B] 7

[C] −7

[D] −49

[E] 14

185. What is the value of p in this equation?

$4p - 8 = -52$

(A) −15

(B) 11

(C) 15

(D) 22

(E) −11

186. If $9h + 12 = 57$, what is 7 less than $4h + 14$?

(A) 27

(B) 34

(C) 45

(D) 14

(E) 20

187. What is the value of w in this proportion?

$\frac{20}{w} = \frac{10}{2}$

(A) 2

(B) 4

(C) 20

(D) 40

(E) 5

188. What is the solution to this equation?

$8j - 3 = 10j + 4$

(A) 3.5

(B) 2

(C) 0.5

(D) −3.5

(E) 3

189. If $2x + 4y = 32$ and $x - 2y = -12$, which of the following is true?

(A) $x + y = 10$

(B) $5x - y = 3$

(C) $8x + y = 26$

(D) $3x - 2y = -11$

(E) $x - y = -2$

190. What is the value of u in this equation?

$-3u + 14 = 8u - 30$

(A) 4

(B) 1

(C) 7

(D) 3

(E) 0

191. If $2q + 5 = 19$, what is the value of $-4q - 5$?

(A) 41

(B) −22

(C) 16

(D) 15

(E) −33

192. If $10a + 2b = 14$ and $-5a - 7b = 11$, what is the value of $7a - (-8b)$?

(A) −10

(B) 22

(C) 6

(D) −3

(E) 14

193. If $3^x = 27$ and $4^y = 16$, what is the value of $7x - 2y$?

(A) 25

(B) 8

(C) 12

(D) 17

(E) 10

194. If $|x| = 9$, what value could x have?

Select all that apply.

[A] 18

[B] 0

[C] 9

[D] −9

[E] −18

195. If $3p - 10q = 4r$, which of the following is equal to the value of p?

(A) $\dfrac{4r - 10q}{3}$

(B) $\dfrac{4r + 10q}{3}$

(C) $4r + 10q$

(D) $4r - 10q$

(E) $2qr$

196. If $2x + 6y = 58$ and $5x + 2y = 41$, what is the solution to the system of equations?

(A) $(8, 5)$

(B) $(5, 3)$

(C) $(-8, 5)$

(D) $(4, -3)$

(E) $(5, 8)$

197. If $\dfrac{2k + 4}{m} = \dfrac{3k - 13}{m}$, what is the value of $k - 17$?

(A) 0

(B) −17

(C) 17

(D) 15

(E) −8

198. What is the value of h in this equation?

$15h + 12 = 11h - 9$

(A) $-\dfrac{21}{26}$

(B) $\dfrac{-21}{4}$

(C) $\dfrac{5}{6}$

(D) $\dfrac{12}{17}$

(E) $\dfrac{26}{21}$

199. If $x + 2y = 22$ and $7x - 3y = 1$, which of the following numbers is NOT between the values of x and y?

(A) 6

(B) 8

(C) 5

(D) 3

(E) 7

200. If $a = b$, what is the value of a in the equation $9a - 2b + 2 = a + 3b$?

(A) $-\dfrac{3}{2}$

(B) $\dfrac{2}{11}$

(C) $-\dfrac{2}{11}$

(D) $\dfrac{3}{2}$

(E) $-\dfrac{2}{3}$

201. What is the solution of this inequality?

$4x + 5 < 17$

(A) $x < 3$

(B) $x > 3$

(C) $x < 5\dfrac{1}{2}$

(D) $x > 5\dfrac{1}{2}$

(E) $x < 12$

202. If $8w - 14 \geq 26$, which of the following could be the value of w?

(A) 4

(B) 2

(C) 3

(D) 1

(E) 6

203. What is the solution to this inequality?

$-9u + 7 > u + 57$

(A) $u < -8$

(B) $u < -5$

(C) $u > -8$

(D) $u > -5$

(E) $u < 8$

204. What is the solution to the following inequality?

$x + 7 < 14$

(A) $x > 7$

(B) $x < 7$

(C) $x > 21$

(D) $x < 21$

(E) $x > 28$

205. If $9j - 13 \geq 4j + 17$, which of the following CANNOT be the value of j?

(A) 6

(B) 7

(C) 5

(D) 9

(E) 8

206. Which of the following graphs represents the inequality $x > 4$?

(A)

(B)

(C)

(D)

(E)

© John Wiley & Sons, Inc.

207. What is the solution to the following inequality?

$12 - 6x < 2x + 12$

(A) $x > 0$

(B) $x < 0$

(C) $x \leq 6$

(D) $x \geq 3$

(E) $x \leq -3$

208. Which of the following is the solution to this inequality?

$8w + 14 - 7w \geq 6w + 3 + 2w$

(A) $w \leq \dfrac{11}{7}$

(B) $w \geq 2$

(C) $w \leq -2$

(D) $w \geq -\dfrac{11}{7}$

(E) $w \geq -11$

209. If $10x + 1 < 8x + 31$, then $5 + x$ would have to be less than which number?

(A) 5

(B) 15

(C) −15

(D) −20

(E) 20

210. What is the solution to the following inequality?

$$-\frac{3}{4}h - 2 + \frac{1}{2}h \le 3h - 11$$

(A) $h \le \frac{13}{36}$

(B) $h \le -\frac{13}{36}$

(C) $h \ge -3$

(D) $h \ge \frac{36}{13}$

(E) $h \le 3$

211. Which inequality does the following graph represent?

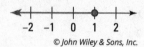

© John Wiley & Sons, Inc.

(A) $x < 1$

(B) $x > 1$

(C) $x \le 1$

(D) $x \ge 1$

(E) $x \le 0$

212. If $q + 2$ is added to the left side of this inequality and $2q - 3$ is added to the right side, and a true inequality is the result, which of the following could NOT be a value of q?

$$-3q - (-2q) + 5 \ge -8q - 2$$

(A) 1

(B) -2

(C) 0

(D) -1

(E) -4

213. If $8x + 13 \ge 2x + 15$, which of the following could be a value of x?

(A) 0

(B) -1

(C) $-\frac{3}{2}$

(D) $\frac{2}{7}$

(E) $\frac{4}{9}$

214. What is the solution to the following inequality?

$$2.5y + 3.7 < 1.7y - 2.1$$

(A) $y > -0.2$

(B) $y < -7.25$

(C) $y < -5.8$

(D) $y > -7.25$

(E) $y < 0.2$

215. If $2.8m + 5.6 - 9.8m \ge 12.2m - 5.2$, then m could NOT be equal to which of the following?

(A) -0.7125

(B) 0

(C) -0.7625

(D) 0.5626

(E) -0.51

216. Two consecutive integers have a sum of 15. What is the greater of the two integers?

(A) 1

(B) 8

(C) 15

(D) 0

(E) 7

217. Two consecutive odd integers have a sum of 28. What is the lower of the two integers?

(A) 13

(B) 15

(C) 28

(D) 2

(E) 17

218. Two consecutive even integers have a sum of 18. What is the product of the two integers?

(A) 10

(B) 100

(C) 80

(D) 8

(E) 18

219. Four more than twice a number is 12 less than 3 times the number. What is the number?

(A) 36

(B) 8

(C) 3

(D) 16

(E) 18

220. If 7 is taken from 5 times a number, the result is 21 more than the number. Which of the following is 11 more than 6 times the number?

(A) 5

(B) 14

(C) 53

(D) 7

(E) 28

221. Fourteen more than twice the sum of a number and 10 is at least 2 more than 10 times the number. Which of the following could be the number?

Select all that apply.

[A] 4

[B] 3

[C] 9

[D] 6

[E] 7

222. Twice the sum of a number and 6 is no more than 3 times the number. Which of the following CANNOT be the number?

(A) 12

(B) 11

(C) 13

(D) 16

(E) 15

223. Jason is 3 years older than Bethany. The sum of their ages is 81. What is Jason's age?

(A) 39

(B) 42

(C) 31

(D) 40

(E) 28

224. Casey's age is 7 years less than twice Kellie's age. In 12 years, Kellie's age will be 10 greater than Casey's current age. How old was Kellie 8 years ago?

(A) 1

(B) 9

(C) 11

(D) 2

(E) 12

225. If half a number is increased by twice the number, the result is 6 more than 2 times half the number. Which of the following is 8 less than 5 times the number?

(A) 4

(B) 28

(C) 2

(D) 27

(E) 12

226. If 11 less than a number is not as much as 3 less than a third of the number, which of the following could NOT have a value that is 26 higher than the number?

(A) 37

(B) 39

(C) 35

(D) 28

(E) 24

227. The product of two numbers is 15. The sum of one of the numbers and 14 is 2 more than 5 times the number. What is the other number?

(A) 3

(B) 5

(C) 15

(D) 12

(E) 2

228. Two numbers are opposites. Their product is −81. The higher number is 3 more than twice *y*. What is the value of *y*?

(A) −3

(B) 9

(C) −6

(D) −243

(E) 3

229. Which of the following is a counterexample to this statement?

If four less than the square of a number is more than five, the number is greater than three.

(A) −2

(B) 1

(C) −4

(D) 0

(E) −1

230. John has 8 less than twice as many four-wheeler wheels attached to his four wheelers as Elizabeth has to hers. However, they have the same number of four wheelers. How many four wheelers does John have?

(A) 16

(B) 4

(C) 2

(D) 8

(E) 3

231. Two numbers have a sum of 17. The greater number minus the smaller number is 7. What is the greater number?

(A) 12

(B) 24

(C) 5

(D) 22

(E) 10

232. A classroom with 28 students has 4 more boys than girls. How many girls are in the classroom?

(A) 12

(B) 16

(C) 4

(D) 28

(E) 24

233. The price of student tickets to a school play is $3, and the price of non-student tickets is $5. David sold 61 tickets for a total price of $251. How many student tickets did David sell?

(A) 34

(B) 22

(C) 17

(D) 27

(E) 81

234. Alex has only $10 and $20 bills in his wallet. The total number of bills in his wallet is 18, and the amount of money in the wallet is $290. How many $20 bills does Alex have?

(A) 4

(B) 220

(C) 70

(D) 7

(E) 11

235. In 17 years, Danforth's age will be 1 more than three times what it is now. How old will Danforth be in 30 years?

(A) 12

(B) 42

(C) 38

(D) 35

(E) 8

236. Is the relation $\{(2,5), (3,7), (4,1), (8,1)\}$ a function?

(A) The relation is a function because no element of the range is paired with more than one element of the domain.

(B) The relation is a function because no element of the domain is paired with more than one element of the range.

(C) The relation is NOT a function because 1 is paired with both 4 and 8.

(D) The relation is NOT a function because no element of the domain is paired with more than one element of the range.

(E) The relation is NOT a function because 2 is paired only with 5.

237. Does the following table represent a function?

x	y
−8	7
−2	4
3	8
−2	14

(A) Yes

(B) No

238. Which of the following relations is a function?

(A) $\{(-8,7), (-3,1), (7,6), (7,8)\}$

(B) $\{(1,2), (3,4), (5,6)\}$

(C) $\{(0,0), (2,2), (0,2), (2,0)\}$

(D) $\{(1,2), (1,3)\}$

(E) $\{(0,1), (1,2), (1,3)\}$

239. Which of the following relations is NOT a function?

(A) $\{(-1,-3), (2,4), (5,10)\}$

(B) $\{(0,1), (1,2), (2,3), (3,4)\}$

(C) $\{(5,5)\}$

(D) $\{(1,1), (2,2), (3,3), (4,4), (5,5)\}$

(E) $\{(-4,5), (2,6), (8,3), (2,7), (5,10)\}$

240. Does the following mapping represent a function?

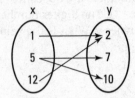

(A) It does represent a function because each number in the domain is paired with at least one number in the range.

(B) It does represent a function because each number in the range is paired with at least one number in the domain.

(C) It does NOT represent a function because 2 is paired with both 1 and 12.

(D) It does NOT represent a function because 5 is paired with both 7 and 10.

(E) It does represent a function because no number is listed more than once in the left column.

241. If $f(x) = x - 2$, what is the value of $f(3)$?

(A) 1

(B) 4

(C) 3

(D) 0

(E) 2

242. For the following function, what is the value of $g(7)$?

$$g(x) = x^2 - 2x + 14$$

(A) 7

(B) 77

(C) 63

(D) 35

(E) 49

243. If $p(x) = -4x^3 + 9x - 15$, what is the value of $p(2)$?

(A) −29

(B) −32

(C) 29

(D) 2

(E) 32

244. If $f(x) = 2x + 7$ and $g(x) = -x - 1$, what is the value of $f(4) - g(10)$?

(A) 15

(B) 26

(C) −11

(D) 4

(E) 9

245. If $q(x) = 1 - 3x$ and $r(x) = 5x - 1$, what is the product of $q(-6)$ and $r(-9)$?

(A) 19

(B) −270

(C) −874

(D) −46

(E) 471

246. For the two following functions, what is the value of $f\big(g(1)\big)$?

$$f(x) = 8x^2 - 2x + 12$$
$$g(x) = 3x + 5$$

(A) 508

(B) 415

(C) 29

(D) 580

(E) 18

Geometry

247. Which of the following is NOT a labeled point on the line in this diagram?

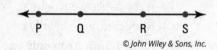

© John Wiley & Sons, Inc.

(A) P

(B) Q

(C) R

(D) S

(E) T

248. Which of the following qualifies as a name of this line, based solely on what is presented?

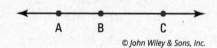

© John Wiley & Sons, Inc.

Select <u>all</u> that apply.

[A] $\overline{AB}$

[B] $\overline{BC}$

[C] $\overline{CD}$

[D] $\vec{B}$

[E] $\overline{CA}$

249. Which of the following qualifies as a name of this ray?

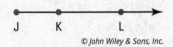

© John Wiley & Sons, Inc.

Select <u>all</u> that apply.

[A] $\overline{KJ}$

[B] $\overline{LJ}$

[C] $\overrightarrow{JK}$

[D] $\overline{KL}$

[E] $\overline{JL}$

250. What is the difference between a ray and a line?

(A) A line has at least one endpoint.

(B) A ray has two endpoints.

(C) A ray is infinite in only one direction.

(D) A line is infinite in only one direction.

(E) A line has two dimensions.

251. A segment is named using which of the following?

(A) Its midpoint

(B) One endpoint

(C) Its distance

(D) Its area

(E) Both endpoints

252. What is indicated by the vertical marks on the two following line segments?

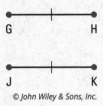

© John Wiley & Sons, Inc.

(A) They are opposite sides of the same polygon.

(B) They are diameters of the same circle.

(C) They have unequal measures.

(D) They are congruent.

(E) Their ratio is π.

253. Which of the following does NOT qualify as a name of the angle below?

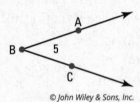

© John Wiley & Sons, Inc.

Select <u>all</u> that apply.

[A] $\angle ABC$

[B] $\angle ACB$

[C] $\angle 5$

[D] $\angle A$

[E] $\angle B$

254. When can an angle NOT be named by its vertex alone?

(A) Any angle can always be named by its vertex alone.

(B) No angle can ever be named by its vertex alone.

(C) An angle cannot be named by its vertex alone when its vertex is the vertex of more than one presented angle.

(D) An angle can be named by its vertex alone when the vertex is a letter from *A* to *D*.

(E) An angle can be named by its vertex alone only if the angle is obtuse.

255. Which of the following could be a name for the plane below?

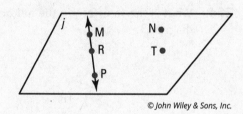

© John Wiley & Sons, Inc.

Select all that apply.

[A] Plane *j*

[B] Plane *MNR*

[C] Plane *MRP*

[D] Plane *RNT*

[E] Plane *PTN*

256. How many points are on a plane?

(A) 0

(B) 2

(C) 3

(D) 4

(E) ∞

257. Which of the following statements is NOT true about the line shown below?

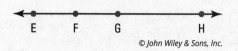

© John Wiley & Sons, Inc.

(A) $\overline{FG}$ is a segment on the line.

(B) The measure of $\overline{EF}$ plus the measure of $\overline{FH}$ is equal to the measure of $\overline{EH}$.

(C) The line's endpoints are *E* and *H*.

(D) $\overline{EF}$ is part of $\overline{EG}$.

(E) *F* is a point on the line.

258. Which type of angle is ∠7?

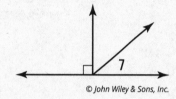

© John Wiley & Sons, Inc.

(A) Acute

(B) Obtuse

(C) Right

(D) Straight

(E) Reflex

259. What is the measure of ∠4 in the following diagram?

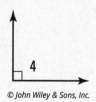

© John Wiley & Sons, Inc.

(A) 360°

(B) 45°

(C) 0°

(D) 180°

(E) 90°

260. If two angles are supplementary, what is the sum of their measures?

(A) 360°

(B) 45°

(C) 0°

(D) 180°

(E) 90°

261. In the following diagram, what is the measure of ∠ABD?

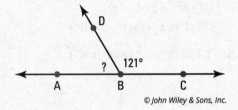

© John Wiley & Sons, Inc.

(A) 121°

(B) 31°

(C) 59°

(D) 61°

(E) 149°

262. If ∠DEF and ∠GHI are complementary angles and the measure of ∠GHI is 54°, what is the measure of ∠DEF?

(A) 36°

(B) 126°

(C) 54°

(D) 34°

(E) 326°

263. What is the value of x in the following diagram?

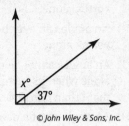

© John Wiley & Sons, Inc.

(A) 143

(B) 53

(C) 233

(D) 37

(E) 63

264. What is the value of y in the following diagram?

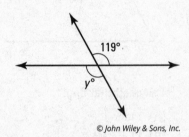

© John Wiley & Sons, Inc.

(A) 61

(B) 119

(C) 29

(D) 151

(E) 74

265. What is the value of w in the following diagram?

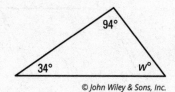

© John Wiley & Sons, Inc.

(A) 52

(B) 128

(C) 142

(D) 38

(E) 146

266. What is the value of k in the following diagram?

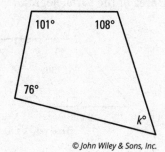

© John Wiley & Sons, Inc.

(A) 15

(B) 105

(C) 285

(D) 35

(E) 75

267. What is the value of n in the following diagram?

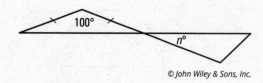

© John Wiley & Sons, Inc.

(A) 80

(B) 140

(C) 120

(D) 65

(E) 40

268. What is the value of x in the following diagram?

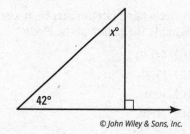

© John Wiley & Sons, Inc.

(A) 48

(B) 103

(C) 42

(D) 46

(E) 138

269. Circle *K* has a diameter of 8 cm. What is the circumference of Circle *K*?

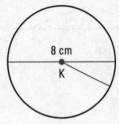

© John Wiley & Sons, Inc.

(A) 8π cm

(B) 64π cm

(C) 8 cm

(D) 64 cm

(E) 4π cm

270. A circle has a circumference of 20π in. What is the radius of the circle?

(A) 4.5 in.

(B) 15 in.

(C) 10 in.

(D) 20 in.

(E) 17.5 in.

271. The two circles have congruent radii. If the radius of one circle is 3 m, what is the area of the other circle, rounded to the nearest hundredth?

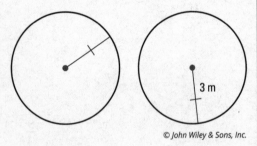

© John Wiley & Sons, Inc.

(A) 6π m²

(B) 18π m²

(C) 14.31 m²

(D) 28.26 m²

(E) 18.35 m²

272. The perimeter of the parallelogram is 50 units. What is the value of *x*?

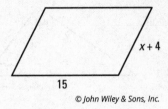

© John Wiley & Sons, Inc.

(A) 10

(B) 7

(C) 12

(D) 15

(E) 6

273. A base of the parallelogram is 9 cm. The corresponding height is 12 cm. What is the area of the parallelogram?

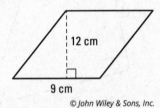

© John Wiley & Sons, Inc.

(A) 21 cm²

(B) 108 cm²

(C) 1.3 cm²

(D) 81 cm²

(E) 144 cm²

274. What is the perimeter of the triangle?

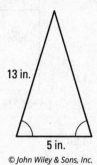

13 in.

5 in.

© John Wiley & Sons, Inc.

(A) 36 in.

(B) 26 in.

(C) 28 in.

(D) 31 in.

(E) 65 in.

275. What is the area of the triangle?

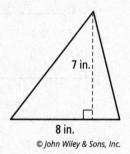

7 in.

8 in.

© John Wiley & Sons, Inc.

(A) 15 in.²

(B) 1 in.²

(C) 14 in.²

(D) 56 in.²

(E) 28 in.²

276. For right triangle ABC, what is the measure of side $\overline{AB}$?

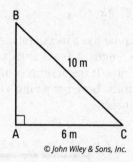

B

10 m

A   6 m   C

© John Wiley & Sons, Inc.

(A) 64 m

(B) 36 m

(C) 18 m

(D) 4 m

(E) 8 m

277. What is the area of the right triangle?

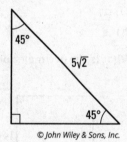

45°

$5\sqrt{2}$

45°

© John Wiley & Sons, Inc.

(A) 25 square units

(B) 12.5 square units

(C) 6.25 square units

(D) 7.5 square units

(E) 10 square units

278. A 30°-60°-90° triangle has a hypotenuse of 16 micrometers. What is the triangle's area?

(A) $32\sqrt{3}$ square micrometers

(B) $32\sqrt{2}$ square micrometers

(C) $8\sqrt{3}$ square micrometers

(D) 32 square micrometers

(E) 12 square micrometers

279. A triangle has sides of 24 dm, 10 dm, and 26 dm. Is the triangle a right triangle?

(A) Yes

(B) No

280. Jamie has a rectangular garden that has a length of $4x+5$ units and a width of 11 units. If the perimeter of the garden is 64 units, how many units is the length of the garden?

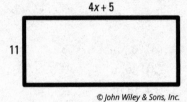

4x + 5

11

© John Wiley & Sons, Inc.

(A) 22

(B) 4

(C) 21

(D) 17

(E) 8

281. What is the perimeter of the square?

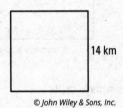

14 km

© John Wiley & Sons, Inc.

(A) 28 km

(B) 56 km

(C) 42 km

(D) 196 km

(E) 140 km

282. What is the area of the square?

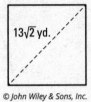

$13\sqrt{2}$ yd.

© John Wiley & Sons, Inc.

(A) 13 yd.²

(B) $169\sqrt{2}$ yd.²

(C) 26 yd.²

(D) 169 yd.²

(E) 52 yd.²

283. The trapezoid has base measures of 4 mm and 6 mm. The area of the trapezoid is 15 mm². What is the height of the trapezoid?

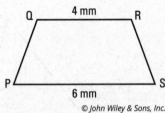

Q   4 mm   R

P   6 mm   S

© John Wiley & Sons, Inc.

(A) 10 mm

(B) 7 mm

(C) 3 mm

(D) 6 mm

(E) 4.5 mm

284. Every square qualifies as which of the following?

Select all that apply.

[A] Quadrilateral

[B] Parallelogram

[C] Rectangle

[D] Trapezoid

[E] Rhombus

285. The area of a square is 100 m². What is the square's perimeter?

(A) 20 m

(B) 60 m

(C) 75 m

(D) 40 m

(E) 25 m

286. A side of an equilateral triangle is 14 ft. What is the perimeter of the triangle?

(A) 84 ft.

(B) 12.5 ft.

(C) 196 ft.

(D) 27.5 ft.

(E) 42 ft.

287. In the diagram, a triangle and a square share two vertices. What is the area of the composite figure formed by the triangle and the square?

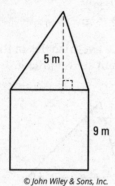

© John Wiley & Sons, Inc.

(A) 103.5 m²

(B) 81 m²

(C) 22.5 m²

(D) 58.5 m²

(E) 108 m²

288. In the figure, the semicircle has points that are the vertices of a rectangle, and the semicircle and rectangle share a side. What is the area of the composite figure formed by the semicircle and rectangle, rounded to the nearest hundredth?

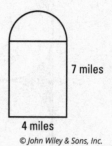

© John Wiley & Sons, Inc.

(A) 28 square miles

(B) 21.72 square miles

(C) 14 square miles

(D) 34.28 square miles

(E) 37 square miles

289. In the diagram, the white triangle shares two vertices with a rectangle and has its other vertex at a side of the rectangle. What is the area of the shaded region?

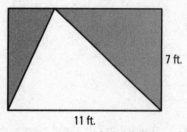

© John Wiley & Sons, Inc.

(A) 77 ft.²

(B) 38.5 ft.²

(C) 35 ft.²

(D) 115.5 ft.²

(E) 28.7 ft.²

290. In the diagram, two circles are inscribed in a rectangle, and the circles share a point. What is the exact area of the shaded region? Write your answer.

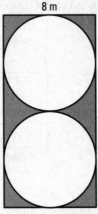

8 m

© John Wiley & Sons, Inc.

291. The two triangles in the following diagram are similar. What is the value of x?

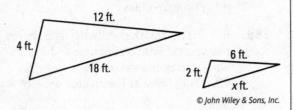

12 ft.

4 ft.

18 ft.

6 ft.

2 ft.

x ft.

© John Wiley & Sons, Inc.

(A) 9

(B) 2

(C) $\frac{1}{3}$

(D) 36

(E) 3

292. Quadrilaterals 1 and 2 are similar. A side of Quadrilateral 1 is 16 dm, and that side's corresponding side in Quadrilateral 2 is 4 dm. What is the scale factor from Quadrilateral 1 to Quadrilateral 2?

(A) 4

(B) $\frac{1}{2}$

(C) $\frac{1}{4}$

(D) 2

(E) 8

293. The two parallelograms in the following diagram are similar. $\overline{BD}$ corresponds to $\overline{FH}$, and $\overline{AB}$ corresponds to $\overline{EF}$. What is the measure of $\overline{EF}$?

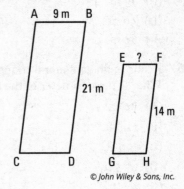

A 9 m B

E ? F

21 m

14 m

C D G H

© John Wiley & Sons, Inc.

(A) $\frac{2}{3}$ m

(B) 126 m

(C) 12 m

(D) $\frac{1}{6}$ m

(E) 6 m

294. The two triangles in the following diagram are congruent.

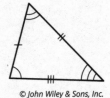

© John Wiley & Sons, Inc.

Which of these statements is true? Select all that apply.

[A] All pairs of corresponding angles are congruent.

[B] All pairs of corresponding sides are congruent.

[C] All corresponding parts are congruent.

[D] The two triangles' perimeters are equal.

[E] All pairs of corresponding angles are congruent, but none of the pairs of corresponding sides are necessarily congruent.

295. What is the surface area of the following cube?

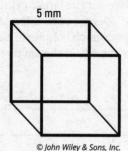

5 mm

© John Wiley & Sons, Inc.

(A) 125 mm²

(B) 150 mm²

(C) 25 mm²

(D) 100 mm²

(E) 50 mm²

296. The following figure is a right rectangular prism. What is its surface area?

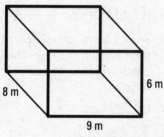

8 m

6 m

9 m

© John Wiley & Sons, Inc.

(A) 266 m²

(B) 144 m²

(C) 246 m²

(D) 432 m²

(E) 348 m²

297. What is the volume of the following cube?

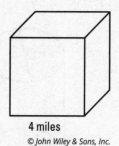

4 miles

© John Wiley & Sons, Inc.

(A) 64 cubic miles

(B) 16 cubic miles

(C) 32 cubic miles

(D) 24 cubic miles

(E) 128 cubic miles

298. A triangular prism has two triangular bases that both have an area of 19 square units. The prism has a height of 8 units. What is the volume of the prism?

(A) 604 cubic units

(B) 76 cubic units

(C) 27 cubic units

(D) 152 cubic units

(E) 228 cubic units

299. What is the surface area of the following right cylinder?

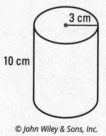

3 cm

10 cm

© John Wiley & Sons, Inc.

(A) 9π cm²

(B) 78π cm²

(C) 90π cm²

(D) 30π cm²

(E) 270π cm²

300. What is the surface area of the following right cylinder?

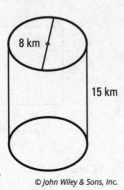

(A) 152π km^2

(B) 304π km^2

(C) 76π km^2

(D) 480π km^2

(E) 240π km^2

301. A right cylinder has a height of 10 micrometers. The cylinder's volume is 490π cubic micrometers. What is the cylinder's radius?

(A) 49 micrometers

(B) 14 micrometers

(C) 21 micrometers

(D) 7 micrometers

(E) 35 micrometers

302. In the following diagram, a cylinder is on the interior of another cylinder. The bases of the interior cylinder are parts of the bases of the larger cylinder. The centers of the bases are shared by the cylinders. How much volume of the larger cylinder is outside of the smaller cylinder?

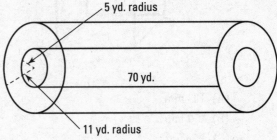

(A) $8,470\pi$ yd.^{3}

(B) $1,750\pi$ yd.^{3}

(C) $6,720\pi$ yd.^{3}

(D) 96π yd.^{3}

(E) $1,190$ yd.^{3}

303. A cone has a lateral area of 54π cm^2 and a base area of 100π cm^2. How many square centimeters is the surface area of the cone?

(A) 254π cm^2

(B) 46π cm^2

(C) $5,400\pi$ cm^2

(D) 208π cm^2

(E) 154π cm^2

304. The following composite figure is formed by a right cone and right cylinder that share a base. What is the surface area of the composite figure?

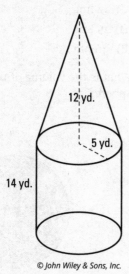

12 yd.

5 yd.

14 yd.

© John Wiley & Sons, Inc.

(A) 65π yd.^{2}

(B) 190π yd.^{2}

(C) 230π yd.^{2}

(D) 255π yd.^{2}

(E) 305π yd.^{2}

305. What is the volume of the following cone?

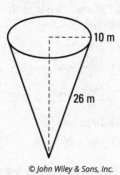

10 m

26 m

© John Wiley & Sons, Inc.

(A) 500π m^3

(B) 800π m^3

(C) $2,400\pi$ m^3

(D) 333π m^3

(E) $19,200\pi$ m^3

306. How many times greater is the volume of a cylinder than a cone that shares its base and has the same height?

(A) $\frac{1}{3}$

(B) 2

(C) 3

(D) r

(E) π

307. The following pyramid has a rectangular base. What is the surface area of the pyramid?

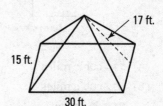

17 ft.

15 ft.

30 ft.

© John Wiley & Sons, Inc.

(A) 1,215 ft.^{2}

(B) 1,980 ft.^{2}

(C) 1,125 ft.^{2}

(D) 450 ft.^{2}

(E) 900 ft.^{2}

308. What is the surface area of a right pyramid with a base area of 92.38 m^2 and a lateral area of 124.19 m^2?

(A) 308.95 m^2

(B) 333.14 m^2

(C) 216.57 m^2

(D) 340.76 m^2

(E) 248.38 m^2

309. By what value must a prism's volume be multiplied to get the volume of a pyramid that shares its base and has the same height?

(A) 3

(B) 9

(C) $\frac{1}{9}$

(D) 1.5

(E) $\frac{1}{3}$

310. The following composite figure is formed by a square pyramid on top of a cube. The pyramid and cube share a base. The height of the pyramid is 9 miles, and the height of the cube is 9 miles. What is the volume of the composite figure?

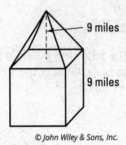

9 miles

9 miles

© John Wiley & Sons, Inc.

(A) 729 cubic miles

(B) 972 cubic miles

(C) 81 cubic miles

(D) 648 cubic miles

(E) 1,458 cubic miles

311. What is the surface area of the following sphere?

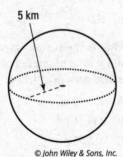

5 km

© John Wiley & Sons, Inc.

(A) 50π km^2

(B) 25π km^2

(C) 166.7π km^2

(D) 100π km^2

(E) 200π km^2

312. A sphere has a surface area of 36π hm^2. What is the diameter of the sphere?

(A) 6 hm

(B) 3 hm

(C) 12 hm

(D) 15 hm

(E) 36 hm

313. What is the volume of the following sphere?

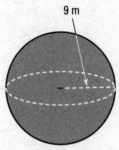

9 m

© John Wiley & Sons, Inc.

(A) 972π m

(B) 144π m

(C) 72π m

(D) 288π m

(E) 546.75π m

314. A spherical bubble has a surface area of 100 km^2. What is the volume of the bubble?

(A) 300π km^3

(B) $\dfrac{100\pi}{3}$ km^3

(C) $\dfrac{500\pi}{3}$ km^3

(D) 100π km^3

(E) 30π km^3

315. What is the lateral area of a cube in which each side is 2 inches?

(A) 20 in.^{2}

(B) 24 in.^{2}

(C) 12 in.^{2}

(D) 16 in.^{2}

(E) 8 in.^{2}

316. Mrs. Gray is using the following rectangular prism storage tank to store liquid nitrogen. How much liquid nitrogen can fit in the tank?

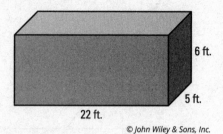

6 ft.

5 ft.

22 ft.

© John Wiley & Sons, Inc.

(A) 132 ft.³

(B) 330 ft.³

(C) 660 ft.³

(D) 324 ft.³

(E) 544 ft.³

317. What ordered pair is represented by point *C*?

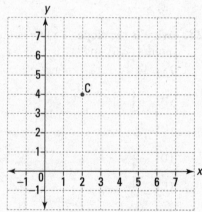

© John Wiley & Sons, Inc.

(A) $(2, 4)$

(B) $(4, 2)$

(C) $(2, 2)$

(D) $(4, 4)$

(E) $\left(\frac{2}{4}, \frac{4}{2}\right)$

318. What is the distance between points *A* and *B*?

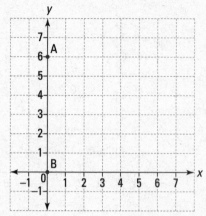

© John Wiley & Sons, Inc.

(A) 36

(B) 3

(C) 6

(D) 12

(E) 8

319. What is the distance between the points $(2, 8)$ and $(4, 10)$ on the coordinate plane, rounded to the nearest tenth?

(A) 7.3

(B) 2.83

(C) 8

(D) 4.2

(E) 2.8

320. What is the midpoint between points G and H on the following coordinate plane?

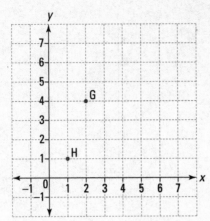

© John Wiley & Sons, Inc.

(A) $(3, 5)$

(B) $\left(\frac{3}{2}, \frac{5}{2}\right)$

(C) $(5, 3)$

(D) $\left(\frac{5}{2}, \frac{3}{2}\right)$

(E) 3.16

321. What is the midpoint between the points $(-5, 14)$ and $(7, -4)$ on the coordinate plane?

(A) $(-1, 5)$

(B) $(5, 1)$

(C) $(-5, -1)$

(D) $(1, 5)$

(E) $(-1, -5)$

322. What is the slope of the following line?

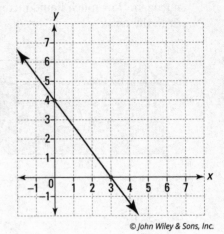

© John Wiley & Sons, Inc.

(A) $\frac{3}{4}$

(B) $-\frac{4}{3}$

(C) $\frac{3}{8}$

(D) $\frac{4}{3}$

(E) $-\frac{3}{4}$

323. What is the slope of a line containing the points $(2, 5)$ and $(17, 9)$?

(A) $\frac{15}{4}$

(B) $-\frac{4}{15}$

(C) $\frac{4}{15}$

(D) $-\frac{15}{4}$

(E) $-\frac{4}{11}$

324. What is the slope of the graph of $y = -\frac{3}{16}x + 75$? Write your answer.

325. Which of the following is true about a line containing points *A* and *B*?

Select all that apply.

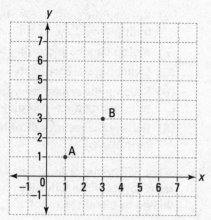

© John Wiley & Sons, Inc.

[A] The line represents all ordered pairs that make its equation true.

[B] The line represents the ordered pairs that make its equation false.

[C] The ordered pair $(1, 1)$ is a solution to the equation of the line.

[D] The ordered pair $(3, 3)$ is NOT a solution to the equation of the graph.

[E] The ordered pair $(3, 3)$ is a solution to the equation of the line.

326. Which of the following is a solution to the equation of the graphed line?

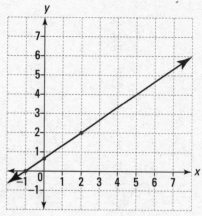

© John Wiley & Sons, Inc.

(A) $(2, 2)$

(B) $(0, -1)$

(C) $(1, 3)$

(D) $(5, 0)$

(E) $(1, 2)$

327. What is the only point that is a solution to both equations that are graphed that follows?

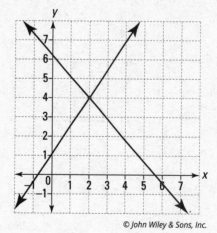

© John Wiley & Sons, Inc.

(A) $(2, 1)$

(B) $(2, 4)$

(C) $(3, -1)$

(D) $(-3, 5)$

(E) $(1, -10)$

328. What will be the endpoints of the following segment if it is translated 5 units right and 7 units down?

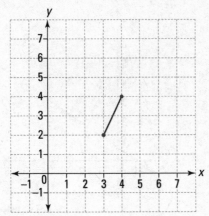

© John Wiley & Sons, Inc.

(A) (8, –5) and (–1, –3)

(B) (–2, 9) and (–3, 11)

(C) (8, –5) and (9, –3)

(D) (–2, 9) and (9, –3)

(E) (5, –7) and (–5, 7)

329. Which of the following will be a vertex of the following triangle if it is reflected over the y-axis?

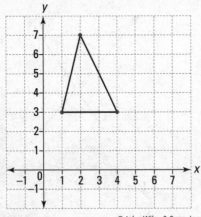

© John Wiley & Sons, Inc.

(A) (1, 3)

(B) (–4, 3)

(C) (–3, 4)

(D) (3, –1)

(E) (2, –7)

330. If a polygon in the coordinate plane is reflected over the x-axis, which of the following can be done to the coordinates of the vertices of the polygon to get the coordinates of its new vertices?

(A) Keeping the same y-coordinates and multiplying the x-coordinates by –1

(B) Multiplying both coordinates by –1

(C) Switching the coordinates

(D) Keeping the same x-coordinates and multiplying the y-coordinates by –1

(E) Getting the reciprocals of the coordinates

331. What will be the ordered pair for the top right vertex of the following square if it is dilated by a scale factor of 7?

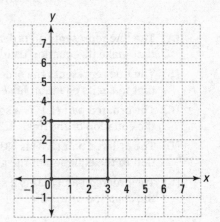

© John Wiley & Sons, Inc.

(A) (3, 7)

(B) (9, 9)

(C) (7, 1)

(D) $(\frac{3}{7}, \frac{3}{7})$

(E) (21, 21)

332. Which aspect of a figure on the coordinate plane always changes as a result of a dilation, unless the scale factor is 1?

(A) Shape

(B) Position

(C) Side of the x-axis

(D) Side of the y-axis

(E) Size

333. Which of the following will be an endpoint of the following segment if the segment is rotated 90° counterclockwise about the origin?

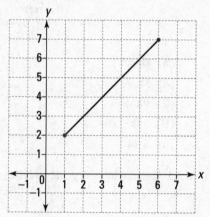

© John Wiley & Sons, Inc.

(A) (6, −7)

(B) (−7, 6)

(C) (1, −2)

(D) (−2, −1)

(E) (1, 7)

334. Which of the following will NOT be a vertex of the following pentagon if it's rotated 180° counterclockwise about the origin?

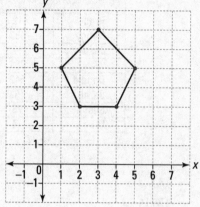

© John Wiley & Sons, Inc.

(A) (−1, −5)

(B) (−3, −7)

(C) (−3, −4)

(D) (−2, −3)

(E) (−5, −5)

Statistics

335. The following table shows the weights of three members of the same family. How many more pounds is Jeffrey than Drew?

Player	Weight (Pounds)
Drew	175
Jeffrey	348
William	217

© John Wiley & Sons, Inc.

(A) 131

(B) 72

(C) 173

(D) 170

(E) 137

336. The following table indicates the numbers of cars sold in a year by various sales-people. How many of the salespeople sold more cars than Nancy?

Salesperson	Cars Sold
Brad	12
Nancy	458
Jason	17
Willy	754
Donald	542
Sarah	152
Susan	75
Luke	74

© John Wiley & Sons, Inc.

(A) 2

(B) 5

(C) 458

(D) 296

(E) 742

337. The following bar graph shows the mile-run times of five runners. Who ran the second best time of the five competitors?

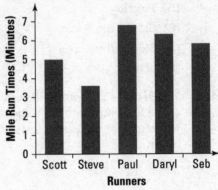

© John Wiley & Sons, Inc.

(A) Daryl

(B) Steve

(C) Paul

(D) Seb

(E) Scott

338. Of the five towns listed in the following bar graph, which has the lowest yearly average temperature?

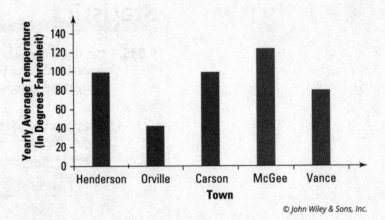

© John Wiley & Sons, Inc.

(A) Henderson

(B) Vance

(C) McGee

(D) Orville

(E) Carson

339. The following line graph shows Chris's annual income for various years. How many of the years listed did Chris have a higher income than his income of 2014?

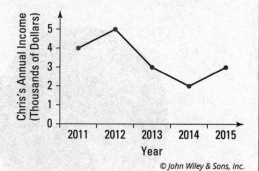

© John Wiley & Sons, Inc.

(A) Three

(B) Four

(C) Zero

(D) Two

(E) One

340. The following line graph shows the numbers of votes Ted received in different elections. In which election did Ted receive the greatest drop in votes from the previous election?

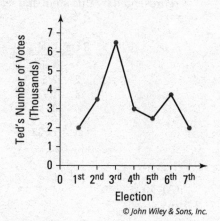

© John Wiley & Sons, Inc.

(A) Fourth

(B) Second

(C) Fifth

(D) Seventh

(E) Third

341. The following line graph shows the relationship between an independent variable and a dependent variable. According to the graph, which of the following statements is true?

Select all that apply.

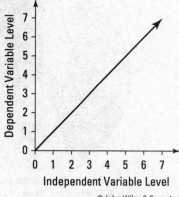

© John Wiley & Sons, Inc.

[A] The correlation between the independent variable and the dependent variable is positive.

[B] The correlation between the independent variable and the dependent variable is negative.

[C] No correlation exists between the independent variable and the dependent variable.

[D] As the independent variable increases, the dependent variable increases.

[E] As the independent variable increases, the dependent variable decreases.

342. The following circle graph indicates the percentages of the population of Spencerton that use each of the phone companies in the town. If the population of Spencerton is 1,700, how many residents use either Mackenco or AB&C?

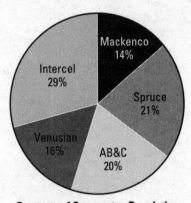

**Percents of Spencerton Population
Using Various Phone Companies**

© John Wiley & Sons, Inc.

(A) 238

(B) 595

(C) 578

(D) 612

(E) 340

343. According to the following circle graph, how much more of a percent of the Squirrel Club's total budget goes to parties than the sum of its public activism and charity benefit budgets?

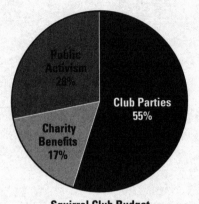

Squirrel Club Budget

© John Wiley & Sons, Inc.

(A) 45%

(B) 55%

(C) 100%

(D) 10%

(E) 11%

344. Which of the following numbers is represented by this stem and leaf plot?

Stem	Leaf
1	4 5 8
2	2 5
3	1 7 9
4	0

Key: 3|5 = 35

© John Wiley & Sons, Inc.

(A) 16

(B) 35

(C) 41

(D) 21

(E) 37

345. Which of the following numbers is NOT represented by the following stem and leaf plot?

Select all that apply.

Stem	Leaf
0	1 2 4 8
2	0 4 5 7
5	0 1 2 5 8
7	1 1 2
8	5

Key: 8|5 = 850

© John Wiley & Sons, Inc.

[A] 40

[B] 140

[C] 400

[D] 71

[E] 840

346. What is the highest number in the set of data represented by the following box and whisker plot?

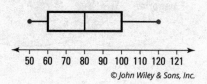

© John Wiley & Sons, Inc.

(A) 121

(B) 120

(C) 100

(D) 50

(E) 60

347. From the lowest number to the highest number, how much of the number line does the data in the following box and whisker plot represent?

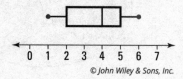

© John Wiley & Sons, Inc.

(A) 3

(B) 4

(C) 6

(D) 5

(E) 7

348. Which of the following is indicated by the following Venn diagram?

© John Wiley & Sons, Inc.

(A) Kiss is a country act.

(B) Led Zeppelin is NOT a rock act.

(C) Robert Wilkins is a rock act and a blues act.

(D) Jimi Hendrix is NOT a blues act.

(E) The Marshall Tucker Band is both a country act and a rock act.

349. The following Venn diagram shows the numbers of people in a club who are in at least one of three given occupations. According to the Venn diagram, how many people in the club are professors or preachers but not biologists?

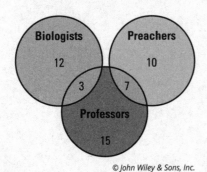

© John Wiley & Sons, Inc.

(A) 25

(B) 10

(C) 32

(D) 15

(E) 7

350. Which of the following is indicated by the following Venn diagram?

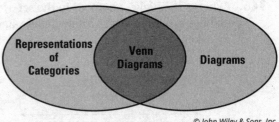

© John Wiley & Sons, Inc.

(A) Venn diagrams are NOT diagrams.

(B) Representations of categories CAN-NOT be diagrams.

(C) Venn diagrams are both diagrams and representations of categories.

(D) Venn diagrams are NOT representations of categories.

(E) Diagrams CANNOT be representations of categories.

351. Which of the following is NOT indicated by the following scatterplot?

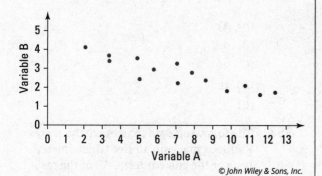

© John Wiley & Sons, Inc.

(A) A negative correlation exists between Variable A and Variable B.

(B) As Variable A increases, Variable B tends to decrease.

(C) The higher Variable B is, the lower Variable A tends to be.

(D) Some increases in Variable A are accompanied by increases in Variable B.

(E) An increase in Variable A is always accompanied by an increase in Variable B.

352. Is the correlation between amount of time in the Stud Challenge Training Program and average endurance test score a positive or negative correlation?

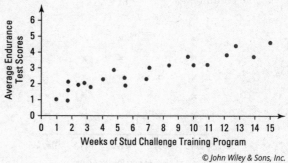

© John Wiley & Sons, Inc.

353. According to the following line plot, how many more first place jousting ribbons did Mosi win than Aaron?

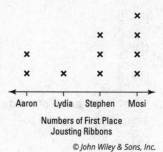

© John Wiley & Sons, Inc.

(A) 4

(B) 2

(C) 3

(D) 1

(E) 6

354. The following line plot shows the number of pies Spike ate on certain days. What is the simplest form of the ratio of the number of pies Spike ate on Day 4 to the number of pies he ate on Days 2 and 5 combined?

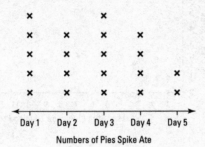

Numbers of Pies Spike Ate

© John Wiley & Sons, Inc.

(A) $\frac{4}{6}$

(B) $\frac{2}{3}$

(C) $\frac{6}{4}$

(D) $\frac{2}{1}$

(E) $\frac{3}{2}$

355. What is the mean of a data set containing two numbers, 4 and 10?

(A) 6

(B) 7

(C) 14

(D) 40

(E) 2.5

356. What is the mean of the following set of data?

0   8   12   8

(A) 8

(B) 12

(C) 7

(D) 4

(E) 0

357. What is the mean of the following set of data?

4   8   11   14   3   26

(A) 23

(B) 9.5

(C) 26

(D) 11

(E) 3

358. The following data figures are the scores Kathleen made on all five trigonometry tests of the current term. All of the tests are worth the same number of points. What does Kathleen need to make on the next test to have a test average of 70?

54   80   61   72   58

(A) 94

(B) 70

(C) 78

(D) 95

(E) 67

359. What is the mean of the first seven prime numbers?

(A) $8\frac{2}{7}$

(B) $8\frac{1}{7}$

(C) 6

(D) $3\frac{6}{7}$

(E) 8

360. What is the mean of the data represented by the following table?

Player	Quiz Score
Ware	92
Leigh Ann	84
Christian	92
Elizabeth	96
Meredith	82

© John Wiley & Sons, Inc.

(A) 92

(B) 14

(C) 89.2

(D) 96

(E) 82

361. What is the median of the following set of data?

1   2   3

(A) 2

(B) 1

(C) 3

(D) 6

(E) $\frac{1}{6}$

362. What is the median of the following set of data?

7   12   15   8   1

(A) 14

(B) 8.6

(C) 1

(D) 15

(E) 8

363. What is the median of the following set of data?

9   4   1   20   5   1

(A) $6\frac{2}{3}$

(B) 19

(C) 4.5

(D) 1

(E) 9

364. Malloy made the following scores in four games of golf. What is the median of his scores for the four games?

72   80   68   74

365. What is the median of the first five composite numbers?

(A) 8

(B) 6

(C) 7.4

(D) 5.8

(E) 4.2

366. What is the median of the set of data represented by the following stem and leaf plot?

Stem	Leaf
0	1 2 4 8
2	0 4 5 7
5	0 1 2 5 8
7	1 1 2
8	5

Key: 5|2 = 52

© John Wiley & Sons, Inc.

(A) 71

(B) 84

(C) 39.76

(D) 50

(E) 85

367. What is the mode of a set of data?

(A) The sum of the numbers in a data set, divided by the number of numbers in the set

(B) The number that appears the most often in the set

(C) The middle number or the mean of the two middle numbers of a data set, in terms of value

(D) The difference between the greatest and the smallest numbers in a data set

(E) A number far greater or far less than the general vicinity of most of the numbers in a data set

368. What is the mode of the following set of data?

1   3   4   3

(A) 2.75

(B) 2

(C) 1

(D) 4

(E) 3

369. What is the mode of the following set of data?

7   7

(A) 0

(B) 7

(C) 14

(D) 49

(E) 1

370. Rick scored the following numbers of points for ten basketball games. What is the mode of the numbers of points Rick scored for the ten games?

12 14 12 6 12 14 18 28 14 12

(A) 12

(B) 14

(C) 13

(D) 14.2

(E) 22

371. The numbers of students in seven classrooms are 24, 31, 17, 19, 31, 24, and 31. What is the mode of the numbers of students in the seven classrooms?

(A) 24

(B) 25.3

(C) 31

(D) 14

(E) 48

372. What is the mode of the set of data represented by the following line plot?

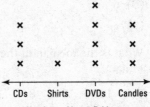

Numbers of Items Bridgette
Bought Yesterday

© John Wiley & Sons, Inc.

(A) 1

(B) 3

(C) 5

(D) $2\frac{3}{4}$

(E) 4

373. What is the range of a set of data? Select all that apply.

[A] The middle number or the mean of the two middle numbers in the set

[B] The numerical distance covered by the set

[C] The difference between the highest number and the lowest number in the set

[D] The number that could be subtracted from the highest number to get the lowest number

[E] The number that could be added to the lowest number in the set to get the highest number

374. What is the range of the following set of data?

0   10

(A) 10

(B) 5

(C) 0

(D) 1

(E) 100

375. What is the range of the following set of data?

2   5   3   8   4   11   4   9

(A) 4.5

(B) 4

(C) 5.75

(D) 11

(E) 9

376. Sophia got six speeding tickets in one week. The following set of data reflects the speeds at which she was clocked driving to get the tickets. What is the range of the six speeds Sophia was caught driving?

91   104   122   85   98   158

(A) 101

(B) 73

(C) 109.667

(D) 158

(E) 85

377. Prince Rogers Nelson passed away at the age of 57. What is the range of all of the ages, in terms of whole numbers of years, Prince ever was?

(A) 57

(B) 29.5

(C) 28.5

(D) 0

(E) 1

378. What is the range of the set of data represented by the following box and whisker plot?

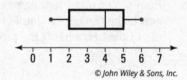

© John Wiley & Sons, Inc.

(A) 4

(B) 2

(C) 5

(D) 1

(E) 6

379. If a quarter is flipped in a way that will cause it to land randomly, what is the probability that it will land on heads?

(A) $\frac{2}{1}$

(B) $\frac{1}{2}$

(C) $\frac{1}{4}$

(D) $\frac{4}{1}$

(E) $\frac{2}{2}$

380. A bag contains 3 orange marbles, 4 blue marbles, and 2 yellow marbles. If Melissa randomly pulls a marble out of the bag, what is the probability that the marble will be blue?

(A) $\frac{4}{9}$

(B) $\frac{9}{9}$

(C) $\frac{2}{9}$

(D) $\frac{1}{3}$

(E) $\frac{9}{4}$

381. A teacher writes the names of five different students on small pieces of paper and puts them in a hat. One of the names is Joseph. The other four names are different. If the teacher randomly pulls a name out of the hat, what is the probability that it will be Joseph?

(A) $\frac{2}{5}$

(B) $\frac{1}{5}$

(C) $\frac{5}{5}$

(D) $\frac{5}{1}$

(E) $\frac{5}{2}$

382. A number wheel has the natural numbers 1 through 8 on it. Each number covers the same amount of room that is met by the arrow. If someone spins the wheel and the arrow randomly lands on a number, what is the probability that the number will be 3?

(A) $\frac{8}{1}$

(B) $\frac{8}{8}$

(C) $\frac{1}{4}$

(D) $\frac{1}{8}$

(E) $\frac{3}{8}$

383. A die has six faces, and each face displays a different natural number from 1 to 6. The die is rolled at a table in a way that it lands randomly on a face. What is the probability that the die will land on 4 or 5?

(A) $\frac{1}{6}$

(B) $\frac{1}{2}$

(C) $\frac{2}{3}$

(D) $\frac{4}{5}$

(E) $\frac{1}{3}$

384. The city of Barnville has 1,548 residents. Twenty-two of the residents have the last name Johnson, and 14 of the residents have the last name Dean. If the mayor of Barnville randomly picks a resident to be on his float in the town's Family Day parade, what is the probability that the person he picks will have a last name of Johnson or Dean?

(A) $\frac{22}{774}$

(B) $\frac{1}{43}$

(C) $\frac{1}{1,548}$

(D) $\frac{36}{43}$

(E) $\frac{5}{1,548}$

385. Beth, Michelle, Tekeeta, and Pam are four friends who bought raffle tickets for a drawing. Others also bought raffle tickets for the same drawing. The following table shows the numbers of raffle tickets bought by each of the four friends as well as the number bought by others. One ticket will be randomly drawn to decide the winner. What is the probability that the winner will be Beth, Michelle, Tekeeta, or Pam?

Participant	Number of Raffle Tickets
Beth	4
Michelle	1
Tekeeta	7
Pam	3
Others	875

© John Wiley & Sons, Inc.

(A) $\frac{1}{178}$

(B) $\frac{3}{890}$

(C) $\frac{1}{15}$

(D) $\frac{3}{178}$

(E) $\frac{3}{875}$

386. The numbers of students running for student council in each of four third-period classes in a small hallway of a school are indicted by the following line plot. Thirty-seven students not represented by the line plot are also running. Based on only this much information, what is the probability that one of the students in Class B or Class D will get elected to be on student council?

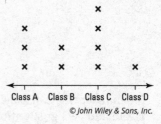

© John Wiley & Sons, Inc.

(A) $\frac{3}{40}$

(B) $\frac{3}{37}$

(C) $\frac{1}{40}$

(D) $\frac{3}{47}$

(E) $\frac{1}{3}$

387. Madison bought a bag of pool balls. Each ball is marked with a number from 1 to 15, and each number is used only once. The bag also contains a cue ball, which has no number on it. The balls are randomly arranged in the bag. If Madison reaches into her new bag of pool balls and randomly pulls one out, what is the probability that she will pull the 8 ball or the cue ball?

(A) $\frac{1}{15}$

(B) $\frac{2}{15}$

(C) $\frac{1}{8}$

(D) $\frac{1}{4}$

(E) $\frac{2}{5}$

388. A basket contains plastic chips of equal size and shape, and each chip has a different prime number that's less than 20 painted on it. If John randomly pulls a chip out of the bag, what is the probability that it will have a number on it that's NOT 5 or 7?

(A) $\frac{3}{4}$

(B) $\frac{1}{4}$

(C) $\frac{1}{8}$

(D) $\frac{3}{7}$

(E) $\frac{1}{7}$

389. If a number wheel displaying only composite numbers greater than 6 and less than 30 is spun, what is the probability that the wheel will land on a composite number between 17 and 25?

(A) $\frac{1}{4}$

(B) $\frac{5}{17}$

(C) $\frac{1}{3}$

(D) $\frac{5}{16}$

(E) $\frac{1}{5}$

390. A skydiver who has lost control of his parachute will happen to randomly land in a rectangle that is divided into ten smaller rectangular sections of equal length and width. Each section is labeled with a different number, as shown in the following figure. The section where most of the skydiver's body is when he lands will determine the official section of his landing. What is the probability that the skydiver will land in the section labeled with the number 8?

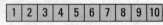

(A) $\frac{1}{8}$

(B) $\frac{1}{5}$

(C) $\frac{10}{10}$

(D) $\frac{1}{10}$

(E) $\frac{3}{10}$

391. A probability is always greater than or equal to one number and less than or equal to another number. What are the two numbers?

(A) −1 and 1

(B) 0 and 2

(C) −∞ and ∞

(D) 0 and ∞

(E) 0 and 1

392. If a day of the week is chosen at random, what is the probability that it will be Wednesday or Saturday?

(A) $\frac{1}{7}$

(B) $\frac{5}{7}$

(C) $\frac{2}{7}$

(D) $\frac{7}{2}$

(E) $\frac{7}{5}$

393. If a natural number from 1 to 12 is chosen at random, what is the probability that the number will be 4 or an odd number?

(A) $\frac{1}{12}$

(B) $\frac{7}{12}$

(C) $\frac{1}{2}$

(D) $\frac{2}{7}$

(E) $\frac{5}{12}$

394. If a natural number from 1 to 20 is chosen at random, what is the probability that it will be 7 or a multiple of 5?

(A) $\frac{1}{5}$

(B) $\frac{1}{4}$

(C) $\frac{5}{12}$

(D) $\frac{4}{7}$

(E) $\frac{12}{5}$

395. A pet store has 8 snakes, 5 dogs, 2 birds, and 3 cats. If a child has one of those animals randomly selected by a computer, what is the probability that the animal will NOT be a dog or a bird?

(A) $\frac{7}{18}$

(B) $\frac{18}{11}$

(C) $\frac{7}{11}$

(D) $\frac{11}{18}$

(E) $\frac{11}{7}$

396. If a penny is flipped twice, what is the probability that it will land on tails both times?

(A) $\frac{1}{4}$

(B) $\frac{1}{8}$

(C) $\frac{3}{8}$

(D) $\frac{1}{2}$

(E) $\frac{3}{4}$

397. If a penny is flipped twice, what is the probability that it will land on heads the first time and tails the second time?

(A) $\frac{1}{8}$

(B) $\frac{1}{4}$

(C) $\frac{3}{8}$

(D) $\frac{7}{8}$

(E) $\frac{2}{3}$

398. A weatherman accurately determined that there's a $\frac{3}{7}$ chance of rain in Jackson today and that if there is rain in the city today, there will be a $\frac{4}{9}$ probability of lightning. There will be no lightning if there is no rain. What is the probability that there will be lightning in Jackson today?

(A) $\frac{55}{63}$

(B) $\frac{12}{27}$

(C) $\frac{1}{9}$

(D) $\frac{8}{63}$

(E) $\frac{4}{21}$

399. Two dice each have six faces, with each face having a different number from 1 to 6 on it. What is the probability of getting a sum of 7 from a random roll of those dice?

(A) $\frac{2}{11}$

(B) $\frac{1}{6}$

(C) $\frac{1}{11}$

(D) $\frac{7}{12}$

(E) $\frac{2}{11}$

400. Robert is a contestant on the game show Price of Fortune. He has a 72% chance of making it to the second round. If he makes it to the second round, he will have a 41% chance of reaching the final round. If he makes it that far, he will have a 21% chance of winning a brand-new blender. What is the probability that Robert will win the brand-new blender?

(A) 29.52%

(B) 61,992%

(C) 86.1%

(D) 8.61%

(E) 6.1992%

401. What is 3.45×10^3 in standard form?

(A) 3,450

(B) 345

(C) 34.5

(D) 0.03450

(E) 0.003450

402. Which of the following is the standard form of 9.452137×10^5?

(A) 945.2137

(B) 0.00009452137

(C) 0.0009452137

(D) 945,213.7

(E) 9,452.137

403. Which of the following expresses 2.54802×10^7 in standard form?

(A) 25,480.2

(B) 0.00000025480200

(C) 0.25480200

(D) 0.000025480200

(E) 25,480,200

404. What is 8.0534×10^{-2} in standard form?

(A) 0.0080534

(B) 0.00080534

(C) 805.34

(D) 0.080534

(E) 80,534

405. Which of the following represents 1.24×10^{-3} in standard form?

(A) 0.00124

(B) 0.124

(C) 0.000124

(D) 124

(E) 1,240

406. What is the standard form of 7.248094×10^{-5}?

(A) 0.0007248094

(B) 0.7248094

(C) 724,809.4

(D) 0.00007248094

(E) 7,248,094

407. Which of the following expresses 6.889357×10^8 in standard form?

(A) 688,935,700

(B) 0.00000006889357

(C) 0.0000006889357

(D) 68,893,57

(E) 6,889.357

408. What is 3.211×10^{-7} in standard form? Write your answer.

409. Which of the following is equal to 6.433052×10^1 in standard form?

(A) 0.6433052

(B) 64,330.52

(C) 0.06433052

(D) 643.3052

(E) 64.33052

410. The Andromeda galaxy has approximately 1.0×10^{12} stars. Which of the following expresses that figure in standard form?

(A) 1,000,000,000,000

(B) 0.000000000001

(C) 0.00000000001

(D) 100,000,000,000

(E) 1,000,000,000

411. What is 827 in scientific notation?

(A) 8.27×10^{-2}

(B) 8.27×10^1

(C) 8.27×10^2

(D) 82.7×10^2

(E) 827×10^{-2}

412. What is 0.48 in scientific notation?

(A) 4.8×10^1

(B) 4.8×10^2

(C) 0.48×10^0

(D) 48.0×10^{-1}

(E) 4.8×10^{-1}

413. Which of the following is the scientific notation form of 7,942.0548?

(A) 0.79420548×10^4

(B) 7.9420548×10^3

(C) 79.420548×10^3

(D) 7.9420548×10^{-3}

(E) 7.9420548×10^{-2}

414. Which of the following is 0.00056 in scientific notation?

(A) 5.6×10^4

(B) 0.56×10^{-3}

(C) 5.6×10^5

(D) 5.6×10^{-4}

(E) 56.0×10^{-4}

415. Which of the following represents 839.002 in scientific notation?

(A) 83.9002×10^1

(B) 839.002×10^{-2}

(C) 8.39002×10^{-2}

(D) 8.39002×10^2

(E) 8.39002×10^3

416. What is 0.00003544 in scientific notation?

(A) 3.544×10^6

(B) 3.544×10^{-5}

(C) 35.44×10^4

(D) 3.544×10^{-6}

(E) 354.4×10^{-2}

417. A centigram is 1.0×10^{-5} kilograms. Write the number of kilograms in a centigram in standard form.

418. Which of the following represents 50,000,000 in scientific notation?

(A) 5.0×10^{-7}

(B) 5.0×10^6

(C) 50.0×10^6

(D) 5.0×10^{-6}

(E) 5.0×10^7

419. What is the product of 5.647×10^8 and 6.287×10^4 in standard form?

(A) 35,502,689,000,000

(B) 200,483,684,783

(C) 35,502,689

(D) 20,048,368,478,300

(E) 0.002048368478

420. What is the scientific notation form of the product of 3.53451×10^5 and 8.2457×10^3?

(A) $2.9144509107 \times 10^{-9}$

(B) 2.9144509107×10^8

(C) 29144509.107×10^5

(D) 2.9144509107×10^9

(E) 29.144509107×10^2

421. Which of the following expresses the product of 15,527 and 2,548,054 in scientific notation?

(A) $3.9563634458 \times 10^{10}$

(B) 3.9563634458×10^1

(C) 3.9563634458×10^8

(D) $39.563634458 \times 10^{11}$

(E) 395.63634458×10^9

422. The statistics and probability section of a practice test has 88 questions. What is the scientific notation form of that number?

(A) 8.8×10^3

(B) 0.88×10^2

(C) 88.0×10^0

(D) 8.8×10^1

(E) 8.8×10^{-1}

Chapter 2
Reading Comprehension

The reading comprehension questions really focus on two different types of reading skills: comprehension, yes, but also critical thinking. These reading questions ask you to read the lines and read *between the lines*. That often means deciding what the author might be subtly implying with word choice, nuances in the language, and the types and content of the sources used.

A reading comprehension passage may contain two or more paragraphs or may be an excerpt that's only a few lines in length. All questions are based on what's stated or implied in the passage. You don't need to know anything about the subject outside of the given text. If you're familiar with the topic, you may easily comprehend the passage, but be careful not to mix your own knowledge of the topic with what you read on the test.

The Problems You'll Work On

When working through the questions in this chapter, be prepared to

>> Read text on varied topics

>> Find the main idea and message of the text

>> Find key details

>> Find out the meanings of words or phrases (most of the time, you can use context clues to define unknown words)

>> Determine an author's purpose and the audience

>> Choose the best answer from a multiple-choice selection

>> Use the process of elimination

What to Watch Out For

Trap answers include the following:

>> Facts that aren't mentioned in the passage

>> Things that are true but don't answer the question

>> Terms that twist the facts around, such as *never* for *always*

Set 1

People often comment on the irony of the fact that Alfred Nobel, the man who endowed the famous Nobel Prizes, spent his life inventing military explosives. Fewer people, however, know how directly related Nobel's two legacies actually were: when a French newspaper believed him dead and mistakenly printed his obituary in 1888, Nobel was horrified to see himself referred to as "the merchant of death." In an effort to make amends for the harm his inventions had caused, he changed his will, leaving nearly his entire estate to endow the famous prizes in Peace, Literature, and various natural sciences that now bear his name.

423. According to the passage, the Nobel Prizes were created in order to

(A) save money

(B) save lives

(C) change a rule

(D) change an image

(E) correct an inaccuracy

It's certainly an exciting time for killer whales — or, at least, for the marine biologists who study them. It's only in the last couple of decades that genetic testing has revealed killer whales to be a large species of dolphin, much more closely related to those cute fellows than to the "great" whales. We've also learned that there are at least three, and possibly as many as six, subspecies of killer whales that diverged from one another around two million years ago, and all have distinct markings, diets, and systems of communication. Even the name "killer whale" is falling out of fashion, as most scientists now prefer to use the term "orca."

424. In composing this passage, the author's intention was presumably to

(A) distinguish between the opinions of biologists and those of whales

(B) explain precisely what distinguishes a whale from a dolphin

(C) summarize the recent scientific literature concerning orcas

(D) alert readers to the fact that the term "killer whale" is now objectionable

(E) announce the invention of a new method of genetic testing

The archaeological excavation of Göbekli Tepe in southeastern Turkey in the 1990s revolutionized our knowledge about early human civilization. Not only are the site's stone pillars larger and heavier than those at the more famous Stonehenge in England, but they also have meticulous artwork carved into them that is clearly the work of specialist craftsmen. The place was obviously labored over in a highly organized fashion for many years, beginning around 10,000 BCE, and yet it contains no residences or any evidence of permanent human habitation — humans had not yet invented agriculture and were still nomadic, so Göbekli Tepe must have been a place of worship to which people returned at important times of the year. This is the first confirmation that early humans built elaborate structures for their gods before they even built permanent homes for themselves.

425. According to the passage, archaeologists came to a conclusion about the purpose of Göbekli Tepe primarily by using

(A) the largest and most advanced equipment

(B) specialized artistic analysis

(C) comparisons with and contrasts to Stonehenge

(D) agricultural evidence

(E) a process of elimination

The ABC hit drama *Lost* speaks to our deepest fear: the fear of being cut off from everything we know and love, left to fend for ourselves in a strange land. This fear is a philosophical fear, because it speaks to the human condition. It forces us to confront profound questions about ourselves and the world: Why am I here? Does my life matter? Do I have a special purpose? Can I make a difference?

426. In this passage, the author implies that the "human condition" is essentially

(A) rooted in fear

(B) a quest for answers

(C) the ability to love oneself

(D) unexplainable by art

(E) the drive to make a difference

X-Men comics were one of the first Marvel series to feature female characters as the leads in multiple storylines. X-Women are shown as strong and powerful, equal to the men around them. X-Men comics also developed a diverse population of mutant superheroes that included African characters such as Storm, Native Americans like Dani Moonstar and Thunderbird, and Asian characters such as Jubilee and Lady Deathstrike. Originally, Stan Lee named the comic "The Mutants," a less gender-specific title, but his editor thought the audience would not understand what or who a mutant was, so Lee suggested X-Men because the main characters had "extra" powers and were led by a man named Professor X. That was also a rather new concept: having a handicapped leader in Professor X, who, despite being wheelchair-bound, is still one of the most powerful, influential heroes in the X-Men series. Here, too, we can see the underlying philosophical spirit of the X-Verse: All of our traditional hierarchies are scrutinized, questioned, and reimagined.

427. The author's analysis of X-Men comics would best be summed up by saying that these comics

(A) work to subvert dated paradigms

(B) pose challenges to newfangled ethics

(C) sacrifice good storytelling to a political agenda

(D) demonstrate tonal inconsistencies over time

(E) merely pay lip service to multiculturalism

There are serious problems with the idea that God dictates the meaning of our lives. Think of great scientists, who better our lives with their discoveries. Or humanitarians, who tirelessly work to improve the world. Or entertainers even, who make our lives more enjoyable. Do we really want to say that if there's no God, then these accomplishments don't count?

428. It can safely be assumed that the author of this passage believes that

(A) all religion is inherently harmful

(B) entertainers do more good than scientists

(C) it is impossible ever to know whether God exists

(D) free will does not truly exist

(E) human existence has meaning unto itself

Questions 429–431 are based on the following passage.

Myths abound about Shakespeare in part because of half-remembered or out-of-date scholarship from schooldays, because Shakespeare the man is such an elusive and charismatic cultural property, and because innovations in Shakespeare studies, particularly biographical and theatrical ones, make headline news: witness the "authorship question" or speculation about Shakespeare's sexuality. Put simply, myths are told and retold about Shakespeare because no other writer matters as much to the world: nineteenth-century Germany had a flourishing academic Shakespeare criticism before England did; India had a Shakespeare Society before England; Shakespeare is regularly performed at amateur and professional levels, in translation, worldwide. Shakespeare is not just English. Thus myths about Shakespeare go some way toward telling us stories about ourselves.

429. One aspect of the author's argument is the claim that

(A) Shakespeare's plays work at least as well in translation as in English

(B) most schoolchildren do not pay very close attention when studying Shakespeare

(C) several other writers should matter more to the world than Shakespeare

(D) new ideas about Shakespeare pop up to suit each generation's concerns

(E) Shakespeare may not actually have been born in England

430. In calling Shakespeare a "charismatic cultural property," the author most nearly means that Shakespeare is

(A) a mysterious symbol of the elite

(B) a private language of the popular

(C) an attractive communal touchstone

(D) an elaborate means of showing off

(E) a frustrating marker of intelligence

431. As it is used by the author, the word *abound* refers to something that is

(A) ubiquitous

(B) limited

(C) ancient

(D) false

(E) infuriating

Questions 432–434 are based on the following passage.

Often named as one of the greatest female sculptors of all time, Malvina Hoffman was born in New York City in 1887. Early in her career she studied under the famous Auguste Rodin, as well as with Gutzon Borglum, the Danish-American who would go on to create Mount Rushmore. Hoffman's crowning achievement was a series of bronze sculptures commissioned by the Field Museum of Natural History in Chicago, exploring physical and cultural differences among humans. She traveled extensively in order to study her subjects in life and eventually produced 105 spectacularly detailed and lifelike pieces depicting people from all over the world. Hoffman's sculptures were a centerpiece of the 1933 Chicago World's Fair, and an entire hall at the Field Museum was dedicated to their subsequent display. By the 1960s, however, the notion of physical differences among various types of humans had become a touchy subject, and some argued that Hoffman's work was racist. Three years after her death in 1966, the Field Museum moved most of Hoffman's work into basement storage. A few pieces remain displayed without fanfare in select corners of the museum, but the vast majority of the masterpiece collection of this pioneering artist has not been seen in nearly 50 years.

432. The author presumably hopes that, upon reading the passage, the reader will

(A) agree with his opinion about whether Hoffman's work was racist

(B) understand the many ways in which Hoffman influenced modern sculpture

(C) be more informed about Hoffman herself and the significance of her work

(D) object to the arbitrary policies of Chicago's Field Museum

(E) suspect that Hoffman may have had some influence in creating Mount Rushmore

433. The author most probably uses the word "crowning" in the third sentence to mean

(A) final

(B) greatest

(C) boldest

(D) most controversial

(E) only original

434. Based on the passage, it can most safely be assumed that Malvina Hoffman

(A) was overrated as a sculptor

(B) held unorthodox political views

(C) had been largely forgotten by the time of her death

(D) enjoyed a privileged education

(E) never married or had any children

Everyone knows that the Renaissance was an explosion of artistic brilliance and scientific advancement in the Europe of the 15th and 16th centuries and that it was especially welcome after the preceding centuries of ignorance and violent political oppression now referred to as the Dark Ages. But why did the Renaissance happen when it did? For that matter, why did it happen at all? Believe it or not, this European golden age we call the Renaissance may simply be the term we've given to the direct aftereffects of Europe's worst nightmare: the Black Plague.

Originating in the plains of central Asia, the Black Death hit Europe in 1347 when merchant ships laden with Asian goods landed in southern Italy, unwittingly bringing along the rats whose fleas carried the deadly plague bacteria. By the end of the century, more than 50% of Europe's total population had died. This time must have been indescribably horrific to live through, but those who did were changed by the experience: desperation to stop the devastation had gotten people thinking seriously about science and medicine, and daily confrontation with so much death focused their hearts and minds on the human experience and the things that made life worth living. Perhaps most importantly of all, the Black Death meant the collapse of the feudal system. The masses of commoners who had been bound to work the lands of their lords as serfs had been too badly decimated for the arrangement to remain feasible, and the survivors were allowed to buy their freedom and go into business for themselves as skilled tradesmen, leading to the emergence of a middle class and the birth of our modern free-market economic system. In a multitude of ways, human life was suddenly more valuable than ever before.

435. How might the structure and intent of the passage most fully be described?

(A) Multiple periods in history are analyzed with respect to the role played by disease.

(B) A controversial theory concerning the Black Plague is meticulously rebutted.

(C) A multifaceted historical phenomenon is ultimately attributed to a sole root cause.

(D) Reasons why the feudal system was suddenly outlawed are delineated.

(E) The Renaissance is claimed not to have actually happened, for various reasons.

436. The passage could reasonably be taken to imply that some phenomenon other than the Black Death could presumably have brought an end to the feudal system as long as it

(A) prompted advancements in ethical philosophy

(B) focused people's hearts and minds on the human experience

(C) inspired thinkers to adhere to the scientific method

(D) brought valuable goods to Europe from Asia

(E) drastically reduced the population

437. As it is used in the opening sentence, "explosion of" can be taken to mean

(A) destruction of

(B) overhauling of

(C) battle for

(D) opposition to

(E) proliferation of

438. Which most accurately describes the passage in terms of tone and likely intended audience?

(A) It mocks an outdated viewpoint for an audience of intellectual rebels.

(B) It efficiently describes a new theory for an audience of educated non-experts.

(C) It defends a conspiracy theory to an audience of stubborn skeptics.

(D) It seeks to resolve a controversy for an audience of partisans.

(E) It offers a lighthearted gloss of a traditional viewpoint for a general audience.

439. The passage implies that "desperation to stop the devastation" would have taken the form of people looking for

(A) means of treatment for or prevention of the Black Death

(B) someone to blame for causing the Black Death

(C) artistic insights into the human experience

(D) a sweeping overthrow of ignorance and violent oppression

(E) an economic system that could feasibly replace feudalism

Questions 440–442 are based on the following passage.

Perhaps no term that has entered mainstream discourse via the language of philosophy is more misunderstood than *nihilism*. The word conjures up images of melancholy iconoclasts dressed in black, and it is doubtlessly largely for that reason that it has become something of a byword among rebellious youngsters. Even more serious and educated people frequently seem to believe that "nihilism" is a philosophy built around the idea that life is meaningless and that there is therefore no such thing as morality. But in actuality, not only does "nihilism" not mean that, but it isn't even a term for a school of philosophy at all. All the philosophers who have used the term "nihilism" — even Friedrich Nietzsche, with whom it is most closely

associated — have not espoused it themselves but rather used it pejoratively to describe other philosophies with which they disagreed. Used properly, "nihilistic" is an insult for a philosophical viewpoint that (in the speaker's opinion) sucks all the significance out of life due to some massive flaw or contradiction. While certain philosophers like Nietzsche and Kierkegaard claimed that they "welcomed" nihilism, this was because they saw nihilism not as an end in itself but rather as a necessary step on the path toward creating greater significance.

440. The principal purpose of the passage is presumably to

(A) define a meaningless term

(B) resolve an endless debate

(C) shed light on a source of confusion

(D) dramatize an unpopular viewpoint

(E) satirize a ridiculous objection

441. According to the passage, "nihilism" is all of the following EXCEPT for

(A) a term that serious and respected philosophers use

(B) a buzzword thrown around by uninformed amateurs

(C) a phrase sometimes taken to mean that life is meaningless

(D) a state that certain geniuses have seen as an end in itself

(E) a charge leveled against inferior philosophers

442. The mood of the passage, as established by the author, can best be described as one of

(A) mildly amused didacticism

(B) justifiably irate condescension

(C) utterly bemused concern

(D) suspiciously confident optimism

(E) wildly biased partisanship

ASMR, or "Autonomous Sensory Meridian Response," is a pleasant trancelike state that some people claim to experience as a result of exposure to auditory "triggers" such as the sounds of whispering, nail tapping, paper crinkling, or gum chewing. Over the last few years, hundreds of ASMR videos designed to help viewers fall asleep or reduce stress have popped up on YouTube, and some of the more prolific and creative "ASMRtists" have become minor Internet celebrities. Professional psychologists have largely declined to comment on whether there is a scientific basis for the effects that ASMR enthusiasts, known as "tingleheads," are purported to experience, but by the standards of pop psychology, the ASMR movement is one of the most coherent and fast-growing we've seen in years.

443. Various terms in the passage are placed in quotation marks in order to indicate that they are

(A) grammatically incorrect

(B) likely new to a general readership

(C) used ironically to signify their opposites

(D) incompatible with the passage's scholarly tone

(E) loanwords

The tiny dunnart of Australia is casually referred to as a "marsupial mouse," but of course, it isn't really a mouse at all. As a marsupial, it is necessarily more closely related to all other marsupials — to the kangaroo, for example, or to the koala or Tasmanian devil — than it is to any non-marsupial mammal, such as a mouse. So why does it look exactly like a mouse? Because of a process called *convergent evolution*. The fact is that there are good reasons for animals to have the forms that they have. A mammal that is the size of a mouse and fulfills a mouselike niche will likely also have a stocky body, big ears, a longish snout, and so forth. In other words, it will end up looking like a mouse even though it isn't one.

444. In composing the passage, the author's intent was presumably to

(A) confirm the fact that marsupials count as mammals

(B) debunk a frustratingly persistent piece of misinformation

(C) compare and contrast the dunnart with marsupials

(D) suggest that mice should be classified as marsupials

(E) illustrate a principle by proceeding from an example of it

As far as the public is concerned, 1941's *Chaplinsky v. New Hampshire* might well be the most misunderstood Supreme Court case of all time. While it's true that *Chaplinsky* established the famous "fighting words" doctrine, it's also true that this doctrine doesn't mean what many people think it does. The decision is often taken to imply that a citizen has the right to physically assault another citizen who gravely insults him, but anyone who tries to use that defense in court will be in for a rude awakening. All the Supreme Court actually did in this case was uphold the right of a police officer to arrest a citizen who had verbally abused him, in accordance with a New Hampshire state law that the defendant subsequently tried to argue was unconstitutional. Ironically, in light of the fact that *Chaplinsky* has come to be known as "the 'fighting words' decision," no fight actually took place, and no one has ever successfully used *Chaplinsky* as a defense for a violent response to an insult.

445. The passage characterizes *Chaplinsky v. New Hampshire* as

(A) a rare instance of a governmental body condoning violence

(B) a potentially unconstitutional judicial misstep

(C) a dangerous decision to comprehend poorly

(D) an overlooked source of possible defenses

(E) a rude awakening for numerous legal scholars

Questions 446–448 are based on the following passage.

Claude Nicolet has described the Roman Principate as a significant stage on the road to the modern state. On the other hand, several features that marked this new version of the imperial order seem to undermine this claim. The autocratic power center was adapted to republican institutions in ingenious and effective ways but, by the same token, suffered from a certain under-institutionalization of its more innovative aspects — hence the overpowering emphasis on the person of the ruler and a corresponding weakness of the foundations for continuous and impersonal statehood.

446. In simple terms, the passage can accurately be described as comparing and contrasting

   (A) two different viewpoints on a single period in history

   (B) two different periods in the history of a single place

   (C) a single form of government as it existed in two different places

   (D) two different historical influences on the modern state

   (E) various methods of adapting republican institutions

447. The passage characterizes ancient Imperial Rome in all of the following ways EXCEPT to say that it

   (A) relied heavily on a cult of personality centered on the leader

   (B) established key inroads to present concepts of government

   (C) involved clever adaptations of a more representative form of government

   (D) failed to officially shore up its progress with laws and bureaucracies

   (E) was markedly lacking in innovative aspects

448. The author is primarily concerned with a debate over whether the Roman Principate was

   (A) as obsessed with "the person of the ruler" as some historians have claimed

   (B) more or less under-institutionalized than the preceding republic had been

   (C) more ingenious than effective with respect to its autocratic power center

   (D) more structurally similar to a contemporary government or to other ancient ones

   (E) doomed to failure from the start or merely made fatal errors along the way

If deciding and acting don't change the future, what about changing the past? Although the difference between eternalism and presentism divides philosophers into two heavily armed camps, the question of whether the past can be changed is, relatively speaking, a side issue. Almost all philosophers are in agreement: No, sir, it cannot. Aristotle regarded the past as necessary, and St. Augustine (354–430 C.E.) thought that not even God can change the past. Surprisingly for philosophy, almost everyone who has thought about the matter has followed suit.

449. At some point in the passage, the author makes which of the following implications?

   (A) The debate between eternalism and presentism is the most contentious in all of philosophy.

   (B) Aristotle was the first philosopher to extensively analyze the past.

   (C) It is only slightly easier to change the future than to change the past.

   (D) Almost all philosophers are in agreement about the nature of God.

   (E) It is unusual for philosophers to be in agreement about anything.

Though it is the most famous and most cherished of the rights guaranteed by the U.S. Constitution, freedom of speech is quite possibly also the most misunderstood. When a celebrity or other public figure lands in hot water over controversial comments, his or her supporters will inevitably take up the cry of "free speech" — but such a reaction bespeaks a fundamental misunderstanding of both constitutional law and the Founders' intent. Freedom of speech does not, and was never intended to, mean that no one is allowed to criticize you for what you say — only that the government is not allowed to imprison you for it. Far from being something it intended to prevent, heated debate among the citizenry is the very outcome that the First Amendment was designed to ensure.

450. The author seeks to correct a misunderstanding of

(A) the Founders' intent on the part of the present government

(B) the Constitution on the part of many citizens

(C) the First Amendment on the part of a specific public figure

(D) a public figure's comments on the part of the media

(E) one of his previous writings on the part of his readers

Though King Richard I of England — famously known as "the Lionheart" — remains popular in the U.K. and is one of the few Medieval British monarchs whose name is widely known even in America, his golden reputation is based more on romantic wishful thinking than historical fact. He wasn't a bad king, but this is mainly because he wasn't much of a king at all. During the ten years of Richard's reign, he spent only six months in England and most of his time acting as a military commander in the Crusades rather than concerning himself with the business of government. The idealization of Richard largely comes courtesy of the fact that his inept younger brother John — the sinister "Prince John" of so many Robin Hood films — watched over England in Richard's absence, and so Richard's popularity skyrocketed based on little aside from the fact that he was not John. Perhaps the greatest irony is that this archetypal English King, born less than a century after the Norman Conquest, spoke no English, a fact that popular culture understandably glosses over.

After all, it simply wouldn't do to have Good King Richard return at the end of the Robin Hood movie and speak French.

451. Which of the following claims about King Richard the Lionheart is implicitly made by the passage?

(A) He was the only English king who did not speak English.

(B) He is known in America only because of the movies.

(C) He was probably not actually Prince John's brother.

(D) His good reputation is based almost wholly on conjecture.

(E) His supposed military acumen is predominantly wishful thinking.

Questions 452–454 are based on the following passage.

He is arguably the most famous and influential fictional character ever created, so it usually surprises people to learn that the world's greatest detective, the peerless Sherlock Holmes, was essentially a rip-off. Years before Arthur Conan Doyle published the first Sherlock Holmes adventure in 1887, the American master of horror, Edgar Allan Poe, published a trilogy of short stories featuring his own detective character, Auguste Dupin. Debuting in 1841's "The Murders in the Rue Morgue," Dupin shares many similarities with the later and far more famous Holmes even beyond the fact that he is a master amateur sleuth whom the police consult when they are baffled: he smokes a pipe, he lives with a best friend who narrates his adventures, and he has a tendency to go on at length about logic in a condescending and socially oblivious manner. Conan Doyle himself always admitted the obvious influence and gave Poe credit for inventing the detective genre, but the question remains: Why did Sherlock Holmes immediately become a popular literary phenomenon, when a nearly identical character who debuted half a century earlier did not? Perhaps Poe and his Dupin were simply ahead of their time.

452. The best description of the structure of the passage would be to say that it

(A) states a personal opinion and attempts to support it with evidence

(B) presents a series of facts that culminates in a mystery

(C) resolves a quandary by citing newly discovered data

(D) makes an accusation that is eventually revealed to be in jest

(E) analyzes a real-life issue as though it were a work of literature

453. According to the passage, Arthur Conan Doyle's attitude toward Edgar Allan Poe and his influence can best be described as

(A) ornery

(B) evasive

(C) conciliatory

(D) inflammatory

(E) erratic

454. The author concludes the passage by positing that Poe's Auguste Dupin stories were

(A) quixotic

(B) insouciant

(C) subversive

(D) melodramatic

(E) avant-garde

Questions 455–458 are based on the following passage.

The going idea in English departments of American colleges when it comes to the teaching of "freshman comp" — the introductory writing courses that virtually all incoming students are required to take — is that instructors are supposed to grade and correct student work based on the students' writing alone, without attempting to change or influence the students' opinions. This is a polite notion, and for that reason it is popular with administrators, whose primary motivation is to avoid controversy. But there are more than a few problems with this nice-sounding idea. The

first is that, in practice, it's impossible, rather like the paradox from the climax of Shakespeare's *The Merchant of Venice,* where Shylock is challenged by the disguised Portia to take a pound of flesh without spilling a drop of blood. If a student's opinion, or any of the supposed facts cited in support of it, is objectively false, then how can the organization of the argument be analyzed as a discrete aspect of the paper?

More importantly and more dangerously, such a yardstick carries the implication that *everything* is simply a matter of opinion, which of course is not true. Although it might well lead to more tension in the classroom and more hurt feelings on the parts of some students, the inescapable fact is that there are simply better reasons to believe some things than there are to believe other things. If "politeness" dictates that this fact cannot be acknowledged, even at the college level, then the students are being taught far less than they could or should be, and the function of the professor is demoted to that of a simple proofreader.

455. The "going idea" mentioned in the opening sentence is one that the author

(A) prefers to the idea he goes on to analyze

(B) feels regret for initially championing

(C) composed the passage primarily to oppose

(D) supposes to have been influenced by the works of Shakespeare

(E) used to believe before his circumstances changed

456. The word "paradox," as it is used in this passage, most nearly means

(A) mystery

(B) contradiction

(C) ceremony

(D) rule

(E) denouement

457. Based on the passage, it can be assumed that the proponents of the standards analyzed herein are largely

  (A) students and administrators

  (B) parents and professors

  (C) professors and administrators

  (D) students and proofreaders

  (E) politicians and poets

458. The passage can fairly be taken to imply that the author believes professors

  (A) should begin to respectfully accuse administrators of plagiarism

  (B) focus too highly on literature, at the expense of logic and science

  (C) are no longer sufficiently familiar with Shakespeare's plays

  (D) have both the right and the duty to disparage false theses

  (E) must continue to be paid more highly than proofreaders

Questions 459–461 are based on the following passage.

It's the most famous series of words ever composed in the English language. Everyone has heard of it, and most people even know a little bit of it by heart, regardless of whether they ever made a deliberate effort to commit it to memory. And virtually everyone, including many English teachers and a fair number of the actors who have delivered it on stage, is dead wrong about what it means. The plain fact is that Hamlet's "To be or not to be" soliloquy is *not* about whether to commit suicide. Hamlet already flatly ruled out suicide on ethical grounds in his first soliloquy back in Act One. The immortal showstopper from Act Three is about something much more complex and much more deeply related to the grander themes of the play than that. When the melancholy prince asks "Whether 'tis nobler in the mind to suffer / The slings and arrow of outrageous fortune / Or to take arms against a sea of troubles," he is not debating whether to cash in his chips but instead pondering an eternal paradox of morality: Should a good

person "turn the other cheek" in the face of evil, or should he attempt to make the world a better place by actively combating the wicked, running the risk not only of dying in the process but — even more troublingly — of becoming just as bad as the people he seeks to oppose?

459. The author's argument about the "To be or not to be" soliloquy includes the assertion that

  (A) only English teachers understand it fully

  (B) it addresses a perennial ethical quandary

  (C) it is entirely devoted to opposing suicide

  (D) it contains a central flaw that is impossible to resolve

  (E) it is somewhat more famous than it deserves to be

460. According to the author, Hamlet is _____ pacifism.

  (A) unsure about

  (B) opposed to

  (C) influenced by

  (D) advocating

  (E) satirizing

461. It can be assumed that, in composing the passage, the author's motivation was to

  (A) correct a prior view of his that he now believes was mistaken

  (B) advocate the teaching of Shakespeare's *Hamlet* in philosophy classes

  (C) investigate why the "To be or not to be" soliloquy in particular is so well known

  (D) direct readers to what he sees as the true core of the "To be or not to be" soliloquy

  (E) explain how modern ideas have caused most people to misunderstand Shakespeare

Founded in 1994 by philosophers Peter Singer and Paola Cavalieri, the Great Ape Project is an international organization that lobbies for a United Nations Declaration of the Rights of Great Apes. These proposed rights would include not only life but also liberty, meaning that great apes could no longer be experimented upon or even kept in zoos. The reasoning goes that, since great apes are intelligent enough to understand their status as captives in a zoo, keeping them in one would be morally equivalent to imprisoning a human who has committed no crime.

462. According to the passage, assertions of the rights of Great Apes are predicated upon

    (A) the philosophical works of Peter Singer and Paola Cavalieri

    (B) the legislative authority of the United Nations

    (C) the differences between Great Apes and human beings

    (D) moral opposition to the practice of animal experimentation

    (E) claims about their capacity for awareness

The words "rabbit" and "hare" are often used interchangeably (especially in the titles of Bugs Bunny cartoons), but the two animals are quite different. Hares live and bear their young in nests, not in underground burrows like rabbits do, and those young are born already furred and able to see, as opposed to blind and hairless like newborn rabbits. Unlike rabbits, who live in groups, hares are loners. A hare has 48 chromosomes to the rabbit's 44, and its jointed skull is unique among mammals. Hares and rabbits really aren't that difficult to tell apart if you know what to look for, although it doesn't help that the animal known as a jackrabbit is actually a hare and that the pet breed called a Belgian hare is really a rabbit.

463. According to the passage, which of the following is true of rabbits?

    (A) They build nests in which to bear their young.

    (B) They are more social animals than hares.

    (C) They have a greater number of chromosomes than do hares.

    (D) They are especially different from the Belgian hare.

    (E) They have jointed skulls.

Questions 464–466 are based on the following passage.

Are time machines and time travel possible? Many physicists, including the great Stephen Hawking, now say yes. But before you get too excited, understand that there is a lot of fine print. Firstly, virtually all authorities on the subject agree that time travel to the past is an impossibility. Traveling backward in time would open the door to all sorts of insoluble conundrums, such as the famous Grandfather Paradox ("What if you went back in time and killed your own grandfather, thereby preventing yourself from ever existing in the first place?"). As Hawking succinctly explains, when it comes to physics, things that would create paradoxes tend not to happen — not directly because they would create the paradoxes, but rather because the paradoxes indicate that they must be impossible for some other reason. Time travel to the future, however, is eminently possible — even if the process is less exciting than in the movies. All you'd have to do is move really fast.

As Einstein discovered, time slows down for moving objects as they approach the speed of light. A traveler in a spaceship moving at half the speed of light would experience the passing of only one day for every two days that passed on Earth. Speed up to 99% of the speed of light, and a year would pass on earth for every day on the ship. So if you want to travel through time, all you'd have to do is build a spaceship that can go *really* fast and then hang around in space for a while, going really fast. When you came back to Earth, you would indeed have traveled into the future — simply because less time had passed for you than it had for everyone else. A "time machine," then, is just anything that can move fast enough to function as one.

464. Which of the following questions is most fully answered by the passage?

(A) What would happen if you traveled back in time and killed your grandfather?

(B) Why does time slow down as one approaches the speed of light?

(C) Why do we suspect that time travel to the past is impossible?

(D) Who first came up with the concept of a time machine?

(E) Why is Stephen Hawking so preeminent among modern physicists?

465. The phrase "there is a lot of fine print," as it is used in this passage, most nearly means

(A) a great deal of training is necessary

(B) the following explanation is highly___ technical

(C) many intelligent people disagree about this

(D) the ensuing claims are not completely serious

(E) this comes with numerous qualifications

466. The explanation of time travel to the future, as given in the passage, indicates something about the relationship between

(A) time and speed

(B) gravity and light

(C) the present and the speed of light

(D) the Earth and the sun

(E) matter and the past

Questions 467–472 are based on the following passages.

Passage 1

The theory that the Cretaceous-Paleogene Event — the mass extinction 65 million years ago that is most famous for having killed the dinosaurs, although many other species disappeared as well — was caused by an asteroid impact is now so widely accepted, it can be hard to believe that the idea was little more than a rogue hypothesis until fairly recently. Although paleontologists had previously realized that the extinction would be compatible with an asteroid impact, there was no hard evidence for one until 1980, when Luis Alvarez and his team discovered that the geologic record contains massive levels of iridium, an element rare on Earth but plentiful in asteroids, at the Cretaceous-Paleogene Boundary. As for the fact that the actual location of the impact was the Chicxulub Crater in Mexico's Yucatan Peninsula, this wasn't established until 1990.

Passage 2

Increasing numbers of paleontologists are leaning toward the idea that the scientific community was too hasty in ascribing the extinction of the dinosaurs solely to an asteroid impact. After all, doing so involves writing off the idea that any role in the mass dying was played by the Deccan Traps, a nearly 200,000 square-mile grouping of volcanic flood basalts in what is now India. We know that they formed between 60 and 68 million years ago, releasing huge amounts of lava and toxic gases in the process. No one is denying that the Chicxulub asteroid impact did in fact occur and that it almost certainly played a substantial role in the extinction, but there is also no good reason to insist that the Cretaceous-Paleogene Event had only a single cause.

467. Which best describes the relationship between Passage 1 and Passage 2?

(A) Passage 1 and Passage 2 present different counterarguments to a single theory.

(B) Passage 1 and Passage 2 agree about an event but disagree about when it took place.

(C) The theory in Passage 2 sees the theory in Passage 1 as limited.

(D) The theory in Passage 1 sees the theory in Passage 2 as outdated.

(E) The theory in Passage 2 sees the theory in Passage 1 as fraudulent.

468. As it is used in Passage 1, the phrase "rogue hypothesis" most nearly means

(A) principled objection

(B) previous realization

(C) uncommon notion

(D) inherent contradiction

(E) accepted revision

469. Which of the following statements accurately describes how the Chicxulub asteroid is regarded by the authors of the two passages?

(A) At least one author is not 100 percent sure that it really existed.

(B) The two authors disagree about where it struck Earth but not about when.

(C) The author of Passage 2 believes that the Chicxulub asteroid struck the Deccan Traps.

(D) The two authors agree that it had a hand in the Cretaceous–Paleogene Event.

(E) Only the author of Passage 1 believes that it explains the iridium levels in the geologic record.

470. Which of the following statements accurately identifies one difference between the two passages?

(A) Only the author of Passage 2 champions a single cause of the Cretaceous–Paleogene Event.

(B) Only the author of Passage 1 explains how his supporting evidence was obtained.

(C) Only the author of Passage 2 questions whether the Chicxulub asteroid hit the Earth.

(D) Only the author of Passage 1 posits that some dinosaurs may have escaped extinction.

(E) Only the author of Passage 2 discusses an event that affected the entire Earth.

471. The attitude of the author of Passage 1 toward the content of Passage 2 is presumably that it is

(A) superfluous

(B) outdated

(C) self-contradictory

(D) unfalsifiable

(E) offensive

472. Neither passage appears to be especially concerned with data regarding

(A) whether the Cretaceous–Paleogene Event had multiple causes or a single one

(B) when the Deccan Traps came into existence

(C) which species of dinosaurs went extinct before others

(D) the location of the impact of the Chicxulub asteroid

(E) the typical chemical composition of asteroids

Ask any schoolchild (or virtually any adult) to draw a picture of a Medieval knight, and the odds are that you'll wind up with a depiction of someone encased from head to foot in a suit of armor. This is one of the most widespread misconceptions about history. The iconic "suit of armor" that we now associate so closely with the period actually didn't develop until the tail end of the Middle Ages, and it didn't become commonplace on the battlefield until well into what we would now call the Renaissance. European warriors of the true Medieval period, even the wealthier and more aristocratic ones like knights, would have worn scattered pieces of plate armor over chain-mail suits but not "suits of armor" as we now picture them.

473. The author largely takes for granted the fact that the reader already knows that

(A) Europeans did not actually wear suits of armor

(B) knights were generally wealthier than common soldiers

(C) the word "Renaissance" is a recently invented term

(D) the Renaissance preceded the Middle Ages

(E) the "Middle Ages" and the "Medieval Period" are the same thing

People often prickle at evolutionary or instinctual explanations for human behavior based on the idea that it's been a long time since humans lived in a state of nature. But this depends upon a rather sizeable misapplication of the phrase "a long time." When we speak of "human civilization" — meaning the existence of permanent settlements, agriculture, and some rudimentary form of government — we are talking about things that appeared only about 10,000 years ago. Conversely, the first humans — meaning members of the genus *Homo* — reared their heads just over two million years ago. We were evolving for a heck of a long time before we were "civilized."

474. One implication definitively made by the passage is that

(A) the term "human civilization" cannot be usefully defined

(B) hardly anyone is upset by instinctual explanations for human behavior

(C) the bulk of human evolution took place in a state of nature

(D) there are humans who did not belong to the genus *Homo*

(E) permanent settlements and agriculture brought a halt to human evolution

The title of "the southernmost city in the world" is valuable bait when it comes to attracting tourists, but the question of which burg — and, accordingly, which nation — can boast it is not such an easy matter to settle. It all comes down to the fact that there is no hard-and-fast definition of what counts as a "city." Ushuaia, the southernmost city in Argentina, has a population of 64,000. Just across the Beagle Channel, however, lies Chile's Puerto Williams — farther south but with a population of only about 3,000. Does that make it populous enough to count as a city? Unsurprisingly, Chile says yes, and Argentina says no.

475. The specific information presented by the passage serves as an example of what general principle?

(A) Cartography (that is, map-making) is a surprisingly inexact discipline.

(B) The attempt to impose definitions on elements of existence is sometimes futile.

(C) Borders between nations can sometimes be a matter of perspective.

(D) Cardinal directions (e.g., "north" or "south") ultimately do not exist in nature

(E) There is in fact no such thing as a "city."

Questions 476–480 are based on the following passage.

You don't hear the name of William Tyndale every day, but if you speak English, he probably had a greater influence on the words that come out of your mouth than anyone besides William Shakespeare. An English Protestant reformer of the early 1500s, Tyndale was the first since the invention of the printing press to translate the Bible into English (John Wycliffe's handwritten translations of the 1300s were quickly banned and easily destroyed by authorities, as the process of producing them was so laborious). This was an act punishable by death, as the ability of the common man to read scripture in his own language would weaken the power of the Church, and so Tyndale had to do his work in hiding on continental Europe.

He was captured in 1535 and executed the following year, but ironically, Tyndale's Bible became the standard in England soon afterward, when Henry VIII broke with Rome. The more famous King James Bible of 1611, finalized by a committee of scholars, is largely just a revision of Tyndale's single-handed work, which established the tone and conventions of literary Early Modern English. As the formulator of such famous idioms as "eat, drink, and be merry," "fight the good fight," and "salt of the earth," Tyndale is surpassed in the coining of English expressions only by Shakespeare, who developed his own ear for literary English by reading Tyndale's Bible as a schoolboy.

476. Which of the following best describes the relationship between the two paragraphs of the passage?

(A). The first paragraph compares William Tyndale with John Wycliffe, and the second compares William Tyndale with William Shakespeare.

(B) The first paragraph offers a brief biography of William Tyndale himself, and the second delineates how his life's work came to be as influential as it was.

(C) The first paragraph focuses on William Tyndale's role in the invention of the printing press, and the second explains his role in Henry VIII's break with Rome.

(D) The first paragraph concentrates on William Tyndale's education, and the second, on his influence.

(E) The first paragraph argues that William Tyndale influenced the Church, and the second argues that he influenced William Shakespeare.

477. The passage mentions William Shakespeare multiple times with the implication that

(A) many phrases that the average person believes to have been invented by him were actually invented by William Tyndale

(B) he may have secretly collaborated with William Tyndale on the King James version of the Bible

(C) his own personal religious views were heavily influenced by William Tyndale

(D) it is widely accepted, and justifiably so, that he had the single greatest influence on the English language of any one person

(E) it should be more widely disputed whether he had the single greatest influence on the English language of any one person

478. The passage implies that "the tone and conventions of Early Modern English" were established in

(A) the early 16th century

(B) the late 16th century

(C) the early 17th century

(D) the late 17th century

(E) the 14th century

479. One question that the passage does NOT address is whether

(A) there were ultimately political reasons for the influential nature of Tyndale's Bible

(B) William Shakespeare was able to understand Early Modern English

(C) William Tyndale considered himself a Catholic

(D) the phraseology of William Tyndale's Bible was influenced by that of John Wycliffe's

(E) there was any special reason William Tyndale left England

480. The word "laborious" is roughly synonymous with

(A) illegal

(B) subversive

(C) primitive

(D) depressing

(E) time-consuming

Set 2

Questions 481–483 are based on the following information and graphic.

The following line graph compares the relative populations of two wolf packs in Oregon over the last several years, along with the total wolf population of the state.

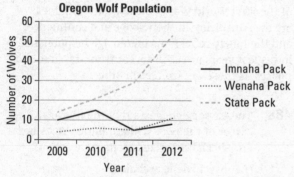

© John Wiley & Sons, Inc.

481. According to the information contained in the graph, the total number of wolves in the state of Oregon declined from

(A) 2009 to 2010

(B) 2010 to 2011

(C) 2011 to 2012

(D) It declined over the entire graph.

(E) It never declined at any point on the graph.

482. The year in which the Wenaha pack comprised its greatest percentage of the total number of wolves in the state of Oregon was

(A) 2009

(B) 2010

(C) 2011

(D) 2012

(E) It is impossible to discern this based on the graph.

483. Among the following choices, the largest difference is between

(A) the numbers of Imnaha wolves in 2010 and 2011

(B) the numbers of Wenaha wolves in 2009 and 2012

(C) the total numbers of wolves in 2011 and 2012

(D) the total numbers of wolves in 2009 and 2011

(E) the number of Imnaha wolves in 2010 and Wenaha wolves in 2012

Questions 484–487 are based on the following passage.

We've all heard the terms, but what, if anything, is the actual difference between a *psychopath* and a *sociopath?* The average person's confusion on this point is forgivable, because the fact is that psychologists and neurologists themselves disagree: Some consider the terms interchangeable, others favor dispensing with both in favor of the more modern diagnosis of *antisocial personality disorder* (which fits in more neatly with the spectrum of other personality disorders), and even the professionals who favor the continued and distinct use of both terms cannot form an agreement about what the difference is. Adding to the confusion is the fact that psychopaths and/or sociopaths are notably hard to study. For obvious reasons, an individual being screened for psychopathy is likely to lie, and so it takes a highly skilled professional to make such a diagnosis concerning a living person. Diagnosing psychopathy and/or sociopathy post-mortem is comparatively simpler, as there is agreement that the conditions involve observable differences in brain structure, but an autopsy cannot reveal whether such differences were present at birth or acquired, nor (obviously) can it tell us very much about the individual's subjective experience of the condition — and it is in this subjective experience that most agree the difference between psychopathy and sociopathy probably lies. At the moment, traction is being gained by the viewpoint that, although a psychopath and sociopath will both have a highly reduced or virtually absent capacity for empathy, a psychopath has *no* sense of morality, whereas a sociopath has a *twisted* one. In other words, a psychopath does not know or care whether his or her actions are right or wrong; a sociopath, meanwhile, believes his or her actions to be right but has a definition of "right" that the average person would find horrifying.

484. According to the passage, the opinion described in the closing sentence is

(A) now the majority opinion

(B) becoming increasingly popular

(C) about to be proved by new data

(D) about to be disproved by new data

(E) a popular viewpoint with little basis in fact

485. It can reasonably be assumed that the author composed the passage for an audience of

(A) psychological professionals

(B) general readers with no interest in psychology

(C) decently educated and curious general readers

(D) law-enforcement officials

(E) medical students studying the structure of the brain

486. The word "interchangeable" most nearly means

(A) meaningless

(B) technical

(C) vague

(D) synonymous

(E) confusing

487. According to the passage, something upon which all professionals agree is that psychopathy and sociopathy both involve

(A) observable differences in brain structure

(B) the uncontrollable impulse to lie

(C) the absence of a belief in right and wrong

(D) inborn genetic differences from the average person

(E) a spectrum of personality disorders

The poetry of William Butler Yeats, who became in 1923 the first Irishman to receive the Nobel Prize for Literature, went through so many distinct phases during his long career that to read him is almost to read several different poets. The mystical and deliberately archaic-sounding verse of his early books borders on the psychedelic; the strident political poems he produced at the time of the First World War and the Irish "Troubles" are awe-inspiring in their scope and confidence; and the lonely reflections on old age he published in his last years are as different from the first two phases as those are from each other.

488. The passage suggests that the literary career of the poet William Butler Yeats is largely characterized by its

(A) psychedelic archaisms

(B) lonely reflections

(C) political iconoclasm

(D) strident mysticism

(E) stylistic detours

Popular tradition holds that celebrities die in groups, but all superstition aside, is it sometimes the case that one famous individual is too lightly mourned by the culture due solely to the bad luck of having passed away in too close proximity to another. Perhaps no great American ever received a more insufficient send-off than show-business legend Groucho Marx, who happened to leave us on August 19, 1977, only three days after the death of Elvis Presley. Granted, Presley's death was both untimely and mysterious, whereas Groucho was an elderly man — but still, it is lamentable that the national hysteria over the King of Rock and Roll should have prevented the King of Comedy from getting his due.

489. The passage opens by citing and then reflects on an example of

(A) an objectionable superstition

(B) a majority opinion

(C) a folk truism

(D) an irreconcilable paradox

(E) an instance of déjà vu

The etymology of vulgar or profane words is a subject of both frustration and amusement for linguists. Since "dirty" words tend to be used in speech for a considerable length of time before they are ever used in print, their origins are often a subject of controversy. Often, urban legend will hold that a particular four-letter word originated as an acronym, but such after-the-fact explanations — jokingly dubbed "backronyms" — are inevitably spurious.

490. The closing expression "inevitably spurious" can best be taken to mean

(A) always untrustworthy

(B) deliberately complex

(C) deceptively revealing

(D) likely to be offensive

(E) never traceable

Though most people believe that the famous British monument of Stonehenge was built by the druids as a site for their mysterious rituals, this idea is wrong on several fronts. First of all, we now know that Stonehenge is much older than was long supposed. The first megaliths were raised sometime between 3000 and 2500 BCE, meaning that Stonehenge considerably predates the druids and may even be older that the Great Pyramid of Egypt. As for what Stonehenge was used for, the answer may very well be "nothing." Most anthropologists now believe it was a sacred *necropolis*, or "city of the dead," which stood on lands believed to be occupied by the spirits and strictly forbidden to the living.

491. Based on the information about it presented by the passage, which of the following statements about Stonehenge is presumably true?

(A) The method by which humans raised the megaliths remains a mystery.

(B) Archaeologists have found no evidence of human habitation in it.

(C) Its layout is in keeping with certain druidical ceremonies.

(D) It was used only at certain times of the year.

(E) Its design influenced that of the Great Pyramid of Egypt.

Questions 492–496 are based on the following passage.

When the Frankish king Charlemagne was crowned emperor on Christmas Day, 800, this was the final step in a centuries-long process during which the Franks assumed Rome's inheritance in Western Europe. Ever since they made their first historical appearance in northeastern Gaul, the Franks had been in close contact with the *Imperium Romanum*, and after the collapse of its western half in 476, they had conquered large parts of northern, central, and finally southern Europe. Already in the sixth century, their kingdom had become the dominant power in the West (Geary 1988; Wood 1994). Despite several crises, it succeeded in maintaining this position until the end of the seventh century and moved on to further expansion during the eighth.

The Franks were Rome's heirs not only in a geographical sense but also concerning the internal constitution of their realm. Their kings were not the only ones in the former imperial territories to imitate the Roman mode of rule, but especially in religious matters they adapted much more thoroughly, and from the beginning, to the Roman population majority than did any of the other German states. Apart from a favorable geographical position at a safe distance from Byzantium and the Arabs, this was the main reason why the Frankish realm survived its many inner crises and proved capable of extending its power to Italy, including Rome.

492. The primary purpose of the first paragraph of the passage is to

(A) pose a question regarding a historical mystery

(B) compare two viewpoints on a historical event

(C) reject a traditional historical explanation

(D) establish the facts of a historical situation

(E) enumerate the causes of a historical crisis

493. The primary purpose of the second paragraph of the passage is to

(A) unpack the mechanics of the state of affairs described in the first paragraph

(B) answer the questions posed by the first paragraph

(C) provide a counterargument to the claims made in the first paragraph

(D) illuminate the logic connecting the first paragraph's reasons to its claims

(E) undermine an opinion concerning the importance of an event mentioned in the first paragraph.

494. Based on the information in the passage, it can be assumed that political entities who were contemporaneous with the rising Frankish empire but were even more powerful would have included

(A) northeastern Gaul

(B) the *Imperium Romanum*

(C) the other German states

(D) Byzantium

(E) Italy

495. Overall, the passage implies that the Franks were able to

(A) defeat the Roman Empire militarily by adopting its methods of warfare

(B) assume the mantle of Roman power by assimilating themselves into it

(C) outlast the Roman Empire due to a favorable geographical position

(D) attract Roman citizens with more favorable laws and policies

(E) evade Roman attention by always remaining on the move

496. The phrase "internal constitution" should be taken to refer to

(A) a codified set of governing rules and regulations

(B) the geographical borders marking a sphere of influence

(C) the organization of an administrative bureaucracy

(D) a set of influences on the aesthetics of a government

(E) the religious justification for the use of governmental power

Though popular culture often still regards them as the quintessential aspect of the test, analogies were actually removed from the SAT in 2005. The decision to axe the series of questions that simultaneously tested vocabulary knowledge and critical-thinking skills (e.g., "cat is to kitten as goose is to...") was a relief to many but a cause for outrage and suspicion to others. Though the College Board never issued a full explanation for the decision, education insiders indicated that the analogies were dumped in response to complaints that logical reasoning was an inborn skill that couldn't be studied (meaning that these questions rewarded natural aptitude rather than diligent preparation) and that the vocabulary words were biased towards certain ethnic or socioeconomic groups (one recent question had infamously employed the word *regatta*, a type of sailing race). Fans of the analogies section countered that the entire point of the test was for smart kids to do well and that students of any ethnic group or socioeconomic class could have learned a word from reading, regardless of their life experience.

497. The passage directly answers which of the following questions?

(A) When was the first time that the format of the SAT was changed?

(B) What is the etymology of the word "analogy"?

(C) What argument might be used to defend the SAT analogies section?

(D) How do we know that logical reasoning is an inborn skill?

(E) When were the first complaints about the SAT analogies section made?

Questions 498–500 are based on the following passage.

The fact that Europa, a moon of the planet Jupiter, spins on its axis at a rate faster than that at which it orbits the planet probably wouldn't cause many people to leap from their chairs with excitement. But perhaps it should: Such an orbital eccentricity indicates that Europa is likely to have a sizeable layer of liquid between its frozen outer crust and dense core, and the fact that the liquid in question is almost certainly water means that Europa is now the top candidate in our solar system for an extraterrestrial body that contains life. A subsurface ocean would receive little if any of the sunlight that was long thought to be a prerequisite for life, but scientists now know that life can originate in and be supported by the chemical disequilibrium created by undersea volcanoes, a feature that Europa's hidden sea is likely to contain. We may find out conclusively in our lifetimes, though we will have to have a bit of patience: the Jupiter Icy Moon Explorer (JUICE) satellite will launch in 2022 and reach the Jupiter system in 2030.

498. Which of the following, if true, would decrease the probability of there being life on Europa?

(A) A serious malfunction in the JUICE satellite after it launches

(B) The discovery of liquid water containing bacteria on the planet Mars

(C) A political battle over the JUICE satellite's funding before it launches

(D) The confirmation of below-freezing temperatures throughout its interior

(E) The revelation that the planet Saturn's rings are not actually composed of ice

499. The information about Europa's possible undersea volcanoes is crucial because the passage establishes that Europa's water does not receive enough

(A) life

(B) heat

(C) liquid

(D) chemicals

(E) sunlight

500. Which phrase from the passage is MOST crucial to the theory that Europa might contain life?

(A) "spins on its axis"

(B) "dense core"

(C) "extraterrestrial body"

(D) "a prerequisite for life"

(E) "chemical disequilibrium"

Questions 501–506 are based on the following passages.

Passage 1

Even among people who comprehend and accept the basics of the theory of evolution, a common misunderstanding involves the belief that evolution is *goal-oriented* or somehow "destined" to arrive at one and only one "right" outcome — e.g., the belief that mice are *supposed to be* fast, or that wolves are *supposed to be* vicious, or that human beings are *supposed to be* intelligent. Although it is indisputably true that the traits of speed, aggression, and intelligence have *thus far* been beneficial adaptations for the animals that became mice, wolves, and humans, we must not fall victim to the fallacy of *retrospective determinism* — i.e., the idea that just because something *did* happen, it must have been *meant* to and must therefore *always* be that way.

Passage 2

Pop sociologists love to talk about how factors like matchmaking websites or the troubled economy are affecting people's love lives, but those minor changes are nothing compared to the "dating revolution" that's been recently observed in the African elephant population. For untold generations, the male elephant with the biggest, baddest set of tusks has been the elephant equivalent of the captain of the football team, calling the shots among males and making all the lady elephants swoon. In comparatively recent history, of course, tusks are also a liability, as any elephant with an impressive pair is a target for human ivory poachers. And although we're still not sure whether an elephant "never forgets," it now appears clear that an elephant — a female one, anyway — is smart enough to understand both the motivation behind poaching and a little bit of genetics as well. In what could only be the result of an effort to keep her eventual offspring from becoming the victims of poachers, female elephants are now seeking out smaller-tusked or entirely tuskless males, a phenomenon that has been jokingly but not inaccurately described as the biggest "Revenge of the Nerds" ever witnessed in the animal kingdom.

501. The function of Passage 2 is principally to
   (A) demonstrate the accuracy of Passage 1
   (B) present hard data that falsifies Passage 1
   (C) explain what Passage 1 means by *retrospective determinism*
   (D) resolve a contradiction found in Passage 1
   (E) Passage 2 is largely unrelated to Passage 1

502. The terms that appear in quotation marks in Passage 1 are placed in quotation marks in order to indicate that they are
   (A) direct quotations
   (B) mocking the opinions they represent
   (C) examples of dramatic irony
   (D) examples of situational irony
   (E) humorous popular references

503. The terms that appear in quotation marks in Passage 2 are placed in quotation marks in order to indicate that they are
   (A) direct quotations
   (B) mocking the opinions they represent
   (C) examples of dramatic irony
   (D) examples of situational irony
   (E) humorous popular references

504. Passage 1 and Passage 2
   (A) present the same data at two different reading levels
   (B) address different subjects but in a similar tone
   (C) address a common subject but differ in tone
   (D) champion two mutually exclusive theories
   (E) are by a single author who has changed his mind

505. Which of the following accurately describes the disciplines concerned by both passages?
   (A) Both Passage 1 and Passage 2 concern biology.
   (B) Passage 1 concerns biology, and Passage 2 concerns psychology.
   (C) Passage 1 concerns politics, and Passage 2 concerns culture.
   (D) Passage 1 concerns rhetoric, and Passage 2 concerns economics.
   (E) Passage 1 concerns psychology, and Passage 2 concerns organic chemistry.

506. Neither of the two passages contains any examples of

(A) official terms from argumentative rhetoric

(B) grammatically incorrect words used for humorous effect

(C) symbolic logic

(D) references to proverbs

(E) Latin abbreviations

We had not even a good laboratory at that time. We worked in a hangar where there were no improvements, no good chemical arrangements. We had no help, no money. And because of that the work could not go on as it would have done under better conditions. I did myself the numerous crystallizations which were wanted to get the radium salt separated from the barium salt with which it is obtained out of the ore. And in 1902 I finally succeeded in getting pure radium chloride and determining the atomic weight of the new element radium...

507. The primary purpose of this passage is

(A) to persuade the reader that the sacrifices made in the interest of science are worthy.

(B) to argue that radium is a difficult element to study and adapt for use.

(C) to present background information about the writer's experience.

(D) to praise scientists who work for little money.

(E) to complain how the sacrifices and challenges the author had to endure.

But we must not forget that when radium was discovered no one knew that it would prove useful in hospitals. The work was one of pure science. And this is a proof that scientific work must not be considered from the point of view of the direct usefulness of it. It must be done for itself, for the beauty of science, and then there is always the chance that a scientific discovery may become like the radium a benefit for humanity.

But science is not rich, it does not dispose of important means, it does not generally meet recognition before the material usefulness of it has been proved. The factories produce many grams of radium every year, but the laboratories have very small quantities. It is the same for my laboratory and I am very grateful to the American women who wish me to have more of radium and give me the opportunity of doing more work with it.

508. What is one way to tell the difference between the contributions of science and the commercialism of science, according to the author of this passage, Dr. Marie Curie?

(A) All scientific efforts are meant to prove valuable to humans and to enhance life.

(B) If a scientific endeavor can be a benefit for humanity, the results should be shared commercially so the greatest number of people can have access to it.

(C) Scientific work should be considered only from the point of view of usefulness. If a product cannot be useful, scientists should not, ethically, attempt to experiment with it.

(D) Although scientists work for the purity of the scientific process, some consequences prove to be valuable and useful in human settings. If scientific efforts begin to create income for those using it, the scientific community can lose access to continued work with the product.

(E) Scientific work should be considered only from the point of view of commercial benefit. If a product cannot be commercially viable, it will not be used by the populace at large.

Questions 509–512 refer to the following passage.

Perhaps there are but few persons who have read Poe's "Raven" or Dickens's "Barnaby Rudge" who have not felt some curiosity to learn why ravens and crows, more than any other birds, should be invested with characters so ominous and demoniacal. And not only do these birds bear this ominous reputation in poetry and fiction, and in the legends and folklore of many of the nations of the earth, but by the unlearned they are still looked upon as too weird and uncanny for ordinary birds; and many a person can be found even in this age of positivism who would consider a crow lighting upon his house-top as certain a harbinger of evil as Hesiod did, when he said to his brother Perses, "Nor when building a house, leave it not unfinished, lest, mark you, perching upon it, the cawing crow should croak."

In this age, our plane of thought is so far above that of our rude and ignorant ancestors that their superstitions and myths seem too puerile to merit notice; but when we study them attentively, with the light which comparative mythology is able to throw upon them, we find that what at first seemed only childish fables are really the degraded fragments of the religion of our forefathers, and as such they are surely worthy of the attention of their descendants.

509. According to this passage, why do humans still have a curiosity about ravens and crows?

(A) Ravens and crows frequently appear in famous literature, and readers should know the difference between them.

(B) Ravens and crows have long been seen as ominous symbols in literature and folklore.

(C) Only unlearned humans are curious about ravens and crows. Learned humans understand these are just animals that cannot bring messages of evil.

(D) Ravens and crows are so similar that ancient people could not tell them apart, and thus they came to be seen as changeling creatures who worked for the devil.

(E) Authors frequently use these creatures as symbols, and readers puzzle over their meaning in their modern lives.

510. In this passage, "puerile" is used most nearly to mean

(A) superstitious

(B) ancient

(C) silly

(D) important

(E) frightening

511. In analyzing literary works that include ravens and crows, the author is implying that

(A) modern man has largely forgotten the important symbols used just a short time ago

(B) only literary authors think mythological stories are important

(C) the use of symbolism is important only in stories, not in real life

(D) all stories are retold myths from our ancient ancestors

(E) ravens and crows must have some latent power; otherwise, they wouldn't be in so many myths and folk stories

512. The author's opinion is that

(A) our ancestors were so ignorant that their ideas should no longer be considered valid

(B) our ancestors believed that ravens and crows were part of an important religion and should be considered holy animals

(C) mythological stories of ravens and crows most likely have their basis in religious contexts and should be considered worthy of study and attention

(D) the superstitions and myths concerning ravens and crows hearken back to fantastic mythological beginnings and should be seen for what they are: just stories

(E) more scientific study should be spent to best understand the psychological implications of such symbols

We can clearly understand why a species when once lost should never reappear, even if the very same conditions of life, organic and inorganic, should recur. For though the offspring of one species might be adapted (and no doubt this has occurred in innumerable instances) to fill the exact place of another species in the economy of nature, and thus supplant it; yet the two forms—the old and the new—would not be identically the same; for both would almost certainly inherit different characters from their distinct progenitors. For instance, it is just possible, if our fantail-pigeons were all destroyed, that fanciers, by striving during long ages for the same object, might make a new breed hardly distinguishable from our present fantail; but if the parent rock-pigeon were also destroyed, and in nature we have every reason to believe that the parent-form will generally be supplanted and exterminated by its improved offspring, it is quite incredible that a fantail, identical with the existing breed, could be raised from any other species of pigeon, or even from the other well-established races of the domestic pigeon, for the newly-formed fantail would be almost sure to inherit from its new progenitor some slight characteristic differences.

513. The author, Charles Darwin, most probably uses the word "supplant" to mean

(A) to supersede by force or treachery

(B) to suddenly uproot and eradicate

(C) to take the place of and serve as a substitute for

(D) to displace or dislodge

(E) to become more important than

514. Which of the following best states the main idea of this passage?

(A) When a species is lost due to natural selection, that particular species will not reappear naturally.

(B) New species are so similar to previous generations that differences can hardly be noted, and the two species should be considered to be the same without considering why such changes occurred.

(C) Domesticated species can be bred to exactly duplicate those species that are in danger of extinction.

(D) Only species that can adapt to their environment will survive.

(E) New breeds of species will exterminate the older versions because they are hardier.

515. The author mentions fantail pigeons most likely in order to

(A) bring awareness to the species before it becomes extinct

(B) provide an example to more clearly illustrate the scientific points being made

(C) provide a clear example of human and species interaction and to show how natural selection can be manipulated

(D) give a fascinating example of how nature doesn't always neatly follow proposed theories

(E) illustrate what is lost when a species becomes extinct

516. What does Darwin imply about rock pigeons?

    (A) Rock pigeons are the "parents" of fantail pigeons and will eventually be taken over by new breeds.

    (B) Future generations of rock pigeons, because they are domesticated, will exactly duplicate their "parents."

    (C) Rock pigeons and fantail pigeons are the same creature, but the fantail is the new and improved form.

    (D) All future generations of rock pigeons will inherit some slight characteristic differences.

    (E) If these types of pigeons are to survive, breeders must create new and better versions.

Questions 517–521 refer to the following passage.

Enjoying [the TV show] *Lost* means having a deep, existential experience: in other words, one that connects with the themes basic to our human experience. *Lost* produces this kind of experience in an especially clear and direct way and so can help us understand why other shows appeal to us so much, especially the many detective and puzzle-solving shows that continue to keep our interest.

Cultural critics sometimes compare contemporary Western culture unfavorably with ancient Greek culture, whose storytelling art did not mainly provide a means of escape from life, but instead was a standard way of experiencing deep questions about it. I suggest, however, that one of the lessons of *Lost* is that our culture's standard, supposedly escapist entertainment is sometimes also that kind of deep art.

We may not be conscious of our depth, but that doesn't mean it goes away. Whether we know it or not, we never stop being entirely who we are and in one way or another experiencing and living our all of who we are. This is also true in our various forms of entertainment, where we are their creators or their audience. It is true, as well, whether the entertainment is a famous public effort or simply our chatting with one another in our every-day lives.

517. Which of the following best describes the organization of this passage?

    (A) An unresolved problem is pointed out, and then a possible solution is given.

    (B) An unknown theory is given, and then definitions are provided in order to give basis to the theory.

    (C) A controversy is presented, and then evidence is given to support the argument.

    (D) A universal truth is given, and then examples are provided as evidence.

    (E) An alternate theory is presented, and then the author shows why the prevailing theory is weak.

518. The author gives the example of ancient Greek cultural entertainment primarily in order to

    (A) persuade the readers that TV shows like *Lost* are not so different from what is considered artistic forms of storytelling

    (B) show a flaw in the reasoning of counterarguments that Greek storytelling is better than American storytelling

    (C) provide a worldwide perspective that shows the topic has importance outside the U.S.

    (D) solve the problem of comparisons with TV watching versus watching theater

    (E) illustrate how poorly modern entertainment compares to classical entertainment

519. The word "existential" most nearly means

    (A) ethically and morally correct

    (B) approved of by common consent

    (C) considered to be the most usual or normal form according to human existence

    (D) considered to be the established authority

    (E) being in the moment

520. It can be inferred that the author views the TV show *Lost* as

(A) a deeply personal experience that will vary for each person watching it

(B) an artistic experience that is similar to the aesthetic joy one might receive when watching artistic forms of theater

(C) so similar to mystery shows that everyone watching those genres would also love *Lost*

(D) an experience that will cause human connections, as the message will have us question who we are as humans

(E) the best show on TV and one that everyone should watch

521. The passage suggests that escapist entertainment is important because

(A) it allows us to escape from the rigors of life, a common need that all humans have

(B) it allows those who have stressful lives to escape those situations and become someone else

(C) it allows us to escape from our own time period and imagine what life was like in another time period

(D) TV, the best format for this, is also in the puzzle-solving and mystery genre

(E) people don't watch theater anymore, so TV serves as the only form of escapist entertainment

Questions 522–525 refer to the following passage.

The early republic faced intense outside pressure and domestic conflict. In the late sixth century, Rome was by far the largest and most powerful of the Latin communities, with whom it was linked in a loose "league," perhaps hardly inferior to some of the Etruscan city-states to the north. The sanctuaries it built for its gods and the mansions of its elite on the Palatine attest to prosperity; the temple of Jupiter on the capital, dedicated soon after the fall of the monarchy, was at the time one of the largest in central Italy. Rome was ideally located on well-defensible hills on the edge of the Latin plain, where an island in the Tiber offered the first opportunity to cross the river, and where the navigable section of the Tiber ended, at the intersection of the route along the river, linking the interior (the Tiber valley and Sabine country), with the coast and salt pans at Ostia, and an important trade route skirting the hills in safe distance from the coast and connecting Campania and Latium with Etruria. It maintained a net of international relations, including Massilia and Carthage; an early treaty with the latter seems to acknowledge Rome's predominance among the Latins.

522. In this passage, the author implies that Rome's location was ideal in what ways?

(A) It was north of other Etruscan city-states.

(B) It could be easily defended, and a navigable water source was nearby.

(C) It was the most powerful Latin community.

(D) It was close to fresh water sources, which was important for crops.

(E) It was the largest Latin community.

523. According to the passage, which of these details supports the idea that Rome was a wealthy and powerful Latin community?

(A) It was the most well-known community in the area in the late sixth century.

(B) Rome's sanctuaries, mansions, and temples were some of the largest in central Italy and were used by the elite.

(C) Its location served as the first opportunity to cross the Tiber River.

(D) It was a safe distance from the coast and served as a connection point to outlying towns and villages.

(E) It formed international treaties.

524. The passage suggests which of the following?

    (A) The salt pans at Ostia were used to build Rome's wealth.

    (B) The followers of Jupiter overthrew the monarchy of Rome in order to more fully establish their religion.

    (C) Roman citizens were more educated, making them superior to the other Etruscan city-states to the north.

    (D) Rome's location was ideal for defending against enemies.

    (E) Rome was in league with other Etruscan city-states and received support from them.

525. This passage is primarily concerned with

    (A) explaining the intense outside pressure that Rome had to overcome in order to thrive

    (B) explaining the domestic pressures that caused a strain on the newly forming public

    (C) explaining how Rome got to be such an important community

    (D) explaining why it was necessary for Rome to maintain international connections

    (E) explaining what Rome needed in order to survive its eventual fall

Even so it proved a difficult war, marked by major setbacks. Creating a system of colonies that divided their enemies and constructing the first "highway" from Rome to Capua (the Via Appia), the Romans eventually prevailed.

526. The use of quotation marks suggests which of the following?

    (A) An authority has used the term "highways," and the author must use quotation marks in order to correctly cite the source of the term.

    (B) The first highway actually had the name Via Appia.

    (C) The word "highways" is an overgeneralization, and our modern idea of highways is the best way to illustrate the concept, although the two versions of highways are quite different.

    (D) Romans were far ahead of the technological advances of other civilizations and created the first highways the world had ever known.

    (E) The author coined this term and wants to receive credit for any future use of the term.

Scholars debate to what extent the structures Rome created to control Italy reflect the beginnings of imperial rule rather than a hegemonial alliance. However that may be, there is no question that the foundations of those later successes were laid much earlier. The main factors that made it possible, despite often almost insurmountable difficulties, to increase communal power steadily and to meet every enemy in a spirit of united resolve and superior resources were created in the first 150 years of the republic: determined leadership by a strong and cohesive aristocracy, solid and socially as well as religiously sanctioned ties between elite and non-elite, the resolution of domestic conflicts, a gradual and eventually massive expansion of Rome's own territory and citizen population, and a sound and mutually beneficial strategy of alliance building.

527. The author of this passage is primarily concerned with

(A) a comparison of the political structures of imperial rule and hegemonial alliance

(B) the historical basis on which Rome was strongly influenced by imperial rule

(C) establishing that the republic of Rome had its first beginnings 150 years earlier

(D) the fact Rome almost did not survive the almost insurmountable difficulties to create a communal power

(E) examining the debates scholars have over Rome, both the beginning and ending of the society

Now for the first time, man is beginning to grasp the key which may solve the question of whether or not life in some form exists on the other celestial bodies of our solar system. The key is, of course, the technology of space exploration. The question of extraterrestrial life and the question of the origin of life are interwoven. Discovery of the first may very well unlock the riddle of the second.

528. The author suggests which of the following about extraterrestrial life?

(A) Space exploration is the key to discovering the origin of life, which will also tell us about extraterrestrial life.

(B) Man may never be able to solve the questions concerning extraterrestrial life, but he can solve the riddle of the origin of life.

(C) Some form of life already exists on other celestial bodies in our atmosphere, and exploring those will answer questions about intelligent extraterrestrial life.

(D) Man already holds the key to solving the question of extraterrestrial life.

(E) Man will never know the answer to whether extraterrestrial life exists.

Questions 529–532 refer to the following passage.

Important as the ideas are in Shakespeare's plays, we are on far less simple ground in attempting to determine which of them are specifically his own. Do Shakespeare's characters sometimes serve as mouthpieces for his own personal beliefs? The notion is attractive because the things that are said by Hamlet, or Macbeth, or just about any other thoughtful character are so wise and stimulating and eloquently expressed that we like to imagine that we can hear the author himself. Yet, we must be vigilantly aware that each speaker is a narrative voice, even in the Sonnets and other nondramatic poems. If that is true in nondramatic verse, it is insistently more true in drama. Knowing as little as we do about Shakespeare's personal views outside of his writings, we must exercise great care in assuming that we can hear him asking 'To be or not to be' with Hamlet or endorsing Macbeth's nihilistic conclusion that 'Life's but a walking shadow'. One can as easily and fruitlessly generalize on the basis of Puck's 'Lord, what fools these mortals be!' in *A Midsummer Night's Dream*. Shakespeare's utterances often achieve the status of proverbial speech because they are so persuasively and exquisitely worded.

529. The passage suggests that

(A) readers and audience members like to imagine the voice and person of Shakespeare speaking through his characters

(B) Shakespeare's writing is so persuasive that it encourages readers and audience members to believe what the characters believe

(C) those who pay careful attention to the language of Shakespeare will find hidden meanings

(D) Shakespeare's true character can be found in his works, both dramatic and nondramatic

(E) if one pays close enough attention and studies the text, one can see Shakespeare's viewpoints on issues of the time

530. Why does the author say that some of Shakespeare's lines have reached proverbial status?

    (A) Because most of the statements are nihilistic and point to universal truths

    (B) Because Shakespeare was such a master wordsmith and wrote beautifully

    (C) Because Shakespeare used his works to persuade readers to believe in certain things about how the world works and how men operate

    (D) Because Shakespeare used general language that appealed as much to the common man as to the richer and more learned members of his audience

    (E) Because Shakespeare was a learned man who desired to pass along his wisdom and viewpoints to those who came after

531. The primary purpose of this passage is

    (A) to introduce readers to the most well-known speeches in the works of Shakespeare

    (B) to persuade readers that Shakespeare's nondramatic works are just as important as his dramatic works

    (C) to encourage readers to look more deeply at the characters' speeches to determine what Shakespeare's political thoughts and feelings might have been

    (D) to caution readers against putting much meaning into the characters' words and believing them to be the voice of the author himself

    (E) to encourage readers to view the sonnets and nondramatic poems as worth philosophical study in the same way that his drama is worthy of such study

532. Which of these statements is true according to the passage?

    (A) Shakespeare's sonnets and poems are just as important as his drama.

    (B) Each work of an author and each character in that work has its own narrative voice.

    (C) Shakespeare wrote as many nondramatic works as he did dramatic works.

    (D) It is a worthwhile endeavor to imagine Shakespeare speaking in his plays because that adds to the pleasure of reading or viewing them.

    (E) *Macbeth* and *Hamlet* are different from Shakespeare's other, lesser works because they hold more symbolic meaning.

Questions 533–536 refer to the following passage.

Archimedes lived a life entirely devoted to mathematical research. Incidentally he made himself famous by a variety of ingenious mechanical inventions. These things were however merely the "diversions of geometry at play," and he attached no importance to them. In fact he wrote only one such mechanical book, *On Sphere-making*.

Some of his mechanical inventions were used with great effect against the Romans during the siege of Syracuse. Thus he contrived catapults so ingeniously constructed as to be equally serviceable at long or short ranges, machines for discharging showers of missiles through holes made in the walls, and others consisting of long moveable poles projecting beyond the walls which either dropped heavy weights upon the enemy's ships, or grappled the prows by means of an iron hand.

Archimedes died, as he had lived, absorbed in mathematical contemplation. Livy says simply that, amid the scenes of confusion that followed the capture of Syracuse, he was found intent on some figures which he had drawn in the dust, and was killed by a soldier who did not know who he was. In illustration of his entire preoccupation by his abstract studies, we are told that he would forget all about his food and such necessities of life, and would be drawing geometrical figures in the ashes of the fire, or, when anointing himself, in the oil on his body.

533. The author's attitude can best be described as

(A) effusive in admiration

(B) cleverly nonjudgmental

(C) essentially negative

(D) grudgingly appreciative

(E) staidly impersonal

534. The term "mathematical contemplation" refers to which of the following?

(A) Archimedes' rough drafts and the sketch works he left behind

(B) Living a life entirely devoted to mathematical research

(C) Thinking of mathematical concepts continuously, to the point of distraction

(D) Working to bring mathematical concepts to fruition for usefulness in the real world

(E) Archimedes' mathematical concepts that will never see the light of day because of his untimely death

535. In the second paragraph, the author suggests that

(A) the work of Archimedes was instrumental in helping to win battles

(B) Archimedes' true calling was building instruments of war

(C) his enemies were so fearful of his works that they held off for a long siege instead of fighting directly against his machines

(D) Archimedes' works were not used for the purposes with which he had designed them

(E) if not for Archimedes, the Romans would have prevailed during the siege of Syracuse

536. The author would most likely agree with which of the following statements?

(A) Archimedes felt that mathematics was a game and didn't care if his works were useful or not.

(B) Archimedes felt he had a divine gift to give to the world through his understanding of mathematical concepts.

(C) Archimedes felt his inventions could change the world for the better.

(D) Archimedes was a great teacher and left the world a more fruitful place because of his works and inventions.

(E) Archimedes wanted to spend his life in mathematical contemplation and rejected humanity's intrusions into his life's work.

In his works, William Shakespeare cites Aristotle twice in throwaway comments. He never mentions Plato or his academy. Socrates appears once by name as the hapless henpecked husband of Xantippe (*The Taming of the Shrew*). Shakespeare's four references to Pythagoras seem to regard his ideas as a bizarre joke.

537. It can be inferred from the passage that which of the following statements is true?

(A) Shakespeare felt that philosophy was important but that his own ideas on the subject should be considered as the final authority.

(B) Shakespeare felt all philosophers were fools, full of bizarre ideas.

(C) Shakespeare does not discuss philosophers very often and may not have read them widely.

(D) Philosophy plays no part in any of Shakespeare's works.

(E) Shakespeare felt Socrates was a philosopher worth quoting, while Plato was beneath his notice.

Set 3

There is no more familiar and possibly more important figure in the history of Latin learning during the 12th century than Peter Abelard who flourished at its beginning. His career, set forth in his own words, illustrates educational conditions in Gaul at that time. His brilliant success as a lecturer on logic and theology at Paris reveals the great medieval university of that city in embryo. His pioneer, *Sic et Non*, set the fashion for the standard method of presentation employed in scholasticism.

538. The passage provides information for answering which of the following questions most fully?

   (A) Which person has most helped shape Latin learning and scholasticism?

   (B) Who was the most influential figure in 12th-century educational endeavors?

   (C) What contributions did Peter Abelard make to logic and theology in 12th-century Paris?

   (D) Who would be considered the most important figure of Latin learning during 12th-century Gaul, and what contributions did he or she make?

   (E) Who did more to influence and enhance Latin learning during the 12th century?

Questions 539–542 refer to the following passages.

Philosophically, the idea that someone is meant to be in a particular place at a particular time could be a description of the theory of fate or determinism.

Passage 1

Fatalism is the idea that no matter what choices a person makes, a certain thing will happen to him or her.

The most famous story concerning fate is *Oedipus Rex*. Oedipus is told that his fate is to kill his father and sleep with his mother. He desperately wants to avoid this and so leaves what he thinks is his family. Even though he does everything he can to prevent these events from coming to pass, his rash nature makes him kill a stranger who has insulted him at a crossroad and marry a woman who turns out to be the stranger's widow.

Passage 2

Determinism is the idea that every event (including thoughts and actions) is necessitated by previous events and natural laws.

An example of this would be with a man being on a flight that crashed. So we might say that his being on the flight was determined, not because he would have been on the flight no matter what decision he made, but because given certain facts about the kind of man he is, his choice to fly during that time for whatever reason was itself inevitable.

539. Both passages are primarily concerned with

   (A) divine providence

   (B) coincidence

   (C) determinism

   (D) fatalism

   (E) fate

540. The primary purpose of the first paragraph of the entire passage is to

   (A) analyze the specific parameters under which coincidences have been characterized

   (B) summarize both Passage 1 and Passage 2

   (C) identify the context in which theory examples are explanatory

   (D) discuss conflicting theories of coincidental situations

   (E) introduce the prevailing theories of fate and determinism

541. Which of the following, if true, would suggest an alternative to the theories of coincidence as given in the passages?

(A) The Earth will one day be subjected to another geologic Ice Age.

(B) Lord Voldemort began his own demise when he attacked and marked the child Harry Potter, fulfilling a prophecy that a boy born in July would have the power to defeat Lord Voldemort.

(C) God has a plan for all of us, and what happens is providential and happens under the watchful eye of a divine creator.

(D) Julius Caesar was warned by his wife and by a soothsayer to beware the Ides of March, but he chose to fulfill his political duties and didn't take the warnings seriously.

(E) In Nicholas Sparks' novel *The Notebook*, it is clear that the two main characters, Allie and Noah, are meant to be together because no obstacle stops their happy ending.

542. Which best describes the relationship between Passage 1 and Passage 2?

(A) Both passages describe a relationship that is presented in the introduction.

(B) Passage 1 presents a viewpoint that is undermined by the arguments in Passage 2.

(C) Passage 2 disagrees about the reliability of the evidence discussed in Passage 1.

(D) Passage 1 defines a term that is discussed in greater detail in Passage 2.

(E) Passage 2 supports the ideas presented in Passage 1 and gives further examples on the same topic.

543. "Byzantine society was neither static nor even at times particularly stable."

In the context in which it appears, "static" most nearly means

(A) relating to or producing stationary charges of electricity

(B) characterized by a lack of change

(C) being at rest

(D) fluid

(E) resistant to change

Questions 544–547 refer to the following passage.

I have heard it asserted by some, that as America hath flourished under her former connection with Great Britain, that the lame connection is necessary towards her future happiness and will always have the same effect. Nothing can be more fallacious than this kind of argument: we may as well assert that because a child hath thrived upon milk, that it is never to have meat, or that the first twenty years of our lives is to become a precedent for the next twenty. But even this is admitting more than is true, for I answer, roundly, that America would have flourished as much, and probably much more had no European power taken any notice of her.

Alas! We have been long led away by ancient prejudices and made large sacrifices to perdition. We have boasted the protection of Great Britain, without considering, that her motive was *interest* not *attachment*; that she did not protect us from our enemies on our account, but from her enemies on her own account. Let Britain waive her pretensions to the continent, or the continent throw off the dependence, and we would be at peace with France and Spain were they at war with Britain.

544. Which of the following, if true, would most strengthen the argument presented in the passage?

(A) Great Britain has always kept sovereignty over its protectorates for their own good, even at the expense of war.

(B) America relies on its allies — Britain, France, and Spain.

(C) Great Britain ruled India for hundreds of years, yet the country flourished only after that rule ceased.

(D) Change in governmental leadership provides societies a chance to grow and embrace change for the good of all people.

(E) Should Great Britain have continued its protection of America, that fledgling nation would have been much stronger and more powerful than it is.

545. Thomas Paine, the author, most likely mentions "milk" and "meat" in order to

(A) strengthen the claim that such change is necessary for growth

(B) change the topic to the weakened American economy under Britain's rule

(C) weaken the claim of British supporters, that Britain is the sole reason for America's prosperity

(D) elaborate on the relevance of independence by giving an example of the common man

(E) bring attention to American national products that are of better quality than those same British products

546. The passage indicates which of the following about patriotism?

(A) Patriotism to a country includes both interest in the good of the people and attachment to political motives.

(B) True patriotism will cause a nation to protect its own interest against common enemies of rivals.

(C) Patriotism should not be rooted in old habits but should be motivated by current interest.

(D) Patriotism should be an example to other countries and should be proclaimed across the continents through a show of force.

(E) Patriotism cannot take into account the needs, strengths, or weaknesses of other nations; it should focus on the country of one's patriotic attention.

547. Which of the following does Paine NOT discuss as a possible indicator of American strength and independence?

(A) Whether America's connection to Britain is strong enough

(B) Whether American citizens support such a move

(C) Whether Britain is holding America back from greatness

(D) Whether Britain truly protects American interests

(E) Some citizens feel that British support has been beneficial

In May of 1860, Mr. Milton Bradley founded his one-man company at 247 Main Street in a building facing Court Square in Springfield. Throughout its history of becoming the leader in the manufacturing of toys, games, and educational materials, Milton Bradley Company has supported every business, civic, and cultural effort undertaken to make Greater Springfield a better place in which to live, to work, and to play. Today, this commitment to our employees and the citizens of Greater Springfield is reinforced by our unreserved approval and support of "The Master Plan" for Downtown Springfield. Its fruition will bring a more productive environment for all of us.

548. The author mentions the company name Milton Bradley primarily in order to

- (A) persuade readers to support "The Master Plan"
- (B) inform readers about a new program in the downtown area
- (C) explain to readers a history of the downtown area of Springfield
- (D) instill a sense of civic pride in the town of Springfield
- (E) inspire confidence by naming a well-known businessman who got his start in Springfield

The most obvious element of any urban renewal effort is attracting new businesses. They are needed to fill the vacant buildings and the empty lots. Officials from Springfield Central and the City have been making a determined attempt to convince existing Downtown enterprises to expand their operations and new ones to locate here. Recent newspaper headlines show that this effort is bearing fruit.

549. This passage suggests that which of the following probably occurred?

- (A) Attempts made by the town to convince new businesses to locate there have been somewhat successful.
- (B) If urban renewal is to be successful, new businesses must be attracted to the downtown area.
- (C) Existing downtown businesses and new businesses will be in direct competition with one another for consumer traffic.
- (D) The downtown area has many vacant buildings and empty lots, which detracts from new businesses relocating to the area.
- (E) There are so many vacant buildings and empty lots because Springfield has not always been supportive of new business and plans to change their business development processes.

In Don Marquis' work, *As They Liked It*, he writes a scene of William Shakespeare in a tavern, discussing his writing life with these lines: what they want / is kings talking like kings / never had sense enough to talk / and stabbings and stranglings / and fat men making love. . . Shakespeare laments, 'give them a good ghost / or two', or 'kill a little kid or two a prince', 'a little pathos along with the dirt'.

550. It can be inferred from the passage that which of the following statements is true concerning how Marquis felt about Shakespeare?

- (A) A public artist in Shakespeare's situation needed to cater to the tastes of his public.
- (B) Shakespeare got away with inappropriate content because of his famous name.
- (C) Shakespeare was a true artist who was allowed to create content according to his wild and artistic nature.
- (D) Today, Shakespeare would most certainly be criticized for his "art."
- (E) Shakespeare saw above man's trifling concerns to the more important issues of the day that shaped his existence.

Questions 551–554 refer to the following passages.

Passage 1

In Shakespeare's *The Taming of the Shrew*, the shrewish Katherine is described in animal terms: she is a wasp, a wildcat, a shrew. At the start of the play Shakespeare presents a binary view of women. Society divides women into silent (and therefore marriageable) and talkative (or therefore unmarriageable). Despite this apparent sympathy for Katherine, the last scene presents her as a dutiful wife. She gives a long speech—her longest in the play—explaining that a wife owes obedience to her husband.

Shakespeare may well have sensed a particular constituency in his audience to which he wished especially to address the concerns embedded in his plays. London was of course not of one mind about matters of sexuality. Many ordinary citizens tended to endorse the church's insistence on sexual restraint before marriage and fidelity within the marriage contract.

An instance of this gentle expurgating is to be found in the plot of *The Taming of the Shrew*. This delightful comedy features two plots. One is the better known story of Petruchio's taming of the shrewish Kate. The other centres on Kate's younger sister, Bianca, who, as the attractive and seemingly mild-mannered of the wealthy Baptista Minola, is sought after by several wooers.

551. The reference to *The Taming of the Shrew* in both passages serves to

(A) emphasize that Shakespeare's ideas on gender were thinly veiled barbs at Elizabethan attitudes toward sexuality

(B) indicate examples of Elizabethan attitudes toward sex and gender as seen through a playwright who lived at that time

(C) illustrate that Shakespeare had prejudicial attitudes toward gender and used sexual situations to point to what he considered the weaker sex

(D) highlight Shakespeare's most important works, which preached modern (at that time) thoughts on sex and gender

(E) demonstrate that Shakespeare's works are immortal, in that the concerns of Elizabethans are similar to the concerns of modern man

552. Which adjective best characterizes how both authors seem to feel about how the Elizabethans viewed women?

(A) supportive

(B) indifferent

(C) antagonistic

(D) sympathetic

(E) misogynistic

553. Both authors do which of the following?

(A) Acknowledge Shakespeare's contributions to the dramatic world as a view piece for Elizabethan attitudes

(B) Provide clear examples of Shakespeare's subservient attitude toward the wants of his audience and the needs of his acting company

(C) Reference personal examples of Shakespeare's life and attitudes that can be clearly seen in his plays

(D) Offer a societal view of women that was ingrained and not likely meant to be seen as a political statement

(E) Use *The Taming of the Shrew* as evidence of Shakespeare's personal attitude about women and their role in society

554. Which of the following best describes the relationship between Passage 1 and Passage 2?

(A) Passage 1 presents a viewpoint that is undermined by the argument in Passage 2.

(B) Passage 2 presents a viewpoint that is undermined by the argument in Passage 1.

(C) Passage 1 offers evidence of prejudicial treatment of women matter-of-factly as seen in a popular play of the time, while Passage 2 offers evidence that that prejudicial treatment should be viewed within the larger constructs of religious training and beliefs.

(D) Passage 2 disagrees on the reliability of the evidence discussed in Passage 1.

(E) Passage 2 only summarizes *The Taming of the Shrew*, while Passage 1 provides a literary discussion of symbolic elements of the play.

During the 1890s, the opening of Coney Island amusement park encouraged new values for fast-paced entertainment, glorified adventure, and a free, loose social environment. If Central Park reinforced self-control and delayed gratification, Coney Island stressed the emerging consumer-oriented values of extravagance, gaiety, abandon, revelry, and instant gratification.

555. The author mentions Central Park in order to

(A) provide a contrast in entertainment forms during this time period

(B) criticize the emergence of a "Coney Island" mentality

(C) suggest that Central Park could serve as a similar example of consumerism

(D) point out that one has stood the test of time and the other, Coney Island, was a flash in the consumer pan

(E) provide further examples of entertainment options available to New Yorkers in the 1890s

The urban tabloid was the first instrument of modern mass culture. Popular newspapers began to differ dramatically from the staid, upper-class newspaper that dominated late nineteenth-century journalism: They featured banner headlines; a multitude of photographs and cartoons; an emphasis on local news, crime, society news, and sports; and large ads, which made up half of a paper's content. To make them easier to read on a subway or streetcar, page size was cut, stories shortened, and the text heavily illustrated with drawings and photographs.

556. The final sentence in the passage suggests that which of the following is true?

(A) Newspapers changed formats in order to more fully appeal to the reader.

(B) The change in ad size and content was designed to appeal to advertisers.

(C) Modern mass culture was changed according to the whims of society.

(D) As people became more dependent on drawings, photographs, and cartoons, their literacy levels began to require easier formats in what they read.

(E) Newspapers were originally for upper-class society, and they had to lower their standards in order to appeal to other classes

Questions 557–559 refer to the passage below.

Grammar schools were so called because what they taught was grammar. The grammar taught was Latin. School started at 6 a.m. and continued until 6 p.m., followed by homework, and, as the boys moved into higher forms, the language in which they conversed and in which they were instructed was Latin. It is often said, without exaggeration, that by the time a grammar-school boy left school he had as much classical education as a university student of Classics today.

But grammar meant much more than just the parsing of sentences. Grammar was a part of rhetoric; and rhetoric had many branches, all rooted in stylistic awareness.

557. The function of the second sentence is

(A) to explain that the situation is likely unfamiliar to the reader because it takes place in another country and uses another language

(B) to illustrate why such learning conditions were necessary

(C) to denigrate the modern educational system by comparing it to the more stringent conditions of schooling in another century

(D) to inform the reader that the grammar of the time period differed from the reader's likely conception of "grammar"

(E) to differentiate the type of language discussed in this passage

558. Which of the following best describes Latin grammar school?

(A) It is similar to modern university courses.

(B) It was long days of study and years dedicated to learning.

(C) A separate school was necessary because Latin is the hardest language to learn.

(D) Only those learning Latin could hope to get a job as a scholar.

(E) This was the only choice available to young boys if they chose not to apprentice at a skill.

559. The author most probably uses the word "rhetoric" to mean

(A) language that may not be honest or reasonable

(B) the art or skill of speaking or writing

(C) a lofty or pompous manner in speaking

(D) the exaggerated talk of someone who is trying to sound very proud

(E) insincere or meaningless written or spoken persuasive language

Questions 560–563 refer to the following passage.

We have called this body of knowledge "myths." We were drawn to the term because "myth" foregrounds the act of storytelling; because it underlines the cultural work these stories do rather than their accuracy; because it is not about a specific point of origin but about accepted beliefs; because it is about the people who accept or invent or need these stories as much as it is about the stories themselves. Not all of our myths are untrue: in calling these beliefs "myths" we are less interested in stigmatizing them as foolish or unsubstantiated than we are concerned to understand how they become ossified and block our interpretation of works.

Karen Armstrong's *A Short History of Myth* (2005) offers some pithy observations. Myths are dynamic: they change over time, they adapt themselves to cultural and historical developments, they have accretions and deletions, they iron out—or accumulate—contradictions. Myths are not historically accurate: they do not work by being factual; they are interested in what an event meant, not in what actually happened; they are designed to be effective, not true. And, she argues, humans are myth-seeking creatures. That is to say we are creatures drawn to stories. Myth, from the Greek *muthos,* is something that is told, a speech, a narrative, a fiction, a plot.

560. The author mentions Karen Armstrong's book most likely to

(A) provide more evidence and another example of how people view the topic

(B) show that a well-known authority figure agrees with the author's theories of myths

(C) find common ground between the reader and the topic and draw on common knowledge

(D) show this topic is so important that many books have been written about it

(E) provide an example of an alternate theory

561. The author would most likely agree with which of the following statements?

(A) Myths are meant for entertainment and should not be studied too closely.

(B) Studying myths will bring us closer to understanding our own history because myths are based in fact.

(C) Myths serve as a culture's way of remembering important events.

(D) Myths are either based in fact or are false; they are either true or untrue.

(E) Myths are more important for their storytelling components than for their historical accuracy.

562. When the author states that humans are "myth-seeking creatures," what does she mean?

(A) That myths focus only on topics concerning humanity and what it means to be human

(B) That humans seek to understand their world and remember their histories as interesting stories rather than dry recordings of fact

(C) That our natural world can best be explained through blends of factual accuracy and storytelling

(D) That myths are created by humans and have dynamic, changing natures according to human whims

(E) That humans like stories better and are more apt to remember stories rather than a complicated litany of historical facts

563. It can be inferred from the passage that the author would probably *disagree* that which of the following statements is a myth?

(A) Johnny Appleseed wandered across America during pioneer times and planted orchards of apple trees.

(B) Paul Bunyan was a giant lumberjack who did superhuman feats accompanied by Babe the Blue Ox.

(C) Thomas Jefferson is known today for his views of equality, but he kept several slaves and even had many children by a slave.

(D) George Washington chopped down his father's cherry tree and, when threatened with severe punishment, owned up to his faults with the famous statement "I cannot tell a lie."

(E) In a race against a steam-powered hammer, John Henry beat the machine only to die when his heart burst from the effort.

Philosophers who think that life is meaningless are called nihilists. To avoid nihilism, it seems we should stop worrying about God and the afterlife and instead try to find meaning in our finite lives in the natural world.

How about how we *feel* about our actions? Does that matter? If a person feels that she's not accomplishing her goals, for example, or not having a positive impact on society, she might feel that her life has little or no meaning. But if she feels good about what she's doing, if it matters *to her,* might we not say that she's leading a meaningful life?

No, this is too easy.

564. The author finds fault with the connection between how one feels and living a meaningful life for its failure to answer which of the following questions?

(A) Is meaningful equal to getting what you want?

(B) Is meaningless the same as not getting what you want?

(C) If what a person wants is trivial, irrational, or evil, can this add up to a meaningful life?

(D) Personal feelings equate with the larger topics of God and the afterlife and can lead to a deeper understanding of life.

(E) What can one do to lead a more meaningful and full life?

Socrates (469–399 BCE), the first hero of Western philosophy, was found guilty of corrupting the youth of Athens and not believing in the gods. For his crime, he was condemned to death. In actuality, Socrates was being punished for his habit of questioning others and exposing their ignorance in his search for truth.

565. Which of the following could be substituted for the phrase "In actuality" in this passage with the least change in meaning?

(A) Figuratively,

(B) Symbolically,

(C) Literally,

(D) In reality,

(E) Hypothetically,

While extraordinarily important in itself, self-consciousness is also essential to the development of an objective identity. To have a self means to have in one's mind an objective sense of oneself, a sense of one's characteristics, aptitudes, and likes and dislikes. Jean-Paul Sartre does not believe that individuals can develop selves on their own, but rather argues that others play an integral role in the consolidation of personal identity. As Sartre states, "The Other holds. . . the secret of what I am."

566. By using Sartre's example, the author means to say that

(A) developmentally speaking, individuals obtain their sense of self initially through the assimilation of objective characterizations supplied by others

(B) self-consciousness means learning to live with an objective sense of oneself and live above the thoughts and opinions of others

(C) those who are self-conscious develop this sense of self because they initially learned to reject the objective characterizations supplied by others

(D) only others can reveal the true sense of a person; a self-conscious person is unable to realize the truth about him- or herself

(E) individuality can be obtained only when one seeks to shun the attitudes of others in order to develop a sense of oneself

Questions 567–570 refer to the following passage.

In the past decade, considerable advances have been made in our knowledge of the probable processes leading to the origin of life on Earth. A succession of laboratory experiments has shown that essentially all the organic building blocks of contemporary terrestrial organisms can be synthesized by supplying energy to a mixture of the hydrogen-rich gases of the primitive terrestrial atmosphere. It now seems likely that the laboratory synthesis of a self-replicating molecular system is only a short time away from realization. The syntheses of similar systems in the primitive terrestrial oceans must have occurred—collections of molecules which were so constructed that, by the laws of physics and chemistry, they forced the production of identical copies of themselves out of the building blocks in the surrounding medium. Such a system satisfies many of the criteria for Darwinian natural selection, and the long evolutionary path from molecule to advanced organism can then be understood. Since nothing except very general primitive atmospheric conditions and energy sources are required for such syntheses, it is possible that similar events occurred in the early history of Mars and that life may have come into being on that planet several billions of years ago. Its subsequent evolution, in response to the changing Martian environment, would have produced organisms quite different from those which now inhabit Earth.

567. The passage indicates which of the following about manufacturing the building blocks for primitive Earth creatures in a laboratory setting?

(A) Man has been unsuccessful in creating these building blocks, and biological advances have eluded scientists.

(B) Man has used this process to understand the origin of life on Earth.

(C) Through these experiments, scientists have learned that life on Earth involved a process of applying energy to a mixture of hydrogen-rich gases available in the primitive atmosphere.

(D) Creating such building blocks is hampered by ethical concerns and legislation opposing such a process.

(E) Man is capable of building complicated terrestrial organisms from the manufacture of these building blocks.

568. The author suggests that which of the following explains the potential for life on Mars?

(A) The Martian atmosphere does not currently, and did not formerly, provide the necessary materials for the growth and development of life.

(B) Life must have existed on Mars several billion years ago, but finding evidence of that can be done only through laboratory experiments that duplicate that exact environment.

(C) Life has never existed on Mars because of the primitive atmospheric conditions.

(D) Although life on Mars and Earth might share a similar evolutionary process, Mars creatures would have produced organisms dissimilar to Earth creatures because of natural selection.

(E) Repopulation of Mars is possible with the eventual creation of primitive life forms in Earthen laboratories.

569. By using the phrase "criteria for Darwinian natural selection," the author means to say that

(A) all creatures must adhere to a set of criteria in order to be considered a life form

(B) Darwin suggested a set of criteria for life forms which has since become established scientific practice

(C) Darwin's theory of natural selection can be applied to these collections of molecules because they followed the same path as all life forms, reproducing in order to endure

(D) extraterrestrial life forms do not comply with the same theories as those on Earth

(E) it is unknown how Martian natural selection would have occurred because Darwinian natural selection can be applied only to life forms on Earth

570. The passage states that we can know which of the following to be true?

(A) Atmospheric conditions and energy sources are necessary for life.

(B) Self-generating molecular systems can be re-created in a laboratory setting.

(C) Life on Mars occurred several billion years ago.

(D) The evolutionary processes on Mars predate those same processes on Earth.

(E) The primitive conditions on Mars were the same as those on primitive Earth, and these similar conditions would have led to similar life forms.

Fantasy and science fiction provide an escape from the normal, allowing us to imagine the richness of a life that is enhanced by having special abilities and extraordinary experiences. We imagine the great and wonderful things we could do if only we weren't so limited, so ordinary. And it is no mere stereotype that the creators of works in speculative fiction and film have themselves often felt as if they didn't fit into society, thus turning to worlds in which characters who did not fit in were magnificent and enviable.

571. One way to distinguish between fantasy and realistic fiction is that

  (A) fantasy provides an escape from the real world, while realistic fiction cannot do that

  (B) fantasy has unlimited plotlines, while realistic fiction is limited and ordinary

  (C) fantasy provides a richness of a life where characters can act outside of known rules of how the world works, while realistic fiction has to follow known truths

  (D) the creators of fantasy fiction and film have often felt left out of society and created works to correct that, while the creators of realistic fiction and film have had no such experiences

  (E) realistic fiction helps viewers fit into society, while fantastic fiction focuses only on qualities that make reality difficult to endure

Questions 572–575 refer to the following passage.

For starters, there are only a limited number of ways to be normal: to fall within a small range around the average score for various traits, whether physical, mental, or social. But there are an unlimited number of ways to be abnormal.

Here the basic paradox of normality in the human species arises. On the one hand, we are social beings who feel a strong need to fit into a group (even "nonconformists" usually hang out with similar "nonconformists"), so there is a powerful desire to fit within an acceptable range. You don't want to stand out. On the other hand, we also want to attract attention to distinguish ourselves from others, so that we don't get ignored. These conflicting desires may both stem from a basic evolutionary pressure: the drive to be seen as reproductively attractive.

But we also want to attract more attention than our competitors and indicate that we have some advantage over others—we have better genes or more social status.

It's a conundrum of the human condition: we want to fit in and we want to stand out. But there are lots of ways to stand out, some ways better than others. Some of these ways indicate to others that we are desirable; some indicate that we are undesirable.

572. What is an important distinction the author makes between conformity and nonconformity?

  (A) Humans have a desire to be both conformists and nonconformists.

  (B) Some nonconformity can be desirable.

  (C) Conformity includes a limited and accepted range of abilities, while nonconformity is unlimited.

  (D) A standard of conformity never changes, while nonconformity can vary from generation to generation and from situation to situation.

  (E) Animal species do not have issues of conformity or nonconformity.

573. Which of the following best describes the organization of this passage?

  (A) A sociological theory is presented and then illustrated with examples.

  (B) A debate is summarized from one point of view, and a counterposition is defeated.

  (C) It's a classic compare-and-contrast essay, with two terms fully explained and defined.

  (D) It's a challenge of previous accepted thought with a controversial new theory.

  (E) A theory is given, and then an alternate theory is proven to be illogical in comparison.

574. Which of the following is presented by the passage as a key question that cannot be answered?

(A) What are the acceptable things we can do to be considered normal?

(B) Why do we feel the need to fit in a group and yet still value the qualities that make us unique?

(C) Why are nonconformists ostracized for their dress or behavior?

(D) How can we seem more desirable to the opposite sex?

(E) How can humans ignore the desire to conform?

575. As it is discussed in this passage, the issue of conforming is important because

(A) it allows us to attract competitors and have advantages over others

(B) it is a socially powerful viewpoint that can be used to advantage in matters of sex, politics, and business

(C) it is a paradox that provides new avenues for future research

(D) it raises sociological questions and then discusses possible answers

(E) it allows humans to constantly strive for perfection and enhance standards of desirability

---

Questions 576–578 refer to the following information.

Following is a chart showing the schedule of a wedding planner for one business week.

Time	Monday	Wednesday	Thursday	Friday
9–11 a.m.	Pink Orchid Events Team presentation (Las Vegas Resort, Rm. 14)	Jacklyn Frank Photography presentation	French Tips Designs wedding nails presentation	Lions' ceremony and reception setup for Sat. event
11 a.m.–1 p.m.	Sweet Nothing wedding cakes lunch catering presentation	Trish T. hair and makeup consultation	Trip to Oswald Nature Park for meeting with park ranger	Richards' ceremony and reception setup for Sat. event
2–3 p.m.	Trina C. bridesmaid dress consultation	Jennifer W. hair and makeup consultation	Felicia's Hair Salon presentation	Paul's ceremony and reception setup for Sat. event
3–5 p.m.	Sanders' Party pre-ceremony photos — groom's party	Delaine G. wedding dress shopping	Sanders' Party pre-ceremony photos — bride's party	Sanders' ceremony and reception setup for Sat. event

576. Samantha is the owner of Wedding Warriors, a wedding consultant business. Given the information provided, which best accounts for the absence of presentations on Friday?

(A) This Friday seems to be an unusual occurrence. Normal schedules would allow for presentations.

(B) After the Oswald park setting is secured, Samantha must ensure that the decorations are set up immediately because it's an outside location.

(C) Fridays are reserved for setting up weddings, which typically happen on Saturdays.

(D) Consultants typically do not work Fridays.

(E) Friday is Samantha's personal day off.

577. Which of the statements about Samantha's routine is best supported by the information provided?

(A) Samantha schedules the bride's and groom's photography on the same days.

(B) Samantha participates in presentations more than any other activity.

(C) Samantha regularly has lunch catered.

(D) Samantha always makes businesses who want to present come to her office.

(E) Samantha would prefer to do presentations at her place of business.

578. Which of the following activities does Samantha participate in at least three times?

(A) Makeup presentations/sessions

(B) Dress consultations

(C) Photography sessions/presentations

(D) Site visits to wedding locations

(E) Sander's party pre-ceremony photos

Questions 579–582 refer to the following passage.

Wars are functions of social systems. Peoples in Western society do not go to war for the same causes as those which actuated the early Hindus; in fact, with the rise of capitalist civilization, the nations of Western society began to go to war on different grounds from those which incited the rulers of medieval society.

This latest period involves the struggle between social systems. Thus, World War II began and ended, although wars continue around the world; and imminent civil strife in almost every Middle Eastern country concerns immediately the fate of the political class adjustment within the major powers of the world. This is not the old relatively static, imperialistic era; it is something new in history. Frequently, it has been asserted that "the next war will end civilization."

Although a recognition of the fact may be distasteful, it is necessary to realize that capitalist civilization received a tremendous shock from World War I, and, at the same time, the democratic movement was invigorated. World War II concluded another capitalist crisis—so much so that in all the world only the system as it now exists in the United States can stand unaided upon its own feet. And yet it is currently believed by some leaders of great political power that only World War III could restore the system to a healthy, peaceful existence.

579. What is a key detail of this passage?

(A) It is only through war that civilizations undergo drastic but needed change.

(B) The reasons for war vary from generation to generation and differ according to ideological beliefs.

(C) The rise of capitalistic civilization has changed the tenor and reasoning for going to war.

(D) The United States has the only civilization that would survive the next world war.

(E) World War III is necessary in order to restore a healthy and peaceful existence to worldwide social systems.

580. According to this passage, modern capitalistic civilization differs from the imperialistic era in that

(A) imperialistic societies focused on struggles for dominance, while democratic societies are concerned with issues of individual rights

(B) imperialistic societies focused on international concerns, while capitalistic civilizations focus on political-class wars

(C) imperialistic societies waged wars for ethical, moral, or religious reasons; capitalistic societies wage wars for political and economic reasons

(D) modern capitalistic civilizations focus on international consequences and sensitivity, while the imperialistic era focused on domestic and nationalistic concerns

(E) World War II effectively ended imperialistic society concerns and ushered in a worldwide capitalistic view

581. Concerning the author's attitude, the author most likely

(A) considers war an important social determinant that ushers in change for the good

(B) believes that only war can bring a new social order to the world

(C) feels as if a new world war will drastically change our current notions of civilization

(D) feels the previous world wars were necessary to end civil strife and helped to strengthen worldwide democracy

(E) feels that war is inevitable in any civilized society

582. Presumably, the author alludes to Hindus in order to

(A) introduce an examination of the differences between religious war and imperialistic wars

(B) contrast Eastern and Western thoughts and beliefs

(C) support assertions that Western thought regarding wars are of more serious concern

(D) prevent the audience from confusing medieval wars with Hindu wars

(E) present a nonexample of a warring society

Questions 583–584 refer to the following passage.

In attempting a discussion of the caste system, one is usually confronted at the very outset with the persistent query: What is a caste? Many earnest inquirers will not listen further to the caste theorist unless he states precisely, in the beginning, what he means by the word "caste." The expert, thus cornered, is naturally tempted, in the interest of the discussion, to submit some hastily considered definition, hoping that it will be forgotten forthwith. But he seldom settles the matter so lightly. His abbreviated picture of caste usually remains to haunt all future commitments about the phenomenon.

583. This passage is primarily concerned with

(A) attempting to convince readers that many have the wrong definition of the term "caste"

(B) defining the term "caste"

(C) helping the reader to understand that this term can have many meanings, depending on the context in which it is used

(D) arguing that the author's definition should be considered the correct definition for the term "caste"

(E) suggesting how the caste system might be changed or modified to his improved version

584. In the passage, the tone adopted by the author with regard to the topic of "caste" is one of

(A) dispassionate explanation

(B) playful mockery

(C) authoritative condescension

(D) grudging admiration for other viewpoints

(E) frustrated acceptance

The Spanish *conquistador*, reckless of native life in his eager quest of gold, and the Spanish-preaching friar, often yielding himself to death for the spread of the Gospel, are the two types of men most impressively delineated in the pages of the first decades of Spain's history in America, illustrating the complex and conflicting motives which urged the great adventure.

585. One way to distinguish between the Spanish conquistadors and friars is that

(A) both spoke Spanish and looked for adventure in the new world

(B) both types of men were important in the role of Spain's history in the Americas

(C) the conquistadors sought gold, and the friars sought souls for the Gospel

(D) both were reckless, one throwing his life away for the attainment of gold and the other giving himself to death in order to spread the Gospel

(E) only the friars are remembered by history with respect; the conquistadors are seldom mentioned in important annals of history

Questions 586–589 refer to the following passage.

When it first aired in the fall of 2004, the Fox series *House* seemed an unlikely hit. Focusing its attention on the brilliant but deeply unlikeable Dr. Gregory House, it left little room for the audience to see the show's protagonist as anything but a jerk. But several years and several Golden Globes later, *House* is a huge success. What is the source of *House*'s appeal? As a medical drama, it draws upon our deep-seated cultural interest in medicine. Centered on the investigation of mysterious maladies with a protagonist modeled on the legendary Sherlock Holmes, it also satisfies our long-standing fascination with detective stories. But *House* is more than another *ER*, more than another *CSI*. Its singularity lies primarily in its surprising protagonist, a man who simultaneously inspires interest and loathing. *House* is like a car wreck—you can't help but look. While, thankfully, most of us don't come upon car wrecks every day, *House* illustrates something we do encounter daily: irritating people.

Ultimately, *House* illustrates the antagonistic nature of social relations primarily through the means of its misanthropic protagonist, Dr. Gregory House. It illustrates the dependency we have on others through the medium of medicine. *House* reinforces the message that humans need others not only in obvious physical ways, but also in more subtle, but equally important, psychological ones. While others engender anxiety, they also define who we are.

586. The passage indicates which of the following about the popularity of the TV series *House*?

(A) The protagonist of *House* is a flawed man who appeals to viewers because of those very flaws and failures.

(B) Viewers enjoy watching deeply unlikeable characters getting what they deserve.

(C) Viewers are more interested in shows about medicine than mystery.

(D) Watching the TV show *House* is like watching a car wreck.

(E) No one is really quite sure why *House* has become so popular.

587. The author's attitude is best described as one of

(A) disdain

(B) disgust

(C) admiration

(D) puzzlement

(E) detachment

588. In analyzing the mystery genre in relation to the medical drama, the author's main concern is

(A) the ways in which the drama satisfies the same cultural interest and fascination viewers and readers seem to have with puzzles

(B) the unique place of *House* in this particular genre

(C) ascertaining that medical dramas are more popular and well-watched or well-read than mystery dramas

(D) comparing Dr. Gregory House to Sherlock Holmes

(E) that medical dramas such as *House* don't realistically portray actual medical knowledge and issues

589. The author begins the last paragraph with the word "ultimately" in order to

(A) emphasize that his last point is the most important one

(B) point out that the final test of this show is how many awards it has won, thereby defending its status as worthy of acclaim

(C) transition to another show in the medical drama with just as much appeal, supporting the argument that the medical genre is more enjoyable than the mystery genre

(D) summarize the author's main point that *House* meets more needs than just being entertained

(E) end the discussion with the most important point emphasized

The full significance of Wounded Knee emerged in time: it was the conclusion of a four-century-long struggle with America's First Nations. That struggle had embroiled the United States for longer than a century and, before that, the European imperial powers for almost three centuries. It epitomized the greatest reality of the American Indian experience during that four-century-long struggle: the unalterable reality of white dominance over the continent and the lives and destinies of its indigenous peoples.

590. The author logically implies which of the following about the Wounded Knee incident?

(A) Now that the struggle was over, the U.S. could deal with issues of national importance, such as the settlement of new citizens in the lands west of the Mississippi.

(B) Wounded Knee effectively ended the rebellion of Native Americans and established white dominance in the U.S.

(C) Wounded Knee lasted for so long that America was unable to achieve the same imperial powers as European countries.

(D) Wounded Knee was a tragic incident, but it closed an unfortunate situation and allowed Native Americans and the white men to settle amicably.

(E) Wounded Knee was more of an American concern than a European issue.

Questions 591–592 are based on the following passage.

Though the ring-tailed lemur of Madagascar, with its striped tail, pointy snout, and cuddly four-legged body, may look like some exotic type of raccoon, it is actually much more closely related to humans than it is to those nocturnal trash-can robbers of America. Lemurs, like their close relatives the tarsiers and lorises, are classified as *prosimians* — the nearest nonhuman relatives of apes and monkeys — and as *primates*, along with apes, monkeys, and us.

591. According to the passage, which of the following is true?

(A) Monkeys live in Madagascar.

(B) Lemurs live in America.

(C) Apes are not prosimians.

(D) Raccoons are prosimians.

(E) Tarsiers and lorises are types of monkeys.

592. The passage characterizes lemurs and raccoons as sharing a

(A) superficial resemblance

(B) wariness of primates

(C) nocturnal hunting practice

(D) surprisingly human diet

(E) rapidly vanishing habitat

Questions 593–594 are based on the following passage.

Of all the numerous conspiracy theories postulating that the name of "William Shakespeare" was actually a front for some other writer, the idea that the Bard's ill-fated contemporary Christopher Marlowe actually faked his death only to resurface under his supposed rival's name may be the most plausible. After all, the first printed work that identified Shakespeare as the author did pop up in bookshops mere weeks after Marlowe was supposedly killed in a bar brawl on May 30, 1593. The theory has a fatal stylistic flaw, however, in addition to numerous historical ones: during his acknowledged lifetime, Christopher Marlowe dealt exclusively in bloody tragedies, whereas the majority of the plays attributed to Shakespeare are comedic in nature. Why would faking his death have suddenly turned Marlowe funny?

593. Which of the following is *alluded to* but NOT *explained* in the passage?

(A) Circumstantial evidence in favor of the idea that Shakespeare was Marlowe

(B) The historical objections to Shakespeare as a front for Marlowe

(C) The "fatal stylistic flaw" in the theory that Marlowe was Shakespeare

(D) The date of the first theory postulating that Marlowe was Shakespeare

(E) The scientific evidence that William Shakespeare really existed

594. The name William Shakespeare appears in quotation marks because

(A) the author of the passage does not believe that Shakespeare really existed

(B) the author of the passage believes that Shakespeare existed but did not really write his plays

(C) the name itself is so exalted and famous

(D) it is the first time that the name is used in the passage

(E) the name is being referred to as a name

Set 4

When John McCain lost the 2008 presidential election to Barack Obama in a landslide, political pundits attributed the results to popular dissatisfaction with the Republican Party after the presidency of George W. Bush, to Obama's historic status as an African-American candidate, and to a variety of other factors. But perhaps they should have laid the blame on McCain's parents: alone among the five major parties in American history, the Republicans have never won the presidency with a candidate named John.

595. In this passage, the author presumably seeks to

    (A) defend an unorthodox theory about presidential elections

    (B) explain the reasons for George W. Bush's unpopularity

    (C) celebrate the achievements of Barack Obama

    (D) facetiously introduce a mildly interesting factoid

    (E) analyze a growing trend in American politics

Questions 596–599 are based on the following passage.

Whenever I watch a detective show or mystery movie, I always figure out who did it (and why) pretty early. My friends tell me I should be a detective, but there are a lot of differences between solving crimes on TV and solving crimes in real life. A detective show always presents the viewer with background information and a finite number of suspects, all of whom are good enough to discuss their alibis at length. The detective – or a clever fan – then deduces the culprit either by noticing an inconsistency in someone's story or by bringing an obscure bit of trivia to bear on the facts of the case. If you're a real investigator, on the other hand, your list of suspects is infinite, and most people don't especially want to talk to you.

Mystery screenwriters always use this trick wherein a vital piece of information you'll need later is revealed during the funny part, so most of the audience doesn't pay it any mind. But looking out for this wouldn't help you if you were a real detective: actual police investigations, not having been scripted by writers, aren't conveniently divided into "funny parts" and "serious parts." That only happens on TV. What my friends think is my knack for solving crimes is really just an eye for characterization, suspense, irony, misdirection, thematics, and all the other tools of the trade that writers use to craft compelling storylines. The trick to solving crimes on TV shows isn't to think like a detective – it's to think like a TV writer!

596. The author's principal intent in composing the passage was presumably to

    (A) boast about what a good detective he would make

    (B) explain why most TV shows are so unrealistic

    (C) provide a counterargument to a popular theory

    (D) distinguish between one skill set and another

    (E) resolve two seemingly contradictory opinions

597. In the context of the first paragraph, "culprit" appears to mean something like

    (A) objective

    (B) alibi

    (C) perpetrator

    (D) enigma

    (E) sleuth

598. Which of the following does the author NOT present as a reason why solving crimes on fictional TV shows is easier than solving crimes in real life?

(A) Real-life criminals have incomprehensible motives.

(B) Screenwriters present clues at predictable moments.

(C) Real-life suspects are less forthcoming in interviews.

(D) Episodes of TV shows are built around themes.

(E) TV mysteries present a limited number of suspects.

599. By the end of the passage, the author has characterized the advice given to him by his friends in the second sentence as

(A) sardonic

(B) ironic

(C) laconic

(D) loquacious

(E) anachronistic

Questions 600–602 are based on the following passage.

When it comes to English history, the convention solidified by so many Robin Hood films that the people loved "Good" King Richard the Lionheart but justly despised his despotic brother John is far more cinematic than historical. The problem isn't that John wasn't an inept and unpopular king, but that Richard himself wasn't much better. He spent nearly all of his reign conducting foreign wars rather than in England, first in the Middle East and then in France, and the necessity of funding these campaigns led him to levy taxes just as oppressive as any that were ever ordered by John of his own device. But unlike John, who was as lackluster a warrior as he was an administrator, Richard was redeemed in the popular imagination by both his military prowess and the convenient fact of his absence. Had he remained at home and made any attempts to actually run the country, his policies might well not have been any fairer or more popular than were those of his younger brother.

600. Which of the following best describes the purpose and organization of the passage?

(A) It uses new research to bolster one side of a seemingly endless debate.

(B) It cleverly equivocates to avoid partisanship with regard to a controversial issue.

(C) It defends a cherished traditional viewpoint against biased revisionism.

(D) It offers an unproven but potentially illuminating resolution to a paradox.

(E) It brings careful distinctions to bear against a rose-tinted oversimplification.

601. The passage characterizes

(A) Richard as a cipher and John as a good king who is unjustly maligned

(B) Richard as a competent administrator and John as a coward

(C) Richard as the beneficiary of doubt and John as bad but not uniquely so

(D) John as a misunderstood genius and Richard as supremely lucky

(E) John as a cunning military strategist and Richard as a financial wizard

602. As it is used in this passage, "lackluster" most nearly means

(A) zealous

(B) manipulative

(C) innovative

(D) reluctant

(E) unimpressive

Questions 603–606 are based on the following passage.

I love it when people ask me what my favorite fruit is, because I get to savor the looks of confusion and suspicion on their faces when I say "olives." If they think I'm messing with them and ask again, so much the better, because it *really* drives them crazy when I say "cucumbers." I'm not messing with them, of course — I just happen to know that, even though people tend to think of "fruits" as being sweet and brightly colored, the word actually refers to the seed-bearing structure of any flowering plant.

603. The author characterizes his responses to the question "What is your favorite fruit?" as

(A) facetious

(B) earnest

(C) equivocal

(D) evasive

(E) philosophical

604. In a sense, the passage illustrates the difference between

(A) prescription and description

(B) allegory and symbolism

(C) belief and actuality

(D) situational irony and dramatic irony

(E) a metaphor and a simile

605. The personality of the passage's author could accurately be described as

(A) didactic

(B) iconoclastic

(C) devious

(D) mercurial

(E) neurotic

606. The purpose and tone of the passage could best be described as

(A) adorably confused

(B) satirically melancholy

(C) ironically modest

(D) whimsically self-satisfied

(E) aggressively paranoiac

Questions 607–610 are based on the following passage.

It is yet another testament to Shakespeare's genius (as though we don't have enough of these already) that his comedies are still so funny despite the fact that most of what his audience was actually laughing at has almost certainly been lost to history. The texts of Shakespeare's plays — in other words, the actors' lines — are what has survived, but just as with a modern comedic movie, the wording of the lines doesn't account for everything the audience laughs at, no matter how cleverly written they are. It was almost certainly the case that Shakespeare and his actors crafted certain characters as parodies of various famous contemporaries, and that the performances would have reflected this, with the actors doing impressions of people that the audience would have recognized. Because all we know now is *what* was said, and not *how* it was said, or *who* was being sent up, a lot of the comedy Shakespeare so carefully crafted is simply gone for good.

607. According to the passage, which of the following is true?

(A) The texts of many of Shakespeare's greatest comedies have been lost.

(B) Shakespeare crafted his texts with specific actors and their performances in mind.

(C) There is no difference between Shakespeare's comedies and modern comedic movies.

(D) Shakespeare never intended for the texts of his plays to be published.

(E) Modern audiences are doomed to misunderstand the true moral of a Shakespearean comedy.

608. The parenthetical statement in the opening sentence can be taken to indicate that the author believes which of the following?

(A) Most students are rightfully sick of hearing about how brilliant Shakespeare was.

(B) It is a daunting task for one person to read every single play Shakespeare ever wrote.

(C) Far too much scholarship is devoted to Shakespeare and not enough to other playwrights.

(D) The case for Shakespeare as a great genius is often offputtingly overstated.

(E) Shakespeare was so good at so many things that it is mind-boggling.

609. It is reasonable to assume that, in writing the passage, the author's intention was at least partially to

(A) acquaint the reader with certain peculiarities of 16th-century acting styles

(B) argue that all of Shakespeare's plays are comedic on at least some levels

(C) make recommendations about how Shakespeare's comedies should be performed today

(D) suggest that Shakespeare's comedies are actually not as clever as many people assume

(E) acknowledge that a common facet of comedy would have applied to Shakespeare too

610. As it is used in this passage, the phrase "sent up" most nearly means

(A) remembered

(B) celebrated

(C) lampooned

(D) entertained

(E) ignored

Questions 611–616 are based on the following pair of passages.

Passage 1

The steroid scandal has been a blight on Major League Baseball for nearly 20 years now. Fans are beyond disgusted with the rampant cheating of their former heroes, and nobody even blinks an eye anymore when the inevitable news comes out that the most recent record-breaker has tested positive for performance-enhancing substances. It's good news that MLB has finally begun to actually enforce its historically laughably lax steroid policies, but policing, no matter how vigorous, isn't going to clean up the mess by itself. Players need to start putting honor and a sense of fair play above their individual quests for personal glory and remember that they are role models representing America's pastime rather than cutthroat businessmen looking to exploit every advantage imaginable.

Passage 2

If you think performance-enhancing drugs in baseball are a recent development, then I have a bridge to sell you. It's a documented fact that players were injecting themselves with pig testosterone back in the 1890s, for Pete's sake. The stars of the 1950s and '60s were popping amphetamines at a pace that would have put Elvis to shame. Modern steroids have been common since the 1970s. For over a century, it's been a safe bet that as soon as any chemical cocktail that's even rumored to give an athlete an edge is invented, baseball players will be lining up around the block for it. The only difference nowadays is that people suddenly care — or *pretend* to care, rather like Claude Rains being "shocked, *shocked*" to find that gambling is going on at Rick's Café in *Casablanca* (right before an attendant brings him his winnings). You want to make baseball fair? Drop the charade and let the players juice themselves up with whatever they want.

611. Which statement accurately characterizes the relationship between the two passages?

    (A) Passage 1 demonstrates idealism, whereas Passage 2 demonstrates realism.

    (B) Passage 2 advocates an unorthodox solution, whereas Passage 1 suspects no solution is possible.

    (C) Both passages are primarily concerned with the past rather than with the present.

    (D) Neither author sees steroid use as a bigger problem in baseball than it is in other sports.

    (E) Both authors take careful steps to protect themselves against accusations of sexism.

612. As it is used in Passage 2, the famous movie line "shocked, *shocked*" functions as an accusation of

    (A) cluelessness

    (B) avarice

    (C) flip-flopping

    (D) disingenuousness

    (E) paranoia

613. Which of the following statements accurately describes a point of agreement *and* a point of disagreement between the two authors?

    (A) They agree that steroids should be banned, but they disagree about how harmful they are.

    (B) They agree that steroid use is a new problem, but they disagree about how common it is.

    (C) They both believe in the concept of fairness, but they characterize it very differently.

    (D) They both believe in the need for accountability, but they disagree about enforcement.

    (E) They agree that baseball is waning in popularity, but they disagree about how to promote it.

614. The author of Passage 2 would be most likely to accuse the author of Passage 1 of

    (A) elitism

    (B) hypocrisy

    (C) insincerity

    (D) prejudice

    (E) naïveté

615. Much more so than the author of Passage 2, the author of Passage 1 prioritizes the status of professional baseball players as

    (A) businessmen

    (B) role models

    (C) skeptics

    (D) performers

    (E) philosophers

616. The author of Passage 1 would be most likely to accuse the author of Passage 2 of

    (A) defeatism

    (B) mercilessness

    (C) obstructionism

    (D) casuistry

    (E) sophistry

Questions 617–618 are based on the following passage.

Was the much-maligned phenomenon of "bronies" — adult male fans of the children's cartoon series *My Little Pony: Friendship Is Magic* — really a "terrifying new trend" and an exercise in "creepy immaturity," as the website Big Hollywood alleged, or were the media once again stirring up a tempest in a teacup? There have long been grown-up fans of cartoons intended for kids, going back to the critically praised *Animaniacs* or *Batman: The Animated Series* in the 1990s. The alarmism over the crossover audience for *MLP:FIM* can largely be attributed to two things: firstly, the fact that it is much easier for mockery of fan communities to spread and intensify in the Internet Age, and secondly, the fact that grown fans of a show intended for girls tend to seem "creepier" than do grown fans of a show intended for boys, even (lamentably) to people who consider themselves progressive.

617. It can safely be assumed that the author of the passage believes that

   (A) it is always at least a little bit creepy when adults are fans of a children's cartoon show

   (B) adult male fans of *My Little Pony: Friendship Is Magic* probably do not really exist

   (C) mockery of "bronies" is largely motivated by sexism, however unconsciously

   (D) the "Internet Age" has made adult television viewers less mature

   (E) *Batman: The Animated Series* was a better show than *My Little Pony: Friendship Is Magic*

618. As it is used in this passage, the expression "a tempest in a teacup" most nearly means

   (A) an overreaction to a trivial matter

   (B) a deliberate deception for monetary gain

   (C) a dishonest profession of neutrality

   (D) an old story dressed up as a new one

   (E) an imperfectly remembered anecdote

Questions 619–621 are based on the following graph.

The bar graph concerns the types of video games made by a particular company.

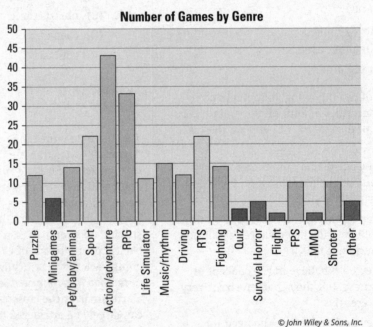

Number of Games by Genre

619. Based on the information in the graph, which of the following statements is NOT true?

  (A) The company makes about twice as many driving games as minigames.

  (B) Roughly a third of the games the company makes are RPGs (role-playing games).

  (C) The company does not make more than 50 of any one genre of game.

  (D) The company makes fewer than 20 fighting games.

  (E) The company does not make the exact same number of games in any two genres.

620. The percentage of games made by this company that are puzzle games is

  (A) 12%

  (B) 24%

  (C) 6%

  (D) none of the above, but possible to calculate based on the information in the graph

  (E) not possible to calculate based on the information in the graph

621. The fraction of the company's total games that are action/adventure games is closest to

  (A) one-half

  (B) one-sixth

  (C) one-tenth

  (D) one-sixteenth

  (E) This is not possible to calculate based on the information in the graph.

Questions 622–623 are based on the following passage.

Purring and roaring aren't just sounds that cats make when they're happy or angry — these sounds are actually how we classify cats into different types. No individual member of the family *Felidae* can both purr and roar. Smaller cats of the *Felis* genus, such as housecats, can purr but not roar, and the big cats of the *Panthera* genus — the lion, tiger, leopard, and jaguar — can roar but not purr. Although we know this to be the case, we're not sure why it is the case. For years, biologists believed that the ability to purr or to roar resulted from complete or partial (respectively) ossification of the hyoid bone in the throat — but it's been recently discovered that the snow leopard can purr but not roar, despite possessing a partially ossified hyoid.

622. The purpose of the passage is to

  (A) explain why some cats can purr but not roar or roar but not purr

  (B) distinguish between cats belonging to *Felidae* and cats belonging to *Panthera*

  (C) clarify the fact that the lion, tiger, leopard, and jaguar are classified as big cats

  (D) highlight both the importance and the mystery of the abilities to purr and to roar

  (E) inform the reader that only members of the cat family possess a hyoid bone

623. The word "respectively" is placed in parentheses in this passage in order to indicate

  (A) that the theory being explained has been overturned

  (B) that the remainder of the sentence includes scientific terminology

  (C) that the concepts being analyzed are worthy of respect

  (D) the relationships between the preceding pairs of words

  (E) no identifiable idea, and therefore it should be deleted

Though we associate Roman numerals with the ancient world, as their name would imply, these symbols that we see today only in the names of kings, queens, and movie sequels remained the standard numerical notation in Europe well into the second millennium CE. If you think you hated math class in school, just imagine how much more difficult it would have been if you'd had to use Roman numerals! Besides the obvious stumbling block of large numbers taking a lot of time and space to write, the system also lacked a symbol to represent zero. The numbers that we use today, called Arabic numerals, were developed in India around 500 CE and soon spread to the Middle East. Their prior adoption in that region is one of the main reasons why so many important advances in mathematics and astronomy were made by Arabic scholars while Europeans were still comparatively ignorant in these disciplines (as well as why so many common mathematical terms, such as *algebra* or *algorithm,* are derived from Arabic). The numbers we consider "normal" today were unknown in Europe until the Italian mathematician Fibonacci, who had spent time in Africa as a youth, introduced them in the early 13th century, and their use didn't become common until the 15th — so the characters in popular historical movies like *Braveheart* or *A Knight's Tale* would have lived their whole lives without ever having seen modern numbers!

624. Based on the information in the passage, which of the following is true?

(A) Many mathematical concepts were invented by the Arabs, but Arabic numerals were not.

(B) The use of Roman numerals enabled many important scientific advances in the ancient world.

(C) Roman numerals are never seen by the average person today in any context.

(D) The number system we are familiar with today has been around longer than most people believe.

(E) It was the Romans who first developed the mathematical concept of zero.

625. Based on the information in the passage, it can be gleaned that "the second millennium CE" began

(A) about 500 years ago

(B) about 1,000 years ago

(C) in the 13th century

(D) in the 15th century

(E) It is impossible to deduce this based on the information in the passage.

Literary critic Adam Gopnik, in a phrase that attained unusually quickly the status of conventional wisdom, once referred to the "three perfect books" of American literature as being Mark Twain's *The Adventures of Huckleberry Finn,* F. Scott Fitzgerald's *The Great Gatsby,* and J. D. Salinger's *The Catcher in the Rye.* The analysis is surprisingly difficult to disagree with — it rings with a sense of Jeffersonian "self-evident" truth — but it does make one wonder whether it is possible to write a "perfect" novel about anything other than a sharp-minded young man's loss of innocence.

626. The author of the passage characterizes the opinion referred to in the opening sentence as being

(A) pointless to discuss because literature is so subjective

(B) potentially politically controversial for complex reasons

(C) plagiarized by Adam Gopnik from earlier literary critics

(D) obviously false for reasons of narrow-mindedness

(E) obviously true for reasons that are largely ineffable

627. The phrase "self-evident" appears in quotation marks because

(A) it is being emphasized especially strongly

(B) it is being used ironically to signify its opposite

(C) it is a reference to a phrase from a famous text

(D) it is a technical term from philosophy

(E) It is in quotation marks for no clear reason, and the quotation marks should be deleted.

Questions 628–630 are based on the following passage.

If a friend told you that he'd just invented a new method of foretelling the future, you'd almost certainly be highly skeptical, as would anyone with half a brain. So why do so many people lend credence to the same patently ridiculous notion as long as the method in question is described as "ancient"? The reason is unclear, but the fact remains that they do, which is probably why most divination methods are talked up as being a lot older than they really are. Tarot cards are actually a more recent design than normal playing cards, and they didn't even appear in their current form until 1909. As for Ouija boards, they're a simple board game like any other, first appearing in 1890. (Think about it: if they were really "ancient," then how could both the design and the name *Ouija board* itself be copyrighted by Parker Brothers?) The lesson here is as clear as it is depressing: if you want people to fall for a bunch of bull, pretend it's *old* bull.

628. The author's primary motivation in composing the passage was presumably to

(A) point out that many popular games are much older than most people realize

(B) make a statement concerning puzzling inconsistencies in copyright law

(C) present logical arguments against the veracity of astrology

(D) encourage people to examine their own occasional fallacious reasoning

(E) instruct clever readers in a way to make their tricks seem more plausible

629. As it is used in this passage, the word "divination" most nearly means

(A) prank

(B) prophecy

(C) popularity

(D) prefabrication

(E) progress

630. Which of the following does the author of the passage admit he doesn't know?

(A) How the design of Ouija boards can be copyrighted

(B) Whether tarot cards are actually an accurate method of foretelling the future

(C) Why it is persuasive to some people when a silly idea is presented as "ancient"

(D) Why most people are reluctant to believe unorthodox ideas, even from their friends

(E) What percentage of the population claims to be able to predict the future

Questions 631–633 are based on the following passage.

Edna St. Vincent Millay became the third woman to win the Pulitzer Prize for Poetry in 1923, at the age of only 31, and throughout the nineteen-twenties and thirties was arguably the most widely known American poet. Today, however, she is read and discussed far less and is virtually never studied as part of poetry curricula in schools. The reasons for Millay's decline in visibility are manifold. The accessible and traditionally formal style that made her broadly popular in her day came to be seen as quaint and dated when compared to the aggressive experimentalism of modernist poets like T. S. Eliot and Gertrude Stein. The patriotic poems Millay wrote late in her career upon the outbreak of World War II made her appear "square" to many critics. And perhaps most significantly, the image of a scandalous seductress that the famously beautiful Millay cultivated did not sit well with subsequent generations of feminist poets and critics.

631. Which of the following claims does the passage NOT make?

   (A) Millay was one of the most widely known American poets in the 1930s.

   (B) Millay's poetry was less stylistically innovative than that of Gertrude Stein.

   (C) Millay's celebrity status in her heyday was due in part to her physical appearance.

   (D) Millay was the most talented woman ever to win the Pulitzer Prize for Poetry.

   (E) Millay's poetry is currently out of fashion thanks in part to feminist critics.

632. As it is used in this passage, the word "manifold" most nearly means

   (A) numerous

   (B) unfortunate

   (C) old-fashioned

   (D) emotional

   (E) unclear

633. Which of the following, if added to the passage, would make the author's position stronger?

   (A) Information about the first two women to win the Pulitzer Prize for Poetry

   (B) Further analysis of the work of T. S. Eliot and Gertrude Stein

   (C) Quotations from Millay's allegedly "square" patriotic poems

   (D) A brief list of which poets are most often studied in schools today

   (E) An artistic defense of what makes Millay's poetry good in and of itself

---

Questions 634–635 are based on the following passage.

A popular urban legend holds that the French word *bistro*, signifying a sidewalk café and eatery, derives from the Russian occupation of Paris in 1815. According to the legend, Russian soldiers, who were forbidden to drink alcohol on duty, would sneak into corner bars when their commanding officer's back was turned and try to grab a drink before they were missed, always crying "*bystro, bystro*" — Russian for *quickly*. Despite the lack of an alternate explanation for the term's etymology, however, most French linguists dispute the veracity of this tale, noting that there are no written records of the term's use until close to the end of the 19th century.

634. Based on the passage, which of the following is the most likely NOT to be true?

   (A) Russian soldiers occupied Paris in 1815.

   (B) "*Bystro*" is Russian for "quickly."

   (C) Russian soldiers in Paris covertly drank on duty.

   (D) A small French eatery is called a *bistro*.

   (E) The French word *bistro* did not appear in writing until the late 19th century.

635. Which of the following phrases from the passage is most useful to the argument for the *truth* of the "urban legend" mentioned at the start of the passage?

   (A) "who were forbidden to drink alcohol on duty"

   (B) "the lack of an alternate explanation for the term's etymology"

   (C) "most French linguists dispute the veracity of this tale"

   (D) "there are no written records of the term's use"

   (E) "derives from the Russian occupation of Paris in 1815"

Santa Claus had better start packing: it's recently been discovered that the North Pole is moving and that humans are the cause. While both the North and South rotational poles (as distinct from the magnetic poles) have always changed location at the rate of a few centimeters per year, it's only in the last couple of decades that scientists have observed the *direction* in which the poles move suddenly changing. The Earth, of course, is not a perfect sphere: geographical features such as mountains, as well as deposits of both liquid and frozen water, are unevenly distributed across its surface, and changes in their locations (i.e., changes in the distribution of mass) will cause the angle at which Earth rotates to shift slightly this way and that. Our planet has passed into and out of naturally occurring ice ages before as well as seen the positions of the continents shift due to plate tectonics, and the rotational poles shifted accordingly. The recent rapid melting of polar ice due to the effects of human industry on the environment is partly responsible for the recent about-face of the poles' directions, but it's not the only cause: the fresh water storage necessitated by the ever-increasing human population has actually reached the point where the mass of the stored drinking water is causing the planet to tip over. Even if it's only by a few centimeters, that's still pretty freaky.

636. Which of the following best describes the style and likely intended audience of the passage?

(A) It is written in an unadorned technical style for an audience of scientific professionals.

(B) It is written in a silly and entertaining style for an audience of schoolchildren.

(C) It is written in an intelligent yet casual style for an educated general audience.

(D) It is written in a persuasive and evidentiary style to convince a skeptical audience.

(E) It is written in an alarmist and exhortatory style to inspire action in its audience.

637. The content of the passage can best be described as

(A) mostly the author's opinions, as based on a smattering of facts

(B) mostly a catalogue of facts, with some colorful touches thrown in

(C) equally devoted to presenting original arguments and overturning counterarguments

(D) inclusive of a few facts but principally aimed at entertaining the reader

(E) a series of careful distinctions between credible and biased evidence

638. Based on the information in the passage, which of the following is true?

(A) There is ultimately no such thing as the North Pole.

(B) The North Pole is really the South Pole, and vice versa.

(C) The exact location of the North Pole has only recently been determined.

(D) The Earth might someday no longer have a North Pole.

(E) The Earth technically has two North Poles.

639. Based on the information in the passage, which of the following is NOT true?

(A) Before humans existed, the Earth was a perfect sphere.

(B) The continents have not always been in their present locations.

(C) The locations of the magnetic poles have always shifted.

(D) Earth's ratio of frozen to liquid water has changed many times.

(E) Most frozen water is located at or near the poles.

640. The use of the term "about-face" in this passage constitutes an example of

    (A) metaphor

    (B) personification

    (C) allegory

    (D) euphemism

    (E) stichomythia

Questions 641–644 are based on the following passage.

Despite the irritating persistence of an urban legend to that effect, mascara does not actually contain bat feces. Presumably, the confusion came about because *guanine,* one of the typical ingredients in the popular everyday cosmetic, has a name that looks similar to *guano,* a highfalutin term for the droppings of bats and birds. While it's true that the chemical (one of the four nucleobases in DNA, as signified by the letter "G" in strings of genetic code) *can* be extracted from bat droppings, and that its name was indeed originally derived from this fact, it is plentiful in nature and can be extracted from any number of other sources as well. The guanine found in mascara is actually derived from fish scales. It *is* recommended not to continue using a mascara tube or brush for longer than three months because of a slight risk of bacterial growth in the substance, but bat poop has nothing to do with this.

641. The author's motivation for composing the passage was presumably to

    (A) bemoan the persistence of urban legends

    (B) criticize the cosmetics industry

    (C) provide information about guanine

    (D) correct a widespread misunderstanding

    (E) express disapproval of a childish joke

642. Which of the words in the passage is italicized for purposes of emphasis?

    (A) guanine

    (B) guano

    (C) can

    (D) All three of these words are italicized for purposes of emphasis.

    (E) None of these words is italicized for purposes of emphasis.

643. Which of the following is NOT true, according to the passage?

    (A) Many people believe that mascara contains guano.

    (B) DNA can be found in guanine.

    (C) Guanine can be found in guano.

    (D) An ingredient in mascara is derived from animals.

    (E) *Guanine* and *guano* are etymologically related.

644. Which of the following is the most accurate description of the balance of fact and opinion in this passage?

    (A) The passage contains solely the author's opinions.

    (B) The passage contains solely facts.

    (C) The passage contains roughly equal amounts of fact and opinion.

    (D) The passage contains mostly facts with one educated guess.

    (E) The passage contains mostly the author's opinions with one verified statistic.

Is the ubiquitous children's rhyme "Ring Around the Rosie" actually a macabre reference to the Black Death, the plague that swept Europe in the Late Middle Ages, as many often claim? The supposition seems to work: a ringed and rosy rash was a symptom of the plague, flower petals (a "pocket full of posies") were carried and sniffed to ward off the "bad air" thought to bring the deadly infection, and cremation of the plentiful dead would certainly have resulted in "ashes, ashes." But not every explanation that looks plausible is true. Folklorists point out that the rhyme did not appear in English until the 19th century, that it was clearly derived from a German verse that originally mentioned only flowers and nothing about "falling down," and that the "ashes, ashes" bit only appears in the version popular in America, a country that never experienced the Black Death. People can find an eerie and persuasive coincidence anywhere, if they look hard enough.

645. Which best describes the organization of the passage?

(A) A fallacious argument is followed by an analysis of its central fallacy.

(B) A vicious rumor is followed by a demand for contrition.

(C) The basis for a legend is followed by contradictory facts.

(D) The author's claim is followed by his opponents' counterclaims.

(E) A populist opinion is followed by an elitist dismissal of it.

646. The closing sentence of the passage could most accurately be described as

(A) a maxim

(B) a caveat

(C) an idiom

(D) an allusion

(E) a kenning

647. Which of the following pairs of words from the passage are most nearly synonymous?

(A) plentiful, persuasive

(B) ubiquitous, macabre

(C) ubiquitous, persuasive

(D) persuasive, popular

(E) macabre, eerie

How did Valentine's Day — the February 14th feast day of an obscure Catholic Saint martyred in the third century — come to be associated with celebrations and professions of romantic love? A popular tradition holds that the custom is derived from the ancient Roman *Lupercalia* festival — but, although Lupercalia was celebrated on February 14th, Roman culture didn't hold it to have very much to do with love. Even if it did, the connection with our idea of Valentine's Day would still likely be a coincidence, as there are no subsequent mentions of the day being an occasion for sweethearts until the late 1300s, when the English poet Geoffrey Chaucer wrote *Parlement of Foules,* a humorous poem about mating birds. Medieval tradition (incorrectly) held that birds paired off in mid-February, and so Chaucer picked Valentine's Day for his setting based on the convenient date and pretty name. Well-read and witty people began to make references to "coupling up" on Valentine's Day based on the poem, and the rest is history. So our yearly celebration of love actually has nothing to do with saints or ancient Romans — it's merely the result of a medieval poet being poorly informed about birds.

648. The author's central argument is essentially that

(A) Valentine's Day does not really exist

(B) birds do not really choose mates in mid-February

(C) the Lupercalia festival had nothing to do with love

(D) the modern Valentine's Day has mildly humorous origins

(E) our idea of Valentine's Day was deliberately crafted by Chaucer

649. As it is used in the opening sentence, "professions" most nearly means

(A) occupations

(B) declarations

(C) conceptions

(D) obsessions

(E) inventions

650. The passage characterizes Chaucer's selection of Valentine's Day as the setting for his poem *Parlement of Foules* as being largely based on

(A) artistic concerns

(B) theological ideas

(C) ancient philosophy

(D) romantic science

(E) political subversiveness

651. Suppose it were discovered that many ancient Romans did in fact celebrate romantic love on the date of Lupercalia. How would this discovery affect the author's argument?

(A) The author's argument would be mostly unaffected.

(B) The author's argument would be severely weakened.

(C) The author's argument would be substantially strengthened.

(D) The author's argument would be conclusively proven.

(E) The author's argument would be conclusively disproved.

Set 5

Questions 652–655 are based on the following passage.

The typical Western diet contains a lot of poultry, and most Americans would doubtless be more amenable to eating birds themselves than their nests. Bird's-nest soup is considered among the most supreme delicacies in the cuisine of Southeast Asia, however, with a bowl of the most rarefied kind going for up to $100 US dollars per bowl. The labor-intensive treat is made not from the nest of any old birds but specifically from those of a species of cave-dwelling swiftlet. These birds construct their nests out of saliva, and they dissolve into a delicious gelatin in hot water, but gathering them is no simple task. The red nests used in the most prized soups are made by a subspecies of the bird that dwells only on one island off the coast of Thailand and affixes its nests to dangerously steep and high rock walls. Selling for $10,000 per kilogram, these red swiftlet nests are the most expensive foodstuff in the world.

652. The purpose of the passage is principally to

(A) criticize the Western diet

(B) criticize the practice of making bird's-nest soup

(C) lament the expensiveness of bird's-nest soup

(D) provide interesting information that will teach a valuable lesson

(E) provide interesting information merely for the sake of doing so

653. As it is used in this passage, the word "rarefied" most nearly means

(A) nearly impossible to safely obtain

(B) mysterious and closely guarded

(C) emblematic of the elite and privileged

(D) precisely proper and traditional

(E) central to many sacred illusions

654. Which of the following can be logically assumed based on the information provided by the passage?

(A) The people who pick these nests for a living become wealthy.

(B) Most bird's-nest soup is made from nests of a color other than red.

(C) Most bowls of bird's-nest soup are purchased with American money.

(D) The swiftlets that make these nests are becoming endangered.

(E) The best bird's-nest soup can be eaten only in Thailand.

655. As it is used in the context of the passage, which of the following terms could be considered an example of foreshadowing?

(A) "more amenable"

(B) "labor-intensive"

(C) "cave-dwelling"

(D) "delicious gelatin"

(E) "dangerously steep"

Questions 656–660 are based on the following passage.

The 1869 invention of margarine, a butter substitute made from concentrated vegetable oils, presented a potential nightmare for the dairy industry. Because margarine is both cheaper and healthier than butter, easier to make, and tastes pretty much the same, butter manufacturers knew they were in for the fight of their lives. They had only one option: pressuring politicians into making life tough for the margarine industry. Dairy's advantage was that it employed a lot of workers. Because dairy farmers put out of work by a margarine boom would mean votes against the politicians who let it happen, legislators bent over backwards to placate the butter barons. In addition to taxing it, and to requiring expensive licenses for makers and sellers, one peculiar method of discouraging margarine consumption became commonplace: forbidding manufacturers to add the yellow coloring necessary to make margarine (which is naturally pearly in color, hence its name, from the Greek for "pearl-oyster") *look* like delicious butter. Margarine might have passed out of history altogether, if not for the dairy shortages and rationing required by the two World Wars, during which it gained the upper hand in its battle with butter. Even so, laws against adding yellow coloring remained widespread. Gradually, most were overturned, but yellow margarine is banned in the state of Missouri to this very day!

656. It can be assumed that the closing sentence of the passage ends with an exclamation point because

(A) the author wishes to express his disapproval over the fact it relates

(B) the author is trying to liven up an otherwise dull ending to the passage

(C) the author is assuming that the reader will find its content surprising

(D) the passage had implied that Missouri would be unlikely to ban yellow margarine

(E) the last sentence finally answers a question alluded to early in the passage

657. The passage establishes that most of the early opposition to margarine came from people who were

(A) genuinely unsure about what its long-term effects would be

(B) acting out of concern for people's health

(C) acting out of concern for the economic stability of the nation

(D) acting purely out of self-interest

(E) initially merely misinformed and later sorry for it

658. The reader is led to assume that the reason it was so important to add yellow coloring to margarine was that

    (A) people had to be tricked into thinking it was butter

    (B) politicians passed laws that required this

    (C) of a demand on the parts of dairy farmers

    (D) it substantially improved the taste of margarine

    (E) margarine simply looked gross without it

659. Which of the following claims does the passage NOT make, either directly or indirectly?

    (A) The invention of margarine was an accidental occurrence.

    (B) Margarine might be unknown today if not for wartime rationing.

    (C) More people are necessary to make butter than to make margarine.

    (D) Policies intended to discourage margarine consumption were initially successful.

    (E) There are many good reasons to eat margarine instead of butter.

660. The phrase "legislators bent over backwards to placate the butter barons" is most strongly an example of

    (A) simile

    (B) personification

    (C) anaphora

    (D) stichomythia

    (E) alliteration

Questions 661–664 are based on the following passage.

Fans of *Star Wars* watch the films not just for the entertainment value but also for their supposed philosophical insights about the nature of good and evil. The movies' ethical prescriptions, however, are often set aside for the sake of cinematic excitement. For example, although Jedi Master Yoda frequently warns that anger leads to the Dark Side, the films contain several scenes where a good character is only able to defeat an evil one after something happens to make him sufficiently angry. Furthermore, the ethics of the prequels seem to contradict those of the original trilogy. In *Return of the Jedi*, we admire Luke Skywalker for tossing aside his lightsabre and refusing to kill an unarmed Darth Vader, but in *Revenge of the Sith*, it is wrong of Anakin to stop Mace Windu from executing a weakened Palpatine and a big mistake for Obi-Wan to walk away without finishing off a defeated Anakin! Perhaps the single most unsatisfying thing about the prequels is that they ignore the central lesson of the original trilogy: stick by the people you love, no matter what. In *The Empire Strikes Back*, Luke Skywalker disobeys Master Yoda and abandons his training on Dagobah when he senses that his friends are in danger. Naturally, this turns out to be the right decision, because as wise as Yoda is, Luke was following his heart. But then in the prequels, Anakin's making the exact same decision ends up turning him into a monster!

661. Based on the passage, it can be safely assumed that the author believes which of the following?

    (A) The *Star Wars* films are not actually as entertaining as they seem.

    (B) Anger can often lead to positive results in life.

    (C) It's a bad idea to try to learn philosophy from movies.

    (D) Friends are more important than wisdom is.

    (E) Movie series should be very careful not to contradict themselves.

662. Based on the analysis in the passage, the author seems to think that the ethical philosophy of the *Star Wars* films struggles to find a balance between

(A) wisdom and love

(B) honor and pragmatism

(C) strength and education

(D) innocence and experience

(E) logic and art

663. In terms of identity, the passage's author can most logically be assumed to be

(A) an educated *Star Wars* fan who has thought deeply about the films

(B) an expert in philosophy who sees *Star Wars* as only one example of his main concern

(C) a screenwriter who thinks the *Star Wars* films are a bad influence on writers

(D) a moralist who is generally skeptical of the movies' influence on people's behavior

(E) someone who hates the *Star Wars* films and wishes to criticize them for his amusement

664. As it appears early in this passage, the phrase "ethical prescriptions" most nearly means

(A) uncompromising demands

(B) illuminating subtext

(C) intended audience

(D) advice about how to behave

(E) rules about how to succeed

Questions 665–667 are based on the following passage.

Perhaps the 20th century's greatest paleontologist, Roy Chapman Andrews was born into modest circumstances in Wisconsin in 1884. As a boy, Andrews's favorite pastime was to explore the forests near his house, and his fascination with nature led him to teach himself taxidermy, a skill he subsequently used to put himself through college. After graduation, Andrews relocated to New York City to seek a job at the famous American Museum of Natural History. Told that there were no openings, he worked as a janitor while simultaneously earning a degree in mammalogy from Columbia University. He married in 1914, and together the Andrewses set out to explore the remote areas of northwest Asia. It was in Mongolia's Gobi Desert that his team made the discoveries for which Andrews became most famous: fossil remains of several previously unknown species of dinosaur, including the famous *Velociraptor*, as well as the first-ever discovery of fossilized dinosaur eggs. Andrews went on to serve as director of the very museum where he had once been a janitor and to write many books about his adventures in the dangerous Mongolian desert. These tales sparked the imaginations of generations of young readers, and it's said that, over twenty years after his death in 1960, Roy Chapman Andrews provided the inspiration for the movies' most dashing archeologist, Indiana Jones.

665. Which of the following is an ambiguity that the author might be well advised to clear up in a revision of the passage?

(A) Where Andrews went to college

(B) Whether the American Museum of Natural History is located in New York City

(C) Whether Andrews's wife was a partner in his scientific work

(D) The process by which dinosaur eggs become fossilized

(E) Whether the makers of the *Indiana Jones* films ever acknowledged that Andrews was an influence

666. The closing sentence contains an example of what undesirable rhetorical device?

(A) hyperbole

(B) mixed metaphor

(C) weasel words

(D) archaism

(E) equivocation

667. It can most safely be assumed that the author of the passage set out to compose

(A) an interesting and inspiring biographical text

(B) a well-researched and persuasive exhortatory text

(C) a historically based literary text

(D) an encyclopedia entry about Roy Chapman Andrews

(E) an obituary for Roy Chapman Andrews

Questions 668–671 are based on the following passage.

Many schools of thought are controversial, but few have been called "the World's Most Dangerous Idea." Transhumanism, the belief that scientific techniques both could and should transform us to a point where we are no longer human but "posthuman," has been described by a number of pundits as such. But many on the other side insist that such well-intentioned fears are unfounded. Why, they argue, should procedures like extending human memory capacity or screening embryos for predisposition to disease be regarded any differently than organ transplants, hip-replacement surgery, or pacemaker implantation? Granted, parental selection of infant eye color or other physical traits appears shallow and takes all the surprise out of reproduction — but then again, if the technology exists, and the parents have both the desire to use it and the ability to afford it, should the government have the right to tell them no? It is on this point, however, that one of the chief criticisms — known as the "*Gattaca* argument," after the 1997 science-fiction film — of Transhumanism is based: if genetic enhancement is only an option for the wealthiest of us, then rich and poor might slowly but surely become two different species.

668. What can logically be assumed about the author's stance on the issue described in the passage?

(A) The author is clearly a supporter of transhumanism.

(B) The author is firmly opposed to transhumanism.

(C) The author appears to be undecided about transhumanism.

(D) The author does not believe that transhumanism is really possible.

(E) The author has invented the idea of transhumanism as satire.

669. All of the instances of quotation marks in the passage occur because the terms are either

(A) direct quotation or ironic

(B) direct quotation or jargon

(C) direct quotation or highly emphasized

(D) ironic or highly emphasized

(E) ironic or jargon

670. The concerns raised by the passage relate to a perceived need to balance

(A) scientific advances with spirituality

(B) parental rights with parental responsibilities

(C) scientific advances with parental rights

(D) equality with wisdom

(E) freedom with equality

671. Which of the following provisions would resolve a criticism made in the passage?

(A) A constitutional amendment legalizing transhumanism

(B) Requiring schools to teach courses on the ethics of transhumanism

(C) Providing law-enforcement agencies with registries of posthumans

(D) Requiring insurance providers to cover transhumanist procedures

(E) Requiring transhumanist scientists to watch the movie *Gattaca*

Attacked on all sides by everyone from religious leaders to feminists, Sigmund Freud is typically introduced to students these days via someone complaining about the things he got wrong. We've all heard about his embarrassing missteps, like the theory of "penis envy" or the fact that, as a young man, he briefly advocated cocaine as a wonder drug. I just can't believe that students aren't also taught about all the amazing things he got right. Freud not only invented psychoanalysis pretty much single-handedly but also developed many of its core theories, including those of repression, transference, and the subconscious. Broadly speaking, we are indebted to him for the very idea that how we behave as adults depends largely on our experiences as children, a notion now universally accepted. So it seems very silly indeed to dismiss him based on a few isolated paragraphs found in one or two of his sixteen major works. It really is curious that people are so reluctant to admit the many ways in which Freud's ideas have shaped modern society. In fact, I can't help but wonder what Freud would say about it!

672. The author of the passage can safely be assumed to believe which of the following?

(A) Modern attitudes toward the work of Sigmund Freud are largely unfair.

(B) Sigmund Freud made important contributions to both religious studies and feminism.

(C) Sigmund Freud's most infamous "wrong" ideas are actually the most likely to be true.

(D) The vast majority of Sigmund Freud's works contains no errors whatsoever.

(E) Others were actually to blame for Sigmund Freud's most notable mistakes.

673. The closing sentence of the passage functions as

(A) a thesis statement that ties together the passage as a whole

(B) a bit of sarcasm that lightens up an otherwise dry rant

(C) a witticism that also underscores the author's point

(D) a piece of personal information that serves to humanize the author

(E) an admission that the author is not actually an expert on Freud

674. Based on this passage, it might fairly be assumed that the author believes that

(A) psychology is the most important of the sciences

(B) education today is less rigorous than it used to be

(C) religious leaders and feminists are usually wrong

(D) traditional ideas are sometimes prematurely dismissed

(E) all children are born without behavioral inclinations

Both Rory Kinnear's *Hamlet* (2010) and David Tennant's (2008) were placed in similarly effective modern dress settings. When Ophelia appeared (in the Tennant *Hamlet*) in her mad scene wearing only her underwear—an innocent floral cotton starter-bra and mini-shorts—the social impropriety and personal vulnerability of her uncontrolled behavior was portrayed more powerfully than a bawdy song alone could. A teenager talking (or singing) about sex does not shock us today or invite our concern; a teenager appearing in public in underwear does (Gertrude compassionately covered Ophelia with her pashmina). In the Kinnear *Hamlet* Claudius's spy-state was conveyed by besuited officials with clipboards and walkie-talkies exchanging information and receiving instructions. Similarly, when Romeo climbs the orchard walls of the Capulet estate in *Romeo and Juliet,* it is hard for us to appreciate the danger he runs in entering enemy territory. Banks of CCTV security monitors and patrol-guards with Alsatian dogs, as in Baz Luhrmann's film *Romeo + Juliet,* set the scene and create the atmosphere in ways we instantly comprehend. Today we understand the social statements made by modern dress when we no longer know how to "read" the sartorial status of codpieces.

675. In the preceding passage, the authors' intent is to

   (A) persuade readers that modern versions of Shakespeare are even better than the originals because of modern costuming

   (B) rebut the assertion that Shakespeare should never be modernized in film

   (C) analyze the idea that modernized versions can make Shakespeare still relevant to audiences

   (D) explain how Shakespeare has changed in regard to modern tastes

   (E) satirize a silly film that showed Ophelia wearing modern teenaged-girl underwear

676. As used in the last sentence of the passage, "sartorial" means

   (A) sarcastic

   (B) inappropriate

   (C) professionally costumed for drama

   (D) relating to clothing

   (E) ironic

677. When the authors write, "Today we understand the social statements made by modern dress when we no longer know how to 'read' the sartorial status of codpieces," they mean to say

   (A) codpieces were as inappropriate on the stage in Shakespeare's time as training bras are today

   (B) codpieces were necessary costuming components, although modern viewers don't know what these are

   (C) costuming in modern retellings changed to reflect current social statements in the same way that original costuming reflected those times and beliefs

   (D) in order to understand Shakespeare's work, an understanding of all the nuances of a play — such as costuming — must be taken into consideration

   (E) codpieces were considered bawdy long ago, even though modern audiences would think such things silly

678. When the authors describe "patrol-guard" and Alsatian dogs in regard to Romeo and Juliet, they most likely do this in order to support the idea that

   (A) small details can be changed in the play to make it more realistic and understandable to modern readers

   (B) a historical Romeo and Juliet most likely existed, although in another country

   (C) every culture has a different myth surrounding the story of Romeo and Juliet

   (D) *Romeo and Juliet* is an unlikely tale because so many necessary details were left out of the story

   (E) *Romeo and Juliet* would likely have ended much differently had there been a different setting

679. Which of the following examples would provide the most compelling support for the authors' argument?

(A) *Hamlet* being performed on a street corner by a troupe of traveling actors

(B) *Macbeth* being performed in Scotland on the site of Macbeth's actual castle

(C) Leonardo DiCaprio and Claire Danes starring in a modern remake of *Romeo and Juliet* updated with hip, modern costuming and music

(D) a public school reading the original *Julius Caesar*

(E) *A Midsummer Night's Dream* as retold through Tchaikovsky's ballet

Questions 680–682 are based on the following passage.

For more than one hundred years, films have been the most influential instrument of mass culture in the United States. As America's "dream factory," which manufactures fantasies and cultural myths much as a Detroit automaker produces cars, Hollywood has shaped the very way that Americans look at the world. Hollywood's films have played a pivotal role in "modernizing" American values. They have been instrumental in shaping Americans' deepest presuppositions about masculinity, femininity, race, ethnicity, and sexuality. Movies have helped form Americans' self-image and have provided unifying symbols in a society fragmented along lines of race, class, ethnicity, region, and gender. In certain respects subversive of traditional cultural values, movie culture created a mythic fantasy world that has helped Americans adapt to an ever-changing society.

680. The central idea of the passage is to argue that

(A) American values are portrayed in films

(B) American values shape the nature of films

(C) films have shaped American values

(D) films are nothing more than honest portrayals of American life and do not emphasize any particular moral or value

(E) filmmakers purposely change the culture of America by instilling their own hidden agendas in their works

681. As it is used in this context, the phrase "cultural myths" seems most nearly to mean

(A) a fiction or half-truth, especially one that forms an ideology

(B) a fictitious story that is made up in order to stress a point

(C) a popular belief about a cultural idea

(D) a traditional story that is used to explain certain aspects of the natural world

(E) a truth that has become so accepted that most people believe it is a myth

682. It is fair to assume that part of the author's goal in composing the passage was to encourage his readers to consider that Hollywood movies have had the positive effect of

(A) shaping Americans' self-images into more acceptable forms across all segments of society

(B) unifying members of society who would otherwise have been divided along the lines of sex, class, and ethnicity

(C) equating traditional cultural ideas with more subversive ideas about sex, class, and race

(D) providing an escape from the realities of life into a rich fantasy world

(E) bringing American values into a more modern reference

Questions 683–686 are based on the following passage.

Toward the end of the nineteenth century, a New York neurologist named George M. Beard coined the term "neurasthenia" to describe a psychological ailment that afflicted a growing number of Americans. Neurasthenia's symptoms included "nervous dyspepsia, insomnia, hysteria, hypochondria, asthma, sick-headache, skin rashes, hay fever, premature baldness, inebriety, hot and cold flashes, nervous exhaustion, brain-collapse, or forms of 'elementary insanity.'" Among those who suffered from neurasthenia-like ailments at some point were Theodore Roosevelt, settlement house founder Jane Addams, psychologist William James, painter Frederic Remington, and novelists Owen Wister and Theodore Dreiser.

According to medical experts, neurasthenia's underlying cause was "over-civilization." Stress, overstimulation, the frantic pace of modern life, and emotional repression produced debilitating bouts of depression or attacks of anxiety and nervous prostration. Fears of "over-civilization" pervaded late nineteenth-century American culture. Many worried that urban life was producing a generation of pathetic, pampered, physically and morally enfeebled 98-pound weaklings — a far cry from the stalwart Americans who had tamed a continent.

683. The passage presents the term "over-civilization" as all of the following EXCEPT a

(A) bona fide medical condition

(B) controversy

(C) paradox

(D) buzzword

(E) mixed blessing

684. The author suggested using the term "neurasthenia" when referring to people with a tendency to

(A) find clever ways to avoid doing hard work

(B) find medical excuses to avoid the draft

(C) become overstimulated by their busy lifestyles

(D) seek medical care for any ailment

(E) look for the newest and latest fashionable "disease"

685. Why does the author mention Theodore Roosevelt, Jane Addams, and other famous names from that time period?

(A) To suggest that the condition would affect those who truly did work hard and could not apply to other segments of the population who did not have such pressing matters to deal with

(B) To give medical credence to the ailment

(C) To show how common the condition was by suggesting that many people suffered from it

(D) To show that the condition was truly a farce because only famous people suffered from it

(E) To show how the disease affected these personalities in certain consequences of their lives

686. Which of the following best describes the organization of the passage?

(A) A medical condition is mercilessly analyzed for errors in judgment.

(B) A loaded term is judiciously unpacked.

(C) A traditional phrase is redefined for a new era.

(D) A theoretical concept is put into actual practice.

(E) A sarcastic label is reexamined in seriousness.

In 1898, the National Biscuit Company (Nabisco) launched the first million-dollar national advertising campaign. It succeeded in making Uneeda biscuits and their waterproof "In-Er-Seal" box popular household items. During the 1880s and 1890s, patent medicine manufacturers, department stores, and producers of low-price, packaged consumer goods (including Campbell Soups, Heinz Ketchup, and Quaker Oats) developed modern advertising techniques. Where earlier advertisers made little use of brand names, illustrations, or trademarks, the new ads employed snappy slogans and colorful packages. As early as 1900, advertisements began using psychology to arouse consumer demand by suggesting that a product would contribute to the consumer's social and psychic well-being. For purchases to be promoted, observed a trade journal in 1890, a consumer "must be aroused, excited, terrified." Listerine mouthwash promised to cure "halitosis"; Scott tissue claimed to prevent infections caused by harsh toilet paper.

687. The author's tone in the passage can best be characterized as

(A) largely theoretical but consistently open-minded

(B) primarily informative but somewhat humorous

(C) primarily explanatory but subtly critical

(D) largely analytical and mildly biased

(E) primarily skeptical but ultimately forgiving

688. The primary purpose of the final sentence of the passage is presumably to

(A) emphasize how ridiculous some advertising campaigns were

(B) surprise the reader by linking an unknown product from long ago to a well-known modern product

(C) provide a hint as to what the next paragraph will be about

(D) definitively answer a question posed earlier in the passage

(E) imply that some advertising campaigns were actually truthful

689. According to the passage, the most likely reason that the products of some companies, such as Nabisco and Campbell Soup Company, became successful is that

(A) those companies spent millions of dollars on advertising

(B) the companies offered unique patented and packaged consumer goods, such as goods sold in watertight packaging

(C) the products and ads made use of colorful packaging and snappy slogans

(D) the ads promised to aid a consumer's social and psychic well-being

(E) the ads promised relief from common medical ailments, such as halitosis

Of all the differences between the nineteenth and twentieth centuries, one of the most striking involves the rapid growth of commercialized entertainment. For much of the nineteenth century, commercial amusements were viewed as suspect. Drawing on the Puritan criticisms of play and recreation and a republican ideology that was hostile to luxury, hedonism, and extravagance, American Victorians associated theaters, dance halls, circuses, and organized sports with such vices as gambling, swearing, drinking, and immoral sexual behavior. In the late nineteenth century, however, a new outlook that revered leisure and play began to challenge Victorian prejudices.

During the first 20 years of the new century, attendance at professional baseball games doubled. Vaudeville, too, increased in popularity, featuring singing, dancing, skits, comics, acrobats, and magicians. Amusement parks, penny arcades, dance halls, and other commercial amusements flourished.

690. In context, the "commercialized entertainment" referred to in the passage is best exemplified by

(A) luxury, hedonism, and extravagance

(B) gambling, swearing, drinking, and immoral sexual behavior

(C) Victorian prejudices

(D) theaters, dance halls, circuses, and organized sports

(E) Puritan criticisms of play and recreation

691. Which of the following questions is directly answered by the passage?

(A) Why did the Victorian point of view and moral code start to decline in the early 20th century?

(B) What did people do for fun during those time periods — the 19th and 20th centuries?

(C) What is one of the biggest differences between prevailing attitudes of the 19th and 20th centuries?

(D) Exactly how did entertainment change between the 19th and 20th centuries?

(E) How does social entertainment in the 19th century compare to the 20th century in regard to commercial entertainment?

692. Which of the following words or phrases from the passage is used most nearly as a synonym for "hedonism," as it appears in this passage?

(A) republican ideology

(B) revered leisure

(C) vices

(D) immoral sexual behavior

(E) prejudices

Questions 693–695 are based on the following passage.

We don't want to blame someone for something that isn't his fault—something beyond his control. We can call this the Control Principle. But, paradoxically, we blame people more when their actions cause serious harm than when those same actions, through sheer luck, cause no harm at all. For example, a drunk driver who kills someone has done something far worse, we feel, than a drunk driver who does not kill anyone. This paradox—that we are responsible only for what we control, and yet we are also responsible for things beyond our control—is known in philosophy as the problem of "moral luck." It complicates our ideas about how moral responsibility is supposed to work.

693. According to the passage, the Control Principle is

(A) being responsible only for what is within our control

(B) blaming people less when their actions cause serious harm

(C) blaming people more when sheer luck causes great harm

(D) being responsible only for things beyond our control

(E) a code of moral responsibility

694. The primary purpose of this passage is to

(A) persuade people to subscribe to the Control Principle so they can alleviate feelings of guilt

(B) discern why events beyond a person's control occur

(C) explain a theory regarding why humans feel certain ways about events that cause harm

(D) argue that the Control Principle can eliminate unnecessary feelings of guilt when people blame themselves for events beyond their control

(E) provide information about how to act when a person encounters trauma during both controllable and uncontrollable events

695. The author characterizes the paradox of the Control Principle as

(A) an inevitable conclusion to traumatic events

(B) the surprising effect of undergoing a traumatic event

(C) the fault of the person who caused a tragic event

(D) an emotional reaction to unforeseen circumstances

(E) an attempt to reduce personal responsibility

Questions 696–698 refer to the following passage.

Gottfried Wilhelm Leibniz, a seventeenth-century German philosopher, wrote, "Nothing takes place without sufficient reason, that is... nothing happens without it being possible for someone who knows enough things to give a reason sufficient to determine why it is so and not otherwise." Later Leibniz added that we often do not know these reasons. This principle of sufficient reason (PSR) flatly rejects the possibility of random or unexplainable events. Even if we are not aware of the reason behind a particular event, it is nevertheless true that there's a reason that fully explains why the event took place.

696. The author of the passage uses the word "sufficient" most nearly to mean

(A) adequate

(B) qualified

(C) competent

(D) enough to meet the needs of a situation

(E) proficient

697. The organization of the passage can best be described by which of the following?

(A) A compromise is reached by the author in allowing some exceptions to the presented theory.

(B) A popular misconception is corrected.

(C) A problematic theory is more fully explained.

(D) A tricky question is analyzed for a general audience.

(E) A comparison is made between this theory and a similar one.

698. In this passage, the author's tone can best be described as

(A) paranoid hypothesizing

(B) self-justification

(C) defensiveness

(D) rational philosophizing

(E) blissful ignorance of reality

Questions 699–702 refer to the following passage.

But not all of the anxiety about the uncanny and the extraordinary is science fiction. What about the real-world attempt to use technology to change into something extraordinary? Is such a desire understandable, even praiseworthy? Or is such a desire to be met with skepticism, horror, or even condemnation? We live on the edge of a world in which genetic engineering, pharmacological manipulation, and cybernetic implants open up the opportunity for a person to become something like a real mutant. Soon, perhaps, we may be able to alter ourselves to achieve what some fictional mutants possess: greater strength, intelligence, agility, immunity, longevity (though probably not weather control). Is this a bad thing? Is it wrong to push ourselves outside the limits of what is human?

Transhumanists don't think so. The transhumanist movement wants to use technology to enhance human beings, to push us beyond our biological limits until we become something grander and more transcendent.

Contrasting with transhumanists are "bioconservatives," who advocate conserving the normal biological status of human beings. One group of bioconservatives consists of natural law theorists. "Natural law" argues that morality comes from the given needs, abilities, and limitations we have as humans and says that trying to change human nature is the worst sort of pride and arrogance.

699. In this passage, the phenomenon of science fiction is characterized by

    (A) anxiety about extraordinary events or traits

    (B) a desire to use technology to change the world, for good or evil

    (C) a transgression against natural law

    (D) an attempt to use technology to change the "real world" as we currently know and understand it

    (E) an attempt to use technology to change the biological status of humans

700. Which of the following best describes the organization of the passage?

    (A) It raises a philosophical question and then gives a series of possible answers to the questions.

    (B) It identifies a misconception and then analyzes more logical explanations.

    (C) It defines a sociological term and then illustrates it with a series of examples.

    (D) It compares and contrasts two viewpoints of an issue.

    (E) It challenges the reader's assumptions about previously held beliefs.

701. As discussed in this passage, the central contrast of transhumanists and bioconservatives is that

    (A) one group argues that the use of technology in enhancing humans is immoral, and the other feels that morality plays no part in the discussion

    (B) one group believes technology should be used to enhance humanity, and the other feels humanity should be conserved in its pure form with no technological enhancements

    (C) one group feels that enhancing humans with technology is simply another step in natural selection, and the other believes that natural law is being violated

    (D) one group argues that mutantism is actually a form of natural law, and the other feels such instances are not "true" examples of natural skill or ability

    (E) one group feels that the use of technology to enhance humans will make for better biological humans, and the other feels such use will weaken humanity and that future generations will not be able to survive without continued enhancement

702. According to the natural law theorists, the implied relationship between technological enhancements of humans and the concept of morality is that

(A) morality is tied not to biological functions but to emotional responses

(B) morality doesn't play a part in the issue of biological and technological enhancements

(C) morality is formed from human responses to the environment, and destroying that environment will likely negatively affect morality

(D) pride and hubris will eventually end the discussion as those who are technologically enhanced will create their own downfall through their arrogance

(E) if such technological enhancements were to take place in the larger world, man might no longer be seen as the ultimate predator because his own sense of morality would be destroyed; instead, other life forms would be able to develop moral codes and thus reasoning skills

---

Questions 703–708 are based on the following passage.

Although creator Stan Lee once claimed that the "X" in the X-Men's title stood for their "extra" power, the letter might as well have stood for "existential." The doubt, struggle, fear, and absurdity at the heart of existentialism are also the reasons why we respond so viscerally to the X-Men. But like the X-Men, existentialism isn't purely negative. Quite the contrary, existentialism can be a way to make sense of, and assign responsibility in, a world where God seems to be gone. But even more, to understand the X-Men it may be helpful to think of existentialism as a body of literature, a way of reading and writing, perhaps the most influential and important intellectual movement of the last century.

The X-Men's stories, then, may be best understood as literary examples of existential crisis. The mutant experience is anguished and absurd, a never-ending struggle not only to defeat bad guys — those staples of superheroism — but for safety and tolerance from the very people mutants protect. As each crisis passes, with another villain imprisoned, Magneto defeated (or killed or cloned or brainwashed or transported in space-time), yet another crisis inevitably begins, as the cycle has continued now for a half-century. Is the X-Men's eternal labor merely the nature of the serial narrative, the franchise in need of the next installment? Or has it come to represent the boundless, meaningless pursuit that is life?

703. This passage is primarily concerned with

(A) explaining the philosophical model that Stan Lee based the X-Men series on

(B) attempting to explain how the X-Men series is an example of existentialism

(C) correcting what appears to be a misconception about the X-Men series created by Stan Lee

(D) arguing that the X-Men series is a perfect example of existentialism

(E) criticizing those who have never watched or read the X-Men series by pointing out exactly what they have been missing

704. A paradox raised in the passage concerns the question of

(A) whether the X-Men ought to keep saving a human race who is not grateful for their sacrifices

(B) whether the X-Men are the evil superheroes and whether the bad guys are really the staples of society

(C) the fact that the X-Men struggle just as valiantly to defeat bad guys as they do to protect themselves from humans, the very creatures they are trying so hard to protect

(D) whether the X-Men and their challenges really just represent the meaninglessness of human life and the constant struggle against prevailing issues of morality

(E) whether the X-Men, in their quest to save humanity, become less human because of the bad guys they must constantly destroy

705. According to the information in the passage, existentialism can best be defined as

(A) simply a way of reading and writing

(B) the most profound thought development to occur in the last century

(C) a means through which literary criticism can have more meaning

(D) a theory to help explain man's existence and struggle in an uncaring world

(E) an explanation of man's continued anguish when life doesn't go as planned

706. According to the passage, the author believes

(A) that the X-Men contradict the theory of existentialism

(B) that the X-Men could find relief from their plight if they subscribed to the theory of existentialism

(C) that the X-Men's continued failure is the perfect example of the negativity of existentialism

(D) that the X-Men's eternal struggle is a lesson best seen through existentialism as they constantly question their own existence

(E) that people overthink comic books topics and X-Men should be seen as only a story

707. Based on the passage, the author most likely suggests which of the following is a lesson that can be learned from reading *X-Men*?

(A) Admit that society is a constant competition and only those who win will receive the accolades of society.

(B) Accept that the necessity of daily life is the struggle to constantly prove your worth as a human.

(C) Abandon your true desires, because little of what you do actually matters.

(D) Understand that all people, even heroes, struggle with the desire to understand man's very existence.

(E) Understand that life is a meaningless pursuit and your actions will have no effect on others around you.

708. According to the passage, the X-Men are caught in a cycle of

(A) wins and losses

(B) beginnings and endings

(C) plot repetitions

(D) instances of life events that give us meaning versus dry spells of a meaningless existence

(E) successfully conquering evil only to be conquered by evil in the next storyline

Set 6

Questions 709–714 are based on the following passage.

An inevitable problem in dealing with the peoples I am writing about is how to refer to them. The difficulty began with Christopher Columbus, who demonstrated the enormous creative fertility of error. Upon reaching the Caribbean, Columbus, mistakenly believing that he was near the East Indies, called the locals whom he met *indios,* which translated from Spanish into English as *Indians.* And this is what almost all of the native people of North America have been called by English-speaking people ever since. In recent decades, the term *Native Americans* has come into common usage among educators, publishers, the media, and various other well-intentioned, and in some cases guilt-driven, folks. Currently, the terminology most acceptable to native people themselves is *American Indians* — this, interestingly, disquiets many white people. American Indians more commonly refer to themselves by their tribal name: Mohawk, Cherokee, Pawnee, Cheyenne, Hopi, and so forth. The term *Native American* has almost become lost by Indian people since a great many individuals born in the United States contend correctly that they are native Americans. An emerging trend in terminology is *First Nations* or *indigenous Americans, Native people,* or *Indigenous Nations.* This reflects a growing movement for Indian studies programs looking for parallels and common themes among the many groups of indigenous peoples throughout the western hemisphere and in other parts of the world.

709. The passage is primarily concerned with

(A) aesthetically comparing terminology to collectively describe a group of people

(B) analyzing the specific effect that words have on the people whom those words describe

(C) criticizing people who make sweeping generalizations with terminology, when the terms are specific indicators that could be used to separate the groups

(D) suggesting better terms to describe a group of people who have been historically suppressed

(E) providing examples of how some words are better than others to describe groups of people

710. According to the passage, the terminology regarding American Indians differs in that

(A) well-intentioned people have sought to label them in a way that better fits who they are and what they want to be called

(B) historical terminology is no longer appropriate because research has led to a greater understanding of their cultural backgrounds

(C) this group of people now insists on a label that more accurately represents their heritage

(D) society always seeks to use the best "politically correct" term of the times, whatever that may be

(E) modern terms take into account the vast difference among the tribes rather than collectively grouping them

711. The author's attitude toward the subject matter most nearly appears to be one of

(A) indignant incredulousness at history

(B) satisfied acceptance of the final solution to the problem

(C) firm conviction in his proposal

(D) rueful nostalgia for the good old days

(E) respectful but aloof discussion of the topic

712. According to the passage, *Native* differs from *native* in that

(A) there are no differences in the meaning of the word

(B) one is more politically correct than another

(C) one is a common usage that refers only to American Indians while the other refers to a person born in America

(D) one refers only to American Indians while the other terms refer to all peoples born in America, Caucasian or otherwise

(E) one term is more preferred by American Indians, while the other is more preferred by the larger segment of society

713. The passage directly answers which of the following questions?

(A) What was the official explanation for the change in terminology from the term "Indians"?

(B) What are the criteria used to determine which term should be used?

(C) What are some of the complaints American Indians had with different terms to refer to their race?

(D) What do American Indians prefer to call themselves in this naming debate?

(E) How will this debate affect future terms when referring to American Indians?

714. The author most likely includes the sentences about the reasoning behind Columbus's term "Indian" in order to

(A) draw a more exact comparison between the terms being used

(B) explain why there is a debate about such terminology

(C) appeal to readers and get them interested in American Indian rights

(D) address an anticipated objection from more-informed readers

(E) establish the inherent racism in the older terms

Questions 715–719 are based on the following maps and refer to information provided about the loss of American Indian lands.

1783
Acres seized since 1776:
0

Indian homelands
Reservations

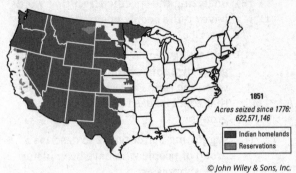

1851
Acres seized since 1776:
622,571,146

Indian homelands
Reservations

© John Wiley & Sons, Inc.

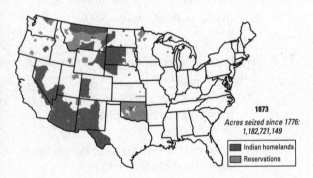

1873
Acres seized since 1776:
1,182,721,149

Indian homelands
Reservations

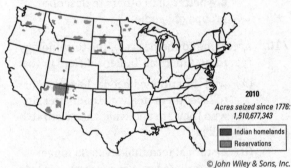

2010
Acres seized since 1776:
1,510,677,343

Indian homelands
Reservations

© John Wiley & Sons, Inc.

715. Based on the information from all four maps, the biggest drop-off in acreage of Indian homelands occurred roughly

(A) before 1783

(B) from 1783 to 1841

(C) from 1851 to 1873

(D) from 1873 to 2010

(E) after 2010

716. Based on information from all four maps, the largest increase in reservations occurred roughly

(A) before 1783

(B) from 1783 to 1841

(C) from 1851 to 1873

(D) from 1873 to 2010

(E) after 2010

717. What is the only state that was almost entirely set aside for reservations?

(A) California

(B) Oklahoma

(C) Montana

(D) Arizona

(E) Kentucky

718. The American government, in a quest to expand the population of white citizens westward, created the Bureau of Indian Affairs to settle the "Indian Question," or what to do with American Indians. Based on the maps, which of the original proposals did the government agency decide to do?

(A) Create a frontier line along the Appalachian Mountains, with one side for the American Indians and the other side for white settlers

(B) Take some land but allow the American Indians to maintain their accustomed way of life in the West, free from white encroachment

(C) Co-exist peacefully without the need for specific rules or boundaries and allow future disputes to be handled individually

(D) Create geographic boundaries that would separate American Indian lands from the government lands

(E) Culturally assimilate the American Indians into dominant society

719. Currently, which of the following states has the highest amount of acreage set aside for reservation use?

(A) South Dakota

(B) Oklahoma

(C) Montana

(D) Arizona

(E) Nevada

Questions 720–723 are based on the following passage.

American Indians were a preliterate people. No tribe had ever fashioned a writing system to express their oral language. This feat was the work of an individual named Sequoyah. Sequoyah was born sometime around 1770 in present-day Tennessee. In adulthood, he, his wife, and their children moved to Cherokee County, Georgia. There Sequoyah began work on developing a Cherokee writing system in 1809. His efforts are all the more remarkable because, far from being a student of linguistics or even phonetics, he had no formal education and spoke no language but his native Cherokee. Sequoyah nonetheless worked to isolate the complex sounds of the Cherokee tongue and endowed each with an identifying letter. The letters were of his own devising and not merely adopted from existing scripts. The Cherokee nation adopted his alphabet in 1825. Historian Arrell Morgan Gibson reported that the Cherokees achieved near total literacy in their own language in less than half a decade. This was the only time in recorded history that a member of a preliterate people independently created an effective writing system.

720. The passage directly answers which of the following questions?

(A) What are the criteria used to determine what constitutes literacy?

(B) How did the development of a writing system change the Cherokee nation?

(C) How was this alphabet and writing system taught to the Cherokee peoples?

(D) What is one of the greatest single and personalized achievements in the development of literacy?

(E) Why did Sequoyah feel the need to create an alphabet and writing system for the Cherokee peoples?

721. According to the author, the passage functions overall as an example of

(A) news reporting about other cultures being offensively oversimplified

(B) outdated beliefs standing in the way of progress

(C) an individual meeting his desire to improve the lives of his community members with creativity and vision

(D) the only example of American Indian achievement in the area of literacy

(E) a lack of understanding on the part of the American Indians about cultural assimilation

722. The author suggests that Sequoyah's feat was even more amazing because

    (A) the Cherokee had never valued written communication prior to this point

    (B) Sequoyah had no formal training in linguistics

    (C) Sequoyah had limited script available to help with translations

    (D) American English is so dissimilar from the Cherokee language

    (E) the Cherokee resisted learning the language

723. Which of the following best describes the relationship between the first and last sentences of the paragraph?

    (A) The first sentence describes a misconception, and the last sentence corrects it.

    (B) The first sentence introduces a general idea, and the last sentence supports it with specifics.

    (C) The first sentence states a historical perspective, and the last sentence presents a different perspective based on chronological events.

    (D) The first sentence raises a question, and the last sentence attempts to answer it.

    (E) Both sentences present different perspectives on a single issue.

Questions 724–729 are based on the following passages.

Passage 1

The relationship of the name of Shakespeare's son, Hamnet, to the tragic hero, Hamlet, comes into [the] pleasurable category of seeing or seeking equivalence. Sigmund Freud, for one, was confident that the son and the prince were the same. In *The Interpretation of Dreams* (1900) he wrote:

> it can of course only be the poet's own mind which confronts us in Hamlet. I observe in a

book on Shakespeare. . . a statement that *Hamlet* was written immediately after the death of Shakespeare's father (in 1601), that is, under the immediate impact of his bereavement and, as we may well assume, while his child-hood feelings about his father had been freshly revived. It is known, too, that Shakespeare's own son who died at an early age bore the name of "Hamnet," which is identical with "Hamlet."

Passage 2

But how, if at all, did Shakespeare respond to that horror of Hamnet's death when it occurred? Did he use his chief vehicle of expression, the drama, to reflect on what such a death meant to him? He certainly used the sonnet form to urge to his gentlemanly friend the vital importance of bearing a son, though once again these writings may well precede the death of Hamnet in August of 1596. We know that in October of 1596 Shakespeare insti-tuted proceedings to obtain a coat of arms for his father John Shakespeare, so that the father (who was to die in 1601) could style himself a gentleman. Yet despite the seemingly huge importance of the father–son relationship to Shakespeare, nothing emerges in the plays of 1596 and immediately afterwards.

724. What best describes the relationship between Passage 1 and Passage 2?

    (A) Passage 2 provides further examples of the viewpoint of Passage 1.

    (B) Passage 2 issues a counterargument to a viewpoint that is presented in Passage 1.

    (C) Passage 2 provides more up-to-date information than is presented in Passage 1.

    (D) Passage 1 provides an authoritative expert to support a claim made, while Passage 2 is pure conjecture.

    (E) The arguments of Passage 1 and 2 are largely unrelated.

725. In the context in which it appears in Passage 1, the phrase "pleasurable category of seeing or seeking equivalence" most likely means

(A) needing to find symbolism in all of life's events

(B) enjoying the symmetry and circularity of events

(C) a literary critic's method of attributing life events to literature, even though the author himself might have been unaware of the instance

(D) the psychoanalytical process of explaining seemingly random events with hidden agendas

(E) the interpretative nature of assigning names to children

726. What does the reference to Shakespeare's purchasing of a coat of arms for his father suggest about the relationship between the two, according to information from both passages?

(A) That Shakespeare hoped his estrangement with his father could be ended

(B) That the two had not seen one another in a long time

(C) That family was important to Shakespeare and family names should have honor

(D) That Shakespeare felt the relationship with his father was important only after Hamnet's death

(E) That Shakespeare cared more for his father than his son

727. Compared with Passage 1, the purpose and tone of Passage 2 is

(A) equally argumentative but more explanatory

(B) equally open-minded but more jocose

(C) equally educated but less scientific

(D) equally analytical but more skeptical

(E) equally angry but less forgiving

728. Both authors do which of the following?

(A) Gently mock those who disagree with their theory

(B) Discuss recent evidence to prove their particular viewpoint

(C) Make reference to the works of Shakespeare to prove their point

(D) Reference several examples to prove their point

(E) Criticize Shakespeare's unfeeling nature

729. Both passages are primarily concerned with

(A) disputing common objections about the man who was Shakespeare

(B) dispelling common misconceptions about the man who was Shakespeare

(C) seeking to know more about the man Shakespeare by looking at his works as evidence of his true character

(D) explaining basic facts about the topic to an unknowledgeable audience

(E) expanding general interest in the topic of the symbolism and meaning that can be found in Shakespeare's works

Questions 730–733 are based on the following passage.

After half a century has been spent in the investigation and improvement of our indigenous Materia Medica, Prof. Wood... says, "the present standard remedies, have for the most part been gathered from all quarters of the globe, have gone through every variety of trial, have been sifted out from an immense mass of materials, and hence stood the test of experience, which for thousands of years has been in the course of accumulation." Conceding all this however, it must be admitted, that from custom, or indolence, or want of thought, or some other cause, we are too much in the habit of depending on foreign countries for our supplies of vegetable medicines, such, even, as we could furnish ourselves in a far purer and fresher state. And when we take into consideration, the immense amount of old, decayed, deteriorated, effete and adulterated stuff, cast upon our shores from foreign countries, said to be at a cheap rate, but which, in the end, would be dear, even if they paid us for using it, at the rate we charge our patients; it is surprising, that long ere this, we had not opened our eyes to the imposition, and learned to rely on the rich resources of our own country.

730. It can be inferred from the passage that the author would agree with which of the following statements?

(A) Pharmaceutical companies should always seek to purchase materials at the lowest price so those cost savings can be passed on to the consumer.

(B) People would do well to research their own back woods and yards for common plants that have been known to contain healing properties.

(C) There should be no cost consideration if a plant could be used to heal a sick or dying person.

(D) America does not have to rely on other countries for medicinal plants, as many of the same things can be easily and more freshly grown here.

(E) Scientific modifications have improved natural plants.

731. Which of the following examples would serve as a counterargument to the theory that America could best represent her own medicinal needs?

(A) Medicinal use of marijuana to treat seizures, cancer, etc.

(B) The use of tansy as a bug repellent or in flavoring beers

(C) Rotating between crops of soy and corn to enrich the soil

(D) Drinking mint tea to settle digestion

(E) The founding of the Terra Nova ethno-medicinal Rainforest Reserve to ensure rare tropical plants are available for medical research

732. According to the author, why don't American pharmaceutical companies devote more money to indigenous plant research?

(A) The high cost of development

(B) Laziness and lack of creativity

(C) Rising healthcare costs due to the medical profession

(D) Lack of resources

(E) Quality of the product received from foreign vendors

733. The author of the passage advises that more medicinal products could be developed in the U.S. What reason does the author give to make consumers feel safe when making this decision?

(A) The consumer can never be really sure what is in the products from foreign markets.

(B) Decades of research, trials, and tests have determined the validity of indigenous plant material.

(C) Plants could be grown more cheaply here.

(D) Modern research has confirmed American products are just as effective as products produced elsewhere.

(E) Foreign products have a harder time passing FDA regulation.

Questions 734–738 are based on the following passage.

These jungle stories [*Man-Eaters of Kumaon*] by Jim Corbett merit as much popularity and as wide a circulation as Rudyard Kipling's *Jungle Books*. Kipling's *Jungle Books* were fiction, based on great knowledge of jungle life; Corbett's stories are fact, and fact is often stranger than fiction. These stories should prove of entrancing interest to all boys and girls who like exciting yarns; they should be of equal interest to all who take any interest in the wild life of the jungle; they should prove of great value to any genuine sportsman who wishes to earn by his own efforts the credit of shooting a tiger; they will be of interest even to the so-called sportsman who feels some pride in killing a tiger when all that he has done is to fire straight from a safe position on a *machan* or on the back of a staunch elephant, when all the hard work involved in beating up a tiger to his death has been done by others.

Corbett's description of his campaign against the man-eaters of the Kumaon Hills shows the qualities that a successful *shikari* needs, physical strength, infinite patience, great power of observation, and power not only to notice small signs but also to draw the right inference from those signs. To these must be added great courage.

734. The purpose of the first paragraph of the passage is to

(A) explain how the author knows Corbett's stories are based on fact

(B) establish that Corbett's stories should be believable

(C) raise the question of whether Corbett's stories are true

(D) explain why Corbett's stories should be read

(E) inform the reader about Corbett's credentials

735. The author of the passage mentions Rudyard Kipling and the *Jungle Books* in order to

(A) establish Corbett's prominence among other literary figures

(B) compare another key influence on the adventure/jungle genre of literature

(C) introduce an influence on Corbett's writing style

(D) consider all similar authors and styles to set the preference for Corbett's writing

(E) show envy toward Kipling's success and encourage readers to give Corbett's writing the same consideration

736. The first sentence of the passage suggests which of the following is true of Corbett's work *Man-Eaters of Kumaon*?

(A) It is as worthy of acclaim as Kipling's more popular work.

(B) It is just as popular as Kipling's work.

(C) It is just as well-read and circulated as Kipling's work.

(D) Rudyard Kipling does not deserve the acclaim and popularity his work receives.

(E) The lack of Corbett's financial and literary success can be attributed to the popularity of Kipling's *Jungle Books*.

737. The author would most likely agree with which of the following about *Man-Eaters of Kumaon*?

(A) It is a fantastical account of tiger hunting.

(B) It more accurately depicts life in the jungle than Kipling's *Jungle Book*.

(C) In order to fully understand *Man-Eaters of Kumaon*, readers need some knowledge of jungle life, such as that depicted in *Jungle Book*.

(D) Sportsmen will be able to learn how to shoot tigers from a *machan* or from the back of an elephant.

(E) Corbett's unique religious outlook adds a level of interest to the book not available in Kipling's works.

738. According to the passage, why is Corbett uniquely qualified to write this work?

    (A) His writing style is as good as that of another author who enjoys worldwide acclaim.

    (B) He has much experience with tiger hunting in the jungle and is an expert on the subject.

    (C) Corbett brings personal experience to the subject due to traumatic life events.

    (D) Corbett's work as a *shikari* provided him with the strength, patience, and courage to tackle such a tremendous feat as killing man-eating tigers — and to write about it.

    (E) Corbett's work as a tiger hunter made him a hero in the area for having rid the area of Kumaon of the fierce beasts.

Questions 739–742 are based on the following passage.

The store in which the Justice of the Peace's court was sitting smelled of cheese. The boy, crouched on his nail keg at the back of the crowded room, knew he smelled cheese, and more: from where he sat he could see the ranked shelves close-packed with the solid, squat, dynamic shapes of tin cans whose labels his stomach read, not from the lettering which meant nothing to his mind but from the scarlet devils and the silver curve of fish — this, the cheese which he knew he smelled and the hermetic meat which his intestines believed he smelled coming in intermittent gusts momentary and brief between the other constant one, the smell and sense just a little of fear because mostly of despair and grief, the old fierce pull of blood. He could not see the table where the Justice sat and before which his father and his father's enemy (*our enemy* he thought in that despair; *ourn! mine and hisn both! He's my father!*) stood, but he could hear them, the two of them that is, because his father had said no word yet.

739. How does the author develop the narrator's point of view?

    (A) By using a limited narrator and stating only the boy's thoughts and feelings directly

    (B) By using an omniscient narrator and allowing the reader to see into the minds of all the characters and understand their thoughts and feelings

    (C) By using a detached narrator who has very little voice or interest in the story

    (D) By using a commentator as a narrator so that unbiased observations can be made and the decisions can be left to the reader

    (E) By using a secondary character so that the reader can experience the action first-hand but not be held to the feelings and views of those directly involved in the conflict

740. Why did Faulkner begin the story with such a rich description of the setting?

    (A) Faulkner's style is to provide rich description of each aspect of the stories that he writes.

    (B) The reader can see how hungry the boy is, and the reader is led to believe the judgment will be an important one in the boy's life.

    (C) By using a boy, Faulkner had to think like a boy and write like a boy, which meant simple descriptions of food and his surroundings.

    (D) Because the work was written about historical times, Faulkner had to let the reader know why a Justice of the Peace was in a store.

    (E) It sets the scene for the boy's thievery in order to save his family from starvation after his father is sent to jail.

741. Which of the following could be inferred about the boy's father?

    (A) He has been unjustly accused of a crime he didn't commit.

    (B) The wealthy Justice of the Peace has a vendetta against the boy's father.

    (C) The father likely committed the crime of which he is being accused.

    (D) The father is in court for a trivial incident.

    (E) The father is silent because he doesn't want to cause his son further grief.

742. How does Faulkner use the thoughts of the boy to develop a tone in this introduction to the story with his use of words such as "hisn" and "ourn"?

    (A) Faulkner uses these speech patterns to show that the boy comes from an uneducated Southern family, one likely to be taken advantage of by a more educated and richer political system.

    (B) The boy's thoughts are an example of his innocence and helplessness at his father's presence in the court.

    (C) The use of such diction shows the story will be told from the point of view of a boy, and the misspellings point more to his extreme youth than to other considerations.

    (D) The speech patterns show only that the boy is terrified and are not meant to provide more meaning to the reader.

    (E) The difference between the perfectly grammatical thought patterns and the speech diction point to the character being an unreliable narrator, one whom the reader cannot trust.

Questions 743–746 are based on the following passage.

In May 1946, *The New Yorker* sent John Hersey, journalist and author of *A Bell for Adano*, to the Far East to find out what had really happened at Hiroshima: to interview survivors of the catastrophe, to endeavor to describe what they had seen and felt and thought, what the destruction of their city, their lives and homes and hopes and friends, had meant to them — in short, the cost of the bomb in terms of human suffering and reaction to suffering. He stayed in Japan for a month, gathering his own material with little, if any, help from the occupying authorities; he obtained the stories from actual witnesses. The characters in his account are living individuals, not composite types. The story is their own story, told as far as possible in their own words. On August 31st, 1946, Hersey's story was made public. For the first time in *The New Yorker*'s career, an issue appeared which, within the familiar covers, bearing — for such covers are prepared long in advance — a picnic scene, carried no satire, no cartoons, no fiction, no verse or smart quips or shopping notes: nothing but its advertisement matter and Hersey's 30,000-word story [*Hiroshima*].

743. It can be inferred that the author would be inclined to make what criticism of the news outlets' presentation of Hiroshima?

    (A) It is often difficult for the audience to fully understand the complicated stories of Hiroshima because the news outlets focused on the scientific facts of the atomic bomb.

    (B) The rigidity of the news made it unlikely that the viewers were able to understand the importance of the event, which effectively ended the war.

    (C) The news stories were unimaginative, and the author wanted readers to have better descriptions of what the setting looked like before and after the event.

    (D) The news was too harsh toward U.S. involvement in the event.

    (E) The news focused on the celebratory nature of the event from the American perspective and little, if anything, was shown about the tragic effect on the Japanese citizens.

744. Based on the passage, which of the following descriptions are likely to appear in Hersey's work?

(A) Perspectives of the soldiers who dropped the bomb and the guilt they feel at causing such destruction

(B) Viewpoints of the developers of the bomb and opinions on the consequences of how the bomb was used

(C) Interviews with the original correspondents on why their portrayal included only certain aspects of the event

(D) An editorial by *The New Yorker* staff concerning why they decided to publish Hersey's work

(E) First-person accounts from actual witnesses and victims of the event

745. Based on the passage, the mostly likely assumption about the reason *The New Yorker* broke with its traditional publishing and ran the story as a stand-alone instead of a serial is that

(A) *The New Yorker* felt like it would lose advertising and readership

(B) the subject matter was such that respect for the lives lost was more important than traditional routine and formatting

(C) Hersey's work would have been hard to serialize

(D) *The New Yorker* editors felt the U.S. government might have censored future stories because of sensitive war information that could be leaked to the enemy

(E) Hersey took so long to write and research the story, they felt such respect was owed to the author

746. What is meant by the term "composite types"?

(A) A piecing together of different stories and personalities to get an overall idea

(B) A blending of all the interviews into one long interview

(C) Fictionalizing historical events and personages

(D) The analysis of each person being interviewed so the reader gets a better idea of the psychological damage

(E) Infusing Hersey's own thoughts and opinions in the story

Questions 747–750 are based on the following passage.

Estimates of woman are as varied as the minds which cherish them. The beautiful see the beautiful, and the base, the base. Men portray their own characters by the manner in which they portray the characters of others, and this is especially true with regard to their judgment of women. If they have treated them as toys and playthings, they esteem them frivolous and empty. If they have used them lawlessly, they write them down as base. If, on the other hand, they have honoured and cherished them, as every true man should, guarding their weakness and reverencing their purity, they will hold them as superior to themselves in all finer human qualities nearer, indeed, to the divine and the heavenly. "We pity the man," says Richter, "for whom his own mother has not made all other mothers venerable."

Woman, however, need not be discouraged by the unjust things which have been said of her by men, since it is certain that the good things said about her far outnumber and outweigh the evil things. Furthermore, we have observed that as a man rises in nobleness, his estimate of woman rises with him, and it is also true that the wisest and noblest men have cherished the most exalted views of woman.

747. Which of the following could be substituted for the term "venerable" in the first paragraph with the least change in meaning?

(A) reputable

(B) revered

(C) respectable

(D) discreditable

(E) admirable

748. Which of the following accurately describes the author's views on women?

(A) Women are only as good as the man they are with.

(B) All women should be cherished and honored in the same way that one cherishes and honors his own mother.

(C) Women should not believe the lesser judgment of themselves, as most of those judgments instead reflect on the men who make them.

(D) All women should aspire to be the same type and mold of woman as the author's own mother.

(E) Women should be individually judged, and not lumped together in collective categories of "good" or "bad."

749. Which of the following accurately describes the author's views on men, in regard to women?

(A) Women are only as good as the man they are with.

(B) A man will treat women in the same manner as he treats his mother.

(C) A man's judgments of women more accurately reflect his own manner and morals than those of the women he is judging.

(D) A man can be only as good as the women he associates with.

(E) Men should not judge women collectively, as each is an individual, and some are "good" while others are "bad."

750. In the last paragraph, the author implies which of the following about men of character?

(A) Men who are noble in character often have better views of those who are around them.

(B) Men can improve the lives of the women around them by acting more nobly.

(C) Such men learned these valuable lessons at the feet of worthy mothers.

(D) Men will become nobler if they dramatically change how they view and treat women.

(E) Men who are not noble in character can blame this on their mothers, who have failed in their maternal responsibilities.

Questions 751–754 are based on the following passage.

Ethnology is in the sadly ludicrous, not to say tragic, position, that at the very moment when it begins to put its workshop in order, to forge its proper tools, to start ready for work on its appointed task, the material of its study melts away with hopeless rapidity. Just now, when the methods and aims of scientific field ethnology have taken shape, when men fully trained for the work have begun to travel into savage countries and study their inhabitants — these die away under our very eyes.

The research which has been done on native races by men of academic training has proved beyond doubt and cavil that scientific, methodic inquiry can give us results far more abundant and of better quality than those of even the best amateur's work. Most, though not all, of the modern scientific accounts have opened up quite new and unexpected aspects of tribal life. They have given us, in clear outline, the picture of social institutions often surprisingly vast and complex; they have brought before us the vision of the native as he is, in his religious and magical beliefs and practices. They have allowed us to penetrate into his mind far more deeply than we have ever done before.

751. In the first sentence, the phrase "sadly ludicrous" is intended to imply

(A) a joke that no one thinks is funny

(B) a joke in poor taste

(C) a ridiculous waste of time

(D) a frustrating but expected situation, considering all the time and effort spent

(E) a signal that ethnology has outlived its usefulness

752. Which of the following best describes the definition of "ethnology," as described in the passage?

(A) The science that deals with the study of magic and religion in other cultures

(B) The science that deals with the study of the origins of races of people

(C) The science that deals with the study of the characteristics of specific races of people

(D) The science that deals with the study of the relations of human beings

(E) An analytical study of all of the above

753. According to the passage, studying native races is important to the larger world because

(A) of the views of a vast and complex social community that was previously unknown to the world

(B) of the secrets that such communities have hidden and the idea that these secrets will be forever lost

(C) the religious and magical beliefs of these societies point to truths in our own religions

(D) a greater understanding of such races confirms that these people are not the savages others suppose

(E) ethnologists have no other avenues of study should these races disappear forever

754. The primary purpose of the passage is to

(A) humorously humanize the work of ethnologists

(B) persuade readers to understand that many cultures are disappearing before they can be studied

(C) explain both the value of and the difficulty of ethnology in studying populations of native tribes

(D) explore the ways that ethnologists can expand and perfect their work before the purpose of study ceases to exist

(E) report on new and exciting discoveries being made by ethnologists in the field

Questions 755–758 are based on the following passage.

If Picasso is applauded for painting pictures which do not represent anything he has hitherto seen, if Schoenberg can pen a score that sounds entirely new even to ears accustomed to listen to modern music, why should an employer of English words be required to form sentences which are familiar in meaning, shape, and sound to any casual reader? Miss Stein herself implies somewhere that where there is communication (or identification) there can be no question of creation. This is solid ground, walked on realistically, as anyone who has been exposed to performances of music by Reger, for example, can readily testify. However, it must be borne in mind that composers and painters are not always inspired to *absolute* creation: Schoenberg wrote music for *Pelleas et Mélisande* and the tuneful *Verklaerte Nacht,* while Picasso had his rose and blue and classic periods which are representational. Like the composer and painter Miss [Gertrude] Stein has her easier moments (*The Autobiography of Alice B. Toklas,* for instance, is written in imitation of Miss Toklas's own manner) and even in her more "difficult" pages there are variations, some of which are in the nature of experiment.

755. According to the passage, the reader can infer the author feels that

(A) Stein's work is just as creative and masterful as the works of Picasso and Schoenberg, albeit in a different genre

(B) Stein's work with *The Autobiography of Alice B. Toklas* shouldn't be taken as an example of her finest work

(C) Stein's work with *The Autobiography of Alice B. Toklas* should be taken as a definitive representation of her creative talent

(D) The creative nature of artists cannot be limited by the works they create

(E) Stein's work with *The Autobiography of Alice B. Toklas* is an example of artistic experimentation and creativity and should be seen as such

756. The principal intent of the passage is to

(A) justify Stein's work as being worthy of being read

(B) prepare the reader for *The Autobiography of Alice B. Toklas,* which might be different from expectations

(C) offer a professional and personal biography of Stein and brief summary of *The Autobiography of Alice B. Toklas*

(D) argue that Stein's work should enjoy more acclaim than it currently does

(E) explain why some people were offended by *The Autobiography of Alice B. Toklas*

757. The author most probably uses the term "absolute creations" to mean

(A) work that is representative of the artist's principal style

(B) work that should be viewed independently, with no thought to other works by the same artist

(C) work that is considered total and complete by the author, regardless of how it is perceived by the public

(D) work that is not diminished even though it is not the "best" example of an author's style

(E) work that is wholly original and not to be thought of as representative of an author's style

758. The paradox raised by the passage concerns the need to balance

(A) the cultural values of art with the need for creativity

(B) multicultural sensitivity to different genres without a need to compare one form of art to another

(C) the dispensing of labels when reviewing creative works

(D) the difficulty of competing with those who are considered "masters" when attempting a new type of artistic creation

(E) intentionalist artistic criticism with interpretive artistic criticism

Chapter 3

Grammar and Writing

I n addition to gauging your grammar, usage, and punctuation skills, this part of the test asks you to detect writing problems in sample rough drafts.

Note: The sample rough drafts in this chapter come from our sample responses to some of the Argumentative Essay prompts in Chapter 4. If you'd like to write your own essays before you read these drafts, see Questions 990–992 in Chapter 4 before tackling the "Revising in Context" questions.

The Problems You'll Work On

Your challenge is to find the error in the sentence — or the lack of one — or to choose the best version of a sentence or phrase. When working through the chapter, be prepared to do the following:

>> Recognize whether phrases and clauses are used correctly

>> Choose the right words, including in idioms

>> Select the proper punctuation, particularly with commas, semicolons, and apostrophes

>> Decide whether a sentence should be cut from a passage

What to Watch Out For

Concerning grammar and punctuation, pay attention to these areas:

>> **Matters of agreement:** Agreement problems make up a large part of this section of the Praxis.

>> **Contractions:** Whenever you see a contraction, sound it out: *it's = it is, they're = they are,* and so on.

>> **Commas:** Longer sentences don't necessarily require more punctuation, especially commas, than shorter ones. If the Praxis asks you to consider punctuation, locate the sentence's main subject and verb and go from there.

Correcting Sentences

Select the error or choose the best version of the sentence.

759. Research (A) <u>shows</u> that two (B) <u>out of</u> seven people (C) <u>who</u> take tests turn out to be (D) <u>a very diligent student</u>. (E) <u>No error</u>

760. (A) <u>As she came down the stairs</u>, the books Mariah (B) <u>carried</u> (C) <u>proved to be</u> more than she could (D) <u>handle; she</u> dropped them. (E) <u>No error</u>

761. (A) <u>Howard's boss</u> not only requires employees (B) <u>to be</u> at work by eight (C) <u>but asks</u> them (D) <u>to stay</u> after six. (E) <u>No error</u>

762. Only a few years ago, Pluto's status was (A) <u>that of a planet</u>, but now (B) <u>it's status</u> is that of a dwarf (C) <u>planet; the problem</u>, it seems, is the fact that other objects share (D) <u>Pluto's orbit</u>. (E) <u>No error</u>

763. In (A) <u>the mid-1850s</u>, relatives of a Revolutionary War militiaman (B) <u>painstakingly wrote</u> down his war (C) <u>experience because</u> they knew of no other way to record (D) <u>, to them</u> as well as others, priceless information. (E) <u>No error</u>

764. Of all the bulbs Mildred planted last fall, (A) <u>only the daffodils</u> came up, and she (B) <u>thinks</u> the many neighborhood squirrels (C) <u>must be eating</u> (D) <u>her</u> bulbs. (E) <u>No error</u>

765. The doctor (A) <u>himself</u>, busy as the (B) <u>busiest</u> of doctors, (C) <u>stop in</u> to check on the progress of (D) <u>each patient</u>. (E) <u>No error</u>

766. (A) <u>This</u> often (B) <u>frustrates people</u> (C) <u>who find such</u> (D) <u>interruptions</u> hard to believe. (E) <u>No error</u>

767. Seward's Folly, the (A) <u>so-called</u> mistake (B) <u>Secretary of State</u> William Seward made by purchasing Alaska for $7 million from Russia (C)<u>,</u> turned out to be (D) <u>anything but</u> folly when gold was discovered in the Klondike. (E) <u>No error</u>

768. (A) <u>Making up the story as he went</u>, Paul's lies became (B) <u>a problem that snowballed</u>; (C) <u>however,</u> he eventually stayed out of trouble by telling the truth, (D) <u>unglamorous</u> as it was. (E) <u>No error</u>

769. The twins (A) <u>Alicia and Tomas</u> are on (B) <u>their</u> way to learning responsibility, but each of them (C) <u>need</u> (D) <u>to consider</u> the consequences of actions. (E) <u>No error</u>

770. The way to succeed in a hobby is (A) <u>through practice</u> (B)<u>, so you should start</u> (C) <u>spending</u> time in a fun activity and continue as time (D) <u>allows</u>. (E) <u>No error</u>

771. When a student signs up for a class that has (A) <u>always</u> been popular, (B) <u>they</u> usually are correct (C) <u>in thinking it</u> (D) <u>will be</u> enjoyable. (E) <u>No error</u>

772. It is very important to (A) <u>both</u> Mr. Sigurian and (B) <u>myself</u> that all correspondence be (C) <u>attended to</u> (D) <u>promptly</u>. (E) <u>No error</u>

773. The (A) <u>incessantly</u> bickering (B) <u>of the couple</u> became (C) <u>increasingly</u> annoying to everyone around (D) <u>them</u>. (E) <u>No error</u>

774. A (A) <u>senator</u> usually has more to do than (B) <u>he or she</u> alone can accomplish (C)<u>; thus</u>, several (D) <u>aids</u> are often employed. (E) <u>No error</u>

775. (A) <u>Playwrights</u> of (B) <u>ancient Greece</u> had a specific (C) <u>effect</u> in mind when (D) <u>they</u> created plays, which were either comedies or tragedies. (E) <u>No error</u>

776. In (A) <u>Bloom's</u> taxonomy (B)<u>, the</u> highest level in the new version is Create (C)<u>; but</u> in the old version, it (D) <u>was</u> Evaluation. (E) <u>No error</u>

777. After (A) <u>scenting the food</u> the cat (B) <u>leapt</u> (C) <u>onto the counter</u> as though it were (D) <u>only</u> a foot high. (E) No error

778. A (A) <u>lose</u> cannon was (B) <u>originally</u> just that: a (C) <u>ship's</u> cannon (D) <u>whose</u> moorings became undone. (E) <u>No error</u>

779. The miniature poodle was a cute dog, but it barked continually, <u>which drove its owners crazy</u>.

(A) which drove its owners crazy

(B) which drove it's owners crazy

(C) which always drove its owners crazy

(D) a habit which drove its owners crazy

(E) a habit which drove it's owners crazy

780. <u>In spite of the fact that she still did not trust the hostess</u>, Belinda plans on attending the party.

(A) In spite of the fact that she still did not trust the hostess

(B) In spite of the fact that she still does not trust the hostess

(C) Despite the fact that she still did not trust the hostess

(D) Still not trusting the hostess anyway

(E) Accepting the fact that she still did not trust the hostess

781. <u>The childrens' reading hour had come to an end; however,</u> the babysitter knew Clara and Evan remained attentive and so read for another thirty minutes.

(A) The childrens' reading hour had come to an end; however,

(B) The childrens' reading hour had come to an end, however,

(C) The childrens' reading hour had come to an end; but,

(D) The children's reading hour had come to an end; but,

(E) The children's reading hour had come to an end; however,

782. When Geraldo and Miguel ran onto the field and met the opposing team's players, <u>they were more than a little uncertain</u>.

(A) they were more than a little uncertain

(B) they were more than a little frightened

(C) Geraldo and Miguel were more than a little uncertain

(D) they were more confidant

(E) Geraldo and Miguel feel more than a little uncertain.

783. <u>In science, the process of compiling data and reporting the results are important steps of the scientific method.</u>

(A) In science, the process of compiling data and reporting the results are important steps of the scientific method.

(B) In science, the processes of compiling data and reporting the results are important steps of the scientific method.

(C) In science, the process of compiling data and reporting the results is an important step of the scientific method.

(D) In science, the processes of compiling data and reporting the results is an important step of the scientific method.

(E) In science, the act of compiling data and reporting the results are important steps of the scientific method.

784. Silvio decided to switch to a different approach <u>because he constantly found impediments</u> in the job-search path he was on.

(A) because he constantly found impediments

(B) because he constant found impediments

(C) , because he found constant impediments

(D) because he constantly was finding impediments

(E) because he constantly found implements

785. <u>Although not sure that the voters would except such action</u>, the senators gave themselves a raise.

(A) Although not sure that the voters would except such action

(B) Not at all sure that the voters would except such action

(C) Although not sure that they would accept such action

(D) Although not sure that the voters would accept such action

(E) Not even sure that the voters would except such action

786. The salesclerk sold the fifteen extra-large blue T-shirts faster than she thought possible.

(A) The salesclerk sold the fifteen extra-large blue T-shirts faster than she thought possible.

(B) The salesclerk sold the fifteen, extra-large, blue T-shirts faster than she thought possible.

(C) The salesclerk sold the fifteen extra-large blue T-shirts faster than they thought possible.

(D) The salesclerk sold the fifteen, extra-large, blue t-shirts faster than she thought possible.

(E) The salesclerk sold the fifteen extra-large blue T-shirts faster then she thought possible.

787. The wire services just reported that the jury has finally reached their decision.

(A) that the jury has finally reached their decision

(B) that the jury has finally reached its decision

(C) , that the jury has finally reached their decision

(D) , that the jury has finally reached a decision

(E) that the jury has reached their decision finally

788. They took their walk through a wild-flower field, a hundred yards away from the river that was formed during the Ice Age.

(A) that was formed during the Ice Age

(B) that was formed during the ice age

(C) that had been formed during the Ice Age

(D) that had been formed during the ice age

(E) which was formed during the Ice Age

789. Increasingly higher levels of carbon dioxide causes more and more heat to be trapped in the atmosphere.

(A) causes more and more heat to be trapped

(B) causes more heat to be trapped

(C) cause problems

(D) is a problem

(E) cause more and more heat to be trapped

790. The infestation approaches the park, and the caretakers think that each species of bird, mammal, and amphibian have to be watched carefully.

(A) that each species of bird, mammal, and amphibian have to be watched carefully

(B) that each species of bird, mammal, and amphibian have to be carefully watched

(C) that each bird, mammal, and amphibian have to be watched carefully

(D) that each species of bird, mammal, and amphibian has to be watched carefully

(E) , that each species of bird, mammal, and amphibian has to be watched carefully

791. When you want to experiment with clothing styles, it's best if we get friends' opinions first before buying a lot of clothes or venturing out.

(A) it's best if we get friends' opinions first

(B) it's best if you get friends' opinions first

(C) its best if you get friends' opinions first

(D) it's better if we get friends' opinions first

(E) it's best if you get friend's opinions first

792. The spectators trembled watching the male tiger prowl back and forth in his cage, so he stood back to be at a safer distance.

(A) The spectators trembled watching the male tiger prowl back and forth in his cage, so he stood back to be at a safer distance.

(B) The spectators trembled watching the male tiger prowling back and forth in his cage, so he stood back to be at a safer distance.

(C) The spectators trembled watching the male tiger prowl back and forth in his cage, so they stood back to be at a safer distance.

(D) The spectator trembled watching the male tiger prowl back and forth in his cage, so he stood back to be at a safer distance.

(E) The spectators trembled watching the male tiger prowl back and forth in his cage; he stood back to be at a safer distance.

793. Critics hailed the movie as an artistic masterpiece worth seeing once if not twice; unfortunately, the public didn't agree.

(A) ; unfortunately, the public didn't agree

(B) , unfortunately, the public didn't agree

(C) ; unfortunately, the public don't agree

(D) ; but the public didn't agree

(E) ; but moviegoers didn't agree

794. Day after day in class, I didn't sit next to anyone beside Jonah.

(A) , I didn't sit next to anyone beside Jonah

(B) ; I didn't sit next to anyone beside Jonah

(C) I didn't sit next to anyone beside Jonah

(D) , I sat next to everyone but Jonah

(E) , I didn't sit next to anyone besides Jonah

795. Rounding out the top ten songs, which surprisingly represented a diversity of styles, more or less.

(A) Rounding out the top ten songs, which surprisingly represented a diversity of styles, more or less.

(B) Rounding out the top ten songs, which surprisingly represented a diversity of styles, more or less, was the song "Rock On."

(C) Rounding out the top ten songs, which surprisingly represented a diversity of styles, more-or-less.

(D) Rounding out the top ten songs, which surprisingly represented a diversity of styles, more or less, the station aired "Rock On."

(E) It rounded out the top ten songs, which surprisingly represented a diversity of styles, more or less.

796. An interesting fact about Robert Lincoln who was the only son of Abraham Lincoln to survive into adulthood, is that Robert was rescued from a train accident by Edwin Booth, John Wilkes Booth's brother.

(A) An interesting fact about Robert Lincoln who was the only son of Abraham Lincoln to survive into adulthood,

(B) An interesting fact about Robert Lincoln who was the only son of Abraham Lincoln to survive into adulthood;

(C) An interesting fact about Robert Lincoln the only son of Abraham Lincoln to survive into adulthood,

(D) An interesting fact about Robert Lincoln, who was the only son of Abraham Lincoln to survive into adulthood,

(E) Robert Lincoln, who was the only son of Abraham Lincoln to survive into adulthood,

797. At the end of the day, <u>neither Nathan or Natasha wanted anything to do with Niles</u>.

   (A) neither Nathan or Natasha wanted anything to do with Niles

   (B) neither Nathan or Natasha wanted nothing to do with Niles

   (C) neither Nathan nor Natasha wanted anything to do with Niles

   (D) either Nathan or Natasha wanted anything to do with Niles

   (E) neither Nathan or Natasha wanted a thing to do with Niles

798. Of all the cats I ever owned, two Siamese <u>remain my favorites, they were</u> beautiful!

   (A) remain my favorites, they were

   (B) remained my favorites, they were

   (C) remain my favorites they were

   (D) remand my favorites; they were

   (E) remain my favorites; they were

799. <u>The Mayor of the little town of Bloomsburg likes to have lunch at the diner on Main Street.</u>

   (A) The Mayor of the little town of Bloomsburg likes to have lunch at the diner on Main Street.

   (B) The mayor of the little town of Bloomsburg likes to have lunch at the diner on Main Street.

   (C) The mayor of the little town of Bloomsburg likes to have lunch at The Diner on Main Street.

   (D) The Mayors of the little town of Bloomsburg liked to have lunch at the diner on Main Street.

   (E) The Mayor of the small, little town of Bloomsburg likes to have lunch at the diner on Main Street.

800. <u>Chen and Yvonne thought going to see their legislators was a capitol idea.</u>

   (A) Chen and Yvonne thought going to see their legislators was a capitol idea.

   (B) Chen and Yvonne thought going to see their legislators was a capital idea.

   (C) Chen and Yvonne thought going to see their senators was a capitol idea.

   (D) Chen and Yvonne thought going to see their legislators was a Capitol idea.

   (E) Chen and Yvonne thought going to see there legislators was a capitol idea.

801. <u>Travelling along the crowded, busy thoroughfare</u> at a high rate of speed was not wise, Luke reasoned.

   (A) Travelling along the crowded, busy thoroughfare

   (B) Traveling along the crowded, busy thoroughfare

   (C) Traveling along the crowded, busy throughfare

   (D) Travelling along the crowded thoroughfare

   (E) Traveling on the crowded, busy thoroughfare

802. Looking through her coat pockets when she got home, Sarah <u>discovered a gold woman's bracelet and knew</u> she'd taken the wrong coat.

   (A) discovered a gold woman's bracelet and knew

   (B) discovers a gold woman's bracelet and knows

   (C) discovered a woman's gold bracelet and knew

   (D) discovered a gold woman's bracelet, and she knew

   (E) discovered a woman's gold bracelet and new

803. Why should our taxes go to old, harmful forms of energy; we should invest in new, environmentally friendly ones.

(A) Why should our taxes go to old, harmful forms of energy; we should invest in new, environmentally friendly ones.

(B) Why should our taxes go to old, harmful forms of energy; we should be investing in new, environmentally friendly ones.

(C) Why should our taxes go to old, harmful forms of energy? Invest in new, environmentally friendly ones!

(D) Why should our taxes go to old, harmful forms of energy; however, we should invest in new, environmentally friendly ones.

(E) Why should our taxes go to old, harmful forms of energy? We should invest in new, environmentally friendly ones.

804. We experienced some difficult times, but the hardest thing for Dona and I was when I lost my job.

(A) but the hardest thing for Dona and I was when I lost my job

(B) however, the hardest thing for Dona and I was when I lost my job

(C) the hardest thing for Dona and I was when I lost my job

(D) but the hardest thing for Dona and me was when I lost my job

(E) but the hardest year for Dona and I was when I lost my job

805. After hibernating through an exceptionally long winter, the bear's hunger drove it far down the slope, which led to the river.

(A) the bear's hunger drove it far down the slope, that led to the river

(B) the bear's hunger drove it far down the slope that led to the river

(C) the bear wanted to eat and so began wandering far down the slope, which led to the river

(D) the bear, driven by hunger, ranged far down the slope, which led to the river

(E) the bear's hunger drove it farther down the slope, which led to the river

806. Some people have a hard time deciding between the Bolshoi and Kirov as to which ballet company is the most artistic.

(A) between the Bolshoi and Kirov as to which ballet company is the most artistic

(B) among the Bolshoi and Kirov as to which ballet company is the most artistic

(C) between the Bolshoi and Kirov as to which ballet company is the more artistic

(D) between (the Bolshoi and Kirov) as to which ballet company is the most artistic

(E) among the Bolshoi and Kirov as to that ballet company is the most artistic

807. <u>When she received her test results, Clarissa heartily congratulated herself for having studied so diligently.</u>

(A) When she received her test results, Clarissa heartily congratulated herself for having studied so diligently.

(B) When she received her test results, Clarissa heartily congratulated her for having studied so diligently.

(C) When she received her test results, Clarissa heartily congratulated herself for having studied so diligent.

(D) When she received her test results, Clarissa was heartily congratulating herself for having studied so diligently.

(E) When she received them, Clarissa heartily congratulated herself for having studied so diligently.

808. <u>The Northern section of North Korea, far from being flat, is largely hilly and mountainous.</u>

(A) The Northern section of North Korea, far from being flat, is largely hilly and mountainous.

(B) The Northern section of North Korea, far from South Korea, is largely hilly and mountainous.

(C) The Northern section of North Korea, far from being flat, is large hilly and mountainous.

(D) The northern section of North Korea, far from being flat, is largely hilly and mountains.

(E) The northern section of North Korea, far from being flat, is largely hilly and mountainous.

809. (A) <u>Even though</u> interest rates are low, loan requirements are so (B) <u>stringent</u> (C) <u>anymore</u> (D) <u>that</u> many people don't qualify for a loan. (E) <u>No error</u>

810. (A) <u>It was raining and</u> instead of (B) <u>whining</u>, Lorraine and Rico began (C) <u>to go</u> through (D) <u>their</u> closets to find clothes that their mother could donate. (E) <u>No error</u>

811. As much as Rosa did not (A) <u>identify with</u> the (B) <u>disco era</u>, she now (C) <u>readily</u> admits that she (D) <u>found</u> some of the music to be toe-tapping. (E) <u>No error</u>

812. Farah and Theo, (A) <u>having studied</u> a complicated painting, (B) <u>reflects on</u> different parts of it (C) <u>later,</u> (D) <u>once</u> they are home. (E) <u>No error</u>

813. Rather than do (A) <u>further</u> damage, Juan stopped chipping off the (B) <u>peeling</u> varnish and began (C) <u>sanding</u> the (D) <u>decorative</u> legs of the old table. (E) <u>No error</u>

814. A student in computer (A) <u>programming</u> must study (B) <u>hard</u> even though (C) <u>they're</u> in demand and (D) <u>should be able</u> to get a job. (E) <u>No error</u>

815. Sarah had (A) <u>too</u> many things to do and was (B) <u>multitasking</u> all the (C) <u>time; even so,</u> she made sure her department ran (D) <u>smooth</u>. (E) <u>No error</u>

816. A baker does not (A) <u>need</u> to use white or brown (B) <u>sugar,</u> (C) <u>he or she</u> may use honey or (D) <u>apple-juice</u> concentrate. (E) <u>No error</u>

817. The (A) <u>expression</u> *the acorn does not fall far from the oak* is a cliché (B)<u>, true,</u> but (C) <u>it</u> (D) <u>conveys</u> an important point. (E) <u>No error</u>

818. Feeling (A) <u>badly</u> about her earlier comment, (B) <u>Trina</u> found the (C) <u>extern</u> after lunch and (D) <u>genuinely</u> apologized to her. (E) <u>No error</u>

819. Hannah and Tyron voted for Ling, the new Senior Class (A) <u>President</u>, but (B) <u>they</u> did not want to (C) <u>abide with</u> her (D) <u>latest</u> decision. (E) <u>No error</u>

820. Unfortunately, (A) <u>Rita's late,</u> (B) <u>overdue</u> term paper had many errors that (C) <u>careful</u> proofreading (D) <u>would have caught</u>. (E) <u>No error</u>

821. The members of the audience (A) <u>was</u> pleased with the (B) <u>actors'</u> performances (C)<u>;</u> <u>thus,</u> the audience gave (D) <u>them</u> a standing ovation. (E) <u>No error</u>

822. When the painting was completed but still drying (A)<u>,</u> we requested that the artist give (B) <u>it</u> to (C) <u>ourselves</u> so we could begin (D) <u>to enjoy</u> it. (E) <u>No error</u>

823. Neither the teenage children (A) <u>nor</u> I (B) <u>were</u> able to figure out the instructions; (C) <u>however,</u> my mother (D) <u>was</u> — go figure! (E) <u>No error</u>

824. The (A) <u>timely</u> rain (B) <u>had brought</u> the farmers a welcome (C) <u>relief from</u> worry; however, the relief proved to be (D) <u>short-lived</u>. (E) <u>No error</u>

825. I have always tried (A) <u>to leave</u> for an appointment (B) <u>several</u> minutes early; (C) <u>you</u> never know when (D) <u>those</u> extra minutes will come in handy. (E) <u>No error</u>

826. The (A) <u>illusion</u> Nathan (B) <u>made</u> to a certain magazine, on top of being rude, was (C) <u>too</u> obscure to have the desired (D) <u>impact</u>. (E) <u>No error</u>

827. Some citizens take the right to vote for (A) <u>granted,</u> (B) <u>but,</u> at least in a year of a (C) <u>presidential</u> election, there should be a good percentage of (D) <u>voter's</u> ballots. (E) <u>No error</u>

828. (A) <u>Surprisingly,</u> all three of the mutts became (B) <u>a star pupil</u> at obedience school (C)<u>;</u> the teacher did not let breed (D) <u>affect</u> her basic teaching philosophy. (E) <u>No error</u>

829. <u>The Olympic marmot, digging out a burrow before the snows come and hibernating through a seven-month winter.</u>

- (A) The Olympic marmot, digging out a burrow before the snows come and hibernating through a seven- month winter.
- (B) The Olympic marmot, digging out a burrow before the snows come, hibernating through a seven month winter.
- (C) The Olympic marmot, digging out a burrow before the snows come; hibernating through a seven-month winter.
- (D) The Olympic marmot, digging out a burrow before it starts snowing and hibernating through a seven-month winter.
- (E) The Olympic marmot, digging out a burrow before the snows come, hibernates through a seven-month winter.

830. <u>Crawling along the ocean floor, the submersible spotted a species of starfish it believed to be unidentified.</u>

- (A) Crawling along the ocean floor, the submersible spotted a species of starfish it believed to be unidentified.
- (B) Crawling along the ocean floor, a species of starfish was spotted by a submersible, which believed the species to be unidentified.
- (C) Scientists in a submersible spotted a species of starfish, which they believed to be unidentified, crawling along the ocean floor.
- (D) Crawling along the ocean floor, the submersible spotted a species of starfish that the scientists believed to be unidentified.
- (E) Crawling along the ocean floor, the scientists in a submersible spotted a species of starfish that they believed to be unidentified.

831. The play, _The Mousetrap_, is the longest-running play on record, having run continually in London's West End since 1952.

(A) The play, _The Mousetrap_, is the longest-running play on record, having run continually in London's West End since 1952.

(B) The play, _The Mousetrap_, is the longest running play on record, having run continuously in London's West End since 1952.

(C) The play _The Mousetrap_ is the longest-running play on record, having run continually in London's West End since 1952.

(D) The play _The Mousetrap_ is the longest-running play on record, having run continuously in London's West End since 1952.

(E) The play _The Mousetrap_, the longest-running play on record, having run continuously in London's West End since 1952.

832. Far from being boring the mens' relay race captured everyones' attention, and that's saying something.

(A) Far from being boring the mens' relay race captured everyones' attention, and that's saying something.

(B) Far from being boring, the men's relay race captured everyone's attention, and that's saying something.

(C) Far from being boring the mens' relay race captured everyone's attention, and thats saying something.

(D) Far from being boring, the men's, relay race captured everyone's attention, and that's saying something.

(E) Far from being boring, the men's relay race captured everyone's attention and that's saying something.

833. Just between you and me, the new Governor is in for trouble; the legislative members are not known for being cooperative.

(A) Just between you and me, the new Governor is in for trouble; the legislative members are not known for being cooperative.

(B) Just between you and I, the new Governor is in for trouble; the legislative members are not known for being cooperative.

(C) Just between you and I, the new Governor is in for trouble, the legislative members are not known for being cooperative.

(D) Just between you and me, the new governor is in for trouble; the legislative members are not known for being cooperative.

(E) Just between you and me, the new governor is in for trouble, the legislative members are not known for being cooperative.

834. The early blooming of the cherry blossoms', disappointed the tourists, who had made there travel plans long ago.

(A) The early blooming of the cherry blossoms disappointed the tourists who had made there travel plans long ago.

(B) The early blooming of the cherry blossoms' disappointed the tourists, who had made their travel plans long ago.

(C) The early blooming of the cherry blossoms disappointed the tourists, who had made their travel plans long ago.

(D) The early blooming of the cherry blossoms, disappointed the tourists, who had made their travel plans long ago.

(E) The early blooming of the cherry blossoms, disappointing the tourists, who had made there travel plans long ago.

835. Tamara's and Don's cold, hers with accompanying aches and his with a runny nose, does not seem to have come from the same source.

(A) Tamara and Don's cold, hers with accompanying aches and his with a runny nose, does not seem to have come from the same source.

(B) Tamara's and Don's cold, hers with accompanying aches and his with a runny nose, do not seem to have come from the same source.

(C) Tamara's and Don's cold, hers with accompanying aches and his with a runny nose, is not likely to have come from the same source.

(D) Tamara's and Don's colds, hers with accompanying aches and his with a runny nose, do not seem to have come from the same source.

(E) Tamara and Don have colds, hers with accompanying aches and his with a runny nose, which does not seem to have come from the same source.

836. Even though he thought the task seemed daunting, Josiah was determined in his mind to read the complete works of Milton.

(A) Even though he thought the task seemed daunting, Josiah was determined in his mind to read the complete works of Milton.

(B) Even though the task seemed daunting, Josiah was determined in his mind to read the complete works of Milton.

(C) Although he thought the task seemed daunting, Josiah was determined in his mind to read the complete works of Milton.

(D) Even though he thought the task seemed daunting Josiah was determined to read the complete works of Milton.

(E) Even though the task seemed daunting, Josiah was determined to read the complete works of Milton.

837. In order to finish the assignment on time, Flora started working on it three weeks before it was due.

(A) In order to finish the assignment on time, Flora started to work on it three weeks before it was due.

(B) In order to finish the assignment on time, Flora, working on it three weeks before it was due.

(C) In order to finish the assignment on time, Flora started working on it well in advance, three weeks before it was due.

(D) In order to finish the assignment on time, she started working on it three weeks before it was due.

(E) In order to finish the assignment on time, Flora started working on it previously.

838. Whether she said something positive, stated correctly or incorrectly, heard by one person or many.

(A) Whether Inga said something positive, stated correctly or incorrectly, heard by one person or many.

(B) Whether she said something positive, stated correctly or incorrectly, heard by one person or many, Inga thought she should say something.

(C) Whether she said something positively, stated correctly or incorrectly, heard by one person or many.

(D) Inga said something positive, stated correctly and heard by many people.

(E) Whether she said something positive, stated correctly or incorrectly.

839. Made from the forces of heating and cooling, it's easy to see why igneous rocks are found near volcanoes.

(A) Made from the forces of heating and cooling, it's easy to see why igneous rocks are found near volcanoes.

(B) Made from the forces of heating and cooling; it's easy to see why igneous rocks are found near volcanoes.

(C) Made from the forces of heating and cooling, it's easy to find igneous rocks near volcanoes.

(D) It's easy to see igneous rocks made from the forces of heating and cooling near volcanoes.

(E) It's easy to see why igneous rocks, made from the forces of heating and cooling, are found near volcanoes.

840. Harriet Tubman, who guided many African-Americans to freedom in the years before the Civil War, is perhaps the most famous of the "conductors" of the Underground Railroad.

(A) Harriet Tubman, who guided many African-Americans to freedom in the years before the Civil War, is perhaps the most famous of the "conductors" of the Underground Railroad.

(B) Harriet Tubman who guided many African-Americans to freedom in the years before the Civil War is perhaps the most famous of the "conductors" of the Underground Railroad.

(C) Harriet Tubman, guiding many African-Americans to freedom in the years before the Civil War, and becoming perhaps the most famous of the "conductors" of the Underground Railroad.

(D) Harriet Tubman, which guided many African-Americans to freedom in the years before the Civil War, is perhaps the most famous of the "conductors" of the Underground Railroad.

(E) Harriet Tubman, whom guided many African-Americans to freedom in the years before the Civil War, is perhaps the most famous of the "conductors" of the Underground Railroad.

841. The book, *The Two Towers,* is the second of J.R.R. Tolkien's famous trilogy, *The Lord of the Rings.*

(A) The book, *The Two Towers,* is the second of J.R.R. Tolkien's famous trilogy, *The Lord of the Rings.*

(B) The book *The Two Towers* is the second of J.R.R. Tolkien's famous trilogy *The Lord of the Rings.*

(C) The book, *The Two Towers,* is the second of J.R.R. Tolkien's famous trilogy.

(D) The book *The Two Towers* is the second of J.R.R. Tolkien's famous trilogy, *The Lord of the Rings.*

(E) The book *The Two Towers,* the second of J.R.R. Tolkien's famous trilogy, *The Lord of the Rings.*

842. The marathoner, running for all she was worth, legs feeling like lead and breath very hard to come by.

(A) The marathoner, running for all she was worth, legs feeling like lead and breath very hard to come by.

(B) The marathoner, running for all she was worth, worried because her legs felt like lead and her breath was very hard to come by.

(C) The marathoner, running for all she was worth, worrying because her legs felt like lead and her breath was very hard to come by.

(D) The marathoner, running for all she was worth, legs felt like lead and breath very hard to come by.

(E) The marathoner who was running for all she was worth, legs feeling like lead and breath very hard to come by.

843. The old, Dodge truck, far from being troublesome, provided Armand with steady transportation.

(A) The old, Dodge truck, far from being troublesome, provided Armand with steady transportation.

(B) The old Dodge truck, far from being troublesome provided Armand with steady transportation.

(C) The old Dodge truck, far and away troublesome, provided Armand with steady transportation.

(D) The old, Dodge truck, far from being troublesome, provided Armand with steady transpiration.

(E) The old Dodge truck, far from being troublesome, provided Armand with steady transportation.

844. Clara didn't want to admit it, but she was real angry with the other women for not being supportive of her when she needed them to be.

(A) Clara didn't want to admit it, but she was real angry with the other women for not being supportive of her when she needed them to be.

(B) Clara didn't want to admit it, but she was real angry with the other women for not supporting her when she needed them to be.

(C) Clara didn't want to admit it, but she was really angry with the other women for not being supportive of her when she needed them to be.

(D) Clara didn't want to admit it, but she was really angry with the other women; not being supportive of her when she needed them to be.

(E) Clara didn't want to admit it but she was really angry with the other women for not being supportive of her when she needed them to be.

845. George marked the online textbook until way passed midnight with the online highlighter.

(A) George marked the online textbook until way passed midnight with the online highlighter.

(B) George marked the online textbook with the online highlighter until way past midnight.

(C) George marked the online textbook until way past midnight with the online highlighter.

(D) George marked the online textbook, until way past midnight with the online highlighter.

(E) George marked the online textbook until way passed midnight and he used an online highlighter.

846. When Maury finally woke up and saw that it was 10:00 a.m., he knew he should of read the instructions for his new alarm.

(A) When Maury finally woke up and saw that it was 10:00 a.m., he knew he should of read the instructions for his new alarm.

(B) When Maury finally woke up and saw that it was 10:00 a.m. he knew he should of read the instructions for his new alarm.

(C) When Maury finally woke up, and saw that it was 10:00 a.m., he knew he should of read the instructions for his new alarm.

(D) When Maury finally woke up and saw that it was 10:00 a.m., he knew he should have read the instructions for his new alarm.

(E) When Maury finally woke up, and he saw that it was 10:00 a.m., he knew he should of read the instructions for his new alarm.

847. It was April, and the birds sang <u>gloriously; and Fiona knew</u> today was the day to go for a long walk.

(A) gloriously; and Fiona knew

(B) gloriously, Fiona knew

(C) gloriously, knew

(D) gloriously; Fiona knew

(E) gloriously; knew

848. Pablo <u>lay down the books</u> and decided he would finish reading it later.

(A) lay down the books

(B) lied down the books

(C) laid down the books

(D) laying down the book

(E) laid down the book

849. If you want <u>to wet your appetite</u>, try walking into a kitchen where garlic and onions simmer in olive oil.

(A) to wet your appetite

(B) to wet you're appetite

(C) to whet your appetite

(D) to whet you're appetite

(E) to wit your appetite

850. <u>"Why don't you have a go at it?," Sylvia finally said,</u> having already shown Helga how to create the hairstyle.

(A) "Why don't you have a go at it?," Sylvia finally said,

(B) "Why don't you have a go at it?" Sylvia finally said,

(C) "Why don't you have a go at it," Sylvia finally said,

(D) "Why don't you have a go at it?," Sylvia finally said

(E) "Why don't you have a go at it? Sylvia finally said,

851. On foot in Hanoi, where he'd never been, Rashad <u>proceeded uncertainly into the Old Quarter</u>.

(A) proceeded uncertainly into the Old Quarter

(B) proceeded uncertain into the Old Quarter

(C) preceded uncertainly into the Old Quarter

(D) preceded uncertain into the Old Quarter

(E) proceeded uncertainly for the Old Quarter

852. Evelyn knew that if the workers <u>cooperated together, it</u> would get more accomplished.

(A) cooperated together, it

(B) cooperated together, they

(C) cooperated; it

(D) cooperated, they

(E) cooperated, it

853. <u>Because Hansel and Gretel could not find</u> the bread crumbs they had left; the birds had eaten all the crumbs.

(A) Because Hansel and Gretel could not find

(B) Hansel and Gretel could not find

(C) Hansel and Gretel, looking for

(D) Because Hansel and Gretel were looking

(E) Hansel and Gretel, not finding

854. Edith Hamilton<u>, whose *Mythology* was read by countless students,</u> published her first book when she was 62.

(A) , whose *Mythology* was read by countless students,

(B) , whose *Mythology* was read by countless students

(C) , whose Mythology was read by countless students

(D) , whose Mythology was read by countless students,

(E) , who's *Mythology* was read by countless students,

855. Before she stopped to stretch, Ursula took another deep breath and continued weeding in the garden.

   (A) continued weeding in the garden

   (B) continually weeded in the garden

   (C) continued to weeding in the garden

   (D) began weeding again in the garden

   (E) began weeding the garden again

856. There is no sense in fighting city hall this bit of old wisdom is still true.

   (A) this bit of old wisdom is still true

   (B) , this bit of old wisdom is still true

   (C) , this old bit of wisdom is still true

   (D) ; this is still true

   (E) ; this bit of old wisdom is still true

857. The varied results of the test were surprising; it caught everybody off-guard.

   (A) ; it caught everybody off-guard

   (B) , it caught everybody off-guard

   (C) ; they caught everybody offguard

   (D) ; they caught everybody off-guard

   (E) , and it caught everybody off-guard

858. Everyone became amazing quiet when the principle entered the classroom.

   (A) amazing quiet when the principle

   (B) amazingly quiet when the principle

   (C) amazingly quiet when the principal

   (D) amazing quiet when the principal

   (E) amazed and quiet when the principle

859. (A) Unknowingly, it was Van (B) who tripped the alarm when, (C) having lost his key, he (D) pried open the window. (E) No error

860. Rochelle didn't think that Texas (A) was bigger (B) then Alaska (C), but for some reason (D) in class she said that it was. (E) No error

861. No matter how many times Lawrence argued (A) his point, (B) most of the audience members disagreed with him (C), it made (D) him feel frustrated. (E) No error

862. Each of them (A) says that the message (B) only reaches a few people (C), and so (D) it shouldn't be sent. (E) No error

863. Both Arlo and Holly (A) want to see the new candidate elected (B), but neither (C) wants to use the energy to campaign for (D) her. (E) No error

864. (A) Instead of looking (B) happy, the people (C), boarding the plane, look angry and (D) understandably confused. (E) No error

865. Trevon (A), an expert in native art, (B) knew that all totems are (C) not rare, but he liked (D) looking at them all, anyway. (E) No error

866. When you want to (A) site information from the (B) Internet, (C) first make sure the information is (D) reliable. (E) No error

867. Feeling (A) exhausted, Beth (B) lay down for just a few minutes on a couch in the (C) teachers' lounge (D); the short rest worked like magic. (E) No error

868. (A) Finding many clothes she liked, the store continued to be one of (B) Paula's favorites, (C) to the extent that she considered applying for a job (D) there. (E) No error

869. Every singer (A), no matter how old, no matter how experienced, must (B) study and practice (C) in order to keep (D) their skills sharp. (E) No error

870. Settling on a career can be difficult (A), especially in (B) today's fluid economy (C), you have to be (D) prepared for changes. (E) No error

871. A major part of the (A) <u>theory of evolution</u> is that (B) <u>a species</u> will (C) <u>adopt</u> to the conditions in (D) <u>its</u> environment. (E) <u>No error</u>

872. Behind the tree stump, crouched and (A) <u>silent</u>, (B) <u>the zebra</u> was (C) <u>stealthily</u> observed by the lions (D) <u>that</u> stalked it. (E) <u>No error</u>

873. (A) <u>A fear of closed-in spaces</u>, Felix is (B) <u>deeply</u> troubled by claustrophobia (C)<u>;</u> he is seeking help with (D) <u>this fear</u>. (E) <u>No error</u>

874. (A) <u>Quick</u> solutions to money problems can (B) <u>seem</u> like (C) <u>superb</u> ideas (D)<u>;</u> however, usually not very economical in the long run. (E) <u>No error</u>

875. (A) <u>Deciding to come to their senses</u>, Orrin and Pablo began (B) <u>to talk</u> over (C) <u>their</u> differences and (D) <u>accept</u> each other almost unconditionally. (E) <u>No error</u>

876. (A) <u>Even though</u> they tried several different strategies (B)<u>,</u> the negotiators didn't (C) <u>even</u> achieve one (D) <u>of their goals</u>. (E) <u>No error</u>

877. (A) <u>In order to avoid hurting themselves</u>, athletes always try to (B) <u>if possible</u> stretch and (C) <u>warm up</u> before a (D) <u>meet or match</u>. (E) <u>No error</u>

878. Chas, (A) <u>who's</u> excellent recommendation letter (B) <u>just</u> came in from (C) <u>his</u> professor, was feeling (D) <u>good</u> about his application package. (E) <u>No error</u>

879. I felt very honored that my fellow students <u>gave the award to both Ivan and myself</u>.

   (A) gave the award to both Ivan and myself

   (B) had given the award to both Ivan and myself

   (C) gave the award to both me and to Ivan

   (D) gave the award to both Ivan and me

   (E) gave the award to both Ivan and I

880. Mosquitos are known to be carriers of the Zika virus<u>; this is true regarding yellow fever, too</u>.

   (A) ; this is true regarding yellow fever, too

   (B) ; this spreading of a disease by mosquito bites is true regarding yellow fever, too

   (C) , this is true regarding the spreading of yellow fever, too

   (D) ; this is true regarding the spreading of yellow fever, too

   (E) , this spreading of a disease by mosquito bites is true regarding yellow fever, too

881. By the time the professor arrived, thirty minutes late<u>, all but a few of the students left</u>.

   (A) , all but a few of the students left

   (B) ; all but a few of the students left

   (C) , only a few of the students left

   (D) ; all but a few of the students had left

   (E) , all but a few of the students had left

882. <u>Carmen wanted to be Mayor when she grows up;</u> her parents are involved in city politics, and she likes and understands the concept of acting locally.

   (A) Carmen wanted to be Mayor when she grows up;

   (B) Carmen wants to be Mayor when she grows up;

   (C) Carmen wants to be mayor when she grows up;

   (D) Carmen wanted to be mayor when she grows up,

   (E) Carmen wanting to be mayor when she grows up;

883. Both of the foals that Helga entered in the rural Wisconsin fair was later sold to the biggest of the two nearby farms.

(A) was later sold to the biggest of the two

(B) were later sold to the bigger of the two

(C) was later sold to the bigger of the two

(D) were later sold to the biggest of the two

(E) were latter sold to the bigger of the two

884. Each type of print medium, including books, magazines, and newspapers, has something significant to offer.

(A) Each type of print medium,

(B) Each type of print media,

(C) Each kind of print media,

(D) Each type of print medium

(E) Each type of print media

885. Speaking clearly, Luann respectively submitted their opinion to the professors that their scoring of her orals examination was unfair.

(A) Luann respectively submitted their opinion

(B) Luann respectively submitted her opinion

(C) Luann respectfully submitted their opinion

(D) Luann respectfully submitted her opinion

(E) Luann respected submitted her opinion

886. Not having dressed for the weather, the sleet dripped inside Willa's collar, chilling her to the bone.

(A) , the sleet dripped inside Willa's collar

(B) , the sleet dripped inside Willas' collar

(C) , Willa felt the sleet drip inside her collar

(D) Willa felt the sleet drip inside her collar

(E) , Willa's collar was soaked from the sleet

887. You know your in trouble when heat raises off the pavement and you didn't drink enough water.

(A) You know your in trouble when heat raises

(B) You know you're in trouble when heat rises

(C) You know your in trouble when heat rises

(D) You know you're in trouble when heat raises

(E) You know you're into trouble when heat rises

888. "Its more than I myself can cope with," Brianna thought morosely.

(A) "Its more than I myself can cope with,"

(B) "Its more than I can cope with,"

(C) "It's more than I myself can cope with,"

(D) "It's more then I myself can cope with,"

(E) "It's more than I can cope with"

889. Wanting to provide the students with hands-on experience; they wanted their lessons to be meaningful, to provide learning.

(A) Wanting to provide the students with hands-on experience;

(B) Wanting to provide the students with hands on experience;

(C) The teachers, wanting to provide the students with hands-on experience;

(D) The teachers wanted to provide the students with hands on experience;

(E) The teachers wanted to provide the students with hands-on experience;

890. Beginning to lose patience, Sean started pacing; soon, he was huffing and muttering to himself.

(A) Beginning to lose patience, Sean started pacing;

(B) Beginning to loose patience, Sean started pacing;

(C) Beginning to lose patience, Sean started to paced;

(D) Beginning to lose patience, Sean started pacing,

(E) Beginning to lose patients, Sean started pacing;

891. In setting up a budget, Quinn was concerned with the basic essentials: food, clothing, shelter, transportation, and communication (a longer list than his grandfather's).

(A) Quinn was concerned with the basic essentials:

(B) Quinn was concerned with the essentials:

(C) Quinn was concerned with the basic essentials;

(D) Quinn, concerned with the basics:

(E) Quinn, concerned with the basic essentials:

892. Of all the lesser-known Greek Gods, Aether, also known as Acmon, is Grace's favorite; Aether's name means *light*.

(A) Of all the lesser-known Greek Gods,

(B) Of all the lesser-known Greek Gods

(C) Of all the lesser-known Greek gods,

(D) Of all the lesser known Greek Gods,

(E) Of all the lesser known Greek gods,

893. Jules wanted to stop, but Arlo wanted to go farther down the road, so they talked until they came to a compromise.

(A) farther down the road, so they talked

(B) farther down the road; so they talked

(C) further down the road, so they talked

(D) further down the road; so they talked

(E) further down the road; so it was talked about

894. Anna was late and had to take a seat in the back; she couldn't hardly hear the professor.

(A) ; she couldn't hardly hear the professor

(B) , and she couldn't hardly hear the professor

(C) ; and she couldn't hardly hear the professor

(D) ; she could hardly here the professor

(E) ; she could hardly hear the professor

895. Two witnesses described the suspect as a six-foot-tall man with a beard weighing 180 pounds.

(A) a six-foot-tall man with a beard weighing 180 pounds

(B) a 180-pound, six-foot-tall man with a beard

(C) a six-foot tall man with a beard weighing 180 pounds

(D) a 180-pound weighing six foot tall man with a beard

(E) a 180-pound man with a beard six-foot-tall

896. Famous for having sewn the first American flag, Betsy Ross who had an upholstery business made extra money during the Revolutionary War by mending blankets, tents, and uniforms for the Continental Army.

(A) Betsy Ross who had an upholstery business made extra money during the Revolutionary War

(B) Betsy Ross who had an upholstery business, made extra money during the Revolutionary War

(C) Betsy Ross, who had an upholstery business made extra money during the Revolutionary War

(D) Betsy Ross, who had an upholstery business, made extra money during the Revolutionary War

(E) Betsy Ross who had an upholstery business made extra money, during the Revolutionary War

897. Some track athletes from the country of Jamaica trains for the winter sport of bobsledding, which requires a good running start.

(A) Some track athletes from the country of Jamaica trains

(B) Some track athletes, from the country of Jamaica, trains

(C) Some track athletes from the country of Jamaica train

(D) Some track athletes from the country of Jamaica training

(E) Some track athletes, from the country of Jamaica, train

898. Many solutions have been proposed for the city's congestion problems; not one of the solutions have been chosen by the city council.

(A) ; not one of the solutions have been chosen by

(B) , not one of the solutions have been chosen by

(C) , not one of the solutions has been chosen by

(D) , but not one of the solutions have been chosen by

(E) ; not one of the solutions has been chosen by

899. All the added work at the end of the semester had a strange effect on the new teacher: she found more discipline than she thought she had.

(A) All the added work at the end of the semester had a strange effect on the new teacher: she found more discipline than she thought she had.

(B) All the added work at the end of the semester had a strange affect on the new teacher: she found more discipline than she thought she had.

(C) All the added work at the end of the semester had a strange effect on the new teacher, she found more discipline than she thought she had.

(D) All the added work at the end of the semester strangely effected the new teacher: she found more discipline than she thought she had.

(E) All the added work at the end of the semester, having a strange effect on the new teacher: she found more discipline than she thought she had.

900. Studies showed that vehicles drove too fast along the busy street, so traffic engineers recommended adding an additional traffic light.

(A) Studies show that vehicles drove too fast along the busy street, so traffic engineers recommended adding an additional traffic light.

(B) Studies showed that vehicles drove too fast along the busy street, so traffic engineers recommended adding a traffic light.

(C) Studies show that vehicles driving too fast along the busy street, so traffic engineers recommended adding an additional traffic light.

(D) Studies showing that vehicles drove too fast along the busy street, so traffic engineers recommended adding a traffic light.

(E) Studies showed that vehicles drove too fast along the busy street, so traffic engineers highly recommended adding an additional traffic light.

901. Xavier and Tony spent three hours trying to resolve the problem, but they couldn't agree; however you looked at the situation.

(A) Xavier and Tony spent three hours trying to resolve the problem, but they couldn't agree; however you looked at the situation.

(B) Xavier and Tony spent three hours trying to resolve the problem, but they couldn't agree; however they looked at the situation.

(C) Xavier and Tony spent three hours trying to resolve the problem, but they couldn't agree, however you looked at the situation.

(D) Xavier and Tony spent three hours trying to resolve the problem, but they couldn't agree, however they looked at the situation.

(E) Xavier and Tony spent three hours trying to resolve the problem; but they couldn't agree, however you looked at the situation.

902. The ability to initiate a national revenue bill is one of the many things that sets the House apart from the Senate.

(A) The ability to initiate a national revenue bill is one of the many things that sets the House apart from the Senate.

(B) The ability to initiate a national revenue bill is one of the many things that sets the house apart from the senate.

(C) The ability to initiate a national revenue bill is one of the many things that set the House apart from the Senate.

(D) The ability to initiate a national revenue bill is one of the many things that set the house apart from the senate.

(E) The ability to initiate a national revenue bill is one of the many things which sets the House apart from the Senate.

903. Darla had ordered tulip bulbs from a well-known farm; she read the package many times but couldn't figure out how deeply they wanted her to plant the bulbs.

(A) Darla had ordered tulip bulbs from a well-known farm; she read the package many times but couldn't figure out how deeply they wanted her to plant the bulbs.

(B) Darla had ordered tulip bulbs from a well-known farm; she read the package many times but couldn't figure out how deep they wanted her to plant the bulbs.

(C) Darla had ordered tulip bulbs from a well known farm; she read the package many times but couldn't figure out how deeply they wanted her to plant the bulbs.

(D) Darla had ordered tulip bulbs from a well-known farm; she read the package many times, but the growers couldn't figure out how deeply they wanted her to plant the bulbs.

(E) Darla had ordered tulip bulbs from a well-known farm; she read the package many times but couldn't figure out how deeply the growers wanted her to plant the bulbs.

904. Trevor reflected that it was extremely difficult for Hannah and himself to come to terms with their new responsibilities as first-time parents.

(A) Trevor reflected that it was extremely difficult for Hannah and himself to come to terms with their new responsibilities as first-time parents.

(B) Trevor reflected that it was extremely difficult for Hannah and himself to come to terms for their new responsibilities as first-time parents.

(C) Trevor reflected that it was extremely difficult for Hannah and he to come to terms with their new responsibilities as first-time parents.

(D) Trevor reflected that it was extremely difficult for Hannah and him to come to terms with their new responsibilities as first-time parents.

(E) Trevor reflected that it was extremely difficult for Hannah and them to come to terms with their new responsibilities as first-time parents.

905. An adult *Stegosaurus* weighed over three tons and was 26–30 feet long, amazingly, its brain was the size of a walnut.

(A) An adult *Stegosaurus* weighed over three tons and was 26–30 feet long, amazingly, its brain was the size of a walnut.

(B) An adult *Stegosaurus* weighed over three tons and was 26–30 feet long, amazingly, it's brain was the size of a walnut.

(C) An adult *Stegosaurus* weighed over three ton's and was 26–30 feet long; amazingly, its brain was the size of a walnut.

(D) An adult *Stegosaurus* weighed over three tons and was 26–30 feet long; amazingly, its brain was the size of a walnut.

(E) An adult *Stegosaurus* weighed over three tons and was 26–30 feet long; amazingly, it's brain was the size of a walnut.

906. According to the American Diabetes Association, common symptoms of type 1 diabetes can include the following: feeling very thirsty, feeling very hungry, blurry vision, and cuts or bruises that are slow to heal.

(A) According to the American Diabetes Association, common symptoms of type 1 diabetes can include the following: feeling very thirsty, feeling very hungry, blurry vision, and cuts or bruises that are slow to heal.

(B) According to the American Diabetes Association, common symptoms of type 1 diabetes can include the following; feeling very thirsty, feeling very hungry, blurry vision, and cuts or bruises that are slow to heal.

(C) According to the American Diabetes Association, common symptoms of type 1 diabetes can include the following: extreme thirst, extreme hunger, blurry vision, and cuts or bruises that are slow to heal.

(D) According to the American Diabetes Association, common symptoms of type 1 diabetes can include the following: very thirsty, very hungry, blurry vision, and cuts or bruises that are slow to heal.

(E) According to the American Diabetes Association, common symptoms of type 1 diabetes can include the following, feeling very thirsty, feeling very hungry, blurry vision, and cuts or bruises that are slow to heal.

907. When George, hands covered in chalk dusk, finished demonstrating the equation on the old blackboard, he ran his hands through his hair; using the old teaching tools had turned him into an old man.

(A) When George, hands covered in chalk dusk, finished demonstrating the equation on the old blackboard, he ran his hands through his hair; using the old teaching tools had turned him into an old man.

(B) When George, hands covered in chalk dusk, finished demonstrating the equation on the old blackboard; he ran his hands through his hair; using the old teaching tools had turned him into an old man.

(C) When George's hands, covered in chalk dusk, finished demonstrating the equation on the old blackboard, he ran his hands through his hair; using the old teaching tools had turned him into an old man.

(D) When George, hands covered in chalk dusk, finished demonstrating the equation on the old blackboard and running his hands through his hair; using the old teaching tools had turned him into an old man.

(E) When George, hands covered in chalk dusk, finished demonstrating the equation on the old blackboard, he ran his hands through his hair; using the old teaching tools and turning him into an old man.

908. For most of his life, Byron had found it easier to explain his actions in writing than talking to people directly.

(A) For most of his life, Byron had found it easier to explain his actions in writing than talking to people directly.

(B) For most of his life Byron had found it easier to explain his actions in writing than talking to people directly.

(C) For most of his life, Byron had found it easier to explain his actions in writing, than talking to people directly.

(D) For most of his life, Byron, finding it easier to explain his actions in writing than talking to people directly.

(E) For most of his life, Byron had found it easier to explain his actions in writing than to talk to people directly.

909. (A) Having new windows or putting plastic over old ones can help (B) you save money during the winter (C), additionally, you might try (D) closing off a room when it's not in use. (E) No error

910. It was quite a (A) complement, Yvonne knew (B), for her classmates to ask her to speak on (C) their (D) behalf, but still it made her unsettled. (E) No error

911. Chico and Louisa (A), taking turns tossing a bean bag into the (B) game-board hole (C), (D) likes this activity more than any other at the center. (E) No error

912. Alicia (A), careening down the hallway, and before she knew it, (B) rounding the corner, she (C) collided with the woman (D) carrying her laundry. (E) No error

913. You can't go back to the past (A), and (B) whose to know if trying (C) to undo something would solve a problem or create (D) one? (E) No error

914. Sven, with his (A) newly designed skateboard (B), went to several different skateboard (C) parks' (D) to test the design in different situations. (E) No error

915. Donna wasn't trying to deceive anyone (A), and (B), in fact, she truly loved her husband, even though he was quite a bit older (C) <u>than</u> (D) <u>her</u>. (E) <u>No error</u>

916. Fran felt she (A) <u>should have</u> known how to repair her (B) <u>frayed</u> (C) <u>friend's</u> dress since (D) <u>Fran's</u> mother was a dressmaker. (E) <u>No error</u>

917. In order to (A) <u>adapt</u> to the changing economic realities (B), (C) <u>Councilman Johnson</u> explained, the city must begin (D) <u>to encourage</u> small businesses. (E) <u>No error</u>.

918. Feeling (A) <u>well</u>, even though two (B) <u>days</u> ago he'd had a fever, James (C) <u>proceeded</u> to work a full day and not worry about any negative side (D) <u>effects</u>. (E) <u>No error</u>

Revising in Context

Read the passage. Then answer the questions, considering each sentence in context.

Questions 919–934 refer to the following passage.

(1) The problem of homelessness is something many cities face. (2) Unfortunately, there are some cities that ignore the problem. (3) To solve the problem, many cities are employing different methods. (4) One of these methods is the controversial tent city.

(5) What is a tent city, you may ask? (6) A tent city is a homeless encampment, an area set aside and supervised by a city where the homeless can camp out, using there own tarps or tents. (7) Obviously, a tent city wouldn't work in a part of the country that experiences cold winters. (8) That's not the only problem.

(9) Tent cities let local governments become distracted from the real solution, permanent housing. (10) These governments put public funds into the encampments, such as for portable toilets, but the problem isn't solved. (11) The homeless are still

homeless. (12) They're basically living outside. (13) In some places there are even children living in the tent cities. (14) It's causing public health and safety concerns.

(15) Some people feel that tent cities should be okay because at least the homeless are off the street. (16) When they're off the street, they're warmer and safer at night. (17) Tent cities are better than nothing and should be maintained until permanent housing can be arranged.

919. In context, what is best to do with sentence 2 (reproduced below)?

Unfortunately, there are some cities that ignore the problem.

(A) Leave it as it is.

(B) Take it out.

(C) Begin the sentence with "Of course."

(D) Take out "ignore" and replace it with "overlook."

(E) Insert "major" between *some* and *cities*.

920. Which is the best way to revise and combine sentences 3 and 4 (reproduced below) at the underlined portion?

To solve the problem, many cities are employing different <u>methods. One of these methods is</u> the controversial tent city.

(A) methods, one of which is

(B) methods, and this includes

(C) methods; this includes

(D) methods, including

(E) methods, which can sometimes be

921. In context, which is the best version of the underlined portion of sentence 4 (reproduced below)?

One of these methods is the controversial <u>tent city</u>.

(A) and so-called tent city

(B) and so-called *tent city*

(C) *tent city*

(D) and argument-starting tent city

(E) and argument-starting *tent city*

922. In context, which sentence provides the best conclusion to the first paragraph?

(A) What would you do if you were the mayor of a city faced with such a situation?

(B) For all the problems it may solve, though, a tent city should not be considered a permanent solution.

(C) As it turns out, there are many different approaches to homelessness that can prove successful.

(D) Using a tent city as a solution to homelessness has stirred up a lot of controversy.

(E) The mayor and city council of each major city should work together to end homelessness instead of working for political gain.

923. In context, what is best to do with sentence 5 (reproduced below)?

What is a tent city, you may ask?

(A) Leave it as it is.

(B) Take it out.

(C) Replace it with "What might a person find in a tent city?"

(D) Put the term *tent city* in italics.

(E) Insert "well" between *may* and *ask*.

924. In context, which is the best version of the underlined portion of sentence 6 (reproduced below)?

A tent city is a homeless encampment, an area set aside and supervised by a city where the homeless can camp out, using there own tarps and tents.

(A) [Leave it as it is.]

(B) [Take it out.]

(C) using there own flimsy tarps and tents

(D) using their own tarps and tents

(E) doing so by using their own tarps and tents

925. In context, which is the best transitional word/phrase to add at the beginning of sentence 8 (reproduced below)?

That's not the only problem.

(A) However,

(B) Ironically,

(C) But

(D) On the other hand,

(E) In addition,

926. In context, which is the best way to modify the underlined portion of sentence 8 (reproduced below)?

That's not the only problem.

(A) That's

(B) That is

(C) Climate is

(D) This is

(E) This problem

927. In context, which is the best transitional word/phrase to add at the beginning of sentence 9 (reproduced below)?

Tent cities let local governments become distracted from the real solution, and that would be permanent housing.

(A) In other words,

(B) Specifically,

(C) Indeed,

(D) Another key point is that

(E) To begin with,

928. In context, which is the best way to modify the underlined portion of sentence 9 (reproduced below)?

Tent cities let local governments become distracted <u>from the real solution, permanent housing</u>.

(A) [Leave it as it is.]

(B) [Take it out.]

(C) from the real solution, and that would be permanent housing

(D) from the real and only solution, permanent housing

(E) from what they should be paying attention to

929. In context, which is the best way to modify the underlined portion of sentence 14 (reproduced below)?

<u>It's</u> causing public health and safety concerns.

(A) It's

(B) This is

(C) People, not to mention children, essentially living outside are

(D) The entire scope of the homelessness problem is

(E) The local governments' support of these tent cities is

930. In context, what is best to do immediately following sentence 14 (reproduced below)?

It's causing public health and safety concerns.

(A) Restate the thesis.

(B) Begin a new paragraph and start the conclusion.

(C) Make a connection with an earlier point.

(D) Add a sentence with a long introductory clause for sentence variety.

(E) Insert an explanation and examples.

931. Which version of sentence 15 (reproduced below) would make the best beginning to the fourth paragraph?

Some people feel that tent cities should be okay because at least the homeless are off the street.

(A) Some people feel that tent cities should be okay because at least the homeless are off the street.

(B) Conversely, some people feel that tent cities should be okay because at least the homeless are off the street.

(C) Conversely, some people feel that tent cities should be allowed because at least the homeless are off the street.

(D) In spite of these concerns, some people feel that tent cities should be allowed because at least the homeless are off the street.

(E) Equally important, some people feel that tent cities should be allowed because at least the homeless are off the street.

932. Which is the best way to revise and combine sentences 15 and 16 (reproduced below) at the underlined portion?

Some people feel that tent cities should be okay because at least the homeless are off the <u>street. When they're off the street</u>, they're warmer and safer at night.

(A) street, at which point

(B) street, where

(C) street, where, first of all,

(D) street, and

(E) street; thus,

933. In context, what is best to do immediately following sentence 16 (reproduced below)?

When they're off the street, they're warmer and safer at night.

(A) Restate the thesis.

(B) Begin a new paragraph and start the conclusion.

(C) Make a connection with an earlier point.

(D) Insert details and examples.

(E) Introduce another major point.

934. Which version of sentence 17 (reproduced below) would make the best conclusion to the last paragraph?

Tent cities are better than nothing and should be maintained until permanent housing can be arranged.

(A) Tent cities are better than nothing and should be maintained until permanent housing can be arranged.

(B) Notwithstanding their problems, tent cities are better than nothing and should be maintained until permanent housing can be arranged.

(C) Although this may indeed be true, tent cities are better than nothing and should be maintained until permanent housing can be arranged.

(D) Cities, take notice: Tent cities are better than nothing and should be maintained until permanent housing can be arranged.

(E) Tent cities are indeed better than nothing and should be maintained until permanent housing can be arranged.

Questions 935–951 refer to the following passage.

(1) If facing a choice between wild salmon having habitat and you get to use electricity, which would you choose? (2) Almost all of us would choose electricity. (3) But choosing electricity, in some places, means losing wild salmon. (4) This is because the power comes from dams that block the salmon runs. (5) I say, save electricity *and* save the salmon — its a win-win situation.

(6) Everybody knows there are ways to cut back on electricity. (7) Most utility companies even have suggestions on their websites. (8) You can turn off power strips when you aren't using the appliances plugged into them. (9) If you have electric heat, try setting the thermostat just one or two degrees lower. (10) If the thermostat's lower and you're cold, put on a sweater. (11) Some health officials believe it's healthier anyway not to have the heat up too high.

(12) From a salmon's point of view, it's healthier for them to be able to swim upstream! (13) If there's a dam in the way, the salmon can't lay and fertilize their eggs. (14) The salmon run — the path salmon take from when they hatch, swim out to the ocean, and return to spawn — is effectively destroyed. (15) Another route, more vital habitat, for the wild salmon is lost, and their numbers decrease.

(16) Many organisms depend on the returning salmon. (17) Bears catch the salmon live. (18) The salmon die after they spawn. (19) The decaying salmon feed scavengers as well as provide nutrients for plants and trees along the stream.

(20) Don't put up dams where the salmon run. (21) If there is such a dam, take it down and find ways to conserve energy. (22) Long live the wild salmon!

935. In context, what is best to do with sentence 1 (reproduced below)?

If facing a choice between wild salmon's having habitat and you getting to use electricity, which would you choose?

(A) Leave it as it is.

(B) Take it out.

(C) Take out "If" and replace it with "Image you are."

(D) Take out the first "you" and replace it with "your."

(E) Insert the word "necessary" between *having* and *habitat*.

936. Which is the best way to revise and combine sentences 2 and 3 (reproduced below) at the underlined portion?

Almost all of us would choose electricity. But choosing electricity, in some places, means losing wild salmon.

(A) electricity, but this

(B) electricity; however, this choice

(C) electricity, unfortunately, this choice

(D) electricity; however, choosing electricity

(E) electricity, but this, of course

937. In context, which is the best version of the underlined portion of sentence 4 (reproduced below)?

This is because the power comes from dams that block the salmon runs.

(A) This is because the power comes from

(B) This loss is a result of the hydroelectric power generated by

(C) Some people accept this loss as a trade-off for the hydroelectric power generated by

(D) There are some people who believe this loss is an effect of the hydroelectric power generated by

(E) This loss is simply a trade-off for the hydroelectric power generated by

938. In context, what is best to do with sentence 5 (reproduced below)?

I say, save electricity *and* save the salmon — its a win-win situation.

(A) Leave it as it is.

(B) Take it out.

(C) Remove the italics from *and*.

(D) Insert a comma and the word "too" after *salmon*.

(E) Change "its" to "it's."

939. In context, which is the best transitional word/phrase to add at the beginning of sentence 6 (reproduced below)?

Everybody knows there are ways to cut back on electricity.

(A) Alternately,

(B) To begin with,

(C) As it turns out,

(D) In addition,

(E) In reality,

940. In context, what is best to do with sentence 7 (reproduced below)?

Most utility companies even have suggestions on their websites.

(A) Leave it as it is.

(B) Take it out.

(C) Replace it with "Most areas even have suggestions on the utility company's website."

(D) Begin the sentence with "For example."

(E) Insert "large-city" between *most* and *utility*.

941. Which is the best way to revise and combine sentences 9 and 10 (reproduced below) at the underlined portion?

If you have electric heat, try setting the thermostat just one or two degrees lower. If the thermostat's lower and you're cold, put on a sweater.

(A) lower, because if

(B) lower; however, if

(C) lower; supposing

(D) lower; if

(E) lower; but if

942. In context, which is the best transitional phrase to add at the beginning of sentence 11 (reproduced below)?

Some health officials believe it's healthier anyway not to have the heat up too high.

(A) An added benefit of this method of saving electricity is that

(B) Additionally, by saving electricity

(C) On the other hand,

(D) By saving electricity here,

(E) An added benefit of wearing a sweater here is that

943. In context, which is the best way to modify the underlined portion of sentence 12 (reproduced below)?

From a salmon's point of view, it's healthier for them to be able to swim upstream!

(A) From the point of view of most salmon

(B) Correspondingly, regarding the salmon

(C) Regarding the best interests of the salmon

(D) Thinking about what salmon would rather do

(E) Speaking in regard to what's best for the salmon

944. In context, what is best to do with sentence 13 (reproduced below)?

If there's a dam in the way, the salmon can't lay and fertilize their eggs.

(A) Leave it as it is.

(B) Take it out.

(C) Replace "lay and fertilize their eggs" with "spawn."

(D) Begin the sentence with "For example."

(E) Insert "reach the area where they" between *can't* and *lay.*

945. In context, which is the best version of the underlined portion of sentence 15 (reproduced below)?

Another route, more vital habitat, for the wild salmon is lost, and their numbers decrease.

(A) [Leave it as it is.]

(B) their numbers decreasing

(C) and unfortunately their numbers decrease

(D) and they die

(E) and wild salmon are lost forever

946. In context, which sentence provides the best introduction to paragraph 4?

(A) It's not just people who lose out.

(B) It's not just people who are affected by this dwindling food source.

(C) It's not just people who are the only losers in this matter.

(D) Furthermore, it's not just people who lose out.

(E) As the following examples illustrate, it's not just people who lose out.

947. In context, what is best to do with sentence 16 (reproduced below)?

Many organisms depend on the returning salmon.

(A) Leave it as it is.

(B) Change "organisms" to "animals."

(C) Insert "for sustenance" at the end.

(D) Begin the sentence with "Equally important."

(E) Insert "food-wise" between *depend* and *on.*

948. In context, which is the best transitional phrase to add at the beginning of sentence 17 (reproduced below)?

Bears catch the salmon live.

(A) Notably,

(B) As any scientist could tell you,

(C) As you may not know,

(D) For example,

(E) As much dramatic film from the wild has shown,

949. In context, what is best to do with sentence 18 (reproduced below)?

The salmon die after they spawn.

(A) Leave it as it is.

(B) Change "salmon" to "fish."

(C) Insert "Then" at the beginning.

(D) Replace it with "After the salmon spawn, they die."

(E) Insert "slowly" between *salmon* and *die.*

950. In context, which is the best way to modify the underlined portion of sentence 19 (reproduced below)?

The decaying salmon feed scavengers as well as provide nutrients for plants and trees along the stream.

(A) The dead salmon feed scavengers

(B) The dead salmon feed scavengers such as raccoons and eagles

(C) The decaying salmon feed scavengers such as raccoons and eagles

(D) The dead and decaying salmon feed scavengers such as raccoons and eagles.

(E) The dead and decaying salmon feed scavengers such as insects, raccoons, and eagles.

951. In context, what is best to do with sentence 22 (reproduced below)?

Long live the wild salmon!

(A) Leave it as it is.

(B) Take it out.

(C) Insert "And so" at the beginning.

(D) Change "wild salmon" to "salmon."

(E) Insert "still" between *the* and *wild.*

Questions 952–969 are based on the following passage.

(1) Genetically altering food is unnatural and unhealthy, and people shouldn't do it unless they have to.

(2) True, if you're starving, you aren't going to be picky. (3) Many believe that genetically modified organisms (GMOs) are the best choice in some people's minds because they can be made drought-resistant. (4) In California, for example, where drought has been a problem for many years now, crops that need less water can be very helpful. (5) Additionally, crops can be made resistant to insects or other organisms that would otherwise attack them.

(6) Also, some GMOs can be made sweeter, such as corn or tomatoes. (7) Foods such as peppers can be spicy. (8) If you never liked the taste of Brussels sprouts, a genetically altered variety might be popular.

(9) A final benefit involves adding vitamins and minerals. (10) They can be added to crops in poor countries. (11) They can help ensure that people get the essential nutrition they need that they would not otherwise get.

(12) However, there are basic and fundamental reasons to avoid GMOs. (13) Ninety percent of the soy and canola products in the U.S. are genetically altered. (14) Eighty-five percent of the corn is. (15) Most people do not even know when they are consuming such foods.

(16) GMOs may make sense in some places, but there are unhealthy affects associated with these altered foods. (17) Care should be taken when deciding to grow GMOs.

952. Which version of sentence 1 (reproduced below) would make the best opening to the first paragraph?

Genetically altering food is unnatural and unhealthy, and people shouldn't do it unless they have to.

(A) Genetically altering food is unnatural and unhealthy, and people shouldn't do it unless they have to.

(B) For all the problems it may solve, genetically altering food should not be considered a permanent solution.

(C) While there are some benefits to genetically altering food, it is unnatural and unhealthy and should be considered a last resort.

(D) Genetically altering food is unnatural and unhealthy, and considering it is a last resort.

(E) You may like the way it tastes, but genetically altered food is not good for you.

953. In context, which statement is the best version of the underlined portion of sentence 2 (reproduced below)?

True, if you're starving, you aren't going to be picky.

(A) you aren't going to be picky

(B) you aren't going to care

(C) you may not even know about genetically altered foods

(D) genetically altered foods may be a good solution for you

(E) you may be allergic to genetically altered foods

954. In context, what is best to do immediately following sentence 2 (reproduced below)?

True, if you're starving, you aren't going to be picky.

(A) Add a statement as to the point.

(B) Add a statement of the essay's position.

(C) Add a reference to the thesis.

(D) Add a transition.

(E) Add an explanation and at least one supporting detail.

955. In context, what is best to do at the beginning of sentence 3 (reproduced below)?

Many believe that genetically modified organisms (GMOs) are the best choice in some people's minds because they can be made drought-resistant.

(A) Start a new paragraph.

(B) Restate the thesis.

(C) Explain what GMOs are.

(D) Explain how the foods are genetically altered.

(E) Remind the reader of the importance of the topic.

956. In context, which is the best version of the underlined portion of sentence 3 (reproduced below)?

Many believe that genetically modified organisms (GMOs) are the best choice in some people's minds because they can be made drought-resistant.

(A) [Leave it as it is.]

(B) [Take it out.]

(C) according to some

(D) in *some* people's minds

(E) according to experts

957. In context, what is best to do with sentence 4 (reproduced below)?

In California, for example, where drought has been a problem for many years now, crops that need less water can be very helpful.

(A) Leave it as it is.

(B) Take it out.

(C) Begin the sentence with "Nevertheless."

(D) Take out "drought" and replace it with "lack of rainfall."

(E) Replace "in California" with "in some places."

958. In context, which is the best way to modify the underlined portion of sentence 5 (reproduced below)?

Also, crops can be made resistant to insects or other organisms that would otherwise attack them.

(A) that would otherwise attack and damage them

(B) which would otherwise attack them

(C) which would otherwise attack and damage them

(D) that would otherwise attack and damage the crops

(E) that would otherwise severely harm the crops

959. In context, what is best to do immediately following sentence 5 (reproduced below)?

Also, crops can be made resistant to insects or other organisms that would otherwise attack them.

(A) Add a statement as to the point.

(B) Add a statement of the essay's position.

(C) Add an explanation and at least one supporting detail.

(D) Add a reference to the thesis.

(E) Add a transition.

960. In context, which is the best way to modify the underlined portion of sentence 6 (reproduced below)?

Also, some GMOs can be made sweeter, such as corn or tomatoes.

(A) In other words,

(B) An additional benefit is that

(C) Indeed,

(D) Furthermore,

(E) One can see by way of explanation that

961. In context, which is the best way to modify the underlined portion of sentence 7 (reproduced below)?

Foods such as peppers can be spicy.

(A) [Leave it as it is.]

(B) could perhaps be made spicy

(C) will be spicier

(D) could perhaps be made spicier

(E) can be spicier

962. Which version of sentence 8 (reproduced below) would make the best conclusion to its paragraph?

If you never liked the taste of Brussels sprouts, a genetically altered variety might be popular.

(A) If you never liked the taste of Brussels sprouts, a genetically altered variety might be popular.

(B) And for making food generally tastier, a genetically altered variety of Brussels sprouts might be popular.

(C) If you wanted something tasty, a genetically altered variety of Brussels sprouts might be popular.

(D) If you wanted something tastier, a genetically altered variety of Brussels sprouts might be popular.

(E) If you could imagine food being made tastier, could you imagine tasty Brussels sprouts?

963. Which is the best way to revise and combine sentences 9 and 10 (reproduced below) at the underlined portion?

A final benefit involves adding vitamins and <u>minerals. They can be added to</u> crops in poor countries.

(A) minerals to

(B) minerals, which can be added to

(C) minerals, where they can help

(D) minerals, a good addition for

(E) minerals; they can be added to

964. Which version of sentence 11 (reproduced below) would make the best conclusion to its paragraph?

They can help ensure that people get the essential nutrition they need that they would not otherwise get.

(A) They can help ensure that people get the essential nutrition they need that they would not otherwise get.

(B) These benefits can help ensure that people get the essential nutrition they would not otherwise get.

(C) These countries can help ensure that people get the essential nutrition they would not otherwise get.

(D) They can help ensure that people receive the essential nutrition they might not otherwise get.

(E) These alterations to food can help ensure that people receive the essential nutrition they might not otherwise get.

965. Which version of sentence 12 (reproduced below) would make the best introduction to its paragraph?

However, there are basic and fundamental reasons to avoid GMOs.

(A) However, there are basic and fundamental reasons to avoid GMOs.

(B) However, there are fundamental reasons to avoid GMOs.

(C) In spite of these benefits, there are fundamental reasons to avoid GMOs.

(D) In addition to these benefits, there are fundamental reasons to avoid GMOs.

(E) However one may extol the virtues of GMOs, there are fundamental reasons to avoid them.

966. In context, what is best to do immediately preceding sentence 13 (reproduced below)?

Ninety percent of the soy and canola products in the U.S. are genetically altered.

(A) Restate the thesis.

(B) Begin a new paragraph and start the conclusion.

(C) Make a connection with an earlier point.

(D) State a reason.

(E) Insert details and examples.

967. In context, what is best to do with sentence 15 (reproduced below)?

Most people do not even know when they are consuming such foods.

(A) Leave it as it is.

(B) Take it out.

(C) Begin the sentence with "Additionally."

(D) Take out "most" and replace it with "some."

(E) Insert "today" between *people* and *do*.

968. In context, what is best to do between the second-to-last and final paragraphs?

    (A) Add reasons and supporting details to develop the main point stated in sentence 12.

    (B) Add more statistics to accompany those of sentences 13 and 14.

    (C) Add a sentence that restates the thesis and makes the author's position clear.

    (D) Add a transition that connects the second main point to the thesis.

    (E) Add a transition that connects the first main point to the second main point.

969. In context, what is best to do with sentence 16 (reproduced below)?

GMOs may make sense in some places, but there are unhealthy affects associated with these altered foods.

    (A) Leave it as it is.

    (B) Take it out.

    (C) Change "affects" to "effects."

    (D) Replace "altered foods" with "GMOs."

    (E) Change "these altered foods" to "them."

Chapter 4

Research and Essays

From answering research–skills questions to writing your own essays, you'll be up to your ears in the nuts and bolts of composition. The graders of the Praxis Core exam don't expect perfection, but they do expect you to know what you're writing about and to support your ideas.

The Problems You'll Work On

When working through the questions involving research skills and when crafting your essays, be prepared to

>> Make choices regarding the reliability and appropriateness of sources, the components of a citation, and what makes a good research strategy

>> Understand an essay's focus, organization, support, and correctness and facility of language

>> Recognize how these areas might be improved

What to Watch Out For

Your challenge is to think like — in turn — a research librarian, a writer, and an editor. Remember the following:

>> The steps of the research process may be intuitive, so you may not need to memorize them. Such is not the case, however, with the parts of a citation.

>> Stay focused on your position. Before you begin writing, think about your viewpoint; then create a rough outline by jotting down a thesis and the reasons you have that particular view.

>> Avoid redundancy.

>> Include logical connections and transitions where appropriate.

>> When considering whether you have enough support for a point or reason in your essay, make sure you haven't left someone wondering what your point is.

>> You get only 30 minutes to produce a logical, well-developed, well-supported, mostly error-free essay. Practice organizing your thoughts in 10 minutes, writing for 15 minutes, and proofreading in the last 5 minutes.

Research Skills

970. Which of the following shows the best order for engaging in the initial steps of the research process?

    (A) Ask questions, start search, find sources, settle on topic.

    (B) Ask questions, start search, settle on topic, find sources.

    (C) Settle on topic, start search, ask questions, find sources.

    (D) Start search, find sources, ask questions, settle on topic.

    (E) Find sources, start search, settle on topic, ask questions.

971. Which of the following is a general database?

    (A) PubMed

    (B) ERIC

    (C) Web of Science

    (D) ProQuest

    (E) PsycINFO

972. Which two citation formats are most commonly used in American schools?

    (A) APA and IGA

    (B) URL and MLA

    (C) APA and MLA

    (D) MLA and MRI

    (E) CWA and SLR

973. Which of the following best explains the value of a primary source?

    (A) It allows the student to focus on the main topic.

    (B) It allows the student to examine original research on a topic.

    (C) It allows the student to read what experts have to say about others' research.

    (D) It allows the student to find sources.

    (E) It allows the student to narrow the topic.

974. In a citation, which of the following should appear in italics, not quotation marks?

    (A) The title of a newspaper article

    (B) The title of a newspaper

    (C) The title of a chapter of a book

    (D) The title of an episode of a TV show

    (E) The title of a poem

975. A student wants to put a comment in a footnote to note another source that contradicts the one cited. Which of the following should the student use to introduce the contradicting source?

    (A) N.B.

    (B) ibid.

    (C) sic

    (D) cf.

    (E) et al.

976. For a research paper, a student has selected the topic "What programs exist to help alcoholics?" Which of the following suggestions will a librarian most likely make?

    (A) Make the topic narrower and more interesting.

    (B) Make the topic narrower.

    (C) Make the topic broader.

    (D) Make the topic more significant.

    (E) Make the topic more historical.

977. When initially scanning a database for articles, which of the following is NOT something to keep in mind?

    (A) The title of the article

    (B) The date of the article

    (C) The volume number of the article

    (D) The title of the periodical

    (E) The length of the article

978. If you're using data, why would you want to get it from a primary source?

(A) Relevancy issues are more likely to arise in a secondhand report.

(B) Scholarly issues are more likely to arise in a secondhand report.

(C) The library probably has only primary sources.

(D) It will be easier to find.

(E) Mistakes are more likely to be made in a secondhand report.

979. The current MLA citation format no longer requires a Works Cited page to list the URL for a web page because

(A) researchers can more easily find sources through author or title searches via a search engine

(B) researchers have less time than before to look up someone else's sources

(C) a Works Cited page has different standards for electronic sources than it does for paper sources

(D) a Works Cited page is less important now than it used to be

(E) professors and other reviewers trust students and researchers to be accurate in the use of electronic sources

980. In the following APA citation, what does "n.d." stand for?

American Psychological Association. (n.d.). Recovering emotionally from disaster. Retrieved from `http://www.apa.org/ helpcenter/recovering-disasters. aspx`

(A) New data

(B) Not done

(C) No date

(D) New decision

(E) No decision

981. Following APA format, what would you do to reference a web source that has no page numbers?

(A) Just leave that part out.

(B) Use the abbreviation *no pag.*

(C) Find another source that does have page numbers.

(D) Use the abbreviation *n.p.*

(E) Use a paragraph number.

982. When, in your research, you find a source that disagrees with most of your other sources, you should

(A) discard it but keep a note of where you can find it

(B) consider including it in the bibliography but not the Works Cited

(C) eliminate it as a point of view that is probably too radical

(D) assess its argument for possible inclusion as an in-text reference

(E) use it only if it does not contradict your working thesis

983. When you're initially skimming for possible sources, what two criteria should you use to decide sources' probable usefulness?

(A) relevance and timeliness

(B) nationality and relevance

(C) reliability and relevance

(D) reliability and timeliness

(E) association and reliability

984. When evaluating web sources for reliability, researchers should consider

(A) author, title, audience and purpose, and age

(B) title, sponsor, audience and purpose, and age

(C) graphics, sponsor, audience and purpose, and age

(D) author, sponsor, audience and purpose, and age

(E) author, sponsor, audience and purpose, and length

985. A student is writing a paper on the role of large banks in the financial crisis of 2007–8. Which of the following is LEAST likely to appear on the Works Cited page?

(A) An article by a retired bank manager

(B) The website of a major bank

(C) A book by an independent financial expert

(D) The website of a public television station

(E) An interview with a lending specialist

986. Which of the following shows the best order for engaging in the final steps of the research process?

(A) Read and take notes, write draft, write working thesis and outline, revise with more research (if necessary).

(B) Write working thesis and outline, read and take notes, write draft, revise with more research (if necessary).

(C) Read and take notes, write working thesis and outline, write draft, revise with more research (if necessary).

(D) Write working thesis and outline, write draft, read and take notes, revise with more research (if necessary).

(E) Read and take notes, write working thesis and outline, revise with more research (if necessary), write draft.

987. If you're doing historical research and need articles written prior to 1980, which of the following is the best strategy?

(A) Search a general database.

(B) Search a subject-specific database.

(C) Consult your professor.

(D) Consult a print index.

(E) Change the paper's topic.

988. Which of the following is NOT a clue to a source's probable scholarly nature?

(A) Quotations from primary sources

(B) Footnotes or a bibliography

(C) The academic or scientific credentials of the author

(D) Formal language

(E) The journalistic credentials of the author

989. The following MLA citation has two dates. What information do they contain?

Roberts, Johnnie L. "Big Media, R.I.P.: Media Conglomerates Were Supposed to Takeover the World. So Why Are They Dying?" *Newsweek.* Newsweek, 5 May 2009. Web. 6 May 2009.

(A) The first date is when the article was published, and the second is when it was accessed on the web.

(B) The first date is when the article was published, and the second date is when it was revised on the web.

(C) The first date is when the author submitted the article, and the second date is when it was accepted for publication on the web.

(D) The first date is that of the print article, and the second date is that of the article's publication on the web.

(E) The first date is that of the author's copyright, and the second date is that of the magazine's copyright.

Argumentative Essays

990. Discuss the extent to which you agree or disagree with this point of view. Support your position with specific reasons and examples from your own experience, observations, or reading.

"Tent cities, or places set aside where the homeless can camp out using tents or tarps, are not a good solution to the problem of homelessness. Conditions in tent cities are often unsafe and unsanitary."

991. Discuss the extent to which you agree or disagree with this point of view. Support your position with specific reasons and examples from your own experience, observations, or reading.

"An unusual choice being faced by some areas is having to choose between providing electricity to people or habitat to wild salmon. The culprit in this dilemma is a dam, built for hydroelectric power but making it impossible for salmon to reach their spawning grounds, where they lay and fertilize their eggs. It's time for the dams to come down."

992. Discuss the extent to which you agree or disagree with this point of view. Support your position with specific reasons and examples from your own experience, observations, or reading.

"While it's true there are benefits from genetically modified organisms (GMOs), the hazards definitely outweigh these benefits. You may get sweeter corn and juicier tomatoes, but you may also get food-based allergies you never had."

993. Discuss the extent to which you agree or disagree with this point of view. Support your position with specific reasons and examples from your own experience, observations, or reading.

"Online learning delivers a clearer message than face-to-face learning. When you just want to get the work done, online learning is so much easier. Everybody can manage his or her own time."

994. Discuss the extent to which you agree or disagree with this point of view. Support your position with specific reasons and examples from your own experience, observations, or reading.

"It's time for everyone to give up paperback books for digital versions. As the world's population increases and its natural resources decrease, everyone must find ways to reduce their use of these resources. Giving up paperback books is one such way, and it doesn't really involve a sacrifice."

995. Discuss the extent to which you agree or disagree with this point of view. Support your position with specific reasons and examples from your own experience, observations, or reading.

"Making athletes who cheat with drugs relinquish their records is unrealistic. Many athletes cheat, but not all the cheaters are caught. Therefore, why should the ones caught be the only ones whose statistics don't count?"

Informative/Explanatory Essays

996. The following sources address different aspects of the benefits of arts education. Read the two passages carefully and then use information from both to discuss the most important concerns relating to the issue and explain why these concerns are important. When paraphrasing or quoting, cite each source by referring to the author's last name, the title, or any other clear identifier. You may also draw on your own experiences, observations, or reading.

Source 1

Adapted from: Bryant, Bob. "The Importance of Fine Arts Education." Fine Arts Department, Katy Independent School District. Fine Arts Department. Web. 30 Mar. 2016.

Evidence from brain research is only one of many reasons education and engagement in fine arts is beneficial to the educational process. The arts develop neural systems that produce a broad spectrum of benefits ranging from fine motor skills to creativity and improved emotional balance. One must realize that these systems often take months and even years to fine-tune. In a study conducted by Judith Burton, Columbia University, research evidenced that subjects such as mathematics, science, and language require complex cognitive and creative capacities "typical of arts learning" (Burton, Horowitz, & Abeles, 1999). "The arts enhance the process of learning. The systems they nourish, which include our integrated sensory, attentional, cognitive, emotional, and motor capacities, are, in fact, the driving forces behind all other learning" (Jensen, 2001).

Today's students are inundated with data but are starving for meaningful learning. Workplace demands are for students to understand how to solve problems, what makes arguments plausible, how to build teams and coalitions, and how to incorporate the concept of fairness into the everyday decisions. Students need to be thinkers, possess people skills, be problem-solvers, demonstrate creativity, and work as a member of a team. We need to offer more in-depth learning about the things that matter the most: order, integrity, thinking skills, a sense of wonder, truth, flexibility, fairness, dignity, contribution, justice, creativity and cooperation. The arts provide all of these.

Source 2

Adapted from: Hulbert, Ann. "Drawing Lessons." The New York Times. 27 April 2008. Web. 30 Mar. 2016.

In a scrupulous review of 50 years of research into the academic impact of studying the arts, Ellen Winner, a Boston College professor of psychology, and Lois Hetland, who teaches at Massachusetts College of Art and Design, searched mostly in vain for evidence of a causal influence on school success. There is indeed a correlation between, for example, how many years students spend in arts classes and their SAT scores; more art, higher scores. But that doesn't prove that it's the added exposure to the arts that boosts verbal or math performance.

As unsatisfied with wafty promises that arts learning inspires "creativity" as with pledges that it boosts scores, the researchers videotaped several very different classrooms in two schools with intensive arts instruction. They watched teachers imparting techniques and introducing students to the world of the visual arts, and saw certain cognitive "dispositions" being elicited by the interactions: persistence in tackling problems, observational

acuity, expressive clarity, reflective capacity to question and judge, ability to envision alternative possibilities and openness to exploration.

These mental habits are clearly valuable in pursuing all kinds of academic (and other) endeavors, not just in tackling a canvas or a lump of clay. But Winner et al. caution that exercising them in an arts course doesn't ensure their automatic transfer to, say, the school lab.

997. The following sources address different aspects of energy drinks. Read the two passages carefully and then use information from both to discuss the most important concerns relating to the issue and explain why these concerns are important. When paraphrasing or quoting, cite each source used by referring to the author's last name, the title, or any other clear identifier. You may also draw on your own experiences, observations, or reading.

Source 1

Adapted from: Doheny, Kathleen. "Pros and Cons of the Caffeine Craze." WebMD 2006. Web. 4 Apr. 2016.

So what's the harm, ask caffeine fans, who point to studies showing the benefits of caffeine, such as boosting memory and improving concentration and perhaps lowering risks of diseases such as Alzheimer's and liver cancer. But others are alarmed by what they say is an increasingly overcaffeinated nation; they are concerned by studies finding too much caffeine can set you up for high blood pressure, high blood sugar, and decreased bone density — not to mention jangled nerves.

Caffeine abuse by young people alarms some experts. It was the cause of many calls to an Illinois Poison Center over a three-year tracking period, a team of doctors reported at the American College of Emergency Physicians annual meeting in New Orleans.

"Hidden" caffeine is a growing danger, say scientists at the Center for Science in the Public Interest (CSPI), a nonprofit health advocacy organization. In 1997, the CSPI petitioned the FDA to label the caffeine content of foods, noting that the amount of caffeine varies widely among food products.

Source 2

Adapted from: Nordqvist, Christian. "Energy Drinks Help Heart Function." MedicalNewsToday 28 August 2012. Web. 4 Apr. 2016.

Energy drinks improve the contractions of both the left and right ventricles of the heart; they have a beneficial effect on myocardial function, Dr. Matteo Cameli, from University of Siena, Italy, explained at the European Society of Cardiology 2012 Congress, in Munich, Germany. Dr. Cameli added that energy drinks raise the risk of cardio-metabolic diseases.

"Taken together these results show that energy drinks enhance contractions of both the left and right ventricles, thereby delivering a positive effect on myocardial function," said Dr. Cameli.

He continued: "Our study was performed in young healthy individuals at rest. Future studies need to focus on whether such benefits persist after long term consumption of energy drinks, and what the effects are of consuming these drinks during physical activity. It will also be important to determine which of the effects are induced in patients with cardiac disease to further our understanding of the potential benefits or risks of energy drink consumption."

998. The following sources address strengths or weaknesses of standardized tests. Read the two passages carefully and then use information from both to discuss the most important concerns relating to the issue and explain why these concerns are important. When paraphrasing or quoting, cite each source by referring to the author's last name, the title, or any other clear identifier. You may also draw on your own experiences, observations, or reading.

Source 1

Adapted from: Jouriles, Greg. "Here's Why We Don't Need Standardized Tests." Education Week. 8 Jul 2014. Web. 4 Apr. 2016.

Standardized tests are unnecessary because they rarely show what we don't already know. Ask any teacher and she can tell you which students can read and write. That telling usually comes in the form of letter grades or evaluations that break down progress on skills. So trust the teacher. Publish grade distributions. Locally publish a compilation of evaluation reports. Release a state or national report reviewed and verified by expert evaluators with legislative oversight.

Even if standardized testing were not only desirable to give the public a picture of basic competencies, but also an efficient way to do so, the costs have been too great.

Many have previously made cogent arguments (unrealistic definitions of achievement, skewed instructional schemes, inequitable curricular offerings, inevitable corruption, perverted charter school missions, alienation, disempowerment, and embarrassment of educators, etc.) in this vein, but let's think about a supposed example of success on this front — a school with the high test scores.

In general, such a school has a compliant or affluent population. Test scores are a point of pride. The school has a good reputation. But, when you go in and observe, the teaching and learning do not impress.

Source 2

Adapted from: Almagor, Lelac. "The Good in Standardized Testing." Boston Review. 2 Sept. 2014. Web. 4 Apr. 2016.

Testing doesn't produce the staggering gaps in performance between privileged and unprivileged students; historical, generational, systemic inequality does. Testing only seeks to tell the truth about those gaps, and the truth is that the complex tasks of the Common Core are a better representation of what our students need to and ought to be able to do. I'm all for measuring that as accurately as we can. In recent years our schools have in fact made huge gains in helping our students tackle real complexity. I'd love to take genuine pride in our scores, knowing they reflect those strides toward rigor.

If we could give these harder tests internally and get back detailed results — share them only with parents, and use them only to improve our own planning — many more teachers would embrace them. Liberated from the testing tricks and stamina lessons, we would embrace more honest feedback about where our students are and how they still need to grow.

The trouble is that we know the scores can and will be used against us and our students. Those who interpret the results in public don't focus on the needs of the individual. Nor do they seek to identify and propagate the most effective instructional practices. Instead they use the scores to judge who is capable and incapable; to bar access to opportunity; to dismiss and diminish our successes; to justify rather than fight against educational inequality.

In this atmosphere of fear, it is difficult to look forward to more-rigorous tests and the detailed results they produce. Our instinct is to shield our students — and ourselves. Instead of dropping test prep from the schedule, we are tempted to push it to the point of absurdity, in case those old tricks might serve us better than the truth.

999. The following sources address aspects of music censorship. Read the two passages carefully and then use information from both to discuss the most important concerns relating to the issue and explain why these concerns are important. When paraphrasing or quoting, cite each source by referring to the author's last name, the title, or any other clear identifier. You may also draw on your own experiences, observations, or reading.

Source 1

Adapted from: Sanneh, Kelefa. "Don't Blame Hip-Hop." The New York Times. *25 Apr 2007. Web. 6 Jun. 2016.*

The [hip-hop] genre has already acquired (and it's fair to say earned) a reputation for bad language and bad behavior. Oprah Winfrey organized a two-show "town meeting" on what's wrong with hip-hop — starting with the ubiquity of the word "ho" and its slipperier cousin, "bitch" — and how to fix it.

Consumers have learned to live with all sorts of semi-voluntary censorship, including the film rating system, the F.C.C.'s regulation of broadcast media and the self-regulation of basic cable networks. Hip-hop fans, in particular, have come to expect that many of their favorite songs will reach radio in expurgated form with curses, epithets, drug references and mentions of violence deleted.

One of hip-hop's many antecedents is the venerable African-American oral tradition known as toasting; those toasts are full of those three words. Hip-hop took those rhymes from the street corner to the radio, and those old-fashioned dirty jokes are surely meant to shock people like Ms. Winfrey. Once upon a time, such lyrics (if they had been disseminated) might have been denounced for their moral turpitude, but now they're more likely to be denounced for their sexism. Both verdicts are probably correct, and each says something about mainstream society's shifting priorities and taboos. Maybe dirty jokes never change, only the soap does.

On BET's "106 & Park," one of hip-hop's definitive television shows, you can watch a fresh-faced audience applaud [clean-cut] songs, cheered on by relentlessly positive hosts. For all the panicky talk about hip-hop lyrics, the current situation suggests a scarier possibility, both for hip-hop's fans and its detractors. What if hip-hop's lyrics shifted from tough talk and crude jokes to playful club exhortations — and it didn't much matter? What if the controversial lyrics quieted down, but the problems didn't? What if hip-hop didn't matter that much, after all?

Adapted from: Strauss, Neil. "Better Songs Through Censorship." The New York Times. 12 Mar. 2000. Web. 6 Jun. 2016.

LISTENING to rap radio is often like reading a declassified government document in which thick black lines obscure the most tantalizing parts. Except that instead of black marker, rap singles are doctored for the public with sound-effects CD's. Gunshots, sirens, car screeches, turntable scratching and lyrics played backward conceal words deemed dirty, derogatory or harmful to minors. Some songs, especially ones with obscene words as their chorus, become so bowdlerized that their meaning is no longer even fathomable on the radio.

Typically, the notion of artists changing their music to please the prudish and commercial elements of society is odious to critics, but in the case of several recent singles, the editing has actually improved the song. In a pop landscape in which the crude come-on has replaced the sly innuendo, some remakes are bringing a touch of subtlety back to urban music.

While it is interesting to see how these artists respond when confronted with the content limitations of radio, re-rapping songs is a strange practice that supporters of artistic freedom might compare to painting clothes on nudes before they can be displayed in a museum where children might see them. Though I'll take modified lyrics over obscuring sound effects in my rap any day, I'd also like to see the process work the other way around. If albums with curse words are deemed dirty and must be presented in clean versions, why can't albums that are clean to begin with (Celine Dion, 'N Sync, Barney) be remade into dirty versions for those who don't like their pop so tame?

1,000. The following sources address aspects of plastic surgery. Read the two passages carefully and then use information from both to discuss the most important concerns relating to the issue and explain why these concerns are important. When paraphrasing or quoting, cite each source used by referring to the author's last name, the title, or any other clear identifier. You may also draw on your own experiences, observations, or reading.

Source 1

Adapted from: Rappaport, Norman, M.D. "5 Benefits of Plastic Surgery." Houston Center for Plastic Surgery. 2 Jul 2015. Web. 6 Jun. 2016.

When you look good, you feel good. Improvements to appearance naturally translate to increased self-confidence for most people, which means a greater willingness to try new things or open up in social situations. You may also be willing to wear certain types of clothing or participate in activities you tended to avoid before your surgery, due to your discomfort with your appearance.

Some plastic surgery procedures can improve your physical health as well as your looks. For example, rhinoplasty or nose reshaping surgery may improve breathing at the same time it improves the aesthetics of the nose.

Mental health benefits can be gained from plastic surgery procedures as well. Some people see a reduction in social anxiety after their surgery, due to the new feelings of self-confidence their new look inspires. It is not unusual to feel greater control over your life, become more willing to take on new challenges, or take charge of your life in a whole new way.

Some studies suggest that people that are more attractive may enjoy more professional and personal opportunities. A 2012 study published in Applied Financial Economics found that attractive real estate agents were able to sell properties at a higher price than agents that were not perceived as attractive. Other studies have also found attractive people tend to make higher salaries and get selected for promotions more often.

Patients seeking body contouring, such as liposuction or a tummy tuck, may find it is easier to keep the weight down after their plastic surgery. The positive results of the procedure may motivate the person to maintain a healthy diet and exercise program to keep their weight in check.

Source 2
_____

Adapted from: Ray, Linda. "Positive and Negative Benefits of Plastic Surgery." Livestrong.com. 16 Aug. 2013. Web. 6 Jun. 2016.

While the benefits of cosmetic surgery are widely accepted, patients should consider the positive and negative aspects of plastic surgery before undergoing any treatments.

The bigger the procedure, the higher the risk of complications. Any cut made on the skin is likely to leave a scar. Most procedures however take this into account and skilled cosmetic surgeons take great pains to hide scars in little seen areas, such as under the hair, behind ears and in skin folds. Although steps are taken to reduce the risk of infection, there is always a chance that infection at the site of the incision can occur. Blood clots may spring up following extended periods of surgery, although walking and movement following surgery usually help to remove the risk. Finally, there are the risks associated with anesthesia that need to be talked about with the anesthesiologist before the procedure.

A study performed by a social worker and two psychiatrists reported by the American Psychological Association showed that for the most part, patients felt better about themselves following plastic surgery. Patients reported a boost in self-image

and overall well-being. The same study reported negative responses from those who had high expectations that were not fulfilled by the cosmetic procedure. Patients who were not satisfied with the results of the surgery often went in for additional work. Others experienced periods of depression, isolation and anger towards their doctors. The researchers concluded that more psychological counseling be enacted by plastic surgeons prior to doing the work.

In addition to the time spent, plastic surgery can be expensive, with procedures ranging up to $6,000 or more. Most insurance policies do not cover elective procedures, such as plastic surgery. The money can be thought of as an investment in the future, especially when the improved appearance will help in obtaining a job or promotion.

1,001. The following sources address strengths or weaknesses of mandatory community-service programs for students. Read the two passages carefully and then use information from both to discuss the most important concerns relating to the issue and explain why these concerns are important. When paraphrasing or quoting, cite each source used by referring to the author's last name, the title, or any other clear identifier. You may also draw on your own experiences, observations, or reading.

Source 1
_____

Adapted from: Sparks, Sarah. "Community Service Requirements Seen to Reduce Volunteering." Education Week. 20 Aug 2013. Web. 6 Jun. 2016.

Maryland's statewide requirement that all students complete 75 hours of service learning by graduation led to significant boosts in 8th grade volunteering — generally in school-organized activities — but it actually decreased volunteering among older students, leading to a potential loss in long-term volunteering, according to a study previewed online by the *Economics of Education Review* in June.

"If this is for school, how do we know [students] are considering this as community service, rather than just homework for school?" said the study's author, Sara E. Helms, an assistant professor of economics at Samford University in Birmingham, Ala. "One of the interpretations that is more convincing is, maybe we are substituting this [service requirement] for being self-motivated."

R. Scott Pfeifer, the executive director of the Maryland Association of Secondary School Principals and a former principal of Centennial High School in Howard County, Md., cautioned that the findings may underrepresent subtler volunteer activities among older students because students may be better able to recall and report official school-related volunteer activities, such as those they would pursue during middle school.

"There's a ton of volunteering that goes on," he said, but "kids are social animals. They may not think of their activity in National Honor Society of bringing food to the old-age home as volunteering."

Both Ms. Helms and Mr. Pfeifer agreed that schools' service-learning programs require planning and time for students to reflect on their experiences in order to be meaningful.

And as a tool for engaging students in different subjects, from history to environmental science, Mr. Pfeifer argues that the state's service-learning requirement has been a success.

"Without it, there'd be something lacking in every one of our schools that's there now, a focus," he said. "There'd be something missing if [the service requirement] wasn't there."

Source 2

Adapted from: Bodeeb, Julia. "Should You Have to Volunteer in Order to Graduate?" BrightHubEducation. com. 15 May 2015. Web. 6 Jun. 2016.

With many school districts starting to require community service, it will be interesting to see which way this trend continues.

Most teenagers have a lot of energy and are eager to take on a project to help the community or the world. They like to do group projects and they like to create ideas for new projects. Community service may help teenagers build leadership skills and learn that they have the ability to start a project that will help people tremendously.

When community service is required for graduation it sparks creativity in students and propels them to create projects that may have a profound impact on the local community. Also, when students work with community leaders in public service they start to make connections that may help them later in their careers or life.

Some students have to work after school and weekends to help support their family or to buy the clothes and supplies they need for school. Many high school students have very busy school, work, and sport schedules that barely leave time for sleep. Adding community service requirements would severely stress some high school students who work long hours simply to keep their family financially afloat.

Also take into account students who may just want to volunteer for the sake of helping others and not to get something out of it. To a certain extent, requiring someone to volunteer takes away the whole purpose of volunteerism.

Teachers often see postings in the local paper for high school students seeking help for public service projects. It is awe inspiring to see the good deeds teenagers can do to benefit the local community and the world. Upon seeing the sometimes huge amounts of money raised, or large amounts of items donated to worthy charitable groups, it is easy to think that volunteering surely helps teenagers build skills that will be helpful in future careers.

2

The Answers

IN THIS PART . . .

Review the answers to all 1,001 questions.

Study the answer explanations to better understand the concepts being covered.

Chapter 5
The Answers

Chapter 1

1.   E. 18

> You can use your calculator to find the answer. However, it's good to know how to do this kind of problem without one.
>
> Add the numbers two at a time. Remember that subtracting a negative number is the same as adding a positive one.
>
> $$-3 + 14 - (-7) = 11 - (-7)$$
> $$= 11 + 7$$
> $$= 18$$

2.   A. −18

> Add two numbers at a time:
>
> $$-5 + (-10) + 4 + (-7) = -15 + 4 + (-7)$$
> $$= -11 + (-7)$$
> $$= -18$$

3.   D. 90

> You can do this problem on your calculator, but it may be easier not to use it. This is pure multiplication of factors. Count the number of factors that have negative signs. Because the number of factors with negative signs is even, the product is positive. From there, ignore the negative signs and multiply the numbers. The product is 90.

4. D. –1

You can use your calculator to find the answer, but there's a quicker and easier way. Because the exponent 379 is odd, –1 is multiplied by itself an odd number of times. That means the product will be negative, because –1 is a negative number. No matter how many times 1 is multiplied by itself, the product will be 1; make that negative, and the product here is –1.

5. B. 21

Start by finding the prime factorization — the prime numbers you can multiply by each other to get 63. Note that some prime factors are used more than once.

$$63 = 9 \times 7$$
$$= 3 \times 3 \times 7$$

The prime factorization of 63 is $3 \times 3 \times 7$.

Then determine all the products of the different combinations of the prime factors. The only answer choice that's a product of a combination of those prime factors is 21, which is 7×3.

6. E. 18

You can find all the factors of 42 by getting its prime factorization — the prime numbers you multiply by each other to get 42 — and then finding all the products of the combinations of the factors. In this case, each prime factor is a factor only once:

$$42 = 6 \times 7$$
$$= 3 \times 2 \times 7$$

The only answer choice that isn't a product of a combination of prime factors of 42 is Choice (E), 18. Choice (A) is a prime factor of 42, Choice (B) is 3×2, Choice (C) is 2×7, and Choice (D) is 3×7.

7. C. 370

You can use your calculator and add 53 to itself and keep adding 53 to find its first few multiples. All the choices listed are multiples of 53 except Choice (C); it gets skipped between and 318 and 371.

8.   D. 23

A number is a multiple only of its factors, so this question is really asking which choice is *not* a factor of 90. All the choices are factors of 90 except Choice (D), 23. It doesn't go into 90 a whole number of times.

9.   A. 4

You can use the prime factorizations of 28 and 72 to determine their factors: $28 = 2 \times 2 \times 7$ and $72 = 2 \times 2 \times 2 \times 3 \times 3$, so

Factors of 28: 1, 2, 4, 7, 14, 28

Factors of 72: 1, 2, 3, 4, 6, 8, 9, 12, 18, 24, 36, 72

The largest number that is a factor of both 28 and 72 is 4, so it's their greatest common factor.

10.   E. 21

Use combinations from the prime factorizations of 84 and 144 to determine the factors of each: $84 = 2 \times 2 \times 3 \times 7$ and $144 = 2 \times 2 \times 2 \times 2 \times 3 \times 3$, so

Factors of 84: 1, 2, 3, 4, 6, 7, 12, 14, 21, 28, 42, 84

Factors of 144: 1, 2, 3, 4, 6, 8, 9, 12, 16, 18, 24, 36, 48, 72, 144

The largest number that's a factor of both 84 and 144 is 12, so it's their greatest common factor.

11.   B. 72

You can find the multiples of a number by adding the number to itself repeatedly and taking note of each sum:

Multiples of 18: 18, 36, 54, 72, 90, 108, . . .

Multiples of 24: 24, 48, 72, . . .

The lowest number that's a multiple of both 18 and 24 is 72.

Choices (C) and (D) are a multiples of both numbers but not the lowest common multiple.

12. **A. 12**

Twenty-four is a multiple of only Choices (A), (C), and (E). You can list the first few multiples of those choices and 8 to determine the answer to the question. Here are the multiples of 8 and Choice (A):

Multiples of 8: 8, 16, 24 . . .

Multiples of 12: 12, 24, . . .

Without going any further, you can see that 24 is the least common multiple of 8 and 12, so Choice (A) is correct. In case you're curious, 8, not 24, is the least common multiple of 8 and Choices (C) and (E).

13. **D. 125**

The cube of 5 is 5^3, which is $5 \times 5 \times 5$, or 125.

14. **B. 3**

You can use your calculator and multiply each answer choice as a factor 4 times. You can also stop at Choice (B) because this isn't a "Select all that apply" question, and 3 to the 4th power is 81:

$$3^4 = 3 \times 3 \times 3 \times 3$$
$$= 81$$

The only other number that can be set to the 4th power to get 81 is −3, which isn't one of the choices.

15. **C. 24**

Your calculator on the Praxis Core exam will have a square-root key. However, you can multiply each choice by itself until you find the only one that gives you 576 when squared.

16. **B. 20**

You can find the cube root of 64 by getting its prime factorization (the prime numbers that give you 64 when multiplied by each other) and creating three identical factor groups:

$$64 = 8 \times 8$$
$$= 4 \times 2 \times 4 \times 2$$
$$= 2 \times 2 \times 2 \times 2 \times 2 \times 2$$
$$= (2 \times 2)(2 \times 2)(2 \times 2)$$

The number with a value equal to 2×2 is the cube root of 64. That number is 4.

You can use the prime factorizations of 20 and 45 to find the factors of 20 and 45 and then determine their greatest common factor: $20 = 2 \times 2 \times 5$, and $45 = 3 \times 3 \times 5$, so

Factors of 20: 1, 2, 4, 5, 10, 20

Factors of 45: 1, 3, 5, 9, 15, 45

The greatest common factor of 20 and 45 is 5.

The cube root of 64 times the greatest common factor of 20 and 45 is the product of 4 and 5, which is 20.

---

17. A. 882

Add each number to itself multiple times to find its first few multiples:

Multiples of 14: 14, 28, 42, 56, 60, 74, . . .

Multiples of 21: 21, 42, . . .

You can see that 42 is the least common multiple of 14 and 21. The square of 42 is 42^2, which is 42×42, or 1,764. That number divided by 2, or times $\frac{1}{2}$, is 882.

---

18. E. 64

Work within the innermost grouping symbol first, and then move outward:

$$\left(\left(2 \right)^3 \right)^2 = \left(8 \right)^2$$
$$= 64$$

---

19. D. 36

The square of 6 is 6^2, which is 6×6, or 36. You can find the least common multiple of 8 and 9 by listing their first few multiples and looking for the first one they have in common:

Multiples of 8: 8, 16, 24, 32, 40, 48, 60, 64, 72, 80, . . .

Multiples of 9: 9, 18, 27, 36, 45, 54, 63, 72, . . .

The least common multiple of 8 and 9 is 72.

You can find the greatest common factor of 36 and 72 by listing all their factors and looking for the greatest common one. You can also identify 36 immediately as a factor of 72. Every number is a factor of itself, so 36 is a factor of 36. Thus, the greatest common factor of 36 and 72 is 36.

20.   A. 3

First determine the factors of 24 and 120:

Factors of 24: 1, 2, 3, 4, 6, 8, 12, 24

Factors of 120: 1, 2, 3, 4, 5, 6, 8, 10, 12, 15, 20, 24, . . .

You can stop listing factors of 120 at 24 because that's the highest factor of 24. You can see that 3 is a factor of both 24 and 120, and 3 is an odd number. It's therefore a counterexample to the statement that all factors of 24 and 120, other than 1, are even. The example of 3 proves the statement wrong. The other choices are even, except Choice (D), which is not a factor of 24 or 120.

21.   B. $\frac{3}{4}$

To simplify a fraction, first find the greatest common factor (GCF) of the numerator and denominator. Then divide both by their greatest common factor. The greatest common factor of 12 and 16 is 4:

$$\frac{12}{16} = \frac{12 \div 4}{16 \div 4}$$
$$= \frac{3}{4}$$

Choice (C) is a reduced form of $\frac{12}{16}$, but it isn't fully reduced. It's the result of dividing the numerator and denominator by 2. If you divide by a factor that isn't the GCF, you need to divide the top and bottom by a common factor again until the GCF of the numerator and denominator is 1.

22.   C. $\frac{2}{7}$

Divide both the numerator and the denominator by their greatest common factor, 10:

$$\frac{20}{70} = \frac{20 \div 10}{70 \div 10}$$
$$= \frac{2}{7}$$

23. C. $\frac{28}{49}$

You could simplify every choice until you find that one of them is equal to $\frac{4}{7}$. However, there's a quicker and easier method. Because this is a multiple-choice question, you can look for a fraction in which the numerator is a multiple of 4 and the denominator is a multiple of 7. When the numerator and denominator of $\frac{4}{7}$ can be multiplied by the same number to get a fraction that is one of the choices, that choice is the correct answer. Because 4 can be multiplied by 7 to get 28 and 7 can be multiplied by 7 to get 49, the correct answer is $\frac{28}{49}$:

$$\frac{4(7)}{7(7)} = \frac{28}{49}$$

24. E. $\frac{5}{9}$

This question is essentially asking which choice is equal to $\frac{55}{99}$. The only common factor of 55 and 99 is 11. If you divide both the numerator and denominator by 11, you get $\frac{5}{9}$.

25. B. $\frac{6}{17}$

The numerator and denominator in the fraction are such big numbers that you most likely can't immediately determine whether they have a GCF other than 1. Because the digits of 324 have a sum that is a multiple of 3 and the same is true of 918, both numbers are divisible by 3. You can follow this pattern and continue to divide by common factors for as many steps as necessary:

$$\frac{324}{918} = \frac{108}{306}$$
$$= \frac{36}{102}$$
$$= \frac{18}{51}$$
$$= \frac{6}{17}$$

Another option is to write the prime factorization of both numbers in their places in the fraction and cancel each case of a prime factor that's in the numerator and denominator. That's just a different version of the same general process.

26. **A. Yes**

You can divide 84 by 14 and see whether you get the same result when you divide 96 by 16. Because $84 \div 14 = 6$ and $96 \div 16 = 6$, the two fractions are equal:

$$\frac{84}{96} = \frac{84 \div 6}{96 \div 6}$$
$$= \frac{14}{16}$$

27. **C. $\frac{42}{5}$**

To convert a mixed number to an improper fraction, multiply the denominator of the fraction by the whole number and then add the numerator to the result. Put the number you get over the denominator:

$$8\frac{2}{5} = \frac{5(8)+2}{5}$$
$$= \frac{40+2}{5}$$
$$= \frac{42}{5}$$

28. **$\frac{75}{8}$**

Multiply the 8 that is in the denominator by the whole number, 9, and add 3 to the product. The result is 75. Put 75 over the denominator, 8:

$$9\frac{3}{8} = \frac{8(9)+3}{8}$$
$$= \frac{72+3}{8}$$
$$= \frac{75}{8}$$

29. **E. $-\frac{43}{10}$**

Multiply 10 by 4, add 3 to the product, and put that sum over the denominator; put the negative sign before the fraction. Make sure you don't multiply 10 by −4 before adding 3; the negative sign applies to both the whole number and the fractional part of the mixed number, so it's best to keep the negative sign out in front.

$$-4\frac{3}{10} = -\frac{10(4)+3}{10}$$
$$= -\frac{40+3}{10}$$
$$= -\frac{43}{10}$$

30. D. $10\frac{1}{8}$

To convert an improper fraction to a mixed number, divide the numerator by the denominator. The integer that results is the integer in the mixed number. The remainder is the numerator of the fraction, and the denominator remains the denominator.

$$\frac{81}{8} = 10 \text{ R } 1$$
$$= 10\frac{1}{8}$$

31. E. $18\frac{1}{2}$

Divide 37 by 2. The quotient is 18 with a remainder of 1. The 18 is the whole number in the mixed number, and the remainder, 1, is the numerator in the fraction. The 2 is the denominator in both forms.

$$\frac{37}{2} = 18 \text{ R } 1$$
$$= 18\frac{1}{2}$$

32. C. 7

Divide 77 by 11. The result is 7, with no remainder:

$$\frac{77}{7} = 11$$

33. E. $3\frac{3}{5}$

To add a fraction and a mixed number, convert the mixed number to an improper fraction. Then add the improper fraction and the first fraction. If necessary, you can convert the resulting improper fraction to a mixed number.

$$\frac{2}{5} + 3\frac{1}{5} = \frac{2}{5} + \frac{5(3)+1}{5}$$
$$= \frac{2}{5} + \frac{16}{5}$$
$$= \frac{18}{5}$$
$$= 3\frac{3}{5}$$

34.   **B.** $-2\dfrac{2}{15}$

To combine mixed numbers, convert them to improper fractions. Then combine the fractions:

$$\begin{aligned}
5\frac{2}{3} - 7\frac{4}{5} &= \frac{17}{3} - \frac{39}{5} \\
&= \frac{17(5)}{3(5)} - \frac{39(3)}{5(3)} \\
&= \frac{85}{15} - \frac{117}{15} \\
&= -\frac{32}{15} \\
&= -2\frac{2}{15}
\end{aligned}$$

35.   **D.** $-4\dfrac{1}{2}$

To multiply mixed numbers, convert them to improper fractions and then multiply the improper fractions. If necessary, convert the resulting improper fraction to a mixed number.

$$\begin{aligned}
2\frac{5}{8} \times \left(-1\frac{5}{7}\right) &= \frac{8(2)+5}{8} \times \left(-\frac{7(1)+5}{7}\right) \\
&= \frac{21}{8} \times \left(-\frac{12}{7}\right) \\
&= -\frac{252}{56} \\
&= -\frac{63}{14} \\
&= -4\frac{1}{2}
\end{aligned}$$

36.   **A.** $\dfrac{20}{531}$

To divide a fraction by a mixed number, convert the mixed number to an improper fraction. Then divide the first fraction by the second fraction. To do so, multiply the first fraction by the reciprocal of the second fraction.

$$\begin{aligned}
\frac{4}{9} \div 11\frac{4}{5} &= \frac{4}{9} \div \frac{5(11)+4}{5} \\
&= \frac{4}{9} \div \frac{59}{5} \\
&= \frac{4}{9} \times \frac{5}{59} \\
&= \frac{20}{531}
\end{aligned}$$

37. $\dfrac{237}{250}$

Convert both mixed numbers to improper fractions. Divide the first improper fraction by the second.

$$-9\frac{7}{8} \div \left(-10\frac{5}{12}\right) = -\frac{8(9)+7}{8} \div \left(-\frac{12(10)+5}{12}\right)$$
$$= -\frac{79}{8} \div \left(-\frac{125}{12}\right)$$
$$= -\frac{79}{8} \times \left(-\frac{12}{125}\right)$$
$$= \frac{948}{1,000}$$
$$= \frac{237}{250}$$

38. A. 0.8

To convert a fraction to a decimal, divide the numerator by the denominator. You can use your calculator to divide 4 by 5. The result is 0.8.

39. D. 0.125

All the choices are in decimal form, so convert the fraction to a decimal. To do so, divide the numerator by the denominator. You can use your calculator: 1 divided by 8 is 0.125.

40. A. $\dfrac{17}{50}$

To convert a decimal to a fraction in simplest form, first write the fraction that the decimal represents. Because the 3 in 0.34 represents tenths and the 4 represents hundredths, 0.34 represents 34 hundredths, or $\dfrac{34}{100}$. That fraction isn't in simplest form, so reduce it by dividing the numerator and denominator by their greatest common factor, which is 2:

$$\frac{34}{100} = \frac{34 \div 2}{100 \div 2}$$
$$= \frac{17}{50}$$

41. E. 75%

To convert a decimal to a percent, move the decimal point two places to the right and put % after the result:

$$0.75 = 75\%$$

Both forms represent 75 hundredths.

42. D. 25%

To convert a fraction to a percent, first convert it to a decimal by dividing the numerator by the denominator:

$$\frac{1}{4} = 0.25$$

Then convert the decimal to a percent by moving the decimal point two places to the right and putting % after the result:

$$0.25 = 25\%$$

43. C. $\frac{21}{50}$

First, write the percent as the fraction it represents. Remember that % means "hundredths":

$$42\% = \frac{42}{100}$$

Then simplify the fraction by dividing the numerator and denominator by their greatest common factor, which is 2:

$$\frac{42}{100} = \frac{42 \div 2}{100 \div 2}$$
$$= \frac{21}{50}$$

44. E. 0.34848

To convert a percent to a decimal, drop the % and move the decimal point two places to the left. These values are equal because including a % symbol and moving a decimal point two places to the left are both forms of dividing by 100.

$$34.848\% = 0.34848$$

45. E. 4.96032

Drop the % and move the decimal point two places to the left:

$$496.032\% = 4.96032$$

46. A. −2.125

First, put the mixed number in improper fraction form:

$$-2\frac{1}{8} = -\left(\frac{8(2)+1}{8}\right)$$
$$= -\frac{16+1}{8}$$
$$= -\frac{17}{8}$$

Next, convert the fraction to a decimal by dividing the numerator by the denominator:

$$-\frac{17}{8} = -2.125$$

47. **E. 840%**

The first step is to write the mixed number as an improper fraction:

$$8\frac{2}{5} = \frac{5(8)+2}{5}$$
$$= \frac{40+2}{5}$$
$$= \frac{42}{5}$$

The next step is the write the improper fraction as a decimal by dividing the numerator by the denominator:

$$\frac{42}{5} = 8.4$$

From decimal form, you can convert to percent form by moving the decimal two places to the right and putting % after the result. Remember that after the last nonzero digit after a decimal point, you can add as many zeros as you need to.

$$8.4 = 8.40$$
$$= 840\%$$

48. **E. 3.261**

The answer choices are in decimal form, so put $\frac{1}{12}$ in decimal form by dividing 1 by 12:

$$\frac{1}{12} = 1 \div 12$$
$$= 0.08333\ldots$$

The quotient has 3 repeated infinitely after the decimal point. When that happens, you can round to the nearest ten-thousandth (four places after the decimal point) to make reliable calculations for the Praxis Core exam:

$$0.08333\ldots \to 0.0833$$

Now you can add 8.3333 to 3.178, which is already in decimal form:

$$0.0833 + 3.178 = 3.2613$$

The question asks for the sum rounded to the nearest thousandth, which is three places past the decimal point. Because the fourth digit after the decimal point is 3, round down by dropping the last 3 and keeping the 1:

$$3.2613 \to 3.261$$

49.   **D. 15.5**

All the choices are in decimal form, so convert 46.893% to decimal form by dropping the % and moving the decimal point two places to the left:

$$46.893\% = 0.46893$$

Now add 0.46893 to 15.0723. You can use your calculator.

$$0.46893 + 15.0723 = 15.54123$$

A number rounded to the nearest tenth has one digit after the decimal point. Because the next digit after the decimal is less than 5, round down: Keep the 5 after the decimal point and drop the other digits.

$$15.54123 \rightarrow 15.5$$

50.   **C. −2.16**

All the choices are in decimal form (Choices (B) and (C) have understood decimal points, not visible ones), so you want both factors in decimal form. You can convert $\frac{3}{20}$ to decimal form by dividing 3 by 20:

$$\frac{3}{20} = 3 \div 20$$
$$= 0.15$$

Next, multiply 0.15 by −14.4. You can use your calculator.

$$0.15(-14.4) = -2.16$$

51.   **B. 0.76**

To compare numbers, put them in the same form. Decimal form is generally best (though there are exceptions, such as when fractions can easily be given a common denominator). You can convert $\frac{3}{4}$ to decimal form by dividing the numerator by the denominator:

$$\frac{3}{4} = 0.75$$

Because 0.76 is greater than 0.75, 0.76 is greater than $\frac{3}{4}$.

52. E. $\frac{16}{5}$

You can convert all the numbers to decimal form and then compare them:

$$\frac{25}{8} = 3.125$$

$$3\frac{1}{9} = 3.\overline{1}$$

$$3.1 = 3.1$$

$$3.11 = 3.11$$

$$\frac{16}{5} = 3.2$$

Of all those decimal forms, 3.2 is the greatest, so $\frac{16}{5}$ has the greatest value.

53. A. $-\frac{3}{8}$

You can get the absolute values of the numbers by simply dropping all negative signs. Then you can put all the absolute values in decimal form and compare them:

$$-\frac{3}{8} \rightarrow 0.375$$

$$\frac{23}{50} \rightarrow 0.460$$

$$-0.47 \rightarrow 0.470$$

$$0.471 \rightarrow 0.471$$

$$\frac{5}{12} \rightarrow 0.41\overline{6}$$

To make the comparison easier, you can put extra 0s at the end of some decimals so all values have three digits after the decimal point. You can see that the lowest of all the absolute values in decimal form is 0.375, so of the numbers in the question, the one with the lowest absolute value is $-\frac{3}{8}$.

54. **C.** 134%, $\frac{27}{20}$, 1.36, $1\frac{9}{20}$, $1\frac{7}{10}$

Convert all the numbers to the same form. You can use a calculator, so decimal form may be easiest:

$$\frac{27}{20} = 1.35$$

$$1\frac{9}{20} = 1.45$$

$$134\% = 1.34$$

$$1.36 = 1.36$$

$$1\frac{7}{10} = 1.70$$

All the decimal forms are 1 followed by a decimal point and two digits. Look at the two digits after the decimal point in each converted form and determine their order. From least to greatest, the order is 1.34, 1.35, 1.36, 1.45, 1.70. Therefore, the order of the forms in the question, from least to greatest, is 134%, $\frac{27}{20}$, 1.36, $1\frac{9}{20}$, $1\frac{7}{10}$.

55. **E.** $\frac{105}{25}$, $4\frac{3}{20}$, $\frac{411}{100}$, 4.1, 409%

You can convert all the numbers to decimal form:

$$4.1 = 4.10$$

$$\frac{411}{100} = 4.11$$

$$\frac{105}{25} = 4.20$$

$$4\frac{3}{20} = 4.15$$

$$409\% = 4.09$$

Based on the converted forms of the numbers, the order of the forms in the question from greatest to least is $\frac{105}{25}$, $4\frac{3}{20}$, $\frac{411}{100}$, 4.1, 409%.

56. **B.** $-12\frac{11}{16}$

Convert the number in the question and the answer choices to decimal form. You can get the magnitudes (absolute values) of the converted forms by leaving out negative signs.

$$-12\frac{5}{8} \rightarrow 12.6250$$

$$1{,}250\% \rightarrow 12.5000$$

$$-12\frac{11}{16} \rightarrow 12.6875$$

$$12\frac{13}{24} \rightarrow 12.5416$$

$$-12.51 \rightarrow 12.5100$$

$$\frac{23}{2} \rightarrow 11.5000$$

From the magnitudes of the converted forms, you can see that the only choice with a greater magnitude than $-12\frac{5}{8}$ is $-12\frac{11}{16}$.

57. **A.** $-5\frac{4}{25}$, 5.14, $-\frac{128}{25}$

You can convert each number form in the question to decimal form, or you can easily convert each to mixed-number form with 100 in the denominator. You can find absolute values by simply dropping all negative signs.

$$5.14 \rightarrow 5\frac{14}{100}$$

$$-5\frac{4}{25} = -5\frac{4(4)}{25(4)}$$
$$= -5\frac{16}{100}$$
$$\rightarrow 5\frac{16}{100}$$

$$-\frac{128}{25} = -5\frac{3}{25}$$
$$= -5\frac{3(4)}{25(4)}$$
$$= -5\frac{12}{100}$$
$$\rightarrow 5\frac{12}{100}$$

Based on these conversions, the order of the absolute values of the number forms in the question, from greatest to least, is $-5\frac{4}{5}$, 5.14, $-\frac{128}{25}$.

58. **E.** 18

The distance is the same from one labeled coordinate to the next in every case. Some of the labels indicate that each coordinate is 3 units away from the adjacent ones. The number that's 3 more than 15 and 3 less than 21 is 18.

59. **E.** 1.1

The number that's halfway between two numbers, or the midpoint between them on a number line, is their average (mean):

$$\frac{-5.2+7.4}{2} = \frac{2.2}{2}$$
$$= 1.1$$

You can also test each choice by finding its distance from −5.2 and 7.4. The distance equals the higher number minus the lower one. The only choice that's the same distance from −5.2 and 7.4 is Choice (E).

60. **A. 18**

You can figure out the distance from P to S if you determine the distance from P to Q, because the distance from P to S is that distance, plus twice that distance, plus twice that.

The distance from P to R is 6 because $10 - 4 = 6$. Q is in a position in which its distance from P is half its distance from R. The sum of those distances is 6. Therefore, the distance from P to Q is a number that can be added to twice itself to get 6. That number is 2.

$$2 + 2(2) = 6$$

You could use algebra to determine that, but it's not necessary. Because the distance from P to Q is 2, you know that the distance from Q to R is 4 and that the distance from R to S is 8. The coordinate of P is 4, so the coordinate of S is $4 + 2 + 4 + 8$, or 18.

61. **E. The distance from A to B is equal to the distance from C to D.**

Drawing a number line with points A, B, C, and D is helpful for this problem.

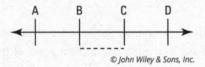

© John Wiley & Sons, Inc.

You can divide AC (the distance from A to C) into AB (the distance from A to B) and BC (the distance from B to C). The two distances are equal: $AB = BC$. You can also divide BD (the distance from B to D) into BC and CD. Those two distances are also equal: $BC = CD$. Because BC is equal to both AB and CD, AB and CD are equal to each other.

62. **A. 3.5**

The number that's halfway between two numbers, which is their midpoint on a number line, is the average (mean) of the two numbers. The average of two numbers is half their sum. The coordinate of M is 2, and the coordinate of W is 5. The average of 2 and 5 is 3.5:

$$\frac{2+5}{2} = \frac{7}{2}$$
$$= 3.5$$

Therefore, the coordinate of T is 3.5.

63. C. 29

After the first term, each term is 4 greater than the previous one. Four terms are shown. The seventh term is three terms past the fourth term, which is 17. That means 4 is added three more times after 17:

$$17 + 4 + 4 + 4 = 29$$

The seventh term is therefore 29.

64. B. 20

The second term is 3 more than the first, but that doesn't mean the sequence is arithmetic. However, you can test it to see if it is. If you add 3 to 17, you get 20. If you add 3 to that, you get 23. That justifies adding 3 each time to get the next term. It also proves that adding 3 to 17 to get the missing term is the correct method, so the answer is 20.

65. D. 3

In this sequence, adding the same number each time does not give you the next term. However, multiplying by 2 each time does. The sequence is therefore geometric. The number that can be multiplied by 2 to get 6 is 3.

66. E. 3

You can test each choice to see whether it works. If you start with 1 and multiply by the same number repeatedly to get four more terms, with the last one being 81, the number by which each term is multiplied can only be 3. The only choice that works is Choice (E).

$$1 \times 3 \times 3 \times 3 \times 3 = 81$$

67. A. Arithmetic

Each term after the first one is 5 greater than the preceding term. Because each term is the same number greater than the preceding one (after the first term), the sequence is arithmetic. If the sequence were geometric, each term would be multiplied by the same number in each case to get the next term.

68. **D. 15**

You can put the entire expression into your calculator and push the =
button. However, working out the problem on your own is great practice.
Your calculator won't understand expressions with exponents or variables.

Follow the order of operations by using GEMDAS (grouping symbols and
exponents, multiplication and division, and addition and subtraction):

$$2+3\times4+1=2+12+1$$
$$=14+1$$
$$=15$$

69. **A. Multiplying 5 by 2**

The G in GEMDAS stands for grouping symbols, such as parentheses.
Within the parentheses, there are no grouping symbols or exponents (the
E in GEMDAS). There is multiplication (the M), so the first step in
evaluating the expression is to multiply 5 by 2. The other choices violate
the correct order of operations.

70. **E. −3**

Follow the order of operations by using GEMDAS (grouping symbols and
exponents, multiplication and division, addition and subtraction).

$$\left(3\times8+2^2-4\times6\right)\times\left(-1\right)+1=\left(3\times8+4-4\times6\right)\times\left(-1\right)+1$$
$$=\left(24+4-24\right)\times\left(-1\right)+1$$
$$=\left(4\right)\times\left(-1\right)+1$$
$$=-4+1$$
$$=-3$$

The other choices can result from using false orders of operations and
other miscalculations.

71. **C. −30**

You can put the expression into your calculator, but using the traditional
method is good practice for order of operations situations in which you
can't.

Follow the order of operations by using GEMDAS:

$$-5\times4\div2+1+\left(-3\right)-24\div4\times3=-20\div2+1+\left(-3\right)-6\times3$$
$$=-10+1+\left(-3\right)-18$$
$$=-9+\left(-3\right)-18$$
$$=-12-18$$
$$=-30$$

72. B. 4

Follow the order of operations by using GEMDAS. Keep in mind that a fraction bar is a grouping symbol. It groups the numerator and also groups the denominator.

$$\frac{3\times2-1+3}{9-(6\times2-5)} = \frac{6-1+3}{9-(12-5)}$$

$$= \frac{8}{9-(7)}$$

$$= \frac{8}{2}$$

$$= 4$$

73. E. 21

Follow the order of operations by using GEMDAS. This problem has grouping symbols within grouping symbols. In such instances, work with the innermost grouping symbols first:

$$4\left(8-\left(2\times4-7\right)^3-5\right)^2+5 = 4\left(8-\left(8-7\right)^3-5\right)^2+5$$

$$= 4\left(8-\left(1\right)^3-5\right)^2+5$$

$$= 4\left(8-1-5\right)^2+5$$

$$= 4\left(2\right)^2+5$$

$$= 4\left(4\right)+5$$

$$= 16+5$$

$$= 21$$

74. A. 15

You can use your calculator for this problem. If you don't, follow the order of operations by using GEMDAS:

$$15\div3+2\times5 = 5+2\times5$$

$$= 5+10$$

$$= 15$$

75. C. $30\frac{2}{3}$

You can use your calculator for this problem, putting fractions in parentheses and using the ÷ in place of a fraction bar. Otherwise, follow the order of operations by using GEMDAS:

$$\frac{2}{3}+\frac{3}{4}(10\times3+10)=\frac{2}{3}+\frac{3}{4}(30+10)$$
$$=\frac{2}{3}+\frac{3}{4}(40)$$
$$=\frac{2}{3}+\frac{3(40)}{4}$$
$$=\frac{2}{3}+\frac{120}{4}$$
$$=\frac{2}{3}+30$$
$$=30\frac{2}{3}$$

76. B. $\frac{3}{4}$

You can use your calculator for this. Fractions can be put in parentheses, and the division symbol works as a substitute for the fraction bar.

Without using the calculator, you can follow the order of operations by using GEMDAS. Remember that fractions in final answers must be in simplest form.

$$\frac{1}{2}+\frac{5}{8}\times\frac{2}{5}=\frac{1}{2}+\frac{5(2)}{8(5)}$$
$$=\frac{1}{2}+\frac{10}{40}$$
$$=\frac{1(20)}{2(20)}+\frac{10}{40}$$
$$=\frac{20}{40}+\frac{10}{40}$$
$$=\frac{30}{40}$$
$$=\frac{3}{4}$$

77. D. −10

You can use the Praxis Core calculator to find the value of the expression, or you can strengthen your skills by following the order of operations with GEMDAS:

$$3+4-5\times6\div3-2+4\div2-7=3+4-30\div3-2+2-7$$
$$=3+4-10-2+2-7$$
$$=7-10-2+2-7$$
$$=-3-2+2-7$$
$$=-5+2-7$$
$$=-3-7$$
$$=-10$$

78.   **B. 52.59%**

Because the school has 110 boys and 122 girls, the total number of students is 232. Therefore, the portion of students who are girls is $\frac{122}{232}$. To convert that fraction to a percent, first convert it to a decimal by dividing the numerator by the denominator. The quotient, rounded to a few decimal places, is 0.52586. To convert that decimal to a percent, move the decimal point two places to the right and put a % after the result:

$$0.52586 = 52.586\%$$

When rounding to the nearest hundredth, you want to end up with two digits after the decimal point. Because third digit in 52.586% is greater than 5, round up:

$$52.586\% \rightarrow 52.59\%$$

Choices (A) and (E) were derived incorrectly, and they are also rounded to the nearest thousandth. The other choices are rounded quotients of false combinations of numbers involved in the problem.

79.   **E. 2%**

Before the change, Joe had 400 records in his collection. After the change, he had 408. That means the number of records in his collection went up by 8. The original number was 400, so the collection increased by $\frac{8}{400}$. To convert that portion to a percent, first convert it to a decimal by dividing the numerator by the denominator:

$$\frac{8}{400} = 0.02$$

To convert 0.02 to a percent, move the decimal point two places to the right and put a % after the result.

$$0.02 = 2\%$$

Joe's record collection went up by 2%.

80.   **C. 25% decrease**

The number of cookies went down by 10, so the change was a decrease. The amount of the decrease is 10 out of the original number, so it's $\frac{10}{40}$. To convert that fraction to a percent, first convert it to a decimal by dividing 10 by 40:

$$\frac{10}{40} = 0.25$$

You can convert that decimal form to percent form by moving the decimal point two places to the right and putting a % after what results:

$$0.25 = 25\%$$

The change was therefore a 25% decrease.

81. A. 40%

To convert a fraction to a percent, first convert the fraction to a decimal by dividing the numerator by the denominator:

$$\frac{2}{5} = 0.4$$

You can convert the decimal form to a percent by moving the decimal two places to the right and putting a % after the number:

$$0.4 = 40\%$$

82. A. $\frac{7}{50}$

Because 14% of the officers are rookies, $\frac{14}{100}$ of the officers are rookies. You can simplify that ratio by dividing the numerator and denominator by their greatest common factor, 2:

$$\frac{14}{100} = \frac{14 \div 2}{100 \div 2}$$
$$= \frac{7}{50}$$

83. A. $\frac{7}{8}$

The ratio of the number of miles Sebastian ran the first week to the number of miles he ran the second week is 42 to 48, which you can write in fraction form as $\frac{42}{48}$. You can simplify the fraction by dividing the numerator and denominator by their greatest common factor, which is 6:

$$\frac{42}{48} = \frac{42 \div 6}{48 \div 6}$$
$$= \frac{7}{8}$$

The simplest form of the fraction is Choice (A).

84. D. $\frac{1}{24}$

Because 2 U.S. states are not on the U.S. mainland and the country has 50 states, the U.S. has 48 states on its mainland: $50 - 2 = 48$. Therefore, the ratio of U.S. states not on the mainland to U.S. states that are on the mainland is $\frac{2}{48}$, which can be simplified to $\frac{1}{24}$.

85. B. $\frac{11}{2}$

The ratio of Dave's age to Luca's age is 66 to 12, or $\frac{66}{12}$. To put that fraction in simplest form, divide the numerator and denominator by their greatest common factor, 6:

$$\frac{66}{12} = \frac{66 \div 6}{12 \div 6}$$
$$= \frac{11}{2}$$

86. A. $\frac{13}{12}$

The ratio of Johnny's golf score on the first day to his score on the second day is 78 to 72, or $\frac{78}{72}$. To write that fraction in simplest form, divide the numerator and denominator by their greatest common factor, which is 6:

$$\frac{78}{72} = \frac{78 \div 6}{72 \div 6}$$
$$= \frac{13}{12}$$

87. C. $\frac{11}{12}$

The ratio of Trace's comedy videos to his drama videos is 132 to 144, or $\frac{132}{144}$. To put that in simplest form, divide 132 and 144 by their greatest common factor, 12:

$$\frac{132}{144} = \frac{132 \div 12}{144 \div 12}$$
$$= \frac{11}{12}$$

88. E. $\frac{61}{77}$

Because the number of football players in the first classroom is 8 and there are 30 students in the classroom, the ratio of students who play football to students who do not is $\frac{8}{22}$, which can be reduced to $\frac{4}{11}$. In the second classroom, 3 of the 10 students play football, so 7 do not. The ratio of students who play football to students who do not in that classroom is $\frac{3}{7}$. You can add the two ratios to get their sum:

$$\frac{4}{11} + \frac{3}{7} = \frac{4(7)}{11(7)} + \frac{3(11)}{7(11)}$$
$$= \frac{28}{77} + \frac{33}{77}$$
$$= \frac{61}{77}$$

89.   B. $\frac{2}{15}$

To find how much greater the Jar 1 ratio is than the Jar 2 ratio, subtract the Jar 1 ratio from the Jar 2 ratio. To do that, the fractions need to have the same denominator. Remember that multiplying a fraction's numerator and denominator by the same number is equivalent to multiplying the fraction by 1, and doing that doesn't change the value of the fraction.

$$\frac{1}{3} - \frac{1}{5} = \frac{1(5)}{3(5)} - \frac{1(3)}{5(3)}$$
$$= \frac{5}{15} - \frac{3}{15}$$
$$= \frac{2}{15}$$

90.   B. 984

To find 41% of 2,400, multiply 41% by 2,400. The easiest way to do that is to convert 41% to a decimal and multiply the decimal form by 2,400. To convert a percent to a decimal, drop the % and move the decimal point two places to the left. Remember that moving a decimal point two places to the left is the same as dividing by 100, so it compensates for a missing %.

$$0.41 \times 2,400 = 984$$

91.   B. 50%

The ratio of honor roll students on the track team to members of the track team is 11 to 22, or $\frac{11}{22}$. To convert that fraction to a percent, first convert it to decimal form by dividing 11 by 22:

$$\frac{11}{22} = 0.5$$

To convert the decimal form to percent form, move the decimal point two places to the right and put a % after the result. Moving a decimal point two places to the right is the same as multiplying by 100, and that compensates for introducing a %, which is a way of dividing by 100.

$$0.5 = 0.50$$
$$= 50\%$$

92.   E. 33

The sum of 4 and 7 is $4+7$. Triple that is 3 times that, or $3(4+7)$. To find the value of that expression, you can use the order of operations:

$$3(4+7) = 3(11)$$
$$= 33$$

93. **D. 99**

In mathematical language, 17 decreased by 8 is $17-8$, which has a value of 9. If 9 is multiplied by 2 more than itself, it is multiplied by 11. The product of 9 and 11 is 99.

94. **D. Sixteen more campers went rock climbing than canoeing.**

To find the number of campers who did each activity, multiply the percent for the activity by 400. You can multiply by the percents by converting the percentages to decimals.

$$\text{Canoers:} \quad 34\% \times 400 = 0.34 \times 400$$
$$= 136$$
$$\text{Hikers:} \quad 21\% \times 400 = 0.21 \times 400$$
$$= 84$$
$$\text{Rock climbers:} \quad 38\% \times 400 = 0.38 \times 400$$
$$= 152$$
$$\text{Birdwatchers:} \quad 17\% \times 400 = 0.17 \times 400$$
$$= 68$$

With those numbers, you can make calculations to determine which of the answer choices is true. The only true choice is Choice (D). The number of campers who went rock climbing is 152, and the number of campers who went canoeing is 136:

$$152 - 136 = 16$$

95. **D. 228**

The best way to answer this question is to first find the difference between the percent of students not in a listed political party and students who are in a listed political party. The number of students not in a listed political party is 54%. That is stated directly in the table. The number of students in a listed political party is the sum of 22%, 16%, and 8%. That sum is 46%. The difference between 54% and 46% is $54\% - 46\%$, or 8%. Because the difference is 8%, you can find the number of students by multiplying 8% by the number of students at the college. To do that, first convert 8% to a decimal; then multiply:

$$8\% \times 2,850 = 0.08 \times 2,850$$
$$= 228$$

96. **A. 927**

To find the number of penguins that left the island the first time, subtract $\frac{1}{4}$ of 824 from 824:

$$824 - \frac{1}{4}(824) = 824 - \frac{824}{4}$$
$$= 824 - 206$$
$$= 618$$

Immediately after the first penguin departure, 618 penguins remained on the island. For that number to increase by $\frac{1}{2}$, $\frac{1}{2}$ of 618 must be added to 618:

$$618 + \frac{1}{2}(618) = 618 + \frac{618}{2}$$
$$= 618 + 309$$
$$= 927$$

97. **D. 24**

To find $\frac{4}{7}$ of 42, multiply $\frac{4}{7}$ by 42:

$$\frac{4}{7} \times 42 = \frac{4}{7} \times \frac{42}{1}$$
$$= \frac{4(42)}{7(1)}$$
$$= \frac{168}{7}$$
$$= 24$$

98. **B. $\frac{34}{45}$**

To find the total portion of the book Karen read, add to portions for each day:

$$\frac{5}{9} + \frac{1}{5} = \frac{5(5)}{9(5)} + \frac{1(9)}{5(9)}$$
$$= \frac{25}{45} + \frac{9}{45}$$
$$= \frac{34}{45}$$

99. **B. 680**

All 34 team members have 5 stripes, and every one of those stripes has 4 stars. Put another way, there are 34 sets of 5 sets of 4 stars. The total number of stars is therefore the product of 34, 5, and 4:

$$34 \times 5 \times 4 = 680$$

100. E. $\frac{5}{84}$

The portion of the members of the organization who are women from Texas who ride a bus to work is $\frac{5}{8}$ of $\frac{3}{7}$ of $\frac{2}{9}$ of the people in the organization. A fraction of another number is the same as the fraction times the other number, so $\frac{5}{8}$ of $\frac{3}{7}$ of $\frac{2}{9}$ is equal to $\frac{5}{8} \times \frac{3}{7} \times \frac{2}{9}$:

$$\frac{5}{8} \times \frac{3}{7} \times \frac{2}{9} = \frac{5 \times 3 \times 2}{8 \times 7 \times 9}$$
$$= \frac{30}{504}$$
$$= \frac{15}{252}$$
$$= \frac{5}{84}$$

101. E. 227

At 5:15 p.m., it was an hour after 4:15 p.m., so the number of customers in the grocery store was 37×5, and the number customers in the decoration store was $12 \times 3\frac{1}{2}$. The sum of the number of customers in the grocery store and the number of customers in the decoration store at 5:15 p.m. was therefore the sum of 37×5 and $12 \times 3\frac{1}{2}$.

You can multiply by $3\frac{1}{2}$ if you convert it to an improper fraction, or you can convert $3\frac{1}{2}$ to the decimal 3.5, because $\frac{1}{2}$ is 0.5. If you go that route, you can use your calculator to do the calculations.

$$37 \times 5 + 12 \times 3\frac{1}{2} = 185 + 12 \times \frac{7}{2}$$
$$= 185 + \frac{84}{2}$$
$$= 185 + 42$$
$$= 227$$

102. A. $560

At exactly a year, the amount of interest accrued for the savings account is 12% of $500:

$$12\% \times 500 = 0.12 \times 500$$
$$= 60$$

The interest is $60. That amount is added to the account on top of the $500 that was already there:

$$500 + 60 = 560$$

The amount of money in the account exactly a year after Edward put $500 in it is $560.

103. C. $60.48

The total price of the hat is $56 plus 8% of $56:

$$56 + 8\%(56) = 56 + 0.08(56)$$
$$= 56 + 4.48$$
$$= 60.48$$

The total price of the hat is $60.48.

104. A. Yes

You can see whether two fractions are equal by making a proportion with them (or setting them equal to each other) and testing the proportion by cross-multiplying. For a true proportion, the cross products are equal. In other words, the product of the numerator of one fraction and the denominator of the other fraction is the same in both possible cases:

$$\frac{3}{11} \overset{?}{=} \frac{9}{33}$$
$$3(33) \overset{?}{=} 9(11)$$
$$99 = 99$$

The cross products of the proportion are equal, so the proportion is true. Therefore, the two fractions are equal.

Another approach is to have both fractions in simplest form and see whether the simplest form is the same for both.

105. E. 0.148

There are several ways to work problems like this. However, time matters a great deal on the Praxis Core exam, so here's what might be the fastest and easiest method for working these problems.

In the metric system, converting units involves simply moving the decimal point. You need to determine two things:

- **The direction the decimal point needs to be moved:** Because a meter is longer than a centimeter, there are fewer meters in a given distance than there are centimeters, so the number gets smaller when you convert from centimeters to meters. Because the number gets smaller, move the decimal point to the left.

- **How many places you need to move the decimal point:** Move it the number of places *centi-* and the base unit (meter, gram, liter) are from each other on the metric prefix chart. *Centi-* is two places from the base unit, so move the decimal point two places to the left.

Therefore, 14.8 cm = 0.148 m.

106.   B. 571

A deciliter is smaller than a hectoliter, so there are more deciliters than hectoliters in a given volume. Therefore, the number needs to get bigger. You thus need to move the decimal point to the right. *Deci-* and *hecto-* are three places apart on the metric prefix chart, so move the decimal point three places to the right:

$$0.571 \text{ hL} = 571 \text{ dL}$$

107.   A. 4,932.7

There are more centigrams in a given mass than decagrams because a centigram is smaller than a decagram. Therefore, the answer to this problem is greater than 4.9327, so you need to move the decimal point to the right. The number of places you should move the decimal point to the right is three because *deka-* and *centi-* are three places apart on the metric prefix chart.

$$4.9327 \text{ dag} = 4,932.7 \text{ cg}$$

108.   E. 54,000,000

There are a lot more millimeters than kilometers in a given distance, so the number you're looking for is a lot bigger than 54. That means you need to move the decimal point (54 = 54.0) to the right. Because *kilo-* and *milli-* are six places apart on the metric prefix chart, you need to move the decimal point six places to the right:

$$54 \text{ km} = 54,000,000 \text{ mm}$$

Alexia drove 54,000,000 millimeters (probably give or take a few!) on the Natchez Trace.

109.   B. 0.00038

There are fewer kiloliters in a given volume than there are liters, so you need to move the decimal point to the left. *Kilo-* and base units are three places apart on the metric prefix chart, so move the decimal point three places to the left:

$$0.38 \text{ L} = 0.00038 \text{ kL}$$

110.   D. 48

A quick and simple method you can use is to replace the word "feet" with "12 inches," because a foot is 12 inches. You're looking for the number of inches in this problem, so you want to work with "inches" instead of converting an inch to $\frac{1}{12}$ feet, which you could do if you were looking for a number of feet.

111.   A. $\frac{1}{3}$

In this problem, you're looking for a number of feet, so work with "feet":

$$4 \text{ inches} = 4 \times \frac{1}{12} \text{ feet}$$
$$= \frac{4}{12} \text{ feet}$$
$$= \frac{1}{3} \text{ feet}$$

112.   D. 72

Because a gallon contains 16 cups, you can replace "gallons" with "16 cups":

$$4.5 \text{ gallons} = 4.5 \times 16 \text{ cups}$$
$$= 72 \text{ cups}$$

113.   A. 0.28125

You're looking for a number gallons here, so work with gallons. A cup is $\frac{1}{16}$ of a gallon, so replace "cups" with "$\frac{1}{16}$ gallon":

$$4.5 \text{ cups} = 4.5 \times \frac{1}{16} \text{ gallon}$$
$$= \frac{4.5}{16} \text{ gallon}$$
$$= 0.28125 \text{ gallon}$$

114.   A. 3.456

Because you're looking for a number of kilometers, you need to express the two parts of the full distance in kilometers. The first part is already in kilometers. The second one isn't.

Because there are fewer kilometers in a given distance than meters, you need to move the decimal point in 456.0 (that's what 456 is) to the left. The base unit (*meter*) and *kilo-* are three places apart in the metric prefix chart, so move the decimal point three places to the left. The result is 0.456 kilometers. Now that you have both parts in kilometers, you can combine them:

$$3 + 0.456 = 3.456$$

Simon walked a total of 3.456 kilometers.

If you know the general difference between a kilometer and a meter, you can answer this question without doing the calculations. Adding a few hundred meters isn't going to increase the number of kilometers by an order of magnitude (from 3 to 30, 300, or 3,000), so Choice (A) is the only reasonable answer.

115. **B. 1.103**

The choices are in kiloliters, so convert 42.79 hectoliters to kiloliters. The number of kiloliters in a volume is less than the number of hectoliters, so move the decimal point to the left. *Kilo-* and *hecto-* are one place apart on the metric prefix chart, so move the decimal point one place to the left. The result is 4.279 kiloliters. Next, subtract 4.279 from 5.382. You can use your calculator.

$$5.382 - 4.279 = 1.103$$

What remains in the drum is 1.103 kiloliters of the chemical.

116. **B. 804.07 decigrams**

The choices are in decigrams, so make sure your addition involves only decigrams for mass units. You need to convert 0.08 kilograms to a number of decigrams. Because the number of decigrams in a given volume is greater than the number of kilograms, you need to move the decimal point to the right. *Deci-* and *kilo-* are four places apart on the metric prefix chart, so move the decimal point four places to the right. A mass of 0.08 kilograms is a mass of 800 decigrams. The sum of 800 and 4.07 is 804.07, so the mass of the frog after the growth is 804.07 decigrams.

117. **C. 36 feet**

The choices are in feet, so convert 7 yards to a number of feet and then add it to 15 feet. A yard is 3 feet.

$$7 \text{ yards} = 7 \times 3 \text{ feet}$$
$$= 21 \text{ feet}$$

The sum of 15 feet and 21 feet is 36 feet, so the tower is 36 feet tall.

118. C. 42 feet south

You need to work with one type of unit so you can compare the two distances. All the choices are in feet, so convert the given distances to feet:

$$2{,}088 \text{ inches} = 2{,}088 \times \frac{1}{12} \text{ feet}$$
$$= \frac{2{,}088}{12} \text{ feet}$$
$$= 174 \text{ feet}$$

$$72 \text{ yards} = 72 \times 3 \text{ feet}$$
$$= 216 \text{ feet}$$

Because the snail went 174 feet north and then 216 feet (a greater distance) south, it ended up south of its starting point. The distance south of the starting point is the difference between 216 feet and 174 feet:

$$216 - 174 = 42$$

The snail's final position is 42 feet south of its starting point.

119. C. 14

The number of 2-pint bottles that can be filled is the number of sets of 2 pints that are in 3.5 gallons. First convert 3.5 gallons to pints:

$$3.5 \text{ gallons} = 3.5 \times 8 \text{ pints}$$
$$= 28 \text{ pints}$$

The number of 2-pint sets in 28 pints is equal to 28 divided by 2:

$$28 \div 2 = 14$$

Therefore, 3.5 gallons can fill 14 2-pint bottles.

120. C. 5 miles per hour

The problem gives you a distance and a time, and it asks for a rate. You thus need to use the distance formula:

$$\text{distance} = \text{rate} \times \text{time}$$
$$d = rt$$

Replace each variable with its known value, where possible, and then solve for r, the rate (speed). The value of d is 15 miles, and the value of t is 3 hours.

$$d = rt$$
$$15 \text{ miles} = r \times 3 \text{ hours}$$
$$\frac{15 \text{ miles}}{3 \text{ hours}} = \frac{r \times 3 \text{ hours}}{3 \text{ hours}}$$
$$5 \text{ miles/hour} = r$$

121. D. 5.7

The speed (rate) at which the trains are moving apart is the sum of 56 kilometers per hour and 72 kilometers per hour, or 128 kilometers per hour. The distance in question is 729.6 kilometers. The problem asks how long the trains take to cover this distance. You can use the distance formula to determine the time. Substitute the known values in for the variables and solve for t:

$$d = rt$$
$$729.6 = 128t$$
$$\frac{729.6}{128} = \frac{128t}{128}$$
$$5.7 = t$$

Because the calculations involve kilometers per hour, the value of t is in hours.

122. A. 24.6 inches per second

You can find the answer by converting 41 yards to inches and a minute to seconds:

$$41 \text{ yards} = 41 \times 3 \text{ feet}$$
$$= 41 \times 3 \times 12 \text{ inches}$$
$$= 1,476 \text{ inches}$$

$$1 \text{ minute} = 60 \text{ seconds}$$

Therefore, 41 yards per minute is equal to $\frac{1,476 \text{ inches}}{60 \text{ seconds}}$, which you can reduce to 24.6 inches per second.

123. E. 1,714.29 feet per minute

The question asks for a rate in feet per minute, so convert 40 yards to feet and 4.2 seconds to minutes:

$$40 \text{ yards} = 40 \times 3 \text{ feet}$$
$$= 120 \text{ feet}$$

$$4.2 \text{ seconds} = 4.2 \times \frac{1}{60} \text{ minutes}$$
$$= \frac{4.2}{60} \text{ minutes}$$
$$= 0.07 \text{ minutes}$$

Now, write a ratio of those quantities and reduce it:

$$\frac{120 \text{ feet}}{0.07 \text{ minutes}} = 1,714.285714\ldots \text{ feet/minute}$$

Round to the nearest hundredth, which is two places after the decimal point. The third place after the decimal point is 5, so round up:

$$1,714.285714 \rightarrow 1,714.29$$

The correct answer, rounded to the nearest hundredth, is 1,714.29 feet per minute.

124. B. 26xy

The two terms are like terms because they have the same variables with exponents of 1. To combine like terms, add the coefficients and put the sum next to the variable-and-exponent combination:

$$12xy + 14xy = (12 + 14)xy$$
$$= 26xy$$

125. E. $w^2 + 3w - 10$

To multiply binomials, use the FOIL (First terms, Outer terms, Inner terms, Last terms) technique:

$$(w-2)(w+5) = w(w) + 5(w) + (-2)(w) + (-2)(5)$$
$$= w^2 + 5w - 2w - 10$$
$$= w^2 + 3w - 10$$

126. A. $4a + 3b$

Because a represents 2 pounds, $4a$ represents 8 pounds (because 4 is the number by which 2 must be multiplied to get 8). Because b represents 4 ounces, 3 times that represents 12 ounces. Thus, $3b$ is equivalent to 12 ounces. An amount of 8 pounds and 12 ounces is therefore symbolized by $4a + 3b$.

127. D. $-4p^3q^5r$

The two terms are like terms because they have the same combination of variables and exponents. The sum of like terms is the sum of their coefficients, followed by their variable-and-exponent combination:

$$3p^3q^5r + (-7p^3q^5r) = (3-7)p^3q^5r$$
$$= -4p^3q^5r$$

128.   **B.** $jw^{15}x^{30}y^{15}$

When terms with exponents are raised to powers, multiply the exponent representing the power-raise by each exponent in the term. Remember that a variable written without an exponent is understood to have an exponent of 1.

$$j\left(\left(wx^2y\right)^3\right)^5 = j\left(wx^2y\right)^{3(5)}$$
$$= j\left(wx^2y\right)^{15}$$
$$= jw^{1(15)}x^{2(15)}y^{1(15)}$$
$$= jw^{15}x^{30}y^{15}$$

129.   **C.** $-17x^2y^2$

All the choices except Choice (C) have the same variable-and-exponent combination as $-17x^4y^2$. The x in $-17x^2y^2$ has 2 for an exponent instead of 4, so Choice (C) is the correct answer.

130.   **D.** $\dfrac{6}{35}a^2b^2$

To multiply fractions, write the product of the numerators over the product of the denominators. Then reduce if necessary. To multiply variables, add each variable's exponents.

$$\frac{2}{5}ab \times \frac{3}{7}ab = \frac{2(3)}{5(7)}a^{1+1}b^{1+1}$$
$$= \frac{6}{35}a^2b^2$$

131.   **A.** $72f^9g^9h^7$

To multiply terms, multiply their coefficients, and multiply their variables by adding the exponents for each variable:

$$\left(9f^4g^4h^7\right)\left(8f^5g^5\right) = (9)(8)f^{4+5}g^{4+5}h^7$$
$$= 72f^9g^9h^7$$

132. B. k

Because j, k, and m are consecutive integers in order from least to greatest, k is 1 more than j and m is 2 more than j. You can therefore represent k as $j+1$ and m as $j+2$. To find one-third of the sum of the integers, add those three expressions and divide by 3:

$$\frac{j+k+m}{3} = \frac{j+j+1+j+2}{3}$$
$$= \frac{3j+3}{3}$$
$$= \frac{3j}{3} + \frac{3}{3}$$
$$= j+1$$

Because $j+1$ is how you defined k, the answer is k. None of the other choices are equal to $j+1$.

133. D. x^2y^2z

The product of Bill's and Michael's ages is the product of xy and xyz. To multiply terms, first multiply their coefficients. To multiply variables, add the coefficients for each variable. (Remember that a variable with no written coefficient has an understood coefficient of 1, and a variable without a written exponent is understood to have an exponent of 1.)

$$(xy)(xyz) = (1)(1)x^{1+1}y^{1+1}z$$
$$= 1x^2y^2z$$
$$= x^2y^2z$$

134. A. $q+4$

There are more complicated methods, but you can multiply $p-7$ by each choice until you find the correct one. The only choice that will result in the product in the question is Choice (A). Because all the choices are binomials, you can use the FOIL (First terms, Outer terms, Inner terms, Last terms) technique:

$$(p-7)(q+4) = p(q) + p(4) + (-7)(q) + (-7)(4)$$
$$= pq + 4p - 7q - 28$$

135.

B. $-22\left(2g^4h^3j^{14}g^4h\right)$

Multiply the coefficients of the terms and then multiply the variables by adding the exponents for each variable. Write the coefficients' product next to the variables' products.

$$4g^3h^2j^6\left(-11g^5h^2j^8\right)=4(-11)g^{3+5}h^{2+2}j^{6+8}$$
$$=-44g^8h^4j^{14}$$

Next, determine which choice is equal to $-44g^8h^4j^{14}$ by using the same multiplication method for each choice until you find the answer. The only choice that is equal to $-44g^8h^4j^{14}$ is Choice (B):

$$-22\left(2g^4h^3j^{14}g^4h\right)=-22(2)g^{4+4}h^{3+1}j^{14}$$
$$=-44g^8h^4j^{14}$$

136.

E. $\sqrt{pr}=\pm q$

You can write ratios as fractions, and when two ratios are equal, their cross products are equal. Set up the proportion $\dfrac{p}{q}=\dfrac{q}{r}$ and find the cross products. (A *cross product* is a product of the numerator of one fraction and the denominator of the other fraction.) In this case, the cross products are $p(r)$ and $q(q)$. They're equal. Thus, $pr=q^2$. You can use that equation to determine which choice is correct.

Because $pr=q^2$ and the square of a number is always equal to the square of its opposite, $\sqrt{pr}$ is equal to either q or $-q$. Square roots always have positive numerical values, but q could be a negative number. Thus, $-q$ could be a positive number.

137.

E. $2m$

All the terms in the expression are like terms because they all have only m for a variable, and m has an understood exponent of 1 in every term. A term with no written coefficient has an understood coefficient of 1. To combine like terms, add the coefficients and put the result next to the variable-and-exponent combination:

$$5m-m+m-m-2m=(5-1+1-1-2)m$$
$$=2m$$

The other choices have the correct variable component but wrong coefficients.

138.   **A.** $3jk - 7$

Think about what happens when you add or multiply even and/or odd numbers:

- **Even sum:** The sum of two even numbers or two odd numbers is always even.

- **Odd sum:** The sum of an even number and an odd number is always an odd number. Because 1 more than an even number is an odd number, any odd number added to an even number results in an odd number.

- **Even product:** An even number times an even or odd number is always even. Multiplication is a matter of adding a number a given number of times. Adding 2 to an even number results in an even number, so adding any multiple of 2 to an even number results in an even number.

- **Odd product:** An odd number times an odd number is always odd. Every odd number is 1 more than an even number, and that extra 1 must be added an odd number of times to get an even number. That's why the product of two odd numbers is odd in every case.

Because of these principles and the fact that j is an even number and k is an odd number, the only choice that represents an odd number is Choice (A). The product of j and k is even, and an odd number times an even number is even. The difference of an even number minus an odd number is odd.

There's another way to approach this problem: Because the rules discussed here are universal, you can make up values for j and k and put them into each choice. If you give j an even value and k an odd value and your calculations are correct, you'll see that only Choice (A) has an odd value.

139.   **B.** $(c+4)(c+3)$

Because the trinomial in question has only integer exponents for the one variable, which has a highest exponent of 2, you may be able to perform reverse FOIL. As it turns out, you can. You can use trial and error and see that the full factorization of $c^2 + 7c + 12$ is $(c+4)(c+3)$, but there's a shortcut. The question is multiple-choice, and you can perform FOIL on the choices given until you find the choice that is equal to $c^2 + 7c + 12$:

$$(c+4)(c+3) = c(c) + c(3) + 4(c) + 4(3)$$
$$= c^2 + 3c + 4c + 12$$
$$= c^2 + 7c + 12$$

None of the other choices have a product of $c^2 + 7c + 12$.

140.   B. $10xy\left(5x^2y - y^2 + 4\right)$

The first step in algebraic factoring of multiple-term expressions is to look for a greatest common factor (GCF) and factor it out of the expression if there is one. In this case, you can factor $10xy$ out of every term because every coefficient is divisible by 10 and every term has x and y in it. The lowest exponent for x in the terms is 1, and the lowest exponent of y is 1 (the 1 is understood in both cases). The variables of the greatest common factor are therefore x and y, both understood to have an exponent of 1. The exponent on each variable in the GCF is always the lowest exponent of that variable in the multiple-term expression.

Because $10xy$ is the greatest common factor, factor it out of the expression and put it next to parentheses; inside the parentheses, you need to write the number of times $10xy$ goes into each term. You can figure that out by writing the number of times 10 goes into the coefficient of each term; next to that number, represent each variable with an exponent that's the number that must be added to the exponent in the GCF to get the exponent in the given expression.

There's also an easier route. You can find the product of each choice until you get a product of $50x^3y^2 - 10xy^3 + 40xy$; however, the correct choice must have a greatest common factor of 1 for the expression in the parentheses. The only choice that meets those requirements is Choice (B). You can multiply each choice by using the distributive property:

$$10xy\left(5x^2y - y^2 + 4\right) = 10xy\left(5x^2y\right) - 10xy\left(y^2\right) + 10xy\left(4\right)$$
$$= 10\left(5\right)x^{1+2}y^{1+1} - 10xy^{1+2} + 10\left(4\right)xy$$
$$= 50x^3y^2 - 10xy^3 + 40xy$$

There's an even quicker way to eliminate incorrect answer choices: You can multiply the expression outside the parentheses by the last term and note that Choice (B) is the only one that gives you $40xy$.

141.   D. $5a^4b^3c^{10}$

To find the greatest common factor of the two terms, find the greatest common factor of the coefficients and write it next to each common variable. Give each common variable the lowest exponent it has in the terms. The greatest common factor of 35 and 20 is 5, the lowest exponent of a in the terms is 4, the lowest exponent of b is 3, and the lowest exponent of c is 10. Thus, the greatest common factor of the two terms is $5a^4b^3c^{10}$.

142. B. $5(h-5)(h-4)$

Because the expression has more than one term, first look for a greatest common factor (GCF) for the terms. The GCF is 5, so put it to the left of a set of parentheses and write how many times it goes into each term:

$$5h^2 - 45h + 100 = 5(h^2 - 9h + 20)$$

Because the resulting expression in parentheses is a trinomial in which the variable has all integer exponents and the highest variable exponent is 2, you may be able to factor the expression through reverse FOIL. In fact, you can.

You can also look at the choices and identify the ones in which 5 is beside parentheses. Of those choices, look for the one in which the product of the binomials is $h^2 - 9h + 20$. It's Choice (B). The product of the binomials times 5 equals the trinomial asked about in the question:

$$5(h-5)(h-4) = 5(h(h) + (-4)(h) + (-5)(h) + (-5)(-4))$$
$$= 5(h^2 - 4h - 5h + 20)$$
$$= 5(h^2 - 9h + 20)$$
$$= 5h^2 - 45h + 100$$

143. C. $9m^8 n^{14} p^{11}$

For an algebraic term to be a factor of another term, the coefficient must be a factor and all the variables must have exponents lower than their exponents in the second term. All the choices have coefficients that are factors of 18, but in Choice (C), n^{14} has an exponent of 14, which is larger than n's exponent in $18m^8 n^{11} p^{15}$.

144. $28w^5 x^8 y^5 - 16w^9 x^{10} y^5$

The question implies that the expression in question is a full factorization, so you don't need to make sure it is. To answer this question, multiply the outside term by the inside expression using the distributive property.

$$4w^4 x^7 y^3 (7wxy^2 - 4w^5 x^3 y^2) = 4w^4 x^7 y^3 (7wxy^2) - 4w^4 x^7 y^3 (4w^5 x^3 y^2)$$
$$= 4(7)w^{4+1} x^{7+1} y^{3+2} - 4(4)w^{4+5} x^{7+3} y^{3+2}$$
$$= 28w^5 x^8 y^5 - 16w^9 x^{10} y^5$$

145.   **A.** $(q-8)(q+4)$

The trinomial in question is in the right form, so you can perform reverse FOIL on it. That process involves trying binomial combinations until you find one that gives you the polynomial in question when you perform FOIL. Because you have multiple choices for this question, you can limit your trial-and-error to those options. The only one that works is Choice (A).

$$(q-8)(q+4) = q(q) + q(4) + (-8)(q) + (-8)(4)$$
$$= q^2 + 4q - 8q - 32$$
$$= q^2 - 4q - 32$$

146.   **D.** $42xy^2$

The first thing to look for is which choices have $6xy$ for a factor. $6xy$ must be a factor of a term to be a greatest common factor of it and $24x^2y$. $6xy$ is not a factor of Choice (A) because 6 isn't a factor of 8, and $6xy$ isn't a factor of Choice (B) because y does not go into $12x$. $6xy$ is also not a factor of Choice (C) because x doesn't go into $24y$. And $6xy$ isn't a factor of Choice (E) because 6 isn't a factor of 3.

Alternatively, you can eliminate Choices (A) and (E) because their coefficients, 8 and 3, aren't multiples of 6. And you can eliminate Choices (B) and (C) because the correct answer needs both an x and a y. That leaves Choice (D) to consider. $6xy$ is a factor of $42xy^2$. Because 6 is the greatest common factor of 24 and 42, and because x has a lowest exponent of 1 and y has a lowest exponent of 1 in $24x^2y$ and $42xy^2$, $6xy$ is the greatest common factor of $24x^2y$ and $42xy^2$.

147.   **E.** $7a^2b^5 - 5ab$

You can determine what term $11a^4b$ must be multiplied by to get each term in the binomial. Because 11 is multiplied by 7 to get 77, a^4 is multiplied by a^2 to get a^6 (because $4 + 2 = 6$), and b is multiplied by b^5 to get b^6, you know that $11a^4b$ is multiplied by $7a^2b^5$ to obtain a product of $77a^6b^6$; that narrows down your choices to (D) and (E). By the same rules, $11a^4b$ must be multiplied by $-5ab$ for a product of $-55a^5b^2$. Therefore, $11a^4b$ must be multiplied by $7a^2b^5 - 5ab$ to get a product of $77a^6b^6 - 55a^5b^2$, so the correct answer is Choice (E).

148.   B. $4xyz + 1$

Because 12 goes into 48 four times and into 12 one time, the first term of the answer should begin with 4, and the second term of the answer must begin with 1. The next issue to consider is what exponents the variables in the answer should have. When a variable with an exponent is multiplied by the same variable with an exponent, the product is that variable with the sum of the two exponents. Because 7 is 1 less than 8, 8 is 1 less than 9, and 9 is 1 less than 10, each variable of the first term of the answer needs an exponent of 1. The second term of the binomial in the question is exactly the same as what the question says is factored out of the binomial, and it goes into itself 1 time. Therefore, the number of times $12x^7y^8z^9$ goes into $48x^8y^9z^{10} + 12x^7y^8z^9$ is $4xyz + 1$. Remember that a variable with no exponent presented with it is understood to have an exponent of 1.

149.   A. $3x^2 + 15x - 72$

You can multiply the three products of the expression in the question to find the answer. The question itself implies that the factorization is full. Use FOIL to multiply $(x - 3)(x + 8)$, and multiply the result by 3:

$$3(x-3)(x+8) = 3\big(x(x) + x(8) + (-3)(x) + (-3)(8)\big)$$
$$= 3\big(x^2 + 8x - 3x - 24\big)$$
$$= 3\big(x^2 + 5x - 24\big)$$
$$= 3x^2 + 15x - 72$$

150.   C and E. $7p^9q^5r$ and $14p^8q^7r^{11}$

Choice (C) is correct because 7 is a factor of 28 and each variable in the term has an exponent less than or equal to what it has in $28p^{10}q^7r^{12}$. Choice (E) is right because 14 is a factor of 28 and each variable has an exponent less than or equal to what it has in $28p^{10}q^7r^{12}$.

Choice (A) is incorrect because the exponent for q is greater than q's exponent in $28p^{10}q^7r^{12}$. Choice (B) is wrong because the exponent for p is too high. Choice (D) is incorrect because $28p^{10}q^7r^{12}$ does not have a v in it.

151.   D. $y - 8$

Test each binomial until you find the one that works. You can square the final term of each binomial to see which one has a square of 64, because the last-terms product of FOIL will be the second term of the binomial times itself. That rules out Choices (B) and (C).

Because the given trinomial has a negative term in it, the binomial that is squared to get it must have a negative in it. Choice (A) therefore isn't a possibility.

That leaves Choices (D) and (E). You can square each binomial by multiplying it by itself using FOIL. The choice that works is Choice (D).

$$(y-8)(y-8) = y(y) + y(-8) + (-8)(y) + (-8)(-8)$$
$$= y^2 - 8y - 8y + 64$$
$$= y^2 - 16y + 64$$

152.   A. $27jk^4m^2$

You can determine the greatest common factor of the two terms by finding the greatest common factor of the coefficients and then finding the lower exponent of each variable's exponents. The greatest common factor of 27 and 54 is 27; as for the exponents, 1 is less than 10, 4 is less than 5, and 2 is less than 8. Therefore, the greatest common factor of $27jk^5m^2$ and $54j^{10}k^4m^8$ is $27jk^4m^2$. Choice (A) is correct.

None of the other choices even have the correct coefficient, but Choices (B) and (C) have the right variable-and-exponent combination. The coefficient in Choices (C) and (D) is 54, which is a multiple, not a factor, of 27.

153.   D. $a+7$

You can use try using reverse FOIL to factor the trinomial. It works in this case. Because the coefficient of a^2 in $a^2 + 11a + 28$ is 1, you can simply find two numbers that have a product of 28 and a sum of 11. Those numbers are 7 and 4. Those are what you need to add to a in each set of parentheses:

$$a^2 + 11a + 28 = (a+7)(a+4)$$

You can FOIL to make sure the binomials have the necessary product. Neither of the binomials can be factored further, so they're the only factors of the trinomial, other than 1. The only binomial that's an answer choice is $a+7$.

154.   D. $u+7$

You can eliminate Choice (A), because 1 is always a factor. When factoring an algebraic expression with more than one term, first check for a greatest common factor other than 1. In this case, you can factor 2 out of every term:

$$2u^2 - 8u - 42 = 2(u^2 - 4u - 21)$$

Because 2 is a factor, you can eliminate Choice (E).

Next, factor the trinomial through reverse FOIL. Because u^2 has a coefficient understood to be 1, you can look for two numbers that have a product of -21 and a sum of -4. You'll add those numbers to u in the parentheses. Remember that the result is multiplied by 2 to get the given trinomial:

$$2u^2 - 8u - 42 = 2\left(u^2 - 4u - 21\right)$$
$$= 2\left(u - 7\right)\left(u + 3\right)$$

The result can't be factored further. It shows that the only factors of $2u^2 - 8u - 42$ are 1, 2, $u - 7$, and $u + 3$. The only choice that is not one of those expressions is Choice (D).

155. **B.** $16x - 4$

To simplify the expression, combine the like terms:

$$19x + 4 - 3x - 8 = \left(19 - 3\right)x + \left(4 - 8\right)$$
$$= 16x - 4$$

156. **C.** $5x^2y + 7xy^2$

You can combine the like terms to simplify the expression. *Like terms* have the same variables, and each variable has the same exponent in each of the like terms.

To combine like terms, add their coefficients; the variable-and-exponent combinations that the terms have in common go to the right of the new coefficients:

$$8x^2y - 5xy^2 + 12xy^2 - 3x^2y = \left(8 - 3\right)x^2y + \left(-5 + 12\right)xy^2$$
$$= 5x^2y + 7xy^2$$

157. **E.** $\dfrac{a^4b^3c^3}{5}$

You can reduce the coefficient ratio to $\frac{1}{5}$ and then reduce the variable ratios by subtracting bottom exponents from top exponents:

$$\frac{4a^7b^5c^8}{20a^3b^2c^5} = \frac{1a^{7-3}b^{5-2}c^{8-5}}{5}$$
$$= \frac{a^4b^3c^3}{5}$$

158. **B.** $\frac{x+8}{x-7}$

To determine how the rational expression can be reduced, factor the numerator and denominator. In this case, you can use reverse FOIL. Then cancel any factor that is a factor of both the numerator and denominator.

$$\frac{x^2+6x-16}{x^2-9x+14} = \frac{(x+8)(x-2)}{(x-7)(x-2)}$$
$$= \frac{x+8}{x-7}$$

159. **E.** $2pq$

The terms of the expression are like terms, so they can be combined:

$$9pq - 7pq = (9-7)pq$$
$$= 2pq$$

160. **C.** $4x^2 - 5x + 12$

Subtracting a multiple-term expression involves subtracting the entire expression, not just the first term in it. The minus sign before it applies to every term in the expression. The clearest way to work such a problem is to put a plus sign before the parentheses and change the sign of every term in the expression in parentheses; subtracting a value is the same as adding its opposite. Then you can combine like terms:

$$12x^2 - 3x + 4 - (8x^2 + 2x - 8) = 12x^2 - 3x + 4 + (-8x^2 - 2x + 8)$$
$$= 4x^2 - 5x + 12$$

161. **D.** $\frac{u+8}{u+3}$

Factor the numerator and denominator. Then cancel any expression that's a factor of the numerator and denominator.

$$\frac{u^2+13u+40}{u^2+8u+15} = \frac{(u+8)(u+5)}{(u+3)(u+5)}$$
$$= \frac{u+8}{u+3}$$

162. **E.** $17x - 3y - 5$

Combine like terms by combining their coefficients or constants and keeping the variables (unless a coefficient combination results in 0, which none do in this case).

$$8x - 7 + 2y + 9x - 5y + 2 = 8x + 9x + 2y - 5y + 2 - 7$$
$$= (8+9)x + (2-5)y + (2-7)$$
$$= 17x + (-3y) + (-5)$$
$$= 17x - 3y - 5$$

163. A. –1

Expressions involving subtraction that have reversed minuend and subtrahend are opposites; in other words, when a binomial has a minus sign in the middle, switching the terms on opposite sides of the minus sign results in a binomial of opposite value. Any value divided by its opposite is equal to –1. Therefore, the value of the rational expression in question here is –1. It cannot have any other value.

164. E. $3x^4y$

You can simplify the rational expression by reducing the coefficient ratio and subtracting bottom-variable exponents from top-variable exponents, because the coefficients and variable components are factors.

$$\frac{9x^8y^4z^2}{3x^3y^2z^2} = \frac{3x^{8-4}y^{4-3}z^{2-2}}{1}$$
$$= \frac{3x^4y^1z^0}{1}$$
$$= 3x^4y$$

165. C. $p+2$

The only possibility this rational expression has of being reduced is for a factor of its numerator to also be a factor of the denominator and be canceled from both. The numerator can be factored, and one of its factors is a factor of the denominator:

$$\frac{p^2+7p+10}{p+5} = \frac{(p+5)(p+2)}{p+5}$$
$$= p+2$$

166. D. $\frac{m}{3}$

You can reduce the coefficient ratio and cancel n as a factor from the numerator and denominator:

$$\frac{8mn}{24n} = \frac{1mn}{3n}$$
$$= \frac{m}{3}$$

It isn't necessary to leave 1 presented as a factor of the numerator or denominator unless nothing else is there. It's understood to be a factor of both the numerator and denominator.

167.   **B.** $9x^2 - 30xy + 25y^2 + 2y - 7x - 28$

Square the first expression in parentheses. You can use FOIL to multiply it by itself, and you can use the distributive property to multiply -7 by the last expression in parentheses. Then combine like terms.

$$(3x - 5y)^2 + 2y - 7(x + 4) = (3x - 5y)(3x - 5y) + 2y - 7(x) + 7(4)$$
$$= 9x^2 - 15xy - 15xy + 25y^2 + 2y - 7x + 28$$
$$= 9x^2 - 30xy + 25y^2 + 2y - 7x + 28$$

168.   **C.** $\dfrac{1}{y+7}$

You can factor the denominator and then cancel out $y - 5$, which is revealed to be a factor of both the numerator and denominator:

$$\frac{y-5}{y^2 + 2y - 35} = \frac{y-5}{(y+7)(y-5)}$$
$$= \frac{1}{y+7}$$

169.   **D.** $7b$

You can reduce the coefficient ratio and cancel a from the numerator and denominator because it's a factor of both:

$$\frac{14ab}{2a} = \frac{7ab}{1a}$$
$$= \frac{7b}{1}$$
$$= 7b$$

The other choices have factors in wrong places.

170.   **E.** 5

Substitute 2 in for its corresponding variable. Then simplify the remaining expression:

$$a + 3 = 2 + 3$$
$$= 5$$

171.   **C.** 64

Substitute each variable value in for its corresponding variable. Then simplify the result.

$$7x - 5y + 4z = 7(1) - 5(-5) + 4(8)$$
$$= 7 - (-25) + 32$$
$$= 32 + 32$$
$$= 64$$

172. **A. 72**

Replace each variable with its value. Then simplify the result.

$$6p^2q(8q-10p) = 6(1)^2(2)(8(2)-10(1))$$
$$= 6(1)(2)(16-10)$$
$$= 12(6)$$
$$= 72$$

173. **B. 24**

Because $a = 3$ and $b = 2a - 7$, you know that $b = 2(3) - 7$, or -1. Therefore, $c = 4(-1) + 5$, or 1. You can replace each variable in $5a - 2b + 7c$ with its value and simplify the resulting expression:

$$5a - 2b + 7c = 5(3) - 2(-1) + 7(1)$$
$$= 15 - (-2) + 7$$
$$= 15 + 2 + 7$$
$$= 17 + 7$$
$$= 24$$

174. **E. $\frac{4}{19}$**

Replace each variable with its value and then simplify the resulting expression:

$$\frac{w-x}{y+z} = \frac{8-4}{9+10}$$
$$= \frac{4}{19}$$

175. **D. 28**

Substitute each variable value in for its corresponding variable; then simplify:

$$5(2p - r \cdot q)^2 + pr = 5(2(4) - 5 \cdot 2)^2 + 4(2)$$
$$= 5(8-10)^2 + 8$$
$$= 5(-2)^2 + 8$$
$$= 5(4) + 8$$
$$= 20 + 8$$
$$= 28$$

176. **A. 45**

Because $x = 5$ and $y = x$, you know that $y = 5$. Because $z = 2y$ and $y = 5$, $z = 2(5)$, or 10. You can replace each variable with its numerical value in $3x - 2y + 4z$ and then simplify:

$$3x - 2y + 4z = 3(5) - 2(5) + 4(10)$$
$$= 15 - 10 + 40$$
$$= 5 + 40$$
$$= 45$$

177. **B.** $-\frac{1}{10}$

You can replace each variable with its value and then simplify the resulting expression:

$$2j - 2k = 2\left(\frac{3}{4}\right) - 2\left(\frac{4}{5}\right)$$
$$= \frac{6}{4} - \frac{8}{5}$$
$$= \frac{6(5)}{4(5)} - \frac{8(4)}{5(4)}$$
$$= \frac{30}{20} - \frac{32}{20}$$
$$= -\frac{2}{20}$$
$$= -\frac{1}{10}$$

178. **C.** $-\frac{61}{16}$

You can substitute each variable value in for its corresponding variable and then simplify the resulting rational expression:

$$\frac{7k + 4m - 3n}{(5k - 4m)^2 + 7} = \frac{7(-7) + 4(-10) - 3(11)}{(5(-7) - 4(-10))^2 + 7}$$
$$= \frac{-49 - 40 - 33}{(-35 - (-40))^2 + 7}$$
$$= \frac{-89 - 33}{(-35 + 40)^2 + 7}$$
$$= \frac{-122}{(5)^2 + 7}$$
$$= \frac{-122}{25 + 7}$$
$$= \frac{-122}{32}$$
$$= -\frac{61}{16}$$

179.   B. 20

You can substitute each variable value in for its corresponding variable and then simplify:

$$5\left(x^y\right)^z = 5\left(2^1\right)^2$$
$$= 5\left(2\right)^2$$
$$= 5\left(4\right)$$
$$= 20$$

180.   D. 5

Get the variable by itself on one side of the equals sign by using inverse operations. Add 7 to both sides of the equation to get the $3x$ by itself, and then divide both sides by 3 to isolate the x:

$$3x - 7 = 8$$
$$3x - 7 + 7 = 8 + 7$$
$$3x = 15$$
$$\frac{3x}{3} = \frac{15}{3}$$
$$x = 5$$

To check this answer, you can substitute 5 in for the variable and see that doing so results in a true equation.

181.   A and D. 5 and −5

Because the absolute value of $2u$ is 10, $2u$ has to be equal 10 or −10. You can solve both equations to find the possible values of u.

$$2u = 10$$
$$\frac{2u}{2} = \frac{10}{2}$$
$$u = 5$$

$$2u = -10$$
$$\frac{2u}{2} = -\frac{10}{2}$$
$$u = -5$$

The only two possible values of u are 5 and −5.

182. **C. 8**

You can use the substitution method or elimination method to find the value of one variable and then substitute in that value to find the other variable's value.

With the elimination method, you can add the two equations and get an equation without y:

$$\begin{array}{r} x + y = 12 \\ x - y = 4 \\ \hline 2x = 8 \end{array}$$

You can then solve for x.

$$2x = 8$$
$$\frac{2x}{2} = \frac{8}{2}$$
$$x = 4$$

Now that you know x is 4, you can put 4 in for x in either equation and determine the value of y:

$$x + y = 12$$
$$4 + y = 12$$
$$4 + y - 4 = 12 - 4$$
$$y = 8$$

The other choices can result from incorrect substitution, from miscalculation, or from both. Choice (D) is the value of x, not y.

183. **D. 8**

Because w and y have the same value, you can substitute one in for the other and work with only one variable, which allows for cancelations:

$$\frac{8wy^2}{w^2y} = \frac{8yy^2}{y^2y}$$
$$= \frac{8y^3}{y^3}$$
$$= 8$$

184. **B and C. 7 and −7**

For any true proportion, the cross products are equal. Thus, $ac = b^2$. Because the value of ac is 49, the value of b^2 is 49. Only two numbers can be squared to get 49: They are 7 and −7.

185. E. –11

Get p by itself on one side of the equals sign by using inverse operations. Add 8 to both sides of the equation to get $4p$ by itself, and then divide both sides by 4 to isolate the p. (Make sure you perform those inverse operations to both sides of the equation to keep the sides equal.)

$$4p - 8 = -52$$
$$4p - 8 + 8 = -52 + 8$$
$$4p = -44$$
$$\frac{4p}{4} = -\frac{44}{4}$$
$$p = -11$$

The other answers can result from incorrect operations and calculations.

186. A. 27

First, determine the value of h by solving the equation for h:

$$9h + 12 = 57$$
$$9h + 12 - 12 = 57 - 12$$
$$9h = 45$$
$$\frac{9h}{9} = \frac{45}{9}$$
$$h = 5$$

Next, find the value of $4h + 14$ by substituting 5 in for h:

$$4h + 14 = 4(5) + 14$$
$$= 20 + 14$$
$$= 34$$

Because $4h + 14$ is 34, 7 less than $4h + 14$ is 7 less than 34. The number that is 7 less than 34 is 27. The other answers can result from incorrect substitution or calculations. Choice (B) is the value of $4h + 14$.

187. B. 4

The cross products of a true proportion are equal. You can set the cross products of the proportion here equal to each other and solve for w:

$$\frac{20}{w} = \frac{10}{2}$$
$$20(2) = w(10)$$
$$40 = 10w$$
$$\frac{40}{10} = \frac{10w}{10}$$
$$4 = w$$
$$w = 4$$

The other choices can result from incorrect calculations in the solving process.

188. **D. –3.5**

First, get j on one side of the equation by subtracting one of the j terms (say, $10j$) from both sides. Then, get j by itself on one side by performing inverse operations: Add 3 to both sides of the equation, and then divide both sides by -2 to isolate j:

$$8j - 3 = 10j + 4$$
$$8j - 3 - 10j = 10j + 4 - 10j$$
$$-3 - 2j = 4$$
$$-3 - 2j + 3 = 4 + 3$$
$$-2j = 7$$
$$\frac{-2j}{-2} = \frac{7}{-2}$$
$$j = -\frac{7}{2}$$

Because $-\frac{7}{2}$ is equal to -3.5, the correct answer is -3.5.

189. **B. $5x - y = 3$**

You can use elimination or substitution to solve for x or y. Substitution might be easier because in the second equation, you can easily isolate the x because it doesn't have a written coefficient (and neither variable has two coefficients with the same absolute value, which would be ideal for elimination). To use that method, solve the second equation for x in terms of y:

$$x - 2y = -12$$
$$x - 2y + 2y = -12 + 2y$$
$$x = -12 + 2y$$

Next, substitute $-12 + 2y$ in for x in the other equation, $2x + 4y = 32$. You'll then be working with an equation with one variable, and an equation with one variable can be solved.

$$2x + 4y = 32$$
$$2(-12 + 2y) + 4y = 32$$
$$-24 + 4y + 4y = 32$$
$$-24 + 8y = 32$$
$$-24 + 8y + 24 = 32 + 24$$
$$8y = 56$$
$$\frac{8y}{8} = \frac{56}{8}$$
$$y = 7$$

Now that you know y has a value of 7, you can put 7 in for y in either given equation to find x:

$$2x + 4y = 32$$
$$2x + 4(7) = 32$$
$$2x + 28 = 32$$
$$2x + 28 - 28 = 32 - 28$$
$$2x = 4$$
$$\frac{2x}{2} = \frac{4}{2}$$
$$x = 2$$

To check your answer, you can put 2 in for x in and 7 in for y in the given equations and see that the pair makes both equations true. Next, test each of the choices to see which one is made true by the pair. The only one it works for is Choice (B).

190. A. 4

First, get u on one side of the equation by subtracting either u term from both sides. Then isolate u by using inverse operations.

$$-3u + 14 = 8u - 30$$
$$-3u + 14 - 8u = 8u - 30 - 8u$$
$$-11u + 14 = -30$$
$$-11u + 14 - 14 = -30 - 14$$
$$-11u = -44$$
$$\frac{-11u}{-11} = \frac{-44}{-11}$$
$$u = 4$$

Then check your answer. You can put 4 into the given equation to see that it makes the equation true. None of the other choices do.

191. E. −33

First, solve the given equation for q:

$$2q + 5 = 19$$
$$2q + 5 - 5 = 19 - 5$$
$$2q = 14$$
$$\frac{2q}{2} = \frac{14}{2}$$
$$q = 7$$

Then put the value of q into the expression in question. Because $q = 7$, put 7 in for q in $-4q - 5$:

$$-4q - 5 = -4(7) - 5$$
$$= -28 - 5$$
$$= -33$$

The other choices can result from invalid substitution and miscalculations.

192. **A.** −10

In this case, elimination is the better method of solving the system of equations for most people because there's no variable with a coefficient of 1 (which would make substitution ideal) and the second equation can be multiplied by 2 to make the a coefficients have the same absolute value (so you can eliminate the a's). Multiply the second equation by 2 and add the equations:

$$10a + 2b = 14$$
$$2(-5a - 7b = 11)$$

$$\begin{array}{r} 10a + 2b = 14 \\ -10a - 14b = 22 \\ \hline -12b = 36 \end{array}$$

Now you have an equation with one variable, so it can be solved:

$$-12b = 36$$
$$\frac{-12b}{-12} = \frac{36}{-12}$$
$$b = -3$$

You now have the value of b, and you can put it in for b in either equation and solve for a:

$$10a + 2b = 14$$
$$10a + 2(-3) = 14$$
$$10a - 6 = 14$$
$$10a - 6 + 6 = 14 + 6$$
$$10a = 20$$
$$\frac{10a}{10} = \frac{20}{10}$$
$$a = 2$$

Knowing the values of both a and b, you can put the values in for the variables in the expression $7a - (-8b)$:

$$7a - (-8b) = 7(2) - (-8(-3))$$
$$= 14 - (24)$$
$$= -10$$

193. **D. 17**

Because $3^3 = 27$, $x = 3$. Because $4^2 = 16$, y has a value of 2. You can put those values in for the variables in the expression in question.

$$7x - 2y = 7(3) - 2(2)$$
$$= 21 - 4$$
$$= 17$$

False substitution and miscalculation can lead to the other choices.

194. **C and D. 9 and −9**

Absolute value is a number's positive distance from 0. The absolute value of a positive number is the number, and the absolute value of a negative number is its opposite, or the number you get when you drop the negative sign. Only two numbers have an absolute value of 9. They are 9 and −9. None of the other choices have an absolute value of 9.

195. **B.** $\dfrac{4r + 10q}{3}$

Although the numerical value of p can't be determined, you can determine the value of p in terms of the other variables.

$$3p - 10q = 4r$$
$$3p - 10q + 10q = 4r + 10q$$
$$3p = 4r + 10q$$
$$\frac{3p}{3} = \frac{4r + 10q}{3}$$
$$p = \frac{4r + 10q}{3}$$

196. **E. (5, 8)**

You can use substitution to solve this system of equations, but elimination is easier. You need to multiply one of the equations by a number that allows you to line up coefficients with the same absolute value for one variable. If you multiply the second equation by −3, you can get the y terms to cancel:

$$2x + 6y = 58$$
$$-3(5x + 2y = 41)$$

$$\begin{array}{r} 2x + 6y = 58 \\ -15x - 6y = -123 \\ \hline -13x = 65 \end{array}$$

Then you can solve for x:

$$-13x = -65$$
$$\frac{-13x}{-13} = \frac{-65}{-13}$$
$$x = 5$$

You can put 5 in for x in either original equation (or any equation derived from them with both variables) to determine the value of y:

$$2x + 6y = 58$$
$$2(5) + 6y = 58$$
$$10 + 6y = 58$$
$$10 + 6y - 10 = 58 - 10$$
$$6y = 48$$
$$\frac{6y}{6} = \frac{48}{6}$$
$$y = 8$$

The solution is therefore (5, 8). Remember that in an ordered pair, the first number represents x or whichever other variable comes first alphabetically. You can put that solution into any of the equations with both variables and see that it works. None of the other choices work.

197.   A. 0

You can multiply both sides by m to get rid of m and have a one-variable equation:

$$\frac{2k+4}{m} = \frac{3k-13}{m}$$
$$(m)\left(\frac{2k+4}{m}\right) = \left(\frac{3k-13}{m}\right)(m)$$
$$2k + 4 = 3k - 13$$

Then get k on one side and isolate it by using inverse operations. That can tell you the value of k, which you need to know to figure out the value of $k - 17$.

$$2k + 4 = 3k - 13$$
$$2k + 4 - 2k = 3k - 13 - 2k$$
$$4 = k - 13$$
$$4 + 13 = k - 13 + 13$$
$$17 = k$$

Because k has a value of 17, $k - 17 = 0$. The other choices can result from incorrect substitution and miscalculations. Choice (C) is the value of k, not the value of $k - 17$.

198. B. $\dfrac{-21}{4}$

Subtract an h term from both sides of the equation to get h on one side. Then get h by itself on one side by using inverse operations.

$$15h+12 = 11h-9$$
$$15h+12-11h = 11h-9-11h$$
$$4h+12 = -9$$
$$4h+12-12 = -9-12$$
$$4h = -21$$
$$\frac{4h}{4} = \frac{-21}{4}$$
$$h = -\frac{21}{4}$$

You can put the solution into the equation and see that it makes the equation work. None of the other values do.

199. D. 3

Because the first equation has x with an understood coefficient of 1, you may want to use the substitution method to solve this system of equations. Use the first equation to solve for x in terms of y:

$$x+2y = 22$$
$$x+2y-2y = 22-2y$$
$$x = 22-2y$$

Now substitute $22-2y$ in for x in the other equation, $7x-3y=1$, and solve for y. (Make sure you use the other equation. Using the value of one variable in terms of another in the equation where you found it leads to a dead end.)

$$7x-3y = 1$$
$$7(22-2y)-3y = 1$$
$$154-14y-3y = 1$$
$$154-17y = 1$$
$$154-17y-154 = 1-154$$
$$-17y = -153$$
$$\frac{-17y}{-17} = \frac{-153}{-17}$$
$$y = 9$$

You can now put the numerical value of y in for y in either original equation and determine the value of x:

$$x + 2y = 22$$
$$x + 2(9) = 22$$
$$x + 18 = 22$$
$$x + 18 - 18 = 22 - 18$$
$$x = 4$$

Because you know x is 4 and y is 9, you can determine which choice is not between x and y. The only choice that isn't between 4 and 9 is Choice (D).

200.   E. $-\dfrac{2}{3}$

Because a and b have the same value, you can replace one with the other and have a true equation with one variable. An algebraic equation with one variable can be solved, if a solution exists.

$$9a - 2b + 2 = a + 3b$$
$$9a - 2a + 2 = a + 3a$$
$$7a + 2 = 4a$$
$$7a + 2 - 4a = 4a - 4a$$
$$3a + 2 = 0$$
$$3a + 2 - 2 = 0 - 2$$
$$3a = -2$$
$$\frac{3a}{3} = \frac{-2}{3}$$
$$a = -\frac{2}{3}$$

The other choices are results of miscalculations.

201.   A. $x < 3$

As with an algebraic equation, solve an algebraic inequality by getting the variable by itself on one side. Use inverse operations to isolate the variable. (Remember that the inequality sign must change directions if you multiply or divide both sides by a negative number.)

$$4x + 5 < 17$$
$$4x + 5 - 5 < 17 - 5$$
$$4x < 12$$
$$\frac{4x}{4} < \frac{12}{4}$$
$$x < 3$$

The other choices can result from various errors.

202. E. 6

First, find the solution to the inequality. That will tell you which set of numbers makes the inequality true. Get the variable by itself on one side of the inequality sign by using inverse operations. Do the same thing to both sides with each step to keep the inequalities true. (Remember that the inequality sign must change directions if you multiply or divide both sides by a negative number.)

$$8w - 14 \geq 26$$
$$8w - 14 + 14 \geq 26 + 14$$
$$8w \geq 40$$
$$\frac{8w}{8} \geq \frac{40}{8}$$
$$w \geq 5$$

Because w is either 5 or a number greater than 5, the only choice w might be is Choice (E). All the other choices are less than 5.

203. B. $u < -5$

Get the variable on one side of the inequality sign by subtracting one of the variable terms from both sides. Then isolate the variable by using inverse operations. (Remember that the inequality sign must change directions if you multiply or divide both sides by a negative number.)

$$-9u + 7 > u + 57$$
$$-9u + 7 - u > u + 57 - u$$
$$-10u + 7 > 57$$
$$-10u + 7 - 7 > 57 - 7$$
$$-10u > 50$$
$$\frac{-10u}{-10} < \frac{50}{-10}$$
$$u < -5$$

The other choices can result from various errors.

204. B. $x < 7$

As with equations, get the variable by itself by doing opposite operations. The opposite of adding 7 is subtracting 7, so subtract 7 from both sides:

$$x + 7 < 14$$
$$x + 7 - 7 < 14 - 7$$
$$x < 7$$

Now x is by itself on the left side, and it's only on the left side. The answer is Choice (B).

205.　C. 5

First, get the j terms on one side of the inequality by subtracting either $9j$ or $4j$ from both sides. Then undo everything that's being done to j by performing opposite operations on both sides:

$$9j - 13 \geq 4j + 17$$
$$9j - 13 - 4j \geq 4j + 17 - 4j$$
$$5j - 13 \geq 17$$
$$5j - 13 + 13 \geq 17 + 13$$
$$5j \geq 30$$
$$\frac{5j}{5} \geq \frac{30}{5}$$
$$j \geq 6$$

The last inequality has j on one side and by itself on that side, so it's the solution. Because the value of j is either 6 or something greater than 6, only Choice (C), 5, cannot be the value of j.

206.　E.

Choice (E) is a graph in which the point representing 4 has a clear circle around it, indicating that 4 is a boundary for a region of the graph but isn't part of the region. The line is darkened infinitely to the right of 4, representing all numbers that are greater than 4.

A darkened circle indicates that a number is included in a set, and it's used when "or equal to" ($\leq$ or $\geq$) is involved in an inequality. Choice (D) is the graph for $x \geq 4$ instead of $x > 4$ because the darkened circle shows that 4 is included in the solution set.

207.　A. $x > 0$

Get the x terms on one side by subtracting one of the x terms from both sides. Then use opposite operations to get x by itself:

$$12 - 6x < 2x + 12$$
$$12 - 6x - 2x < 2x + 12 - 2x$$
$$12 - 8x < 12$$
$$12 - 8x - 12 < 12 - 12$$
$$-8x < 0$$
$$\frac{-8x}{-8} > \frac{0}{-8}$$
$$x > 0$$

Note that the direction of the inequality sign switches when both sides are divided by a negative number.

208.

A. $w \leq \frac{11}{7}$

Find the solution to the inequality by getting the variable terms on one side and then using opposite operations to get the variable by itself. Remember that you must reverse the direction of the inequality sign if you multiply or divide both sides by a negative number or you switch the sides.

$$8w + 14 - 7w \geq 6w + 3 + 2w$$
$$w + 14 \geq 8w + 3$$
$$w + 14 - 8w \geq 8w + 3 - 8w$$
$$-7w + 14 \geq 3$$
$$-7w + 14 - 14 \geq 3 - 14$$
$$-7w \geq -11$$
$$\frac{-7w}{-7} \leq \frac{-11}{-7}$$
$$w \leq \frac{11}{7}$$

209.

E. 20

First, solve the inequality by getting the variable on one side and then isolating it:

$$10x + 1 < 8x + 31$$
$$10x + 1 - 8x < 8x + 31 - 8x$$
$$2x + 1 < 31$$
$$2x + 1 - 1 < 31 - 1$$
$$2x < 30$$
$$\frac{2x}{2} < \frac{30}{2}$$
$$x < 15$$

Because x is less than 15, $5 + x$ has to be less than $5 + 15$, which is 20, Choice (E).

210. D. $h \geq \dfrac{36}{13}$

Get the variable terms on one side and then get the variable by itself by performing inverse operations. Remember to switch the direction of the inequality sign when you multiply or divide both sides by a negative number or you switch the sides.

$$-\frac{3}{4}h - 2 + \frac{1}{2}h \leq 3h - 11$$

$$4\left(-\frac{3}{4}h - 2 + \frac{1}{2}h\right) \leq 4(3h - 11)$$

$$-3h - 8 + 2h \leq 12h - 44$$

$$-h - 8 \leq 12h - 44$$

$$-h - 8 - 12h \leq 12h - 44 - 12h$$

$$-13h - 8 \leq -44$$

$$-13h - 8 + 8 \leq -44 + 8$$

$$-13h \leq -36$$

$$\frac{-13h}{-13} \geq \frac{-36}{-13}$$

$$h \geq \frac{36}{13}$$

211. C. $x \leq 1$

The point representing 1 has a solid dot on it. That means 1 is part of the graphed set, so the inequality sign needs to be underlined to indicate "or equal to." The number line is darkened to the left of 1, so the rest of the set is everything less than 1. Therefore, the graph represents the set of numbers less than or equal to 1, symbolized by $x \leq 1$.

212. E. -4

The first step is to solve the inequality. Get the variable terms on one side and then isolate the variable using opposite operations. To keep the resulting inequalities true, perform the same operations on both sides:

$$-3q - (-2q) + 5 + (q + 2) \geq -8q - 2 + (2q - 3)$$

$$-3q + 2q + 5 + q + 2 \geq -8q - 2 + 2q - 3$$

$$7 \geq -6q - 5$$

$$7 + 6q \geq -6q - 5 + 6q$$

$$7 + 6q \geq -5$$

$$7 + 6q - 7 \geq -5 - 7$$

$$6q \geq -12$$

$$\frac{6q}{6} \geq \frac{-12}{6}$$

$$q \geq -2$$

Because q is -2 or a greater number, only Choice (E) couldn't be the value of q.

213. E. $\frac{4}{9}$

Begin by solving the inequality:

$$8x + 13 \geq 2x + 15$$
$$8x + 13 - 2x \geq 2x + 15 - 2x$$
$$6x + 13 \geq 15$$
$$6x + 13 - 13 \geq 15 - 13$$
$$6x \geq 2$$
$$\frac{6x}{6} \geq \frac{2}{6}$$
$$x \geq \frac{1}{3}$$

Therefore, x can only be $\frac{1}{3}$ or a number greater than $\frac{1}{3}$. The only choice that qualifies is Choice (E).

214. B. $y < -7.25$

Find the solution to the inequality by getting the variable terms on one side and then isolating the variable:

$$2.5y + 3.7 < 1.7y - 2.1$$
$$2.5y + 3.7 - 1.7y < 1.7y - 2.1 - 1.7y$$
$$0.8y + 3.7 < -2.1$$
$$0.8y + 3.7 - 3.7 < -2.1 - 3.7$$
$$0.8y < -5.8$$
$$\frac{0.8y}{0.8} < \frac{-5.8}{0.8}$$
$$y < -7.25$$

215. D. 0.5626

The first major step is to solve the inequality. Combine the like terms on the left side, and then subtract one of the m terms in the resulting inequality to get m on one side. Then get m by itself using opposite operations. Remember to change the direction of the inequality sign if you multiply or divide both sides by a negative number or you switch the sides.

$$2.8m + 5.6 - 9.8m \geq 12.2m - 5.2$$
$$-7m + 5.6 \geq 12.2m - 5.2$$
$$-7m + 5.6 - 12.2m \geq 12.2m - 5.2 - 12.2m$$
$$-19.2m + 5.6 \geq -5.2$$
$$-19.2m + 5.6 - 5.6 \geq -5.2 - 5.6$$
$$-19.2m \geq -10.8$$
$$\frac{-19.2m}{-19.2} \leq \frac{-10.8}{-19.2}$$
$$m \leq 0.5625$$

The only choice that m couldn't be is Choice (D), because 0.5626 is greater than 0.5625.

216. B. 8

Because the integers are consecutive, one of them is 1 greater than the other. If you call the lower one x, you can call the higher one $x+1$. Their sum is 15. Express this relationship as an equation and solve for x:

$$x + x + 1 = 15$$
$$2x + 1 = 15$$
$$2x + 1 - 1 = 15 - 1$$
$$2x = 14$$
$$\frac{2x}{2} = \frac{14}{2}$$
$$x = 7$$

The lower number is 7, and the greater one is 1 more than that, so it's 8, Choice (B).

217. A. 13

Consecutive odd integers are always 2 apart from each other. If you use x to represent the lower integer, you can represent the higher one as $x+2$. Their sum is 28. Represent this relationship as an equation and solve for x:

$$x + x + 2 = 28$$
$$2x + 2 = 28$$
$$2x + 2 - 2 = 28 - 2$$
$$2x = 26$$
$$\frac{2x}{2} = \frac{26}{2}$$
$$x = 13$$

The lower odd integer is 13, Choice (A).

218. C. 80

If you represent the lower of the two even integers as x, you can represent the greater one as $x+2$. Now you can set their sum equal to 18 and solve for x to find the lower even integer:

$$x + x + 2 = 18$$
$$2x + 2 = 18$$
$$2x + 2 - 2 = 18 - 2$$
$$2x = 16$$
$$\frac{2x}{2} = \frac{16}{2}$$
$$x = 8$$

Because the lower even integer is 8, the higher one is 10. The product of 8 and 10 is 80, Choice (C).

219. D. 16

You can represent the unknown number with x and translate the given problem into an equation. Twice the number is $2x$, and you add 4 to get four more than that; three times the number is $3x$, and you subtract 12 to get 12 less than that. You can then set these expressions equal to each other solve the equation for x:

$$2x + 4 = 3x - 12$$
$$2x + 4 - 2x = 3x - 12 - 2x$$
$$4 = x - 12$$
$$4 + 12 = x - 12 + 12$$
$$16 = x$$
$$x = 16$$

The number is therefore 16, Choice (D).

220. C. 53

First, you need to find the number. You can represent the number with x (or another variable) and write the given problem as an equation. Translate the English into mathematical language and then solve for x:

$$5x - 7 = x + 21$$
$$5x - 7 - x = x + 21 - x$$
$$4x - 7 = 21$$
$$4x - 7 + 7 = 21 + 7$$
$$4x = 28$$
$$\frac{4x}{4} = \frac{28}{4}$$
$$x = 7$$

The number is 7. However, the question asks for 11 more than 6 times the number, which you can represent as $6x + 11$. Because x is 7, you can replace x with 7 in the expression:

$$6x + 11 = 6(7) + 11$$
$$= 42 + 11$$
$$= 53$$

The expression has a value of 53, Choice (C).

221. **A and B. 4 and 3**

You can represent the number with the variable x and write the scenario using an inequality. The solution to the inequality represents the set of possibilities for the value of the number.

$$2(x+10)+14 \geq 10x+2$$
$$2x+20+14 \geq 10x+2$$
$$2x+34 \geq 10x+2$$
$$2x+34-2x \geq 10x+2-2x$$
$$34 \geq 8x+2$$
$$34-2 \geq 8x+2-2$$
$$32 \geq 8x$$
$$\frac{32}{8} \geq \frac{8x}{8}$$
$$4 \geq x$$
$$x \leq 4$$

The number can be either 4 or a number less than 4. The only choices that work are Choices (A) and (B).

222. **B. 11**

Let the unknown number be x, represent the situation as an inequality, and solve. "A number and 6" is $x+6$, and you multiply that expression by 2 to get twice that.

$$2(x+6) \leq 3x$$
$$2x+12 \leq 3x$$
$$2x+12-12 \leq 3x-12$$
$$2x \leq 3x-12$$
$$2x-3x \leq 3x-12-3x$$
$$-x \leq -12$$
$$-x(-1) \geq -12(-1)$$
$$x \geq 12$$

The number can be 12 or a number greater than 12. It can't be a number that's less than 12, so the answer is Choice (B).

223.   B. 42

If Bethany's age is x, Jason's age is $x+3$ and the sum of their ages is $x+x+3$. You can set that expression equal to 81 and solve for x:

$$x+x+3=81$$
$$2x+3=81$$
$$2x+3-3=81-3$$
$$2x=78$$
$$\frac{2x}{2}=\frac{78}{2}$$
$$x=39$$

Bethany's age is 39, and Jason's age is 3 more than that, so it's 42, Choice (B).

224.   A. 1

First find Kellie's current age. Because Casey's age is described based on Kellie's age, the easiest approach is to represent Kellie's age using a variable. If Kellie's age is x, Casey's age is $2x-7$. Using those representations, Kellie's age in 12 years will be $x+12$ and also $2x-7+10$ (Casey's current age plus 10). The two expressions are equal, so you can set them equal to each other and solve for x to determine Kellie's current age:

$$x+12=2x-7+10$$
$$x+12=2x+3$$
$$x+12-2x=2x+3-2x$$
$$-x+12=3$$
$$-x+12-12=3-12$$
$$-x=-9$$
$$-x(-1)=-9(-1)$$
$$x=9$$

Kellie's age is 9. However, the problem asks for Kellie's age 8 years ago. Because $9-8=1$, Kellie's age 8 years ago was 1, Choice (A).

225.   **E. 12**

First find the number, which you can call x. Write the described scenario as an equation and solve for x:

$$\frac{1}{2}x + 2x = (2)\left(\frac{1}{2}\right)x + 6$$

$$\frac{1}{2}x + 2x\left(\frac{2}{2}\right) = x + 6$$

$$\frac{1}{2}x + \frac{4}{2}x = x + 6$$

$$\frac{5}{2}x = x + 6$$

$$\frac{5}{2}x - x = x + 6 - x$$

$$\frac{5}{2}x - x\left(\frac{2}{2}\right) = x + 6 - x$$

$$\frac{5}{2}x - \frac{2}{2}x = 6$$

$$\frac{3}{2}x = 6$$

$$\frac{3}{2}x\left(\frac{2}{3}\right) = 6\left(\frac{2}{3}\right)$$

$$x = \frac{12}{3}$$

$$x = 4$$

The number is 4. The question asks for 8 less than 5 times the number, which you can express as $5x - 8$. Because x is 4, the expression has a value of $5(4) - 8$. That's $20 - 8$, or 12, which is Choice (E).

226.   **B. 39**

First determine the set of possibilities for the number. Let the number be x and write the described scenario as an inequality; then solve for x:

$$x - 11 < \frac{1}{3}x - 3$$

$$3(x - 11) < 3\left(\frac{1}{3}x - 3\right)$$

$$3x - 33 < x - 9$$

$$3x - 33 - x < x - 9 - x$$

$$2x - 33 < -9$$

$$2x - 33 + 33 < -9 + 33$$

$$2x < 24$$

$$\frac{2x}{2} < \frac{24}{2}$$

$$x < 12$$

Therefore, x can be any real number that is less than 12, so you're looking for real numbers that are less than 26 more than 12, or 38. Because 39, Choice (B), doesn't qualify as less than 38, it couldn't be exactly 26 higher than the number. All the other choices are less than 38.

227. B. 5

Deal with the first sentence after analyzing the rest of the question. Let x represent one of the numbers, and set up an equation based on the scenario described in the rest of the problem:

$$x + 14 = 5x + 2$$
$$x + 14 - x = 5x + 2 - x$$
$$14 = 4x + 2$$
$$14 - 2 = 4x + 2 - 2$$
$$12 = 4x$$
$$\frac{12}{4} = \frac{4x}{4}$$
$$3 = x$$
$$x = 3$$

Because one of the numbers is 3, the other number is 5, Choice (B), because 5 is the number by which 3 must be multiplied to get 15.

228. E. 3

Any two numbers that are opposites have the same absolute value. Because the square root of 81 is 9, the two numbers that are opposites and have a product of −81 are 9 and −9. The higher of the two is the positive one, 9. That is the number that's 3 more than twice y; you can represent this situation with the equation $9 = 2y + 3$ and solve for y:

$$9 = 2y + 3$$
$$9 - 3 = 2y + 3 - 3$$
$$6 = 2y$$
$$\frac{6}{2} = \frac{2y}{2}$$
$$3 = y$$
$$y = 3$$

The value of y is 3, Choice (E).

229. C. −4

Let x represent the number and use an inequality to illustrate the described situation. From that inequality, you can determine that the square of x must be less than 9:

$$x^2 - 4 < 5$$
$$x^2 - 4 + 4 < 5 + 4$$
$$x^2 < 9$$

A counterexample to the statement would have to be a number that makes the inequality untrue. You can use the first inequality or the final one derived from it, but the final one is easier to use. There are techniques for going further with the inequality, but they're beyond the level of the Praxis Core exam, and they aren't necessary here. All you need to do is test each choice until you find one that makes the inequality false. Choice (C) makes it false, so it's a counterexample.

230. C. 2

Let x be the number of attached four-wheeler wheels Elizabeth has. The number of attached four-wheeler wheels John has is therefore $2x - 8$ (eight less than twice as many). This expression and x are equal, so you can set them equal to each other and solve for x:

$$x = 2x - 8$$
$$x - 2x = 2x - 8 - 2x$$
$$-x = -8$$
$$-x(-1) = -8(-1)$$
$$x = 8$$

Elizabeth has 8 attached four-wheeler wheels, and therefore John has $2(8) - 8 = 8$.

You aren't done, because the question doesn't ask how many attached four-wheeler wheels John has; it asks how many four wheelers he has. Because each four wheeler has four wheels, the number of four wheelers John has is a fourth of the number of wheels, or 2.

231. A. 12

Here, you have to use two variables because neither can be expressed in terms of the other in a way that's useful. Because two variables are used, you need to write two equations with them.

Let x represent one number and let y represent the other. Write one equation to show that the sum of the numbers is 17, and write another to show that the greater number minus the smaller number is 7:

$$x + y = 17$$
$$x - y = 7$$

You can use either substitution or elimination with any system of equations, but elimination is probably easier here because the y's cancel out when you add the equations. Line up the variables and constants of the two equations and then add them:

$$\begin{array}{r} x + y = 17 \\ \underline{x - y = 7} \\ 2x = 24 \end{array}$$

Because y is subtracted from x to get a positive number, x must represent the higher number. Use the resulting one-variable equation to solve for x:

$$2x = 24$$
$$\frac{2x}{2} = \frac{24}{2}$$
$$x = 12$$

The higher number is 12, Choice (A). You can check the answer by putting 12 in for x in either equation and seeing that y is 5.

232.   **A. 12**

If x represents the number of girls, the number of boys is $x + 4$. The sum of their ages is 28, and you can represent this relationship using an equation:

$$x + x + 4 = 28$$
$$2x + 4 = 28$$
$$2x + 4 - 4 = 28 - 4$$
$$2x = 24$$
$$\frac{2x}{2} = \frac{24}{2}$$
$$x = 12$$

The number of girls is 12, Choice (A). You can test that by adding 4 more than 12 to 12 to get 28.

233.   **D. 27**

Let x be the number of student tickets. The number of non-student tickets isn't based on the number of student tickets in any way that is helpful, so use another variable. That's fine because two equations can be derived from the given information.

If you use x to represent the number of student tickets and y to represent the number of non-student tickets, the sum of x and y is 61. Also, $3 times the number of student tickets is the amount of money made on selling student tickets. By the same reasoning, $5 times the number of non-student tickets sold is the amount of money made from selling non-student tickets. Thus, $3x + 5y = 251$.

$$x + y = 61$$
$$3x + 5y = 251$$

You can use those two equations to find the values of the variables. In this case, the substitution method may be better because neither variable's coefficients have the same absolute value and because a variable has a coefficient with an absolute value of 1. (In fact, both variables do in the first equation.) Here's the first equation solved for x:

$$x + y = 61$$
$$x + y - y = 61 - y$$
$$x = 61 - y$$

Because x is equal to $61 - y$, you can put $61 - y$ in the other equation and solve for y. (If you put it in the first equation, you'll end up with an equation with no variable and just a number equal to itself.)

$$3x + 5y = 251$$
$$3(61 - y) + 5y = 251$$
$$183 - 3y + 5y = 251$$
$$183 + 2y = 251$$
$$183 + 2y - 183 = 251 - 183$$
$$2y = 68$$
$$\frac{2y}{2} = \frac{68}{2}$$
$$y = 34$$

Now you can put this value in for y in either equation. The first equation is easier:

$$x + 34 = 61$$
$$x + 34 - 34 = 61 - 34$$
$$x = 27$$

Because x represents the number of student tickets sold, the answer is 27, Choice (D).

234. **E. 11**

Let x represent the number of $10 bills in Alex's wallet, and let y be the number of $20 bills. The sum of the variables is 18. The amount of money in $10 bills is $10 times x, and the amount of money in $20 bills is $20 times y.

$$x + y = 18$$
$$10x + 20y = 290$$

You can use substitution or elimination to solve the system of equations. If you use elimination, note that neither variable's coefficients have the same absolute value, so you need to multiply both sides of the first equation by a number that will change that, such as -10:

$$-10(x + y) = -10(18)$$
$$-10x - 10y = -180$$

Line that equation up with the second equation and then add the equations to get rid of x:

$$-10x - 10y = -180$$
$$\underline{10x + 20y = 290}$$
$$10y = 110$$

Then you have a one-variable equation, which you can solve:

$$10y = 110$$
$$\frac{10y}{10} = \frac{110}{10}$$
$$y = 11$$

Because y is represents the number of $20 bills in Alex's wallet and that's what the question asks for, the answer to the question is 11, Choice (E).

235. C. 38

First determine Danforth's current age. Let x represent his age and set up an equation that represents the described situation. Then solve for x:

$$x + 17 = 3x + 1$$
$$x + 17 - x = 3x + 1 - x$$
$$17 = 2x + 1$$
$$17 - 1 = 2x + 1 - 1$$
$$16 = 2x$$
$$\frac{16}{2} = \frac{2x}{2}$$
$$8 = x$$
$$x = 8$$

Danforth's present age is 8. In 30 years, his age will be $8 + 30$, which is 38, Choice (C).

236. B. The relation is a function because no element of the domain is paired with more than one element of the range.

None of the domain numbers (first numbers in the ordered pairs) are paired with more than one range element. In other words, no first number is repeated with a different second number, so the relation is a function.

237. B. No

The relation is not a function, because -2 is a domain element (first number) that is paired with both 4 and 14.

238. B. {(1, 2), (3, 4), (5, 6)}

Choice (B) is the only choice in which no domain element (first number) is paired with more than one range element (second number). In Choice (A), 7 is paired with both 6 and 8. In Choice (C), 0 is paired with 0 and 2, and 2 is paired with 0 and 2. In Choices (D) and (E), 1 is paired with 2 and 3.

239. E. {(−4, 5), (2, 6), (8, 3), (2, 7), (5, 10)}

Choice (E) isn't a function, because 2 is paired as a first number with 6 and 7.

240. **D. It does NOT represent a function because 5 is paired with both 7 and 10.**

The domain element 5 is paired with 7 and 10. It's therefore paired with more than one range element, so it isn't a function. Choices (A), (B), and (E) are incorrect because they have the wrong conclusion and false definitions of *function*. Choice (C) has the right conclusion but a false definition.

241. A. 1

Because $f(3)$ replaces the x in $f(x)$ with 3, put 3 in for x in $x-2$:

$$f(x)=x-2$$
$$f(3)=3-2$$
$$=1$$

242. E. 49

For $g(7)$, 7 replaces the x in $g(x)$, so put 7 in for x in $x^2-2x+14$:

$$g(x)=x^2-2x+14$$
$$g(7)=7^2-2(7)+14$$
$$=49-14+14$$
$$=49$$

243. A. −29

For $p(2)$, put 2 in for x in $-4x^3+9x-15$:

$$p(x)=-4x^3+9x-15$$
$$p(2)=-4(2)^3+9(2)-15$$
$$=-4(8)+18-15$$
$$=-32+18-15$$
$$=-14-15$$
$$=-29$$

244. B. 26

Find the value of $f(4)$ by putting 4 in for x in the $f(x)$ equation:

$$f(x) = 2x + 7$$
$$f(4) = 2(4) + 7$$
$$= 8 + 7$$
$$= 15$$

Find $g(x)$ by using the same method:

$$g(x) = -x - 1$$
$$g(10) = -10 - 1$$
$$= -11$$

Because $f(4)$ is 15 and $g(10)$ is –11, $f(4) - g(10)$ is equal to $15 - (-11)$, which is 26, Choice (B).

245. C. –874

Find the value of $q(-6)$ by putting –6 in for x in $1 - 3x$:

$$q(x) = 1 - 3x$$
$$q(-6) = 1 - 3(-6)$$
$$= 1 - (-18)$$
$$= 1 + 18$$
$$= 19$$

Use the same method to find $r(-9)$:

$$r(x) = 5x - 1$$
$$r(-9) = 5(-9) - 1$$
$$= -45 - 1$$
$$= -46$$

Now multiply 19 and –46 to find the product of $q(-6)$ and $r(-9)$. The product is –874, Choice (C).

246. A. 508

First, find the value of $g(1)$:

$$g(x) = 3x + 5$$
$$g(1) = 3(1) + 5$$
$$= 3 + 5$$
$$= 8$$

Because $g(1)$ is 8, $f\big(g(1)\big)$ is $f(8)$:

$$f(x) = 8x^2 - 2x + 12$$
$$f(8) = 8(8)^2 - 2(8) + 12$$
$$= 8(64) - 16 + 12$$
$$= 512 - 16 + 12$$
$$= 508$$

Therefore, $f\big(g(1)\big)$ is 508, Choice (A).

247. **E. T**

The letter T isn't in the diagram.

248. **A, B, and E. $\overline{AB}$, $\overline{BC}$, and $\overline{CA}$**

A line can be named by any two points on it, in any order. Choices (A), (B), and (E) are all examples of combinations of two points labeled on the line, so they all qualify as names of the line. Choice (D) can't be a name of the line because a line can't be named by just one point on it; every point is on an infinite number of lines.

249. **C and E. $\overline{JK}$ and $\overline{JL}$**

A ray is named by its endpoint followed by any other point on the ray. The endpoint of the ray is J, and the two other labeled points on the ray are K and L. Therefore, $\overline{JK}$ and $\overline{JL}$ both qualify as names of the ray.

250. **C. A ray is infinite in only one direction.**

A line goes infinitely in two directions, and a ray goes infinitely in only one direction. A ray is part of a line, but a ray can never be a complete line because for any ray, another ray sharing the same endpoint and going infinitely in the opposite direction is the rest of the line.

251. **E. Both endpoints**

Segments are named by their endpoints.

252. **D. They are congruent.**

Those marks indicate that segments are congruent, meaning that they have the same measure. Segment congruence can also be indicated by double marks, triple marks, and so on, as long as both or all the congruent segments have the same numbers of identical marks.

253. **B and D.** ∠*ACB* and ∠*A*

If an angle is named after points on it, the vertex must be in the middle. That's why Choice (B) can't be a name of the angle. An angle can't be named by a just a point on one of its sides, so Choice (D) can't be a name of the angle, either.

An angle can be named by a point on one side, then its vertex, and then a point on the other side, so Choice (A) works as the name of the angle. Choice (C) is okay because an angle can be named by a number that's presented inside it (but not by its measure). An angle can be named by its vertex alone as long as the vertex is the vertex of only one angle that's presented. That makes Choice (E) work.

254. **C. An angle cannot be named by its vertex alone when its vertex is the vertex of more than one presented angle.**

An angle can be named by its vertex only when it's completely clear which angle that letter represents.

255. **A, B, D, and E.** Planes *j*, *MNR*, *RNT*, and *PTN*

A plane can be named by a single letter that isn't the name of a point on it, usually in cursive or italics. Choice (A) therefore qualifies. Choices (B), (D), and (E) work because a plane can also be named by any three points on it that aren't collinear (on the same line).

Choice (C) doesn't qualify because three collinear points exist together on an infinite number of planes. Three noncollinear points exist together on exactly one plane, so they can specify the plane.

256. **E.** ∞

Every plane has an infinite number of points. In fact, there are an infinite number of points in every segment, and a plane contains an infinite number of segments. So does a line. The ∞ symbol represents infinity.

257. **C. The line's endpoints are *E* and *H*.**

All the choices are true except Choice (C). A line has no endpoints.

258.   A. Acute

The diagram shows that a right angle forms a linear pair with another angle, which is divided into two angles. Any angle that forms a linear pair with a right angle is also a right angle because angles that form a linear pair are supplementary. A straight angle is 180°, so angles that form a straight angle together have measures with a sum of 180°. Right angles are 90°, and 90° is what must be added to 90° to get 180°. Because the angle that forms a linear pair with the right angle is also a right angle, any angle that partly forms it must be less than 90° but greater than 0°. That makes all such angles acute angles.

259.   E. 90°

The angle is 90° because it's a right angle, as indicated by the small square inside it at the vertex.

260.   D. 180°

If two angles are supplementary, the sum of their measures is 180°.

261.   C. 59°

$\angle ABD$ and $\angle DBC$ form a linear pair, so they're supplementary. Therefore, the sum of their measures is 180°. The measure that must be added to 121° is 59° because $180 - 121 = 59$. Therefore, the measure of $\angle ABD$ is 59°.

262.   A. 36°

Because $\angle GHI$ is 54°, any angle complementary to it has a measure of 36° because $90 - 54 = 36$; 36° must be added to 54° to get 90°.

263.   B. 53

You can work a problem like this by setting up algebraic equation. Here, the sum of x and 37 must be 90 because the two angles are complementary. They form a right angle together, so the sum of their measures is 90°.

$$x + 37 = 90$$
$$x + 37 - 37 = 90 - 37$$
$$x = 53$$

264.   B. 119

The angle labeled $y°$ is a vertical angle to the angle labeled 119°. All pairs of vertical angles are congruent, so both angles are 119°. Therefore, the value of y is 119.

265. A. 52

The interior angles of a triangle have a sum of 180°. Based on that, you can set up an equation for the angles in question here and solve for w.

$$34 + 94 + w = 180$$
$$128 + w = 180$$
$$128 + w - 128 = 180 - 128$$
$$w = 52$$

266. E. 75

The sum of the interior angle measures of a quadrilateral (four-sided polygon) is 360°. Therefore, the sum of 108, 101, 76, and k is 360. You can set up an equation and solve for k.

$$108 + 101 + 76 + k = 360$$
$$285 + k = 360$$
$$285 + k - 285 = 360 - 285$$
$$k = 75$$

267. E. 40

If two sides of a triangle are congruent, the angles opposite those sides are congruent. Therefore, the two triangle angles that aren't labeled with measures have the same measure. Their sum must be 80°, because the sum of the interior angles of the triangle is 180° and the labeled angle is 100°:

$$180 - 100 = 80$$

Because the sum of the two angles is 80° and the two angles have the same measure, each one has to be 40°. One of them is a vertical angle to the $n°$ angle, and vertical angles are congruent, so the $n°$ angle is also 40°. Therefore, the value of n is 40.

268. A. 48

One of the angles of the triangle is labeled as 42°. Another one is 90° because it forms a linear pair with a right angle and is therefore supplementary to it. An angle supplementary to a 90° angle is also 90°:

$$180 - 90 = 90$$

That means one of the interior angles of the triangle is 90° and another one is 42°. The other interior angle of the triangle is x°. The sum of those three measures is 180° because that's always the sum of the interior angle measures of a triangle. You can set up an equation based on that and solve for x:

$$42 + 90 + x = 180$$
$$132 + x = 180$$
$$132 + x - 132 = 180 - 132$$
$$x = 48$$

269. **A. 8π cm**

The circumference of a circle, or distance around it, is the product of the circle's diameter and π:

$$C = \pi d$$
$$C = \pi(8)$$
$$= 8\pi$$

The circumference of the circle is 8π cm.

270. **C. 10 in.**

The circumference of a circle 2 times π times the radius. You can use the formula for circumference, fill in what you know, and solve for r, the radius of the circle:

$$C = 2\pi r$$
$$20\pi = 2\pi r$$
$$\frac{20\pi}{2\pi} = \frac{2\pi r}{2\pi}$$
$$10 = r$$

The radius of the circle is 10 in.

271. **D. 28.26 m²**

The circles' radii are congruent, which means they have the same measure. Because one circle's radius is 3 m, the circle in question has a radius of 3 m. You can use the formula for the area of a circle:

$$A = \pi r^2$$
$$= \pi(3)^2$$
$$= \pi(9)$$
$$= 9\pi$$

Because π rounded to the nearest hundredth is 3.14, you can multiply 9 by 3.14:

$$9 \times 3.14 = 28.26$$

The area of the circle, rounded to the nearest hundredth, is 28.26 m².

272. E. 6

The opposite sides of a parallelogram are congruent, so the side measures for this parallelogram are 15, 15, $x + 4$, and $x + 4$. The perimeter is 50, so you can set the sum of the side measures equal to 50 and solve for x:

$$15 + 15 + x + 4 + x + 4 = 50$$
$$2x + 38 = 50$$
$$2x = 12$$
$$\frac{2x}{2} = \frac{12}{2}$$
$$x = 6$$

273. B. 108 cm²

The area of a parallelogram is the product of one of its bases and the height:

$$A = bh$$
$$A = (9)(12)$$
$$= 108$$

The area of the parallelogram is 108 cm².

274. D. 31 in.

The perimeter of any polygon is the sum of its side measures. If two angles of a triangle are congruent, the sides opposite those angles are congruent. The diagram shows that a 13 in. side is congruent to the unlabeled side. Therefore, the missing side measure for the triangle is 13 in. Thus, the perimeter is the sum of 13 in., 13 in., and 5 in.:

$$P = 13 + 13 + 5 = 31$$

The perimeter of the triangle is 31 in.

275. E. 28 in.²

The area of a triangle is half the product of a base and the corresponding height:

$$A = \frac{1}{2}(8)(7)$$
$$= 4(7)$$
$$= 28$$

The area of the triangle is 28 in.².

276.   E. 8 m

For every right triangle, the square of the hypotenuse is equal to the sum of the squares of its legs. The legs are the sides that form the right angle, and the hypotenuse is the side that's across from the right angle. The formula is commonly represented as $a^2 + b^2 = c^2$, where a and b are the legs and c is the hypotenuse. Fill in what is known and solve for what is unknown:

$$a^2 + b^2 = c^2$$
$$a^2 + 6^2 = 10^2$$
$$a^2 + 36 = 100$$
$$a^2 = 64$$
$$a = 8$$

AB is 8 m.

Tip: Knowing the side lengths of common right triangles can shave off much-needed time. For example, well-known right triangles include the 3-4-5 triangle (and its multiples, such as the 6-8-10 and the 9-12-15), the 5-12-13 triangle, and the 8-15-17 triangle. Based on this information, you could have known the other side length would be 8 without using the Pythagorean theorem.

277.   B. 12.5 square units

Because the triangle is a right triangle, the legs are perpendicular, so one leg can be the base and the other can be the height. The next issue is what those leg measures are. Because the triangle is a 45°-45°-90° triangle, the legs are congruent (they're opposite congruent angles of the triangle) and the hypotenuse is $\sqrt{2}$ times the measure of a leg. You can call either leg x and use that relationship to find the measure of the leg:

$$x\sqrt{2} = 5\sqrt{2}$$
$$\frac{x\sqrt{2}}{\sqrt{2}} = \frac{5\sqrt{2}}{\sqrt{2}}$$
$$x = 5$$

The leg is 5 units, so the other leg is 5 units. Now that you have a base and height to work with, you can use the formula for the area of a triangle:

$$A = \frac{1}{2}bh$$
$$= \frac{1}{2}(5)(5)$$
$$= \frac{1}{2}(25)$$
$$= 12.5$$

The area of the triangle is 12.5 square units.

You can also write the area of a triangle as $\frac{bh}{2}$. Some people find that version easier to work with.

278. **A. $32\sqrt{3}$ square micrometers**

The legs of the triangle qualify as base and height because they're perpendicular and extend from vertices. The shorter leg of a 30°–60°–90° triangle is half the measure of the hypotenuse. Because half of the hypotenuse here is 16 micrometers, the shorter leg is 8 micrometers. The longer leg of a 30°–60°–90° triangle is the shorter leg measure times $\sqrt{3}$, so the longer leg of the triangle in question is $8\sqrt{3}$ micrometers. The area of the triangle is half the product of its base and height:

$$A = \frac{1}{2}bh$$
$$= \frac{1}{2}(8)(8\sqrt{3})$$
$$= 4(8\sqrt{3})$$
$$= 32\sqrt{3}$$

The area of the triangle is $32\sqrt{3}$ square micrometers.

279. **A. Yes**

If the triangle is a right triangle, the Pythagorean theorem applies to it — that is, the sum of the squares of the two leg measures equals the square of the hypotenuse. You can substitute the triangle's measures into $a^2 + b^2 = c^2$ and see whether the equation works:

$$a^2 + b^2 \overset{?}{=} c^2$$
$$10^2 + 24^2 \overset{?}{=} 26^2$$
$$100 + 576 \overset{?}{=} 676$$
$$676 = 676$$

The equation is true, so the triangle is a right triangle.

280. **C. 21**

The perimeter of any polygon is the sum of its side measures. The perimeter of a rectangle is more specifically twice the length plus twice the width, because the opposite sides of a rectangle are congruent:

$$P = 2l + 2w$$
$$64 = 2(4x + 5) + 2(11)$$
$$64 = 8x + 10 + 22$$
$$64 = 8x + 32$$
$$32 = 8x$$
$$\frac{32}{8} = \frac{8x}{8}$$
$$4 = x$$

The length of the garden is $4x + 5$ units, so it's $4(4) + 5$, or 21.

Notice that this question asks for the length of the garden, not the value of x. Make sure you know exactly what a question is asking, especially if it's a geometry question.

281.   B. 56 km

Because all the sides of a square are congruent, you can add 14 km four times to get the perimeter of the square. That's the same as multiplying 14 km by 4:

$$P = 4s$$
$$P = 4(14)$$
$$= 56$$

The perimeter of the square is 56 km.

282.   D. 169 yd.²

A square is also a rectangle, so its area is its length times its width. Because the length and width of a square are the same, you can just square a side measure to get the area of the square.

For this square, you need to determine a side measure. The interior angles of a square are right angles. A diagonal of a square cuts the interior angles in half (bisects them) and cuts the square in half, creating two 45°-45°-90° triangles; the diagonal is the hypotenuse. The hypotenuse of a 45°-45°-90° triangle is $\sqrt{2}$ times the measure of a leg; therefore, because the diagonal here is $13\sqrt{2}$ yd., each side of the square is 13 yd.

The area of a square is the square of one of its sides, so

$$A = s^2$$
$$= 13^2$$
$$= 169$$

The area is 169 yd.².

283.   C. 3 mm

The area of a trapezoid is half the height times the sum of the bases. Fill in the formula with what you know and solve for the height:

$$A = \frac{1}{2}h(b_1 + b_2)$$
$$15 = \frac{1}{2}h(4+6)$$
$$15 = \frac{1}{2}h(10)$$
$$15 = 5h$$
$$\frac{15}{5} = \frac{h}{5}$$
$$3 = h$$

The height of the trapezoid is 3 mm.

284. A, B, C, and E. Quadrilateral, parallelogram, rectangle, and rhombus

A square is a polygon with four sides, so it's a quadrilateral. Both pairs of opposite sides are parallel, so a square is a parallelogram. A square is a quadrilateral with four right interior angles, so it's a rectangle. Also, all four sides of a square are congruent, so a square is a rhombus. Choice (D) is incorrect because a *trapezoid* has exactly one pair of opposite sides that are parallel, but a square has two pairs of opposite sides that are parallel.

285. D. 40 m

To determine the square's perimeter, you first need to find each side measure. The area of a square is the square of one of its side measures, so use that relationship to determine the measure of a side:

$$A = s^2$$
$$100 = s^2$$
$$\sqrt{100} = \sqrt{s^2}$$
$$10 = s$$

Because each side of the square is 10 m and a square has four sides, the perimeter of the square is $10(4)$, or 40 m.

286. E. 42 ft.

The three sides of an equilateral triangle are congruent, so the perimeter of an equilateral is 3 times the measure of a side:

$$P = 3(14) = 42$$

The perimeter of the triangle is 42 ft.

287. A. 103.5 m²

To find the area of the composite figure, find the area of the triangle and the area of the square separately, and then add the areas. The area of the square is the square of a side:

$$A = s^2$$
$$= 9^2$$
$$= 81$$

The square's area is 81 m^2.

The area of the triangle is half its base times its height:

$$A = \frac{1}{2}(9)(5)$$
$$= \frac{1}{2}(45)$$
$$= 22.5$$

The area of the triangle is 22.5 m². The sum of the area of the square and the area of the triangle is 103.5 m².

288. **D. 34.28 square miles**

To find the area of the composite figure, find the area of the rectangle and the area of the semicircle, and then add their areas. The area of the rectangle is its length times its width:

$$A = lw$$
$$= (7)(4)$$
$$= 28$$

The area of the rectangle is 28 square miles.

The area of the semicircle is half the area of a circle with the same radius. The radius is half of 4 miles, so it's 2 miles.

$$A = \frac{1}{2}\pi r^2$$
$$= \frac{1}{2}\pi (2)^2$$
$$= \frac{1}{2}\pi (4)$$
$$= 2\pi$$

The question asks for the area rounded to the nearest hundredth, so use 3.14 as an approximation of π:

$$2 \times 3.14 = 6.28$$

The area of the semicircle, rounded to the nearest hundredth, is 6.28 square miles.

The area of the composite figures is the sum of 28 square miles and 6.28 square miles, or 34.28 square miles.

289. **B. 38.5 ft.²**

The area of the shaded region is the rectangle's area minus the triangle's area. First find the rectangle's area:

$$A = lw$$
$$= (11)(7)$$
$$= 77$$

The area of the rectangle is 77 ft.².

Next, find the area of the triangle:

$$A = \frac{1}{2}bh$$
$$= \frac{1}{2}(11)(7)$$
$$= \frac{1}{2}(77)$$
$$= 38.5$$

The area of the triangle is 38.5 ft.². (Notice that the area of the triangle is half the area of the rectangle. How are their area formulas different?)

The area of the shaded region is the area of the rectangle minus the area of the triangle:

$$77 - 38.5 = 38.5$$

The area of the shaded region is 38.5 ft.². That's equal to the area of the triangle because both the triangle and the shaded region are half the area of the rectangle.

290. $128 - 32\pi$

To find the area of the shaded region, first find the area of the rectangle. Then subtract the areas of the circles.

The width of the rectangle is the same as the diameter of each circle. The length of the rectangle is covered by the diameters of the two circles, so the rectangle's length is twice the diameter of one circle. The length of the rectangle is therefore 16 units. The area of the rectangle is its length times its width:

$$A = lw$$
$$= (16)(8)$$
$$= 128$$

The area of the rectangle is 128 square units.

The area of each circle is π times the square of its radius. The diameter is 8, so the radius is half that, or 4.

$$A = \pi r^2$$
$$= \pi (4)^2$$
$$= 16\pi$$

The area of each circle is 16π, and there are two of them, so the area covered by the circles is $16\pi \times 2$, or 32π.

The area of the shaded region is the rectangle's area minus the circles' total area, so the area of the shaded region is exactly $128 - 32\pi$ square units. Using 3.14 in place of π wouldn't result in an exact answer because 3.14 is merely an approximation of π.

291. **A.** 9

Any two similar triangles have the same shape, so if the triangles are drawn to scale, you can look at the shapes of the triangles to determine which sides correspond. You can also determine which ratios of sides in separate triangles are the same.

The unknown side measure is in the triangle on the right, and its corresponding side in the triangle on the left is 18 ft. You can use either of the other two corresponding side ratios to set up a proportion and solve for x. The cross products of a true proportion are equal.

$$\frac{4}{2} = \frac{18}{x}$$
$$4x = 2(18)$$
$$4x = 36$$
$$\frac{4x}{4} = \frac{36}{4}$$
$$x = 9$$

To check the answer, you can put 9 in for x and see that the two fractions are equal. You can also see that each side in the tringle on the right is $\frac{1}{2}$ its corresponding side measure in the triangle on the right. Because $\frac{1}{2}$ of 18 is 9, the side that corresponds to the 18 ft. side must be 9 ft.

292. **C.** $\frac{1}{4}$

The *scale factor* between similar figures is a ratio of a side measure in one figure to its corresponding side measure in the other figure. Between any two similar figures, there are two scale factors, because either figure's side measures can be put first in the ratio. When a problem asks for a scale factor from one given figure to the other one, you need to find the number by which a side in the first figure must be multiplied to get the corresponding side measure in the other figure.

In this problem, a side in Quadrilateral 1 is 16 dm, and its corresponding side in Quadrilateral 2 is 4 dm. The ratio of the first measure to the second is $\frac{16}{4}$, or 4. However, the scale factor from Quadrilateral 1 to Quadrilateral 2 is the reciprocal of that, because the number 16 can be multiplied by to get 4 is $\frac{1}{4}$. The scale factor from Quadrilateral 1 to Quadrilateral 2 is therefore $\frac{1}{4}$.

Remember: The scale factor from one figure to another is *not* the ratio of a side measure of the first figure to a side measure of the second figure; it's the reciprocal of that. Multiplying a side measure in the first figure by the scale factor must give you the corresponding side measure in the second figure.

293. **E. 6 m**

You can set up a proportion with ratios of corresponding side measures. Use a variable to represent the unknown measure:

$$\frac{9}{x} = \frac{21}{14}$$
$$9(14) = 21x$$
$$126 = 21x$$
$$\frac{126}{21} = \frac{21x}{21}$$
$$6 = x$$

The side measure in question is 6 m.

294. **A, B, C, and D. All pairs of corresponding angles are congruent. All pairs of corresponding sides are congruent. All corresponding parts are congruent. The two triangles' perimeters are equal.**

If two triangles are congruent, they're identical; they're essentially the same triangle in two different places. By definition, all pairs of corresponding parts between two congruent triangles are congruent. That means their corresponding sides are congruent in every case, and their corresponding angles are congruent in every case. Because their corresponding sides are congruent, the sums of their sides are the same, so their perimeters are equal.

Choice (E) isn't true, because all pairs of corresponding sides are congruent in all cases of congruent triangles. Choice (E) is true of similar triangles but not congruent triangles.

295. **B. 150 mm²**

A cube is a type of right rectangular prism, and the surface area of any right prism is the perimeter times the height plus twice the base area: $SA = Ph + 2B$. Every side of a cube has the same measure, so every side of the cube here is 5 mm. Therefore, the perimeter of a base is $4(5)$ mm, or 20 mm, and the height is 5 mm. The area of a base is $5(5)$ mm² because each base area is a side measure times itself.

$$SA = Ph + 2B$$
$$= 4(5)(5) + 2(5)(5)$$
$$= 100 + 50$$
$$= 150$$

The surface area of the cube is 150 mm². Remember that area is a number of square units.

296. **E. 348 m²**

The surface of any right prism is $Ph + 2B$, which is the product of the perimeter of a base and its corresponding height, plus twice the area of the base. Any face of a right rectangular prism can be considered a base, and what you use for height must be the measure of a segment perpendicular to the face you decided to consider a base. For example, if you consider an 8 m × 9 m face a base for the right rectangular prism in this problem, you must consider 6 m to be the height. In that case, the other 8 m × 9 m face is also a base.

$$SA = Ph + 2B$$
$$= (8 + 9 + 8 + 9)(6) + 2(8)(9)$$
$$= (34)(6) + 2(72)$$
$$= 204 + 144$$
$$= 348$$

The surface area of the right rectangular prism is 348 m².

297. **A. 64 cubic miles**

A cube is a type of right rectangular prism. The volume of any prism is the product of a base area and the corresponding height. Because every side of every face of a cube is congruent, every face is congruent; that means you can use any face area and multiply it by the side measure to get the volume. That amounts to multiplying the side measure by itself by itself. In other words, the volume of a cube is the cube of a side measure:

$$V = s^3$$
$$= 4^3$$
$$= 64$$

The volume of the cube is 64 cubic miles, which you can express as 64 mi.³.

298. **D. 152 cubic units**

The volume of any prism is Bh, or base area times the height:

$$V = Bh$$
$$= (19)(8)$$
$$= 152$$

The volume of the prism is 152 cubic units.

299. B. 78π cm^2

The general formula for the surface area of a right cylinder (a term that automatically implies "right circular cylinder") is the same as the surface area formula for a right prism: $Ph + 2B$, or the perimeter of a base times the height plus twice the base area. However, a right cylinder has circular bases, so you use the circumference in place of the perimeter. Use the given measurements to determine the surface area of the cylinder in this problem:

$$\begin{aligned} SA &= Ph + 2B \\ &= 2\pi rh + 2\pi r^2 \\ &= 2\pi(3)(10) + 2\pi(3)^2 \\ &= 60\pi + 2\pi(9) \\ &= 60\pi + 18\pi \\ &= 78\pi \end{aligned}$$

The surface area of the cylinder is 78π cm^2.

300. A. 152π km^2

The radius of a cylinder, as with just a circle, is half its diameter. The radius for the cylinder here is half of 8 km, so it's 4 km. Use the surface area formula for a right prism, where SA is the surface area, P is the perimeter of the base (the circumference in this case), h is the height, and B is the base area:

$$\begin{aligned} SA &= Ph + 2B \\ &= 2\pi rh + 2\pi r^2 \\ &= 2\pi(4)(15) + 2\pi(4)^2 \\ &= 120\pi + 2\pi(16) \\ &= 120\pi + 32\pi \\ &= 152\pi \end{aligned}$$

The surface area of the cylinder is 152π km^2.

301.   D. 7 micrometers

You can use the formula for cylinder volume to find the cylinder's radius. Fill in every variable in the formula with its value and then solve for the variable of unknown value, r:

$$V = Bh$$
$$V = \pi r^2 h$$
$$490\pi = \pi r^2 (10)$$
$$490\pi = 10\pi r^2$$
$$\frac{490\pi}{10\pi} = \frac{10\pi r^2}{10\pi}$$
$$49 = r^2$$
$$7 = r$$
$$r = 7$$

The radius is 7 micrometers.

302.   C. 6,720π yd.³

The amount of volume of the larger cylinder that is outside of the smaller cylinder is the larger cylinder's volume minus the smaller cylinder's volume. To find that difference, first find the larger cylinder's volume:

$$V = Ph$$
$$= \pi r^2 h$$
$$= \pi (11)^2 (70)$$
$$= \pi (121)(70)$$
$$= 8,470\pi$$

The volume of the larger cylinder is $8,470\pi$ yd.³.

Next, find the volume of the smaller cylinder:

$$V = Ph$$
$$= \pi r^2 h$$
$$= \pi (5)^2 (70)$$
$$= \pi (25)(70)$$
$$= 1,750\pi$$

The volume of the larger cylinder is $1,750\pi$ yd.³. The difference between the larger cylinder's volume and the smaller cylinder's volume is $6,720\pi$ yd.³.

303. **E. 154π cm²**

The surface area of a cone is the sum of its lateral area (L) and base area. A cone has only one base, so you add B to the lateral area instead of $2B$.

$$SA = L + B$$
$$= 54\pi + 100\pi$$
$$= 154\pi$$

The surface area of the cone is 154π cm².

304. **C. 230π yd.²**

To find the surface area of the composite figure, add the surface areas of the figure parts. Notice that the base of the cone and one of the cylinder's bases are on the interior of the composite figure; don't include their areas in the calculation of the surface area.

To find the surface area of the cone part, just find the lateral area, $\frac{1}{2}Pl$, where P is the perimeter (or circumference) of the cone:

$$\frac{1}{2}Pl = \frac{1}{2}(2\pi r)l$$
$$= \pi rl$$

The lateral area of a cone is πrl. You can use the Pythagorean theorem to determine the slant height, l. The height of the cone and any of its radii form a right angle, with the slant height as the hypotenuse:

$$5^2 + 12^2 = l^2$$
$$25 + 144 = l^2$$
$$169 = l^2$$
$$13 = l$$

Now you can put 13 in for l to determine the lateral area of the cone:

$$\pi(5)(13) = 65\pi$$

The part of the composite figure's surface area covered by the cone is 65π yd.².

Now find the surface area of the cylinder part. The cylinder part has only one base on the surface, so add B (the base area), not $2B$, to the lateral area (perimeter times height):

$$Ph + B = 2\pi rh + \pi r^2$$
$$= 2\pi(5)(14) + \pi(5)^2$$
$$= 140\pi + 25\pi$$
$$= 165\pi$$

The surface area of the cylinder part of the composite figure is 165π yd.². The total surface area is the sum of the cone part and the cylinder part:

$$65\pi + 165\pi = 230\pi$$

The surface area of the composite figure is 230π yd.².

305. B. 800π m³

The volume of a cone is a third of the product of its base and its height. The height of this cone isn't given, but you can use the Pythagorean theorem to find it. The height, a radius, and the slant height form a right triangle in which the height and the radius are perpendicular and the slant height is the hypotenuse.

$$a^2 + b^2 = c^2$$
$$10^2 + b^2 = 26^2$$
$$100 + b^2 = 676$$
$$b^2 = 576$$
$$b = 24$$

The height of the cone is 24 m. That times a third of the base area is the volume of the cone:

$$V = \frac{1}{3}Bh$$
$$= \frac{1}{3}\pi r^2 h$$
$$= \frac{1}{3}\pi(10)^2(24)$$
$$= \frac{2,400\pi}{3}$$
$$= 800\pi$$

The volume of the cone is 800π m³.

306. C. 3

The volume of a cone is $\frac{1}{3}Bh$, and the area of a cylinder is Bh. That means that if base area and height are the same for a cylinder and a cone, the volume of the cylinder is three times the volume of the cone.

307. A. 1,215 ft.²

The surface area of a pyramid is its lateral area plus its base area, or $\frac{1}{2}Pl + B$. The base perimeter of the pyramid here is the sum of its side measures, so it's 90 ft. The slant height is given as 17 ft. The base area is the product of the length and width of the base, so it's 450 ft.² With those measures, you can determine the surface area of the pyramid.

$$SA = \frac{1}{2}Pl + B$$
$$= \frac{1}{2}(90)(17) + 450$$
$$= \frac{1,530}{2} + 450$$
$$= 765 + 450$$
$$= 1,215$$

The surface area of the pyramid is 1,215 ft.².

308.

C. 216.57 m²

The surface area of a pyramid is the sum of its lateral area and base area.

$$124.19 + 92.38 = 216.57$$

The surface area of the pyramid is 216.57 m².

309.

E. $\frac{1}{3}$

A prism's volume is Bh, and a pyramid's volume is $\frac{1}{3}Bh$. That shows that if a prism and a pyramid have the same base area and height, the prism's volume can be multiplied by $\frac{1}{3}$ to get the volume of the pyramid.

310.

B. 972 cubic miles

The volume of the composite figure is the sum of the volume of the cube and the volume of the pyramid. Find each separately and then add the volumes. The volume of the cube is the cube of its side measure:

$$V = s^3$$
$$= 9^3$$
$$= 729$$

The volume of the cube is 729 cubic miles.

The volume of the pyramid is a third of its base area times its height. Its base is a square, so you can square its side measure to find the base area:

$$9^2 = 81$$

The base area of the pyramid is 81 square miles. With that and the height of the pyramid, you can find the pyramid's volume:

$$V = \frac{1}{3}Bh$$
$$= \frac{1}{3}(81)(9)$$
$$= \frac{729}{3}$$
$$= 243$$

Notice that the volume of the pyramid is $\frac{1}{3}$ times the volume of the cube. That's because they have the same base area and height. The sum of the volume of the cube and the volume of the pyramid is the sum of 729 cubic miles and 243 cubic miles:

$$729 + 243 = 972$$

The volume of the composite figure is 972 cubic miles.

311.   **D. 100π km^2**

The surface area of a sphere is four times the area of its inner circle, or $4\pi r^2$:

$$SA = 4\pi r^2$$
$$= 4\pi(5)^2$$
$$= 4\pi(25)$$
$$= 100\pi$$

The surface area of the sphere is 100π km^2.

312.   **A. 6 hm**

To determine the diameter of the sphere, you can first use the sphere's surface area formula to find the radius:

$$SA = 4\pi r^2$$
$$36\pi = 4\pi r^2$$
$$\frac{36\pi}{4\pi} = \frac{4\pi r^2}{4\pi}$$
$$9 = r^2$$
$$3 = r$$

The radius of the sphere is 3 hm, so the diameter is twice that, or 6 hm.

313.   **A. 972π m**

Use the formula for the volume of a sphere:

$$V = \frac{4}{3}\pi r^3$$
$$= \frac{4}{3}\pi(9)^3$$
$$= \frac{4}{3}\pi(729)$$
$$= \frac{2,916\pi}{3}$$
$$= 972\pi$$

The volume of the sphere is 972π m.

314.   **C. $\frac{500\pi}{3}$ km^3**

You can use the surface area of the bubble to find its radius, which you can use to find the volume. Set up the formula for the surface area of a sphere, fill in all known values, and solve for r:

$$SA = 4\pi r^2$$
$$100\pi = 4\pi r^2$$
$$\frac{100\pi}{4\pi} = \frac{4\pi r^2}{4\pi}$$
$$25 = r^2$$
$$5 = r$$

Now you can put 5 in for r in the sphere volume formula to find the volume of the bubble:

$$V = \frac{4}{3}\pi r^3$$
$$= \frac{4}{3}\pi(5)^3$$
$$= \frac{4}{3}\pi(125)$$
$$= \frac{500\pi}{3}$$

The bubble has a volume of $\frac{500\pi}{3}$ km^3.

315. D. 16 in.²

A cube is a type of right rectangular solid, so its lateral area is the perimeter of one of its bases times the corresponding height. Any face of a cube can be a base. All four sides of each face are 2 in., so every face has a perimeter of $2(4)$ in., or 8 in. Every possible base has a corresponding height of 2 in. because every side is 2 in. Therefore, the lateral area is $2(4)(2)$ in.^{2}, or 16 in.^{2}.

316. C. 660 ft.³

The amount of liquid nitrogen the tank can hold is the same as the volume of the tank. The tank is a rectangular prism, so its volume is Bh (base area times height), which is the same as the product of its length, width, and height:

$$Bh = (lw)h$$
$$= (22)(5)(6)$$
$$= 660$$

The volume of the tank is 660 ft.^{3}, so that's how much liquid nitrogen it can contain.

317. A. (2, 4)

To determine the coordinates of the point, start at the origin and count the number of units you have to move to be lined up with the point vertically. The origin is the point $(0, 0)$. To get directly under point C, you have to move two places in the positive direction, which is to the right. That means the x-coordinate of the point is +2, or 2. Next, count the number of units you have to move from directly under point C to get to it. You have to move up four units. That's four units in the positive vertical direction, so 4 is the y-coordinate of point C. Thus, the ordered pair for point C is $(2, 4)$.

318. C. 6

Point A is $(0, 6)$, and point B is $(0, 0)$. To find the distance between any two points on the coordinate plane, you can use the distance formula. If you consider one ordered pair (x_1, y_1) and the other one (x_2, y_2), you can follow put the corresponding values into the following equation and evaluate it:

$$d = \sqrt{(x_1 - x_2)^2 + (y_1 - y_2)^2}$$
$$= \sqrt{(0 - 0)^2 + (6 - 0)^2}$$
$$= \sqrt{0^2 + 6^2}$$
$$= \sqrt{0 + 36}$$
$$= \sqrt{36}$$
$$= 6$$

The distance between the points is 6. You can also count straight up the y-axis from $(0, 0)$ to $(0, 6)$ and see that the distance is 6 units.

319. E. 2.8

To find the distance between the points, put the coordinates in the distance formula and evaluate the result:

$$d = \sqrt{(x_1 - x_2)^2 + (y_1 - y_2)^2}$$
$$= \sqrt{(2 - 4)^2 + (8 - 10)^2}$$
$$= \sqrt{(-2)^2 + (-2)^2}$$
$$= \sqrt{4 + 4}$$
$$= \sqrt{8}$$
$$= 2.82842712475\ldots$$

The question asks for the distance rounded to the nearest tenth, which means with one digit after the decimal point. The digit that comes after the first digit after the decimal point is 2, so round down:

$$2.82842712475 \rightarrow 2.8$$

The distance between the two points, rounded to the nearest tenth, is 2.8.

320. B. $\left(\dfrac{3}{2}, \dfrac{5}{2}\right)$

Point G is $(2, 4)$, and point H is $(1, 1)$. The midpoint between any two points on the coordinate plane has an x-coordinate that's halfway between the x-coordinates of the given points and a y-coordinate that's halfway between the y-coordinates of the given points. The number that's halfway between two numbers is their average (mean). The midpoint formula is based on that principle. You can put the coordinates of $(2, 4)$ and $(1, 1)$ into the midpoint formula to find the midpoint:

$$\left(\frac{x_1 + x_2}{2}, \frac{y_1 + y_2}{2}\right) = \left(\frac{2+1}{2}, \frac{4+1}{2}\right)$$

$$= \left(\frac{3}{2}, \frac{5}{2}\right)$$

The midpoint between $(2, 4)$ and $(1, 1)$ is $\left(\dfrac{3}{2}, \dfrac{5}{2}\right)$. Notice that the number halfway between 2 and 1 is $\dfrac{3}{2}$, which is $1\dfrac{1}{2}$, and that the number halfway between 4 and 1 is $\dfrac{5}{2}$, which is $2\dfrac{1}{2}$.

321. D. $(1, 5)$

Put the coordinates of the points in the midpoint formula and evaluate:

$$\left(\frac{x_1 + x_2}{2}, \frac{y_1 + y_2}{2}\right) = \left(\frac{-5+7}{2}, \frac{14+(-4)}{2}\right)$$

$$= \left(\frac{2}{2}, \frac{10}{2}\right)$$

$$= (1, 5)$$

The midpoint is $(1, 5)$.

322. B. $-\dfrac{4}{3}$

The slope of a line is the ratio of vertical change to horizontal change between any two points on the line. Two of the points on the line here are $(3, 0)$ and $(0, 4)$. You can use the slope formula, where m is the slope, to find this ratio:

$$m = \frac{y_1 - y_2}{x_1 - x_2}$$

$$= \frac{0 - 4}{3 - 0}$$

$$= \frac{-4}{3}$$

Which y-coordinate is subtracted from the other isn't important, as long as you start with the x-coordinate from the same ordered pair. In other words, you must subtract in the same direction both times.

323.

C. $\frac{4}{15}$

Put the coordinates into the slope formula and evaluate:

$$m = \frac{y_1 - y_2}{x_1 - x_2}$$
$$= \frac{9-5}{17-2}$$
$$= \frac{4}{15}$$

The slope of the line containing $(2, 5)$ and $(17, 9)$ is $\frac{4}{15}$.

324.

$-\frac{3}{16}$

The slope-intercept form of the equation of a line is $y = mx + b$, where m represents slope and b is the y-intercept. For an equation in slope-intercept form, the coefficient of x is the slope of the graph. In $y = -\frac{3}{16}x + 75$, the coefficient of x is $-\frac{3}{16}$.

325.

A, C, and E. The line represents all ordered pairs that make its equation true. The ordered pair (1, 1) is a solution to the equation of the line. The ordered pair (3, 3) is a solution to the equation of the line.

A line on the coordinate plane represents all the x and y combinations that make the line's equation true. Every point represents an ordered pair that's a solution to the equation. That's the purpose and meaning of a linear graph on the coordinate plane. Point A is $(1, 1)$, and point B is $(3, 3)$. Those are therefore both solutions to the equation of the line. Choices (B) and (D) contradict this.

326.

A. (2, 2)

The only choice that's a point on the line is $(2, 2)$, making it a solution to the equation of the line. Putting 2 in for x and 2 in for y makes the equation true. None of the other choices are on the graph, so none of them are solutions to the line's equation.

327.

B. (2, 4)

The lines intersect at $(2, 4)$. That means $(2, 4)$ is a point on both lines, so it's a solution to both equations represented by the lines.

328. C. (8, −5) and (9, −3)

A *translation* is a change in position on the coordinate plane. The segment in this case will look the same, have the same measure, and lean exactly the same way after the translation; it will simply be in a different place — five units to the right and seven units down. That means its x-coordinates will increase by 5 and its y-coordinates will decrease by 7. The endpoints of the segment are currently $(3, 2)$ and $(4, 4)$. After a translation of five units right and seven units down, the endpoints will be $(3 + 5, 2 − 7)$ and $(4 + 5, 4 − 7)$. Those ordered pairs are $(8, −5)$ and $(9, −3)$.

329. B. (−4, 3)

The current vertices of the triangle are $(1, 3)$, $(4, 3)$, and $(2, 7)$. If the triangle is reflected over the y-axis, every point on the triangle will be the same distance from the y-axis but on the other side of it. That's why every x-coordinate will be the opposite but every y-coordinate will be the same. Thus, the vertices of the triangle will switch from $(1, 3)$, $(4, 3)$, and $(2, 7)$ to $(−1, 3)$, $(−4, 3)$, and $(−2, 7)$. The only one of those points that's an answer choice is $(−4, 3)$.

330. D. Keeping the same x-coordinates and multiplying the y-coordinates by −1

When a figure is reflected over the x-axis, it keeps the same horizontal placement but changes to a new vertical level, keeping the same distance (and therefore vertical magnitude) from the x-axis. As a result, the new points keep the same x-coordinates but get the opposite y-coordinates. To find the opposite y-coordinates, multiply the y-coordinates by −1.

331. E. (21, 21)

To dilate a polygon by a scale factor, multiply all the coordinates of its vertices by the scale factor. (Really, all the points on the polygon are multiplied by the scale factor, but you don't need to perform multiplication on an infinite number of points.) If the square graphed here is dilated by a scale factor of 7, both coordinates of each vertex are multiplied by 7. The top right vertex is $(3, 3)$. If the square is dilated by a scale factor of 7, the new coordinates of that vertex will be $(3 × 7, 3 × 7)$, or $(21, 21)$.

332. E. Size

A *dilation* is defined only as a change in size of a figure on the coordinate plane. Choice (B) describes a translation, Choice (C) describes reflection over the x-axis, and Choice (D) describes reflection over the y-axis.

333. B. (−7, 6)

Rotating a figure 90° counterclockwise about the origin involves switching the coordinates of each point and giving the new x-coordinate the opposite sign. The endpoints of the segment in the graph here are currently $(1, 2)$ and $(6, 7)$. After a 90° rotation about the origin, the new coordinates of the endpoints are $(−2, 1)$ and $(−7, 6)$. The only one that's listed as an answer choice is $(−7, 6)$.

334. C. (−3, −4)

The pentagon in this problem has vertices at $(1, 5)$, $(2, 3)$, $(4, 3)$, $(5, 5)$, and $(3, 7)$. A 180° degree rotation of the pentagon about the origin would entail getting new vertices with coordinates that are the opposites of the current ones. Thus, the new vertices would be $(−1, −5)$, $(−2, −3)$, $(−4, −3)$, $(−5, −5)$, and $(−3, −7)$. Every answer choice is one of those points except $(−3, −4)$.

335. C. 173

The table shows that Jeffrey weighs 348 pounds and Drew weighs 175 pounds. Subtract Jeffrey's weight in pounds from Drew's. You can use your calculator.

$$348 − 175 = 173$$

Jeffrey weighs 173 pounds more than Drew.

336. A. 2

The table shows that Nancy sold 458 cars. Only two salespeople sold more: Willie sold 754, and Donald sold 542.

337. E. Scott

The higher a bar is, the higher its corresponding time. The lower a person's time, the faster the person ran the mile. The second lowest bar represents Scott's time, so Scott had the second fastest time. Daryl, Paul, and Seb took longer than Scott to run the mile, and Steve ran a faster mile than Scott.

338. D. Orville

For this graph, the lower a bar is, the lower its corresponding average yearly rainfall is. The lowest bar represents Orville.

339. B. Four

The graph indicates that Chris's annual income was the lowest in 2014, of the five years represented. The lower a dot is, the lower its corresponding income.

340. A. Fourth

You can determine the greatest drop by finding the longest downward sloping "line" (segment) in the graph. The longest one ends at the dot representing the fourth election, so the greatest drop in votes happened from the third election to the fourth. Ted's votes went from a little under 7,000 votes to a little more than 3,000, a drop of nearly 4,000 votes. The only other drops were from the fourth election to the fifth and from the sixth election to the seventh. Neither of those two drops is greater than 2,000 votes.

341. A and D. The correlation between the independent variable and the dependent variable is positive. As the independent variable increases, the dependent variable increases.

The graph shows numbers representing both variables. You can see that as the numbers for the independent variable (on the horizontal axis) increase, the numbers for the dependent variable (on the vertical axis) increase. That fits the definition of a positive correlation. Even if the dependent variable data tends to increase but doesn't increase in every case, a positive correlation exists between the two variables. For a negative correlation to exist, the dependent variable would have to tend to decrease as the independent variable increased.

342. C. 578

Find how many people use Mackenco or AB&C and then add them. Because 14% of the population of Spencerton uses Mackenco and the population is 1,700, the number of residents who use Mackenco is 14% of 1,700:

$$14\% \times 1,700 = 0.14 \times 1,700$$
$$= 238$$

Because 20% of the residents use AB&C, you can multiply 20% by 1,700 to find how many residents use AB&C:

$$20\% \times 1,700 = 0.20 \times 1,700$$
$$= 340$$

The number of Spencerton residents who use AB&C is 340.

The number of residents who use either Mackenco or AB&C is the sum of 238 and 340:

$$238 + 340 = 578$$

343.   **D. 10%**

The circle graph shows that 55% percent of the Squirrel Club's budget goes to parties, 28% goes to public activism, and 17% goes to charity benefits. The sum of the percents of the budget that go to public activism and charity benefits is the sum of 28% and 17%, or 45%. The question asks how much more goes to the party budget. You can find that difference by subtracting 45% from 55%: 55% − 45% = 10%.

344.   **E. 37**

The key indicates that the stems represent tens and the leaves represent ones, because 3|5 = 35. A 3 for a stem with a 7 for a leaf represents 3 tens plus 7 ones, or 37.

345.   **B, C, D, and E. 140, 400, 71, and 840**

The stems represent hundreds and the leaves represent tens. With 0 as a stem and 4 as a leaf, only 40, Choice (A), is represented. The question asks which choices are *not* represented, so Choices (B), (C), (D), and (E) are correct.

346.   **B. 120**

The dot farthest to the right always represents the highest number represented by a box and whisker plot. In this case, that number is 120.

347.   **D. 5**

The highest number represented by the box and whisker plot corresponds to the dot that's farthest to the right, or 6. The lowest number represented corresponds to the dot that's farthest to the left, or 1. The distance from one number on the number line to another is their difference:

$$6 - 1 = 5$$

The distance on the number line from 1 to 6 is 5, which is the range of the represented data.

348.   **E. The Marshall Tucker Band is both a country act and a rock act.**

The Marshall Tucker Band is listed where the country category overlaps with the rock category, suggesting that the Marshall Tucker Band qualifies as both a country act and a rock act.

349. C. 32

The Venn diagram shows that 10 of the people represented are just preachers and 15 of the people represented are just professors. However, these categories also overlap, showing that 7 of the people are both preachers and professors. Therefore, the total number of people who are preachers or professors is the sum of 10, 15, and 7, which is 32.

350. C. Venn diagrams are both diagrams and representations of categories.

The overlap of the category labeled "Diagrams" and the category labeled "Representations of Categories" is labeled "Venn Diagrams." This means that Venn diagrams are in both categories. Venn diagrams are diagrams, and Venn diagrams are representations of categories.

351. E. An increase in Variable A is always accompanied by an increase in Variable B.

The scatterplot shows that as Variable A increases a substantial amount, B decreases. However, not every increase in Variable A is accompanied by a decrease in Variable B; Variable B merely tends to decrease as Variable A increases. That's enough to qualify the correlation between the two variables as negative. The question asks which choice isn't indicated by the scatterplot, so Choice (E) is correct.

352. Positive

As the amount of time in the program increases, the average endurance test scores tend to increase. The test scores don't increase with every addition of time, but they always increase after enough time. That makes the correlation positive. If you were to draw a line, called a *line of fit*, through the inside of the section marked by the dots, the line would go up from left to right. That would show that the correlation is positive.

353. B. 2

The number of first place jousting ribbons a participant won is represented by the number of marks above the person's name. According to the line plot, Mosi won four and Aaron won two. Subtraction shows that Mosi won two more first place jousting ribbons than Aaron:

$$4 - 2 = 2$$

354. B. $\frac{2}{3}$

The line plot indicates that Spike ate four pies on Day 4, four on Day 2, and two on Day 5. Thus, the sum of the pies he ate on Days 2 and 5 is the sum of 4 and 2:

$$4+2=6$$

The ratio of the pies Spike ate on Day 4 to the sum of the pies he ate on Days 2 and 5 is therefore $\frac{4}{6}$, which is $\frac{2}{3}$ in simplest form.

355. B. 7

The mean of a data set is the average of the data set. To find the mean, add all the numbers (elements) of the data and then divide by how many numbers are in the set. The sum of 4 and 10 is 14. There are two numbers in the data set, so divide 14 by 2. The mean is therefore 7.

356. C. 7

To find the mean, add the given numbers and then divide the sum by the number of numbers in the set, which is 4:

$$\frac{0+8+12+8}{4}=\frac{28}{4}$$
$$=7$$

The mean is therefore 7.

357. D. 11

To find the mean, add the numbers and divide the sum by the number of numbers in the set, which is 6:

$$\frac{4+8+11+14+3+26}{6}=\frac{66}{6}$$
$$=11$$

The mean is therefore 11.

358. D. 95

This is a statistics question but also an algebra problem. The necessary score for the sixth test is unknown, so you can use a variable to represent it. You can call it x or another variable of your choosing. If you add it to the sum of the other test scores and divide the new sum by 6, the number of tests after she takes the next test, you get the mean of the set of data. The question is what the sixth test must be for the mean to be 70. Set up an equation for the mean average and then solve for x:

$$\frac{54+80+61+72+58+x}{6} = 70$$

$$\frac{325+x}{6} = 70$$

$$6\left(\frac{325+x}{6}\right) = 6(70)$$

$$325 + x = 420$$

$$325 + x - 325 = 420 - 325$$

$$x = 95$$

The value of the variable is 95, so Kathleen needs to score a 95.

359. A. $8\frac{2}{7}$

The first seven prime numbers are 2, 3, 5, 7, 11, 13, and 17. (Remember that 1 isn't a prime number but 2 is.) The mean of the first seven prime numbers is their sum divided by 7, because there are seven prime numbers in the set:

$$\frac{2+3+5+7+11+13+17}{7} = \frac{58}{7}$$

$$= 8\frac{2}{7}$$

360. C. 89.2

The quiz scores in the data set are 92, 84, 92, 96, and 82. To find the mean of that set, add the elements (numbers) and divide by the number of quiz scores:

$$\frac{92+84+92+96+82}{5} = \frac{446}{5}$$

$$= 89.2$$

361. A. 2

The *median* of a set of data is the middle number when the numbers are in order (unless the data set has an even number of numbers, in which case the median is the mean [average] of the two middle numbers). The numbers are in order, and the middle number is 2.

362. E. 8

The median of a set of data with an odd number of elements is the middle number in value. To find the middle number in value for this set of data, put the numbers in order from least to greatest:

1   7   <u>8</u>   12   15

When the numbers are in order, the middle number is 8.

363. C. 4.5

Put the numbers in ascending order and determine what is in the middle. Because this set has six numbers and six is an even number, there are two numbers in the middle:

1   1   <u>4</u>   <u>5</u>   9   20

The median of the set is the mean (average) of the two numbers in the middle:

$$\frac{4+5}{2} = \frac{9}{2}$$
$$= 4.5$$

364. 73

Put the numbers in order and then identify what is in the middle. Because this data set has an even number of numbers (elements), two numbers are in the middle:

68   <u>72</u>   <u>74</u>   80

The median of the set is the mean (average) of the two numbers that are in the middle:

$$\frac{72+74}{2} = \frac{146}{2}$$
$$= 73$$

365. A. 8

A *composite number* is a positive whole number that has factors other than 1 and itself; in other words, it isn't prime. The first five composite numbers are 4, 6, 8, 9, and 10, in that order. Those numbers are in order, so to find the median, look for what's in the middle:

4   6   <u>8</u>   9   10

The middle number is 8, so 8 is the median of the data set.

366. D. 50

The key indicates that the stems represent tens and the leaves represent ones. Therefore, the number appearances in the data set are the following:

$$1 \quad 2 \quad 4 \quad 8 \quad 20 \quad 24 \quad 25 \quad 27 \quad 50 \quad 51 \quad 52 \quad 55 \quad 58 \quad 71 \quad 71 \quad 72 \quad 85$$

There are 17 numbers in the set, and the numbers are in order. Seventeen is an odd number, so the median is the number in the middle:

$$1 \quad 2 \quad 4 \quad 8 \quad 20 \quad 24 \quad 25 \quad 27 \quad \underline{50} \quad 51 \quad 52 \quad 55 \quad 58 \quad 71 \quad 71 \quad 72 \quad 85$$

That number is 50. It has eight numbers before it and eight numbers after it. *Tip:* To find the number in the middle of a set with an odd number of numbers, add 1 to the number of numbers and then divide that by 2. The middle number will be in that place in the data set.

$$\frac{17+1}{2} = \frac{18}{2}$$
$$= 9$$

$$\frac{x-1}{2} + 1 = \frac{x-1}{2} + \frac{2}{2}$$
$$= \frac{x-1+2}{2}$$
$$= \frac{x+1}{2}$$

For this set, the middle number is the ninth number, which is 50. You can always check your answer by making sure the same number of numbers comes before and after what you identify as the median.

367. B. The number that appears the most often in the set

The *mode* of a set of data is the number that appears the most often in the set. Choice (A) is the mean of a set of data, Choice (C) is the median, Choice (D) is the range of a data set, and Choice (E) is an outlier.

368. E. 3

The *mode* of a set of data is the number that appears the most often. In this case, 3 is in the set twice, whereas the other two numbers appear once each.

369. B. 7

The number that appears the most often in the data set is 7, so 7 is the mode. (It's also the median and the mean.)

370. A. 12

The number that appears most often in the set is 12, so it's the mode.

371. C. 31

The number that appears most often in the set is 31, so it's the mode. Thirty-one appears three times.

372. B. 3

The number appearances that the line plot represents are 3, 1, 4, and 3. The number 3 appears the most often in the set, so it's the mode.

373. **B, C, D, and E. The numerical distance covered by the set; the difference between the highest number and the lowest number in the set; the number that could be subtracted from the highest number to get the lowest number; and the number that could be added to the lowest number in the set to get the highest number**

The *range* of a set of data is defined as the difference that results when the lowest number in the set is subtracted from the highest number. That difference is how far the lowest number is from the highest number. The range is therefore what could be subtracted from the highest number to get the lowest number or the number that could be added to the lowest number to get the highest number. The range of a set of data is all those things because it's the numerical span of the data set. Choice (A) is the median of a set of data.

374. A. 10

The range of the data set is the difference that results from subtracting the lower number from the higher number:

$$10 - 0 = 10$$

375. E. 9

The range of the set of data is the difference of the highest number minus the lowest number:

$$11 - 2 = 9$$

376. B. 73

The range of the data is the numerical distance from the lowest number in the set to the highest number in the set. You can find the range by subtracting the lowest number from the highest number:

$$158 - 85 = 73$$

377. A. 57

The highest age Prince ever was, in terms of a whole number of years, is 57. The lowest age he ever was is 0. The range is the difference that results from subtracting 0 from 57:

$$57 - 0 = 57$$

378. C. 5

The highest number represented by the box and whisker plot is 6. The lowest number is 1. The highest number minus the lowest number is 5, so the range is 5:

$$6 - 1 = 5$$

379. B. $\frac{1}{2}$

The probability of an event is the ratio of the number of qualifying (favorable) outcomes to the number of possible outcomes. For this question, the number of possible outcomes is 2: The coin will land on either heads or tails. Of those possible outcomes, only one qualifies as what's asked about, which is landing on heads. Therefore, the probability that the coin will land on heads is $\frac{1}{2}$.

380. A. $\frac{4}{9}$

The probability that Melissa will pull a blue marble is the ratio of the number of qualifying outcomes to the number of possible outcomes. The number of possible outcomes is 9 because nine marbles are in the bag. Four of those marbles are blue, so the number of qualifying (favorable) outcomes is 4. The ratio of qualifying outcomes to possible outcomes is therefore $\frac{4}{9}$, so that's the probability of picking a blue marble.

381. B. $\frac{1}{5}$

The formula for the probability that a given event will occur is $P(\text{Event}) = \dfrac{\text{number of qualifying outcomes}}{\text{number of possible outcomes}}$. The number of qualifying outcomes is 1 because Joseph's name appears on only one piece of paper. The number of possible outcomes is 5 because there are five names in the hat. The probability that the teacher will pull Joseph's name from the hat is thus $\frac{1}{5}$.

382. D. $\frac{1}{8}$

The number of qualifying outcomes is 1 because the question asks about the probability of landing on one number, which is 3. The number of possible outcomes is 8 because there are eight numbers on which the arrow could possibly land. Therefore, the ratio of the number of qualifying outcomes to the number of possible outcomes is $\frac{1}{8}$.

383. E. $\frac{1}{3}$

The number of qualifying outcomes 2 is because the question asks for a roll of 4 or 5. The number of possible outcomes is 6 because the die has six faces. Thus, the ratio of the number of qualifying outcomes to the number of possible outcomes is $\frac{2}{6}$, which is $\frac{1}{3}$ in lowest terms.

384. B. $\frac{1}{43}$

The number of qualifying outcomes — town residents who have the last name Johnson or Dean — is the sum of 22 and 14, or 36. The number of possible outcomes is 1,548, because that's how many people the mayor can randomly choose from. The ratio of qualifying outcomes to possible outcomes is $\frac{36}{1,548}$, which simplifies to $\frac{1}{43}$.

385. D. $\frac{3}{178}$

The number of qualifying outcomes is the sum of the numbers of raffle tickets bought by Beth, Michelle, Tekeeta, and Pam:

$$4 + 1 + 7 + 3 = 15$$

That's a total of 15 qualifying outcomes. The number of possible outcomes is that sum plus the rest of the raffle tickets that were bought. The "Others" category has 875 raffle tickets, so you get

$$15 + 875 = 890$$

The number of possible outcomes is 890. The ratio of qualifying outcomes to possible outcomes is thus $\frac{15}{890}$, which is $\frac{3}{178}$ in lowest terms.

386. D. $\frac{3}{47}$

The number of qualifying (favorable) outcomes is the sum of the students in Class B and Class D who are running for student council. According to the line plot, two students in Class B and one student in Class D are running for student council, so the sum is 3. The number of possible outcomes is the sum of the numbers of students running in the four classes listed in the line plot and the other 37 students who are running:

$$3+2+4+1+37 = 47$$

The ratio of qualifying outcomes to possible outcomes is therefore $\frac{3}{47}$.

387. C. $\frac{1}{8}$

Use the probability formula, $P(\text{Event}) = \dfrac{\text{number of qualifying outcomes}}{\text{number of possible outcomes}}$. The number of qualifying outcomes, or the number of outcomes that would qualify as the 8 ball or the cue ball, is 2 because that's a total of two balls. The number of possible outcomes is 16 because the number of balls numbered 1 through 15 is 15, and there's another ball in the bag — the cue ball. Any of those balls could be chosen, so there are 16 possible outcomes. The ratio of qualifying outcomes to possible outcomes is thus $\frac{2}{16}$, which you can reduce to $\frac{1}{8}$.

388. A. $\frac{3}{4}$

The first thing to determine is the number of chips that are in the basket. The prime numbers less than 20 are 2, 3, 5, 7, 11, 13, 17, and 19, for a total of eight numbers. Because 5 and 7 are two of those numbers, there are six numbers that qualify as *not* 5 or 7. Thus, the number of qualifying outcomes in this situation is 6. The number of possible outcomes is 8 because there are eight chips in the basket. The ratio of qualifying outcomes to possible outcomes is therefore $\frac{6}{8}$, which you can simplify as $\frac{3}{4}$.

389. D. $\frac{5}{16}$

First, determine how many composite numbers (numbers with more than two positive factors) are greater than 6 and less than 30. You can start by listing those numbers: 8, 9, 10, 12, 14, 15, 16, 18, 20, 21, 22, 24, 25, 26, 27, and 28. The list includes 16 numbers, so the number of possible outcomes is 16. The wheel could land on any of those numbers. The number of qualifying outcomes is the number of those numbers that qualify as between 17 and 25. Note that "between" indicates that 17 and 25 can't be included. (If the question had asked about numbers "from 17 to 25," then 25 would be included, though 17 wouldn't because it isn't a composite number.) The listed numbers that are between 17 and 25 are 18, 20, 21, 22, and 24, for a total of five numbers. The number of qualifying outcomes is 5 and the number of possible outcomes is 16, so the ratio of qualifying outcomes to possible outcomes is $\frac{5}{16}$.

390. D. $\frac{1}{10}$

The skydiver has lost control of his parachute, so his landing spot in the larger rectangle will be random. The number of qualifying outcomes is 1, because landing in rectangle 8 is the only outcome that qualifies. The number of possible outcomes is 10 because there are 10 sections. Therefore, the ratio of qualifying outcomes to possible outcomes is $\frac{1}{10}$.

391. E. 0 and 1

Probability is the ratio of the number of qualifying (favorable) outcomes to the number of possible outcomes. The number of qualifying outcomes can never be greater than the number of possible outcomes, so the ratio can never be greater than 1. However, the number of qualifying outcomes can be 0. It wouldn't make sense for a number of qualifying or possible outcomes to be negative.

392. C. $\frac{2}{7}$

The number of qualifying outcomes is 2 because there are two days that qualify — Wednesday and Saturday. The number of possible outcomes is 7 because there are seven days that can be picked. The probability that Wednesday or Saturday will be randomly chosen is therefore $\frac{2}{7}$.

393. B. $\frac{7}{12}$

The odd numbers from 1 to 12 are 1, 3, 5, 7, 9, and 11, for a total of six numbers; 4 is another qualifying number, so the number of numbers from 1 to 12 that are odd or 4 is $6+1$, or 7. The number of possible outcomes is 12 because the number of natural numbers from 1 to 12 is 12. The ratio of qualifying outcomes to possible outcomes is thus $\frac{7}{12}$.

394. B. $\frac{1}{4}$

The number of multiples of 5 from 1 to 20 are 5, 10, 15, and 20, for a total of four numbers; 7 is another qualifying number, so the number of natural numbers from 1 to 20 that qualify as either 7 or a multiple of 5 is $4+1$, or 5. The number of possible outcomes is 20 because the number of natural numbers from 1 to 20 is 20. The ratio of qualifying outcomes to possible outcomes is $\frac{5}{20}$, which you can reduce to $\frac{1}{4}$.

395. D. $\frac{11}{18}$

The number of animals is $8+5+2+3$, or 18, so the number of possible outcomes is 18. The number of those animals that aren't dogs or birds is the sum of snakes and cats, or $8+3=11$. The ratio of qualifying outcomes to possible outcomes is therefore $\frac{11}{18}$.

396. A. $\frac{1}{4}$

The probability that two events will both happen is the product of their individual probabilities. The probability that the coin will land on tails the first time is $\frac{1}{2}$. The probability is the same for the second flip, so the probability that the coin will land on tails both times is

$$\frac{1}{2} \times \frac{1}{2} = \frac{1}{4}$$

397. B. $\frac{1}{4}$

The probability that the penny will land on heads the first time is $\frac{1}{2}$. The probability that the penny will land on tails on the second flip is also $\frac{1}{2}$.

The two probabilities are independent, so the probability that both will happen is the product of their individual probabilities:

$$\frac{1}{2} \times \frac{1}{2} = \frac{1}{4}$$

398. E. $\frac{4}{21}$

The probability that both events will happen is the product of their individual probabilities. That's because the number of qualifying outcomes is 3×4 and the number of possible outcomes is 7×9. When you multiply the individual probabilities, you get a true ratio, but you have to simplify it:

$$\frac{3}{7} \times \frac{4}{9} = \frac{12}{63} = \frac{4}{21}$$

399. B. $\frac{1}{6}$

For each of the six numbers the first die could land on, there are six possible numbers the other die could land on. Therefore, the number of possibilities for how the two dice could land together is 6×6, or 36. That's the number of possible outcomes.

You can find the number of qualifying (favorable) outcomes by matching each possible first-die number with the number the second die would need to have to give you a sum of 7. There are exactly six possible ways a sum of 7 can be achieved: 1 and 6, 2 and 5, 3 and 4, 4 and 3, 5 and 2, and 6 and 1.

Thus, the ratio of the number of qualifying outcomes to the number of possible outcomes is $\frac{6}{36}$, which reduces to $\frac{1}{6}$.

400. E. 6.1992%

For Robert to win the brand-new blender, the first two events must happen. At that point, his probability of winning the blender is 21 percent, no matter how the first two events happened. The same is true with the second event in regard to the first: It doesn't matter how the previous event happened, as long as it happened. The event probabilities are therefore independent. Dependent probabilities are more advanced and aren't on the Praxis Core exam.

Although the individual probabilities are expressed as percentages, they represent ratios: A percent expresses a ratio of a number to 100. You can multiply the three probabilities to determine the probability that all three will happen:

$$
\begin{aligned}
72\% \times 41\% \times 21\% &= 0.72 \times 0.41 \times 0.21 \\
&= 0.061992 \\
&= 6.1992\%
\end{aligned}
$$

401. A. 3,450

To convert from scientific notation to standard form, move the decimal point the number of places equal to the 10's exponent. In this case, that exponent is 3. That's a positive number, so move the decimal point to the right, the positive direction. Drop the 10 and its exponent.

$$3.45 \times 10^3 = 3,450$$

402. D. 945,213.7

To convert an expression in scientific notation to standard form, move the decimal point the number of places indicated by the 10's exponent. For this problem, that's five places to the right. Positive exponents indicate that the decimal needs to be moved to the right, the positive direction. The 10 with an exponent is no longer needed at that point.

$$9.452137 \times 10^5 = 945,213.7$$

403. E. 25,480,200

The 10's exponent is 7, so move the decimal 7 places to the right. Drop the 10 and its exponent.

$$2.54802 \times 10^7 = 25,480,200$$

Remember that the last nonzero digit after a decimal point is understood to have an infinite number of zeros after it. They just aren't all presented. Because of that, you can use as many zeros as you need to after the last nonzero digit.

404. D. 0.080534

The 10's exponent in this case is negative, so the decimal point needs move in the negative direction, which is left. The exponent is −2, so move the decimal point two places to the left. Drop the 10 with its exponent.

$$8.0534 \times 10^{-2} = 0.080534$$

405. A. 0.00124

The 10's exponent is negative, so move the decimal to the left, the negative direction. Because the exponent is −3, move the decimal point three places to the left. When you do that, the 10 with its exponent is no longer necessary.

$$1.24 \times 10^{-3} = 0.00124$$

406. D. 0.00007248094

The 10's exponent is −5, so move the decimal point five places to the left. Drop the 10^{-5}.

$$7.248094 \times 10^{-5} = 0.00007248094$$

407. A. 688,935,700

The 10's exponent is 8, a positive number, so move the decimal point eight places in the positive direction, which is to the right. Get rid of 10 with its exponent.

$$6.889357 \times 10^8 = 688,935,700$$

408. 0.0000003211

The 10's exponent is −7, so move the decimal point seven places in the negative direction, which is to the left. Drop the 10 and its exponent.

$$3.211 \times 10^{-7} = 0.0000003211$$

409. E. 64.33052

The 10's exponent is 1, so move the decimal 1 place to the right. Drop the 10 and its exponent.

$$6.433052 \times 10^{1} = 64.33052$$

410. A. 1,000,000,000,000

The 10's exponent is 12, a positive number, so move the decimal point 12 places in the positive direction, which is to the right. Drop the 10^{12}.

$$1.0 \times 10^{12} = 1,000,000,000,000$$

That's 1 trillion stars.

411. C. 8.27×10^2

To convert a decimal number to scientific notation, move the decimal point so it has exactly one nonzero digit before it. Then multiply the resulting number by 10 with an exponent. The scientific notation form has to equal the original number, so give 10 an exponent that makes up for the change in decimal place.

Although no decimal point is shown in 827, it's understood to be after the last digit. The number 827 is the same as 827.0. The decimal point needs to be moved two places to the left so it has exactly one digit before it, and moving a decimal to the left decreases a number, so give 10 an exponent that makes up for the difference. That exponent is 2.

$$827.0 = 8.27 \times 10^2$$

Any 0 after the last nonzero digit after a decimal is unnecessary.

Technical Stuff: Every time a decimal point is moved one place to the left, the number is divided by 10. For every expression in which a number is multiplied by 10, giving 10 one higher exponent is the same as multiplying by 10. Dividing by 10 and multiplying by 10 cancel or balance each other. That's why if you divide a number by 10 and then multiply it by 10, the value is unchanged; 827.0×10^0 and 8.27×10^2 have the same value.

412. E. 4.8×10^{-1}

To get exactly one nonzero digit in front of the decimal point, move the decimal point one place to the right. That creates a number that's 10 times greater. To compensate for that movement, multiply the result by 10^{-1}.

$$0.48 = 4.8 \times 10^{-1}$$

413. B. 7.9420548×10^3

Move the decimal point three places to the left to get it after only one nonzero digit. To make up for making the number that much smaller, multiply it by 10 with an exponent of 3.

$$7,942.0548 = 7.9420548 \times 10^3$$

414. D. 5.6×10^{-4}

Move the decimal point so it comes after exactly one nonzero digit. To put it after the 5, you move the decimal point four places to the right. To balance out multiplying by 10 a total of four times, multiply the result by 10^{-4}.

$$0.00056 = 5.6 \times 10^{-4}$$

415. D. 8.39002×10^2

Move the decimal point two places to the left so it follows only the 8. Make up for that movement by multiplying the result by 10 to the power of 2.

$$839.002 = 8.39002 \times 10^2$$

416. B. 3.544×10^{-5}

Move the decimal five places to the right so it follows just the 3. That results in a greater number. Compensate for that change by multiplying the resulting number by 10^{-5}.

$$0.00003544 = 3.544 \times 10^{-5}$$

417. 0.00001 kg

Because 10's exponent is −5, move the decimal point five places in the negative direction, which is to the left. Then drop the 10^{-5}.

$$1.0 \times 10^{-5} = 0.00001$$

418.

E. 5.0×10^7

Move the decimal point (which is merely understood to be there) so it follows just one nonzero digit, the 5. That's a movement of seven places to the left, resulting in a smaller number. Make up for that change by multiplying the new number by 10^7. You need only one 0 after the decimal point because no nonzero numbers come after it.

$$50,000,000 = 5.0 \times 10^7$$

419.

A. $35,502,689,000,000$

Multiply the decimals by each other, and multiply the 10s with exponents by each other (by adding the exponents). To put the answer in standard form, move the decimal point 12 places to the right and drop the 10^{12}:

$$\left(5.647 \times 10^8\right)\left(6.287 \times 10^4\right) = \left(5.647 \times 6.287\right)\left(10^8 \times 10^4\right)$$
$$= \left(35.502689\right)\left(10^{8+4}\right)$$
$$= 35.502689 \times 10^{12}$$
$$= 35,502,689,000$$

420.

D. 2.9144509107×10^9

Multiply the decimal numbers by each other, and multiply the 10s with exponents by each other. Then convert the result to scientific notation:

$$\left(3.53451 \times 10^5\right)\left(8.2457 \times 10^3\right) = \left(3.53451 \times 8.2457\right)\left(10^5 \times 10^3\right)$$
$$= \left(29.144509107\right)\left(10^{5+3}\right)$$
$$= 29.144509107 \times 10^8$$
$$= 2.9144509107 \times 10^9$$

421.

A. $3.9563634458 \times 10^{10}$

You can multiply the numbers and then convert their product to scientific notation.

$$15,527 \times 2,548,054 = 39,563,634,458$$
$$= 3.9563634458 \times 10^{10}$$

422.

D. 8.8×10^1

Move the decimal point one place to the left so that only one digit comes before the decimal point. Compensate for that move by multiplying the result by 10^1.

$$88 = 8.8 \times 10^1$$

Chapter 2

423.   D. change an image

The passage states that Nobel intended to "make amends for the harm his inventions had caused" — in other words, to change his public image.

The right answer isn't Choice (A), because endowing the prizes is something Nobel *spent* money on — it didn't *save* him any. Choice (B) is wrong because creating the prizes didn't save any lives (although Nobel did feel guilty about causing deaths). The right answer isn't Choice (C), because what "rule" was changed? Nobel changed his *will* to endow the prizes, but doing this didn't change any rule. And the right answer isn't Choice (E), because although Nobel wanted to change the meaning of his life and do good for the world, this wouldn't be described as correcting an *inaccuracy*: The things he did before may have been morally questionable, but they really happened.

424.   C. summarize the recent scientific literature concerning orcas

The passage is more or less a list of recently established facts — a summary of recent findings. No more ambitious response is warranted.

The right answer isn't Choice (A), because since when do whales have opinions? If you picked this answer, you must not have read it very carefully. Choice (B) is incorrect because the passage doesn't explain the distinction at any point. The right answer isn't Choice (D), because the passage never goes as far as to imply that the term *killer whale* is considered objectionable (that is, offensive); it merely mentions that scientists no longer use it. Choice (E) is incorrect because although the passage refers to "genetic testing," it doesn't refer to any *new* method for it.

425.   E. a process of elimination

Researchers came to the conclusion that Göbekli Tepe was a religious structure based on the absence of any evidence that it could have been used for any other purpose.

Choice (A) is incorrect because although the passage mentions the stone pillars of the site itself being large, it doesn't refer to any large and advanced scientific equipment. Choice (B) is wrong because although the passage mentions that the ancient art on the site itself is the work of specialists, it doesn't refer to scientists using "specialized artistic analysis" (a term that doesn't make much sense). The right answer isn't Choice (C), because there's only one brief mention of Stonehenge, and that's just for a size comparison. And the right answer isn't Choice (D), because the passage mentions that there *wasn't* agriculture when Göbekli Tepe was built.

426. B. a quest for answers

In the passage, the "human condition" is represented by the series of rhetorical questions at the end.

The right answer isn't Choice (A), because although the passage mentions a fear related to the human condition, it never implies that the human condition is only ever about fear. Choice (C) is wrong because although the passage mentions that being cut off from everything we love is scary, it doesn't concentrate solely on the love of self. Choice (D) is incorrect because although art may ultimately be unable to explain the human condition, the passage doesn't necessarily confirm this viewpoint. It details only one artistic attempt to address the human condition. Finally, Choice (E) relates to only the last of several rhetorical questions about the human condition, so it's incorrect.

427. A. work to subvert dated paradigms

The passage praises the X-Men comics for their social and political progressiveness — their work to *subvert* (that is, overturn) *dated* (old-fashioned) *paradigms* (traditions or viewpoints).

The right answer isn't Choice (B), because the author praises the X-Men comics for challenging old ideas, not new ones. Choice (C) is wrong because although the author characterizes the X-Men comics in a political way, he thinks this is a good thing — he doesn't say that the comics are worse because of this. Choice (D) is incorrect because the passage never addresses anything about the X-Men comics changing in tone. And the right answer isn't Choice (E), because to "pay lip service" to an idea is to pretend to support it while not really doing anything helpful, and the author thinks the comics really do champion multiculturalism instead of merely pretending to do so.

428. E. human existence has meaning unto itself

As clearly stated in the closing lines (via a rhetorical question), the author's point is that human actions can be assigned significance independently of the existence of a deity, *without* making a judgment either way about whether one exists.

The right answer isn't Choice (A), because the author never implies anything antireligious — only that human existence can be said to have meaning in other terms. Choice (B) is incorrect because the passage never says who does more good than whom; it merely acknowledges that many different types of people do good. Choice (C) is incorrect because the passage doesn't make the agnostic argument that the existence of a deity is unknowable; it merely asserts that answering this question isn't necessary in order to assign meaning to existence. And the right answer isn't Choice (D), because the passage never says, or even implies, anything about the existence of free will one way or the other.

429.   D. new ideas about Shakespeare pop up to suit each generation's concerns

The "innovations" mentioned in the opening sentence, as well as the closing sentence suggesting that Shakespeare tells us about ourselves, support the idea that (consciously or not) we continuously present Shakespeare in new ways to suit our own times.

Choice (A) isn't the right answer, because although the passage mentions examples of Shakespeare working well enough in translation to be appreciated, it never says that Shakespeare works just as well or better in translation than in English. The right answer isn't Choice (B), because although it may well be true that most students don't pay close attention to Shakespeare, the passage's point doesn't rest on this idea. The right answer isn't Choice (C), because although the author definitely says that no writer matters more than Shakespeare, he never says that any should. He presumably agrees with Shakespeare's preeminent status. And the right answer isn't Choice (E), because when the author says, "Shakespeare is not just English," he's speaking metaphorically to imply that Shakespeare's works belong to the world.

430.   C. an attractive communal touchstone

The author means to say that Shakespeare is fascinating and belongs to every culture. (Note that the author clearly likes Shakespeare, and Choice (C) is the only one of the answer choices that's complimentary.)

Choice (A) is wrong because the passage implies that Shakespeare is accessible, more so than mysterious, and there's nothing in the passage about elitism. Choice (B) is practically nonsense: What does "a private language of the popular" even mean? The right answer isn't Choice (D), because *charismatic* does not mean *elaborate*, and there's nothing in the passage about "showing off." Finally, the right answer isn't Choice (E), because although fully appreciating Shakespeare certainly does take some intelligence, the author doesn't seem to find this frustrating.

431.   A. ubiquitous

When something *abounds*, it's all over the place, which is what the adjective *ubiquitous* means.

Choice (B) is incorrect because *abounding* is the opposite of being *limited*. Choice (C) is wrong because whether something is ancient is unrelated to whether it's all over the place. Choice (D) is wrong because something can abound whether it's true or false. And Choice (E) is wrong because although myths can certainly be *infuriating*, this isn't what it means for something to abound.

432. **C. be more informed about Hoffman herself and the significance of her work**

The passage merely presents information about Hoffman. There's no reason to gamble on a more ambitious answer choice when this one will do.

Choice (A) is incorrect because the author doesn't present his own opinion; he merely reports the opinions of others. Choice (B) is wrong because the passage doesn't discuss any influence Hoffman had on modern sculpture (she presumably had some, but it isn't mentioned here). Choice (D) is wrong because the author doesn't make an argument about whether the Field Museum's decision was right or wrong; he is only reporting, not arguing. And Choice (E) is wrong because the passage only mentions that Hoffman studied with the man who designed Mount Rushmore; the passage doesn't suggest she influenced its creation.

433. **B. greatest**

Your *crowning* achievement is your greatest achievement, as a crown marks a king or queen as the greatest and most powerful person.

The right answer isn't Choice (A), because although the paragraph doesn't mention a subsequent work of Hoffman's, *crowning* doesn't mean final. And although it's true that Hoffman's work in question was *bold* and *controversial*, these aren't what *crowning* means, so Choices (C) and (D) are wrong. The right answer isn't Choice (E), because the passage doesn't imply that Hoffman's other work was unoriginal, and in any case, *crowning* doesn't mean unoriginal either.

434. **D. enjoyed a privileged education**

The second sentence of the passage mentions Hoffman's studying under two very famous sculptors early in her career, which constitutes a privileged education.

The right answer isn't Choice (A), because the passage never implies that Hoffman's work wasn't good, merely that it was controversial. Choice (B) is incorrect because although the passage establishes that her work became politically controversial, the passage says nothing about Hoffman's own political views. Choice (C) is incorrect because the passage states that Hoffman's masterpieces were still prominently displayed at the Field Museum until *after* her death. And the right answer isn't Choice (E), because although the passage never mentions Hoffman marrying or having children, that doesn't necessarily mean she didn't — the passage is about her professional life, not her personal life.

435. C. A multifaceted historical phenomenon is ultimately attributed to a sole root cause.

The "multifaceted historical phenomenon" is the Renaissance, and the "sole root cause" is the Black Plague. The passage does describe these things in this way, and because this answer choice asserts nothing else, it can't be wrong.

The right answer isn't Choice (A), because only one period in history (the Renaissance) is analyzed. The right answer isn't Choice (B), because the author is advancing a theory about the Black Plague, not rebutting one. Choice (D) is wrong because the passage doesn't say that the feudal system was outlawed; it says that the system collapsed for natural reasons. Choice (E) is wrong because the passage doesn't say that the Renaissance never happened; it advances a theory of *why* the Renaissance happened.

436. E. drastically reduced the population

The passage argues that most of the Black Death's role in the precipitation of the Renaissance was a result of its reducing the population.

Choices (A), (B), and (C) are wrong because the passage presents the focus on ethical philosophy, the new concern for the human experience, and the new focus on science as *secondary* effects of all the death caused by the Black Plague. Choice (D) is wrong because trade ships traveling from Asia to Europe are what caused the Black Plague itself, not what caused the Renaissance directly.

437. E. proliferation of

The idea is that artistic brilliance and scientific advancement increased in frequency and visibility. There was "an explosion" of them in the sense that they *proliferated*.

Choice (A) is wrong because these things became more widespread, not less widespread. Choice (B) is wrong because these things came into a new existence; they weren't merely being revised. Choice (C) is wrong because these things were created, not fought over. And Choice (D) is wrong because just the opposite is true: These elements of society were finally *not* being opposed and repressed.

438. B. It efficiently describes a new theory for an audience of educated non-experts.

The passage does describe a new theory, and the presumed audience must be educated because the reading level is high, but they must also not be experts in this specific area of history because things that experts would already know are explained (such as the definition of *feudalism*).

The right answer isn't Choice (A), because the passage isn't mocking or sarcastic in tone. Choice (C) is incorrect because the passage doesn't present a conspiracy theory, just a regular theory. Choice (D) is wrong because the passage presents a single idea, not two opposing sides. And Choice (E) is wrong because the passage is hardly "lighthearted"; it's about the devastating effects of the deadliest epidemic in history.

439. A. means of treatment for or prevention of the Black Death

The context of the sentence as a whole establishes that stopping the devastation would have involved looking for some type of preventive measure or cure (simple logic also establishes this, as "science and medicine" would be the only means of stopping a disease).

Choice (B) is incorrect because blaming someone for a disease doesn't stop it. Similarly, Choice (C) wouldn't stop a disease; it would just help the survivors deal with their feelings. Choices (D) and (E) are wrong because the "devastation" in question refers to the Black Plague itself, not to the political conditions of the Dark Ages or to feudalism.

440. C. shed light on a source of confusion

If a passage explains something that people need explained to them, as this one does, then it must be clearing up "a source of confusion."

The right answer isn't Choice (A), because the passage doesn't say that the term *nihilism* is meaningless; it says that most people don't know what it really means. Choice (B) is wrong because philosophers don't debate the meaning of *nihilism*; rather, the problem is that regular people are uninformed about what nihilism means. Choice (D) is wrong because the passage doesn't dramatize anything and because the viewpoint it presents isn't unpopular so much as it's not commonly known. And Choice (E) is wrong because the passage doesn't satirize anything, nor does it present objections from any other viewpoints; it merely gives accurate information from the author's own viewpoint.

441. D. a state that certain geniuses have seen as an end in itself

The passage explicitly states that, contrary to popular belief, no actual philosophers have seen nihilism as an end in itself.

Choice (A) is wrong because the passage explains that real philosophers do use the term *nihilism*; they just don't use it to mean what most people think it means. Choice (B) is wrong because the passage explains that uninformed people often use *nihilism* casually and inaccurately (hence all the confusion about its actual definition). Choice (C) is wrong because the passage explains that nihilism is sometimes (incorrectly) used to mean that life is meaningless — for example, by the uninformed people mentioned in Choice (B). And Choice (E) is wrong because the passage explains that real philosophers do use the term *nihilism* as a pejorative way of describing the ideas of other philosophers with whom they disagree.

442.   A. mildly amused didacticism

The author is indeed *mildly amused* (he occasionally speaks with a degree of levity), and he is indeed being *didactic* (that is, trying to teach people something).

Choice (B) is wrong because although you could argue that the author is being condescending, he doesn't seem irate (angry). Choice (C) is incorrect because although the author might well be concerned about how many people misunderstand this idea, he isn't *bemused* (that is, confused); on the contrary, he's well informed. The right answer isn't Choice (D), because why would it be suspicious that the author is confident? He clearly knows what he's talking about. And the right answer isn't Choice (E), because the author is neither biased nor partisan — he's presenting accurate information, not taking one side in a conflict.

443.   B. likely new to a general readership

Think about it this way: Did *you* know all those terms already? If not, then they must be "likely to be new to a general readership."

The right answer isn't Choice (A), because although these terms may be unfamiliar or informal, that isn't the same thing as being grammatically incorrect. Choice (C) is incorrect because there's no indication that these words mean their opposites — if the reader is unfamiliar with these terms, as he or she is likely to be, then the reader wouldn't even know what their opposites are! Choice (D) is wrong because the passage doesn't have a scholarly tone; it's written in a friendly style for a popular audience. Finally, Choice (E) is wrong because *loanwords* are words borrowed from another language, and those words are all clearly English (plus, italics, not quotation marks, would generally be used for foreign words).

444.   E. illustrate a principle by proceeding from an example of it

The point of the passage is ultimately to explain the concept of *convergent evolution*, and the passage begins by establishing that the dunnart is a good example of it.

Choice (A) is wrong because there's no argument about whether marsupials count as mammals — they are mammals, and the passage proceeds from this assumption. Choice (B) is wrong because although the passage does explain a piece of information, there's no corresponding piece of disinformation that it argues against. Choice (C) is wrong because, as the passage explains, the dunnart *is* a marsupial (you can't "compare and contrast" something with itself). And the right answer isn't Choice (D), because the passage clearly explains that true mice are *not* marsupials.

445. **C. a dangerous decision to comprehend poorly**

As the phrase "rude awakening" implies, the passage explains that anyone who thinks he can get out of trouble for physically attacking someone by citing *Chaplinsky v. New Hampshire* is unlikely to succeed with this defense.

Choice (A) is wrong because the passage explains that (contrary to some people's beliefs) the Supreme Court did *not* actually allow any acts of violence through this decision. Choice (B) is wrong because the passage explains that the *Chaplinsky* case was about whether a particular New Hampshire law was unconstitutional; it doesn't say the Supreme Court's decision in the case was unconstitutional itself. Choice (D) is wrong because the point of the passage is that the *Chaplinksy* decision would *not* make a very good legal defense. And Choice (E) is wrong because the passage explains that legal scholars are not the ones who misunderstand the meaning of *Chaplinksy*; regular people are.

446. **A. two different viewpoints on a single period in history**

The passage compares two viewpoints on one period in history — that of Imperial Rome.

Choice (B) is wrong because the passage concerns only one period in Roman history (the Empire), not two. Choice (C) is wrong because the passage concerns only one place, Rome. Choice (D) is wrong because the passage concerns only one influence on the modern state (Rome), although it presents different viewpoints from which to evaluate that influence. And Choice (E) is wrong because although the passage briefly mentions Imperial Rome's "adapting" things "to republican institutions," this is unrelated to the main idea. (Watch out for this trick, in which an answer choice simply copies a memorable phrase from the passage at random.)

447. **E. was markedly lacking in innovative aspects**

The passage says that Imperial Rome adapted earlier aspects of government in "ingenious and effective ways," which is the opposite of saying that it lacked innovative aspects.

The right answer isn't Choice (A), (B), (C), or (D), because the passage *does* clearly state that Imperial Rome did these things.

448.

D. more structurally similar to a contemporary government or to other ancient ones

The opening sentence of the passage establishes that the central question concerns how similar Imperial Rome was to a modern country.

Choice (A) is wrong because the passage presents this emphasis as a simple fact, not a source of contention among historians. Choice (B) is wrong because although the passage does characterize Imperial Rome as under-institutionalized, it never compares that government to the preceding Roman Republic with respect to this idea. Choice (C) is practically nonsense; it's a random assortment of phrases from the passage. Choice (E) is wrong because the passage never brings up this question in any way.

449.

E. It is unusual for philosophers to be in agreement about anything.

By beginning with the phrase "surprisingly for philosophy," the closing sentence implies that unanimous (or even nearly unanimous) agreement among philosophers is rare.

Choice (A) is wrong because although the passage states that this debate is contentious, it doesn't say that this debate is the most contentious one in all of philosophy (beware of extremes in answer choices). Choice (B) is incorrect because although the passage states that Aristotle philosophized about the past, it never says he was the first to do so. Choice (C) is wrong because it's obviously easier to change the future than the past, even to philosophers! And Choice (D) is wrong because the passage only briefly mentions God in a reference to a maxim of Aristotle's, and it doesn't say anything about any philosophical agreement about God's nature.

450.

B. the Constitution on the part of many citizens

The passage explains what freedom of speech does and does not really mean; it never implies that anyone misunderstands this except private citizens.

Choices (A) and (D) are incorrect because the passage says that regular people misunderstand freedom of speech, not that the government or the media does. Choice (C) is wrong because the passage uses an example in which a hypothetical public figure's *supporters,* not the public figure himself, misunderstand freedom of speech. Choice (E) is wrong because the passage contains no reference to the author's previous writings.

451.
D. His good reputation is based almost wholly on conjecture.

Conjecture is synonymous with the "wishful thinking" mentioned in the first sentence.

The right answer isn't Choice (A), because although the passage states that Richard the Lionheart did not speak English, it never says he was the only English king who didn't. Choice (B) is wrong because although the passage states that Richard the Lionheart is often depicted in movies, it never implies that Americans know about him only from movies. The right answer isn't Choice (C), because the passage contains no implication whatsoever that Richard and John weren't really brothers. And Choice (E) is incorrect because the "wishful thinking" refers to Richard's good reputation as a king; it's accepted fact that he was an effective military commander, and the passage states this.

452.
B. presents a series of facts that culminates in a mystery

The passage states a series of facts, and the concluding "mystery" is why Holmes became so popular a character whereas the very similar Dupin had not.

Choice (A) is wrong because the influence that Dupin had on Holmes is more than the author's personal opinion; the passage states that even Arthur Conan Doyle acknowledged it. Choice (C) is incorrect because there's no "newly discovered data" in the passage — it's entirely concerned with books that are over a century old! The right answer isn't Choice (D), because although "rip-off" could be construed as an accusation, there's no indication that the author is joking. And the right answer isn't Choice (E), because the passage analyzes literature, not real life.

453.
C. conciliatory

The passage states that Conan Doyle "always admitted the obvious influence and gave Poe credit" — in other words, he was being *conciliatory*.

Choice (A) is incorrect because *ornery* means bad-tempered or combative, whereas the passage describes Conan Doyle as speaking well of Poe. Choice (B) is wrong because *evasive* means that someone is dodging the issue, whereas the passage states that Conan Doyle freely admitted Poe's influence. Choices (D) and (E) are wrong because *inflammatory* signifies rhetoric that's designed to stir up trouble and *erratic* signifies behavior that changes from one moment to the next, whereas the passage describes Conan Doyle as giving Poe credit.

454.
E. avant-garde

Avant-garde is an artistic term signifying work that is ahead of its time.

Choice (A) is wrong because *quixotic* means paradoxical or nonsensical, Choice (B) is wrong because *insouciant* means unconcerned or indifferent, and Choice (C) is wrong because *subversive* signifies work that is designed to attack dominant political ideas, and the passage doesn't describe Poe's stories as political. Finally, the right answer isn't Choice (D), because although Edgar Allan Poe's work was frequently melodramatic, the passage doesn't specifically describe his detective stories in this way.

455. C. composed the passage primarily to oppose

The subsequent introduction of the phrase "but there are more than a few problems with this" signals that the rest of the passage argues in opposition to the practice described at the beginning.

The right answer isn't Choice (A), because there is no other idea that the passage "goes on to" analyze. Choices (B) and (E) are wrong because the author never says that he ever agreed with the practice that he attacks in this passage. Choice (D) is incorrect because the passage's reference to Shakespeare is an analogy used to describe the idea that the author attacks — Shakespeare isn't named as the source of that idea.

456. B. contradiction

The word *paradox* describes something that is inherently impossible or self-contradictory — as, for example, in the scene from Shakespeare the passage references.

Choice (A) is wrong because although a paradox may well be mysterious, *contradiction* is a more exact synonym. Choices (C), (D), and (E) are wrong because although the scene from *The Merchant of Venice* involves a ceremony, refers to a rule, and occurs during the *denouement* (ending) of the play, those aren't what the word *paradox* means.

457. A. students and administrators

The passage states that the practice in question is "popular with administrators," and obviously anything that keeps students from being criticized is going to be popular with the students!

Choices (B) and (C) are wrong because the passage describes professors as being against this practice, and it never mentions parents at all. The right answer isn't Choice (D), because no actual proofreaders are discussed in the passage — the author *contrasts* the job of a professor with that of a proofreader. And the right answer isn't Choice (E), because neither politicians nor poets are mentioned in the passage (a work by Shakespeare is referenced, but Shakespeare's opinions about college pedagogy are never analyzed).

458. D. have both the right and the duty to disparage false theses

Although phrased in the form of a question, the closing sentence of the first paragraph is essentially the author's thesis statement, and this answer choice closely paraphrases it.

Choice (A) is wrong because the passage doesn't concern plagiarism, and even if it did, the students, not administrators, would be the ones committing it. Choice (B) is wrong because literature versus logic is not the issue at play here; the passage concerns argumentative thesis papers and uses a device from Shakespeare as an analogy to describe the problem. Choice (C) is incorrect because although the author is evidently familiar with Shakespeare, he never accuses anyone else of being insufficiently familiar with Shakespeare's work. And Choice (E) is wrong because the author contrasts professors and proofreaders in terms of their job duties, not in terms of how much money they make.

459. B. it addresses a perennial ethical quandary

The author says that the soliloquy concerns "an eternal paradox of morality" — a very close paraphrase of this answer choice.

Choice (A) is wrong because the passage states that many English teachers do not understand the "To be or not to be" speech properly. Choice (C) is wrong because the passage doesn't argue that "To be or not to be" is a speech devoted to *opposing* suicide — just that it isn't about considering suicide (that is, the speech is about something else entirely). Choice (D) is wrong because the author doesn't say there's a flaw in the speech that's impossible to resolve; he says the speech is about a problem that's impossible to resolve. And Choice (E) is wrong because although the author does go on at length about how famous the speech is, he never says that it shouldn't be this famous; presumably, he thinks the speech's fame is well deserved.

460. A. unsure about

The author's analysis figures Hamlet is "unsure about pacifism" — that is, he is confused about whether it's better to fight evil or to oppose fighting for any reason.

Choices (B), (C), and (D) are wrong because the passage describes Hamlet not as being opposed to, being influenced by, or advocating *pacifism* (the philosophy of nonviolence in all cases) but rather as trying to figure out where he stands on it. The right answer isn't Choice (E), because the passage never implies that the "To be or not to be" speech is satirical.

461. D. direct readers to what he sees as the true core of the "To be or not to be" soliloquy

The author merely intends to explain what he believes to be the true meaning of the "To be or not to be" speech.

Choice (A) is incorrect because the author never says there was a time when he himself misunderstood the "To be or not to be" speech. Choice (B) is wrong because although it may well be the case that the author thinks *Hamlet* should be taught in philosophy classes, he never says so here. Choice (C) is incorrect because although the author begins by establishing that the "To be or not to be" speech is famous, the function of the passage is not to investigate *why* it is so. Choice (E) is wrong because although the author does say that most people misunderstand this particular work of Shakespeare's, he never blames any "modern ideas" for this.

462. E. claims about their capacity for awareness

The closing sentence of the passage explicitly states that the issue is Great Apes' capacity to understand that they are being held in captivity.

The right answer isn't Choice (A), because the passage states that these two philosophers founded the Great Ape Project, not that the project's platform is based on their own works. Choice (B) is wrong because the passage states that proponents want the United Nations to afford rights to Great Apes, not that the United Nations is the *reason* that Great Apes have rights in the first place. Choice (C) is wrong because the passage's point concerns the similarity between Great Apes and humans, not the differences. And the right answer isn't Choice (D), because the passage doesn't concern the practice of animal experimentation generally, only its application to Great Apes.

463. B. They are more social animals than hares.

The passage states that rabbits "live in groups" and that "hares are loners."

Choices (A) and (E) are wrong because the passage states that hares, not rabbits, build nests and have jointed skulls. Choice (C) is wrong because the passage states that hares have 48 chromosomes, and rabbits, 44. Choice (D) is wrong because the passage states that the Belgian hare *is* a rabbit.

464. C. Why do we suspect that time travel to the past is impossible?

The passage explains that natural events that would create paradoxes do not happen and cites time travel to the past as an example of such an event.

The right answer isn't Choice (A), because the passage states that traveling back in time (and killing your grandfather) is impossible, so the passage can't possibly be said to explain what would happen if you did.
Choice (B) is wrong because the passage indeed states that time slows
down as one approaches the speed of light but doesn't explain *why* this is.
Choice (D) is incorrect because the passage never addresses the subject of
who first conceptualized the idea of a time machine. And the right answer
isn't Choice (E), because although the passage implies that Hawking is a
preeminent physicist by calling him "the great Stephen Hawking," it
doesn't specifically explain what he has done to earn this reputation.

465. E. this comes with numerous qualifications

The expression "fine print" (such as is found at the bottom of a contract)
generally means that there are a lot of "*ifs, ands,* or *buts,*" as the saying
goes, and this is what the phrase means here, as signaled by the qualifier
"before you get too excited."

The right answer isn't Choice (A), because the passage concerns not how
much "training" someone would need to travel through time but
whether it's possible to do so at all, so there's no implication that "fine
print" indicates training. Choice (B) is wrong because the passage is
written for a general audience, not an audience of experts, so the explanation is not in fact "highly technical." Choice (C) is wrong because the
passage doesn't describe any disagreement among scientists about this
subject; rather, it implies a general consensus. And Choice (D) is wrong
because there's never the slightest hint that the author is joking.

466. A. time and speed

The passage states that time and speed are *inversely correlated* — that is,
that time slows down as speed increases.

Choice (B) is wrong because the passage discusses light but not gravity.
Choice (C) is wrong because the passage relates the speed of light to the
concept of time broadly, not specifically to the present. Choice (D) is
incorrect because the passage never implies that the principles discussed
are specific to the gravitational bond between the Earth and the sun —
rather, the passage implies that these principles are broadly true
throughout the universe. Choice (E) is wrong because the passage
explains that time travel to the past is impossible.

467. C. The theory in Passage 2 sees the theory in Passage 1 as limited.

Passage 2 acknowledges that the event discussed in Passage 1 (the asteroid impact) played a role in the extinction of the dinosaurs but argues
that it wasn't the *only* cause.

The right answer isn't Choice (A), because there isn't a third idea that both passages are arguing against. Choice (B) is incorrect because both passages cite the same time frame for the extinction event. Choice (D) is wrong because it's clear that the theory discussed in Passage 1 precedes the ideas presented by Passage 2. And Choice (E) is incorrect because Passage 2 doesn't argue that the ideas presented in Passage 1 are false, only that they're incomplete.

468. C. uncommon notion

Based on the structure of the sentence as a whole, you can see that the phrase "rogue hypothesis" is contrasted with the phrase "widely accepted." The implication is that it must mean the opposite of this — that is, "uncommon notion."

Choice (A) is incorrect because a hypothesis doesn't have to constitute an objection — the term can refer to any idea. Choice (B) is wrong because a "rogue" idea doesn't have to precede something else; the word only means that something is rebellious or unusual. Choice (D) is wrong because the fact that the theory eventually became accepted means that it couldn't possibly be inherently contradictory. Finally, Choice (E) is wrong because something described as "rogue" must be unusual rather than already accepted.

469. D. The two authors agree that it had a hand in the Cretaceous–Paleogene Event.

Passage 1 argues that the asteroid was the sole cause of the Cretaceous–Paleogene Event, and Passage 2 argues that it was one of several causes; therefore, both authors agree that it played a role.

The right answer isn't Choice (A), because both authors agree that the asteroid existed and struck Earth. Choice (B) is incorrect because the authors agree about the location of the asteroid impact (they both call it the *Chicxulub* asteroid, referring to where it landed). Choice (C) is wrong because Passage 2 doesn't argue that the asteroid hit the Deccan Traps; it argues that the formation of the Deccan Traps occurred independently and simultaneously. The right answer isn't Choice (E), because although the author of Passage 2 doesn't specifically mention iridium, you have no reason to believe that he disputes the asteroid-based explanation for iridium's presence in the Cretaceous–Paleogene geologic boundary. If he wanted to argue against it, then he would have brought it up.

470. B. Only the author of Passage 1 explains how his supporting evidence was obtained.

Passage 1 details the research and discoveries that went into the asteroid hypothesis. Passage 2 doesn't explain the genesis of the Deccan Traps idea.

Choice (A) is wrong because the author of Passage 1, not Passage 2, champions a single cause of the Cretaceous-Paleogene Event. Choice (C) is incorrect because both authors agree that the Chicxulub impact took place. Choice (D) is wrong because neither author mentions anything about any dinosaurs escaping extinction. (You can argue that some dinosaurs did escape extinction if you classify birds as an extant form of dinosaur, but still, neither author mentions this.) Choice (E) is wrong because both passages concern the Cretaceous-Paleogene Event, which affected the entire Earth.

471.   **A. superfluous**

If the author of Passage 1 believes that the asteroid impact was the sole cause of the Cretaceous-Paleogene Event (which he does), then he would consider the ideas in Passage 2 about the Deccan Traps to be unnecessary or extra — that is, *superfluous*.

The right answer isn't Choice (B), because the ideas in Passage 1 are older than the ideas in Passage 2; the theory in Passage 2 is a response to that of Passage 1. Choice (C) is incorrect because there's no indication that the author of Passage 1 believes the ideas presented in Passage 2 are impossible (indeed, he never discusses them at all). The right answer isn't Choice (D), because Passage 2 presents a scientific hypothesis, so the author of Passage 1 presumably believes there would be a way to test its veracity, even if it hasn't been tested yet. Choice (E) is wrong because there's no indication that either author sees the other's ideas as offensive; this is a scientific disagreement, not a political one.

472.   **C. which species of dinosaurs went extinct before others**

Neither passage gets into the specifics of which species of dinosaurs disappeared first. No specific dinosaur species are mentioned by name in either passage.

Choice (A) is wrong because it notes what the entire debate between the passages is about. Choice (B) is wrong because Passage 2 gives a date for the Deccan Traps. Choice (D) is wrong because both passages mention and agree about the location and impact of the asteroid. And Choice (E) is wrong because Passage 1 discusses the chemical composition of asteroids and Passage 2 does not dispute it.

473.   **E. the "Middle Ages" and the "Medieval Period" are the same thing**

The author uses these two terms interchangeably with no explanation; therefore, he's assuming the reader already knows that they refer to the same historical period.

Choice (A) is wrong because the entire passage concerns Europe. Europeans did wear suits of armor, and only *when* they wore them is in question here. Choice (B) is wrong because the author bothers to explain that knights were generally wealthier, so he isn't assuming that the reader already knows it. Choice (C) is wrong because there's no indication in the passage that the term *Renaissance* is a recent invention. It isn't, so this isn't something the author assumes the reader knows. Finally, Choice (D) is wrong because the Renaissance didn't precede the Middle Ages; it's the other way around.

474. **C. the bulk of human evolution took place in a state of nature**

The closing sentence of the passage — essentially its thesis statement — is a close paraphrase of this answer choice.

Choice (A) is incorrect because instead of arguing that this term can't be defined, the passage specifically defines it. Choice (B) is wrong because the passage opens by stating the reverse of this (*prickle* means "to be annoyed by" in this context). Choice (D) is wrong because the passage makes clear that the genus *Homo* by definition refers to any and all humans. And Choice (E) is wrong because the passage explains that permanent settlements and agriculture define the start of civilization rather than the end of evolution.

475. **B. The attempt to impose definitions on elements of existence is sometimes futile.**

The passage hinges on the idea that there's no exact definition of what constitutes a "city" (in terms of population size), and Choice (B) identifies the general principle underlying this problem.

Choices (A) and (C) are wrong because the passage doesn't argue that we don't know where these cities are or which countries they're in. Choice (D) is wrong because the passage doesn't argue that the terms *north* and *south* are unclear. And Choice (E) is wrong because the passage doesn't say there's no such thing as a city — rather, it argues that although there are definitely cities, we don't always know what counts as one.

476. **B. The first paragraph offers a brief biography of William Tyndale himself, and the second delineates how his life's work came to be as influential as it was.**

The first paragraph explains who Tyndale was and what he did, and the second discusses why his work was important historically.

Choice (A) is incorrect because although the passage does compare Tyndale with both of these people, the paragraph division isn't based on this (Shakespeare is mentioned in both paragraphs). Choice (C) is wrong because the passage doesn't say that Tyndale invented the printing press (he didn't). Choice (D) is wrong because there's nothing about Tyndale's education in the first paragraph. And Choice (E) is incorrect because the first paragraph explains that the Church was strongly opposed to Tyndale's work.

477. **D. it is widely accepted, and justifiably so, that he had the single greatest influence on the English language of any one person**

The opening sentence of the passage states (by implication) that Shakespeare had the single greatest influence on the development of modern English.

The right answer isn't Choice (A), because the passage doesn't state that we mistake Tyndale's phrases for Shakespeare's — only that Tyndale, like Shakespeare, also coined many famous phrases. Choice (B) is wrong because the passage establishes that Tyndale died before Shakespeare was born and long before the King James Bible was written. Choice (C) is incorrect because the passage discusses Tyndale's influence on Shakespeare's literary style, not on his religious beliefs (which are largely unknown). And Choice (E) is wrong because the passage concedes that Shakespeare had the greatest influence on the English language; the passage is concerned only with arguing that Tyndale is in second place.

478. **A. the early 16th century**

The second paragraph states that "Tyndale's work . . . established the tone and conventions of literary Early Modern English," and the passage states that he did his work in the early 16th century (he died in 1535).

Choices (B), (C), and (D) are wrong because the passage establishes that Tyndale was dead by the late 16th century. Choice (E) is wrong because the passage states that John Wycliffe, not William Tyndale, lived in the 14th century.

479. **D. the phraseology of William Tyndale's Bible was influenced by that of John Wycliffe's**

The passage never addresses (and perhaps it should have) whether Tyndale had read Wycliffe's translation of the Bible and whether his own was similar.

Choice (A) is wrong because the passage explains that Tyndale's Bible became the standard after the English government broke with the Catholic Church. Choice (B) is wrong because the passage makes clear that Shakespeare wrote in Early Modern English (which means he could obviously understand it). Choice (C) is wrong because the passage states that Tyndale was a Protestant. And Choice (E) is wrong because the passage explains that Tyndale had to leave England because his work was illegal there.

480. **E. time-consuming**

You can safely assume that having to write every copy of your book by hand over and over would be time-consuming (note the root of *laborious* is *labor*, meaning "work").

Choices (A), (B), (C), and (D) are wrong because although the process being described was also illegal, subversive (of the Church's power), somewhat primitive (in the sense that a printing press wasn't used), and perhaps depressing (Wycliffe was working hard in secret at something punishable by death), those aren't what *laborious* means.

481. **E. It never declined at any point on the graph.**

The line representing the total number of wolves never slopes downward.

482. **A. 2009**

The distance between the lines is shortest at the 2009 point. Though the Wenaha pack's population was higher in 2012 than at any other point on the graph, the total wolf population was also much higher at that time, making the percentage lower.

483. **C. the total numbers of wolves in 2011 and 2012**

Of the answer choices, the line connecting the total numbers of wolves in 2011 and 2012 has a larger change in the wolf population: from approximately 28 to 53, a difference of 25. The rest differ by only 10 or 15 units.

484. **B. becoming increasingly popular**

The penultimate sentence states that "traction is being gained" by this viewpoint — that is, it's becoming more popular but isn't necessarily the dominant viewpoint.

Choice (A) is wrong because the passage neither states nor implies that most psychologists now see things this way. Choice (C) is incorrect because the passage never addresses questions of proof, only of the opinions of qualified professionals (proof in the sense of law and logic is rare in psychology). Choice (D) is wrong because the passage never implies the existence of any data likely to falsify this idea — on the contrary, this viewpoint is described as being increasingly accepted. Choice (E) is wrong because although the passage describes this viewpoint as becoming more popular, it never implies that this is unjustified.

485. **C. decently educated and curious general readers**

The passage is written at a high reading level, so the intended readers must be educated, yet the readership is still presumed to be general rather than expert, because psychological terminology is explained as it would be to an outsider.

Choice (A) is wrong because the passage explains psychological terminology for outsiders. Choice (B) is wrong because why would people with *no* interest in psychology read an essay about psychology? The passage never tries to persuade anyone to be interested in it. Choice (D) is wrong because although we do associate psychopaths and sociopaths with the commission of crimes, the passage focuses on the psychology of these conditions, not on crime. Choice (E) is wrong because the passage offers very little about the structure of the brain, and the language doesn't seem to be aimed at an audience of medical students.

486. D. synonymous

Terms that are *interchangeable* mean essentially the same thing — that is, this is a synonym for *synonymous*.

Choice (A) is wrong because context clues don't indicate that psychologists consider these terms meaningless; rather, psychologists can't agree on what these terms mean. Choices (B) and (E) are wrong because although these terms are technical and the passage does describe people as being confused by these terms, *interchangeable* doesn't mean *technical* or *confusing*. Choice (C) is incorrect because the inability of experts to agree on a definition doesn't necessarily mean that a term is vague.

487. A. observable differences in brain structure

The passage explicitly states that both *psychopathy* and *sociopathy* (whatever the official differences between them might be) both involve alterations in brain structure that are observable in an autopsy.

Choice (B) is wrong because although the passage refers to sociopaths and psychopaths lying in certain situations, this is presented as something done deliberately to gain a calculated advantage, not as an uncontrollable impulse. Choice (C) is wrong because whether this absence is the case with one, both, or neither of these disorders is one of the things that the passage presents as being under debate. Choice (D) is incorrect because the passage explicitly states that "an autopsy cannot reveal whether such differences were present at birth or acquired." Finally, Choice (E) is wrong because the passage says that psychopathy and sociopathy are *located on* a spectrum of personality disorders, not that they both involve a spectrum of personality disorders (that is, that each is only one disorder unto itself).

488. E. stylistic detours

The principal message of the passage is that Yeats changed his style several times over the course of his career.

Choice (A) is wrong because the passage characterizes only Yeats's early work along these lines. Choice (B) concerns Yeats's late work, and Choice (C) characterizes work from the middle of Yeats's career. Choice (D) is wrong because it combines terms from characterizations of two different periods in Yeats's career.

489.   C. a folk truism

The idea that "celebrities die in groups" is a *folk truism* — that is, a popular thing that the common people hold to be true (but isn't necessarily true).

Choice (A) is incorrect because although the idea that opens the passage is a superstition, there's nothing objectionable about it. Choice (B) is wrong because the passage never states that a majority of people believe this, just that many people do. Choice (D) is wrong because the mere fact that something isn't really true doesn't make it a paradox — a paradox is contradictory rather than merely false. Choice (E) is wrong because the passage never refers to déjà vu (the inexplicable sensation that present events have happened before).

490.   A. always untrustworthy

The fact that the passage characterizes such explanations as "urban legend" is a clue to the fact that "inevitably spurious" means "always untrustworthy."

Choices (B), (C), (D), and (E) are wrong because *spurious* refers to a claim's being deceitful or inaccurate rather than complex, revealing, offensive, or obscure in origin.

491.   B. Archaeologists have found no evidence of human habitation in it.

If archaeologists had found any evidence that Stonehenge was inhabited, then they wouldn't have concluded that it was "forbidden to the living."

Choice (A) is wrong because the fact that the passage doesn't say how people raised the stones doesn't necessarily mean we don't know how they did. Choice (C) isn't right because the passage states that Stonehenge is too old to have been built by the druids. Choice (D) is wrong because the passage states that Stonehenge wasn't really "used" for much of anything, regardless of the time of year. And Choice (E) is wrong because even if Stonehenge is older than the Great Pyramid of Egypt, the Egyptians still couldn't possibly have known about it.

492.   D. establish the facts of a historical situation

Does the first paragraph establish facts? Yes, clearly it does. The answer choice asserts nothing beyond this.

Choice (A) is incorrect because the first paragraph doesn't pose any questions; it only makes statements. Choices (B) and (C) are wrong because the first paragraph doesn't compare any viewpoints or assert or reject any explanations; it only states facts. Choice (E) is wrong because the first paragraph doesn't describe any "crisis" — on the contrary, it describes the establishment of a period of historical stability.

493. **A. unpack the mechanics of the state of affairs described in the first paragraph**

The first paragraph explains what happened, and the second explains how it happened.

Choice (B) is wrong because the first paragraph doesn't pose any questions. Choices (C) and (D) are wrong because the first paragraph doesn't make any debatable claims; it only states facts. And Choice (E) is wrong because the passage doesn't respond to any other author's claims, be it to "undermine" them or otherwise — the passage's argument is self-contained.

494. **D. Byzantium**

The fact that the passage describes the Franks as being "at a safe distance" from Byzantium implies that Byzantium was a force to be reckoned with.

The right answer isn't Choice (A), because northeastern Gaul was simply the region where the Franks lived, not the name of a competing power. Choice (B) is wrong because the *Imperium Romanum* was the Roman Empire, which the Franks replaced, not a competing power from the same historical period. Choice (C) is wrong because the passage implies the other German states were eclipsed in power by the Franks instead of being a serious threat to them. And Choice (E) is wrong because the passage states that the Franks eventually conquered Italy.

495. **B. assume the mantle of Roman power by assimilating themselves into it**

From first to last, the passage describes the Franks as succeeding the Western Roman Empire by imitating it.

Choice (A) is wrong because the passage never says that the Franks fought directly against the Roman Empire in war. Choices (C) and (D) are wrong because the passage establishes that the Franks came after the Roman Empire instead of "outlasting" it or attracting Romans to move away from it. Similarly, Choice (E) is wrong because if the Franks came after the Roman Empire, they didn't need to evade its attention.

496. **C. the organization of an administrative bureaucracy**

The fact that the subsequent sentences describe the organization of Frankish government establishes that the phrase "internal constitution" refers to the setup of the Frankish political administration.

Choice (A) is wrong because although the word *constitution* can refer to a written set of laws, the context establishes that this isn't what the word means here. Choice (B) is incorrect because the geographical boundaries of the Frankish Empire are not what the next few sentences go on to describe. Choice (D) is incorrect because this part of the passage describes the Frankish government's organization, not its aesthetics. And Choice (E) is wrong because Frankish religious institutions are only briefly alluded to here, so they aren't the focus of this section of the passage.

497. **C. What argument might be used to defend the SAT analogies section?**

The closing sentence of the passage explicitly presents just such an argument in detail.

The right answer isn't Choice (A), because although the passage mentions that the test was changed in 2005, it never says this was the first time the SAT was changed. Choices (B), (D), and (E) are wrong because this information is wholly absent from the passage.

498. **D. The confirmation of below-freezing temperatures throughout its interior**

Below-freezing temperatures throughout Europa's interior would mean that Europa has no liquid water (because it would be ice instead).

Choices (A) and (C) are wrong because a problem with the satellite wouldn't affect the probability of there being life on Europa — just the chances of our finding out about it. Choice (B) is wrong because although this would increase the probability of there being life on Mars, that wouldn't decrease the probability of there being life on Europa; there's no rule that says life can be only in one other place! Choice (E) is wrong because this fact about Saturn wouldn't affect conditions on Europa in any way.

499. **E. sunlight**

The passage states that sunlight was "long thought to be a prerequisite for life" but then explains that Europa's volcanoes provide a possible alternate condition under which life could arise.

Choice (A) is wrong because the *conditions necessary* for life to arise are in question here. Choice (B) is wrong because the passage doesn't say that heat is directly necessary in order for life to arise (it probably is, but that isn't the specific thing that this passage discusses). The right answer isn't Choice (C), because how could water not "receive enough" liquid? Water *is* liquid. (If it weren't, we would call it *ice* or *steam*, not *water*.) Choice (D) is wrong because the passage establishes that what matters is not the receipt of chemicals but rather what happens to the chemicals that are already present.

500. **E. "chemical disequilibrium"**

The passage states that life might arise from "chemical disequilibrium" and that this can be caused by Europa's undersea volcanoes.

Choices (A), (B), and (C) are wrong because the passage doesn't connect these terms to the conditions necessary for life to arise. Choice (D) is wrong because the phrase "prerequisite for life" itself doesn't explain what the prerequisite for life in question *is*.

501. **A. demonstrate the accuracy of Passage 1**

Although written in a different style, Passage 2 still presents a specific example that illustrates the general principle discussed in Passage 1.

Choice (B) is wrong because Passage 2 doesn't argue against Passage 1. Choice (C) is incorrect because Passage 2 doesn't explain or even reference *retrospective determinism*. Choice (D) is wrong because Passage 2 doesn't even argue that Passage 1 contains any contradictions. Choice (E) is wrong because Passage 2 and Passage 1 are hardly unrelated; on the contrary, they discuss the same topic.

502. **B. mocking the opinions they represent**

The words that appear in quotation marks in Passage 1 ("destined" and "right") signify ideas that the author explains to be severe misunderstandings of the topic at hand.

Choice (A) is wrong because there's no indication that anyone specific is being quoted. Choices (C) and (D) are wrong because both of the answer choices about irony are red herrings — the terms are not used ironically, and the Praxis Reading Test wouldn't expect you to know the difference between dramatic and situational irony. Choice (E) is wrong because there's no indication that these terms are intended to be humorous or that they're referencing anything more specific than an incorrect viewpoint.

503. **E. humorous popular references**

The phrases that appear in quotation marks in Passage 2 ("dating revolution," "never forgets," and "Revenge of the Nerds") bolster the lighter tone of this passage by injecting phrases from popular culture into a discussion of what's actually a fairly complex scientific idea.

Choice (A) is wrong because there's no indication that anyone specific is being quoted. Choice (B) is incorrect because the author of Passage 2 doesn't disagree with these terms — rather, he uses them as explanatory analogies. Choices (C) and (D) are wrong because both of the answer choices about irony are red herrings — the phrases are not used ironically, and the Praxis Reading Test wouldn't expect you to know the difference between dramatic and situational irony.

504. **C. address a common subject but differ in tone**

Passage 1 and Passage 2 discuss the same idea, but the tone of Passage 1 is more scholarly, and that of Passage 2 is more lighthearted.

Choice (A) is wrong because although Passage 1 is written at a slightly harder reading level than is Passage 2, only Passage 2 presents data; Passage 1 only explains a general principle. Choice (B) is incorrect because the passages address the same concept, and they also differ markedly in tone. Choice (D) is wrong because the passages don't disagree with each other; the differences between them are mainly stylistic. Choice (E) is wrong because there's no indication that the two passages are by the same author, and even if they were, the two passages make no mutually exclusive claims, so this author wouldn't have "changed his mind" about anything.

505. **A. Both Passage 1 and Passage 2 concern biology.**

Both passages address the concepts of natural and sexual selection in biology — that is, how living species change and adapt over time.

Choice (B) is wrong because Passage 2 doesn't address psychology (it could be said to address the psychology of elephants, but that would still count as biology from our perspective). The right answer isn't Choice (C), (D), or (E), because both passages are primarily concerned with the principles of the life sciences, or biology.

506. **C. symbolic logic**

Although both passages use logic in the general sense of "a coherent argument involving cause and effect," neither uses *symbolic logic*, which is a form of mathematical notation.

You can eliminate Choice (A) because Passage 1 uses the official rhetorical term *retrospective determinism*. Choice (B) is wrong because Passage 2 uses the word *baddest* for humorous effect. Choice (D) is wrong because Passage 2 references the proverb "an elephant never forgets." And Choice (E) is wrong because Passage 1 uses the Latin abbreviations *i.e.* (*id est*, or "that is to say") and *e.g.* (*exempli gratia*, or "for example").

507. **C. to present background information about the writer's experience.**

In this passage, the author, Dr. Curie, is simply presenting, matter-of-factly, the conditions under which she worked as she experimented.

The right answer isn't Choice (A), because the passage doesn't discuss any sacrifices made by scientists, nor does it discuss how science is a worthy endeavor. Choice (B) is wrong because the passage doesn't indicate that radium was difficult to work with or that it can be adapted for any use. Choice (D) is wrong because no other scientists are discussed and their monetary efforts aren't mentioned. Choice (E) is incorrect because the author doesn't focus on the challenges; she only mentions them briefly.

508. **D. Although scientists work for the purity of the scientific process, some consequences prove to be valuable and useful in human settings. If scientific efforts begin to create income for those using it, the scientific community can lose access to continued work with the product.**

The passage states that the scientific effort to discover and work with radium was of benefit to hospitals. However, the factories that produce the products gained the most riches from it, which led the scientific laboratories to have limited access to the product.

The right answers are not Choices (A) and (C), because the author's opinion is that scientific work must not be considered from the point of view of how useful it might be to humans. Scientific investigation has to be important for its own purposes and what knowledge can be gained from it. The right answer isn't Choice (B), because the passage doesn't claim science should be used commercially or say how scientific endeavors should be shared with great numbers of people. Choice (E) is incorrect because the passage focuses solely on scientific viability, not commercial benefit.

509. **B. Ravens and crows have long been seen as ominous symbols in literature and folklore.**

According to the passage, ravens and crows have had a bad reputation since the most ancient writings and were often been seen as omens of doom.

The right answer isn't Choice (A), because the passage doesn't show any differences between the two birds. Choice (C) is wrong because the author makes a point of saying that we might consider our ancestors ignorant, but when we look more closely at the myths, we should be able to see traces of older religious perspectives. Choice (D) is wrong because that detail isn't in the passage. The passage says nothing about ancient people believing that ravens and crows could change into something else. Choice (E) is incorrect because the passage focuses not on why authors use these symbols but on why these creatures are so prolific as symbols.

510. C. silly

This is just a vocabulary question. *Puerile* is a fancy word for silly or trivial. Saying that such ideas aren't worth notice makes it clear that this word is the right choice.

Choice (A) is wrong because the word *superstitions* was just used, and to say that superstitions are superstitious doesn't really make any sense. The right answer isn't Choice (B). By discussing the topic of mythology, the author suggests that he does think old things are worth studying. To then say that ancient things aren't worth studying makes the whole passage kind of pointless and contradicts the author's main points. The right answer isn't Choice (D), because to say that such things are too important to take any notice of just doesn't make sense. Important things should be noticed. Choice (E) is wrong because the myths and folklore aren't necessarily frightening to people — although ravens and crows alighting atop their houses might be.

511. A. modern man has largely forgotten the important symbols used just a short time ago

By using these examples, and by stating that poetry, fiction, legends, and folklore contain these elements, the author is stating that modern man needs to relook at and rethink symbols used in those texts, especially when — like ravens an crows — the symbols are common in many texts.

The right answer isn't Choice (B). The author refers to the people reading those passages and knows that those works are read widely, which means that the readers must also think those myths are important. The right answer isn't Choice (C). The reference to Hesiod and the quote about building a house shows that many people felt that such symbolism (a raven alighting on the roof of a house) meant doom. This saying is similar to "Don't let a black cat cross your path" or "Don't walk under a ladder." Although many people know these actions don't actually cause bad luck, rare is the person who walks under ladders deliberately . . . just in case. The right answer isn't Choice (D). The author uses the word *might* to make the claim that some myths may have more important meanings and restricts the idea in this passage to crows and ravens. Finally, Choice (E) is wrong because the author isn't suggesting that these birds have secretive powers that have been forgotten over time.

512. C. mythological stories of ravens and crows most likely have their basis in religious contexts and should be considered worthy of study and attention

The passage states that modern myths about ravens and crows can be traced back to early religious beliefs. It suggests that instead of judging all those old myths as silly or superstitious, we should consider the religious aspect important and study it.

Choice (A) is wrong because the end of the passage states the opposite, that our ancestors' ideas are worthy of our attention and need to be considered. Choice (B) is wrong because the article states that ravens and crows might have historic religious significance, not that they were holy animals and were worshipped by our ancestors. Choice (D) is wrong because the author states the birds have a historical meaning that is more symbolic and goes deeper than the literal stories about them. Choice (E) is wrong because the author suggests studying the stories more thoroughly, not investing in scientific study of the symbols' psychological impact.

513. C. to take the place of and serve as a substitute for

The author states that one species, after inheriting different characteristics from its ancestors, is taking the place of another.

Choice (A) is wrong because pigeons are referred to in general animal terms, not in terms of human characteristics like treachery. The new generation of pigeons will not plan a coup or try and trick the others; they'll simply outproduce them. Choice (B) is wrong because two forms of the species could continue. However, the old form, less hardy because of natural selection, will gradually be eradicated by future generations who are more able to survive in the environment. Choice (D) is incorrect because one species wouldn't simply move to a new location. Instead, over time, it would cease to exist. Choice (E) is wrong because the new species isn't necessarily more important than the old.

514. A. When a species is lost due to natural selection, that particular species will not reappear naturally.

Darwin is making the point that natural selection occurs so that more-able forms of the creature can exist. Adapted species do not revert to earlier forms because of the environmental needs of the creature. Any changes in the environment would cause only more changes, not a reversion to old forms.

Choice (B) is wrong because new species are different from earlier forms of the species *because* of those adaptations. Understanding those changes can help people understand how nature affects living creatures. Choice (C) is wrong because the passage makes no mention of species that are in danger of extinction or how to address such a problem. Choice (D) is a correct statement according to Darwin's theory of natural selection, but it isn't the main idea, nor is it discussed in this passage. Choice (E) is wrong because Darwin doesn't suggest the two breeds will compete directly against one another for survival.

515.

B. provide an example to more clearly illustrate the scientific points being made

Darwin provides the example to show how his theory is played out with actual species, and he uses "for instance" to indicate this.

Choice (A) is wrong because there's no indication that fantail pigeons are endangered; this example would instead suggest that the species can survive because of its ability to adapt. (Actually, fantail pigeons are a popular breed.) Choice (C) is wrong because the passage doesn't suggest that humans can influence natural selection, only that they can make breeds similar to those already found in nature. Human interference would not be "natural" by its very definition. Choice (D) is wrong because the example actually *supports* Darwin's theory instead of going against it. Choice (E) is wrong because Darwin states that breeders could "create" a new version of the fantail pigeon should the current version be destroyed.

516.

D. All future generations of rock pigeons will inherit some slight characteristic differences.

Because of natural selection, all future generations will be different in some way from previous generations; they adapt to their environment, which is constantly changing.

Choice (A) is wrong because Darwin's theory doesn't show that one member of a species will survive or supplant another; only new generations of that same species will supplant others. Choice (B) is wrong because Darwin doesn't state that domesticated forms will duplicate their parents. Actually, Darwin says that even domesticated varieties will inherit some slight variations in characteristics. Choice (C) is wrong because Darwin doesn't say these two species are the same; he simply uses both species to illustrate his theories. Choice (E) is incorrect because Darwin doesn't suggest these types of birds are in danger of extinction.

517.

C. A controversy is presented, and then evidence is given to support the argument.

The author begins the passage with a persuasive statement about the quality of a TV show, *Lost*, which many people might argue with. However, the author then provides an example supporting the earlier statements.

Choice (A) isn't correct because no problem is presented, only a theory and opinion about a TV show. There's also no solution given. Choice (B) is wrong because the theory *is* known: the author's belief in the quality of the TV show *Lost*. Choice (D) is wrong because an opinion is not a universal truth (a similar idea held by people from all walks of life). This is just one author's opinion. Choice (E) is incorrect because there is no alternate theory.

518. **A. persuade the readers that TV shows like *Lost* are not so different from what is considered artistic forms of storytelling**

In this passage, the author is trying to persuade readers that the reasons people watch *Lost* (to escape) are not so different from the reasons people watched Greek drama a long time ago. However, one is considered a high form of entertainment and art, and the other is seen "unfavorably."

Choice (B) is incorrect because the passage doesn't suggest any competition between the two national forms of storytelling (Greek versus American). Choice (C) is wrong because the author doesn't suggest that people all over the world should watch this TV show, as they do with Greek theater. The right answer isn't Choice (D), because the author doesn't give a solution. Instead, the author presents an opinion that TV watching is comparable to watching theater and that both should be considered art forms. Choice (E) is incorrect because the author is suggesting that modern TV shows like *Lost* are as good as classical entertainment, such as Greek plays.

519. **C. considered to be the most usual or normal form according to human existence**

The author says "in other words" and gives a definition of *existential:* Watching the TV show is an experience that "connects with the themes basic to our human experience" — themes about the meaning of life and being human and being part of the human race.

Choice (A) is wrong because the author isn't suggesting that only people who watch the show are moral or that watching the TV show is a good ethical decision. It's a form of entertainment. Choice (B) is wrong because although the experience is common to all humans, they haven't arrived at it by consent. People haven't agreed that some themes and topics are appropriate. Choice (D) is wrong for the same reason. There is no consent or authority on existential experiences. These feelings are common to all humans just because they're human.

520. **D. an experience that will cause human connections as the message will have us question who we are as humans**

The author states that the escapist themes in *Lost* cross cultural and time barriers and more deeply connect us as humans because the themes focus on the human experience.

Choice (A) is wrong because the opposite is true: The author is stating that viewers will have similar thoughts, not different ones. Choice (B) is wrong because the author is discussing not the aesthetic pleasure but the philosophical nature of the show. Choice (C) is an overgeneralization.

Although *Lost* is similar to other puzzle-solving shows, such as mysteries, the author doesn't suggest those viewers would also love *Lost*. The author is only suggesting *Lost* would hold a viewer's attention in the same way. Choice (E) isn't right, because the author doesn't actually state how well he likes the show or compare it to other shows on TV.

521. **A. it allows us to escape from the rigors of life, a common need that all humans have**

The author suggests that escapist entertainment has been around a long time and is a common need that all humans have, a "theme that is basic to our human experience."

Choice (B) is wrong because the passage doesn't say that only stressed people feel the need to escape through some form of art. All humans have a need to escape the drudgeries of life. Choice (C) is wrong because the form of escapism the author refers to doesn't involve imagined travels to other time periods. Choice (D) is wrong because TV isn't given as a better form of entertainment. Instead, the author suggests it's as valid a form of entertainment as Greek plays. Choice (E) is incorrect because the author doesn't claim that people no longer watch any forms of theater.

522. **B. It could be easily defended, and a navigable water source was nearby.**

The author says the hills around Rome were "well-defensible" and states that Rome was close to a navigable section of the Tiber River, which was important for its trade route.

Choice (A) is wrong because Rome was located north of those city-states, but the author doesn't say why this was important. Choice (C) doesn't talk about location, which is what the question asked. Choice (D) is wrong because although Rome was close to the Tiber River, the passage doesn't say the proximity was important for crops. The river was important as a trade route. Although Choice (E) is true, Rome's size doesn't answer the question of why the location was ideal.

523. **B. Rome's sanctuaries, mansions, and temples were some of the largest in central Italy and were used by the elite.**

Only a wealthy and powerful community would have the means to build sanctuaries, mansions, and temples.

Choice (A) is wrong because Rome was well-known for reasons besides its wealth. The passage gives many reasons, including Rome's location near a trade route and a navigable river. Choices (C) and (D) are wrong because these facts do not support the idea that Rome was wealthy, only that it was ideally located. Choice (E) may indicate power but not necessarily wealth.

524.

D. Rome's location was ideal for defending against enemies.

The passage states that Rome was located "on well-defensible hills" that had easy access to the coast, the river, and a popular trade route. Therefore, Rome was easy to defend, and the river provided a fast escape route should one be needed.

Choice (A) is wrong because the passage gives no indication that Rome used salt from nearby Ostia to build its own wealth. Choice (B) is wrong because the passage states only that the temple was erected after the monarchy was overthrown, not that the followers of Jupiter led any kind of revolt. Choice (C) is wrong because the passage gives no information about the education of any citizens in the area. Choice (E) is incorrect because although Rome may have been in *league* with other city-states, the passage doesn't state what this means.

525.

C. explaining how Rome got to be such an important community

The entire passage discusses how Rome became an important community and states that location was important, as was the wealth of its citizens.

Choices (A) and (B) are wrong because the passage doesn't explain any outside or domestic pressures that Rome had to overcome. The first sentence mentions such pressures, but the passage doesn't explain them. Choice (D) is incorrect because the passage gives no reasons Rome maintained such international connections. The connections are mentioned in the last sentence but not explained. Choice (E) is wrong because the author doesn't allude to the eventual fall of Rome in any way.

526.

C. The word "highways" is an overgeneralization, and our modern idea of roadways is the best way to illustrate the concept, although the two versions of highways are quite different.

The author uses quotation marks to suggest that the Roman highways are not what the modern term would mean. Although the Roman version was a heavily traveled roadway, it would bear only a slight resemblance to our notions of what highways are today.

Choice (A) is wrong because "highway" is a commonly used term and doesn't need to be cited. Choice (B) is wrong because proper names don't need to point back to common terms with quotation marks. Choice (D) may be a true statement, but it doesn't explain why the word needs to be in quotation marks. Romans didn't coin the term "highway" to refer to their roads. Choice (E) is wrong because "highway" is a commonly used word and couldn't be trademarked for exclusive use by the author.

527. **C. establishing that the republic of Rome had its first beginnings 150 years earlier**

The passage gives examples of how Rome has a historical background that goes back 150 years prior to its emergence as an important city; it gives examples of how the republic was created and how it focused on the rights of all citizens, the elite and non-elite.

Choice (A) is wrong because there are no examples or details about hegemonial rule by Rome or in Rome. Hegemonial alliance is used as a non-example, something Rome didn't exhibit. Choice (B) is wrong because the passage gives historical background information about Rome's penchant toward republican rule rather than imperial rule, and the author states that scholars still debate the issue of imperialism. Although the passage states Choice (D) as a detail, it doesn't give examples or other information that might point to this as the main idea or focus of the passage. Choice (E) is wrong because the author provides no details on the differing viewpoints of scholars, other than saying that scholars debate.

528. **A. Space exploration is the key to discovering the origin of life, which will also tell us about extraterrestrial life.**

The passage states that space exploration is the technology man can use to look for evidence of extraterrestrial life on other planets.

Choice (B) is wrong because the passage states that the origins of life and extraterrestrial life are interwoven, and solving the puzzle to one will help solve the puzzle to the other. Choice (C) is wrong because whether life exists, in some form, on other planets is still in question. Choice (D) is wrong because the passage suggests technology may be the key to finding answers, not that man has already mastered space exploration for the purpose of looking for extraterrestrial life. And Choice (E) is wrong because the author suggests that space exploration may give us the answer.

529. **A. readers and audience members like to imagine the voice and person of Shakespeare speaking through his characters**

The author states that the idea of Shakespeare's characters being his own personal mouthpiece is attractive but probably isn't a careful consideration of the creative art of playwriting, which is making up stories for entertainment.

Choice (B) is incorrect because the passage states that the proverbial speech is persuasive but not to the degree that it would sway audience members or readers to believe everything that every character said. Choice (C) isn't alluded to in the passage; the author says nothing about Shakespeare's words having hidden meanings or symbolism. Choice (D) is wrong because the author states the exact opposite: that Shakespeare's works probably can't tell us who the man Shakespeare was. And Choice (E) is wrong because the passage suggests that you can't find

Shakespeare's views on any subject in his works. Instead, the characters must stand for their own views, not for those of the author who gave them voice.

---

530. **B. Because Shakespeare was such a master wordsmith and wrote beautifully**

According to the author, Shakespeare's lines have achieved "the status of proverbial speech" because they were persuasively and "exquisitely worded."

Choice (A) is wrong because *nihilistic* means negative, and negative ideas don't necessarily point to universal truths. Choice (C) is wrong because the author gives no evidence that Shakespeare wrote for any reason other than entertainment of his audience; in fact, the author argues against assuming Shakespeare was trying to persuade his audience. Although Choice (D) may be true, the passage doesn't discuss his audience's reaction to his plays. The passage cautions modern readers to avoid reading between the lines too much. Choice (E) is incorrect because the author cautions against seeing more to the works than is written there; no deeper meaning or wisdom may exist.

---

531. **D. to caution readers against putting much meaning into the characters' words and believing them to be the voice of the author himself**

The passage cautions readers against thinking that knowledge of the personal beliefs of Shakespeare can be found within his works and suggests that it's impossible to tell which words might actually be his own beliefs and feelings about a topic.

Choice (A) is wrong because so few speeches are given, and many famous speeches are left out. Choice (B) is wrong because the passage gives only a passing mention to Shakespeare's nondramatic works. Choice (C) is wrong because the author states that such a viewpoint should be avoided. No evidence exists that Shakespeare used his plays to make his own beliefs known. Choice (E) is incorrect because the author cautions readers against viewing the drama as worth intense study, and he doesn't suggest that sonnets or nondramatic poems might have deeper meanings.

---

532. **B. Each work of an author and each character in that work has its own narrative voice.**

The passage states that every work of Shakespeare, both dramatic and nondramatic, has its own narrative voice and should not be confused with the voice of the author of the works.

Choices (A) and (C) are incorrect because neither statement is in the passage. The author isn't saying that each work is as important as the others, only that each is individual, and the author doesn't mention the number of works. Choice (D) is wrong because the passage makes no mention regarding what might make reading or listening to Shakespeare more pleasurable. Finally, Choice (E) is wrong because the author uses these two plays as Shakespeare's most famous works, not because they hold deeper symbolic meaning.

533. A. effusive in admiration

The entire passages uses examples to illustrate the positive character of Archimedes and uses terms such as "ingenious." The passage shows multiple examples of how the inventor and mathematician was devoted to his work.

534. C. thinking of mathematical concepts continuously, to the point of distraction

Archimedes' life was one of continuous work and thought about mathematics. However, this constant thinking may have led to his death, as according to one account, he was so distracted by his thoughts of mathematical concepts that he didn't identify himself to a solider.

Choice (A) is wrong because the passage makes no mention of those types of works and states that he wrote only one book. Choices (B) and (D) are wrong because although Archimedes did live a life devoted to mathematics, the word *contemplation* concerns thoughts rather than actions. Choice (E) is wrong because the author doesn't suggest that Archimedes had concepts or work that hadn't been revealed.

535. A. the work of Archimedes was instrumental in helping to win battles

This passage gives Archimedes' inventions, such as catapults, as the reason for Rome's defeat during the siege of Syracuse.

Choice (B) is incorrect because although Archimedes did design inventions that were used for war, the author gives the example to show the man's prowess for creation using mathematical concepts. Choice (C) is wrong because his inventions were used by his country, not used against his personal enemies. Choice (D) is wrong because the passage doesn't suggest that Archimedes didn't want his designs being used this way. Finally, although Archimedes' inventions were said to be used with "great effect," Choice (E) takes things a bit too far.

536. A. Archimedes felt that mathematics was a game and didn't care if his works were useful or not.

The main idea of the passage is that Archimedes constantly thought about and played with mathematical concepts. The first paragraph states that his inventions were merely "diversions of geometry at play" and that he didn't think them important. That's why he left so little written work.

Choices (B) and (C) are wrong because the passage doesn't show that Archimedes felt himself to be a genius or that he felt he owed his gifts to the world; he was only a man who was distracted by math and loved to work with his ideas. Choice (D) is wrong because the passage doesn't show that Archimedes was ever a teacher to those around him; he focused on the pleasure math brought him. Choice (E) is incorrect because the passage gives examples of Archimedes' works being used by humanity. Clearly, he didn't reject intrusions into his work.

537. **C. Shakespeare does not discuss philosophers very often and may not have read them widely.**

The author does note that Shakespeare mentions the most-well quoted philosophers, Socrates and Pythagoras. However, Shakespeare makes few other references to philosophers, and the conclusion is that Shakespeare may not have read this subject very much.

Choice (A) is wrong because the passage gives no evidence on Shakespeare's use of philosophy in his own works. Choice (B) is wrong because the passage states only that Shakespeare used Pythagoras's ideas as bizarre jokes, which may or may not have reflected Shakespeare's personal feelings about all philosophers. Choice (D) is incorrect because the author does give some examples of Shakespeare's references to philosophers. And with only one quote by Socrates in all of Shakespeare's works, Choice (E) simply can't be supported.

538. **D. Who would be considered the most important figure of Latin learning during 12th-century Gaul, and what contributions did he or she make?**

The passage focuses exclusively on Peter Abelard and explains how he became the most familiar and important person in Latin learning, as stated in the topic sentence. The rest of the paragraph names some of his contributions.

Choice (A) is wrong because it asks for an overall analysis of who helped to shape Latin learning, whereas the passage focuses on the 12th century. Similarly, Choice (B) is too broad; it asks for an overall analysis of education in the 12th century, whereas the passage focuses on Latin learning. Choice (C) is wrong because the passage gives no details about Abelard's work in logic or theology; it merely notes that he was a brilliant lecturer. Finally, although Abelard was an important figure, the passage doesn't state that he changed Latin learning during this time. Therefore, Choice (E) is wrong.

539. **B. coincidence**

Both passages seek to provide more specific examples of how coincidence works in situations in which an individual was at a particular place at a particular time.

Choice (A) is wrong because neither passage is about *divine providence*, the idea that things happen according to God's plan. Choice (C) is wrong because only Passage 2 is about determinism, and Choice (D) is wrong because only Passage 1 is about fatalism. Choice (E) is wrong because the passage only briefly alludes to fate in the introduction.

540. **C. identify the context in which theory examples are explanatory.**

The first paragraph is an introduction to the later passages; it offers the reader context, explaining why such specific examples are given.

Choice (A) is wrong because the author sets no parameters for the term "coincidence." Instead, the author proposes a theory about specific areas of coincidence. Choice (B) is wrong because no summary of the passages is given. Choice (D) is wrong because the two examples aren't discussed; they're only introduced in a broad way. Choice (E) is wrong because no prevailing theories are given.

541. **C. God has a plan for all of us, and what happens is providential and happens under the watchful eye of a divine creator.**

These two passages give only two examples of coincidence: fate and determinism. Neither passage mentions a being who controls destiny. Therefore, Choice (C) offers an alternative explanation.

Choice (A) is wrong because it talks about a future event that's based on current scientific data and facts; the explanation concerns a theory of how the world works, not how human events occur. Choice (B) is another example of determinism, an individual causing his own destruction through the choices he makes. Lord Voldemort seizes on the idea that the child Harry Potter will cause his destruction, and Voldemort's destruction is a result of his pursuit of Potter. Choice (D) is another example of fate, an event that occurs even though the individual was warned that it would happen. Caesar was fated, in some way, to have a very bad March 15. The phrase "meant to be together" suggests the theory of fate, so Choice (E) is incorrect.

542. **A. Both passages describe a relationship that is presented in the introduction.**

Both passages further explain and give more specific examples about the author's theory in the first paragraph, the introduction.

Choice (B) is wrong because neither passage undermines the other; both present valid examples of a particular theory. Choices (C) and (D) are wrong because Passage 2 doesn't reference or further define the information in Passage 1. Choice (E) is wrong because Passage 2 discusses determinism, a different topic from Passage 1.

543. **B. characterized by a lack of change**

In the sentence, "[not] static" refers to a movement in society, meaning that many changes were occurring and that those changes were not stable.

Choice (A) is wrong because the passage isn't about electricity. Choices (C) or (D) are wrong because society isn't something that can be at rest or fluid, like a body in motion. There's no context to support that the society resisted change, so Choice (E) is wrong.

544. **C. Great Britain ruled India for hundreds of years, yet the country flourished only after that rule ceased.**

The point of Thomas Paine's passage is that America would have probably done better, as a country, had it not been subjected to British interference and attempts to rule over it. Using India as an example would lend support to this claim.

Choice (A) is wrong because the passage states the opposite: that Britain's interest was strong only because Britain was protecting its own needs and accounts. Choice (B) is wrong because the passage states that only independence from Britain could bring about an alliance with common enemies. Choice (D) is an inference that isn't supported by the passage, which specifically refers to the cause of American independence, not societies in general. Choice (E) is incorrect because Paine suggests that the current support of Great Britain has made America lame, so even more support wouldn't have been a boon to America.

545. **A. strengthen the claim that such change is necessary for growth**

Paine is suggesting that man — and America — must have other experiences and that not to do so would be like a grown man still drinking milk like a baby instead of eating meat like an adult.

Choice (B) is wrong because Paine asserts that America's economy would still have been strong, even if no European country had noticed her. Choice (C) is wrong because British supporters don't claim British rule is the sole reason for America's prosperity; instead, they see British support as vital for continued governance and support of the new nation. Choice (D) is wrong because in this passage, Paine doesn't show that the common man would gain from independence from British rule. Choice (E) is wrong because Paine was speaking figuratively, not literally.

546.
C. Patriotism should not be rooted in old habits but should be motivated by current interest.

Paine tells his readers to shrug off their old prejudices about patriotism to Britain and to consider how those ideals are holding America back.

Choice (A) is wrong because Paine argues that Britain and those who are patriotic to that cause see only the interest to the nation as a whole, not the individual needs of the people. Choice (B) is wrong because Paine was asserting that a focus on American interests by other countries wouldn't cause political allies to suddenly become enemies of either country, America or Britain. A focus on American interests won't cause political allies to become enemies or vice versa. Choice (D) is wrong because Paine argues that Britain asserts its rule and authority as a false flag of power rather than a true show of patriotic authority. Choice (E) is incorrect because Paine isn't suggesting that other nations not be considered within the idea of patriotism; he actually uses other nations to support his ideas.

547.
B. Whether American citizens support such a move

Paine doesn't address whether any other citizens follow along with his arguments, nor does he say how strong the movement toward American independence is. He only gives reasons to strengthen the idea that America should break ties with Britain.

Choice (A) is wrong because Paine does say that America has a "lame" connection with Great Britain. Choice (C) is wrong because Paine states that America would have flourished if Great Britain, or any European country, hadn't noticed her. Choice (D) is wrong because Paine states that Britain doesn't protect American interests, only her own. Finally, Paine alludes to some citizens feeling British support has been beneficial, so Choice (E) is wrong.

548.
D. instill a sense of civic pride in the town of Springfield

In this passage, the author is playing to the feelings of civic pride by reminding those living in Springfield that a famous business was launched in the town and that the town will continue to be a fruitful place to live and work.

Choice (A) is wrong because although the tone is persuasive, the purpose is not to get readers to support the plan. Instead, the passage explains why the town is supporting further growth. Choice (B) is wrong because little information is given about the program, other than that it will improve the town overall. Choice (C) is wrong because the passage mentions only one historical topic, that of a famous and prosperous building. Choice (E) is wrong because although Mr. Bradley did start his company in Springfield, there's no evidence that his company did well due to its location.

549. **A. Attempts made by the town to convince new businesses to locate have been somewhat successful.**

In the last sentence, the author states that recent newspaper articles show that new businesses are locating in the area and that local businesses are expanding.

Choice (B) is wrong because it doesn't focus on events that have occurred; it talks about possible future events. Choice (C) is wrong because the passage doesn't say that businesses will be in competition for consumer traffic. Choice (D) is wrong because the passage gives no suggestion that the vacant buildings are off-putting. Rather, the passage says that new businesses are wanted to fill those spaces. Choice (E) is wrong because the passage doesn't suggest that the town hasn't flourished because of lack of business development from officials.

550. **A. A public artist in Shakespeare's situation needed to cater to the tastes of his public.**

The author suggests that Shakespeare gave his public just what they wanted: "stabbings and stranglings / and fat men making love," without much thought to his own artistic tastes.

Choices (B) and (D) are wrong because there's no hint that the author feels Shakespeare's content was inappropriate, for those times or modern times. Choice (C) is wrong because none of the written lines indicate that Shakespeare was working to fulfill any artistic needs; they suggest only that he was giving in to the audience's desires. Choice (E) is incorrect because this passage seems to focus on "trifling" concerns. No other more important issues are discussed.

551. **B. indicate examples of Elizabethan attitudes toward sex and gender as seen through a playwright who lived at that time**

Both passages show ideas about how women were seen during that time period and use *The Taming of the Shrew* to illustrate these viewpoints.

Choices (A), (C), and (D) are wrong because neither passage suggests that Shakespeare disagreed with the prevailing attitude of the day or used his plays to make political statements. Choice (E) is wrong because the authors aren't trying to show that Shakespeare should be still be read or studied. They clearly feel Shakespeare's value is a given.

552. **B. indifferent**

Both passages simply present the information in an indifferent and scholarly manner. Neither gives personal viewpoints on the role of gender in Elizabethan times.

The absence of tone or persuasive techniques makes all other answers invalid. Choices (A), (C), (D), and (E) call for evidence of emotion.

553. **D. Offer a societal view of women that was ingrained and not likely meant to be seen as a political statement**

Both passages analyze situations in reference to the times in which they were written. Neither passage indicates that Shakespeare wanted to make overt political statements; they note only that he wrote to please his audience and acting company.

Choice (A) is wrong because the analysis looks only at attitudes toward women and present theories, which gives only a limited view of overall Elizabethan attitudes. Choice (B) is wrong because only Passage 2 refers to Shakespeare's toning down his plays for public appeal. Choice (C) is wrong because only Passage 2 gives a connection between Shakespeare and Elizabethan attitudes toward women. Choice (E) is wrong because neither passage focuses on Shakespeare's personal attitude. Rather, both writers see the play as evidence of society's attitude toward women during that time.

554. **C. Passage 1 offers evidence of prejudicial treatment of women matter-of-factly as seen in a popular play of the time, while Passage 2 offers evidence that that prejudicial treatment should be viewed within the larger constructs of religious training and beliefs.**

Passages 1 and 2 use the same play to illustrate different points: One gives an example of stereotypes in a popular play of the time to show that views toward women were prejudicial. The other says that the view toward women should instead be seen as a duality of times, where women were both revered as wives and seen as the weaker sex.

Choices (A) and (B) are wrong because neither passage undermines the other. Choice (D) is wrong because Passage 2 contains no argumentative nature, tone, or wording. Choice (E) is wrong because Passage 2 does more than summarize the play. It also discusses important literary elements.

555. **A. provide a contrast in entertainment forms during this time period**

The author uses Central Park to illustrate how different of an atmosphere Coney Island was. Whereas Central Park was self-controlled, Coney Island was closer to out-of-control fun.

Choice (B) is wrong because the wording or tone doesn't suggest criticism; the passage only reports on the time period and the emergence of a new brand of entertainment. Choice (C) is wrong because the author sees Central Park as an example of delayed gratification, which is the opposite of consumerism. Choice (D) is wrong because the author makes no mention of the legacy left in either location. Choice (E) is wrong because the passage isn't just about the various ways people entertained themselves in the 1890s. If it were, it would have given more than these two examples.

556. **A. Newspapers changed formats in order to more fully appeal to the reader.**

The last sentence suggests that readers wanted newspapers that were more versatile and easier to travel with.

Choice (B) is wrong because the last sentence doesn't mention advertisers. Choice (C) is wrong because it calls for an opinion, but the passage simply relates historical facts. Choice (D) is wrong because the last sentence — indeed, the entire passage — makes no mention of the decreasing literacy levels of readers. Choice (E) is wrong because the passage says that newspapers changed, not that these changes were lowering previous standards according to class structure.

557. **D. to inform the reader that the grammar of the time period differed from the reader's likely conception of "grammar"**

The sentence defines *grammar*, which in modern language means studying how words are used in language, any language. In another time period, studying grammar specifically meant studying Latin.

Choice (A) is wrong because the passage doesn't necessarily refer to any other country and the language of that country. Choice (B) is wrong because the school conditions described were typical for students of that time period seeking higher education, not necessarily because of the difficulty of the topic. Choice (C) is wrong because the author uses a modern university term, "Classics," to show to what degree classical scholars studied their subject. The author isn't saying that educational practices back then were superior to those of modern times. Choice (E) is wrong because Latin was the prevailing language taught at all grammar schools. Differentiating it from other languages wouldn't be necessary.

558. **B. It was long days of study and years dedicated to learning.**

The passage gives details about the length of the school day, followed by more homework, to show how Latin grammar study operated and how the students learned.

Choice (A) is wrong because the passage makes only one comparison, to university "Classics" students. This type of education isn't typical of all university courses. Choice (C) is incorrect because the passage gives no information about the difficulty of learning Latin, only the dedication of the students who were studying it. Choice (D) is wrong because the passage gives no information about how the students might have used such learning. And Choice (E) is wrong because there's no information on how grammar school was a choice different from apprenticeship.

559. **B. the art of skill of speaking or writing**

> Presumably, Latin students studied for such long hours and with dedication in order to read and write better.
>
> Choices (A), (C), (D), and (E) are wrong because each one has a negative aspect: dishonesty, pompousness, insincerity, or exaggeration. The passage was written to show the students' dedication to study. No part of the passage suggests that such study was for negative reasons.

560. **A. provide more evidence and another example of how people view the topic**

> The author cites the work — and uses quotes and examples from it — to provide evidence of how other people view the topic; those ideas are similar to the author's own theories on how myths work in cultural contexts.
>
> Choice (B) is wrong because Armstrong isn't necessarily well-known, nor does writing a book on the topic mean she's an ultimate authority figure. It means only that she has theories and ideas about the same topic as the author of the passage. Choice (C) is wrong because the topic, the telling of and listening to stories, is already common; the author doesn't need to find common ground. Choice (D) is wrong because the passage gives only one book title and doesn't use it as evidence of importance; the author mentions Armstrong's book only to show that others have similar beliefs and ideas about the topic. And Choice (E) is wrong because Armstrong's book supports the original idea of the passage instead of providing another theory.

561. **C. Myths serve as a culture's way of remembering important events.**

> The point of the passage is to present myths as acts of storytelling that blend a culture's history and a culture's belief system and to show that myths are fluid and can mean different things to different people and cultures.
>
> Choice (A) is wrong because the author is trying to make the point that myths can be based in truth and that understanding myths might help us to understand our own beliefs. Choice (B) is wrong because the author states several times that myths aren't always based in fact. Choice (D) is wrong because the passage shows that myths are often blends of truth and storytelling and change over time. Choice (E) is wrong because the author is suggesting that neither storytelling aspects nor accuracy should be considered more important. Instead, the focus should be on the people who created these stories and the need they had for such creations.

562. **B. That humans seek to understand their world and remember their histories as interesting stories rather than dry recordings of fact.**

In the passage, the author states that humans are drawn to stories. Remembering histories is easier and more interesting if they're passed down as stories.

Choice (A) is incorrect because many myths actually describe natural events rather than events that focus solely on "human" interests. Choice (C) is incorrect because the author doesn't state this is the best way to learn and remember myths. Many could argue that in a literate and knowledgeable society, understanding the scientific aspects of how rainbows are formed is much better than reading a myth with fictional elements in it. Choice (D) is wrong because it doesn't explain why humans seek myths; it only describes what humans do with myths. And Choice (E) is wrong because the author doesn't remark on historical facts at all or suggest stories are more fun to remember.

563. **C. Thomas Jefferson is known today for his views of equality, but he kept several slaves and even had many children by a slave.**

Only Choice (C) is based on accurate, historical fact. Thomas Jefferson is known for his ideas of equality, as evidenced by his work on the Constitution. He did own a plantation of slaves, and DNA testing has shown that he fathered several children with a slave he owned.

Choices (A), (B), (D), and (E) are myths. Some are based in fact; others are complete fabrications. The stories have changed over time but still exist as popular American folklore; they exemplify beliefs, including the cultural ideas of prosperity, a spirit of pioneerism, and the importance of truth.

564. **C. If what a person wants is trivial, irrational, or evil, can this add up to a meaningful life?**

Choice (C) focuses on the last sentence in the passage, "No, this is too easy." This suggests that thinking in such simplistic terms of feeling and meaning doesn't take into account the larger moral and ethical views of finding meaning, alluded to in the first paragraph.

Choices (A) and (B) are wrong because they simply rephrase questions asked in the passage. Choice (D) is an evaluative statement, not a question. Choice (E) is wrong because no tips are given on how to lead a more meaningful life.

565.   **D. In reality,**

Socrates was put to death, but his real crime wasn't corrupting the youth. Instead, in reality, his death was meant to serve as a warning to others about what would happen if they questioned those in authority and taught others to do the same.

Choice (A) is wrong because Socrates was actually, not figuratively, punished for questioning authority. Choice (B) is wrong because although his death may have been symbolic, his punishment was not a symbol but a message from those in power. Choice (C) is wrong because he literally was found guilty of corrupting youth, not of questioning others. Questioning others wasn't a crime. Choice (E) is wrong because this event really did happen.

566.   **A. Developmentally speaking, individuals obtain their sense of self initially through the assimilation of objective characterizations of others.**

The passage states that Sartre believes that others play a role in developing one's personal identity, and the quote shows that he believes that people around an individual hold important truths about that person.

Choices (B) and (C) are wrong because the passage doesn't show that self-consciousness develops as a reaction against others' thoughts and opinions; instead, those thoughts and opinions help to form a person. Choice (D) is wrong because although the involvement of others helps to form a person, being self-conscious actually means that a person understands the role others play. Otherwise, a person wouldn't be self-conscious at all. Choice (E) is incorrect because Sartre believed individuality couldn't be developed on one's own.

567.   **C. Through these experiments, scientists have learned that life on Earth involved a process of applying energy to a mixture of hydrogen-rich gases available in the primitive atmosphere.**

The second sentence in the passage states that laboratory experiments have shown that life needed an application of some type of energy in the primitive atmosphere.

Choice (A) is incorrect because the passage says the experiments were successful. Choice (B) is wrong because the passage states that advances have been made to understanding life on Earth, but full understanding hasn't been achieved. Choice (D) is wrong because the passage makes no mention of ethical concerns about the experiments. Choice (E) is wrong because the passage states this is only "likely" and not yet a reality.

568. **D. Although life on Mars and Earth might share a similar evolutionary process, Mars would have produced organisms dissimilar to Earth creatures because of natural selection.**

The passage states that it's possible that similar atmospheric conditions existed on Mars as once existed on Earth. However, natural selection would have rendered any Martian organisms far different from those on Earth because the environmental conditions varied widely between the planets.

Choices (A) and (C) are incorrect because the passage doesn't state that life never occurred on Mars; the author concedes life on Mars as a possibility. Choice (B) is wrong for the same reason: The author only suggests the possibility of life on Mars. Choice (E) is wrong because the passage states that Martian life would have been radically different from terrestrial life forms because of environmental interactions. Therefore, any life created in a lab on Earth wouldn't necessarily be equipped to handle the Martian environment.

569. **C. Darwin's theory of natural selection can be applied to these collections of molecules because they followed the same path as all life forms, reproducing in order to endure**

The author is stating that known theories of life show that Darwin's criteria were satisfied and that understanding this theory helps to show that simple molecules likely developed into more complex forms of life.

Choice (A) is wrong because Darwin's theory of natural selection doesn't address what's considered life. Choice (B) is wrong because the author isn't debating what may be called life, and Darwin never set those criteria. "What is life?" is a debatable topic, but it isn't addressed in this passage. Choices (D) and (E) are wrong because the author claims the opposite: that all forms of life on any planet would follow the same evolutionary process.

570. **A. Atmospheric conditions and energy sources are necessary for life.**

The passage states several times that atmospheric conditions and an energy source are required for the production of life, even in primitive conditions. Without one or the other, life isn't created.

Choice (B) is wrong because the passage states that researchers aren't far from re-creating self-generating molecules; it isn't possible yet. The author says Choices (C) and (D) are likely, but we can't know that they're true. Choice (E) is wrong because the author doesn't state that the conditions on Earth and Mars were very similar or gave rise to similar life forms.

571. **C. fantasy provides a richness of life where characters can act outside of known rules of how the world works, while realistic fiction has to follow known truths**

The author is comparing fantasy to other genres and explaining why fantasy is an enjoyable genre to watch or read. Part of this enjoyment comes from an imagination where anything is possible and the plot doesn't have to rely on what is known and expected about humans or how the world works.

Choice (A) is wrong because realistic fiction can also provide an escape. That escape may not be from the normal, but reading or watching such stories is a means of escape from the real world. Choice (B) is incorrect because the passage makes no mention of the number of plotlines. Choice (D) is wrong because the passage doesn't speculate on how authors of realistic works might have felt. Likely, many also felt (as we've all felt at times) that they didn't fit into society. Choice (E) is wrong because the author doesn't suggest that fantastic fiction makes people unable to fit into society or that other forms of fiction are better at helping people fit in.

572. **C. Conformity includes a limited and accepted range of abilities, while nonconformity is unlimited.**

The passage states that there are a limited number of ways to be normal, or conformist. Being seen as abnormal, or nonconformist, is wildly varied and has unlimited possibilities.

Choices (A) and (B) are wrong because neither answer addresses the distinction between the two terms. Choice (D) just isn't true. Fitting into a group does change from generation to generation and situation to situation. For example, music or clothing that's considered "hip" or "cool" would be seen very differently in another time. Choice (E) is wrong because the passage deals with the paradox of human reflection on the issue of conformity. In the animal kingdom, issues of conformity are evidenced (albinism, for example), but animals don't reflect on the need or desire to conform.

573. **A. A sociological theory is presented and then illustrated with examples.**

Conformity and *nonconformity* are sociological terms that address social questions or issues. The theory presented is that humans want to conform and not conform. Both are needs that humans have.

The correct answer isn't Choice (B), because the passage presents no debate or counterposition. The author presents only his theory. Choice (C) is incorrect because the author doesn't address how the two terms are alike and different. Although the terms can be compared, the author doesn't use this passage to do so. Choice (D) is wrong because the theory presented isn't controversial, and the passage doesn't refer to any previously accepted thoughts about the topic. Choice (E) is wrong because no alternate theory is presented.

574. **B. Why do we feel the need to fit in a group and yet still value the qualities that make us unique?**

The author says the conundrum in normal versus abnormal is that humans want both things: to fit into a group and to stand out.

Choice (A) is wrong because the author doesn't say what defines normal; he says only that what is considered "normal" falls within an average for various traits. Choice (C) is wrong because the author doesn't define what's considered nonconformist, other than to say it's different from normal. The author also makes no statement about how nonconformists are treated by the rest of society. Choice (D) is wrong because the author gives no advice on how to seem more desirable. And Choice (E) is wrong because the author suggests conformity is a common behavior attributable to humans, an evolutionary pressure.

575. **A. it allows us to attract competitors and have advantages over others**

The author emphasizes that this topic points to the evolutionary, reproductive pressure on humans to be seen as the best in a field of competitors.

Choice (B) is wrong because the author doesn't make this statement. It's an inference that takes the author's idea to an extreme. Choice (C) is wrong because the author presents a sociological theory, not necessarily one that can be researched and supported by scientific data. Choice (D) is wrong because the passage doesn't point to any questions raised or discuss answers. It states the issue is a paradox, a puzzle that can't be solved. Choice (E) is wrong because the standards of desirability aren't enhanced in a linear fashion, from one level to the next, so that humans get more and more desirable over time. Rather, according to the passage, there are many ways to stand out.

576. **C. Fridays are reserved for setting up weddings, which typically happen on Saturdays.**

Even if you didn't know that weddings typically happen on Saturdays, a quick glance at the schedule shows the need to set up for the "Sat." event.

Choice (A) is wrong because this Friday actually seems to be the usual occurrence, which is that Samantha spends all day getting ready for the Saturday weddings. Choice (B) is wrong because there's no direct connection noted between the meeting at the park and the Richards' ceremony. The chart presents no information supporting Choice (D). Considering the nature of the business, Wedding Warriors would most certainly be working on the day before weddings. Choice (E) is wrong because Samantha clearly does other work on those days, meaning she didn't take the day off from business.

577. **B. Samantha participates in presentations more than any other activity.**

Samantha has scheduled five presentations, more than any other event.

Choice (A) is wrong because the Sanders' bride and groom photography sessions are on different days. Choice (C) is wrong because a catered lunch happens only once during the week. Choice (D) is wrong because she's seeing the Pink Orchids Event presentation at the Las Vegas Resort, not in her office. Choice (E) can't be supported, because the schedule shows Samantha does travel to engage in presentations.

578. **C. Photography sessions/presentations**

Samantha participates in three events that include photography: the Jaclyn Frank Photography presentation, the Sanders' groom's photography session, and the Sanders' bride's photography session.

There are only two sessions that involve makeup, two sessions that involve dress consultations (one for the wedding dress and one for the bridesmaids' dresses), two sessions involving the Sanders' pre-ceremony photos (one for the groom and one for the bride), and two site visits during the week (it's inferred that one of those is a visit to a potential wedding location).

579. **C. The rise of capitalistic civilization has changed the tenor and reasoning for going to war.**

The passage states that with the rise of capitalistic civilizations, nations began to go to war for reasons different from those in medieval societies.

Choice (A) is an overgeneralization. Although war does change society, the author doesn't state that these changes have been beneficial, only that they've changed civilization in drastic ways. Choice (B) is the main idea of the passage, not a key supporting detail. Choices (D) and (E) are stated as beliefs of some leaders, not necessarily the author; they aren't key details supporting the main idea of the passage.

580. **D. modern capitalistic civilizations focus on international consequences and sensitivity, while the imperialistic era focused on domestic and nationalistic concerns.**

Choice (D) summarizes the main points of the passage, which are that capitalistic concerns change from one civilization to the next and that the imperialistic era focused on how wars would benefit their own nations and people. Other capitalistic civilizations focused on both domestic and international concerns.

Choice (A) is wrong because the passage doesn't mention a democratic society or any society that's focused on issues of individual rights. Choice (B) is wrong because the passage suggests the opposite: that imperialistic societies focused on domestic and nationalistic concerns. Choice (C) is wrong because the passage presents no evidence that imperialistic wars were fought for those reasons. Choice (E) is wrong because the author doesn't suggest which war, if any, ended imperialistic societies or whether those concerns are now concluded at all.

581. **C. feels as if a new world war will drastically change our current notions of civilization**

The entire passage suggests that wars have drastically changed civilizations and that any new wars will do the same, for good or bad.

Choice (A) is wrong because the author doesn't state opinions on how previous wars caused positive change; he says only that they caused important change. Choice (B) is wrong because although the author does state that war brings new social order to the world, he doesn't state that war is the only cause. Rather, war is an effect of a social system. Finally, Choices (D) and (E) are wrong because the author makes no statement that wars were necessary for change or are inevitable. There's also no mention of a "worldwide" democracy; instead, the passage refers to democracy in the Western world.

582. **B. contrast Eastern and Western thoughts and beliefs**

The author is making the point that Western thoughts and imperialistic concerns are very different from those in the Eastern part of the world. Those imperialistic concerns were not a worldwide phenomenon but a Western movement.

Choice (A) is wrong because the passage doesn't address the differences between religious wars and imperialistic wars. Choice (C) is wrong because there's no judgment on the author's part about why some wars are more important than others. The author is simply describing a movement and shift in attitudes toward war. Choice (D) is incorrect because the passage gives no information given on Hindu "wars," nor does the author need to distinguish them from medieval wars. The passage isn't about those wars; it's about wars that happened later, World War I and World War II. Choice (E) is wrong because the Hindus also went to war; they just went for different reasons.

583. **A. attempting to convince readers that many have the wrong definition of the term "caste"**

The author gives an example of how the term is misused, which often leads to confusion in further discussions about the topic.

Choices (B) and (D) are wrong because the author doesn't define the term. Choice (C) is incorrect because the author is only pointing out a source of misdirection that leads to the wrong understanding of the term; he isn't stating that several definitions are correct. Choice (E) isn't right, because the author doesn't present other versions of the caste system. The passage only defines the system.

584. **C. authoritative condescension**

The author spends the passage putting down experts who can't properly qualify the term "caste." He then describes these people as bumbling about; the implication is that the author has more knowledge than they do.

Choice (A) is incorrect because the passage does have emotion, making "dispassionate" the wrong word. Choice (B) is wrong because although the author does mock those "experts," nothing about the tone suggests he's merely teasing. Choice (D) is wrong because the author shows no admiration for these other "experts"; he shows only scorn. Choice (E) is wrong because the author doesn't accept these other, less informed definitions.

585. **C. the conquistadors sought gold and the friars sought souls for the Gospel**

Only Choice (C) makes a distinction between the conquistador and the friar.

Choices (A) and (B) are wrong because they point out only the similarities; they don't distinguish between the two. Choice (D) is wrong because the author doesn't state that both types of men were reckless. He states the conquistadors were reckless but the friars "yielded" themselves to death, implying more respect for that type of man. And Choice (E) is wrong because the passage states that both types of men are "impressively" described in history books.

586. **A. The protagonist of *House* is a flawed man who appeals to viewers because of those very flaws and failures.**

The author says the protagonist is deeply unlikable, even a jerk, but then states that it's for this very reason that viewers enjoy the show.

Choice (B) is wrong because the author gives no evidence that the protagonist suffers justice of any kind for his actions. Choice (C) is wrong because the passage implies that detective stories and medical shows are equally fascinating to viewers. Choice (D) is a statement made in the passage, but it doesn't address or elaborate on why the show was so popular. And Choice (E) is wrong because the author gives several reasons as to why this show became so popular.

587. C. admiration

The author's attitude is one of respect and admiration for the show and the message it gives to viewers. The character is described as "brilliant," and the author lists the awards the show has received.

Choice (A) is wrong because the author feels the show is worthy of the popularity it has received. The author says it meets the needs of the audience and is more than just entertainment. Choice (B) is wrong because the author makes many connections between the show and the cultural truths of human relationships. Choice (D) is wrong because the author clearly explains his theory with relevant details. And Choice (E) is wrong because the author has strong feelings about the show and its entertainment appeal.

588. A. the ways in which the drama satisfies the same cultural interest and fascination viewers and readers seem to have with puzzles

The author directly compares Dr. House to the famous detective Sherlock Holmes. He says that *House* is better than famous mystery shows like *CSI* but that *House* satisfies the same fascination that audiences have with the mystery genre. The appeal of *House* is the same as the appeal of those other famous examples.

Choice (B) is wrong because *House* isn't in the mystery genre. Choice (C) is wrong because the author doesn't make this claim; he actually gives an equal number of examples in the mystery genre. Choice (D) is wrong because the author makes only a general statement comparing House and Holmes. If this comparison were his main concern, the author would give more supporting details. And Choice (E) is wrong because the author addresses only the entertainment aspects of *House*.

589. D. summarize the author's main point that *House* meets more needs than just being entertained

This last paragraph alludes to the author's previous argument and sums up his point about *House:* that it's more than just entertainment because it reinforces sociological and psychological needs.

Choice (A) is wrong because the last paragraph isn't a new point; it's simply a reemphasis and summary of earlier claims. Choice (B) is wrong because the author doesn't address the number of awards won in the last paragraph. Choice (C) is wrong because the author doesn't give information about another medical drama. And Choice (E) is wrong because the last paragraph provides a quick summary of all the important points, with no single one being emphasized as the most important.

590. **B. Wounded Knee effectively ended the rebellion of Native Americans and established white dominance in the U.S.**

The author states that Wounded Knee was the conclusion of Native American rebellions against the U.S. The last sentence states that this incident brought about a reality of white dominance over the indigenous peoples of the U.S.

Choice (A) is incorrect because the author doesn't suggest that other matters, such as colonization of the West, were more important. Instead, the implication is that Wounded Knee was the most important national interest of the time. Choice (B) is wrong because the author mentions European powers only to say that the U.S. accomplished what European imperial powers could not: the ending of the Indians' movement to hold on to their native lands. Choice (D) is wrong because the author doesn't suggest that Wounded Knee was an amicable agreement between Native Americans and white peoples. Instead, he implies that the four centuries were a time of pain, war, and struggle on the part of indigenous peoples of the U.S. Choice (E) is wrong because the author only states that the challenge continued after European concerns were no longer centered in America.

591. **C. Apes are not prosimians.**

The closing sentence states that prosimians are near relatives of apes — in other words, apes *themselves* are *not* prosimians.

Choice (A) is wrong because although the passage never specifies that monkeys *don't* live in Madagascar, it never says that they *do* (only that lemurs do). Choice (B) is wrong because, in context, the phrase "nocturnal trash-can robbers of America" refers to raccoons. Choice (D) is wrong because the passage explains that lemurs aren't very closely related to raccoons, despite bearing a coincidental resemblance to them. And Choice (E) is wrong because the closing sentence states that lemurs, tarsiers, and lorises make up the prosimians and that apes and monkeys are relatives of prosimians, not prosimians themselves.

592. **A. superficial resemblance.**

The passage states that lemurs and raccoons look similar but that this doesn't indicate that they're closely related — in other words, the resemblance is superficial, going only skin-deep.

Choice (B) is wrong because the passage explains that lemurs *are* primates. Choice (C) is wrong because the passage never says that lemurs are nocturnal, only that raccoons are. Choice (D) is wrong because although the passage jokes about raccoons eating discarded human food, it never says anything about the diet of lemurs. Choice (E) is wrong because the passage never says anything about the habitat of either the raccoon or the lemur being threatened.

593. **B. The historical objections to Shakespeare as a front for Marlowe**

The passage explains the "fatal stylistic flaw" but merely refers to the "numerous historical ones" without explaining what they are.

Choice (A) is wrong because the passage does give examples of circumstantial evidence to this effect (for example, the proximity of Marlowe's supposed death and Shakespeare's first publication). Choice (C) is wrong because the last two sentences explain precisely what the "fatal stylistic flaw" in question is. The passage never refers to Choices (D) and (E) at all.

594. **E. the name is being referred to as a name**

Referring to a word or phrase in its capacity as a word or phrase is a valid reason to place the word or phrase in quotation marks.

Choices (A), (B), (C), and (D) are not valid reasons to place a term in quotation marks.

595. **D. facetiously introduce a mildly interesting factoid**

The author doesn't really think that McCain lost the election because his name was John (that would be silly), but he does think it's interesting that every party except the Republicans has produced a president named John. The point of the passage is solely to introduce this bit of trivia.

Choice (A) is wrong because the author isn't seriously advancing a theory about elections here. Choice (B) is wrong because the passage never actually explains Bush's unpopularity; it only alludes to it. Choice (C) is wrong because the passage never mentions any of Obama's accomplishments. And Choice (E) is wrong because although "presidents named John" might technically qualify as a trend, the passage doesn't present it as a growing one.

596. **D. distinguish between one skill set and another**

The passage is organized around the device of repeatedly contrasting real police work with the altogether different skill of figuring out how TV shows will end.

Choice (A) is wrong because the author's central point is that the talent he mentions having wouldn't actually make him a good detective. Choice (B) is wrong because although the passage may allude to some ways in which TV shows are unrealistic, this isn't the author's main argument. Choice (C) is wrong because the author's being occasionally complimented by his friends hardly constitutes a "popular theory." And Choice (E) is wrong because there aren't two "contradictory opinions" that are presented and then resolved in the passage.

597. C. perpetrator

Both *perpetrator* and *culprit* mean "guilty party" — the very thing that the viewers of a whodunit are trying to deduce.

Culprit isn't a synonym for *objective* (goal), *alibi* (a circumstance proving that someone could not have committed a crime), *enigma* (mystery), or *sleuth* (detective), and there are no contextual indications in the passage that might imply that it is.

598. A. Real-life criminals have incomprehensible motives.

The passage never claims that real-life criminals have incomprehensible motives (they do sometimes, but not always, and in any case, the passage never says so).

The passage does name Choices (B), (C), (D), and (E) as reasons.

599. B. ironic

The advice is *ironic*, considering that the author of the passage wouldn't actually make a good detective after all.

Choice (A) is wrong because the author's friends weren't being *sardonic* (sarcastic). They meant their advice; they were just wrong. Choice (C) is incorrect because *laconic* means blunt or concise. Choice (D) is wrong because *loquacious* means talkative. And Choice (E) is wrong because *anachronistic* signifies something that doesn't fit in with a particular time period (for example, someone wearing a digital watch in a movie that's set in the Middle Ages).

600. E. It brings careful distinctions to bear against a rose-tinted oversimplification.

The author presents the popular view of Richard the Lionheart as a rose-tinted oversimplification — that is, unrealistically positive and insufficiently complex — and then seeks to correct it with more precise information.

Choice (A) is wrong because no "new research" comes up in the passage. Choice (B) is wrong because the author takes a firm position instead of equivocating. Choice (C) is wrong because the author is attacking the traditional viewpoint, not defending it. And Choice (D) is wrong because there's no "paradox" that the author is trying to resolve.

601. **C. Richard as the beneficiary of doubt and John as bad but not uniquely so**

The passage argues that Richard was assumed to be good because he barely ran the country and presents John as a bad king but not as bad as many people think.

Choice (A) is wrong because the passage doesn't argue that John was a *good* king. Choice (B) is wrong because the passage points out that Richard's administrative prowess was never really tested. Choice (D) is wrong because the passage never characterizes John as a genius. And Choice (E) is wrong because the passage points out that John was massively unsuccessful in war and that Richard's economic policies were just as bad as John's.

602. **E. unimpressive**

Lackluster is a synonym for *unimpressive,* as the context of the passage indicates.

Lackluster isn't a synonym for *zealous* (eager), *manipulative, innovative* (original), or *reluctant*.

603. **B. earnest**

As per the technical definition of *fruit* offered by the passage, the author is being completely *earnest* (serious) when he says olives are his favorite.

Choice (A) is wrong because the author establishes that he isn't joking when he says olives are his favorite fruit. Choice (C) is wrong because the author is taking a firm position, not being *equivocal* (trying to have it both ways). Choice (D) is wrong because the author is clearly answering the question, not being *evasive* (avoiding giving an answer). Choice (E) is wrong because the author is being scientifically accurate, not philosophical.

604. **C. belief and actuality**

It's clear in the passage that just because a lot of people believe something, it isn't necessarily true.

Choice (A) is wrong because *prescription* refers to an argument advocating a course of action, and *description* to an argument defending an idea. This distinction is irrelevant to the passage. Choices (B) and (E) are wrong because the passage is wholly unrelated to allegory, symbolism, simile, or metaphor. Choice (D) is wrong because none of the various types of irony are relevant to this discussion about the scientific definition of the word *fruit*.

605.   A. didactic

Someone who is *didactic* enjoys teaching people things — clearly, this would be an accurate description of the author of this passage.

Choice (B) is wrong because someone who is *iconoclastic* enjoys mocking or demeaning sacred things, and this idea is irrelevant to the content of the passage. Choice (C) is wrong because someone who is *devious* is dishonest and manipulative, and the author of the passage is being straightforward and honest. Choice (D) is wrong because someone who is *mercurial* changes his mind often, and the author of the passage sticks to one clear idea. Choice (E) is wrong because someone who is *neurotic* is anxious and psychologically troubled, and the author seems to be confident and enjoying himself.

606.   D. whimsically self-satisfied

The author seems to be quite self-satisfied with his knowledge of botany but is also having fun with it — that is, being *whimsical*.

Choice (A) is wrong because the author isn't confused — he possesses more accurate information on this subject than do most people. Choice (B) is wrong because the author doesn't seem at all melancholy (depressed). Choice (C) is wrong because there's nothing ironic about the passage, and the author is boastful, not modest. Choice (E) is wrong because the author isn't paranoid about anything — on the contrary, the passage is light-hearted.

607.   B. Shakespeare crafted his texts with specific actors and their performances in mind.

The passage indicates that Shakespeare wrote his plays intending for certain parts to be played in certain ways by actors he worked with and knew well.

Choice (A) is wrong because the passage argues that we have no knowledge of how Shakespeare's actors originally played certain roles, not that we no longer have the plays themselves. Choice (C) is wrong because the passage mentions only one thing that Shakespeare's plays had in common with modern comic movies; it doesn't argue that they were alike in all respects. Choice (D) is wrong because the passage never says anything about whether Shakespeare wanted his plays to be published. And Choice (E) is wrong because the passage concerns the styles in which Shakespeare's plays were originally performed, not what moral lessons they teach.

608. **E. Shakespeare was so good at so many things that it is mind-boggling.**

The point of the parenthetical comment is to emphasize the astronomical number of things that Shakespeare did brilliantly in his work.

Choice (A) is wrong because regardless of what students may think, the author is clearly a great admirer of Shakespeare and says nothing about him that isn't complimentary. Choice (B) is wrong because the author never says it would be a difficult task to read all of Shakespeare's plays (there are only 38 of them, and lots of people have read them all). Choice (C) is wrong because the author never says too much scholarship is devoted to Shakespeare. And Choice (D) is wrong because there's no indication that the author thinks that Shakespeare's genius is overstated — indeed, he states Shakespeare's genius in this very passage.

609. **E. acknowledge that a common facet of comedy would have applied to Shakespeare too**

The author acknowledges that an element of comedy we recognize today — performances crafted as spoofs of contemporary figures — would have almost certainly been the case in the original performances of Shakespeare's comedies as well.

Choice (A) is wrong because the author focuses on a way in which the performances of Shakespeare's actors would have been similar to modern acting, not on a way they would have been different. Choice (B) is wrong because the author never says that all of Shakespeare's plays were funny; he just happens to be making a point about the ones that were. Choice (C) is wrong because the author doesn't give advice about how Shakespeare's plays should be performed today. Rather, he offers a conjecture about how they would have been performed originally. Finally, Choice (D) is wrong because the author doesn't detract from how cleverly Shakespeare's comedies were written; he merely points out that elements of the way in which they were acted are now lost to us.

610. **C. lampooned**

Someone who is being "sent up" is being mocked, parodied, caricatured, or lampooned.

"Sent up" means made fun of, not remembered, celebrated, ignored, or entertained (though others might be entertained by the mockery).

611. **A. Passage 1 demonstrates idealism, whereas Passage 2 demonstrates realism.**

The claim made by Passage 1 (athletes should be good role models and not take steroids) is idealistic, whereas the claim made by Passage 2 (people are going to cheat no matter what we say, so let's just accept it) is more realistic.

Choice (B) is wrong because although it could be said that Passage 2 advocates an unorthodox solution ("solving" the problem by not caring about it), there's no implication that the author of Passage 1 believes no solution is possible (although the passage doesn't advocate any specific solution). Choice (C) is wrong because although Passage 2 briefly refers to the past, both passages are talking about what should be done in the present. Choice (D) is wrong because both passages discuss baseball without comparing it to any other sports. And Choice (E) is wrong because there's nothing about gender-related issues in either passage.

612. D. disingenuousness

As the passage explains, the point of that line from *Casablanca* is that the character actually knows what's going on and is only pretending to be shocked, so it functions as an accusation of *disingenuousness* (pretending to know less than you really do).

Choice (A) is wrong because the character in the reference is only pretending to be clueless. Choice (B) is wrong because *avarice* means greed, not putting on an act. Choice (C) is wrong because the character in the reference is pretending to believe one thing while he secretly thinks something else, which is different from changing his mind (flip-flopping). Choice (E) is wrong because the character in the reference isn't frightened of something that isn't real; rather, he's pretending not to know something that he actually knows.

613. C. They both believe in the concept of fairness, but they characterize it very differently.

Both characters want the thing they think is fair to happen — they just disagree about what would be fair.

Choice (A) is wrong because the author of Passage 2 doesn't think steroids should be banned. Choice (B) is wrong because the author of Passage 2 points out that steroid use in baseball isn't new. Choice (D) is wrong because the author of Passage 2 doesn't think that any rules against steroids should be enforced at all. And Choice (E) is wrong because neither passage is primarily about how popular baseball is.

614. E. naïveté

The author of Passage 2 adopts the "realistic" perspective that there's no way to effectively stop all athletes from using steroids. Because the author of Passage 1 believes that there is, the author of Passage 2 would consider him naïve.

Choice (A) is wrong because there's no indication that the author of Passage 2 considers an anti-steroid stance to be *elitist* (biased toward the concerns of privileged people). Choice (B) is wrong because the author of

Passage 1 doesn't appear to contradict himself, and the author of Passage 2 doesn't appear to think he does. Choice (C) is wrong because the author of Passage 1 doesn't seem not to really mean what he is saying, and the author of Passage 2 doesn't appear to think so. Choice (D) is wrong because there's no indication that the position of the author of Passage 1 is unfairly biased against any group of people or that the author of Passage 2 thinks he is.

615. B. role models

The author of Passage 1 emphasizes professional athletes' responsibility to act honorably.

Choice (A) is wrong because Passage 1 argues that ball players *shouldn't* just think of themselves as businessmen. Choice (C) is wrong because although the author of Passage 2 is certainly skeptical of Passage 1, Passage 1 doesn't characterize baseball players as skeptics. Choice (D) is wrong because Passage 1 argues that ball players should care about honor and fair play, not just about how well they perform on the field. And Choice (E) is wrong because although the authors of the two passages are philosophizing, the author of Passage 1 doesn't say that baseball players are doing so.

616. A. defeatism

Defeatism refers to the belief that it's pointless to fight because you're going to lose no matter what.

Choice (B) is wrong because the author of Passage 2 isn't advocating punishing anyone, so it would be hard to characterize his position as merciless. Choice (C) is wrong because the author of Passage 2 isn't actively trying to get in the way of a rule's enforcement; he's arguing that the rule should be repealed. Choices (D) and (E) are wrong because the author of Passage 2 really means what he says, whereas *casuistry* and *sophistry* refer to deliberately making an argument you know is wrong. Note that Choices (D) and (E) are synonyms, so neither one could be the answer, because only one answer can be right.

617. C. mockery of "bronies" is largely motivated by sexism, however unconsciously

The passage closes by arguing that it's sexist to consider it weirder for adults to like a girls' show than a boys' show (the fact that it's sexist is why it's "lamentable" when "progressives," who should know better, react this way).

Choice (A) is wrong because the passage argues that this isn't "creepy," even though some people think so. Choice (B) is wrong because the passage explains that these people exist and goes on to analyze the phenomenon. Choice (D) is wrong because the passage doesn't say that the

Internet has made adult viewers less mature, just that it's made it easier to make fun of them. The passage mentions that there were still many adult fans of kids' shows before the Internet existed. Choice (E) is wrong because the passage doesn't directly compare these shows to each other.

618. **A. an overreaction to a trivial matter**

A "tempest in a teacup" is an overreaction to something that isn't a big deal, as the passage indicates by characterizing it as the opposite of something "terrifying."

Choice (B) is wrong because the passage accuses the media of overreacting, not of lying to make money. Choice (C) is wrong because the passage accuses the media of overreacting in an overly critical way rather than pretending to be neutral. Choice (D) is wrong because although the passage characterizes the phenomenon of adults watching kids' shows as old rather than new, the expression "tempest in a teacup" doesn't mean this, and context doesn't indicate that it does. Choice (E) is wrong because nothing in the passage has anything to do with someone messing up the details of a funny story.

619. **B. Roughly a third of the games the company makes are RPGs (role-playing games).**

The chart indicates that the company makes about 33 RPGs. Adding up the numbers shows that the company makes way more than 100 games total, so this statement isn't true.

Choice (A) is a true statement because the graph shows that the company makes about 12 driving games and about 6 minigames. Choice (C) is true because no bar on the graph goes all the way up to the top (the line representing 50). Choice (D) is true because the bar representing fighting games goes up to about 14, which is indeed less than 20. Choice (E) is true because the graph shows that the company makes exactly 10 FPS games and exactly 10 shooter games.

620. **D. none of the above, but possible to calculate based on the information in the graph**

You can calculate the percentage by dividing the number of puzzle games by the total number of games (which you get by adding up the games of each type).

Choice (A) is wrong because the company makes way more than 100 games. Choice (B) is wrong because the company makes way more than 50 games. Choice (C) is wrong because the company makes considerably more than 200 games.

621.

B. one-sixth

Quick estimation and adding shows that the company makes roughly 250 games, so the roughly 43 action/adventure games would make up about one-sixth of these.

622.

D. highlight both the importance and the mystery of the abilities to purr and to roar

The passage explains that cats are classified by whether they purr or roar (which makes this important) but we're not sure why they do one or the other (which makes it a mystery).

Choice (A) is wrong because the passage admits that this is something we don't know. Choice (B) is wrong because the passage explains that *all* cats belong to the family *Felidae* (not to be confused with the genus *Felis*). Choice (C) is wrong because although the passage states this fact, it isn't the point of the whole passage. Choice (E) is wrong because the passage never states that *only* cats have hyoid bones (many animals do, including humans).

623.

D. the relationships between the preceding pairs of words

The word indicates that complete ossification of the hyoid was associated with purring and partial ossification was associated with roaring.

Choice (A) is wrong because although the next sentence explains that the theory in question has indeed been overturned, this has nothing to do with the word *respectively*. Choice (B) is wrong because the word *respectively* doesn't signal upcoming terminology. Why would a word be needed to signal this at all? Choice (C) is wrong because the word *respectively* doesn't have anything to do with *respect* in the sense of reverence. Rather, it signals which concepts relate to which other concepts within a sentence. Choice (E) is wrong because the word does perform an important function within the sentence.

624.

A. Many mathematical concepts were invented by the Arabs, but Arabic numerals were not.

The passage states that the numerals we call "Arabic" were invented in India.

Choice (B) is wrong because the passage explains that it's harder to do complex scientific calculations with Roman numerals (if it were easier, we'd still use them). Choice (C) is wrong because the passage states that Roman numerals are still common in some contexts (for example, in the titles of movie sequels). Choice (D) is wrong because the passage points out that Roman numerals were still in use far later than most people believe. Choice (E) is wrong because the passage states that Roman numerals lacked a symbol to represent zero.

625. B. about 1,000 years ago

"The second millennium CE" refers to the years 1001–2000. This can be deduced from the information that Arabic numerals were invented in 500 CE and introduced to Europe in the 13th century, which the passage describes as "well into" the second millennium CE.

Choice (A) is wrong because although the 15th century was 500 years ago, the passage describes this as "well into" the second millennium CE (it began much earlier). Choices (C) and (D) are wrong because the passage establishes that the second millennium began before the 13th century. Choice (E) is wrong because this information can, in fact, be deduced based on the information provided.

626. E. obviously true for reasons that are largely ineffable

The passage states that the opinion is "difficult to disagree with" but for reasons that are hard to explain ("ineffable").

Choice (A) is wrong because if the author thought the idea was "pointless to discuss," why would he have written the passage about it? Choice (B) is wrong because the passage doesn't characterize the opinion as having anything to do with politics — the allusion to Thomas Jefferson is just a means to employ his famous phrase about truths that are self-evident. Choice (C) is wrong because the passage never suggests that someone other than Gopnik came up with the idea. And Choice (D) is wrong because the author of the passage states that he agrees with Gopnik's opinion.

627. C. it is a reference to a phrase from a famous text

This is a famous phrase from the Declaration of Independence.

Choice (A) is wrong because emphasis is not a reason to place a term in quotation marks. Choice (B) is wrong because there's no suggestion that the author is being ironic; he explains that he agrees with the opinion in question. Choice (D) is wrong because indicating that a term is technical is not a reason to place a term in quotation marks (italics would be preferred in such a situation). Choice (E) is wrong because the quotation marks are indeed used for a specific reason.

628. D. encourage people to examine their own occasional fallacious reasoning

The passage, as a whole, functions as a lament for the fact that so many otherwise bright people still fall for bad arguments and silly ideas under certain circumstances.

Choice (A) is wrong because the author actually makes the opposite point: Certain things that people think are old are actually of recent invention. Choice (B) is wrong because the author makes only one brief mention of copyright law to support a larger idea; copyright law isn't the point of the whole passage. Choice (C) is wrong because astrology isn't mentioned in the passage; the passage concerns other bogus methods of predicting the future. And Choice (E) is wrong because the author doesn't like the fact that people are fooled by such things, so he certainly wouldn't be instructing charlatans in how to get better at fooling people.

629. B. prophecy

Context establishes that *divination* means foretelling the future, as does *prophecy*.

Divination doesn't mean *prank*, *popularity*, *prefabrication* (making something according to a pattern), or *progress*.

630. C. Why it is persuasive to some people when a silly idea is presented as "ancient"

The author asks this in the second sentence of the passage.

Choice (A) is wrong because the author states precisely why Ouija boards are copyrighted (they're by Parker Brothers). Choice (B) is wrong because the author clearly doesn't believe that predicting the future is possible. Choice (D) is wrong because the author bemoans the fact that most people aren't reluctant enough in believing weird ideas. Choice (E) is wrong because the passage never brings this up.

631. D. Millay was the most talented woman ever to win the Pulitzer Prize for Poetry.

The passage states that Millay was the third woman to win the Pulitzer Prize for Poetry, but it never mentions who any of the others were or how their work compares to Millay's.

Choice (A) is wrong because the passage explicitly states this in the first sentence. Choice (B) is wrong because the passage describes Stein's work as aggressively experimental and Millay's as accessible and traditional. Choices (C) and (E) are wrong because the passage states these points in the closing sentence.

632. A. numerous

The fact that the statement is followed by a list of many reasons indicates that *manifold* is a synonym for *numerous*.

633. **E. An artistic defense of what makes Millay's poetry good in and of itself**

This argument that the decline in Millay's popularity is unjustified would benefit from some arguments about why her work is good in and of itself instead of relying solely on impugning the motives of her detractors.

Choices (A), (B), and (D) are wrong because they're unrelated to the work of Millay herself. Choice (C) is wrong because it would make more sense to analyze Millay's celebrated poems than her least respected ones.

634. **C. Russian soldiers in Paris covertly drank on duty.**

The other choices are all stated as facts. This choice may or may not be true.

635. **B. "the lack of an alternate explanation for the term's etymology"**

The absence of any competing theories makes a theory more plausible, simply for lack of a better idea.

Choices (A) and (E) are wrong because although they have to be true for the story to make sense, they don't prove the story in and of themselves (logically speaking, they're necessary but not sufficient conditions). Choices (C) and (D) are wrong because they're arguments against the truth of the story.

636. **C. It is written in an intelligent yet casual style for an educated general audience.**

The passage includes fairly advanced terms and ideas and is not dumbed-down in any way, but it still explains certain things that wouldn't need to be explained to a purely scientific audience; therefore, it's intended for an audience that is intelligent but not specialists.

Choice (A) is wrong because some things are explained more fully than they would need to be for an audience made up of scientists. Choice (B) is wrong because the reading level is too high for an audience of children. Choice (D) is wrong because the passage is purely factual; it doesn't frame any of the information as something people would need to be convinced about. Choice (E) is wrong because the passage states facts instead of proposing action.

637. **B. mostly a catalogue of facts, with some colorful touches thrown in**

Aside from a few turns of phrase intended to make it more entertaining, the passage does nothing but state facts.

Choice (A) is wrong because nothing in the passage is a matter of opinion, be it the author's or anyone else's. Choice (C) is wrong because the passage presents no opposing arguments to overturn. Choice (D) is wrong because the passage is overwhelmingly factual. Only the beginning and the end contain humorous language. Choice (E) is wrong because the passage presents one factual point of view instead of distinguishing between competing points of view.

638. **E. The Earth technically has two North Poles.**

The second sentence alludes to the fact that there are two different definitions of the North Pole (or of the South Pole) — the *rotational* pole and the *magnetic* pole.

639. **A. Before humans existed, the Earth was a perfect sphere.**

The passage explains that geographical features like mountains prevent the Earth from being a perfect sphere, and obviously, there were mountains before there were humans.

640. **B. personification**

Poles don't actually have faces, but humans do, so the application of the expression "about face" (turn around) to the North Pole constitutes an example of *personification*.

641. **D. correct a widespread misunderstanding**

Both the opening and closing sentences restate the main idea that mascara doesn't actually contain bat feces, and the body of the passage explains how this misconception came about. The point of the passage is to correct this widespread misunderstanding.

Choice (A) is wrong because the passage concerns only one urban legend, not urban legends in general. Choice (B) is wrong because the passage doesn't criticize the cosmetics industry; on the contrary, it corrects a rumor about it. Choice (C) is wrong because although the passage defines guanine, it isn't primarily concerned with providing information about this substance itself. Choice (E) is wrong because the idea that mascara contains bat feces is a genuine misunderstanding, not a deliberate joke.

642. **C. can**

Only the word *can* is placed in italics in order to emphasize it. The other words are in italics because they're unfamiliar scientific terms.

643. **B. DNA can be found in guanine.**

The passage explains that guanine is a component of DNA, not the other way around.

644. **D. The passage contains mostly facts with one educated guess.**

The passage is entirely factual except for the lone authorial conjecture about how the urban legend arose in the first place.

645. **C. The basis for a legend is followed by contradictory facts.**

The author explains a myth and then lists various reasons why it's probably untrue.

Choice (A) is wrong because the passage concerns history, not logic. Choice (B) is wrong because the author never demands an apology from anyone. Choice (D) is wrong because the author agrees with the counterarguments to the veracity of the urban legend. And Choice (E) is wrong because although the origin story is popular, that isn't the same thing as *populist* (defending the rights of common people). Furthermore, a historically accurate correction of such a legend is hardly *elitist*.

646. **A. a maxim**

The closing sentence amounts to a *maxim* (a general principle or rule).

The other choices are wrong because a *caveat* is a warning, an *idiom* is a figure of speech, an *allusion* is a reference to another specific work, and a *kenning* is a poetic name for something made up of references to other terms (for example, calling the ocean a "whale-road").

647. **E. macabre, eerie**

The words *macabre* and *eerie* are basically synonyms, as their contexts in the passage indicate.

648. **D. the modern Valentine's Day has mildly humorous origins**

The passage as a whole concerns the origins of Valentine's Day, and this is the only answer choice that refers to this idea.

Choice (A) is wrong because the passage doesn't say that Valentine's Day doesn't exist (clearly, it does). Choices (B) and (C) are wrong because although the passage does point out these ideas, they aren't the point of the whole passage. Choice (E) is wrong because the passage never says that Chaucer deliberately invented the modern Valentine's Day; it's presented as an unintended consequence of his poem.

649. **B. declarations**

Although *professions* can mean more than one thing, the definition that works in this context is *declarations*.

Choice (A) is one definition of the word *professions*, but it doesn't apply in this context. Choices (C), (D), and (E) aren't synonyms for *professions*.

650. **A. artistic concerns**

The passage explains that the "pretty name" of the day had much to do with why Chaucer picked it (as opposed to using some other date around the same time of year).

Choice (B) is wrong because although Valentine's Day was originally a religious holiday, this isn't why Chaucer picked it as the setting for his poem. Choice (C) is wrong because the idea that birds pick mates on Valentine's Day is described as a Medieval idea, not an ancient one. Choice (D) is nonsense. What does "romantic science" even mean? Choice (E) is wrong because the passage doesn't suggest that there was anything political about Chaucer's poem; it's described as romantic and humorous.

651. **A. The author's argument would be mostly unaffected.**

The passage states that even if this were true, our modern Valentine's Day would still be a coincidence, as there were no mentions of February 14th being a day for lovers in the intervening centuries between ancient Rome and Chaucer's time.

652. **E. provide interesting information merely for the sake of doing so**

There's no indication that the author presents this information for any reason other than the fact that it's interesting. He isn't arguing for or against anything.

653. **C. emblematic of the elite and privileged**

Rarefied means fancy or hoity-toity, as the context indicates.

654. **B. Most bird's-nest soup is made from nests of a color other than red.**

The passage establishes that the most expensive and difficult-to-find variety of bird's-nest soup is red, which leads to the assumption that most bird's-nest soup is some other color.

Choice (A) is wrong because there's no reason to assume that the people who pick the nests get to keep most of the profit from the sales. Choice (C) is wrong because the fact that the prices are given in U.S. dollars doesn't mean the soup is usually bought with American money; it just means that the piece was written for American readers. Choice (D) is wrong because there's no mention of the swiftlets being endangered. Choice (E) is wrong because the fact that the best nests for the soups are found in Thailand doesn't mean people can only eat the soup there. Many nests are exported.

655. B. "labor-intensive"

This phrase indicates that it takes a lot of hard work to obtain the nests, a supposition that the passage later confirms.

656. C. the author is assuming that the reader will find its content surprising

The passage characterizes the butter/margarine feud as something from the past, so he prepares the reader to be surprised that a law designed to inconvenience margarine manufacturers is still on the books today.

Choice (A) is wrong because although the author presumably thinks the law in question is silly, the exclamation point isn't intended to express anger. Choice (B) is wrong because the exclamation point is appropriate here; it isn't tacked on in a mere case of wishful thinking. Choice (D) is wrong because the passage hasn't previously mentioned Missouri. Choice (E) is wrong because the sentence doesn't answer any specific previous question.

657. D. acting purely out of self-interest

The opposition to margarine came from dairy farmers who stood to lose profit and from politicians who wanted to be re-elected.

Choices (A) and (B) are wrong because the passage doesn't suggest that anyone thought margarine was dangerous or unhealthy. Choice (C) is wrong because the passage doesn't suggest that margarine would nega-tively affect the nation's economy as a whole. Choice (E) is wrong because the passage doesn't suggest that opposition to margarine came from well-intentioned people who were later sorry.

658. E. margarine simply looked gross without it

The passage establishes that margarine's natural color makes it look unappetizing, so preventing it from being colored yellow was a way for its opponents to reduce its sales.

Choice (A) is wrong because the passage doesn't suggest that there was ever an intent to trick people into actually mistaking margarine for butter. Choice (B) is wrong because politicians actually did the opposite; they passed laws preventing margarine from being colored yellow. Choice (C) is wrong because it was the dairy farmers who opposed margarine being colored yellow. Choice (D) is wrong because the yellow coloring was a purely cosmetic addition; it affected margarine's appearance, not its taste.

659. **A. The invention of margarine was an accidental occurrence.**

The passage provides no information on how margarine was invented.

660. **E. alliteration**

The four words beginning with *b* in that sentence constitute an example of *alliteration*.

Simile is the comparison of two unrelated things, using *like* or *as*. *Personification* attributes human characteristics to nonhuman things. An *anaphora* is a technique of beginning several lines with the same word or words to create parallelism and rhythm, while *stichomythia* is verbal sparring or alternating dialogue in Ancient Greek plays or dramas.

661. **C. It's a bad idea to try to learn philosophy from movies.**

The primary point of the passage is that though the *Star Wars* films are entertaining, they don't present a coherent moral philosophy.

Choice (A) is wrong because the author is clearly a fan of the *Star Wars* series and considers them entertaining as films. Choice (B) is wrong because the author only points out that anger (paradoxically) sometimes has positive results in these movies; he doesn't say it's a good idea in real life. Choice (D) is wrong because the passage never sets up these two concerns in opposition to each other. Choice (E) is wrong because the author doesn't consider it a terribly big deal that these films contradict themselves in terms of their morals; it's just an interesting observation. He's still a fan.

662. **B. honor and pragmatism**

The passage points out that the heroes of these films occasionally achieve desirable results by violating their codes of honor.

663.   **A. an educated *Star Wars* fan who has thought deeply about the films**

The author knows so much about *Star Wars* that he must be a fan, and he's clearly a smart fan who has analyzed the films on a deep level.

Choice (B) is wrong because there's no "main concern" in the passage other than the *Star Wars* movies themselves. Choice (C) is wrong because the author gives no indication that he writes screenplays. Choice (D) is wrong because the author doesn't seem to think that the *Star Wars* movies have been a bad influence on people. Choice (E) is wrong because the author is clearly a big fan of the *Star Wars* movies. He knows a lot about them, and his critique seems affectionate as opposed to mean-spirited.

664.   **D. advice about how to behave**

"Ethical prescriptions" means advice about morality.

665.   **C. Whether Andrews's wife was a partner in his scientific work**

The passage states that Andrews and his wife went to the Gobi desert together, and the reader wonders whether she was also involved in the archaeological work herself, but this is never clarified.

Choice (A) is wrong because the reader has no reason to wonder about this. Choice (B) is wrong because it's clear from context that the museum is in New York. Choice (D) is wrong because the fossilization process is purely scientific information that could easily be looked up elsewhere. Choice (E) is wrong because this is a minor matter that appears at the end and isn't directly relevant to Andrews's life.

666.   **C. weasel words**

The sentence suggests "it's said that" Chapman was the inspiration for Indiana Jones, but exactly who said this is never clarified. This is a deceptive method of suggesting something that might not be true, and it's referred to as *weasel words*.

The other choices are wrong because the last sentence contains no *hyperbole* (exaggeration), *mixed metaphor* (combining elements of two different expressions in a way that makes no sense), *archaism* (obscure outdated words), or *equivocation* (appearing to take both sides of an issue).

667.   **A. an interesting and inspiring biographical text**

The passage is an engaging bit of biography, and there's no reason to assume the author has any more specific intent than this.

Choice (B) is wrong because the passage doesn't encourage *(exhort)* the reader to do anything. Choice (C) is wrong because the passage is factual biography, not historical literature. Choice (D) is wrong because the tone is too emotional for an encyclopedia. And Choice (E) is not the best answer because the passage takes on a tone and style not common in most obituaries.

668. **C. The author appears to be undecided about transhumanism.**

The author never appears to offer his stance on transhumanism one way or the other.

Choices (A) and (B) are wrong because the author never offers his own opinion; he merely reports on what others have said. Choice (D) is wrong because the author reports the information contained in the passage as factual, or at least plausible, with no hint of skepticism on his part. Choice (E) is wrong because it's clear that the passage is serious and that transhumanism is real — there's no tonal indication of jest.

669. **B. direct quotation or jargon**

The phrase "The World's Most Dangerous Idea" is a direct quotation, and the other two terms appearing in quotation marks are buzzwords specific to discussions of transhumanism.

Choices (A), (D), and (E) are wrong because none of the terms appearing in quotation marks is used ironically. Choice (C) is wrong because emphasis is not a valid reason to place a term in quotation marks (italics are preferred to indicate emphasis).

670. **E. freedom with equality**

On one hand, people should have the right to take advantage of transhumanist technology if they choose to, but on the other, it would be unjust for the wealthy to be able to transform themselves into a different species from the less fortunate. Thus, the passage sets in opposition the concerns of *freedom* and *equality*.

Choice (A) is wrong because there's nothing about spirituality in the passage. Choice (B) is wrong because the passage never addresses parental responsibilities. Choice (C) is wrong because scientific advances and parental rights are on the same side in the passage (the right of parents to take advantage of scientific advances), not opposing concerns. Choice (D) is wrong because nothing about wisdom is presented as standing in opposition to equality.

671.

D. Requiring insurance providers to cover transhumanist procedures

This would help the less fortunate take advantage of transhumanist technology and thereby resolve the concerns about equality.

Choice (A) is wrong because the passage doesn't suggest anything about transhumanism being illegal. Choice (B) is wrong because although this may be a good idea, it doesn't resolve any specific objection made in the passage. Choice (C) isn't relevant to anything brought up in the passage. And Choice (E) is wrong because it wouldn't resolve any specific criticism brought up in the passage.

672.

A. Modern attitudes toward the work of Sigmund Freud are largely unfair.

The first three sentences, taken together, establish that this statement is essentially the author's thesis.

Choice (B) is wrong because the passage mentions religion and feminism as institutions that criticize Freud, not as fields he contributed to. Choice (C) is wrong because the author doesn't argue that Freud's infamous wrong ideas are actually true, just that there are few of them compared to the many things he got right. Choice (D) is wrong because the author admits that Freud made some mistakes. And Choice (E) is wrong because the passage never implies that anyone but Freud was responsible for his mistakes.

673.

C. a witticism that also underscores the author's point

By positioning Freud as an authority on people's subconscious motivations, the author cleverly makes a joke at his opponents' expense while emphasizing the importance of Freud at the same time.

Choice (A) is wrong because this comment isn't the thesis of the whole passage. Choice (B) is wrong because although the line is humorous, the author is being earnest when he says it, not sarcastic (plus, the passage is hardly a "dry rant"; it's witty and good-natured). Choice (D) is wrong because although the passage is written in the first person, it doesn't concern the author personally, so humanizing him is not an issue. Choice (E) is wrong because this remark gives no evidence one way or the other about whether the author is an expert on Freud.

674.

D. traditional ideas are sometimes prematurely dismissed

This passage analyzes one specific example of a traditional idea (in this case, Freud's importance) being prematurely dismissed, so the author must believe that this sometimes happens.

Choice (A) is wrong because although the author clearly thinks that psychology is important, he never says it's the most important of all the sciences. Choice (B) is wrong because although the author makes a few criticisms of ideas popular in contemporary education, he never says that education overall is worse than it used to be. Choice (C) is wrong because the author provides only one example of an issue on which he disagrees with religious leaders and feminists; he never implies that he thinks they're wrong most of the time. Choice (E) is wrong because the author says that our personalities are largely, not solely, shaped by life experience — there may still be aspects of our personalities that are matters of instinct.

675. **C. analyze the idea that modernized versions can make Shakespeare still relevant to audiences**

The authors use this passage to explain the idea that through simple changes in costuming, modern retellings can make Shakespeare just as relevant and effective as it was then.

Choice (A) is wrong because the passage doesn't state that any one version — either modern or original — is better. Choice (B) is wrong because the authors never claim Shakespeare shouldn't be modernized. Rather, the authors claim that modern versions of Shakespeare's work can be just as effective. Choice (D) is wrong because the passage only takes a look at modern retellings of Shakespeare. It doesn't show how this is a reflection of modern tastes in film. Choice (E) is wrong because the passage doesn't poke fun at the film.

676. **D. relating to clothing**

The word *sartorial* just means that it relates to clothing.

677. **C. costuming in modern retellings changed to reflect current social statements in the same way that original costuming reflected those times and beliefs**

The authors are stating that costuming had to change with modern retellings. Although today's audience's probably won't know what a codpiece is, having Ophelia appear in a starter-bra is shocking because modern viewers know a teen girl would never appear in public in her underwear.

Choice (A) is wrong because codpieces weren't inappropriate during Shakespeare's time. Indeed, they were used as a gesture of propriety by conspicuously covering the outer garments that already covered male genitalia. Choice (B) is wrong because although both of these statements are true, this isn't the point the authors are trying to make overall. Choice (D) is wrong because the authors don't make such a claim in the entire passage. And Choice (E) is wrong because although codpieces would probably be considered a silly piece of Elizabethan propriety, that isn't what the authors mean by this statement.

678.
A. small details can be changed in the play to make it more realistic and understandable to modern readers

The passage gives several examples of changes that are made in Shakespeare's plays and is pressing home the point that many small changes are necessary in order for modern readers or viewers to fully comprehend the story.

Choice (B) is wrong because the passage describes a modern retelling with walkie-talkies, which certainly never existed in Shakespeare's time. Choice (C) is wrong because the authors aren't suggesting this story came from another culture. Rather, the play has been changed to fit modern times. Choice (D) is wrong because the authors aren't suggesting that the original story should have included Alsatian guard dogs. And Choice (E) is wrong because the authors aren't suggesting that Shakespeare would change his plays if he were alive and writing today. Their point is that modern retellings make changes for the sake of the audience, not because of the creator of such works.

679.
C. Leonardo DiCaprio and Claire Danes starring in a modern remake of *Romeo and Juliet*, updated with hip, modern costuming and music

The authors' argument is that modern retellings are better understood when details are changed, such as costuming, in order to better connect with today's viewers or readers.

Choice (A) is wrong because it doesn't suggest changing the play to connect to a modern audience. Choice (B) seems to show the opposite: that audiences can better understand the work if it's performed in context, on the actual site of the action in the play instead of on a stage. Choice (D) is wrong because it doesn't refer to a performance of a play. It simply refers to the act of reading, which isn't what the passage is about. And Choice (E) is wrong because this format takes the play and turns into a traditional piece of ballet, which isn't a modern take on the play, nor does it make modernized changes.

680.
C. films have shaped American values

The authors argue that films have been "instrumental" in shaping certain American values, such as ideas about ethnicity and sexuality.

Choice (A) is wrong because although the authors wouldn't argue with this statement, it doesn't portray the authors' full point. Choice (B) is wrong because the authors are arguing just the opposite: that values are shaped by the films. Choice (D) is wrong because the authors are arguing that films portray particular things on screen that then shape Americans' self-images and values. And Choice (E) is wrong because the authors aren't suggesting that these Hollywood films serve a subversive purpose. Their influence isn't portrayed as positive or negative.

681. **C. a popular belief about a cultural idea**

> Hollywood creates fantasies on the big screen in much the same way that Detroit makes cars. These myths, or stories told on the silver screen, characterize America's culture.

> Choice (A) is wrong because most American cars *were* made in Detroit. That wasn't a fiction or even half-truth, and it didn't shape an ideology about where cars could, or should, be made. Choice (B) is wrong because the story wasn't made up. The Detroit auto industry has been well-documented. Choice (D) is wrong because the story doesn't explain any aspects of the natural world. And Choice (E) is wrong because most people don't assume that the auto industry of Detroit was a mythical place.

682. **B. unifying members of society who would otherwise have been divided along the lines of sex, class, and ethnicity**

> The author says that one positive effect of Hollywood movies has been a positive force through the unification of symbols that would otherwise have been divided along the lines of class, race, and gender.

> Choice (A) is wrong because although the author does say that Americans' self-images have been positively shaped, he doesn't say that this has translated into a more acceptable form across all segments of society. Choice (C) is wrong because the author doesn't claim that traditional views were equated with subversive ideas from movies. The author is actually saying that some subversive aspects of movies had other consequences that are still shaping the lives of Americans. Choice (D) is wrong because the author gives this as an example of one of those "subversive" consequences. This isn't described as either negative or positive. And Choice (E) is wrong because although Hollywood movies were pivotal in this respect, the author doesn't state the effect was positive overall. The bombing of Pearl Harbor was a pivotal moment in World War II, but it wasn't positive.

683. **E. a mixed blessing**

> The author of the passage has only negative aspects surrounding the term. There's no positive aspect in order to consider it a "mixed blessing."

> Choice (A) is wrong because "over-civilization" isn't the medical condition. Rather, according to the passage, "over-civilization" is the cause of the medical condition neurasthenia. Choice (B) is wrong because the term does suggest controversy when looking at the aspects of weak versus strong Americans in the 19th century. Choice (C) is wrong because the term does suggest a paradox. How could the strongest and richest nation on Earth produce 98-pound weaklings from the segment of society that has had the most advantages? Choice (D) is wrong because the term is a buzzword, a word of jargon that was fashionable to use at this particular time in history.

684.

C. become overstimulated by their busy lifestyles

The author provides evidence that the frantic pace of the 19th-centry lifestyle was overstimulating for some, who sought medical care for their emotional distress.

The correct answer isn't Choice (A) or (B), because the author doesn't suggest the ailment was a way to avoid an unpleasant situation, such as work or being drafted. The correct answer isn't Choice (D) or (E), because the author doesn't suggest the ailment was faked or that those who suffered from the condition were looking to be part of an elite population.

685.

C. To show how common the condition was by suggesting that many people suffered from it

By showing that people from many walks of life — presidents, authors, and so on — suffered from the disease, the author is trying to show that the condition was common.

Choice (A) is wrong because the author isn't suggesting that only hard workers suffered from the condition. Instead, he mentions people with busy lifestyles, which might not equate with hard work. Choice (B) is wrong because the author provides other medical credence, such as statements from medical experts. Choice (D) is wrong because the author doesn't suggest the condition isn't real. Choice (E) is wrong because the author doesn't show any consequences in the lives of those mentioned.

686.

B. A loaded term is judiciously unpacked.

The term *neurasthenia* is discussed in an impartial way, without bringing judgment on either the condition or those who might have suffered from it.

Choice (A) is wrong because the medical condition itself isn't discussed in an analytical way with other scientific data. Choice (C) is wrong because the author doesn't suggest this phrase needs to be used in this era. Choice (D) is wrong because this isn't a theory of the author's; this was considered an actual medical condition in the 19th century. Choice (E) is wrong because the author uses a respectful and explanatory tone throughout.

687.

B. primarily informative but somewhat humorous

The author provides necessary information to make his point but does inject some humor at the end of the passage with the quote about advertising that "aroused, excited, terrified" consumers.

Choice (A) is wrong because the author isn't presenting a theory. He's simply presenting historical facts about advertising. Choice (C) is wrong because the author isn't critical of the advertising successes; he points out no details to suggest the companies shouldn't have succeeded. Choice (D) is wrong because the author shows no bias toward any one company. Choice (E) is wrong because the author doesn't suggest the facts aren't true. He simply presents the information as historically accurate. Furthermore, the new advertising techniques wouldn't need forgiving.

688. **A. emphasize how ridiculous some advertising campaigns were**

By providing the example of an advertising campaign that promised consumers protection from infection simply by using toilet paper, the author is emphasizing how ridiculous advertising campaigns were in attempting to terrify the consumer.

Choice (B) is wrong because the Scott tissue product is still well-known today. Choice (C) is wrong because the end of this passage gives an example to support a point the author just made. It doesn't point to a further explanation of the same topic or to an explanation of a new one. Choice (D) is wrong because the author doesn't pose any questions. Choice (E) is wrong because the author doesn't provide any examples of how these ads might contain the truth. Instead, the author suggests they stretched the truth in order to sell more product.

689. **C. the products and ads made use of colorful packaging and snappy slogans**

The passage states that these companies were successful because they tried more modern advertising techniques to appeal to the consumers, such as using snappy slogans and colorful packaging.

Choice (A) is a true statement, but it isn't mentioned as a reason the campaigns were successful. The campaigns were successful because they appealed to consumers in new ways. Choice (B) is an overgeneralization. Although some features were unique and patented, this wasn't seen as the main cause of the success of the advertising campaigns. Choice (D) was an advertising goal, but it wasn't the specific reason for the success of the companies. Rather, it was an underlying premise for the advertising campaigns. Choice (E) is wrong because not all products made this claim. The author uses this point to illustrate the advertising psychology prevalent at the time. Products could "arouse" or "excite" the consumer in some way other than terror caused by bad breath or infectious toilet paper.

690. **D. theaters, dance halls, circuses, and organized sports**

Choice (D) summarizes the main point of the passage, which is that commercialized entertainment is entertainment that many people pay to see together, generally watching other people perform.

Choices (A) and (B) represent the viewpoint of Victorians toward such activities. Victorians felt these activities were examples of luxury, hedonism, and extravagance, which encouraged gambling, swearing, drinking, and immoral sexual behavior. Choices (C) and (E) are wrong because Victorian prejudices and Puritan criticism aren't examples of commercialized entertainment.

691. **C. What is one of the biggest differences between prevailing attitudes of the 19th and 20th centuries?**

The entire passage shows a shift in attitude from the strict Victorian behavior codes of the 19th century and the more lax, fun-spirited entertainment of the 20th century. The passage uses forms of entertainment to make this point.

Choice (A) is wrong because the author doesn't address why these changes occurred. Choice (B) is wrong because although the passage does answer what people did for entertainment during the 20th century, it doesn't give details for the 19th century. The correct answer isn't Choice (D) or (E), because the passage doesn't give information about the 19th century, so a comparison can't be made. The author states that the differences were striking but doesn't give examples from the Victorian era to illustrate this.

692. **B. revered leisure**

The definition of *hedonism* is the belief that pleasure and happiness are the chief purpose in life. "Revered leisure" comes closest to a synonym, as those words are used in context to illustrate that people considered fun and entertainment to be as important as the previous moral code.

Choice (A) is wrong because "republican ideology" suggests the Victorian and Puritan belief that fun for its own sake leads to immoral behaviors like swearing, drinking, and sexual escapades. Choice (C) is wrong because although hedonists are often accused of poor behavior choices that glorify vices, such as the "immoral sexual behavior" in Choice (D), the term can also be used in a positive light. Choice (E) is wrong because "prejudices" could apply to any word and is neither a synonym nor an antonym. For example, people could have prejudices about fruit because it contains sugar and about rainy weather because it encourages depression.

693.

A. being responsible only for what is within our control

The passage explains this principle more fully, with examples of events outside our control and within our control. The principle suggests that humans are responsible only for what occurs when they're in control of the event or circumstances surrounding the event.

Choice (B) is wrong because the principle states that people shouldn't be blamed based on the amount of harm caused. The correct answer isn't Choice (C) or (D), because these examples go against the principle. People should be blamed less when harm is due to sheer luck, and they shouldn't be blamed at all for things beyond their control. Choice (E) is wrong because the principle doesn't suggest how people should act, nor does it describe moral uncertainties.

694.

C. explain a theory regarding why humans feel certain ways about events that cause harm

This passage explains a theory about why people feel guilty after some events and not guilty after others. It concerns why blame is placed on people in controllable and uncontrollable events.

Choice (A) is wrong because the passage doesn't try to talk readers into believing or disbelieving the theory. The information is simply presented. Choice (B) is wrong because the author doesn't try to explain why uncontrollable events occur — nor, really, could he. After all, knowing about them beforehand would offer some control. These events are most likely just "sheer luck." The correct answer isn't Choice (D) or (E), because the author doesn't show how the theory could be used to eliminate feelings of guilt or give information about how people should act. It only explains why people feel a certain way.

695.

D. an emotional reaction to unforeseen circumstances

Both examples concern unforeseen circumstances, and the author suggests the paradox of our emotions comes from feeling that the person was either in control of the event or not. If the person had control, we feel more likely to place more blame than if the event just simply happened with no human control.

The paradox is that the Control Principle doesn't quite hold up to the emotional response of an unforeseen circumstance. We tend to place blame on people based on the consequences of the circumstance and not just the reality of who was responsible or liable. Choice (B) is wrong because the author doesn't suggest the effects of the principle are surprising. Choice (C) is wrong because it explains only part of the paradox: giving more fault to the person who caused and event. Conversely, if a person committed a crime, such as drunk driving, and no one was injured, the perception is that the crime wasn't as bad even though the same controlling factor was present. Choice (D) is wrong because the author isn't presenting the theory in order to persuade readers that they don't need to feel guilty about an event they had control over.

696. **C. competent**

Although all these words are synonyms of *sufficient*, *competent* implies that all the requirements have been met for a certain judgement.

Choice (A) is wrong because *adequate* implies the level of requirement has barely been met. Choice (B) is wrong because *qualified* implies that a certain level of competency has officially been met, enough to receive a label ascribing professionalism of some sort. Choice (D) implies an amount of some kind must have been submitted (for example, three reasons must be given instead of only one really good reason). Choice (E) is wrong because *proficient* also implies a certain level of competency. Proficiency implies that someone has achieved a skill level above being merely competent.

697. **C. A problematic theory is more fully explained.**

The author explains the principle of sufficient reason in more detail. This theory can be problematic because it attempts to explain a rationale behind unexplainable events.

Choice (A) is wrong because the author presents no exceptions to the theory. Choice (B) is wrong because the theory has no popular misconceptions. Choice (D) is wrong because the author doesn't begin with a question, such as "Why do random events occur, and are they really random?" And Choice (E) is wrong because the author presents no other theories.

698. **D. rational philosophizing**

In this passage, the author presents a theory of philosophy that would help explain why events occur. The tone is rational and assertive.

Choice (A) is wrong because the author shows no paranoia, nor does he present a hypothesis that could be tested. There's no way to prove or disprove the theory. The correct answer is not Choice (B) or (C), because the author isn't defending the theory or justifying the theory from those who might hold a different view, as might be the case with many persuasive or argumentative essays. Instead, the author is simply presenting the theory. Choice (E) is wrong because the author doesn't present a fantastical idea, such as attempting to explain the specific reasons behind a random event, such as the theory that a hurricane hit a particular place because it was a den of iniquity. This would be ignorance of the reality of weather patterns and city planning.

699. **D. an attempt to use technology to change the "real world" as we currently know and understand it**

The passage speaks about one facet of the genre science fiction, the attempts to use technology to change the "real world." Science fiction does have other characteristics, but this is the only one the author focuses on.

Choice (A) is wrong because although some people have anxiety about science fiction becoming reality, many argue in favor of it. Choice (B) is wrong because science fiction doesn't have to be about the *desire* to change the world; it could simply be the changing of the world. For example, some of the mutants in the X–Men comics and movies are natural instead of bioengineered. Choice (C) is wrong because it implies a judgment that the author doesn't seem to share. The author seems fascinated by the possibilities. Choice (E) is wrong because the author gives other examples that don't affect the biological status of humans, such as cybernetic implants and weather control. Although the examples do pertain to humans, they aren't necessarily changing the biology of humans.

700. **D. It compares and contrasts two viewpoints of an issue.**

The author prepares the reader for the issue by giving an explanation and then presents two viewpoints on how people see technology interacting with humans.

Choice (A) is wrong because although the passage raises several questions in the first part of the passage, they're rhetorical. Choice (B) is wrong because there are no misconceptions about the topic, which has no right or wrong answers. The passage simply presents two sides of an issue. Choice (C) is wrong because science fiction isn't necessarily a psychological term; it's a literary term. Although examples of science fiction are briefly given, they serve only to illustrate one facet of the term, that of technology and humans. Choice (E) is wrong because the reader doesn't necessarily have an assumption about science fiction that might disagree with how the author portrays the subject.

701. **B. one group believes technology should be used to enhance humanity, and the other feels humanity should be conserved in its pure form with no technological enhancements**

Transhumanists believe that technology should be used to make a better, "grander" human, and bioconservatives believe that humans should be conserved in their natural state.

Choice (A) is wrong because although one sect of bioconservatives, the natural law theorists, feels that enhancing humans is immoral, the transhumanists do feel that morality comes into play. According to the passage, they don't feel it's wrong for humans to push such boundaries.

Choice (C) is wrong because there's no evidence from the passage that suggests transhumanists believe that technology enhancement is another step in natural selection. Choice (D) is wrong because the issue of mutantism isn't discussed in regard to either transhumanists or bioconservatives. And Choice (E) is wrong because there's no evidence from the passage that bioconservatives believe technology enhancement will have effects on future generations.

702. C. morality is formed from human responses to the environment, and destroying that environment will likely negatively affect morality

These theorists argue that morality is developed from the shortfalls of humanity. If humans no longer encounter such challenges, human nature will begin to show the worst effects of pride and arrogance.

Choice (A) is wrong because the natural law theorists believe morality is tied to biological responses to external stimuli. This belief causes them to argue against transhumanists. Choice (B) is the core of what the natural law theorists believe: that morality could be affected by technological enhancements. Choice (D) is wrong because there's no evidence from the passage to suggest such a dire prediction. The theory states only that there will be a negative effect. Choice (E) is wrong because other life forms aren't discussed.

703. B. attempting to explain how the X-Men series is an example of existentialism

The author suggests that the "X" in X-Men could easily mean "existentialism" because the characters go through a never-ending series of crises.

Choice (A) is wrong because Stan Lee didn't base the series on existentialism. According to the passage, Lee stated the "X" simply meant the characters had something "extra." Choice (C) is wrong because the author offers no example of a common misconception. Choice (D) is wrong because the author doesn't present an argument. He makes a claim. He offers no counterarguments and no reasons his thoughts are the best ones. Choice (E) is wrong because the author doesn't address readers who have never seen the movies or read the comics. Instead, the author simply presents his claim.

704. C. the fact that the X-Men struggle just as valiantly to defeat bad guys as they do to protect themselves from humans, the very creatures they are trying so hard to protect

This paradox — that the X-Men protect the very creatures that then try to destroy them — is a paradox posed in the passage. It's a never-ending struggle: the need to defeat evil and the need to protect oneself from evil in the thing one has sworn to protect.

Choice (A) is wrong because there's never a question that the X-Men would no longer protect humanity. Their commitment to human protection creates the paradox. Choice (B) is wrong because the passage doesn't claim that X-Men are bad guys and doesn't suggest superheroes are staples of society. In the passage, "staples" simply means a constant in the storyline. Choice (D) is wrong because although the author does pose this question at the conclusion of the passage, there are no further details that suggest a paradox. The only paradox might be whether humans should even worry about this stuff or just forget it and focus on enjoying a good read. However, the rest of the passage suggests the author isn't claiming such a thing. Finally, Choice (E) is a paradox, but it isn't discussed in the passage.

705. **D. a theory to help explain man's existence and struggle in an uncaring world**

According to the passage, the X-Men offer a perfect example of existentialism, the belief that man's struggle in an uncaring world causes him to question his own existence and purpose. After all, why do the X-Men get up day after day to battle evil? It's a never-ending struggle for which they never receive any benefits or even goodwill.

706. **D. that the X-Men's eternal struggle is a lesson in existentialism as they constantly question their own existence**

The author is comparing the X-Men's eternal struggle with existence to humanity's: *Why are we here? What purpose do we serve?* The author suggests that the X-Men ask these types of questions, as they're asked by many people about the daily struggle of life.

Choice (A) is wrong because the author is trying to prove the opposite, that the X-Men better explain the theory of existentialism. Choice (B) is wrong because the author isn't giving literary advice or plot advice to Stan Lee. He's using the X-Men to explain a philosophical theory. Choice (C) is wrong because the author doesn't give details about either the positivity or negativity of existentialist theory. And Choice (E) is wrong because the author is suggesting, by the very writing of this passage, that people should explore more theories in literature and how those might influence human thought.

707. **D. Understand that all people, even heroes, struggle with the desire to understand man's very existence.**

The author is suggesting that one can learn lessons from the literary examples of X-Men. In them as heroes, we can see that all humans question their existence and constantly try to discover whether their lives have any meaning in the universe.

Choice (A) is wrong because although the X-Men do ultimately win each battle with evil, they don't receive any accolades from society. Choice (B) is wrong because although the X-Men do feel as if they have to prove their worth, the author doesn't suggest that humans should have to prove their value with good deeds. The correct answer isn't Choice (C). The author doesn't tell the reader to throw in the towel and even remarks that the X-Men are in a constant daily battle, as are we all. He never suggests simply giving up. And Choice (E) is wrong because by using the example of Stan Lee's work, the author is showing this notion false. The actions of one person *do* affect other people.

708. C. plot repetitions

The author states that the characters have had the same plot patterns for a "half-century." After the X-Men capture one bad guy and imprison him, they're called to do so again in the very next story.

Choice (A) is wrong because the passage doesn't mention the X-Men losing a battle. Choice (B) is wrong because the X-Men don't really ever end their duties as superheroes. They're called on again and again to conquer evil, which appears never-ending. Choice (D) is wrong because the author doesn't give any examples of the X-Men finding the meaning of life after saving the world. And Choice (E) is wrong because the author doesn't give any details of the X-Men losing to an evil guy. The passage suggests the X-Men are in a constant struggle to put away bad guys. In this passage, they aren't conquered by evil.

709. A. aesthetically comparing terminology to collectively describe a group of people

The author states that some names are more appealing to certain groups than others and compares the terms that have been used to describe a group of people.

The right answer isn't Choice (B), because the author doesn't give many details about how the terms affect the people involved, other than to state that "many white people" are disquieted by certain terms. Choice (C) is wrong because the author doesn't criticize people who make sweeping generalizations, other than with the example of Christopher Columbus. Choice (D) is wrong because the author doesn't present an opinion on which term to use. Instead, he mentions terms that the specific groups themselves lean toward. Choice (E) is wrong because the author doesn't present a judgment about which terms are better than others.

710. **A. well-intentioned people have sought to label them in a way that better fits who they are and what they want to be called**

The passage points to several groups labeling American Indians, from Christopher Columbus to teachers to those developing Indian studies programs. All these groups sought to give American Indians a name that fit who they were. Modern groups are more concerned with what American Indians want to call themselves.

Choice (B) is wrong because most of the terms (other than Columbus's "Indian") are a matter of choice rather than an appropriate understanding of what to call a group of people. Choice (C) is wrong because the passage states that American Indians prefer to call themselves by this name, not that they insist on it. Choice (D) is wrong because the passage doesn't discuss the implications of political correctness on the debate. The discussion is what American Indians should be called, not on what is politically correct or incorrect about the names. Choice (E) is wrong because modern terms still collectively group all American Indians instead of referring to them by specific tribal name, such as Hopi.

711. **E. respectful but aloof discussion of the topic**

The author maintains a respectful discussion of each group throughout, from Christopher Columbus's misnomer to modern efforts at naming the group. The author doesn't give any term more credence and seems removed from the discussion, other than sparking a debate about the naming of American Indians.

Choice (A) is wrong because the author doesn't present any indignation or surprise at Christopher Columbus's mistake in naming the group "Indian"; he even calls it a "creative fertility of error." The correct answer isn't Choice (B) or (C). The author doesn't provide any proposals to end the ongoing debate and points to the fact that modern groups still struggle with fitting terms. Choice (D) is wrong because the author doesn't suggest times were better when the terms weren't discussed or suggest that changing the terminology is bothersome or negative in any way.

712. **C. one specifically refers to American Indians while the other refers to a person born in America**

The author states that American Indians no longer choose the *Native American* terminology because many people are *native* to America. The term can't necessarily differentiate the group, because it can apply to many people.

Choice (A) is wrong because *Native* specifically refers to what was once referred to as American Indians, while *native* refers to anyone of any race born in America. Choice (B) is wrong because the author doesn't discuss which term is more acceptable to society. Choice (D) is wrong because although *Native Americans* refers only to American Indians, *native* isn't a term commonly used to refer to people born in America. Generally, the term "natural born citizen" is used. Choice (E) is wrong because the author doesn't suggest that society prefers either term. The only suggestion about larger appeal is that many white people are "disquieted" by the term *American Indian*.

713. D. What do American Indians prefer to call themselves in this naming debate?

The passage states that the group prefers the term *American Indian* collectively and refers to themselves by tribal names more specifically.

Choice (A) is wrong because the passage doesn't determine what led to the name change, other than saying the change can be attributed to educators over time. Choice (B) is wrong because the author doesn't suggest any specific criteria in determining which might be more fitting. Choice (C) is wrong because the passage gives no complaints from American Indians about any terminology used. And Choice (E) is wrong because although the author does discuss modern trends in naming, there are no guesses about which name will stick.

714. B. explain why there is a debate about such terminology

By explaining that Christopher Columbus made a mistake concerning the first names given to the group, the author sets the stage for the remainder of the passage, which concerns the debate about better terms to use.

Choice (A) is wrong because there are no specific comparisons made among the terms; the passage notes only the changes in terminology. Choice (C) is wrong because the author is simply providing information about the debate and doesn't call for the reader to choose any particular term, nor does he state that any term is better. Choice (D) is wrong because more-informed readers would already know about Columbus's mistake in naming the group. And Choice (E) is wrong because Columbus didn't name the group *Indians* because of racism. He simply didn't know where he was.

715. C. from 1851 to 1873

Although exact facts and figures aren't given for all the years (because data wouldn't have been kept prior to 1783), a quick study of the charts shows that the most loss of land occurred between the years 1851 and 1873.

Choice (A) is wrong because there was no loss of land prior to 1783. This would be the rough start of data accumulation and is, at best, a guess. Choice (B) is wrong because although American Indians did lose a substantial amount of lands, the exact acreage can't be known. However, a quick glance at the maps shows that this period saw the second largest decrease of lands. Choice (D) is wrong because that number is roughly 300,000,000 acres, which is less than the loss from Choice (C), at roughly 500,000,000. Choice (E) is wrong because no data is available since 2010.

716. **C. from 1851 to 1873**

Although exact figures for the acreage aren't given, a quick glance at the chart shows that as the American Indian lands were being taken away, reservation space was being provided.

Choice (A) is wrong because no reservations were created for American Indian use before 1783, as American Indians had free and unrestricted use of all American lands. Choice (B) is wrong because only parts of three states had lands devoted for reservations at this time. Choice (D) is wrong because the number of reservations decreased during this time period. And Choice (E) is wrong because no data is provided for that time period.

717. **B. Oklahoma**

The 1873 map shows almost the entire state of Oklahoma as being set aside for reservation use.

718. **D. Create geographic boundaries that would separate American Indian lands from the government lands**

Reservations were created to place American Indians within a geographic boundary so that the government could claim other lands for its own use.

Choice (A) is wrong because no such line exists on any of the maps, nor would such a plan be feasible based on current amounts of acreage set aside for reservations. Choice (B) is wrong because the maps shows a continuous encroachment and removal to smaller chunks of land. The correct answer isn't Choice (C) or (E). The use of reservations shows these plans didn't get past the discussion phase.

719. **D. Arizona**

According to the 2010 map, Arizona has the largest shaded section denoting reservation use.

720. **D. What is one of the greatest single and personalized achievements in the development of literacy?**

> Sequoyah's feat is the only noted instance in history where an individual independently created an effective writing system from a preliterate state.

> Choice (A) is wrong because the passage doesn't give specific criteria on what literacy is, other than creation of a writing system. Choice (B) is wrong because the passage gives no information as to the benefits the Cherokee people gained from their writing system. Choice (C) is wrong because the author gives no details about how the alphabet and writing system were taught. And Choice (E) is wrong because the passage doesn't mention Sequoyah's motivation.

721. **C. an individual meeting his desire to improve the lives of his community members with creativity and vision**

> Sequoyah saw a need in his community and worked to accomplish something that had never been done before.

> Choice (A) is wrong because the author's reporting is brief and inoffensive. The language is respectful and in awe of such achievement. Choice (B) is wrong because the opposite is true: Sequoyah had vision to see beyond the beliefs that existed during that time. Choice (D) is wrong because although the author does state Sequoyah's work as a crowning achievement, there's no suggestion this is the only literacy achievement of the Cherokees or any American Indian tribe. Choice (E) is wrong because a smarter inference would be that Sequoyah created the alphabet and writing system in order to help his people culturally assimilate. If two nations had their own writing system, communication between the two parties would be easier and more effective.

722. **B. Sequoyah had no formal training in linguistics**

> The author states that Sequoyah's achievement is even more amazing because he had no formal education and had no training in phonetics or linguistics.

> Choice (A) is wrong because there's no indication the Cherokee didn't value written communication. Choice (C) is wrong because the passage states that Sequoyah had no scripts to work with. Choice (D) is wrong because the passage doesn't give a comparison between the two languages. And Choice (E) is wrong because the passage states that the entire nation learned the language in a short amount of time. Instead of resisting, they seemed to embrace the development.

723. C. The first sentence states a historical perspective, and the last sentence presents a different perspective based on chronological events.

Before Sequoyah, the Cherokee had no system of writing and were considered to be preliterate. After Sequoyah developed a system of writing, the Cherokee people were considered literate.

Choice (A) is wrong because the preliteracy of the Cherokee wasn't a misconception. Literacy simply hadn't yet been developed in a form of writing. Choice (B) is wrong because the last sentence doesn't give more details about preliteracy. Choice (D) is wrong because there's no question or answer in the passage. Choice (E) is wrong because preliteracy isn't a condition to be debated, nor is literacy.

724. B. Passage 2 issues a counterargument to a viewpoint that is presented in Passage 1.

Passage 1 makes the claim that Shakespeare's grief over his son's death is directly evident in his works, whereas Passage 2 makes the claim that no evidence of Shakespeare's grief can be found in his works.

The correct answer isn't Choice (A). If further information linking Hamnet to Hamlet were presented, this might be true. However, Passage 2 states that there's no evidence that Shakespeare used his work as a model for his life. Choice (C) is wrong because there's no evidence that either set of information is more up-to-date than the other. Choice (D) is wrong because although Sigmund Freud would be considered an expert on matters of psychology, he isn't a Shakespeare expert and his viewpoint is just a theory, not proof. Choice (E) is wrong because the two passages address whether Shakespeare's feelings, specifically his family relationships, can be seen in his plays.

725. B. enjoying the symmetry and circularity of events

The author of this passages models Sigmund Freud when she says that he was trying to find a symmetry between the words *Hamnet* and *Hamlet*. Finding those types of events in life, such as knowing that both Shakespeare and Mark Twain died on their birthdays, can be pleasurable. It seems to wrap up things nicely.

Choice (A) is wrong because the name Hamnet isn't explained as a symbol for anything. Choice (C) is wrong because Freud wasn't a literary critic. Choice (D) is wrong because there's no "hidden agenda." Shakespeare might have named the play *Hamlet* after his son regardless of whether the young boy had died. And Choice (E) is wrong because giving children names doesn't have an obvious connection to "seeing or seeking equivalence."

726.   C. That family was important to Shakespeare and family names should have honor

Both passages give examples to prove that Shakespeare considered family to be important. Passage 1 makes that claim that Shakespeare named a major character in his play for his son. Passage 2 makes the claim that a purchase of a coat of arms would honor the family name of Shakespeare because Shakespeare's father could then die as a gentleman.

Choice (A) is wrong because there's no evidence that the two were estranged. Choice (B) is wrong because there's no evidence from either passage that the two hadn't seen one another in a long time. Choice (D) is wrong because the passage does connect the death of Hamnet with the purchasing of a coat of arms, but there's no other evidence to suggest that Shakespeare didn't think family was important before the death. Choice (E) is wrong because neither passage suggests Shakespeare cared more for his father than his son.

727.   D. equally analytical but more skeptical

Both passages analyze whether Shakespeare included details and feelings about his son's death in his dramatic works. Passage 2, however, is more skeptical.

Choice (A) is wrong because Passage 2 gives a few more details, such as the month and year of Hamnet's death, but offers no details focused on the theory. Choice (B) is wrong because the tone isn't necessarily cheerful (jocose). Choice (C) is wrong because neither passage is scientific. And Choice (E) is wrong because Passage 2 isn't angry that a definitive answer can't be found.

728.   C. Make reference to the works of Shakespeare to prove their point

Passage 1 uses the example of the names Hamnet and Hamlet, and Passage 2 suggests Shakespeare's sonnets might have shown his personal feelings about Hamnet's death.

Choice (A) is wrong because neither passage mocks alternative viewpoints. Both writers feel their case has been made. Choice (B) is wrong because, alas, no recent discoveries about Shakespeare's inner thoughts and feelings have been made. People simply continue to debate the issue with his original works as evidence. Choice (D) is wrong because Passage 1 offers only one piece of evidence, and Passage 2 claims there's no evidence — or some evidence, maybe, kind of. Choice (E) is wrong because neither author criticizes the Bard. Both are looking to see how a son's death might have affected his works.

729. **C. seeking to know more about the man Shakespeare by looking at his works as evidence of his true character**

The authors are exploring whether Shakespeare's true feelings about Hamnet's death might have been worked into his creative arts. Both authors are looking through this literary lens in hopes of finding out a bit more about Shakespeare.

Choice (A) is wrong because there are no common objections about the topic of Shakespeare concerning his son's death. (There are many concerns about the legitimacy of his plays, but that isn't the topic here.) Choice (B) is wrong because neither passage dispels the notion that Hamlet was named for Hamnet. Choice (D) is wrong because the authors don't give basic facts to educate. Instead, both just delve into the topic. And Choice (E) is wrong because neither passage addresses what other symbolism or meaning might be found, and Passage 2 suggests that maybe no meaning can be found.

730. **D. America does not have to rely on other countries for medicinal plants, as many of the same things can be easily and more freshly grown here.**

The author proposes that America's resources should be taken into consideration for medicinal plants, especially considering that much of the foreign material is of substandard quality.

Choice (A) is wrong because the author says that purchasing these products "cheap" just results in a higher rate for patients. Therefore, cost probably shouldn't be a consideration. The correct answer isn't Choice (B). It's one thing to say that indigenous products should be used and quite another to send people into the woods to treat themselves. This is definitely not the best answer. Choice (C) is wrong because the author does briefly talk about price considerations but doesn't dwell on the topic enough to support this claim. Finally, Choice (E) is wrong because scientific modifications of plants aren't discussed at all.

731. **E. The founding of the Terra Nova ethnomedicinal Rainforest Reserve to ensure rare tropical plants are available for medical research**

A counterargument to the author's claim that America can do the job better, with purer and richer resources, is that many medicinal plants can't be found in the U.S. Because plants very much depend on climate and temperature, not all American medical needs could be met with products naturally grown without a huge amount of additional cost.

Choice (A) would actually support the author's claim. More research into plants grown in the U.S. might yield better and cheaper alternatives. The correct answer isn't Choice (B) or (C), as these aren't related to the topic of medicinal plants. Choice (D) is wrong because although a common herbal remedy might help to support the author's claim, this example is weak.

732. B. Laziness and lack of creativity

The author states that "custom," "indolence," and "want of thought" have created a reliance on foreign goods.

The correct answer isn't Choice (A) or (C). The passage offers no discussion on cost, other than to say the plants are cheaply secured from foreign sources. Choice (D) is wrong because the author says that America is rich in such resources. Choice (E) is wrong because the author says that foreign product can't be as pure or fresh as that created here. The author calls the other products "old, decayed, deteriorated, effete, and adulterated."

733. B. Decades of research, trials, and tests have determined the validity of indigenous plant material.

The author states that a half century of testing has been spent in investigation of the products to show that standard remedies are okay to use. This would appeal to those who need to feel safe when making such a decision.

The author doesn't give Choice (A) as a reason to back up his claim. Choice (C) is wrong because lower costs wouldn't make consumers feel safer. Choice (D) is wrong because the author doens't give any information on modern research. Choice (E) is wrong because the author gives no information on approval from any government agency.

734. D. explain why Corbett's stories should be read

The author explains to readers that they'll like Corbett's stories if they enjoy reading about adventures or the jungle or if they're sportsmen.

Choices (A) and (C) are wrong because the author simply states the stories are true. Choice (B) is wrong because the author says the story is stranger than fiction, which would make them unbelievable — but the reader should believe in them anyway. And Choice (D) is wrong because the first paragraph gives little information as to why the reader should believe such stories about Corbett, nor does the reader find out much about him, other than the fact that he wrote a book.

735. B. compare another key influence on the adventure/jungle genre of literature

By comparing Corbett's work to the well-known works of Rudyard Kipling, the author is comparing another key influence on the adventure/jungle genre and suggesting that Corbett is in the same category.

Choice (A) is wrong because Corbett doesn't have the same reputation or prominence as Kipling. Choice (C) is wrong because the passage doesn't state that Corbett was influenced by Kipling's stories or style. Choice (D) is wrong because the author suggests Kipling is a similar writer but doesn't state he prefers Corbett's work over Kipling's. Choice (E) is wrong because the author doesn't show that Kipling's success should be envied. He does encourage readers to try the Corbett book but only on its own merits and not to win him similar acclaim.

736. **A. It is as worthy of acclaim as Kipling's more popular work.**

The author is of the opinion that Corbett's work is just as good as Kipling's, although Kipling is read more and is more popular with readers.

Choices (B) and (C) are wrong because Corbett's work isn't as popular or as circulated as Kipling's; otherwise, the author wouldn't say it deserves to be. Choice (D) is wrong because the author doesn't suggest that Kipling's work isn't worthy of its popularity. Choice (E) is wrong because the author doesn't make any claim about Corbett's lack of financial success.

737. **B. It more accurately depicts life in the jungle than Kipling's *Jungle Books*.**

The author states that Corbett's work is based in fact, while Kipling's is based in fiction. He then includes supporting details, such as Corbett's description of hunting tigers on the backs of elephants.

Choice (A) is wrong because the author says the work is based on fact. Choice (C) is wrong because the author doesn't claim readers need knowledge of jungle life. He does compare the works but doesn't encourage the people to read Kipling's *Jungle Books*. Choice (D) is wrong because although the author suggests sportsmen will enjoy the book, he doesn't say that it should be used for learning to hunt. Choice (E) is wrong because the author doesn't compare the religiosity of the two books.

738. **D. Corbett's work as a *shikari* provided him with the strength, patience, and courage to tackle such a tremendous feat as killing man-eating tigers — and to write about it.**

The author states that Corbett's work as a *shikari* gave him a unique background as a hunter and provided him with the exact skills needed to write the story: patience, strength, courage, and powers of observation.

Choice (A) is wrong because the author does suggest that Corbett is on the same level as Kipling but doesn't give specific examples. This isn't the best answer choice. Choice (B) is wrong because the author alludes to Corbett's hunting experience but not to the degree that the reader would automatically assume he's an expert on the subject. More details would be needed to support this claim. Choice (C) is wrong because the author doesn't allude to any traumatic life event. Choice (E) is wrong because the author doesn't give this detail about Corbett's heroism in the passage.

739. **A. By using a limited narrator and stating only the boy's thoughts and feelings directly**

The story is told through the point of view of the boy: What he sees, smells, and thinks is available to the reader. This limits the point of view of the story and doesn't allow the reader to see what other characters think or see.

Choice (B) is wrong because no other viewpoint is seen or described. The reader doesn't know how the Justice or the father feels or what they're thinking. Choice (C) is wrong because the boy is very involved in the story and has great interest in the conflict. You can see this in his despairing thoughts about their common enemy. Choice (D) is wrong because the story is told from the boy's perspective, and he has a biased view of the action because his father is involved. Choice (E) is wrong because it's unclear whether the boy is going to be a secondary character. He's experiencing the action as it occurs and seems to be involved in the conflict because he's attending the session of the Justice of the Peace.

740. **B. The reader can see how hungry the boy is, and the reader is led to believe the judgment will be an important one in the boy's life.**

The lengthy description of the food items surrounding the boy leads the reader to believe that he hasn't eaten well and is distracted by his surroundings. The reader can also see that the boy's focus is also on his father, who is standing before the Justice. Had the boy been rich and well-fed, any judgment might have been bearable, but a boy living in such poverty would depend on his father for his very survival.

Choice (A) is wrong because the reader doesn't have enough information to make a decision about other Faulkner stories. The selection might give an indication of his style, but this isn't the best answer. Choice (C) is wrong because the description doesn't sound like the musings of a young boy. Choice (D) is wrong because there is no evidence Faulkner set the story in the past. At the time the story was written, having legal proceedings outside of a courtroom might well have been common practice according to Faulkner's life experiences. Choice (E) takes imagination a bit too far. The author doesn't give any hints that such a thing will happen.

741. **C. The father likely committed the crime of which he is being accused.**

All inferences about the father have to come from the thoughts of the boy. The boy vehemently denies that his father could be involved, but the author uses the words "despair," "grief," and "fear" to describe how the boy is feeling. The boy, because of his blood ties to his father, is trying to deny whatever happened but knows that his father is likely guilty.

Choice (A) is wrong because the boy is stating the Justice is their common enemy. He knows the father will likely be found guilty, which means he believes his father probably committed the crime. Choice (B) might seem like a good answer because of the word "enemy," but there are no other details to support the idea of a vendetta. Had the boy recalled past instances of his father before the Justice, this answer would make more sense. Choice (D) is wrong because the boy's terror tells readers that the incident isn't trivial. He's so scared he can even smell his fear. Choice (E) is wrong because the reader doesn't know how the father feels. Only the boy's feelings are known.

742.   **A. Faulkner uses these speech patterns to show that the boy comes from an uneducated Southern family, one likely to be taken advantage of by a more educated and richer political system.**

The boy's speech indicates that he likely comes from a poor agrarian Southern family. By calling the judge "*our enemy . . . ourn! mine and hisn both,*" the boy is indicating that the family sees that they're less powerful and at the mercy of the Justice, who is more educated and richer, as are others in the political system.

Choice (B) is wrong because "hisn" and "ourn" don't suggest innocence. Although the boy's helplessness is apparent, this isn't the best answer. Choice (C) is wrong because the diction doesn't necessarily point to the youth of the boy. It's unlikely that a very young boy would understand that his father had an enemy or that a court case, such as this, would be so full of stressful undertones. Choice (D) is wrong because the speech doesn't necessarily show terror. Although the word "enemy" might point to this, the other words point out a cultural difference between the boy's father and the judge. Choice (E) is wrong because the entire passage stays true to the character of a poor boy who is scared that his father has committed a crime. There's no evidence to suggest, at least so far, that the narrator might be unreliable.

743.   **E. The news focused on the celebratory nature of the event from the American perspective and little, if anything, was shown about the tragic effect on the Japanese citizens.**

The author suggests that Hersey wrote the story because other news outlets hadn't shown "what had really happened at Hiroshima." The reader can gather from this that the news outlets focused on the consequences to Americans instead of the people at Hiroshima.

Choice (A) is wrong because nothing in the passage suggests that other news outlets focused on the scientific facts of the bomb. Choice (B) is wrong because the author makes the point that the event was important, so important that a correspondent was sent to write a story for *The New Yorker*. Choice (C) is wrong because although the author did want the truth about the event to come out, the main focus was not on what the city itself looked like. Choice (D) is wrong because nothing in the passage suggests the author feels this way. Rather, the opposite is implied — that news outlets were too forgiving of the U.S. by not truly portraying the full story.

744. E. First-person accounts from actual witnesses and victims of the event

The first part of the passage describes Hersey's efforts to interview those who were actually at the event — who saw and experienced the event firsthand and could give first-person accounts of the bombing of Hiroshima.

Choice (A) is wrong because the passage makes no mention of soldiers or their perspectives. Choice (B) is wrong because the passage doesn't discuss any details about the scientific nature of the bomb. Choice (C) is wrong because the author mentions that Hersey traveled to Japan to find survivors, not the correspondents who wrote the first stories. Choice (D) is wrong because although the author does mention *The New Yorker*, he doesn't give any indication that an editorial would shed more light on the subject, and a staff-written editorial wouldn't be part of Hersey's work.

745. B. the subject matter was such that respect for the lives lost was more important than traditional routine and formatting

By completely changing the normal format of the magazine, *The New Yorker* was making a statement: The subject matter can't be respectfully broken up or be forced to compete with more humorous matter. The reader can assume that by devoting the entire magazine to Hiroshima, the magazine was paying its respects to the victims.

Choice (A) is wrong because the passage doesn't suggest that *The New Yorker* was worried about losing readers and advertising. Actually, because of handling the work in such a manner, the loss of clients and readers was a possibility. *The New Yorker* wasn't *trying* to lose advertising and readers with the story of Hiroshima, however. Choice (C) is wrong because long stories of traumatic events are often *serialized,* or published in pieces over time, if only to give readers smaller doses. Choice (D) is wrong because there's no mention of the U.S. government or possible censorship. Also, the war was definitely over by the time the story was published in 1946. Choice (E) is wrong because the author only mentions that Hersey took a month to interview victims. No mention is made of exactly how long the author took to write the story, but the reader can assume that the story went to press fairly quickly.

746. **A. A piecing together of different stories and personalities to get an overall idea**

Hersey traveled to Hiroshima to get firsthand accounts and told the stories in each person's own words instead of simply combining their thoughts into composites types (for example, the one who suffered the most, the one who saw the bomb drop on a building, and the one who lost a loved one). Hersey simply lets the survivors' stories speak for themselves.

Choice (B) is wrong because the passage doesn't suggest blending the interviews Hersey's intent. The reader can't tell the exact format of the magazine from the description given, but the passage implies that each individual got to tell his or her own story, suggesting the magazine wasn't just one long interview but a series of stories all working together to shed light on the event. Choice (C) is wrong because Hersey's work didn't turn fact into fiction. The passage states that was the real value in Hersey's work: It told the truth. The correct answer isn't Choice (D) or (E). The passage doesn't suggest that Hersey added his own thoughts or psychological analysis.

747. **B. revered**

Venerable is a word that goes above merely showing respect for someone. It takes into account the person's actions, experience, and age and suggests that mothers are more than people to be admired. They deserve greater respect because of all they've done.

Choice (A) is wrong because *reputable* suggests having passed some basic test or achieved a level of moral character. The correct answer is not Choice (C) or (E), because *venerable* suggests a bit more than simple respect or admiration. Choice (D) is wrong because *discreditable* is an antonym, not a synonym.

748. **C. Women should not believe the lesser judgment of themselves, as most of those judgments instead reflect on the men who make them.**

Choice (A) is wrong because the author most certainly doesn't suggest that women are inferior to men or are reflections of men. Choice (B) is wrong because the author doesn't suggest that a man treat all women the same way one treats his own mother. Instead, the author merely says he pities the man who doesn't treat other women with the same respect that a man gives to his own mother. Choice (D) is wrong because the author doesn't specifically describe his own mother or her qualities. Choice (E) is wrong because the author speaks collectively of "women" throughout the entire passage.

749. **C. A man's judgments of women more accurately reflect his own manner and morals than those of the women he is judging.**

The author suggests that when a man judges a woman to be base, his own base view clouds his judgment; he isn't accurately reflecting on who the woman herself might be.

The correct answer isn't Choice (A) or (D). The author actually seems to imply that women are better than men, especially those who would speak ill of women. Choice (B) is wrong because the author would suggest this approach only if the man in question treated his mother well. Choice (E) is wrong because the author speaks collectively of "women" throughout the entire passage.

750. **A. Men who are noble in character often have better views of those who are around them.**

The author suggests that as men become nobler and wiser, their viewpoints of the women they come in contact with are likely to improve.

Choice (B) is wrong because although the author might suggest this advice, this detail isn't included in the passage, nor is any advice explicitly given. The correct answer isn't Choice (C) or (E), because allusions to mothers are in the preceding paragraph, and neither of these details is suggested there, either. Choice (D) goes a step beyond what the author suggests, which is that a man's outlook on feminism improves as he becomes a smarter and better person.

751. **D. a frustrating but expected situation, considering all the time and effort spent**

The phrase doesn't mean either sad or funny but instead focuses on the frustrating experience of spending so much time and money to prepare the study, only to have the subject of the study disappear. Such experts know this is probably going to happen but continue to hope things might be different. When it happens, the researcher can only laugh.

The correct answer isn't Choice (A) or (B), because the author isn't suggesting the first process in the research is a joke. Choice (C) is wrong because the author suggests that such study is valuable but difficult to achieve because the subjects of study keep disappearing. Choice (E) is wrong because even though such communities are disappearing, the author makes statements about how the studies that researchers have been able to do have been very valuable.

752.

E. An analytical study of all of the above

The passage doesn't give the exact definition of *ethnology*. However, the passage does discuss all the answer choices as being part of that study. Therefore, *ethnology* is the science that deals with the analytical study of the division of human beings into races, with specific focus on their origins, religions, and characteristics and the general relationships of those groups.

753.

A. of the views of a vast and complex social community that was previously unknown to the world

The author suggests that learning about these people is important for its own sake, to understand a group of people who have been previously unknown to the world.

Choice (B) is wrong because the author doesn't suggest that any secrets are necessarily hidden. Choice (C) is wrong because the author doesn't compare any details of such religions, nor does he say which religion "theirs" would be compared to (Hinduism? Christianity? Islam?). Choice (D) is wrong because an ethnologist likely would take this concept as a necessity. Having an understanding of the value of other cultures would be a given for that field. Choice (E) is wrong because the field and study of ethnology isn't necessarily dependent on unknown and rare tribes of people in the wild.

754.

C. explain both the value of and the difficulty of ethnology in studying populations of native tribes

The passage begins with an explanation of the difficulty of studying groups of people who disappear as soon as research is ready to begin, and the rest of the passage gives details about why such study is important.

Choice (A) is wrong because although the passage begins with "sadly ludicrous," the passage takes a serious look at the field. Choice (B) is wrong because the author alludes to the disappearance of cultures but doesn't give the reader any notion of having to hurry to complete the work before all such tribes disappear. Choice (D) is wrong because the author doesn't offer suggestions on how to improve the field. And Choice (E) is wrong because the author gives reports on new or exciting discoveries.

755. **E. Stein's work with *The Autobiography of Alice B. Toklas* is an example of artistic experimentation and creativity and should be seen as such**

The author is suggesting that Stein's work should be seen as an example of the author's experimentation and that *The Autobiography of Alice B. Toklas* shouldn't be seen as representative of her entire work.

Choice (A) is wrong because the author doesn't compare the masterfulness of Stein's work with Picasso's and Schoenberg's. He simply uses the comparisons to show other artists experimenting with different ideas. The correct answer isn't Choice (B) or (C), because the author suggests the opposite: that this work should stand on its own as an example of an artist trying something new. The author doesn't suggest anything else about the work. Choice (D) is an overgeneralization of the author's main point.

756. **B. prepare the reader for *The Autobiography of Alice B. Toklas,* which might be different from expectations**

Choice (A) is wrong because the author isn't offering justification for reading Stein so much as explaining why this work might not be like Stein's other work. Choice (C) is wrong because the passage tells the reader little about Stein or the work in question. Choice (D) is wrong because the author seems ambivalent about whether readers will enjoy the experience and seems more concerned that they be open to the idea of reading it. Choice (E) is wrong because although Stein's work achieved some notoriety due to controversies surrounding her lifestyle, the reader wouldn't know this from reading this excerpt.

757. **E. work that is wholly original and not to be thought of as representative of an author's style**

In the passage, an "absolute creation" is one that is wholly original and shouldn't be considered representative of an artist's style. The author contrasts absolute creation with easier-to-understand, more representational work.

Choices (A) and (C) are wrong because the work should not be considered representative of an artist's style or type of work. Choice (B) is incorrect because the absolute creation doesn't have to be viewed separately; it only needs to be understood to be a different type of work than might usually be created. Choice (D) is wrong because these works are not compared to other works by the artist in the passage.

758. **A. the cultural values of art with the need for creativity**

The author is suggesting that some pieces of an artist's work should still be considered valuable because it's only through trying new things that artists can grow. Without such endeavors, other masterpieces might not exist.

Choice (B) is wrong because the author isn't suggesting that art should be compared to music or writing. Choice (C) is wrong because the author isn't describing any types of labels of works. Choice (D) is wrong because the author isn't stating these artists created a new type of art or showing how they competed with "masters." Choice (E) is wrong because the author isn't suggesting criticism. Instead, those judging the work should be more open-minded.

Chapter 3

759. **D. a very diligent student**

More than one person is being referred to *(two)*, so *student* must be plural: *very diligent students*.

Choice (A) is fine because the singular verb *shows* agrees with the singular subject *research*. *Who* is the correct pronoun for *people*, and no comma is necessary when the clause *(who take tests)* provides essential (as opposed to extra) information, so Choice (C) isn't an error.

760. **A. As she came down the stairs**

Mariah came down the stairs, not *the books*, so the opening clause is a misplaced modifier (formerly called a *dangling modifier*). One possible reconstruction of the sentence is *As Mariah came down the stairs, the books she carried proved to be more than she could handle; she dropped them.*

Carried is fine because the use of the past tense is consistent in most of the sentence. Even though the past tense *were* is correct, so too is *proved to be*, used here for effect. The semicolon correctly separates two independent clauses.

761. **C. but asks**

Not only requires the correlative conjunction *but also*. Here, the *also* is missing.

The apostrophe is used correctly in Choice (A), and the infinitive is correct in Choice (B). The answer isn't Choice (D), because the infinitive is in correct parallel structure.

762.   B. it's status

The word *it's* is a contraction of *it is*. The possessive adjective *its* has no apostrophe.

Choice (A) is fine because the underlined portion is the subject complement and so agrees with the singular *status*. In Choice (C), the semicolon is used correctly to separate two independent clauses. The apostrophe is used correctly in Choice (D).

763.   E. No error

There's no error in this sentence.

Choice (D) is okay because the commas correctly set off the clause that modifies and emphasizes the word *priceless*.

764.   C. must be eating

The squirrels' action took place in the past, so they *must have eaten* the bulbs.

765.   C. stop in

The *doctor*, singular, takes the singular verb, *stops (in)*.

766.   A. This

The pronoun *this* is vague, as the noun it refers to (possibly *rudeness*) is missing.

767.   E. No error

There's no error in this sentence.

In Choice (B), the title is correctly capitalized because it precedes the name of a specific official.

768.   A. Making up the story as he went

Paul made up the story, not *Paul's lies*, so the opening clause is a misplaced modifier. One possible reconstruction of the problem is *Making up the story as he went, Paul kept telling lies until they snowballed . . .*

769. **C. need**

The word *each* is singular (each *one*) and so requires the singular verb *needs*.

Choice (A) is fine because a restrictive (essential) clause shouldn't be set off by commas.

770. **E. No error.**

The sentence is correct as written.

771. **B. they**

The singular noun *student* needs a singular pronoun: *he*, *she*, or *he or she*.

772. **B. myself**

The pronoun here is an object of the preposition *to* and so should be in the objective case: *me*. (Check: *It is very important to . . . me.*) The word *myself* may sound more academic, but sounding better here doesn't make it right. As a reflexive pronoun, *myself* needs to reflect upon a subject (here, the word *I*), which isn't present.

773. **A. incessantly**

An adjective *(incessant)* is required to modify the noun *(bickering)*.

774. **D. aids**

Aids is a verb. The word needed here is the noun *aides*.

775. **E. No error**

There's no error in this sentence.

The word *ancient* is a generic descriptor in this case and not an official title. Ancient Greece is not a place; therefore, only *Greece* should be capitalized.

776. **C. ; but**

The two independent clauses here may be joined by a comma + *but* or by a semicolon + *however* (or another appropriate conjunctive adverb).

The right answer isn't Choice (B), because the superlative is correct. Knowing *highest* is right requires also knowing that there are more than two levels in Bloom's taxonomy (otherwise, the *higher* level would be right).

777. A. scenting the food

A comma is needed after the introductory clause, right after *food*.

Note that in American English, either *leapt* or *leaped* is correct. In British English, only *leapt* is correct.

778. A. lose

Lose is a verb. The correct word to use here is the adjective *loose*.

In Choice (D), *whose* is the correct relative pronoun; in English, there is no other choice for inanimate objects.

779. D. a habit which drove its owners crazy

The pronoun *which* requires a noun to refer to. Choice (D) clarifies the pronoun without introducing another error.

780. B. In spite of the fact that she still does not trust the hostess

The tenses of the verbs must be in agreement (here, in the present tense).

The right answer isn't Choice (C), because *despite* and *in spite of* are both correct, but the lack of verb-tense agreement is not. Choice (D) is wrong because the adverb *anyway* (modifying the verb *plans*) would go at the end of the sentence.

781. E. The children's reading hour had come to an end; however,

The word *children* is already plural, so you make it possessive by simply adding *'s*.

The right answer isn't Choice (D), because although the apostrophe is now correctly placed, the coordinating conjunction *but* should be preceded by a comma, not a semicolon, and *but* shouldn't be followed by a comma.

782. **C. Geraldo and Miguel were more than a little uncertain**

The pronoun *they* is ambiguous here: Does it refer to *Geraldo and Miguel* or to *the opposing team's players*? Using a noun provides clarity.

The right answer isn't Choice (E), because although the ambiguity is gone, the shift to present tense (*feel*) is incorrect.

783. **B. In science, the processes of compiling data and reporting the results are important steps of the scientific method.**

Two processes are mentioned: compiling data, reporting results.

The right answer isn't Choice (C), because compiling data and reporting results are two separate steps.

784. **A. because he constantly found impediments**

An adverb is required to modify the verb *found*.

The right answer isn't Choice (B) or (C), because *constant* is used incorrectly. Choice (D) is wrong because the verb tense now is no longer in agreement with *decided*. Choice (E) is wrong because *implements*, meaning *tools*, isn't the right word, whereas *impediments*, meaning *obstacles*, is correct.

785. **D. Although not sure that the voters would accept such action**

In the original sentence, the word *except* is mistakenly used instead of *accept*.

Choice (C) is wrong because it's missing a reference for the pronoun *they* (*they* can't refer to *the senators*).

786. **A. The salesclerk sold the fifteen extra-large blue T-shirts faster than she thought possible.**

Commas aren't used to separate adjectives that are cumulative, that lean on each other. Cumulative adjectives provide different types of information. Here, *fifteen* (number) builds on *extra-large* (size), and *extra-large* builds on *blue* (color). A test for cumulative adjectives is to see whether inserting the word *and* between them makes sense. If it doesn't, they're cumulative.

The right answer isn't Choice (C), because *salesclerk* requires a singular pronoun, not the plural *they*. The lowercase *t-shirt* isn't as common as the uppercase *T-shirt*, but either use is correct; however, the comma in Choice (D) is wrong. Choice (E) is wrong because *than* should be used instead of *then*.

787. **B. that the jury has finally reached its decision**

> The collective noun *jury* is (usually) singular, which you can tell from the use of the singular verb *has*, so the pronoun needs to be singular.
>
> The right answer isn't Choice (D), because the punctuation is wrong.

788. **C. that had been formed during the Ice Age**

> The formation of the river occurred before the action of the walk, so instead of the past tense (as in *took*), the past perfect is used *(had been formed)*.
>
> Choice (D) is wrong because *Ice Age* should be capitalized.

789. **E. cause more and more heat to be trapped**

> The subject is *levels*, which is plural, so the verb must be *cause* (plural).
>
> Choice (C) is wrong because it omits important details; it doesn't express what is presented in the original sentence.

790. **D. that each species of bird, mammal, and amphibian has to be watched carefully**

> The subject *(each) species* requires a singular verb, *has*.
>
> The right answer isn't Choice (E), because the use of a comma before the restrictive (essential) clause is wrong.

791. **B. it's best if you get friends' opinions first**

> The second-person pronoun *you* is needed to agree the *you* in the opening clause.
>
> Choice (E) is wrong because the singular *friend's* would need both the article *a* and the singular *opinion*.

792. **C. The spectators trembled watching the male tiger prowl back and forth in his cage, so they stood back to be at a safer distance.**

> The pronoun must agree in number with the noun *spectators*; as the original sentence stands, *he* refers to the prowling tiger.
>
> Choice (D) is wrong because *he* is closer to *tiger* than *spectator*, and so making *spectators* singular does not make it agree with *he*.

unfortunately, the public didn't agree

... s needed to separate two independent clauses joined by a
... dverb.

... nyone besides Jonah

... side means *next to*, but the meaning here *(in addition to)*
... word *besides*.

**... p ten songs, which surprisingly represented a diversity of
... as the song "Rock On."**

... l sentence is a sentence fragment, lacking both a subject and

... is wrong because the *song*, not the station, rounded out the
... oice (E) is wrong because *It* is a vague pronoun.

---

796. **D. An interesting fact about Robert Lincoln, who was the only son of Abraham Lincoln to survive into adulthood,**

There wasn't more than one Robert Lincoln *who was the only son of Abraham Lincoln to survive into adulthood*, so that italicized phrase is nonessential; an appositive like this is set off by commas.

---

797. **C. neither Nathan nor Natasha wanted anything to do with Niles**

The conjunction *neither* requires the correlative *nor*.

---

798. **E. remain my favorites; they were**

In the absence of a coordinating conjunction (such as *for*), a semicolon is needed to separate the two independent clauses.

---

799. **B. The mayor of the little town of Bloomsburg likes to have lunch at the diner on Main Street.**

The right answer isn't Choice (A), because this is an informal reference to a mayor. If the mayor had been addressed directly or the title were connected to a name, such as Mayor Johnson, then capitalizing "mayor" would have been correct. Keep in mind that the Praxis does not include trick questions to confuse students; it bases answers on the most widely accepted principles of American English.

800. **B. Chen and Yvonne thought going to see their legislators was a capital idea.**

The word *capital* here means *excellent*. The word *capitol* refers to a building.

You might argue that because Chen and Yvonne are most likely going to a capitol building, the use of *capitol* makes a good pun; when taking the Praxis, however, you're better off focusing on standard English rather than amusements, tempting though they may be.

801. **D. Travelling along the crowded thoroughfare**

The use of *crowded, busy* here is redundant. Either *traveling* (American version) or *travelling* (British version) is acceptable.

802. **C. discovered a woman's gold bracelet and knew**

The adjective *gold* modifies *bracelet* and so needs to precede that word, not *woman's*; otherwise, the woman is gold.

803. **E. Why should our taxes go to old, harmful forms of energy? We should invest in new, environmentally friendly ones.**

One independent clause is a question and one is a statement, so they should be in two separate sentences.

Choice (C) is wrong because *our* in the first sentence doesn't agree with *you*, the assumed pronoun in the second sentence.

804. **D. but the hardest thing for Dona and me was when I lost my job**

The preposition *for* requires the object pronoun *me* (as in *the hardest thing for . . . me*).

805. **D. the bear, driven by hunger, ranged far down the slope, which led to the river**

The bear, not the bear's hunger, did the hibernating. The opening clause is a misplaced modifier.

The right answer isn't Choice (C), because the infinitive *(to eat)* and participle *(wandering)* are not parallel forms.

806. **C. between the Bolshoi and Kirov as to which ballet company is the more artistic**

The superlative *(most)* is used to compare more than two things; the comparative *(more)* is used to compare two.

807. **A. When she received her test results, Clarissa heartily congratulated herself for having studied so diligently.**

The original sentence is correct.

808. **E. The northern section of North Korea, far from being flat, is largely hilly and mountainous.**

The word *northern*, meaning simply a direction, is not a proper noun and so is not capitalized.

809. **C. anymore**

The word *anymore* is used in negative contexts: *It wasn't fun anymore.* In positive contexts, use *now* or *today.*

810. **A. It was raining and**

A comma is needed before the conjunction to separate the clauses.

811. **B. disco era**

As a specific period in time, *Disco Era* needs to be capitalized.

812. **B. reflects on**

The verb needs to be the plural *reflect* to agree with the plural subject (*Farah and Theo*).

813. **E. No error**

There is no error in this sentence.

814. **C. they're**

This error is a bit tricky. *They're* would be correct as opposed to *their* or *there*, but *they're* isn't the correct word to use here because it's a vague pronoun reference. Its noun (such as *graduates*) is missing.

815. **D. smooth**

The word needs to be the adverb *smoothly.*

816. **B. sugar,**

The two independent clauses here need to be separated by a semicolon.

Choice (D) is okay because "apple juice" can be hyphenated as a compound adjective here; however, the hyphen isn't necessary, because the adjective is clear.

817. **E. No error**

There are no errors in this sentence.

818. **A. badly**

As opposed to action verbs, verbs that have to do with states of being (*feel, look, smell*) are followed by adjectives (here, *bad*).

Choice (B) is fine because the subject is correctly placed right after its modifier. Choice (C) is okay because *extern* is the correct word. An *extern* usually works for a shorter time period than an intern, has fewer responsibilities, and receives less pay, if any.

819. **C. abide with**

The correct idiomatic phrase is *abide by*.

820. **B. overdue**

After the word *late*, *overdue* is redundant.

821. **A. was**

This verb should be plural to agree with the plural *members*.

Choice (D) is fine because the pronoun *them* may refer to *performances* (although it can't refer to *actors*'; it could refer to *actors* if that word were present).

822. **C. ourselves**

The word is the object of the preposition *to* and so requires the objective pronoun *us*.

823. B. were

When subjects are connected by *or, nor, either . . . or,* or *neither . . . nor,* the verb should agree with the part of the subject closer to the verb. Here, the verb *was* agrees with *I.*

824. E. No error

There are no errors in this sentence.

825. C. you

The pronoun should be in the first person *(I)* to agree with the pronoun at the beginning.

826. A. illusion

The word needed here is *allusion.* An *illusion* is a misconception.

827. D. voter's

There are many voters, so the apostrophe comes after the *s* to denote the plural possessive *(voters').*

828. B. a star pupil

The subject *(three)* requires the plural *(star pupils).*

829. E. The Olympic marmot, digging out a burrow before the snows come, hibernates through a seven-month winter.

The original is a sentence fragment because the *-ing* forms a verbal that doesn't function as the verb of the clause; the clause therefore doesn't have a verb and isn't independent. Choice (E) is the only answer choice that corrects this error.

830. C. Scientists in a submersible spotted a species of starfish, which they believed to be unidentified, crawling along the ocean floor.

This choice fixes both the problem of a misplaced modifier (the submersible was not likely to be crawling) and the problem of the pronoun *it,* which seems to refer to *submersible* (an object that can't believe or not believe). Given a choice between starfish crawling and a submersible or scientists crawling, go with the starfish, the most likely.

831. D. The play *The Mousetrap* is the longest-running play on record, having run continuously in London's West End since 1952.

> The appositive *The Mousetrap* here is restrictive (essential, referring to a specific play) and so is not set off by commas. *Continuously*, meaning *without interruption*, is the correct word. *Continually* means *steadily but with periods of interruption*.

832. B. Far from being boring, the men's relay race captured everyone's attention, and that's saying something.

> This choice fixes the two misplaced apostrophes and adds the necessary comma after the introductory phrase. *Men* is already plural, so the possessive is *men's*, and *everyone* is always singular, so the possessive is *everyone's*.

833. D. Just between you and me, the new governor is in for trouble; the legislative members are not known for being cooperative.

> There are no errors in this sentence.

834. C. The early blooming of the cherry blossoms disappointed the tourists, who had made their travel plans long ago.

> You can say *the cherry blossoms' early blooming*, but with *of*, possession is already indicated, and *blossoms*, a simple plural, does not take the apostrophe. The first comma is incorrect because it separates the subject (*blooming*) from the verb (*disappointed*). The word *there* is the wrong word.

> The comma after *tourists* may or may not be used. Without a comma, the clause refers only to those tourists who made plans long ago.

835. D. Tamara's and Don's colds, hers with accompanying aches and his with a runny nose, do not seem to have come from the same source.

> The original's two errors stem from one cause: There are two colds (Tamara's and Don's, each cold with a different symptom). Therefore, the subject is *colds*; the verb, *do*.

836. E. Even though the task seemed daunting, Josiah was determined to read the complete works of Milton.

> The original's only problem is one of redundancy. *Determined* and *in his mind* say the same thing, and *he thought* is unnecessary.

837. **A. In order to finish the assignment on time, Flora started working on it three weeks before it was due.**

> The sentence is correct. Choice (B) is wrong because it's a fragment, and Choice (C) is redundant. Choice (D) uses the pronoun *she* instead of a name, and *previously* in Choice (E) is poor word choice.

838. **B. Whether she said something positive, stated correctly or incorrectly, heard by one person or many, Inga thought she should say something.**

> The original lengthy clause is a fragment, lacking a main subject *(Inga)* and verb *(thought)*.

> The right answer is not Choice (D) because, although it's grammatically correct, it changes the meaning of the original sentence.

839. **E. It's easy to see why igneous rocks, made from the forces of heating and cooling, are found near volcanoes.**

> The original opens with a misplaced modifier, which needs to be next to the "igneous rocks" it modifies.

> The right answer is not Choice (D), because it changes the sense of the original.

840. **A. Harriet Tubman, who guided many African-Americans to freedom in the years before the Civil War, is perhaps the most famous of the "conductors" of the Underground Railroad.**

> This sentence is correct.

> Choice (B) is wrong because the commas are necessary to set off the appositive; the clause is not essential to identify Harriet Tubman. Choice (E) is wrong because the subject pronoun *who* is correct here.

841. **D. The book *The Two Towers* is the second of J.R.R. Tolkien's famous trilogy, *The Lord of the Rings*.**

> The appositive *The Two Towers* here is restrictive (essential, referring to a specific book) and so is not set off by commas.

842. **B. The marathoner, running for all she was worth, worried because her legs felt like lead and her breath was very hard to come by.**

> This choice fixes the fragment, which lacks a main verb.

843. **E. The old Dodge truck, far from being troublesome, provided Armand with steady transportation.**

There should be no comma between cumulative adjectives or between an adjective (*old*) and the noun (*Dodge*) that follows it.

The right answer is not Choice (B), because a comma is needed after *troublesome* to complete setting off the nonrestrictive, nonessential phrase.

844. **C. Clara didn't want to admit it, but she was really angry with the other women for not being supportive of her when she needed them to be.**

The adverb *really*, not the adjective *real*, is needed here.

845. **B. George marked the online textbook with the online highlighter until way past midnight.**

This version corrects the misplaced modifier (*with the online highlighter* needs to be close to *marked*, not *midnight*) as well as the use of the wrong word (*passed*).

846. **D. When Maury finally woke up and saw that it was 10:00 a.m., he knew he should have read the instructions for his new alarm.**

The use of *should of* is nonstandard for *should have* (sometimes written as the contraction *should've*).

847. **D. gloriously; Fiona knew**

The two independent clauses may be separated here by a comma plus a coordinating conjunction, by a semicolon — as in Choice (D) — or by a semicolon plus a conjunctive adverb followed by a comma.

848. **E. laid down the book**

The transitive verb *lay*, which means to put or place [something], has a simple past of *laid*. *Lay* is the simple past of the verb *lie*, which means to recline or rest.

Choice (C) is wrong because *it* requires *book* to be singular.

849. **C. to whet your appetite**

The idiom is *to whet* (or sharpen) *your appetite*.

850. B. "Why don't you have a go at it?" Sylvia finally said,

Commas are not used with question marks or exclamation points.

851. A. proceeded uncertainly into the Old Quarter

There are no errors in this section.

852. D. cooperated, they

Cooperated together is redundant, and the pronoun *they* is needed to refer to *workers*.

853. B. Hansel and Gretel could not find

The word *Because* makes the first clause dependent. With the semicolon, both the first and second clauses need to be independent.

854. A. , whose *Mythology* was read by countless students,

The original contains no errors.

855. A. continued weeding in the garden

The sentence is correct as written.

856. E. ; this bit of old wisdom is still true

The original is a run-on sentence. The easiest solution is to use a semi-colon to separate the two independent clauses.

Choice (D) is wrong because *this* has become a vague pronoun reference; it doesn't refer to any specific thing.

857. D. ; they caught everybody off-guard

The varied results . . . were describes more than one result, so the pronoun needs to be the plural *they*.

858. C. amazing quiet when the principal

The adverb *amazingly* is required, and the head of a school is the *principal*.

859. **A. Unknowingly**

Unknowingly is a misplaced modifier; it should come right before *tripped*, the verb it modifies.

860. **B. then**

What is needed here instead is the conjunction *than*.

861. **C. , it**

The two independent clauses may be joined by a semicolon or by a comma plus a conjunction.

862. **B. only**

This modifier needs to be next to what it modifies (*a few people*).

863. **E. No error**

There is no error in this sentence.

The right answer isn't Choice (C), because the verb agrees with the singular subject *neither [one]*. The right answer isn't Choice (D), because the pronoun is singular and in the objective case (the pronoun is the object of the preposition *for*). The pronoun's gender shows that the candidate is female. If the candidate were male, the pronoun would be *him*.

864. **C. , boarding the plane,**

This phrase is essential to the meaning (it specifies *which* people), so it shouldn't be set off with commas.

865. **C. not**

The placement of *not* here means that no totems are rare. The modifier (*not*) should be placed before *all*.

866. **A. site**

Site is a noun that usually means place. Here, the correct word is *cite*, a verb.

867. E. No error

There is no error in this sentence.

Choice (A) is fine because adjectives are used with verbs indicating states of being *(feel, look, smell)*. Choice (B) is okay because *lay* is the past tense of *lie*. Choice (C) is fine because the apostrophe is correctly placed for the plural.

868. A. Finding many clothes she liked

Paula, not the store, found clothes she liked, so the opening clause is a misplaced modifier.

869. D. their

The noun *every [one]* is singular, so the possessive adjective referring to *every* must be singular, such as *his or her*.

870. C. ,

A semicolon is needed here to separate the two independent clauses. Alternatively, you can add a conjunction *(because/for)* to go with the comma.

871. C. adopt

The verb needed here is *adapt*.

Choice (A) is fine because the use of lowercase is acceptable here; using lowercase suggests you mean the general theory rather than Darwin's specifically. Choice (B) is fine because the noun *species* may be singular or plural.

872. B. the zebra

The zebra is not crouched and silent; the lions are. *The zebra* needs to be moved and the sentence, reconstructed.

873. A. A fear of closed-in spaces

This modifier (an appositive) should be next to what it modifies, the word *claustrophobia*.

874. D. ;

The semicolon should separate two independent clauses, but there's only one independent clause here. The second part of the sentence is missing a subject *(they)* as well as a verb *(are)*.

875. E. No error

There is no error in this sentence.

876. C. even

This modifier should be next to the word it modifies, *one*.

877. B. if possible

This placement causes an awkward splitting of the infinitive *to stretch*.

The right answer is not Choice (C), because the verb *warm up* has no hyphen. When used as an adjective, as in *warm-up room*, the word is hyphenated. Most sources accept the hyphenation of the noun *(a good warm-up)*.

878. A. who's

The correct word to use here is *whose* (not the contraction for *who is*).

879. D. gave the award to both Ivan and me

Myself is wrong because it's a reflexive pronoun, and the objective pronoun *me* (the object of the preposition *to*) is required. (Check: *gave the award to . . . me.*)

Choice (C) isn't the best choice, because putting others first is customary.

880. B. ; this spreading of a disease by mosquito bites is true regarding yellow fever, too

The pronoun *this* is vague because the noun it refers to *(spreading)* is missing.

881. E. , all but a few of the students had left

The students' leaving occurred before the action of the professor's arrival, so instead of the past tense (as in *arrived*), the past perfect is used *(had left)*.

882. **C. Carmen wants to be mayor when she grows up;**

The first verb should be in the present tense *(wants)* to agree with the other verbs. A professional title is capitalized only when it appears before a name or refers to a specific person.

883. **B. were later sold to the bigger of the two**

There are two foals, so the verb needs to be the plural *were. Biggest* is used to compare more than two things; because there are only two farms, *bigger* is correct.

884. **A. Each type of print medium,**

Each [one] type is singular, so the singular *medium* is used. The comma is the first of a pair used to set off the phrase *including books, magazines, and newspapers.*

885. **D. Luann respectfully submitted her opinion**

The word *respectively* is mistakenly used instead of *respectfully.* The opinion is Luann's, so the possessive adjective should be *her.*

886. **C. , Willa felt the sleet drip inside her collar**

In the original sentence, the opening clause is a misplaced (dangling) modifier. *Willa* needs to be next to the clause *not having dressed for the weather.*

887. **B. You know you're in trouble when heat rises**

Your should be *you're,* the contraction for *you are.* The verb *raise* means to lift [something] up. The verb *rise* means to go up.

888. **C. "It's more than I myself can cope with,"**

The contraction *it's* (for *it is*), not the possessive adjective *its,* is needed here. The use of the intensive *myself* is correct; it emphasizes (intensifies) the *I.*

Choice (E) is wrong because the comma is missing and because taking out *myself* changes the original effect.

889. **E. The teachers wanted to provide the students with hands-on experience;**

Both clauses here (separated by the semicolon) need to be independent, but the first clause is dependent; it's missing its main subject and verb.

The right answer is not Choice (B), because *hands on* is hyphenated when used as an adjective (it modifies *experience*).

890. **A. Beginning to lose patience, Sean started pacing;**

The verb *lose* and the noun *patience* are correct. The semicolon is needed to separate the two independent clauses.

891. **B. Quinn was concerned with the essentials:**

Basic essentials is redundant. A colon may be used before a list.

Choice (D) is wrong because now the main verb is missing.

892. **C. Of all the lesser-known Greek gods,**

Gods should not be capitalized, because it refers to gods in general. *Lesser-known* is an adjective, so it's hyphenated.

893. **A. farther down the road, so they talked**

Farther should be used here because it refers to physical distances. A comma is used with a coordinating conjunction (*so*) to separate two independent clauses.

894. **E. ; she could hardly hear the professor**

Hardly is considered negative, so *couldn't hardly* is a double negative.

895. **B. a 180-pound, six-foot-tall man with a beard**

The beard doesn't weigh 180 pounds; the man does, so the modifier needs to be moved. The use of *weighing* in Choice (D) is unnecessary.

896. D. Betsy Ross, who had an upholstery business, made extra money during the Revolutionary War

There wasn't more than one Betsy Ross who was *famous for having sewn the first American flag,* so the phrase *who had an upholstery business* is an appositive; it's nonessential (not needed to distinguish this Betsy from other people named Betsy Ross), so the phrase is set off by commas.

897. C. Some track athletes from the country of Jamaica train

The plural subject *athletes* requires the plural verb *train.* The phrase *from the country of Jamaica* is essential, so it isn't set off by commas.

898. E. ; not one of the solutions has been chosen by

Not one is singular, so it takes the singular *has.*

899. A. All the added work at the end of the semester had a strange effect on the new teacher: she found more discipline than she thought she had.

Effect is a noun, and *affect* is a verb. Both clauses are independent, so a comma alone isn't enough to separate them.

900. B. Studies showed that vehicles drove too fast along the busy street, so traffic engineers recommended adding a traffic light.

Choice (A) is incorrect because the verb tenses do not agree. *Show* is present tense, while *drove* and *recommended* are past tense. Choice (C) is incorrect because *are* would need to help *driving* for the sentence to flow better.

901. D. Xavier and Tony spent three hours trying to resolve the problem, but they couldn't agree, however they looked at the situation.

However here means *no matter how,* and it's part of a dependent clause; therefore, *however* shouldn't be preceded by a semicolon. The sentence is written in the third person, so *you* (second person) should be *they.*

902. C. The ability to initiate a national revenue bill is one of the many things that set the House apart from the Senate.

Many things set the House apart from the Senate, so the antecedent of *that* is *things,* and the plural *set* is required.

903. E. Darla had ordered tulip bulbs from a well-known farm; she read the package many times but couldn't figure out how deeply the growers wanted her to plant the bulbs.

They is vague; it doesn't have a specific antecedent. The right answer uses *growers*, a specific noun.

904. D. Trevor reflected that it was extremely difficult for Hannah and him to come to terms with their new responsibilities as first-time parents.

The preposition *for* requires the object pronoun *him*.

905. D. An adult Stegosaurus weighed over three tons and was 26–30 feet long; amazingly, its brain was the size of a walnut.

A semicolon is required to separate the two independent clauses. The possessive adjective *its* is correct. In science, the genus name is capitalized and the species is not, and the whole name is in italics, as in *Tyrannosaurus rex.*

906. C. According to the American Diabetes Association, common symptoms of type 1 diabetes can include the following: extreme thirst, extreme hunger, blurry vision, and cuts or bruises that are slow to heal.

Items in a series should be in parallel grammatical structure; otherwise, the phrasing is awkward. At one time the *type* in *type 1 diabetes* was capitalized, but conventions have changed, and it no longer needs to be.

Choice (B) is wrong because the colon, not the semicolon, is used to introduce a list.

907. A. When George, hands covered in chalk dusk, finished demonstrating the equation on the old blackboard, he ran his hands through his hair; using the old teaching tools had turned him into an old man.

The original sentence is correct.

908. E. For most of his life, Byron had found it easier to explain his actions in writing than to talk to people directly.

The two things being compared (*to explain, talking*) should be in parallel grammatical structure (*to explain, to talk*).

909. **C. ;**

You need a semicolon before the word *additionally*, which is acting as a conjunctive adverb connecting two independent clauses.

910. **A. complement**

Complement means something that completes; the word needed here is *compliment*, something flattering.

911. **D. likes**

The main verb needs to be the plural *like* to agree with the plural subject (*Chico and Louisa*).

912. **A. , careening down the hallway**

The clause, a misplaced (dangling) modifier, should be *careened down the hallway*, and it should not be preceded by a comma.

913. **B. whose**

The possessive pronoun *whose* is incorrect here; the sentence needs *who's*, the contraction for *who is*.

914. **C. parks'**

This should be the simple plural *parks* (no apostrophe), as it's the object of the preposition *to* (and not possessive).

915. **D. her**

The subject pronoun is needed here: *older than she [was]*.

916. **B. frayed**

This modifier is misplaced; it's supposed to modify *dress*, not *friend*.

917. **E. No error**

There are no errors in this sentence.

In Choice (C), *Councilman* is connected to a name and so is correctly capitalized.

918. E. No error

As opposed to action verbs, verbs that have to do with states of being (*feel, look, smell*) are followed by adjectives. Here, *well* is an adjective that means in good health.

919. B. Take it out.

The topic is the issue of using tent cities to house the homeless. Sentence 1 provides a general introduction to the issue, but Sentence 2 is off topic — the issue is not cities ignoring the problem.

920. D. methods, including

The phrase "One of these methods" is redundant. You can best revise it by deleting and replacing it with a comma plus *including*.

Choice (A) is not as economical or as direct as Choice (D).

921. C. *tent city*

Tent city is presented as a term, so it should be in italics here (where it's presented and defined).

Choice (B) is wordy, and in Choice (E), "argument starting" is redundant to "controversial."

922. B. For all the problems it may solve, though, a tent city should not be considered a permanent solution.

Choice (B) presents a clear statement of the essay writer's position.

Choice (A) basically restates the opening sentence in question format and doesn't present the essay's position. Choices (C) and (D) are redundant to sentences 3 and 4. Choice (E) is way off task, off the focus of tent cities.

923. B. Take it out.

The phrase *you may ask* is too conversational (and thus informal) for academic writing, and the question isn't economical. The next sentence implies the question and provides the answer.

924. D. using their own tarps and tents

The correct word is the possessive adjective *their*; otherwise, the phrase is fine, presenting important visual details.

925. **A. However,**

After presenting a rather clear problem with a tent city, the essay writer is about to shift to problems that are not so obvious. The word *however* is perfect to indicate this shift.

Choices (C) and (D) indicate a shift like *however* does, but both suggest opposition more than an inclusive shift.

926. **C. Climate is**

Specifying the subject does away with the vague pronoun reference here.

Choice (E) is repetitive and not as clear as Choice (C).

927. **E. To begin with,**

This phrase tells the reader that this problem is the first in a group of related issues (that is, those not about climate).

Choice (A) indicates something already stated, but the first problem/reason hasn't been stated yet. Choice (B) is used to go into detail about something already stated. Similarly, Choice (C) is used to continue a thought. Choice (D) suggests that climate problems are a key point when, in fact, they are not, as the ensuing discussion illustrates.

928. **A. [Leave it as it is.]**

The phrase is clear and economical. Furthermore, it reinforces the essay's position regarding the need for permanent housing.

929. **C. People, not to mention children, living essentially outside are**

Specifying the subject does away with the vague pronoun reference here.

Choice (D) doesn't specifically represent or connect to the preceding sentence; additionally, it's off task, as the essay isn't about the scope of the homelessness problem. Choice (E) is wrong because it's not government support that's causing the concerns; the problem is that people are living essentially outside.

930. **E. Insert an explanation and examples.**

The reason stated is a major one, and it needs to be explained and supported by at least two significant details or examples.

931. **D. In spite of these concerns, some people feel that tent cities should be allowed because at least the homeless are off the street.**

This version thoughtfully connects the sentences coming before and after it and replaces the informal "okay" with "allowed."

Choice (C) is wrong because *conversely* doesn't accurately connect public health and safety concerns with the opposing view of allowing tent cities. Here, *conversely* suggests that the opposing view is against public health and safety concerns. Choice (E) is wrong because it doesn't alert the reader to the major shift in focus from the reasons against tent cities to the reasons for them.

932. **C. street, where, for one thing**

This revision eliminates the repetition (they're *off the street*) and helps make the essay's organization clear by presenting a point (*first of all*).

933. **D. Insert details and examples.**

The reason stated is a major one, and it needs at least two significant details or examples to support it.

934. **B. Notwithstanding their problems, tent cities are better than nothing and should be maintained until permanent housing can be arranged.**

Sentence 17 represents the essay's position and conclusion — it needs to be presented and recognizable as such. Choice (B) accomplishes this goal the best.

Choice (A) is missing a transition at the beginning to clearly establish the essay's position as it involves the main points. Choice (C) is wrong because *this* is vague. Using the word *indeed* here for emphasis is ineffective because with the vagueness of *this*, there's nothing specific to emphasize. Choice (D)'s change in tone does alert the reader to the major shift in focus (that is, to the conclusion), but the tone is new and jarring at this point. Furthermore, Choice (D) is not better than Choice (B) in establishing the essay's position. The right answer is not Choice (E). Although *indeed* is effective here, this version lacks a connection to clearly establish the essay's position as it involves the main points.

935. **D. Take out the first "you" and replace it with "your."**

The sentence provides a nice opening hook, drawing the reader in with a question that presents an essential dilemma of the topic. Choice (D) provides the required possessive form.

936. **B. electricity; however, this choice**

The phrase *choosing electricity* is redundant, and *however* is a good replacement for *but*. Choice (B) is economical and clear.

Choices (A) and (E) are wrong because *this* is a vague pronoun. Although *unfortunately* is a good choice because it clearly suggests the essay writer's opinion, Choice (C) is wrong because a semicolon is needed before *unfortunately*. Choice (D) is as redundant as the original.

937. **C. Some people accept this loss as a trade-off for the hydroelectric power generated by**

The original version contains a vague pronoun reference *(this)* as well as an incompletely explained detail *(power)* and is missing a connection between hydroelectric power and the loss *(as a trade-off)*. Choice (C) addresses all these issues via a clear statement.

Choice (B) is incorrect because the loss is a result not of the hydroelectric power but of the dams. In Choice (D), the word *believe* suggests the salmon loss isn't actually an effect of the dams, which takes the essay off focus, introducing an issue it doesn't address anywhere else. In Choice (E), the word *simply* reduces the problem to one that must simply be accepted, working against the essay writer's position, which is not to simply accept the loss of salmon.

938. **E. Change "its" to "it's."**

The sentence provides a clear statement of the author's position regarding the two issues. All that's needed is to correct the possessive adjective *its* to the contraction *it's*.

939. **B. To begin with,**

Choice (B) connects the introduction to the body paragraphs by alerting the reader that the reasons behind the author's position are coming.

Choice (A) is incorrect because an alternate position isn't being presented. Choice (C) suggests that what follows will have a different effect from what's been previously discussed, which isn't the case; what follows is the beginning of the main discussion. Choice (D) is wrong because the upcoming point is the first of the main points being made, not an additional one. Choice (E) doesn't give the essay the organizational support that Choice (B) does.

940. **A. Leave it as it is.**

Everybody may know there are ways to cut back on electricity, but not everybody will know all or many of the ways. Sentence 7 provides a clearly stated supporting detail that adds to the discussion.

Choice (C) is more awkward than the original. Choice (D) is wrong because the sentence is not an example of something introduced in the preceding sentence (everybody knowing there are ways to cut back on electricity) but a further thought regarding the matter. Choice (E) is unnecessary and likely wrong because it suggests that smaller cities' websites don't have such suggestions.

941. **D. lower; if**

A more complicated wording isn't necessary. This choice is the clearest and the most economical.

942. **A. An added benefit of this method of saving electricity is that**

This transition not only connects the two sentences but also reinforces the part of the thesis pertaining to the benefits of saving electricity.

Choice (E) is incorrect because the thesis is about saving electricity, not wearing a sweater, so Choice (A) is a better option.

943. **C. Regarding the best interests of the salmon**

This transition not only acknowledges the beginning of the paragraph but also makes the connection to the other half of the thesis.

944. **E. Insert "reach the area where they" between** *can't* **and** *lay.*

This phrase makes it clear to the reader, who may have no knowledge of the situation, what the specific problem is.

945. **A. [Leave it as it is.]**

This brief independent clause connects the explanation to the thesis: If salmon numbers decrease, it's not a *win* situation.

Choice (B) lacks the strength and effectiveness of the simple declarative independent clause; Choice (A) has a stronger construction and thus offers stronger support. In Choice (C), the word *unfortunately* works to soften the blow of the loss, which weakens the thesis. Choice (D) is true and direct, but it doesn't have the scope regarding the wild salmon population that Choice (A) does. Choice (E) overstates the situation. The loss of a salmon run doesn't doom the entire species. Exaggerating a point — stretching the truth — doesn't help a thesis but in effect casts doubt on it.

---

946.   **B. It's not just people who are affected by this dwindling food source.**

This sentence is a thoughtful connection, bridging the third and fourth paragraphs in a clear and economical way; additionally, it offers clearly implied support of the thesis (a *dwindling food source* is not a *win*).

The right answer isn't Choice (A), because in focusing on being economical, it sacrifices a clear connection and support for the thesis. Economy isn't about the number of words per se but about what each word contributes.

---

947.   **C. Insert "for sustenance" at the end.**

This brief addition emphasizes an important point and offers an explanation for readers who may not understand or have knowledge of the food web.

The right answer isn't Choice (A), (B), or (D), because they lack the improvement of Choice (C). Additionally, Choice (B) is incorrect because "animals" is a smaller and less accurate classification than "organisms." Choice (D) is incorrect because it suggests that what follows is another reason, but it's the same. Choice (E) does the same things as Choice (C), but the construction is awkward.

---

948.   **E. As much dramatic film from the wild has shown,**

This choice provides not only a transition from the reason to the example but also sentence variety; furthermore, its use of "dramatic" and "wild" are suggestive of the thesis, as is the fact that there's "much" evidence.

Choices (A) and (D) aren't as effective overall as Choice (E), and Choice (B) isn't as specific. Choice (C) is wrong because, in general, it's not a good idea to suggest the audience is ignorant of something, and this choice doesn't support the thesis as well as Choice (E) does.

---

949.   **D. Replace it with "After the salmon spawn, they die."**

Reversing the order provides additional sentence variety.

950. **C. The decaying salmon feed scavengers such as raccoons and eagles.**

Adding the detail about raccoons and eagles helps support the point that many organisms benefit from wild salmon.

The right answer isn't Choice (A) or (B), because "decaying" is important to the end of the sentence — the plants and trees use the nutrients that leave the salmon as they decay. Choices (D) and (E) are redundant; if the salmon are decaying, they're dead.

951. **A. Leave it as it is.**

The tone is not out of place here, as it echoes the "save the salmon" of the thesis statement (sentence 5). Furthermore, the conclusion has already brought closure by restating the thesis and main points; thus, the writer is free to drive his or her point home with the emotional appeal of sentence 22.

Choice (B) is incorrect because removing the sentence would deprive the essay of its emotional call. Choice (D) isn't the best answer, because the sentence is expressly a call *for* the wild.

952. **C. While there are some benefits to genetically altering food, it is unnatural and unhealthy.**

Choice (C) makes the nature of the controversy clearer and improves the wording at the end of the original sentence.

The right answer isn't Choice (A), because although it does state a position, the position isn't as clear as in Choice (C). Choice (B) is wrong because it changes the thesis from a strong comment ("unnatural and unhealthy") to a weaker one ("should not be considered a permanent solution"); "unless they have to" and "not . . . a permanent solution" do not have the same meaning. Choices (D) and (E) don't state the position (embrace the controversy) as completely as Choice (C). Furthermore, the second clause of Choice (D) is awkward, and the style of Choice (E) is too simplistic for academic audiences.

953. **D. genetically altered foods may be a good solution for you**

This choice makes the tone more academic and clarifies the point.

Choices (A) and (B) are nonacademic in style and possibly untrue as well. Choices (C) and (E) change the focus from health and hunger to education and allergies.

954. **E. Add an explanation and at least one supporting detail.**

Sentence 2 makes a point that needs to be supported with an explanation and example.

955. **A. Start a new paragraph.**

Sentences 2 and 3 have different topics and so should be in separate paragraphs.

Neither Choice (B) nor Choice (E) is necessary so near the thesis statement (sentence 1). Choice (C) is wrong because GMOs have already been explained. Choice (D) is off topic.

956. **B. [Take it out.]**

The phrase is redundant to "many believe." It also contains a grammatical error in the pronoun reference: The "they" of the last clause incorrectly refers to "minds."

Choice (D) is redundant as well as snide (due to the italics), which is not an appropriate tone.

957. **A. Leave it as it is.**

Sentence 4 is clear and smooth, and it provides a good explanation and example for the reason stated in sentence 3.

Choice (C) is wrong because it suggests something different will follow, but what actually follows is an example ("drought-resistant" is equivalent to "need less water"). Choice (D) is wrong because there's no need to define *drought* — the replacement is wordy and not as academic. Choice (E) is less specific and therefore less supportive than the original.

958. **D. that would otherwise attack and damage the crops**

"Attack and damage" is more descriptive and to the point than "attack," because insects might attack a GMO without damaging it. Furthermore, with the sentence as written, "them" refers to "organisms," so "them" needs to be replaced with "the crops."

The right answer isn't Choice (A), (B), or (C), because "them" is incorrect. As for Choices (B) and (C), although most writers prefer *that* for an essential (restrictive) clause, *which* isn't wrong. Choice (E) is incorrect because "severely harm" isn't as specific as "attack and damage" in Choice (D), the better choice.

959. **C. Add an explanation and at least one supporting detail.**

Sentence 5 makes a point that needs to be supported with an explanation and example, similar to the explanation and example of sentence 4.

The right answer is not Choice (A), (B), (D), or (E), because what is needed is an explanation and an example following the statement of a reason (point).

960. **B. An additional benefit is that**

This phrase makes a more thoughtful connection than the original. "An additional benefit" refers to the fact that this part of the essay's discussion involves the benefits of GMOs.

Choice (A), "in other words," is used to explain something already stated, but the following benefit/reason hasn't been stated yet. Choice (C), "indeed," is used to go into detail about something already stated. Choice (D) isn't as thoughtful of a connection as Choice (B). Choice (E) is wrong because such a phrase should follow a reason, not be part of one.

961. **E. can be spicier**

The proper construction, parallel to *sweeter*, is *spicier*. Additionally, most peppers are spicy to begin with, so altering them (per this discussion) would make them spic*ier*.

962. **B. And for making food generally tastier, a genetically altered variety of Brussels sprouts might be popular.**

This version states the point (food that is tastier) and supplies the example (altered Brussels sprouts). Though the essay is serious, the humor in this statement is subtle and not out of place.

Choice (A) is incorrect because it doesn't state the point. The right answer isn't Choice (C) or (D), because Choice (C) needs the comparative form of *tasty* and neither choice states the point as directly as Choice (B). Choice (E) shifts the verb tense; furthermore, the tone of Choice (B) is more in keeping with the rest of the essay than Choice (E) or the original is.

963. **A. minerals to**

This revision eliminates the repetition ("they can be added").

964. **E. These alterations to food can help ensure that people receive the essential nutrition they might not otherwise get.**

This version corrects the pronoun-antecedent problem of the initial "they" (which seems to refer to "poor countries," though the subject should refer to "adding vitamins and minerals"). Choice (E) also eliminates the redundancy created by "they need" after "essential."

Choices (B) and (C) are wrong because the initial "they" in the original sentence refers more specifically to food alterations than to "benefits," Choice (B), or to "poor countries," Choice (C). The countries aren't ensuring nutrition; the genetically altered food is.

965. **C. In spite of these benefits, there are fundamental reasons to avoid GMOs.**

This revision eliminates the redundancy (*basic* means *fundamental*) and helps clarify the essay's organization by providing a pivotal and clear connection.

Choice (B) is incorrect because its connection is weak. Choice (D) is wrong because "in addition" is meant to introduce another reason under the same main point, but the second and opposite point is being addressed here. Choice (E) is wrong because the change to third person ("one") disrupts the style, as does the use of the cliché ("extol the virtues of").

966. **D. State a reason.**

Sentence 12 says there are reasons to avoid GMOs, and sentence 13 presents details. Between these two sentences must come one of the reasons to avoid GMOs, a reason supported by the details of sentence 13. Such a reason might be the unknown long-term effects of consuming GMOs in relation to the high percentages of GMOs in soy, canola, and corn.

The right answer isn't Choice (A), (B), (C), or (E), because restating the thesis, beginning a new paragraph and starting the conclusion, making a connection with an earlier point, or inserting details and examples won't clarify the significance of the details of sentence 13.

967. **B. Take it out.**

The topic is reasons to avoid GMOs. Lack of awareness of GMOs isn't a reason to avoid them (in fact, people can't know to avoid them if they're not aware of them), so it's off topic.

968. **A. Add reasons and supporting details to develop the main point stated in sentence 12.**

Sentence 12 presents the essay's second main point, which needs to be supported by at least two reasons; those reasons then need their own explanations and examples in order to fully support the latter half of the thesis. Such additions would involve one or two more paragraphs before the final and concluding one. This lack of development is an indication the writer may have run out of time. Creating an initial rough outline with both main points and supporting reasons could have helped the writer.

969. **C. Change "affects" to "effects."**

Sentence 16 is a good restatement of the thesis; the only correction is changing the verb *affects* to the noun *effects*.

Chapter 4

970. **B. Ask questions, start search, settle on topic, find sources.**

Begin by asking the types of questions you want to answer. Start a wide search, settle on a specific topic, and then find sources for that topic.

971. **D. ProQuest**

As its name suggests, ProQuest is a general database; it provides content on a global scope.

PubMed and PsycINFO are specific to the medical field, ERIC is an educational database, and Web of Science is a science database.

972. **C. APA and MLA**

The format of the American Psychological Association (APA), used in the sciences, and that of the Modern Language Association (MLA), used in the humanities, are the two most common styles in American schools. A third format is Chicago style, which is used in history.

IGA stands for Independent Grocers Alliance, URL stands for uniform resource locator, MRI stands for magnetic resonance imaging, CWA stands for Civil Works Administration, and SLR stands for single lens reflex.

973. **B. It allows the student to examine original research on a topic.**

> The essential definition of a *primary source* consists of the phrase *original research.* Primary sources include journals, letters, speeches, interviews, photographs, and films.

> Choices (A), (D), and (E) describe research strategies, and Choice (C) describes secondary sources.

974. **B. The title of a newspaper**

> A title that represents a whole work, such as a newspaper, appears in italics, whereas a title that represents a part of a whole appears in quotation marks.

> The right answer isn't Choice (A), (C), (D), or (E), because each one represents a part of a complete work (a single poem being part of a book of poems).

975. **D. cf.**

> This abbreviation stands for the Latin *confer*, as in "compare to."

> *N.B.* stands for *note bene*, or "note well," and is used to call readers' attention to a particular fact. *Ibid.* stands for *ibidem* and means "in the same place"; it refers to the work previously cited. *Sic* means *thus* and is put in italics and bracketed (following APA style) to indicate an error or unusual usage in a direct quotation. *Et al.* stands for *et alii*, or "and others"; it's used following the first author's name to save space when a work has (usually) four or more authors.

976. **A. Make the topic narrower and more interesting.**

> Helping alcoholics is a significant topic, but it's broad and bland. A better topic would focus on one type of program and its success, such as "How successful are outpatient rehabilitation programs in helping alcoholics?"

977. **C. the volume number of the article**

> The volume number will be necessary after you've settled on a topic and need to find sources, but the initial *scanning* phase is a wide, general search.

Choices (A), (B), (D), and (E) all help with narrowing the topic. Choice (A) is a clue about relevancy, Choice (B) tells you how current the information is, Choice (D) can tell you whether the information is scholarly, and Choice (E) can tell you how deep the coverage is likely to be.

978. E. Mistakes are more likely to be made in a secondhand report.

Though unintentional, mistakes do happen when data is being copied and pasted or, worse, retyped.

Choice (A) is incorrect because either data is relevant to your topic, or it isn't — where the data appears doesn't affect its relevance. Similarly, Choice (B) is wrong because either the data was obtained in a scholarly (scientific) manner, or it wasn't. Although a peer-reviewed journal is more likely than other publications to have considered and accepted an article's data, where the data appears doesn't affect its validity. Choice (C) is incorrect because a standard college library will have both primary and secondary sources in its stacks and its many databases. Furthermore, just because the library doesn't have a source doesn't mean you should give up trying to find it. Choice (D) is incorrect because a primary source may prove harder to find than a secondary source. In any event, ease of location shouldn't be a criterion for finding data.

979. A. researchers can more easily find sources through author or title searches via a search engine

Web addresses (URLs) can change, and an author or title may appear in more than one database, so to locate the source a writer used — which is the primary purpose of the Works Cited page — having the URL isn't that helpful.

Choice (B) is wrong because looking up someone else's sources can *save* time, as it may lead to valuable sources for your own research. Choice (C) is wrong because the standards are the same for all sources. Choice (D) is wrong because a Works Cited page is still mandatory. Choice (E) is wrong because standards for Works Cited are not based on trust.

980. C. no date

Use *n.d.* in place of the year for an APA citation when no date is listed for the source. Only the date (year) belongs in the second part of a citation, and the absence of a date must be acknowledged.

981.   E. use a paragraph number

At the end of a direct quotation, for example, you would put a parenthetical reference such as *(para. 5)* to show where in the article the quotation occurs.

Choice (A) is incorrect because although the MLA allows for such an omission, the APA does not. Choice (B) is wrong because the APA requires a paragraph reference when no page number exists. Choice (C) is wrong because the absence of page numbers is no reason to discard a vital source; the APA provides for such situations. Choice (D) is wrong because *n.p.* stands for *no publisher*.

982.   D. assess its argument for possible inclusion as an in-text reference

There are points of disagreement in almost all topics worth writing about. Such disagreement should be weighed and welcomed — it often becomes an integral part of not only the discussion but also the thesis.

The right answer isn't Choice (A), because the source should be used (if it's reputable and relevant), not discarded. Choice (B) is wrong because you'll want to use the source for purposes of comparison in the paper, not just mention the source as something that informed your thinking on the topic. Choice (C) is wrong because no source should be automatically eliminated, no matter how radical its position; its argument should be carefully assessed. Choice (E) is wrong because a thesis should change as (relevant and credible) source material does.

983.   C. reliability and relevance

Skimming for sources' reliability and relevance will let you quickly amass sources that are scholarly and that pertain to your topic.

The right answer isn't Choice (A) or (D), because timeliness isn't as initially important as reliability or relevance. The right answer isn't Choice (B) or (E), because neither nationality nor association should be a criterion for exclusion (or inclusion).

984.   D. author, sponsor, audience and purpose, and age

Is there an author? If so, what are his or her credentials? Is there a commercial sponsor, such as for a .com page? Is a specific audience being targeted, and if so, for what purpose? (For example, is the site aimed at a certain group for marketing purposes?) And lastly, how current is the site? Is its material dated and thus potentially no longer credible?

Title, graphics, and length are not criteria affecting a site's reliability.

985.

B. the website of a major bank

Researchers should use unbiased sources, or at least those that have striven for objectivity. A bank isn't likely to readily admit any complicity in something so widespread and devastating (not to mention litigious) as the 2007–8 financial crisis.

Choice (A) is wrong because a retired bank manager may feel able to be honest about his or her role in how questionable lending practices played a part in the crisis. The right answer isn't Choice (C), because such a credible, relevant source would most likely prove very useful. Choice (D) is wrong because such stations seek to present the news objectively. The right answer isn't Choice (E), because although the lender may not be free of bias, he or she, in agreeing to be interviewed, will at least provide an inside opinion. Such a primary source may be very useful.

986.

C. Read and take notes, write working thesis and outline, write draft, revise with more research (if necessary).

After extensive reading and note-taking, derive a working thesis and draft an outline. Then write the rough draft. Finally, determine whether more research is needed and include that in the revised draft.

Choice (A) is wrong because you don't want to write the draft before you have a working thesis and an outline. Even though both the thesis and the outline may change, having them first will make writing the rough draft much, much easier, and it will result in a more focused product.

987.

D. Consult a print index.

Works that predate the electronic age aren't always found in electronic databases. For example, a print index such as the *Agricultural Index* would contain articles about agriculture.

Choice (D) is a better, more direct strategy than consulting your professor. The right answer isn't Choice (E), because you'll likely need to consult a print index for historical research no matter what the topic.

988.

E. The journalistic credentials of the author

Having journalism credentials doesn't make an author an expert in the field (except possibly the field of journalism). All the other clues are indicators of an article's scholarly nature.

Choices (A) and (B) indicate careful and accurately credited research. The right answer isn't Choice (C), because scholarly articles are usually written by academics or scientists. Choice (D) is incorrect because the language in a scholarly article is much more likely to be formal than informal.

Correspondingly, regarding the salmon, it's healthier for them to be able to swim upstream! If there's a dam in the way, the salmon can't reach the area where they lay and fertilize their eggs. The salmon run — the path salmon take from when they hatch, swim out to the ocean, and return to spawn — is basically destroyed. Another route for the wild salmon are lost, and their numbers decrease.

It's not just the salmon that lose out. Many living things depend on the returning salmon for food. For example, bears catch the salmon live. The salmon die after they spawn. The decaying salmon feed such animals as raccoons and eagles as well as provide food for plants and trees along the stream.

Don't put up dams where the salmon run. If there is such a dam, take it down and find ways to save energy. Long live the wild salmon!

Score and Analysis

The following rubric shows why this essay would receive a score of 5:

- **Task:** The essay addresses all the points in the prompt and does so in a manner appropriate for an academic audience.

- **Focus:** The essay begins with a question, effectively drawing the reader in. The introduction explains the situation and includes the position statement. The body paragraphs stay focused on the issue, though the author does need to show how saving electricity relates to providing electricity. The conclusion restates the thesis and main points and ends with an emotional appeal appropriate to the tone of the position statement.

- **Organization:** Each of the body paragraphs contains and supports a main point. Transitions between and within the paragraphs are sufficient but lacking in depth. For example, "Additionally" in the second paragraph would be better as "An added benefit of saving electricity here is that . . ." Similarly, "Correspondingly, regarding the salmon," at the start of paragraph 3, does little beyond what's necessary.

- **Support:** The body paragraphs contain pertinent details and examples. However, the "route" in paragraph 3 needs more explanation, and the writer could mention people using salmon for food, particularly the native tribes who rely on the wild salmon for sustenance, not to mention tradition.

- **Language:** The tone is appropriate for the academic audience. The emotional appeal doesn't override the essay's logic. The language is adequate but doesn't contain the vocabulary of an essay at the 6 level. Similarly, sentences are mostly economical and varied but not at the 6 level.

- **Grammar, Usage, and Mechanics:** The essay has only a few grammar, usage, and mechanical errors. In paragraph 1, "you" should be "your," and "its" should be "it's." In paragraph 2, there should be a semicolon between "lower" and "if." In paragraph 3, "are" should be "is."

992.

Sample Response

While there are some benefits to it, genetically altering food is unnatural and unhealthy and should be considered a last resort.

True, if you're starving, genetically altered foods may be a good solution for you. Genetically modified organisms (GMOs) may provide the best or only nourishment available. Additionally, some GMOs provide higher crop yields and thus more food for more people in developing countries.

Many people believe that GMOs are the best choice because they can be made drought-resistant. In California, for example, where drought has been a problem for many years now, crops that need less water can be very helpful. Additionally, crops can be made resistant to insects or other organisms that would otherwise severely harm the crops. In the United States, two heavily grown crops that sustain such damage are corn and cotton. GMO varieties could cut down on loses.

An additional benefit is that some GMOs can be made sweeter, such as corn or tomatoes. Foods such as peppers can be spicier. And for making food generally tastier, a genetically altered variety of Brussels sprouts might be popular. A final benefit involves adding vitamins and minerals to crops in poor countries. These alterations to food can help ensure that people receive the essential nutrition they might not otherwise get.

In spite of these benefits, there are fundamental reasons to avoid GMOs. The long-term effects of consuming GMOs are unknown, and yet high percentages of them exist in soy, canola, and corn. Data from the Food and Drug Administration shows that 90% of the soy and canola products in the U.S. are genetically altered, and 85% of the corn is. Such GMO foods have been shown to increase food-based allergies. And if a person becomes allergic to GMO corn, for example, and that crop is fed to livestock, then the person can become allergic to the meat. In addition to causing allergies, GMOs may cause intestinal damage. Such has been the case in studies involving animals.

In addition to harming animals and humans, GMOs can cause damage to the environment. A natural, organic plant grows naturally in and as a part of its surroundings. But when a plant is altered, the environment does not necessarily support it, and providing extra support to the plant can upset the natural balance of nature.

GMOs may make sense in some places, but there are unhealthy effects on living things and their environments associated with these altered foods. Care should be taken when deciding to consume or grow GMOs.

Score and Analysis

The following rubric shows why this essay would receive a score of 6:

- **Task:** The essay fully addresses the benefits and hazards mentioned in the prompt and does so in a manner appropriate for an academic audience.

- **Focus:** The essay begins with a clear position statement. Each one of the body (middle) paragraphs pertains to and references a benefit or hazard of GMOs, and the conclusion summarizes the main points and restates the thesis.

- **Organization:** The ideas are logically presented. Paragraph 2 provides a general explanation supported in detail by the examples of paragraph 3. Paragraph 4 concludes the section on benefits, and 5 and 6 cover the main points of the hazards section. Strong, thoughtful connections begin paragraphs 4, 5, and 6. Other connectors help sustain the flow, including "additionally" and "for example."

- **Support:** Many explanations and examples support both the benefits and the hazards sections. Paragraph 5 of the hazards section contains exceptional detail. The idea presented in paragraph 6 is clearly explained.

- **Language:** With the exception of "it" in the first sentence, the language is clear and efficient, and the sentence structure varies. Variety is lacking in the use of connections, as "additionally"/"in addition" is overused. The tone is appropriate for the academic audience.

- **Grammar, Usage, and Mechanics:** The essay is essentially free of grammar, usage, and mechanical errors. The use of the second person at the start of paragraph 2 ("True, if you're starving . . .") is awkward and not in line with the third-person usage in the rest of the essay.

993.

Sample Response

When a wave of the future successfully irrigates the crops, it's time to acknowledge the quality of the water. Such is the case with online learning, which can provide a quality of education often better than that of face-to-face learning.

With online learning, no instructor muddling through a lecture bores the students or leaves them wondering what the point was. Instead, a well-prepared video lecture can deliver the content and make the point(s) clearly. Moreover, the lecturer can provide notes and presentation slides to accompany the video and thus facilitate learning to an even greater extent. Student discussions also tend to be much clearer online than in a face-to-face classroom. The main reason for this improvement is that students in an asynchronous discussion have time to reflect on and craft their thoughts, resulting in focused and well-written responses. Such quality benefits everyone.

While it is true that technical difficulties may arise and cause frustration in online learning, this form of education most often provides students greater ease than face-to-face learning, especially in terms of time and distance. Physically challenged students are able to participate in class more freely. Students with jobs or families also greatly benefit from the accessibility of a virtual classroom. For example, my older sister, with a full-time job and two children, completed her B.A. just last year via online learning. She never had to go back out at night after working all day; she stayed home, with her family. Even full-time students experience the freedom and ease of online learning's accessibility. They may juggle and organize their schedule as best suits them, and they may, if needed, review previous lectures, notes, and discussions before going on. Yes, these students need to work on being self-directed if they aren't already, but the benefits of being self-directed reach beyond those of online learning to improve the quality of life itself.

In addition to clarity and ease, online learning brings equality and student-centered education to the foreground, more so than in face-to-face learning. All online students, regardless of their age, gender, race, ethnicity, or mannerisms, are largely anonymous. The potentially discriminating factors recede, and the focus stays on the content and quality of the discussion. Another quality that comes forward is the interactive nature of online learning as it allows for creative teaching. A virtual classroom, already requiring students to have self-direction, allows for students to follow and control their own interests in smaller discussions that form off the main discussion. Further, students can work with the instructor regarding the direction of their studies and help shape their own learning experience. With the Internet at their fingertips, students can select and follow suggested links to desired supplemental material and their individualized study.

From the clarity of the message to the ease of reaching it, from the equality of participation to its degree of individualization, online learning offers a superbly high quality of education. It's the wave of the future — and it's here.

Score and Analysis

The following rubric shows why this essay would receive a score of 6:

- **Task:** The essay addresses all the points in the prompt and does so in a manner appropriate for an academic audience.
- **Focus:** The essay begins with an engaging metaphor, catching the reader's attention. The position statement follows and is supported throughout. Each one of the body (middle) paragraphs pertains to and references the quality of online learning, and the conclusion restates the thesis and returns to the original metaphor to drive the point home.

- **Organization:** Each of the body paragraphs contains and supports a main point. Transitions between and within the paragraphs summarize when necessary and keep the flow going. For example, the last sentence of paragraph 2 summarizes, as does the first sentence of paragraph 4. Many connectors help sustain the flow, including "moreover" and "also" in paragraph 2, "for example" in paragraph 3, and "in addition," "another," and "further" in paragraph 4.

- **Support:** Paragraph 2 contains an example detailing a video lecture with its accompanying notes and slides as well as an explanation of the benefits of asynchronous discussions. Paragraph 3 addresses objections to the essay's position (that is, potential problems of online learning), simultaneously providing examples — including a detailed example from personal experience — that support the position. Paragraph 4 details added benefits of online learning with explanations and examples.

- **Language:** The language is clear and efficient, and the sentence structure varies. The tone is appropriate for the academic audience.

- **Grammar, Usage, and Mechanics:** The essay is essentially free of grammar, usage, and mechanical errors.

994.

Sample Response

While there are advantages to reading paperbacks, the digital versions offer many more. Some people may feel that giving up paperbacks involves a sacrifice, but sacrificing trees is worse.

One advantage of paperbacks involves the nature of the medium. The paperback needs no battery and won't loose its text to a virus. Furthermore, it won't break if dropped or stop working if caught in the rain.

Perhaps the most often cited advantage of a paperback is the book itself. My grandmother talks about "curling up with a book" and just "liking the feel of the pages" as she turns them. Other people mention the ability to revisit a specific spot. These emotional, tactile issues are very real to people.

E-books, on the other hand, offer more than a few advantages. Once such advantage involves the accessible and condensed nature of digital versions. When traveling, people can carry a dozen books in the space of a slim Kindle or iPad. Magazines or newspapers appear at the touch or swipe of a finger. And the cost of all this digital material is far below the cost of books made of paper.

That brings up perhaps the greatest advantage of e-books: no tree has been cut down for them. As the world's population increases, natural resources dwindle. The overall importance of trees has been well documented, and they cannot be sacrificed for something when a viable alternative exists.

E-books provide additional advantages. There is no need to worry about font size as it is adjustable. Some devices also allow for adjustable screen resolution and lighting. Further, people can increase their vocabulary very easily by looking up words while reading.

Some people may find it hard to give up there paperbacks for digital versions, but they'll find many benefits when they do so. And they won't be sacrificing trees.

Score and Analysis

The following rubric shows why this essay would receive a score of 5:

- **Task:** The essay addresses all the points in the prompt and does so in a manner appropriate for an academic audience.

- **Focus:** Both the introduction and the conclusion state the main points (contrasting advantages of the two media) and the essay's position. Each one of the body (middle) paragraphs pertains to and references these points.

- **Organization:** Each of the body paragraphs pertains to advantages of either paperbacks or e-books. Necessary transitions exist but not particularly thoughtful ones. For example, "That" beginning paragraph 5 could be replaced with a connection such as "The nature of a paperback." Paragraph 6 could begin "In addition to their accessibility, compact size, and resource-saving composition."

- **Support:** Most ideas are explained and supported with examples or details. Paragraph 2 contains explanations but could use more detail. Paragraph 3 needs an explanation and an example following the sentence "Other people mention the ability to revisit a specific spot." Paragraph 5 needs another explanation and significant detail pertaining to trees, as this point regarding the digital advantage is central to the position statement.

- **Language:** The language is clear and efficient; more variety in the sentence structure could be used. For example, the second sentence of paragraph 2 could begin, "As a non-electronic form," adding clarity as well as variety. A synonym or two for "advantage" (*benefit, positive aspect*) — particularly in the topic sentences for the body paragraphs — would also add variety. The tone is appropriate for the academic audience.

- **Grammar, Usage, and Mechanics:** The essay has few grammar, usage, and mechanical errors. In paragraph 2, "loose" should be "lose." In paragraph 5, "that" is a vague pronoun reference, and "there" in the conclusion should be "their."

995.

Sample Response

To say "Making athletes who cheat with drugs relinquish their records is unrealistic" is not only unrealistic itself, it is dangerously short sighted.

Most people know there are athletes who look for whatever edge they can find. High-school athletes aim for prestigious colleges and universities; professional athletes aim for higher salaries and fame. If one athlete is caught cheating with drugs, does that mean he or she is the only one? That's similar to seeing one ant and assuming there aren't any others.

Thus the situation is such that many athletes cheat but only one, let us say, is caught. If that one has to give up his or her records, is that unrealistic or unfair? No, that's life. There are laws, and if people break laws, people suffer the consequences. For example, many people speed, knowing full well they are speeding. If they are caught, they pay a fine appropriate to the offense. Without consequences, or enforcement, there is very little point in having laws. The need for such consequences is a reality of human nature.

Part of the consequences of an athlete's cheating should be the forfeiture of any statistics because they were set under false, drug-enhanced conditions. If a swimmer makes a false (early) start, he or she doesn't get to keep swimming with this advantage and keep whatever time is achieved. The swimmer must return and start again with the others. Similarly, if there's more than a minimal amount of wind at a track meet, the times or distances of certain competitors don't count in terms of records because the wind presents an unfair advantage. Thus, to allow cheaters' statistics to "count" is neither fair nor realistic.

But there is a larger issue here, which must be recognized and goes beyond an athlete keeping statistics. What message do we send our children if athletes' records stand no matter how they were earned? What are we saying if a cheating athlete gets to keep the statistics he or she cheated to get? In essence, we're telling children it's okay for them to steal and keep whatever they've stolen.

We'll never apprehend all the athletes who cheat with drugs, but that's not the issue. The issue is, it's wrong to cheat, and people don't get to keep what they obtained through cheating.

Score and Analysis

The following rubric shows why this essay would receive a score of 6:

- **Task:** The essay fully addresses both concerns mentioned in the prompt — the fact that not all cheaters are caught and the subsequent view that cheaters shouldn't have to relinquish their statistics — and does so in a manner generally appropriate for an academic audience.

- **Focus:** The essay begins with a clear and original position statement. Each of the body (middle) paragraphs explains or exemplifies part of the position, and the conclusion restates the thesis in an effective way.

- **Organization:** The ideas are logically presented. Paragraph 2 provides a general explanation that the examples in paragraph 3 expand on and support in detail. Paragraph 4 concludes the section on the smaller, face-value level of the issue. Paragraph 5 then addresses the larger issue. Strong, thoughtful connections begin paragraphs 3, 4, and 5. Other connectors help sustain the flow, including "for example," "similarly," and "in essence."

- **Support:** Many explanations and examples support the points of the argument. Paragraphs 2, 3, and 4 contain significant examples. The hypothetical situation in paragraph 5 is clearly explained.

- **Language:** The language is clear and efficient, and the sentence structure varies. The tone approaches informality in places but is generally appropriate for an academic audience.

- **Grammar, Usage, and Mechanics:** The essay is essentially free of grammar, usage, and mechanical errors.

996.

Sample Response

Major areas of concern with regard to fine arts education involve the effects it has on other areas of learning as well as in the workplace and whether or not studies have confirmed these effects.

According to Burton, Horowitz, & Abeles (as cited in Bryant) the positive effects of arts education can be seen in classroom subjects such as "mathematics, science, and language." Jensen (as cited in Bryant) makes a broader claim, stating that "the arts enhance the process of learning. The systems they nourish, which include our integrated sensory, attentional, cognitive, emotional, and motor capacities, are, in fact, the driving forces behind all other learning."

In addition to these positive classroom effects, arts education can help students once they enter the workforce. There, these former art students can benefit from knowing "how to solve problems, what makes arguments plausible, how to build teams and coalitions, and how to incorporate the concept of fairness into the everyday decisions" (Bryant).

But not everyone agrees that application in an art class will necessarily lead to creativity or success in other areas. Winner & Hetland (as cited in Hulbert) "searched mostly in vain for evidence of a causal influence [of art classes] on school success." Hulbert emphasizes that the high SAT scores of students who took a lot of art classes does not necessarily mean the two factors are directly connected. The assumption is, one supposes, that the students who got the high scores would have anyway and just happened to like art.

What Hulbert does agree with Bryant on are the benefits of art classes in the art classes themselves. Observing fine arts teachers and their classes, Winner & Hetland (as cited in Hulbert) noted "persistence in tackling problems, observational acuity, expressive clarity, reflective capacity to question and judge, ability to envision alternative possibilities and openness to exploration."

These are fine creative and logical qualities, as both Bryant and Hulbert assert. The point of disagreement, as Hulbert writes, is one of "automatic transfer" from the art class to the world beyond. But both sources agree that, whether for its intrinsic value or for its positive effects beyond its own confines, fine arts education is important.

Score and Analysis

The following rubric shows why this essay would receive a score of 6:

- **Task:** The essay addresses all the points in the prompt, using "information from both sources to discuss the most important concerns relating to the issue" — including the debatable "automatic transfer" — and it does so in a manner appropriate for an academic audience.

- **Focus:** The essay begins with a clear statement regarding the important concerns of fine arts education. Each one of the body (middle) paragraphs pertains to and addresses these concerns; the conclusion summarizes the main points and provides its own insight.

- **Organization:** Topics of the body paragraphs progress logically from broad claims of fine arts education to points of disagreement to points of agreement. The essay synthesizes information from each source, and transitions between and within the paragraphs effectively summarize and link the material. For example, the first sentence of paragraph 3 summarizes what came before as it introduces what follows. Thoughtful connections between sources occur in paragraphs 2, 5, and 6, such as Jensen's making "a broader claim" (paragraph 2).

- **Support:** The essay supports the analysis with material from the sources, incorporating information to establish and explain the concerns. Paragraph 2 contains important explanations. Paragraph 3 offers examples, paragraph 4 explains the significant point of contention, and paragraph 5 notes the point of agreement.

- **Language:** The language is clear and efficient, and the sentence structure varies. The overall tone is appropriate for the academic audience. Paragraph 4's use of "a lot of," "would have anyway," and "just happened to like art" border on the informal but not to the point of distraction.

- **Grammar, Usage, and Mechanics:** The essay correctly integrates and credits information from the sources. The essay is free of grammar, usage, and mechanical errors.

997.

Sample Response

Caffeinated energy drinks offer some benefits while involving risks. Unfortunately, for all the studies that have been conducted, much remains unknown as the need persists for more information regarding these drinks.

According to Doheny, some studies attribute such benefits to caffeine as "boosting memory and improving concentration and perhaps lowering risks of diseases such as Alzheimer's and liver cancer." Also confirming a benefit of energy drinks, a study conducted by Cameli shows that caffeinated drinks "improve the contractions of both the left and right ventricles of the heart" and thus have "a beneficial effect on myocardial [heart muscle] function" (as cited in Nordqvist).

In addition to these documented effects, my own observations confirm a "boost" in energy in general from caffeinated beverages. I have found them to stimulate memory as well as concentration. In layman's terms, the beverages simply help me "think" better. As I observed similar effects in co-workers, I assume the beverages help these people think better as well. At least temporarily.

Unfortunately, fatigue often sets in following these energy boosts. As with the personal boost described above, this fatigue is an observation I have made in myself and in co-workers: it is not a result of a scientific study. But such studies do confirm the existence of risks in energy drinks. For example, Doheny notes studies have found "too much caffeine can set you up for high blood pressure, high blood sugar, and decreased bone density — not to mention jangled nerves." Another study discovered that "energy drinks raise the risk of cardiometabolic diseases" (as cited in Nordqvist). This study, noting that those involved were "young healthy individuals at rest," raised the issue of how energy drinks might affect cardiac patients. It also called into question "whether such benefits [discussed above] persist after long term consumption" (Nordqvist).

In spite of boosts in memory, concentration, and myocardial function, caffeinated drinks pose risks, many involving the heart. Both Doheny and Nordqvist note this duel nature of the beverages, and neither comes out definitively for or against them. This lack of a position, as it were, seems to signal a lack of research, as Cameli notes (above, Nordqvist). Doheny adds the disturbing fact that the FDA does not yet require the labeling of caffeine content, resulting in "hidden caffeine." It is time for the unknown and obscured facts of caffeine to be revealed.

Score and Analysis

The following rubric shows why this essay would receive a score of 6:

- **Task:** The essay addresses the important concerns of the issue, from benefits to problems to the unknown, and it does so in a manner appropriate for an academic audience.

- **Focus:** The essay begins with a clear expression of the concerns and an insightful position statement. Each of the body (middle) paragraphs pertains to and addresses these concerns; the conclusion summarizes the main points and reiterates the position statement.

- **Organization:** Topics of the body paragraphs progress logically from the advantages to the disadvantages of energy drinks. The essay synthesizes information from each source, and the transitions between and within the paragraphs effectively summarize and link the material. For example, the first sentence of paragraph 3 summarizes what came before as it introduces what follows. The phrase "also confirming a benefit of energy drinks" in paragraph 2 makes a thoughtful connection between sources. Other strong connections occur within paragraph 4 and at the start of paragraph 5.

- **Support:** The essay supports the analysis with material from both sources, incorporating information to establish and explain the concerns. Paragraph 2 contains important examples from the sources. Paragraph 3 offers examples from the writer's own observations, and paragraph 4 successfully incorporates the writer's observations with information from the sources.

- **Language:** The language is clear and efficient, and the sentence structure varies. The overall tone is appropriate for the academic audience.

- **Grammar, Usage, and Mechanics:** The essay correctly integrates and credits information from the sources. The essay is largely free of grammar, usage, and mechanical errors. The word "duel" in paragraph 5 should be "dual." The sentence fragment at the end of paragraph 3 is used effectively to make a point and transition to the next main point.

998.

Sample Response

Opinions regarding standardized tests differ in their being categorically unneeded or limitedly useful. Sources agree, however, that the emphasis in schools should be on teaching and learning, not tests.

Both Jouriles and Almagor voice displeasure with how standardized testing turns a classroom's focus away from learning to test-taking. "Alienation [and] disempowerment" are among the many costs to teachers of such an unfortunate focus (Jouriles). The need to do well on tests makes "unrealistic" demands on students, and the material they learn is "skewed" to the test (Jouriles). Many teachers feel compelled to use "testing tricks and stamina lessons," running test-prep lessons "to the point of absurdity" (Almagor). Jouriles concludes by saying that, where schools have achieved high test scores, they are not a result of fine teaching or learning, which on observation "do not impress." High test scores and high standards of education do not equate.

Is there any point to standardized testing? Almagor maintains that the rigors of standards such as the Common Core do have a place in education as long as test scores are not leveraged against all those involved: "If we could give these harder tests internally and get back detailed results — share them only with parents, and use them only to improve our own planning — many more teachers would embrace them." Teachers could "take genuine pride" in student achievement (Almagor) and seemingly pass that good feeling on through their teaching to students.

Jouriles agrees that the focus needs to be on the teachers, who know their students and how they are performing. In place of testing, however, Jouriles encourages systems to "trust the teacher. Publish grade distributions. Locally publish a compilation of evaluation reports. Release a state or national report reviewed and verified by expert evaluators with legislative oversight."

Whether standardized tests should be omitted or reserved only for unofficial use, they should not take the place of well-rounded curricula and learning-based education.

Score and Analysis

The following rubric shows why this essay would receive a score of 5:

- **Task:** The essay addresses the pros and cons of standardized testing, using "information from both sources to discuss the most important concerns," and it does so in a manner appropriate for an academic audience.

- **Focus:** The introduction contains a clear summary of the important concerns regarding standardized tests. Each of the body (middle) paragraphs pertains to and addresses the tests' disadvantages and advantages; the conclusion neatly incorporates the position statement into the summary.

- **Organization:** Topics of the body paragraphs progress clearly from disadvantages to advantages. Points of agreement and disagreement between sources are clear. Some links between ideas are missing. For example, the third sentence of paragraph 2 would be improved if it began, "Additionally." Paragraph 3 needs a better beginning, such as "With such an inadequacy, with teachers disenfranchised and students stressed."

- **Support:** The essay supports the analysis with material from the sources, incorporating information to establish and explain most of the concerns. Paragraph 4 needs an explanation at the close, such as "These methods would serve the purpose of standardized test scores without incurring their costs."

- **Language:** The language is clear and efficient. Variety appears in the sentence structure toward the end of the essay, but the essay lacks variety in the beginning. The overall tone is appropriate for the academic audience.

- **Grammar, Usage, and Mechanics:** The essay correctly integrates and credits information from the sources. The essay is largely free of grammar, usage, and mechanical errors. The hyphen in "test-taking" (paragraph 2) is incorrect.

999.

Sample Response

What does a society lose with music censorship? Can any good come of it?

Perhaps no music genre today has given censors more work than hip-hop. Yet in spite of its admittedly problematic language, raising "moral" and "sexism" issues, hip-hop's roots in a "venerable African-American oral tradition" make it something worth preserving, according to Sanneh. When "a fresh-faced audience applaud [clean-cut] songs, cheered on by relentlessly positive hosts," it's clear to Sanneh that too much "soap" has been applied to the original material. And it's "scary" that a loss of tradition wouldn't matter to "hip-hop's fans [or] its detractors" (Sanneh).

In a similar stand regarding censorship, Strauss admits the very nature of it is "odious." He compares musicians having to re-write songs to painters having to paint "clothes on nudes before they can be displayed in a museum where children might see them." Since society today accepts nudes in painting and sculpture, the unspoken conclusion here is that society today ought to accept songs without their being re-written.

And yet the re-writing of songs, argues Strauss, is not without merit. And as long as we must have censorship, he might say, then let's do it in a good way. Rather than have sound effects laid over a track, "obscuring" the meaning entirely, Strauss much prefers the re-writing of an outrageous lyric to something suggestive. In fact, as he notes, "in the case of several recent singles, the editing has actually improved the song. In a pop landscape in which the crude come-on has replaced the sly innuendo, some remakes are bringing a touch of subtlety back to urban music."

Thus resigned, perhaps, to the censor's control, Strauss finds some good in its having resulted in innuendo, a gentle application of "soap." But, in a toss of his head at the bit in his mouth, Strauss argues that control ought to work both ways. "If albums with curse words are deemed dirty and must be presented in clean versions, why can't albums that are clean to begin with (Celine Dion, 'N Sync, Barney) be remade into dirty versions for those who don't like their pop so tame?"

Ending with a laugh or, in the case of Sanneh, a lament, people find ways to cope with an apparently inescapable fact of life today: for good or ill, with gentle or harsh detergent, music will be censored.

Score and Analysis

The following rubric shows why this essay would receive a score of 6:

- **Task:** The essay addresses the different aspects of music censorship appearing in the sources — including the loss of tradition as well as freedom — and it does so in a manner appropriate for an academic audience.

- **Focus:** The essay begins by expressing the concerns in question format, making use of this technique for a good opener/hook. Each of the body (middle) paragraphs pertains to and addresses the problems as well as the inevitability of censorship, and the conclusion summarizes the main points in an insightful way, effectively using the soap metaphor from one of the sources.

- **Organization:** Topics of the body paragraphs progress logically from losses as a result of censorship to relative gains. The essay synthesizes information from each source, and the transitions between and within the paragraphs effectively summarize and link the material. For example, the first sentence of paragraph 3, in addition to thoughtfully connecting the sources, summarizes what came before as it introduces what follows. Paragraph 4 begins with a strong connection between facets of a source's stance.

- **Support:** The essay supports the analysis with material from the sources, incorporating information to establish and explain the concerns. The close of paragraph 3 provides an insightful explanation, as does paragraph 4's second sentence. The second sentence of paragraph 5 provides an especially insightful explanation.

- **Language:** The language is clear and efficient, and the sentence structure varies. The overall tone is appropriate for the academic audience.

- **Grammar, Usage, and Mechanics:** The essay correctly integrates and credits information from the sources. The essay is largely free of grammar, usage, and mechanical errors. The second sentence of paragraph 2 begins with a dangling modifier: "Issues" should be followed by the (missing) subject of the sentence, "hip-hop," not (hip-hop's) "roots."

1,000.

Sample Response

Major areas of concern with regard to plastic surgery involve the positive and negative effects resulting from the surgery.

According to Rappaport, the positive effects of plastic surgery involve the patient's emotional, physical, and mental health, with benefits extending from the personal to professional. Emotionally, "improvements to appearance naturally translate to increased self-confidence for most people, which means a greater willingness to try new things or open up in social situations" (Rappaport). Confirming this point, one study notes that "patients reported a boost in self-image and overall well-being" (cited in Ray).

Another positive emotional effect leads to a physical benefit as patients who have had weight-reduction surgery may subsequently find new motivation "to maintain a healthy diet and exercise program" (Rappaport). Other physical benefits come as a direct result of surgery, such as in "rhinoplasty or nose reshaping surgery [which] may improve breathing" (Rappaport). Mental benefits bear mentioning, such as people feeling "a reduction in social anxiety after their surgery" or being "more willing to take on new challenges," as reported by Rappaport.

"A 2012 study published in Applied Financial Economics found that attractive real estate agents were able to sell properties at a higher price than agents that were not perceived as attractive" (cited in Rappaport). Ray concurs, noting that the expense of the surgery may be offset "when the improved appearance will help in obtaining a job or promotion."

On the negative side, there are risks involved in the surgery itself, with a bigger surgery potentially leading to bigger risks (Ray). Some of these risks include scars, infections, blood clots, and problems resulting from anesthesia (Ray).

On the negative side emotionally, some patients become depressed if their expectations, which may have been too high, were not met (Ray). Others may experience feelings of "isolation and anger towards their doctors" (Ray).

It's important "that more psychological counseling be enacted by plastic surgeons prior to doing the work" (cited in Ray). This way, patients have a better chance of enjoying the positive effects and escaping the negative ones.

Score and Analysis

The following rubric shows why this essay would receive a score of 5:

- **Task:** The essay addresses the pros and cons of plastic surgery as evidenced in the sources, and it does so in a manner appropriate for an academic audience.

- **Focus:** The essay begins with a clear, if minimal, statement regarding the important concerns. Each of the body (middle) paragraphs pertains to advantages or disadvantages, and the essay ends with a clear position statement.

- **Organization:** The ideas are clearly organized and developed. Some thoughtful connections exist, such as those beginning paragraphs 3 and 5, for all the latter's awkward phrasing. Other connections, however, are missing. For example, the last sentence of paragraph 3 would benefit with an opening phrase such as "While closely aligned with emotional advantages." Similarly, the essay would benefit if paragraph 4 began, "Regarding people's professional life" and if the conclusion started with "As one study found." The connection beginning paragraph 5 is minimal, particularly as it occurs at the major junction between positive and negative effects of plastic surgery. Paragraphs 2 and 4 contain clear links between sources.

- **Support:** The essay mostly supports the analysis with material from the sources, incorporating information to establish and explain the concerns. Paragraph 5 and 6, however, are underdeveloped, lacking full explanation and detail.

- **Language:** The language is mostly clear and efficient. Paragraphs 5 and 6 contain some awkward phrasing. The conclusion's "This way" could be more clearly expressed. The overall tone is appropriate for the academic audience.

- **Grammar, Usage, and Mechanics:** The essay correctly integrates and credits information from the sources. The essay is free of grammar, usage, and mechanical errors.

1,001.

Sample Response

Major areas of concern with regard to mandatory community-service programs for students involve the positive and negative effects of this practice. Some studies have shown a negative effect, yet many sources point out benefits; for the long run, the jury is still out.

A recent study found that mandatory community service led to "significant boosts in 8th grade volunteering — generally in school-organized activities — but it actually decreased volunteering among older students, leading to a potential loss in long-term volunteering" (cited in Sparks). While there is some doubt regarding the older students' understanding of what to record on the survey, the possibility exists that "maybe we are substituting this [service requirement] for being self-motivated" (cited in Sparks). Bodeeb expands on this problem of taking away students' motivation, stating that "to a certain extent, requiring someone to volunteer takes away the whole purpose of volunteerism."

Another disadvantage of a mandatory community-service program is the extra demand on time and energy. Multiple sources "agreed that schools' service-learning programs require planning and time for students to reflect on their experiences in order to be meaningful" (cited in Sparks). Further, "adding community service requirements would severely stress some high school students who work long hours simply to keep their family financially afloat" (Bodeeb). These examples suggest that mandatory service may help the community, but it doesn't help every volunteer.

At the same time, many strong points have been noted regarding these programs. One administrator claims that "as a tool for engaging students in different subjects, from history to environmental science . . . the state's service-learning requirement has been a success," and without it, a "focus" would be "lacking" (cited in Sparks). Others have found that "community service may help teenagers build leadership skills"; in addition, the work "sparks creativity in students and propels them to create projects that may have a profound impact on the local community"

(Bodeeb). Additionally, by working with community leaders now, students may find these service connections "help them later in their careers or life" (Bodeeb).

And that's the final word in terms of a ruling on the pros and cons of the mandatory community-service issue: It will come later. For now, excepting students with outside commitments, they and their communities, at least in the short term, are seeing the benefits.

Score and Analysis

The following rubric shows why this essay would receive a score of 6:

- **Task:** The essay addresses the strengths and weaknesses of mandatory volunteer programs, using "information from both sources to discuss the most important concerns." The discussion is appropriate for an academic audience.

- **Focus:** The introduction provides a clear picture of the main points as well as a position statement. Each of the body (middle) paragraphs presents disadvantages or advantages, and the conclusion summarizes the main points and restates the writer's own position.

- **Organization:** Topics of the body paragraphs progress logically from disadvantages to advantages. The essay synthesizes information from each source, and the transitions between and within the paragraphs effectively summarize and link the material. Paragraphs 3 and 4 begin by summarizing what came before as they introduce what follows. Connections such as "another," "further," and "additional" help sustain the flow.

- **Support:** The essay supports the analysis with material from the sources, incorporating information to establish and explain the concerns. The second sentence of paragraph 2 provides a thoughtful explanation. The last sentence of paragraph 2 begins with an insightful connection. Paragraph 3 provides strong explanations, and paragraph 4 has many significant details.

- **Language:** The language is clear and efficient, and the sentence structure varies. The overall tone is appropriate for the academic audience.

- **Grammar, Usage, and Mechanics:** The essay correctly integrates and credits information from the sources. The essay is free of grammar, usage, and mechanical errors.

Index

area
  of circles, 42, 293
  of composite figures, 45–46, 298–300
  of cubes, 50, 310
  of parallelograms, 42, 294
  of quadrilaterals, 44, 297
  of triangles, 43, 294–296
argumentative essays, 200–201, 473–482
assumptions based on passage, 76, 83, 90–92, 103, 107, 126, 135–136, 143, 157–158, 337, 344, 352–355, 369, 373, 393–394, 401–403, 411, 428–430
audience, 76, 78, 87, 131, 337–339, 349–350, 398
authors
  beliefs and implications of, 75, 77–78, 80, 82, 86–88, 92, 96, 98–99, 101, 103, 111–113, 119, 124, 129–130, 139, 148, 152, 154–155, 157, 159, 161, 335, 338–339, 342–344, 349–351, 355, 360–364, 366, 368–369, 376–377, 379, 386, 391, 397–398, 403–404, 406–407, 417–418, 422, 425, 427, 429–432, 434
  mood and attitude of, 78, 103, 117, 119, 123, 149, 340, 368, 383, 385, 390, 419
  purpose and intention of, 74, 76, 78–81, 83, 94–95, 97–98, 100–102, 104, 106–107, 109–110, 112, 117, 119, 121–124, 127, 129, 132, 134, 138, 140–142, 149, 153–156, 334, 337, 339–342, 346, 354–355, 357, 359, 362–363, 365–372, 374–376, 378, 383–385, 387–388, 390–391, 395–397, 399, 401, 404–405, 407–410, 420, 424, 426–428
averages, 62, 320

B

bar graphs, 56, 126–127, 315, 394–395
"Better Songs Through Censorship" (Strauss), 205
binomials
  identifying, 25–26, 253–255
  multiplying, 23–24, 246, 248
  square of, 25, 254–255
Bodeeb, Julia, 207
box and whisker plots, 59, 65, 317, 324
Bryant, Bob, 201–202

C

capitalization, 168, 170, 180, 183, 441, 443, 454, 456
case, agreement in, 164, 437
characterization, 79–80, 90, 108, 120, 122–123, 125, 128, 145–146, 341, 353–354, 373–374, 386, 388–389, 391–392, 396, 413–415
charts, 115–116, 381–382
circle graphs, 58, 316–317
circles
  area, 42, 293
  circumference, 42, 293
  radius, 42, 293
citation format, 198–200, 468–473
claims, 76, 81, 130, 136, 336, 343, 397, 403
clarity
  essay score and analysis, 474, 477, 479–480, 483, 485, 487–488, 491
  revising in context, 186–187, 189–190, 192, 458–465
Cleveland, Chan, 3
colons, 180, 454
commas, 163–164, 166–167, 170, 172, 175–177, 179–181, 185, 437–439, 441, 443, 446, 448–450, 453–455, 458
"Community Service Requirements Seen to Reduce Volunteering" (Sparks), 206–207
comparatives and superlatives, 169, 179, 442
comparisons and contrasts, 80, 94–95, 108, 114, 117–118, 123, 125, 132, 146, 341, 358–359, 374, 380, 382–384, 389, 392–393, 400, 415–416
complementary angles, 40, 291
composite figures
  area, 45–46, 298–300
  surface, 49, 306
  volume, 50, 308
cones
  surface, 48, 306
  volume, 49, 307
congruent angles, 40–41, 291–292
conjunctions, 164, 168, 435, 441

H

I

numbers (continued)

order of operations, 9, 16–17, 19, 215, 230–232, 236

overview, 2, 7

percentages

converting decimals to, 12, 221

converting fractions to, 12–13, 222–224

converting mixed numbers to, 12, 222–223

converting to decimals, 12–13, 222, 224, 226

converting to fractions, 12, 222

determining, 17, 19, 21, 233–234, 236–237, 239–240

powers

cubes, 9, 214

4th, 9, 214

ratios, 17–18, 234–236

square roots, 9, 214

units of measurement, converting between

linear, 21–22, 240–244

mass, 21–22, 241, 243

speed, 23, 244–246

volume, 21–22, 241–244

O

odd and/or even numbers

adding, 25, 250

multiplying, 25, 250

off topic, 185, 194, 458, 467

online resources

Cheat Sheet (companion to book), 3

online practice access and technical support, 3

opposite numbers, 35, 282

order of operations, 9, 16–17, 19, 23–26, 28, 215, 230–232, 236, 246, 248, 250, 253–256, 259

organization and structure

essay score and analysis, 474–475, 477, 479–480, 482–483, 485–486, 488–489, 491

reading comprehension, 77, 82, 98, 114, 122, 133, 142, 145–146, 337, 343, 362, 380, 388, 400, 410, 414–415

P

paradoxes, 82, 145, 147, 161, 344, 413–414, 416–417, 435

parallel grammatical structure, 164, 177, 183–184, 193, 437, 449, 456, 466

parallelograms

area, 42, 294

defined, 44, 298

length of one side, 46, 302

perimeter, 42, 294

parenthesis, 124, 127, 391, 395

percentages

converting decimals to, 12, 221

converting fractions to, 12–13, 222–224

converting mixed numbers to, 12, 222–223

converting to decimals, 12–13, 222, 224, 226

converting to fractions, 12, 222

determining, 17, 19, 21, 233–234, 236–237, 239–240

perimeter

of parallelograms, 42, 294

of quadrilaterals, 44–45, 297–298

of triangles, 43, 45, 294, 298

person, agreement in, 166, 171, 182, 440, 445, 455, 477

planes

naming, 39, 290

points on, 39, 290

"Positive and Negative Benefits of Plastic Surgery" (Ray), 206

possession, 165, 171–172, 183–184, 186, 188, 438, 445–446, 456–458, 460

powers

algebra, 23, 247

cubes, 9, 214

4th, 9, 214

Praxis Core For Dummies (Kirkland and Cleveland), 1, 4

prisms

surface, 47, 303

volume, 47, 49, 51, 303, 308, 310

W

words

determining meaning of, 76–77, 82, 85–86,
89–92, 96–98, 103, 105, 110–113, 119,
121–122, 124–126, 129–130, 132, 134, 137,
140–142, 144–145, 148–149, 153, 158–161,
336–338, 344, 347–348, 351, 353–354, 356,
360–361, 363, 368, 371, 376–379, 385,
388–389, 391–392, 394, 397, 399, 401, 404,
407, 409–410, 413–414, 417, 419–420, 423,
431–434

misused

correcting sentences, 164–165, 167–168,
170–172, 175–181, 183–184, 436–438,
441–443, 445–446, 448–458

essay score and analysis, 474–475, 480, 485

revising in context, 186, 192, 195, 458, 465,
468

Chapter 2 Sources

Questions	Author	Title	Publisher
423–425, 432–445, 449–491, 497–506, 591–592, 593–594, 595, 596–599, 600–602, 603–606, 607–610, 611–616, 617–618, 619–621, 622–623, 624–625, 626–627, 628–630, 631–633, 634–635, 636–640, 641–644, 645–647, 648–651, 652–655, 656–660, 661–664, 665–667, 668–671, 672–674	Cook, Chris O.	Various writings	
426, 449, 517–521, 539–542	Kaye, S. (Ed.)	*The Ultimate Lost and Philosophy: Think Together, Die Alone*	John Wiley & Sons, Inc.
429–431, 551–554, 560–563, 675–679	Maguire, L. E. and Smith, E.	*30 Great Myths about Shakespeare*	John Wiley & Sons, Inc.
446–448, 492–496, 522–527, 543	Arnason, Johann P. and Kurt A. Raaflaub	*The Roman Empire in Context*	Wiley-Blackwell.
427–428, 699–708, 571–575	Housel, R. & Wisnewski, J.J.	*X-Men and Philosophy: Astonishing Insight and Uncanny Argument in the Mutant X-Verse*	John Wiley & Sons, Inc.
507–508	Curie, M.S.	*The Discovery of Radium*	Vassar College
509–512	Gardner, W.H.	"A Flock of Mythological Crows"	*Popular Science Monthly, 55*
513–516	Darwin, C.	*The Origin of the Species: By Means of Natural Selection*	*John Murray*
528, 567–570	Quimby, F.H	*Concepts for Detection of Extraterrestrial Life*	National Aeronautics and Space Administration
529–532, 537, 550, 724–729	Bevington, D.	*Shakespeare's Ideas: More Things in Heaven and Earth*	John Wiley & Sons, Inc.

Questions	Author	Title	Publisher
533–536	Heath, T.F.	*The Works of Archimedes*	The University Press
538	Thorndike, L.A.	*A History of Magic and Experimental Science*	Northeastern University
544–547	Payne, T.	*Common Sense: Addressed to the Inhabitants of America*	R. Bell
548–549	O'Connell, J. (Eds.)	*TIME for Springfield*	City of Springfield, Massachusetts and Springfield Central
555–556, 557–559, 680–692	Mintz, S., Roberts, R., and Welkly, D. (Eds.)	*Hollywood's America: Understanding History through Film*	John Wiley & Sons, Inc.
579–584	Cox, O.C.	*Caste, Class, and Race: A Study in Social Dynamics*	Monthly Review Press
585	Alexander, H.B.	*The Mythology of All Races*	Marshall Jones
586–589, 564, 526, 565–566, 693–698	Jacboy, H. (Ed.)	*House and Philosophy: Everybody Lies*	John Wiley & Sons
709–723	Weeks, P.	*"Farewell, My Nation": American Indians and the United States in the Nineteenth Century.*	John Wiley & Sons, Inc.
730–733	Bigelow, J. M.	*The Medicinal Plants of Ohio*	J.M. Riley & Co.
734–738	Corbett, J.	*Man-Eaters of Kumaon*	Oxford University Press
739–742	Faulkner, W.	*Collected Stories of William Faulkner*	Random House
743–746	Hersey, J.	*Hiroshima*	Penguin Books
747–750	Downes, R. P.	*Woman: Her Charm and Power*	The Epworth Press.
751–754	Malinowski, B.	*Argonauts of the Western Pacific: An Account of Native Enterprise and Adventure in the Archipelagos of Melanesian New Guinea*	E.P. Dutton & Co.
755–758	Stein, G.	*Selected Writings of Gertrude Stein*	Random House

Notes

Notes

Notes

Notes

Notes

Notes

Notes

About the Authors

Carla Kirkland is founder and CEO of The Kirkland Group, a consulting firm headquartered in Ridgeland, Mississippi, that has provided services to school districts for over 20 years. Mrs. Kirkland is a lifelong educator who has served as a teacher, curriculum specialist, educational consultant, and mentor. Providing professional development, technical assistance, and standardized test preparation to multiple school districts, Mrs. Kirkland speaks to the hearts of teachers and students throughout the country. She resides in Mississippi with her husband.

Chan Cleveland currently serves as executive vice president of The Kirkland Group. Mr. Cleveland has taught elementary, middle, and high school English, and he has worked in several capacities at the Mississippi Department of Education. With over 16 years of experience as an educator, he has created, reviewed, and revised language arts standard documents for multiple school districts and education organizations across the southern region. Mr. Cleveland has assisted students and teachers with attaining positive results on the Praxis, ACT, and subject-area assessments for grades K-12. He holds English degrees from Jackson State University and Mississippi College.

Authors' Acknowledgments

We would like to thank God for the opportunity to write *1,001 Praxis Core Practice Questions For Dummies*. This book would not have been possible without the management and written contributions of Juana Brandon. She worked tirelessly on this project from start to finish. Spencer Powers, Victoria Ford, and C.C. Thomas provided written contributions for this book. We are grateful for Courtnie Mack and Cerissa Neal, who assisted us with editing and revising throughout the entire process. The entire Wiley team is second to no one in quality, professionalism, and support. Tim Gallan, Lindsey Lefevere, and Tracy Boggier of Wiley provided helpful advice and feedback from beginning to end.

Dedications

Carla Kirkland: This book is dedicated to my two children, Malcolm and Alexia. I love you both, and remember to trust in God with all your heart.

Chan Cleveland: This book is dedicated to my four children, Kacie, Cornelius, Dylan, and Jayden. Be strong and courageous. I love you all unconditionally.

Publisher's Acknowledgments

Acquisitions Editor: Tracy Boggier
Project Editor: Tim Gallan
Copy Editor: Danielle Voirol
Technical Reviewer: Carolyn Obel-Omia
Art Coordinator: Alicia B. South

Production Editor: Vasanth Koilraj
Cover Image: © baona/iStockphoto